R. Lek

R. Meuse

R. Rhine

18th ARMY
von KÜCHLER

ARMY GROUP

B

DUTCH

ARMY

9th P.D

BELGIAN

ARMY

Canal

Maastrich

CAVALRY

CORPS

Eban Emael

OUX

LIEGE

Belgian
Ardennes

6th ARMY von REICHENAU
3rd P.D 16th CORPS
4th P.D HOEPPNER

4th ARMY von KLUGE
5th P.D 39th CORPS
7th P.D SCHMIDT
12th ARMY LIST
6th P.D 41st CORPS
8th P.D REINHARDT
16th ARMY BUSCH
1st P.D
2nd P.D 19th CORPS
10th P.D GUDERIAN

A

von RUNDSTEDT
ARMY GROUP

von KLEIST
ARMOURED GROUP

5th
L.C.D. LUXEMBOURG

Treves

Arlen Longwy

Longuyon

1st ARMY
von WITZLEBEN

R. Rhine

Siegfried Line

Maginot

R. Meuse

3rd ARMY
CONDE

St Avold

Maginot Line

METZ

Sarrguemines

4th ARMY
REQUIN

Bitche

RITTER
von LEEB

ARMY GROUP

C

NANCY

Strasbourg

RETELAT
No 2
ARMY GROUP

5th ARMY
BOURRET

7th ARMY
DOLLMANN

R. Moselle

BESSON
No 3 ARMY GROUP

8th ARMY
GARCHERY

6th ARMY
TOUCHON (in reserve)

SIXTY DAYS
THAT SHOOK THE WEST

JACQUES BENOIST-MÉCHIN

Gabriel Paul Michel

SIXTY DAYS
THAT SHOOK
THE WEST

THE FALL OF FRANCE: 1940

Edited with a Preface by
CYRIL FALLS

Translated from the French by
PETER WILES

G. P. PUTNAM'S SONS
NEW YORK

First American Edition 1963

Translated from the French
Soixante Jours qui Ebranlèrent L'Occident

© 1956 BY EDITIONS ALBIN MICHEL, PARIS
ENGLISH VERSION © 1963 BY JONATHAN CAPE LIMITED

Library of Congress Catalog
Card Number: 63-9652

MANUFACTURED IN THE UNITED STATES OF AMERICA

CONTENTS

CONTENTS

CONTENTS

MAPS AND SKETCHES

PREFACE

I WELCOME the opportunity to make better known in this country this remarkable study of the fall of France in 1940, by far the best yet compiled and — it is a hackneyed phrase but appropriate in this connection — 'unlikely to be bettered' by M. Benoist-Méchin or anyone else. He is an experienced historian, but so far less well known on this side of the Channel than on his own. Until today his most valuable work has been his *Histoire de l'Armée Allemande*, a volume on the Imperial Army and a second on the Reichswehr and the National Army to 1939. I mention two other studies because they are of particular interest to our people: his biographies of Mustapha Kemal and Ibn Saud.

His latest work has received warm praise in France. '*Il s'agit ici d'un livre fort. On le lira peut-être avec étonnement et sûrement avec passion*', writes Kléber-Haedens. 'Passion' is the operative word. It has also been hailed for its profound research, its clarity, and its unique documentation. To me it has been an eye-opener, and I suppose I have studied its subject more thoroughly than most people in Britain. Above all it has been belauded in France for its impartiality. Here too I am at one with the critics, though with a few qualifications, I trust not unimportant. Of these I speak later on.

The task of writing even a brief introduction has not been altogether easy, though a trifle by comparison with the editing. The compression has been rigid in the extreme, because it has involved cutting down three substantial volumes into one of approximately the same length. It was something of a nightmare to read the result for the first time, ever apprehensive of jerkiness even more than of gaps. However, I was speedily relieved of anxiety and can now say with conviction that nothing has been lost from the point of view of the English reader. The heaviest risk concerned the third volume of the French edition, dealing as it did with what may be called a postscript, though a very long one, and so perforce the most mutilated. Even here I am pretty well satisfied.

The first volume, concluding on June 4th with the Dunkirk evacuation, has had the lion's share of the available space; the second, that of the lion cub, is essentially that of the armistice. The two other most important and controversial topics are the revision of the Constitution engineered by

Laval, and the tragedy of Mers-el-Kébir. The skill, assurance, and patience of Laval are superbly illustrated, though the formal tribute paid to the oratory and initial prestige of Flandin seems to me inadequate. Still less can I agree with the treatment of Mandel as regards his abortive expedition to North Africa, which appears to me to underrate grossly his shining honesty of purpose, though full justice had earlier been done to his dauntless courage and persistence while the French Army was still fighting. Apart from some reservations concerning the British retreat to the sea and above all the outlook of Jack Dill, this finishes my list of complaints. Dill is portrayed as the anti-French influence in Whitehall. What he was in fact was the most perspicacious soldier on the Allied side. Some time before Hitler's offensive, Dill said to me: 'It's more chancy than I like. The problem of tanks versus anti-tank artillery never was easy to solve, but, compared with now, child's play when the armour came on evenly spread out over the whole front of assault. Now that it concentrates on a single sector or let's call it a couple at the most it's an ugly kettle of fish. It can always break through, always. The only question then is if it can be contained later on.' Here he paused and looked out of the window, his back to me, then switched round looking as though he might have a lot more to say. All he did say was: 'I can't say I'm happy about it. I can't say I like it.'

I agree emphatically with virtually every word uttered by M. Benoist-Méchin about the destruction of the French fleet at Mers-el-Kébir, and of course also its treatment in British ports and at Alexandria, where the courage of Cunningham so narrowly averted a tragedy as great as that of Mers-el-Kébir. I hold that 'one man and one man alone' bears the responsibility, because virtually the whole Cabinet, headed by the late Lord Halifax, if not every man jack, struggled long and painfully to prevent his horrid error. It will perhaps be news to all but a few unusually well-instructed students of this phase of the war that fire was opened after the British Admiral's liaison officer, visiting the French flagship, had read a message from Darlan to the French Admiral which, our naval representative acknowledged, made the dispositions and precautions guaranteed by the Frenchman completely satisfactory.

It may look as though I have given almost as much room to hostile criticism as to friendly, but if one criticizes at all, this is inevitable, because one must support criticism with a few words of detail each time.

I end with the strongest recommendation to read and digest all the praise so amply merited by this work. As the American William L. Langer, here quoted, writes:

PREFACE

Modern history records few events as stupefying as the defeat and collapse of the French Republic in June 1940. Never has a great military power been smashed as quickly and as inexorably since the lightning war of Napoleon against Prussia in 1806. In less than six weeks one of the powers leading the world was literally swept away from the international scene.

We know, of course, that another great power, the Austrian Empire, was defeated severely within roughly the same time in 1866, but it was not swept off the international scene at Königgrätz and remained a great power for over half a century. France has made tremendous efforts to regain that position, but has not succeeded in forty years as well as Austria did when she signed the truce at Prague.

I am confident that English readers will welcome this book. It is at once high drama and good history, a combination rarer than it should be.

CYRIL FALLS

SIXTY DAYS
THAT SHOOK THE WEST

The Fall of France: 1940

I

------◆◆◆◆------

FROM THE OUTBREAK OF WAR TO THE FORMATION OF THE REYNAUD GOVERNMENT

ON September 1st, 1939, at 4.45 a.m., the troops of the Reich invaded Poland. On September 2nd, at the instigation of the Quai d'Orsay, the Italian government suggested convening a four-power conference 'to try and find a peaceful solution to the German-Polish dispute'. But the British government having made it a condition that the Reich should first withdraw its troops from all Polish territories that they already occupied, the suggestion fell through. On September 3rd, at 11 a.m., Great Britain declared herself in a state of war with Germany. Not without diffidence and without consulting Parliament, the French government followed suit at 5 p.m. the same day. The Second World War had begun.

Eighteen days later the Polish army, caught in a state of semi-mobilization, was crushed and the whole country engulfed: in the west by the Wehrmacht, in the east by the Red Army, the two meeting up along a prearranged demarcation line. In less than three weeks Poland had gone under. Thereupon the war's centre of gravity shifted westwards.

What next? The breathtaking incidents that everyone expected somehow failed to materialize. The winter of 1939–40 dragged by uneventfully. Baffled by the inaction at the front that found daily reflection in the monotony of the communiqués, public opinion began to grow restive. Everything about this preventive war, which had been launched too late in the first place, disconcerted the French people — especially the absence of military operations. Not that the thought of fighting was repugnant to them. Their natural impatience was ill suited to the 'cold war', and the memory of their past victories was still alive in their hearts. Besides, it was only a matter of weeks since one of their most eminent military leaders had reassured them with the words:

The French army is stronger than at any other moment in its history; it has top-grade equipment, first-class fortifications, excellent morale

and a remarkable High Command. No one in this country wants
war; but if we are compelled to achieve another victory, achieve it
we shall.

These claims, coming from an illustrious soldier, had bolstered the
nation's courage. But once the echo of them had died away people were
gripped by an indefinable uneasiness. What, they wondered, lay behind
that suspect calm, those silent guns, that clear blue sky untroubled by so
much as the slip-stream of a friendly aircraft? Deprived of firm leadership, perturbed by the growing laxity everywhere about them, they felt
that they were drifting into a situation from which there was no discernible
outcome. In the absence of a solution, public opinion demanded action.
But of what kind? Peace talks? The German Chancellor had suggested
them in his address to the Reichstag on October 6th, 1939, following the
success of his Polish campaign. The King of the Belgians and the Queen of
the Netherlands offered to act as mediators; but other voices declared such
talks unthinkable, since they could serve only to endorse Germany's
victory. Roosevelt sent an envoy to Europe to look into the situation. He
went back to America without completing his round of calls. Since they
could not put an end to it, the French resigned themselves to going on with
the war – this incomprehensible 'phoney war'.

But then came a distraction in the shape of the Russo-Finnish conflict
(November 30th, 1939). People started dreaming of operations other than
those in store for them, of wars other than the one on their doorstep;
that was the last thing they wanted to think about. The young felt drawn
towards a campaign that would couple the pleasures of armed combat with
the delights of winter sports. They got out their skis and pictured themselves banging away in support of a heroic Lotta on the snow-clad
banks of Lake Ladoga, among the sparkling pines and birches ...

Such wonders were not to be. On March 12th Finland, on her last
legs, abruptly put an end to such daydreams by concluding an armistice
with Moscow. The French were brought down to earth with a bump. They
were going to have to fight in the Vosges and along the Rhine, not in
Petsamo or the Karelian plains.

Now France began to question her strength. Was she really equipped to
meet the threat that faced her? Was the High Command ready to stave off
a surprise attack? And the government – what was the government doing?
It gave the impression of floundering and ineffectualness.

Parliamentary circles shared this concern. Meeting in secret session on
March 13th, the Senate displayed for the first time its lack of confidence in

the Daladier government. Dividing, the Upper House accorded it a mere 240 votes. Such hostility was a sign of the times. In the Chamber of Deputies M. Louis Marin tabled a motion on March 19th demanding 'that the war be conducted with increasing vigour' and that the government finally be run 'as a wartime government, determined to exploit the nation's resources methodically and to the full'. The vote of confidence moved by M. Chichery, leader of the Radical-Socialist group, received 239 votes. There were 300 abstentions. On March 21st M. Daladier resigned. At five that afternoon M. Lebrun instructed M. Paul Reynaud to form a new government.

On March 23rd M. Reynaud presented his Cabinet to the Chamber. The new team was greeted 'without warmth, if not with hostility by elements of right, left and centre'. The policy statement was brief. It recorded the new Premier's determination to 'wage war' and wage it with maximum drive and efficiency:

> Everything is at stake in this total war. Winning means saving everything. Succumbing means losing everything ... Parliament, expressing the feelings of the whole country, has fully taken stock of these dreadful facts. So the government that sits before you has no other purpose, and desires no other purpose, than that of rousing, uniting and directing the nation's energies so as to fight and win, and of stamping out treason from whatever source. Thanks to your confidence and with your support we shall accomplish this task.

Though delivered in clarion tones these assurances failed to dispel the Assembly's misgivings. The voting was as follows:

Against ... ... 156 ⎫			...	...	... 267
Abstentions ... ... 111 ⎭					
For 268					

So M. Paul Reynaud had a majority of one.

—•◆••—

2

THE ANGLO-FRENCH AGREEMENT OF
MARCH 28TH, 1940

O N March 27th, four days after his investiture, M. Reynaud went to London for a meeting of the Supreme War Council. With him were General Gamelin and Admiral Darlan. 'It was only wise,' writes General Spears, 'that he should establish contact at the earliest possible moment with his British colleagues and counterbalance by British backing his weakness at home, which was emphasized when, at the last moment, Daladier elected not to accompany him.'

The meeting was in preparation of the Norwegian operation. But it was to be the occasion of a far graver decision.

On March 28th, in fact, the French Premier introduced the idea, readily accepted by the British government, of signing an agreement forbidding either party not merely to conclude a separate peace, but even to embark on negotiations leading towards an armistice, without the consent of her ally. Here is the text of the agreement:

The Government of the French Republic and H.M. Government in the United Kingdom of Great Britain and Northern Ireland mutually undertake that during the present war they will neither negotiate nor conclude an armistice or treaty of peace except by mutual agreement. They undertake not to discuss peace terms before reaching complete agreement on the conditions necessary to ensure to each of them an effective and lasting guarantee of their security. Finally, they undertake to maintain, after the conclusion of peace, a community of action in all spheres for so long as may be necessary to safeguard their security and to effect the reconstruction, with the assistance of other nations, of an international order which will ensure the liberty of peoples, respect for law, and the maintenance of peace in Europe.

Who was the initiator of this agreement — one that was to have incalculable consequences for France? If we are to believe Reynaud, it was his brain-child. Churchill is insistent about it: 'The French government,' he writes, 'had *at their own suggestion* solemnly bound themselves not to make a separate peace.' But, as always, the truth was more complex.

Vacillations in French public opinion had been viewed apprehensively by the British ever since the outbreak of war. In the early days of November, General Spears, in Paris on a special mission for Churchill (then First Lord of the Admiralty), had been struck by how little enthusiasm the war had aroused there. On returning to London he had at once begun to press the idea that France and Britain should undertake not to sign a separate peace. 'It was after all to our advantage to bind the French,' writes Churchill's envoy, 'as they had been uncertain starters and their hearts were certainly not as yet in the war.'

Lord Halifax had told General Spears that he shared his alarm and had discussed it with M. Corbin, the French ambassador. Unfortunately the latter's reaction had been somewhat guarded. Presumably he had promised to refer the matter to Paris.

A month later (December 11th, 1939) Lord Halifax raised the matter again, this time with M. Daladier.

M. Daladier had unburdened himself to General Gamelin: in principle the Premier had no objection to such a declaration, but he would have preferred French and British war aims to be defined and compared beforehand.

A week later (December 19th), during a session of the Supreme War Council attended by M. Reynaud in his capacity as Finance Minister, Mr Neville Chamberlain had asked M. Daladier how things stood with regard to the proposed joint declaration. Such insistence shows clearly which partner was more interested in concluding the agreement. M. Daladier had replied that he was fully prepared to look into the matter, on condition that the text contained a clause 'determining the material guarantees of the security of France' — in other words, specifying Britain's contribution to the common cause. A justifiable precaution — but evidently this was a point on which Great Britain preferred not to make written promises. From that moment the Daladier Cabinet stood condemned in the eyes of the British leaders, who used every means at their disposal to undermine its already tottery authority and get it replaced by a 'sounder' team.

M. Paul Reynaud's appointment as Premier reopened the question.

Did he at least, before appending his signature, consult the military advisers whom he had with him in London? General Gamelin, the French Commander-in-Chief, assures us in his memoirs that he did not:

Away from the conference table, the two governments had decided to publish a joint declaration in which Great Britain and France under-took not to accept a separate peace and jointly to carry the war forward to its victorious conclusion. I do not know whether our war aims had been previously compared, as Premier Daladier had desired. There may have lain his motive, or at least his excuse, for keeping mum. But neither he nor Premier Reynaud confided in me and I did not think it my place to raise the matter with them.

Nor was Admiral Darlan, the French Naval Commander-in-Chief, con-sulted. Post-Captain Auphan, who attended the conference, records:

Of the fourteen pages of notes that I took (in the course of the proceedings) the Joint Declaration occupied only a line and a half. In other words, despite its important bearing on France's foreign policy and the interpretation that was later placed on it, it passed almost unnoticed. None of the officers round me had the impression that the fate of our country, as has since been claimed, had been sealed for evermore by a solemn and considered contract.

Churchill, on his side, confirms Auphan's impression: '*Finally, as an obvious point on which all were at one*, the communiqué stated that the British and French governments had agreed on the following solemn declaration ... '

It may be objected that the agreement of March 28th was a political act, a governmental decision not subject to the approval of military leaders. But what about the Cabinet? What about Parliament? Did M. Paul Reynaud make it his business to sound them, at least, for their opinions?

Again the answer is no. The agreement was never discussed by the Cabinet. Ministers were faced with a *fait accompli*. At no time was it submitted for parliamentary apdroval or even officially communicated to senators and deputies.

The agreement may have been valid from a strictly legal standpoint. But there are conventions termed 'leonine' that even justice refuses to recognize, for the simple reason that they are incompatible with equity. The agreement of March 28th would have been equitable only had it been actuated by the principle of reciprocity and had the obligations that it imposed been equal on both sides. Was that the case?

Far from it. The difference in the geographical positions of the two countries (one exposed on all frontiers, the other protected by the fact of being an island) in itself forbade any comparison between the risks they ran. To be above criticism the agreement of March 28th would have needed to specify:

1. That Britain and France were pursuing identical and clearly defined war aims.
2. That they agreed to abide by a common strategy.
3. That they formally undertook to shoulder the burdens of war evenly and *make equal contributions to its conduct*.

None of these conditions prevailed at the time of the pact's signature. To suppose that M. Reynaud was unaware of the fact would be to insult his intelligence. He had attended the Supreme War Council meeting of December 19th, 1939, and was therefore fully cognizant of the objections raised by M. Daladier. Besides, any lingering doubts that we might have are swept away by the testimony of M. Paul Baudouin who, under the date March 28th, 1940, writes in his memoirs:

I had learned (through a close associate of Paul Reynaud's) of the signing in London that morning of a mutual undertaking by France and Britain not to negotiate or conclude a separate armistice or peace treaty. I was surprised, for I had only recently had the opportunity of discussing this matter with Paul Reynaud who had agreed with me, when I had put it to him, that in my opinion such an undertaking could only be arrived at after a complete agreement as to the terms and conditions for peace and also — the last but not the least[1] — as to the sacrifices that each country would accept in order to win the war.

What, then, was at the back of the French Premier's mind (the British position is clear enough)? Did he mean to bind Britain to France so as to prevent her from negotiating separately with the Reich? It must not be forgotten that at this date Reynaud was dealing, not with Churchill, but with Chamberlain, whose name was synonymous with Munich and appeasement. But another explanation presents itself. Take another look at General Gamelin's words:

... the two governments had decided to publish a joint declaration in which Great Britain and France undertook not to *accept* a separate peace ...

The phrasing indicates the state of mind in which the Declaration was

[1] This phrase appears in English in Baudouin's text.

conceived. The date was March 28th. The war had been on since September but there had been no decisive clash between armies.

At that time Reynaud and Gamelin were obviously convinced that the pact would apply to a 'request' for a separate peace by a defeated Germany. It was this request that Britain and France undertook to 'accept' only by mutual agreement.

THE TOTAL LACK OF BRITISH PREPAREDNESS

I F Britain was perturbed by France's half-heartedness, the French would have been thoroughly alarmed had they known the truth about Britain's war strength. Strictly speaking, it was non-existent. True, her navy was one of the three largest in the world and her fine air force was equipped, albeit inadequately, with excellent machines. But she had no land forces whatever, apart from a small professional army scattered about her Empire. True to her traditions Great Britain had never been willing to introduce conscription at home; thus if she wished to levy divisions she would have neither barracks to house them in, nor equipment to arm them with, nor sufficient trained personnel to instruct them.

Ever since Germany's reoccupation of the Rhineland in 1936 the French High Command had been eager to ascertain the size of Britain's contribution should there be a war. Britain's leaders had constantly evaded the question. They had never agreed to the principle of a joint strategy, nor to the notion of their High Command's forfeiting the right to take independent decisions. They had jibbed at any suggestion that they should alter their view.

In any case, how could Britain's forces be made subordinate to the French High Command when none existed? On September 10th, 1938, at the time of the Sudeten crisis, M. Georges Bonnet asked the British government what forces it could place at France's disposal if there were a war over Czechoslovakia.

The question was put several times without eliciting any response. Finally, the British Cabinet announced that for the first six months of the war all that it could send was a hundred and fifty aircraft and two un-motorized divisions. It can only have been led to advance these laughable figures by the fact that it genuinely had nothing further to offer.

Why, then, had Britain embarked on the risky policy of lavishing pacts and guarantees of independence on the threatened countries of Eastern Europe, knowing full well that she had not the strength to enforce them?

Because she had counted on France to enforce them on her behalf. She had trusted entirely to the French army, treating it as her secular arm.

Some clear-sighted Britons had seen the defects in this reasoning. They had pointed out that in the 1914–18 war France had withstood the German onslaught only with British (and American) support; this time her position would be infinitely more dangerous. For one thing, the force that Britain could afford to send would be much smaller. For another, France would have to face the combined strength of Germany and Italy (population: 125,000,000) and keep careful watch on the Pyrenees – all this without the certain support of her African troops.

There had been the risk that if Britain continued to stand idle France might tire of the policeman's role so generously allotted to her. In order to prevent this, Britain had at last made up her mind to promulgate compulsory military service. The law had been passed on April 27th, 1939 – a mere five months before the outbreak of war. Even then the House of Commons had been reluctant. It had adopted conscription, not so much to increase Britain's military potential as to reassure France and impress the outside world. The law had been applied with extreme slowness. The men had been unconscripted, undrilled, untrained.

Despite the reiterated appeals of the French High Command the War Office remained as casual as ever. A single class of 200,000 men had registered in June 1939. They were to be called up in waves. The first wave, conscripted on July 15th, amounted to only 34,000. And that was a mere six weeks before the outbreak of war!

Did the announcement of hostilities at least have the effect of rousing Britain to action and urging the War Office to make up for lost time? One would like to be able to say so, but it did not. In France one man in eight was called up. In Britain the proportion was one in forty-eight. Her initial aid was very slight: first two, then four, divisions, and 240 planes. No tanks. Even the respite afforded by the 'phoney war' was not turned to account. Between September 1939 and May 1940 she managed to equip only six new divisions, as against forty raised by the Reich in the same period.

On January 16th, 1940, Churchill wrote to the First Sea Lord, Sir Dudley Pound:

Our army is puny as far as the fighting front is concerned; our air force is hopelessly inferior to the Germans ... We maintain an attitude of complete passivity, dispersing our forces ever more widely ... Do you realize that perhaps we are heading for *defeat?*

26

Doubtless the reason for all this lay in the fact that Britain is first and foremost a maritime power and that such powers have always had an idiosyncratic conception of war. As Michel Dacier writes:

> Thucydides has summarized the principles that activate them in the speech that he ascribes to Pericles in the first book of his *History of the Peloponnesian War*. To them time and space are of little consequence. This is due to the wide distribution of their sources of supply, which their enemies can never exhaust. They are adept at striking from a distance. The thraldom of fighting on land does not appeal to them.

Britain under George VI was no exception to this rule. She still ruled the waves and her Home Fleet gave her a sense of security. She placed more reliance upon the effectiveness of blockading and her ability to draw on massive reserves of raw materials all over the world than upon the number of her battalions. Convinced that time was on her side, she was calmly organizing herself behind the French shield.

But that shield was to prove flimsier than she had imagined. At the crucial moment British troops and planes were to be — though not non-existent — far too sparse to avert defeat. And France would have to perform alone the harsh and bloody task of the land fighting.

4

THE TRAGEDY OF FRENCH UNPREPAREDNESS

IN France, civil and military authorities were beset at every level by an unbelievable degree of confusion and unawareness. There were orders and counter-orders, plans and counter-plans, costly schemes set in motion one day only to be scrapped the next — in short, so much overlapping and rescission that the nation's war machine was merely ticking over. Later M. Reynaud could write without exaggeration:

France was no better organized for the preparation and waging of war than she was allied, fortified or armed. We did not think in terms of war. It was because we did not think in terms of it that we had neither allied ourselves, nor fortified ourselves, nor armed ourselves.

How could such a state of affairs have arisen? Had France not realized the dangers confronting her? Had no one spoken out in time? Indeed yes. Paul Reynaud for one — and he was not alone — had delivered warning after warning. In 1936 he had said:

Taken as a whole, our industrial output is 15 per cent lower than in 1928, despite the slight recovery made in the first five months of the year. But we must take a closer look at the figures, for what difference does it make to the supply of munitions that paper production has risen by 78 per cent and the output of 'sundry industries' by 16 per cent? War is not waged with paper streamers or fancy goods. Metal production has dropped by 31 per cent. France is turning out only 40 per cent of the cast iron and a third of the steel produced by Germany.

In 1937 he had said:

Our monthly output of aircraft has fallen from 65 to 35, while our neighbours' figures (Germany 350, Italy 200) have soared. Are our leaders able to sleep at night? What sweeping measures have they adopted? By when do they propose to implement them?

In 1938 he had said:

> Just think! Since the armistice [of 1918] we have spent 372,000,000,000 francs — more than any other country. Yet today we find ourselves lagging behind in every field where there is genuine military rivalry: planes, A.A., tanks. Why? Because we have rashly pursued a policy of pure defence and of maintaining out-of-date equipment.

On December 13th, 1939, two and a half months after the beginning of hostilities, he had said: 'We may easily, very easily, lose the war.'

'Only after war was declared did I begin to speak optimistically,' he writes in his memoirs. Is one to infer that by early 1940 the situation was transformed and gave no cause for anxiety?

No. For a few lines later one is amazed to learn from Paul Reynaud himself that at the time he took over from M. Daladier (March 23rd, 1940) the position was more catastrophic than ever.

Judge from his words:

No Ministry of National Defence

In reality the Ministry of National Defence was a label on an empty bottle ... Daladier was a Minister of National Defence without a Ministry and he coupled the duties of the office with those of War Minister.

No General Staff

We lacked an essential organization of which it may be said that, had it functioned at the right time and been normally constituted, it would have ruled out a military policy as incoherent as ours ... Gamelin was a Chief of Staff of National Defence without a Staff and without powers. In peacetime he had unwillingly coupled his duties as such with those of Commander-in-Chief elect of one of the three armies under him.

No organized High Command

The co-existence of two Commanders-in-Chief, one of whom exercised the real powers while the other was responsible for carrying out the operations defined by the first, sowed misunderstanding and confusion.

No industrial call-up scheme

The industrialization of the army meant that skilled men were needed in the fighting units, so the factories' needs took second place. And the call-up emptied the workshops of France of a large percentage of their charge-hands and trained operators, at the very time when their man-power should have been considerably increased to produce the quantities of arms and ammunition planned for ... In the Renault works man-power fell from 30,000 to 8,000. In a large state-owned factory — the Roanne works, which after three months' delay in starting was required to turn out a third of the 75-mm. shells budgeted for in the production plan — the peacetime skeleton staff was halved by the call-up, whereas it should have been increased twentyfold ... In his report dated March 1st, 1940, discussing the effect of industrial mobilization on aircraft production, the Senator for La Grange was to write: 'The industrial reserve had been neither organized nor equipped ... '

No Air Ministry worthy of the name

In a country threatened with invasion as France was, where all imaginable forces should combine to halt the invader, the creation of an Air Ministry seems to have been a national disaster ... General Vuillemin was hardly guilty of over-confidence, for in a personal and confidential letter to Guy La Chambre on January 15th, 1938, the day on which the latter took over the Ministry, he made the following assessment of the first ten years of its existence: 'The situation is extremely grave. We do not know what the future has in store for us, but I am quite convinced that if war broke out this year France's air power would be crushed within days.' It was an admission of bankruptcy. He was saying much the same thing eight months later, after Munich. On August 26th, 1939 ... he expressed a view that was almost as optimistic as his Minister's: 'Within six months Franco-British air power must succeed in providing a reasonably successful counterbalance to the German and Italian air forces.' Now, eight months — not six — elapsed before the German offensive of May 10th, 1940, and we had only the German air force to reckon with. Yet all who fought at the time aver that the Armée de l'Air was totally inadequate.

No planes in the factories

A few days after we entered the war I was visited one evening by an important aircraft manufacturer who greeted me with tears in his eyes and the words: 'My factory is at a standstill ... ' It occurred to me that events might have got the better of him and I answered: 'Let's go and look.' I saw vast deserted floors where there were barely half a dozen men at work. Next day I called on Daladier and told him: 'That's what I saw last night. Get into your car and go and see for yourself. We're going to lose the war.'

No planes in the sky

So in May 1940 we had only 54 dive-bombers ... As for fighters, our infantrymen and gunners spent their time scanning the skies for them ... Without air reconnaissance our artillery was blind. It did not fire on the Panzer division sweeping along the road through the dense Ardennes forest! Nor were the Panzers attacked by a single bomber or fighter-bomber. How much easier the invasion of France was made!

No anti-aircraft guns

Not till January 1938 was a programme drawn up to provide anti-aircraft cover for the army and the country as a whole. It was high time! Yet owing to production difficulties, manufacture was not really started till 1939. And that was the year the war came. Thus the 90-mm. A.A. guns did not start leaving the factories till two months after the outbreak of hostilities. And that is not all: to manufacture the 25-mm. anti-aircraft gun we had considerably retarded the manufacture of the 25-mm. anti-tank gun.

No anti-tank mines

The most rudimentary, the simplest, the cheapest defensive weapon is the anti-tank mine. Threatened with invasion by the German armoured corps, how badly France needed them! Yet before the war the Directorate of Engineering at the War Ministry had demonstrated its inability to produce any. Such mines were not to appear in any number till May 1940. But in the meantime France was to be overrun by the *Panzerdivisionen* ...

No prototypes, even, in the case of certain weapons

Certain items of equipment, the urgent need for which was obvious, had not even reached the prototype stage when we went to war: e.g. the carriage for the 90-mm. A.A. gun; 210- and 280-mm. delayed-action shells; the machine-pistol; anti-tank mines.

It would be hard to compile a more damning indictment. But that was not all. For nearly ten years France had been spending thousands of millions of francs on her fortifications. All along the Rhine she had erected the powerful bulwark of the Maginot Line, considering it strong enough to discourage any German attempt at invasion. Yet to the north and south of this barrier, between Longwy and the sea and east of the Belfort Gap, there was nothing to impede the enemy's advance — lacunae that passed unnoticed till it was too late.

What made this weakness especially serious was that the building of the Maginot Line, which over the years had become almost a national myth, had deterred France's military leaders from forging the instrument that was to play a decisive role throughout the Second World War: the armoured division.

* * *

What had been France's doctrine with regard to tanks? General Estienne, Fuller, Liddell Hart and Martel had shown the incomparable advantages of this new weapon. By restoring mobility to the battlefield it revived the very essence of the art of war: fluidity, surprise and that bold manoeuvring that allows a break-through to be profitably exploited.

But the lesson was no sooner learned than forgotten. Conservatism or lazy-mindedness had led the General Staff back to the theory of the straight, rigid, unbroken front.

One man had stood out against these old-fashioned notions and tried to rouse the authorities from their torpor: Colonel de Gaulle. He wrote:

As regards National Defence, the chopping and changing of government and the rivalry between the political parties denied those responsible that coherent sequence of uninterrupted planning, decisions fully thrashed-out and measures properly carried through that goes by the name of a policy. That was why the military leadership, which received only spasmodic and contradictory promptings from the State, became so hidebound. The army clung to conceptions that had been in force at the end of the last war.

Thus the notion of the fixed, continuous front dominated the strategy visualized for a future action. Organization, theory, training and armament all sprang directly from this notion. It was understood that in the event of war France would mobilize the bulk of her reserves and man as many divisions as possible — divisions formed with the aim, not of manoeuvring, attacking and exploiting, but of 'holding on to sectors' along our frontiers ... Thus a barrier would be maintained by a nation at arms, the supposition being that she would rest secure behind it till the blockade had drained the enemy's resources and the pressure of the free world had brought about his collapse.

A conception of war such as this suited the mood of the regime. The latter, reduced to stagnation by political wrangling and the weakness of its powers, could not fail to espouse a system that was static to quite this degree ... Everything conspired to make passivity the dominating principle of our National Defence.

In the spring of 1934 de Gaulle published his book *Vers l'armée de métier* ('Towards a Professional Army'). He argued that France could not rely on the defensive powers of insecure formations to bear the brunt of an attack; she needed a tactical force that could be deployed in its entirety at a moment's notice and was characterized by speed, a large measure of independence and maximum penetration; she needed motorization.

To reap full advantage from its expensive and intricate equipment, this shock force would have to be professionally staffed by some 100,000 volunteers serving six-year engagements. Moulded by their long service with crack units, these would later provide leaders for the nation's conscripts and reserves.

Having set forth these principles, Colonel de Gaulle realistically portrayed the staggering effect of this 'strategic battering ram'. He showed how, with the aid of motorization, the forces for an attack could be mustered overnight. He depicted attacks in which three thousand tanks would be launched in echeloned groups; as they advanced, motorized infantry units would move in behind them; it would be possible to make a thirty-mile thrust in the course of a single day's fighting. He enthused over the tremendous opportunities open to the Command once the enemy's defences had been breached:

Often, after achieving success, we shall hurriedly cull its rewards and thrust onwards to where the victor's trophies lie. We shall see capitalization become a fact where it was no more than a dream ... Then we shall be on the road to such great victories as by their profound repercussions provoke a general commotion among the enemy, just as the snapping of a pillar will sometimes bring a cathedral crashing down ... We shall see troops drive fast and deep behind enemy lines, catching him on the raw and ruffling his defences ... Thus that strategic furthering of tactical results will be restored which once constituted the ultimate aim and, so to speak, nobility of the art.

These views differed strongly from those current in France. How were they received? Some politicians – Paul Reynaud, Philippe Serre, Marcel Déat, Léo Lagrange among others – had been quick to see their advantages; they made a point of spreading them among their colleagues and even gaining support for them in Parliament. But the military reaction, on the whole, was one of undisguised hostility. General Debeney, the man behind the 1927 legislation, condemned the scheme outright in the *Revue des Deux Mondes*. In his preface to a book by General Chauvineau (who was to acquire undeserved notoriety on this account) Marshal Pétain claimed that tanks and aircraft did not appreciably alter the basic facts of war, and that the main ingredient of French security was still the continuous front backed by fortifications.

For his part, Léon Blum spoke out strongly against the recruitment of a professional body 'whose mentality, composition and armament would automatically endanger the Republic'. A professional army, in his view, would quickly become subversive. The War Minister, General Maurin, proclaimed before the Assembly: 'After working so hard to construct a fortified barrier, do people really think us mad enough to venture wildly beyond it?'

All the same, General Gamelin was given authority by Daladier in June 1936 to form a dozen battalions of thirty-ton 'B' tanks. But the ordnance branch was distressingly slow to respond. When war broke out three years and three months later there were precisely three battalions in service with the special group at Nancy and one other in preparation.

On December 3rd, 1938, the Army Council finally made up its mind to create two armoured divisions. Was the French armoured corps at last to become fact? That would have been too much to hope. On pretext of saving time, the authorities started wasting it. Instead of going ahead General Gamelin decided to confine himself to setting up the experimental group at Nancy. When he and his colleagues ultimately bowed to the need for establishing the new units, heavy armour was unavailable and remained so till after the industrial call-up and the formation of a Ministry of Munitions.[1] Result: the 1st and 2nd Armoured Divisions were not formed till January 15th, 1940, and had only 120 and 169 tanks respectively (as against the 500 advocated by de Gaulle[2]). Later there was to be a good deal of quibbling over figures; standards and statistics were feverishly compared; there was endless discussion as to whether the Wehrmacht had had more or fewer tanks than the French and whether their armour-plating had been thinner or thicker. None of this can obscure the bald and brutal fact that at dawn on May 10th, owing to her failure to group her tanks properly, France could offer no solid resistance to the onslaught of the German armoured divisions. Such tanks as she possessed were scattered among five different kinds of unit:

a. *Infantry tanks:*
1. Autonomous general reserve battalions, shared between the armies under army tank commanders or in strategic reserve under the commander of general tank reserves;
2. Armoured divisions (the first two formed on January 15th, 1940, and effective as from April 15th; the 3rd formed on March 15th and in theory effective as from June 15th; the 4th improvised by order of May 14th).

b. *Cavalry tanks:*
1. Light cavalry divisions, large composite units consisting of one horse brigade and one motorized brigade (five on May 10th);
2. Reconnaissance groups attached to motorized infantry divisions;
3. Light mechanized divisions (three on May 10th).
This wide dispersal could only lead to terrible weakness.

* * *

In 1918 the French had won the war only because the gap in strength between the Anglo-French forces and the German forces had been filled by the United States army. Twenty years later this gap was even more pronounced, as Paul Reynaud wrote:

Against the hundred and ninety German divisions manned by April 1940, we should be able to pit only a hundred French and ten British,

[1] In other words, after the outbreak of war.
[2] Clearly too many, entailing tremendous expense and unwieldiness; even Guderian considered 350 the absolute maximum.

and things were to go from bad to worse.[1] The French had practically reached their maximum potential; the British were to form only about ten new divisions in the course of the year, whereas the Germans soon exceeded the figure of 248 divisions, which had been their maximum in the previous war. Thus if we could not hope for the support of a third army, as in 1918, it was idle for us to expect to win the war by military means. And was not this third army still far below the horizon?

And the ex-Premier concluded: 'Having failed to shape the army of our policy, we had shaped the policy of our army.' What interpretation are we to place upon these words?

Unless it is just an empty phrase 'shaping the policy of our army' can mean only one thing in relation to those early months of 1940: namely that two courses — and *only* two courses — were open to France:

1. To withdraw from a conflict that had caught her on the hop and re-examine the possibility of coming to terms with the Reich;
2. To remain at war but play for time, using each day of respite to make good her deficiencies and refraining from any action liable to precipitate events.

'A comparison of the forces soon to confront each other,' writes General Gauché, 'certainly did not encourage bold planning. So the French High Command pinned its faith entirely on the solidity of a front that would enable it both to await the help that it anticipated from abroad and to make a belated start to its war production.'

Those were the views of the General Staff about a month before the outbreak of war. The preference for a waiting game was not merely dictated by the static, defensive character imposed on the French army by the laws of 1927 and 1928; it derived equally from a strategic outlook rigidly blinkered by a threefold impossibility: the acknowledged impossibility of crossing the Rhine; the impossibility, likewise acknowledged, of piercing the Siegfried Line; and the moral impossibility of violating Belgian neutrality.

The French 'war plan' — if one can apply the word 'plan' to the slow, gradual alignment of forces along a prepared front — amounted, as Roton put it, to 'a mere collection of defensive reflexes invariably crystallizing and coming to rest on or about the Maginot Line'.

So the General Staff pinned a good deal of hope on the talks that General

[1] The exact figures, on May 10th, 1940, were 131 German, 107 French and 10 British divisions.

Doumenc was having with the Red Army leaders in Moscow, for Germany was far more vulnerable from the east than from the west. The expectation was that the Soviet divisions would come to the aid of the Polish army and thrust forward in the direction of the Oder, across the plains of East Prussia and Posnania. This was another notion borrowed from the 1914 war.

But Stalin was not Nicholas II, nor was Voroshilov Rennenkampf. When the Soviet government signed a non-aggression pact with the Reich, these plans for an eastern offensive went up in smoke. France's military leaders had no option but to devise some other plan. But *what* other plan?

On August 23rd an emergency council of war, prompted by this Russo-German collusion, brought Premier Daladier and M. Georges Bonnet, Minister for Foreign Affairs, face to face with the most eminent military minds of the day.

The minutes of this meeting make painful reading.

The Commander-in-Chief began with the assurance that the army was prepared. But this assertion, dictated by the need to put a bold face on things, was immediately undermined by the statement that 'in the early days of a conflict the army and navy will not be able to do much against Germany'. To sweeten the pill he implied that it would be possible to 'act vigorously' against Italy were that power to enter the war; but he at once added that it would be as well to obtain her absolute neutrality so that France's links with North Africa should not be jeopardized.

Strategically the document contains no allusion to the possibility of offensive action, the guiding principle being to 'gain time'.

The minutes then pay tribute to the efforts made by the air force. But this was merely another euphemism, for they at once go on to emphasize France's weakness in respect of bomber-planes ('which will not be mass-produced till 1940'), anti-aircraft guns ('sacrificed in favour of fighter-planes'[?] and internal air defence ('a source of grave concern').

On September 1st, 1939, fighting broke out. The Wehrmacht had overrun Poland's frontiers. That day the Commander-in-Chief, Land Forces, told Colonel Gauché: 'France is caught in the political mesh; she has her back to the wall and cannot retreat another inch.'

Then, leading the Colonel to a giant wall-map, he laid his right hand on East Prussia and his left on Silesia. With a brisk pincer-like movement he brought them together on the area round Warsaw, and said: 'After that, we shall have the full weight of Germany to contend with; we shall have to hold out alone while the others prepare and move in.'

What an admission of helplessness! Obviously the General Staff had only a strictly defensive plan. And in view of the situation confronting it and the scale of forces at its disposal, it could not conceivably have had any other. Seeing that there was no Polish army left, that United States forces were still 'below the horizon', that Britain would not be ready till 1942, that France's planes and 'B' tanks would not be mass-produced till May 1940, that her industrial call-up was only in its infant stages and that her northern defences were still under construction, the General Staff could hardly be blamed for treading warily.

But if devising a plan of campaign was the High Command's responsibility, it was for the government to safeguard the conduct of the war. Rather late in the day it took stock of the fact that, were the Wehrmacht to invade Belgium and Holland, France would be obliged to lend support to the twenty-two Belgian and ten Dutch divisions that would then be allied, by force of circumstance, to the Anglo-French cause. To provide this support her troops, pivoting upon Givet and Namur, would have to abandon the network of light defences erected along her northern frontier and strike out into the Dutch-Belgian plain. How far were they to advance, and in what circumstances? This was what the General Staff had to determine. There were three possibilities:

a. *The Albert Canal plan:* This consisted of moving French forces as far east as possible along the Albert Canal and the line of fortifications protecting it. This was the solution preferred by the Belgian government, for it would have covered almost the entire area of Belgium.

b. *The Escaut plan:* More cautious, this consisted of moving up the Escaut and forming a kind of shield covering Audenarde, Gand and Anvers. It offered the advantage of avoiding the frontal operation feared by our General Staff and of giving the French units more time to settle in before having to withstand the onslaught of the enemy's forces. On the other hand it aroused no enthusiasm in the Belgians, for it would have protected only a very small part of the country and presupposed the surrender of Brussels. Added to which, it would not have allowed the French forces to link up with the Dutch.

c. *The Dyle plan:* This was a compromise solution. It lay in advancing as far as the river of that name, so as to establish a defensive front along the line Namur–Anvers, covering Brussels. It would

also enable units to strike out towards Breda, on the extreme left
of the line, to reinforce the Dutch.

The General Staff rejected the Albert Canal plan out of hand, as being
too risky. Consulted as to the respective advantages and drawbacks of the
Escaut and Dyle plans, General Gamelin came down on the side of the
latter. General Billotte, the commander of the 1st Group of Armies, was
instructed to make final plans for the operation.

On hearing of this, General Georges protested. 'This is happy-go-lucky,'
he wrote in the margin of the Billotte scheme. 'If the enemy masks Belgium, he can manoeuvre elsewhere. So do not let us pour our resources
into this business. Let us stop dreaming.' Despite this cry of alarm the
Dyle plan was adopted by the British and French governments.

In pursuance of this decision Giraud's 7th Army, which had till then
been held in reserve in the Rheims area and whose considerable manoeuvring power would have been capable of intervening in all directions, was
transferred to the extreme left of the line. It would be the 7th's task, in fact,
to thrust towards Breda and link up with the Dutch — a step that was to
have far-reaching consequences! For from then on General Gamelin had
no manoeuvring power at his disposal.

Once the plan was adopted, the members of the General Staff —
stimulated by Daladier, who readily accused them of being unimaginative
— turned their minds to the following problem: how were they to bring
about the collapse of Germany without exposing themselves to attack by
the Wehrmacht? A ticklish question? Not at all! The solution was simple:
by subjecting her to a stranglehold — in other words, by depriving her of
essential raw materials: Scandinavian iron ore, Russian and Roumanian
oil. A whole series of eccentric operations was dreamed up: the mining
of the Norwegian Leads, if necessary accompanied by the occupation of
Norway itself; a landing at Salonika and the occupation of Greece;
putting the Roumanian oil-fields out of action; mining the Danube;
mining the Black Sea; a thrust into Transcaucasia, with the backing of the
Turks; the bombing of Batum and Baku, supported if necessary by inter-
ventions in Iran and Afghanistan.

This string of impracticable plans takes one's breath away. How could
the General Staff fail to see that these operations could only result in a
fatal dispersal of forces that were already inadequate? How could it fail
to realize that an act of aggression against Russia would instantly trans-
form the Russo-German pact into a military alliance and saddle us with the
whole weight of the Red Army as well as of the Wehrmacht?

But once the General Staff started thinking along these lines, there was no stopping it. It now reasoned that the Reich must be goaded into action and induced to switch from defence to attack at the earliest possible moment, preferably on the Western Front. It was during this period that General Gamelin told General Visconti-Prasca, the Italian military attaché in Paris, that he would willingly give the Germans a billion francs if they would do him the favour of attacking without delay.

'Plainly,' Reynaud was to declare later, 'our High Command was eager to join issue in the role that it considered advantageous: the role of the attacked.'

One would prefer not to believe this. Yet official documents make the truth of Reynaud's assertion only too plain.

On March 16th, 1940, General Gamelin sent a memorandum to M. Daladier summarizing the new arguments of the General Staff. It was a question, he explained, of forcing the Wehrmacht to fight. It must be impelled to go over to the offensive on the Western Front and at the same time open up other theatres of war. This was how it could be done:

1. In the west the blockade must be tightened so that the enemy should have nothing further to gain from handling Belgium and Holland with kid gloves. The object was to 'prompt Germany to precipitate matters and invade the Netherlands and Belgium, which would be of no great use to her economically.'
2. In Scandinavia, supplies of Swedish iron ore must be denied to Germany. 'Faced with such a situation, Germany might decide to react by making an armed intervention in Sweden.'
3. The bombing of the oil-fields at Baku and Batum would in all probability hamper German fuel supplies to a considerable extent ...
4. It would be as well to begin mining operations by air and water-way as soon as possible.

Conclusion: By combining blockading measures with certain military operations the Allies could not merely tighten their economic grip *but induce Germany to stop playing a waiting game.*

Daladier was wisely hesitant about adopting this course. He would have preferred to wait a while. But a few days later (March 22nd) he was toppled from power, and his successor, Reynaud, proved a whole-hearted supporter of the General Staff's projects. On March 27th the new Premier went to London to lay plans with the British for the Norwegian expedition. Twelve days later (April 8th) the operation was launched.

On April 10th Reynaud informed the Senate that action in Scandinavia had begun. 'The iron ore supply route is, and will remain, cut,' he assured its members:

> Our action began at 5 a.m. last Monday. It consisted of sealing off the channel to Norwegian territorial waters with minefields ... We first gave notice of our intentions, then we acted. For this act of war directed against Germany by the Allies the government assumes full responsibility.

Was this the language of a man determined not to precipitate events, so that France should have time to complete her preparations? Definitely not. But let us continue the tale.

Stung by Britain's slowness in undertaking the Norwegian operation (she never does things in a hurry), France called a meeting of the Supreme War Council to put some life into her hesitant partner. It was held in Paris on April 12th. The minutes read:

> General Gamelin stressed how much was to be gained by putting an end to Germany's waiting game and outlined a plan to this effect.
> M. Reynaud in turn insisted ... on the need for striking quickly and firmly. He asked whether it would not be possible to speed things up by adopting the plan mentioned by General Gamelin ...

But the Germans reacted at lightning speed. It very soon became clear that the Norwegian operation would meet with failure. Except at Narvik, where French Chasseurs finally entrenched themselves solidly, the Allies were up against superior air strength from the word go. The High Command promptly turned their minds from the campaign. It was not in Andalsnes and Namsos that the fate of the war would be decided, but along the Franco–Belgian–Dutch front stretching from Basle to the mouth of the Rhine: that was where the decisive clash must be speedily provoked. And rather than wait for an enemy attack it would be better to breach the German lines without delay. In short, the French army, designed for positional warfare, was electing to engage in a mobile war ...

This time Gamelin and Georges came out in favour of the operation. Poor fools! Entirely ignorant of Nazi invasion plans, they did not know that this was just what the enemy was waiting for!

The reason that led Reynaud to adopt a 'resolutely offensive' attitude, in public as well as in the privacy of the Cabinet room, was deeply rooted. It derived from his natural impatience, and also from the fact that he was no longer free to pick and choose. He had set himself up as a forceful, determined figure and he was already a victim of his own legend. He had condemned Daladier's procrastinating policy far too roundly not to embark on the opposite course. To live up to his reputation as a man whom nothing could stop and for whom no responsibility was too great he had no choice but to speed things up and turn the cold war, forthwith, into a hot one. It was essential that his assumption of power should coincide with the ending of the stagnation that had characterized his predecessor's period of office. The 'phoney war' was over and done with! He had bestridden France as though she were a stubborn mare, confident of his power to prevent her from shying at the fence: he would ride her into battle whatever the consequences. Perhaps he experienced a secret tremor of apprehension when the moment came for him to put his arguments into practice. Who can say otherwise? Events are easier to fathom than human hearts. But if he felt any trepidation he showed no sign of it; in any case, it was now too late to turn back. To stay in the saddle and hold on to the power invested in him by a flimsy majority, he would not hesitate to stake the whole life of the nation on a single throw of the dice ...

'Democracy,' General Spears has written, 'is a splendid conception, but has the disadvantage on occasions of placing in the lead men who will ... encompass the defeat of a great nation in the space of a few days.'

5

------◆◆◆◆------

THE THOROUGHNESS OF GERMAN
PREPARATIONS

TURNING our attention to the other side of the Rhine, what do we
find? A nation straining at the leash, convoys of motorized troops
tearing along the autobahns, and an industry whose factories were
working round the clock to create the most powerful war machine that
Germany had ever possessed. But none of this had been achieved overnight.

When Hitler came to power in January 1933 he found a Reichswehr
that was already half evolved. This army of 100,000 professional soldiers,
which von Seeckt allegedly turned into 'an army of 100,000 captains',
was gradually breaking free of the limitations ostensibly imposed by the
Treaty of Versailles. Debarred from increasing its numbers, it had
surrounded itself with a host of para-military organizations that kept the
fighting spirit alive in the youth of Germany. Above all, it had striven
to compensate for its numerical weakness by an intensive study of new
techniques. This had led to the winter manoeuvres of 1923–4, organized
by Lieutenant-Colonel von Brauchitsch, the future Commander-in-
Chief, 'with a view to studying the possibilities provided by the use of
motorized troops in conjunction with planes'. Following these exercises a
young cavalry officer, Captain Heinz Guderian, was appointed lecturer
in tactics and military history at the Reichswehr ministry. His maturity of
outlook and competence in the sphere of motorization had made a
great impression on his superiors.

At that time Guderian had already studied the work of Liddell Hart,
Fuller and Martel, and in particular the book on armoured warfare by the
Austrian General Eimansberger. In his memoirs he writes:

> These perspicacious soldiers were already trying to turn tanks into
> something other than a weapon to be used in support of infantry.
> They viewed them in terms of the increasing motorization of our
> times and thus became pioneers of a new strategy.

From them I learned concentration of armour, as employed by the British in the battle of Cambrai (1917). Moreover, it was Liddell Hart who advocated the use of armoured units for long-distance raids and operations directed against the enemy's communications; it was likewise he who suggested a type of armoured division that would combine tanks with motorized infantry units. These ideas made a deep impression on me and I tried to adapt them to the potentialities of our own army.

From then on Guderian unceasingly urged the use of tanks in any future war, insisting that they would play a similar role to that of Murat's cavalry in the campaign of 1806.

Field-exercises were held during the summer of 1929, but they were unmanned. One of them, organized by Guderian, was based on the use of an armoured division that so far existed only in his imagination. This 'phantom division' came through with flying colours. From then on Guderian was sure that he was on the right lines, even though General Otto von Stulpnagel had forbidden the use, even in theory, of tank combinations numerically superior to a regiment. 'Armoured divisions,' he declared, 'are a dangerous utopia.'

Yet on February 1st, 1931, Major Guderian was appointed commander of a motorized battalion garrisoned at Berlin-Lankwitz. It was nothing to shout about: one reconnaissance company, one motor-cycle company, one anti-tank company and one company of medium tanks. The vehicles were obsolete; the anti-tank guns were made of wood; the tanks were mere mock-ups, with plywood 'armour plating'. Only the motor-cycle company was fully equipped. But what did it matter! It was from this 'first motorized fighting unit that the whole weight of German armour was to emerge, like a mastodon from its embryo'.

Guderian and the other officers in his unit were immediately convinced that tanks were a decisive operational weapon. To achieve maximum results with them it was necessary to group them in divisions and eventually in army corps. But bringing this home to the bigwigs of the Army Staff: there lay the difficulty.

These, like their French counterparts, were filled with an instinctive distrust of the new weapon. Guderian shared de Gaulle's experience of meeting with indifference, scepticism and even hostility from the generals of the old school. Red tape and lazy-mindedness know no frontiers, and it is curious to note the close similarity of the objections put foward to tanks on either side of the Rhine.

44

Although it was the logical outcome of events, the armoured division was accused of having logic and history against it. 'You are too impetuous.' Guderian was told by General Otto von Stulpnagel. 'Neither of us will live to see German tanks in action.' General von Fritsch went one better. 'The armoured corps is just a dream,' he said. 'Those who claim that it has great strategic value are all liars.' But unquestionably the palm goes to General Beck, who asserted categorically: 'The vehicles' armament will not allow them to salute properly on parade; besides, you are too fast: how are you going to direct it all without telephones?' 'By radio,' answered Guderian. 'Nonsense!' retorted Beck, 'a radio will never work in a tank.'

But if armour had its detractors, other generals were favourable to Guderian's theories — notably Blomberg, Reichenau, Lutz and Joachim von Stulpnagel. These went ahead with the motorization of the army, while adhering to the belief that tank units should be employed individually. Plainly, in Germany too, the concept of the 'strategic battering ram' was beyond most people's comprehension.

On January 13th, 1933, Hitler took over the Chancellery. Reichenau became his military adviser and Blomberg was appointed War Minister. These two arranged an interview for Guderian with the new master of the Reich. It occurred at Kummersdorf and lasted a mere half-hour — a half-hour in the course of which Guderian outlined the role of mechanized units to the Führer and staged a demonstration by a motor-cycle detachment, an anti-tank detachment, a detachment of Panzers (in their experimental form) and a detachment of light and heavy reconnaissance tanks. Hitler was instantly captivated by the swift, precise movements of these formations. 'This is what I need!' he exclaimed repeatedly. 'This is what I must have!' In that moment the creation of a massed armoured force was as good as settled.

The rest of the year was given over to the study of the structure and composition of the new units, and of how their various branches were to be synchronized. By 1934 the period of trial and error was over. In the spring, separate headquarters were established, under the command of General Lutz. Guderian became his deputy. In June the first armoured division was formed by amalgamating the small formations already in existence.

On March 16th, 1935, Hitler announced that the Reich was resuming its sovereignty with regard to armaments and reintroducing compulsory military service. The Treaty of Versailles had had its day. The Reichswehr — that interim army which had bridged the gap between the Second and Third Reichs — had fulfilled its purpose. It became incorporated in the new national Wehrmacht.

Thereafter German rearmament was to continue at an ever-increasing pace. Within six months of the revival of conscription, three Panzer divisions had been formed: the first in Weimar, the second in Würzburg and the third in Berlin. Colonel Guderian was placed in command of the second.

Simultaneously, at the prompting of Goering, Udet and Milch, substantial efforts were made to build up Germany's air strength. The Reich endowed itself with an air force that its leaders regarded as the personal achievement of the regime. Milch stressed the need for co-operation between tanks and squadrons of reconnaissance planes and dive-bombers (Stukas). It was the integration of these two weapons that gave rise to the *Panzerdivision* of 1940.

On General Lutz's instructions, Guderian brought out a book in the winter of 1936–7. Entitled *Achtung! Panzer*, it aimed at implanting the notion of armour and spreading its basic principles among the general public. It was the German counterpart of Colonel de Gaulle's book, *Vers l'armée de métier*.

While Guderian was building up the armoured corps, the remainder of the Wehrmacht was not idle. The number of standard divisions rose from twelve to thirty-six, then forty-eight, then sixty-two. A corresponding effort was being made in aviation. In 1936 Goering carried through a programme comprising ninety-three front-line squadrons (fighters, bombers, reconnaissance planes) in anticipation of the tank formations.

On May 1st, 1937, Hitler paraded a complete armoured division in Berlin for the first time. Squadrons of Stukas flew overhead. The line of vehicles extended for several miles, while the roar of aero-engines filled the skies of the capital. 'The impression induced in the spectators,' writes de Gaulle, 'and primarily in M. François-Poncet, the French ambassador, and our military attachés was that of a force which nothing, apart from a comparable strength, could arrest.'

Soon there were not three, but five, divisions in existence; and to these were to be added three light divisions. The number of air squadrons was doubled in the course of 1938; that of standard army divisions rose from sixty-two to ninety-six. So Hitler was not bragging when in his speech at the Berlin Sportpalast on September 26th, 1938 — three days before Munich — he proclaimed: 'Today I can openly admit what you all know already: we have built up an armed strength such as the world has never yet seen.'

How could France continue to act as though she were in ignorance of all this? The scale of German rearmament was no secret to anyone.

The Deuxième Bureau had watched these developments and kept the French General Staff regularly informed. Others had drawn attention, in France and elsewhere, to the growing strength of the Wehrmacht. But none of it seemed to make any impression on the authorities. They remained engrossed in their petty preoccupations and aircraft production proceeded at a snail's pace ...

This was because France was being subjected to conflicting propaganda. On the one hand Germany was depicted as a monstrous force threatening her life, her property and her most sacred possessions; on the other she was assured that the Wehrmacht was nothing to worry about; that her tanks were made of plywood and her fortifications of papiermâché; that Hitler was only bluffing; that his generals loathed him and that it would all fall through the moment the Allies showed their teeth.

Certainly German rearmament had its weaknesses. The more conservative generals remained blind to the possibilities of the armoured divisions and regretted the enormous sums that had gone into their creation and development. They wondered whether they would live up to their promises on the battlefield ...

They were not to be left in the dark much longer. The participation of the Condor Legion in the Spanish Civil War had helped to perfect the tactical liaison between tanks and planes and had shown up the inadequacy of very light tanks; the annexing of Austria and the Sudetenland had allowed the correction of certain technical faults in liaison and transportation. Finally, the Polish campaign had subjected the large armoured units to the baptism of fire. It revealed that the armour-plating was not thick enough and that the light divisions were a mistake. The lesson was not wasted. The light divisions were eliminated, and between October 1939 and April 1940 the heavier divisions' equipment was modified and their structure revised. Experiment had strengthened theory.

On the eve of the Battle of France the Wehrmacht, in addition to a hundred and twenty standard divisions, numbered ten Panzer divisions, representing a total of between two thousand five hundred and three thousand tanks grouped in three independent armoured corps, while two further Panzer divisions were being built up behind the lines.

* * *

German generals are often given credit for a kind of superhuman prescience. An examination of the facts reveals that this is quite false, and that they were as prone to blundering and vacillation as other human beings. Strange as it may seem, once the Polish campaign was over (September 18th, 1939) the German Supreme Command had no clear idea of how it was to continue the war. The prospect of beginning operations in the west did not appeal to it in the very least; it was pinning all its hope on a political compromise with Britain and France. But when Hitler's peace proposals, put forward from the dais of the Reichstag on October 6th, failed to evoke any response, the leaders of the Wehrmacht were compelled to admit that the continuation of hostilities had become unavoidable.

What were they to do? Neither Halder, nor Brauchitsch, nor Stulpnagel, nor Greiffenberg, the Army's director of operations, had drawn up any plan to meet the eventuality of having to clash with the French, British and Belgian forces in the area between the Rhine and the sea. As General von Manstein writes:

> The leaders of the Wehrmacht, and General von Brauchitsch himself, rejected the idea of an offensive in the west, for they did not regard it as the best way of putting an end to hostilities. Furthermore, they did not think the German army capable of striking a decisive blow in the west or of gaining a swift victory over the French forces.

The outlook of the strategists of the Bendlerstrasse, like that of their colleagues in Vincennes, was blinkered by a series of impossibilities: the impossibility of piercing the Maginot Line by frontal attacks; the impossibility of circumventing the Allied fortified positions without invading Belgium or Switzerland, whose neutrality had been recognized by the Reich government.

So they preferred to confine themselves to a defensive strategy. What prompted this attitude?

In the first place, the German generals considered that the Wehrmacht had been built up too swiftly. The feverish haste with which Hitler had set about rearming the Reich was bound to entail loss of quality. They reasoned that a Reichswehr of 100,000 men could not be transformed, within months, into a national army of several millions without something's going amiss. The nucleus was neither large enough nor experienced enough, and many of the newly formed reserve divisions did not seem adequately trained. Besides, the German generals had not forgotten the harsh lessons of the 1914–18 war. They were convinced that General Gamelin was an exceptionally gifted commander, full of resourcefulness and daring. He had made a great impression on General Beck, who had met him shortly before the war. In these circumstances would it not be better to play a waiting game, in the hope that the French would make the first move, then beat them with a counter-attack tailored to the needs of the moment? Did not Hitler himself appear to favour this conception? So far the Führer had issued no order appertaining to the preparation of an offensive in the west. In the course of the winter of 1939–40 General Sperrle, commander of the air forces that were to co-operate with von Rundstedt's group of armies, told General von Manstein that his machines were grounded by the soddenness of the soil. When Manstein expressed surprise and asked why concrete runways had not been laid during the autumn, Sperrle replied that Hitler had 'until recently expressly forbidden the carrying-out of such work'. Yet unless it *were* carried out, the launching of an offensive in the west was quite. impracticable …

But to the impossibilities listed above was now added another: the impossibility of waiting. France might be free to bide her time (since time, in the phrase of the moment, was on her side), but Germany was not. The U.S.S.R. had got all that she could hope to get out of the Reich and would soon be bringing more and more pressure to bear on her. Besides, if time was allowing France to organize, Britain to arm and America to step up her deliveries, it was robbing Germany of the lead she had laboured to acquire during the past few years. She could hardly sit back and watch her enemies increase their war potential and step up their armaments to a level that would shortly exceed her own.

As soon as Hitler's peace offers were rejected it became clear that a deal was impossible, and that Germany was going to have to come to blows with the West. So on October 9th — three days after his Reichstag speech — the Führer instructed the Military Operations Room to plan an offensive through Holland and Belgium, to be executed as early as possible. A date was even set for it: the operation was to be launched on October 15th. When it was pointed out that this was insufficient notice, he agreed to put the date back, but adhered to his decision and specified the objectives that were to be attained. His Secret Instruction stipulated:

The aim of the projected offensive shall be to defeat as many units as possible of the French and Allied armies and to conquer sufficient Dutch, Belgian and French territory for an aerial and naval war to be launched against Britain and for the Ruhr Basin to be sealed off defensively.

Roused to activity, the German Army Staff (O.K.H.) then drew up a plan resembling the Schlieffen plan adopted by the forces of Wilhelm II in August 1914. But this resemblance was only superficial, for the O.K.H.'s scheme was a 'watered-down Schlieffen Plan', to the extent that it envisaged only *partial* results (those that Hitler had prescribed in his note), not a complete encirclement of the Anglo-French forces by a pivoting movement of the German right flank. Were the Allied armies to retreat southwards after moving into Belgium, a continuous front would inevitably be created along the Somme and Aisne, a front that would subsequently be very hard to breach. This would lead to the same fatal stagnation as had characterized the 1914–18 war and to a second Verdun, which would probably turn out just like the first.

On taking stock of these arrangements, one man gave vent to his surprise and disillusion: this was General von Manstein, General von Rundstedt's Chief of Staff. If Guderian was the creator of the armoured corps, and Rommel was to make the most dashing use of it, Manstein was the keenest strategic brain in the Wehrmacht. Endowed with un-common lucidity and quick to form an overall view of events, his logical mind subjected the O.K.H. plan to relentless scrutiny and was quick to spot its weaknesses. As he saw it, the project was 'one of those deadly initial blunders that throw a whole campaign out of gear and have irremediable consequences'.

The scheme struck me as being a copy of the famous Schlieffen Plan adopted in 1914. It was humiliating to find that our generation could devise nothing better than the repetition of an old formula, even one emanating from a man as eminent as Schlieffen. What could one expect from a war-plan taken down from a shelf on which it had lain collecting dust for twenty years, a plan of which the enemy had taken stock at the same time as ourselves and for the repetition of which he was bound to be prepared? It must surely be obvious to any military mind that, having failed to storm the fortified line Verdun–Toul–Nancy–Epinal in 1914, we were even less likely to rush the Maginot Line now.

But my first reaction, dictated as it was by sentiment, was unfair to the O.K.H.: first of all because this plan was born of the con-ceptions put forward by Hitler himself; and also because it was not at all a repetition of the Schlieffen Plan. The widespread view that it *was* such a repetition holds good on only two points of detail. The first is that in 1939, as in 1914, the centre of gravity of the German offensive was to lie on the right wing. The second, that in both cases we were going through Belgium. But in every other respect the 1914 and 1939 plans differed profoundly.

In the first place, the situation was quite different. In 1914 we could still count on the element of surprise — as Schlieffen in fact did — not so much with regard to the thrust through Belgium as in respect of the dominance given to the right flank of our army. In 1939 Hitler's similar intentions could not pass unnoticed by the enemy.

Again, in 1914 we could hope — as Schlieffen did — that the French would play into our hands by launching a premature attack in Lorraine. In 1939, on the other hand, we could not expect favours of this kind ...

I concluded that neither the O.K.H. nor Hitler envisaged a full-scale repetition of the Schlieffen Plan. The latter had aimed at the complete and final destruction of the *whole* of the French forces. By fully extending his right arm, so to speak, he had intended to sweep through Belgium and the whole of northern France, and then, pivoting to the west of Paris, bring the entire French army to bay on the Metz–Voges–Swisss border front and force it to surrender. In doing this he had accepted the risk of initial set-backs in Alsace and even hoped that the enemy would contribute to the complete success of the German encircling movement by launching an attack on Lorraine.

The 1939 plan, on the other hand, nowhere envisaged a knock-out blow. The prescribed objective was merely a *partial* victory over the allied enemy forces operating in Belgium. It was a question of ensuring that we held a coastal sector *large enough to allow us to continue the war against Britain* ... Let it not be supposed, however, that I already had a ready-made plan in mind in October 1939. Mortals never achieve their aims except through strenuous toil and struggle. What they seek does not suddenly emerge from their heads in its finally wrought state, like Pallas Athene from the brain of Jupiter.

As always, the plan was to be conceived in stages and acquired its final form only after a series of rectifications and trial-and-error experiments. Of what did it consist?

Manstein took the view that for the entire strength of the Wehrmacht to strike westwards, the stakes must justify the risk; and the stakes could only justify the risk if they amounted to absolute victory rather than partial success.

To achieve this victory the plan's basic propositions must be reversed and the attack's centre of gravity must lie, not *on the right* of the German line-up (in the sector held by von Bock's Army Group), but *on the left* (in the sector held by von Rundstedt's Army Group). The element of surprise was likewise essential, and Manstein thought of achieving it by launching a powerful thrust in the Sedan area. This would enable the Wehrmacht to breach the Allied front where its northern fortifications met the Maginot Line, thus cutting the French forces in two.

Early in November 1939, he sent for Guderian and asked him whether his armour was capable of putting this operation into effect. After giving the matter due thought, Guderian replied that it was. He imposed only one condition: that the hammer-blow should be delivered by a large number of Panzer divisions — if possible by the *entire* armoured strength of the Wehrmacht.

While Manstein and Guderian were engaged in these preliminary labours — the dates originally fixed for the launching of the offensive had been constantly put back as a result of the bad weather — an utterly unexpected telegram from Hitler arrived at von Rundstedt's headquarters. This was on November 12th; the message read:

> By order of the Führer, a third motorized group will be formed on the southern flank of the 12th Army, or alongside the 16th, and will advance on Sedan using the unwooded strip on either side of Arlon, Tintigny and Florenville. It will be made up of the 19th Army Corps, the 2nd and 10th Panzer Divisions, a motorized division, the Lieb-Standarte Adolf Hitler and the Gross-Deutschland Regiment.
>
> The mission of this group will be as follows:
>
> (a) to beat the enemy's mobile forces advancing northwards through Belgium and thus facilitate the task of the 12th and 16th Armies;
>
> (b) *to reach the west bank of the Meuse to the south-east of Sedan by surprise* and thus create conditions favourable to the continuance of operations, particularly if the Panzer formations attached to the 6th and 4th Armies should not fully succeed in forging ahead.

Who had suggested this idea to Hitler? Was it General Busch, who had recently seen him and was conversant with Manstein's views? Or had it occurred to him without prompting? 'This latter hypothesis cannot be ruled out,' writes Manstein, 'for the Führer had an innate sense of tactical possibilities.' But even thus modified, the projected operations plan was still a long way from the one that Rundstedt's Chief of Staff had in mind.

More than ever convinced that he was on the right track, Manstein then revealed his definitive plan in a memorandum addressed to General von Rundstedt. This was the first sign of the famous 'dummy attack from the south' that was to immortalize his name. On December 4th, 1939, General von Rundstedt forwarded it to the Army General Staff (O.K.H.), recommending it warmly to the heads of the Supreme Command.

The idea of a central thrust struck the adherents of classical strategy, and notably Halder, as insane. The High Command would go no further than envisaging an attack in the region of Arlon, to be carried out by one or two armoured divisions. Guderian declared this inadequate. Manstein stuck to his views. There followed a war of prestige between the 'Staff Plan' and the 'Army Group A Plan'. Manstein persisted in defending his point of view. In the end his doggedness won him the hostility of the heads at Supreme Headquarters. To teach him to be less presumptuous they deprived him of his post as Chief of Staff to General von Rundstedt, who commanded the sector facing the Belgian Ardennes and Luxembourg, and sent him to command the 38th Army Corps at Stettin (January 27th, 1940). Manstein was in disgrace. He asked that he should at least be given charge of an armoured formation; his request was turned down. 'Thus,' writes Guderian, 'our best tactician was to participate in the battle in a corps in the third wave, when the dazzling success of the operation was to be mainly due to his initiative.'

Meanwhile a mishap had occurred. It deserves mention, for it caused quite a stir at the time, though it had no influence on the way things developed. On the morning of January 10th a General Staff liaison plane had run into a snow-storm, strayed over the Belgian border and made a forced landing. The pilot had hurriedly tried to burn the papers that he was carrying, but the Belgian police had forestalled him and seized his dispatch case. It contained the O.K.H. invasion plans and some details of the German line-up. The Belgian intelligence service at once communicated them to the Allies.

Goering was beside himself with rage when he heard the news. The plane belonged to the 2nd Air Wing under Air Marshal Felmy. Both he and his chief of staff, Colonel Kammhuber, were instantly relieved of their posts. They were replaced by General Kesselring and Colonel Speidel.

Gamelin saw this forced landing as merely a German trap. Churchill, on the other hand, regarded it as a genuine accident, and today we know from the Nuremberg documents that he was right. Whatever the truth of the matter, no changes were made in the French line of defence.

On February 7th the advocates of the thrust staged a *Kriegsspiel* in

Mainz, based on a further note that Manstein had addressed to General von Brauchitsch on January 25th. Despite Halder's reservations the exercise yielded such satisfactory results that even the adversaries of the scheme were forced to agree to it. But the manoeuvre highlighted a fact to which Guderian had constantly drawn his chiefs' attention: the need to reinforce the armoured units in the Sedan sector and the impossibility of entrusting the break-through to the 19th Corps alone.

Another *Kriegsspiel* took place on February 14th at 12th Army Headquarters in Mayen. This time Manstein was not present. Closer attention was given to the crossing of the Meuse. The discussion bore on the following point: was the task of crossing the river to be left entirely to the Panzers after they had driven through the Ardennes, or would it be better to wait till the infantry caught up and entrust the operation to the latter? Opinions were divided, for this manoeuvre was without precedent in the annals of strategy. Even Rundstedt was hesitant. He declared that 'to entrust this mission solely to the tanks was altogether too venturesome', and that it would be better to adopt a less risky solution. Whereupon Guderian and General von Wietersheim flew into a rage.

'This discussion shows a complete misconception of the use of tanks!' they exclaimed. 'We can have no faith in the success of the operation if you persist in mounting it in accordance with erroneous conceptions. Are you never going to realize that it is the tanks' job to clear the way for the infantry? Why do you keep putting the cart before the horse?'[1]

'It was at that moment more than any other,' writes Guderian, 'that we could have done with Manstein's support!'

Such support was to come in an unexpected manner. Custom required that any general given command of a large unit should be presented to the Führer before joining his post. On February 17th Manstein was summoned to Berlin with a group of newly promoted generals. Colonel Schmundt, Hitler's aide-de-camp, took advantage of the occasion to secure for Manstein a long interview with the Supreme Commander of the Wehrmacht. Much to his surprise, Manstein discovered that none of his notes had been forwarded by the O.K.H. and that Hitler knew practically nothing of his schemes. Manstein then outlined his plan to the Führer, emphasizing its advantages and exposing the inadequacy of the objectives visualized by the General Staff. Hitler was immediately won over by the scope and the boldness of Manstein's scheme: here at last was someone prepared to

[1] This was the crux of the problem. The notion of employing tanks to exploit a break-through was generally accepted. What disquieted the German High Command was the boldness of Guderian's conception, whereby the break-through itself was to be achieved by the Panzer divisions alone, without infantry support or preliminary infantry action.

abandon the beaten track! He gave orders for the plan to be thoroughly looked into, without a moment's delay.

On March 6th the Führer summoned a full-scale military conference at the Chancellery. Present — in addition to General von Kleist, commander of the armoured group that bore his name, and General Guderian, commander of the 19th Armoured Corps — were General von Rundstedt, commander of Army Group A, and the leaders of the various armies of which it was made up.[1] Hitler was in the chair. One by one his generals outlined how they reckoned to carry out the missions entrusted to them. Guderian spoke last:

'On zero day,' he said, 'I shall cross the border of Luxembourg and then head across southern Belgium to Sedan, my corps advancing in three columns. I expect to reach the Belgian frontier on the first day and I shall cross it that night; on the second day I shall advance to Neufchâteau; on the third I shall reach Bouillon and cross the Semois; on the fourth I shall get to the Meuse; on the fifth I shall cross it. By the evening of the fifth I expect to have established a bridgehead on the other bank.'

He writes in his memoirs:

Then Hitler asked me: 'And what will you do next?' He was the only one who had thought of asking me this leading question. I replied: 'In the absence of orders to the contrary I expect to continue my westward advance on the following day. It is for the Supreme Command to decide whether my target is to be Amiens or Paris. In my opinion, the correct solution would be to march on Amiens so as to reach the Channel.' Hitler nodded but said nothing. General Busch, commander of the 16th Army, which was on my left, was alone in objecting: 'I shall be greatly surprised if you manage to cross the river at the first attempt!' Hitler, with a tense look on his face, glanced at me to see what my answer would be.

Without turning a hair I replied: 'You do your own job and leave me to worry about mine ... '

Hitler made no comment, but after the conference the Manstein Plan was formally adopted.[2] Later, when asked whether he thought that Hitler had any gift as a strategist, he replied: 'Of course! I had the highest opinion of his judgment in military matters, in view of the fact that he adopted my own ideas.' The Führer made two important adjustments,

[1] Manstein did not attend this conference, either. At the time he was inspecting inactive units in Pomerania.

[2] General Warlimont, the Führer's military adviser, also had a hand in getting Hitler to see the advantages of the Manstein Plan.

however. The fact that the break-through was not to be effected in the Sedan sector, by the left flank, made the old O.K.H. plan more or less superfluous; for in that, as in the Schlieffen Plan, the main stress had been laid on the advance through Belgium by the forces situated on the right wing. This advance was now to play only a subsidiary role. But Hitler preferred to combine the two plans. He wanted the advance through Holland and Belgium to be simultaneous with the thrust across the Meuse. This put paid to Guderian's demand that *all* armoured divisions should be massed in the Sedan sector. Of the ten Panzer divisions in the front line, three were to be withdrawn from the main body. One of them would be assigned to von Rüchler's 18th Army, whose objective was Rotterdam; the other two to von Reichenau's 6th Army, whose initial objectives were Maestricht and Liège.

Guderian spoke out against this proposed dispersal of armoured strength, seeing it as a return to the misconceptions of the past. His motto had always been: '*Nicht kleckern, klotzen!*' – by which he meant, 'Don't disperse, concentrate!'

The Führer's reasoning was inspired less by pure strategy than by psychology. The object of the operation was to encircle and destroy the greater part of the Allied forces as swiftly as possible, so as to facilitate the second phase of the battle – the destruction of the remainder of the French army. The Manstein Plan was perfect *provided the Allies swung northwards* and poured the bulk of their forces into Belgium. Who could be sure they would do so? If they withdrew *southwards* the operation would have failed in its principal objective. Everything must be done, therefore, to encourage them to head for the Dyle and the Escaut. To ensure this it was *essential* that part of the Wehrmacht should advance on Rotterdam and Brussels. The three armoured divisions transferred to this sector would lure them into the trap by leading them to suppose that Flanders was to be the main fighting area. Nothing could be further from the truth. The advance of the right wing, borrowed from the Schlieffen Plan, would be just a feint; the essential operation would be the break-through in the centre. General von Manstein's plan was a superb trap in every detail but one: it lacked a bait. Now that bait had been supplied.

The Führer's second adjustment was inspired by caution, not psychology. The weakness of the Manstein Plan was that it exposed the left flank of the Wehrmacht to a French attack from the south. (Throughout the first phase of the campaign Hitler remained obsessed by the possibility of a flank attack from the south.) To guard against this Manstein was of opinion that the motorized divisions advancing westwards in the wake of the Panzers should stay on the move and on the attack throughout the operation, constantly dislocating — by raids on Rethel, Rheims, Laon and Soissons — the line of defence that the French were bound to establish between Longuyon and the Somme. It was essential for this front to remain fluid and for the French reinforcements moving up from the south to be destroyed as they reached the fighting zone.

To this bold conception Hitler preferred a two-part campaign: first the encirclement of the Allied forces in Belgium, then a southward movement culminating in the destruction of the rest of the opposing forces. The campaign was to be divided into two distinct phases: first the Battle in the North, then the Battle of France. One was to follow the other without any break in continuity.

6

THE WEST ON THE EVE OF THE GERMAN
OFFENSIVE

LET us dwell for a moment on those opening days of May 1940 and take a final glance at a West that was never to be seen again. On the eve of one of the greatest battles in history, nearly sixteen million men were under arms and wondering what the hours ahead held in store for them.

Peace had gone, but the real war had not yet come. It was still permissible to be carefree, to dream of love, to enjoy the spring and those radiant orchards that at night provided the only point of light in the landscape now that the towns were sentenced to the black-out. In the evenings the wireless played *Monica* or *J'attendrai*, and thoughts turned sadly to last year's summer holidays ...

But tomorrow? What would tomorrow bring? That was the question a whole generation of men were asking themselves in their service camps or fighting posts, all the way from the North Sea to Flanders and from the Vosges to the Mediterranean.

In Warsaw the spark had died. Far to the north the artillery still rumbled in the Norwegian fjords. But elsewhere all was surprisingly calm. Britain was preparing at her leisure beyond the sea barrier that thudded monotonously against her cliffs. Holland and Belgium were lulling themselves into a false sense of security, quite unaware that they would wake to find their cities ablaze.

Germany was ready for action. The passivity and resignation prevalent at the start of the war — especially among the older generations — had given way to eagerness and seriousness. The *Feldheer* was wholly behind its Führer. The troops' morale was at its peak. They were longing to fight. There was only one lingering doubt in their minds: the Maginot Line. It was said to be impregnable. But was there any obstacle that could not be overcome by men so brimming over with vitality and surrounded by such a show of strength?

There were between a hundred and twenty and a hundred and twenty-five divisions, the bulk of them concentrated between the Moselle and the Rhine. This formidable array of steel and humanity, kept in trim by intensive training, had been untapped by the Norwegian operation. It was ready to move at the first signal from its leaders.

When would this signal be given? Nobody knew. An officer in von Kleist's armoured group wrote:

> We are in May. Whitsun is approaching; often we stare up into the unchanging blue sky and wonder if things may be about to start. But no. Nothing ever happens. Everything is calm, so calm that with luck we might get leave for the holidays.

What about the French?

Eight months of inactivity in the casemates of the Maginot Line or in billets behind the line had scarcely strengthened the reservists' fighting spirit. Winter had seemed long. But now spring, with its week-end passes and variety shows, made life seem less dismal and allowed them to contemplate the future with jauntiness. Outdoor games were organized between the concrete structures of the Maginot Line. 'The good spirits of our soldiers,' declared General Giraud, 'reassures me even more than the stoutness of our fortifications.' Oh, if only the 'phoney war' could last till summer ...

But was the General Staff, at least, conscious of the gravity of the hour? Were its members living and working at full stretch? Apparently not. Its executives went on with their daily tasks in the gloom of the Vincennes Keep with the same presumptuous nonchalance as before. And yet they had plenty of warnings!

Early in March, King Leopold informed G.H.Q. through General Delvoie[1] that 'according to information from a reliable source the German attack will be launched on the Meuse, in the Givet–Longwy area'.

'Patiently established ever since peace-time,' the French high-ups claimed, 'perfectly suited to the terrain, echeloned in ever-increasing depth, roofed and buttressed ever since mobilization, the fortified position defending French territory is wholly capable of withstanding the enemy. The position stretching from Charleville to the Moselle has enjoyed the High Command's particular attention.'

But at this point the teleprinters began to click. Telegrams came from all directions. There was a constant flow of messages that ought surely to have put G.H.Q. on its guard:

[1] Belgian military attaché in Paris.

April 11th: The Intelligence Service reported: 'Western operations imminent; watch out for military movements in the next few days!'
April 20th: 'Staff of German Intelligence pulling out of Belgium!'
May 1st: France's military attaché in Berne wired: 'The German attack will occur between May 8th and May 10th; the main effort will be made on Sedan.' The Deuxième Bureau confirmed this: 'Stand by! In circles close to the German G.H.Q. it is being said that the Wehrmacht will attack along the whole front between May 8th and May 10th and that the area round Sedan, Belgium, Holland and northern France will be occupied within ten days and France within a month.'
May 2nd: 'Closing of Belgian and Dutch frontiers imminent.'
Night of May 5th–6th: 'General offensive embracing Netherlands imminent!'
May 6th: 'Attack ready. It is said in circles close to the German Command that the French army will be incapable of halting the armour in the open country.'
May 9th: 'Stand by! Attack at daybreak tomorrow!'

But none of these cries of alarm had any effect. It is doubtful whether they were even brought to the notice of the Commander-in-Chief. Certainly the Prime Minister was not told of them. So many had come in already that no attention was now being paid to them.[1] They had almost become part of the daily routine ...

On the evening of May 9th Commandant Baril, one of the heads of the Deuxième Bureau, suggested to General Colson's Staff that all troops away on leave should be instantly recalled.

'What on earth for?' he was asked. 'They won't be needed yet awhile! Germany is disintegrating ... '

The Commandant replaced the receiver with a worried frown, for he was convinced that the decisive test was imminent. He would have been even more wrought-up had he known the terrible awakening that was in store for us!

For while the French General Staff was engaged in wool-gathering, scattering its already inadequate forces and cherishing dreams of opening up 'further theatres of war', the Reich was silently assembling its battering ram of Panzer divisions within a few miles of our frontiers, ready to strike in the narrow sector between Givet and Sedan.

[1] True, while they gave indications as to dates they contained no details of the disposition of the enemy's forces.

But of this, France's generals had not the faintest inkling. By the time the scales fell from their eyes it was too late for anyone to ward off the catastrophe.[1] In sixty lightning days history would present the bill for twenty years of blundering.

[1] The French and British navies had taken note of certain warnings. Jacques Mordal tells us that French submarines had been blockading Texel Island since May 6th; on May 9th Admiral Abrial ordered the loading of equipment for the Expeditionary Corps to Flushing.

FIRST PHASE

THE BATTLE IN THE NORTH

(May 10th – June 4th)

MAY 9TH

Calm along the whole front.
The German High Command issued the following order:

Berlin 9.5.40

W.FA/Abt. L.N² 22 — 180/40 gK CHIEFS
The Führer and Supreme Commander has decided:

Zero day 10.5
Zero hour 05.45

    The code-names 'Danzig' or 'Augsburg' will be given to the various sections of the Wehrmacht before 21.30 hours on 9.5.

Head of the Oberkommando of the Wehrmacht,

KEITEL

At 1.30 p.m. all German military formations were ordered to stand by. All senior officers returned to their command posts. At 4 p.m. General Guderian rejoined his armoured corps at Sonnenhof, near Bitburg. General von Rundstedt left his H.Q. at Koblenz and drove to the wooded region ten miles from the centre of Army Group A, of which he was assuming command.

General Rommel, in command of the 7th Panzer Division, hurriedly scribbled this note to his wife:

We are on our way at last. Not for nothing, let us hope. You will get all the news from the papers in the days ahead. Don't worry. Everything will be all right.

At six o'clock in the evening von Kleist's armoured group pulled out. The division advanced along the three highways leading to the west, while the infantry, widely spread out, used all available roads. It was a moonless night; there was not a single light; the going was slow and difficult.

By midnight all German front-line units were at their starting-points.

THE BATTLE IN THE NORTH

POLITICAL SITUATION

In Germany: Hitler left for the front by special train from Berlin.

In Italy: Mussolini decided to join in the war against Britain and France. From now on he was merely biding his time. He instructed Ciano to tell Sir Percy Loraine, British ambassador in Rome, that the Duce intended to abide by the pacts that bound him to Berlin.

In Britain: Prime Minister Neville Chamberlain resigned office on grounds of ill-health. Great Britain was without a government.

In France: At 1 p.m. Premier Reynaud decided to resign following a stormy Cabinet meeting. The subject under discussion had been the dismissal of General Gamelin, who was blamed for the failure of operations in Norway. Daladier had stood out against the move to relieve the C.-in-C. of his command.

M. Albert Lebrun received M. Reynaud in the Elysée Palace at 7 p.m. and asked him to hold on for a few days. He did not want to break the news to the public till it had been possible for a new administration to be formed.

'There is no denying,' writes General Gamelin, 'that we were in a strange pickle for a nation about to go into battle.'

MAY 10TH

MILITARY SITUATION

At 3 a.m. the German government addressed a 'Memorandum' to the Dutch and Belgian governments informing them of the imminent arrival of Wehrmacht forces in their respective countries 'to forestall a projected Anglo-French action'.[1]

At daybreak every available German aircraft took off. The Luftwaffe's targets included Belgian airfields, the Dutch airfields at Waalhaven, Bergen, Schiphot and Kooy, the French airfields at Calais, Dunkirk, Metz, Essey-les-Nancy, Bron and Châteauroux and Valdahon Camp. From the North Sea to the Rhône Valley the sky was filled with a heavy drone. The attack extended two hundred and fifty miles behind the front, destroying planes on the ground and pounding road and railway junctions.

At the same time the Wehrmacht dropped almost the whole of its airborne strength over Holland. The 22nd Airborne Division, comprising twelve thousand men and supported by four thousand paratroops[2] divided into five battalions, swooped on the bridges at Rotterdam, Dordrecht and Moerdijk. Their mission was to seize them before the Dutch had time to destroy them. Surprise won complete success for the operation: it cost the Germans only a hundred and eighty men. 'It was imperative that we should succeed,' states General Student, who was in charge of it. 'A failure by us would have led to the failure of the entire offensive.'

A sixth battalion of airborne troops was landed in the Maestricht area. The Belgian troops mistook the gliders that conveyed them for planes with engine trouble. The battalion seized several bridges along the Meuse —

---

[1] Franco-Belgian military talks had been held on several occasions, in particular on November 15th, 1939, and January 14th, 1940 (following the forced landing of the German aircraft containing the O.K.H. invasion plans). These discussions had been prompted by the growing threat from Germany. They had been resumed in April 1940, but the only upshot had been Belgium's refusal to allow French troops to enter the country. The Germans had obviously known about these talks. None of which alters the fact that their attempt to justify their action — by alleging that Allied forces were about to invade Belgium — was completely without foundation.

[2] According to Marshal Kesselring, these paratroops numbered 4,500. Four thousand of them were dropped over Holland and five hundred on the Belgian fortress at Eben-Emaël.

notably at Veldwergelt and Ursenhaven — without firing a shot, and then immediately crossed the Albert Canal, establishing several small bridge-heads on the west bank. Simultaneously, paratroops dropped on to the turret of the fort at Eben-Emaël, the key position in the defence of Liège, and began to invest it.

While these preliminary operations were going on, the vanguard of von Kleist's armoured group, comprising between twelve and fifteen hundred tanks, was advancing in dense waves through the Grand Duchy of Luxembourg.[1] The tanks were moving in very close columns, rigidly shepherded through the hearts of the valleys. 'These three blocks were positioned one behind the other in a kind of giant phalanx,' claims General Blumentritt. 'They stretched back for a hundred miles, the rear rank lying fifty miles to the east of the Rhine. Had this mass formation of Panzers been placed in single file, the tail-end would have been in Königsberg, in East Prussia, and the head of the column in Trèves.' This mass of armour comprised:

Schmidt's 39th Armoured Corps	{ 5th P.D.
	7th P.D.
Reinhardt's 41st Armoured Corps	{ 6th P.D.
	8th P.D.
Guderian's 19th Armoured Corps	{ 1st P.D.
	2nd P.D.
	10th P.D.

The three Panzer divisions that made up Guderian's Corps advanced in the following manner:

> *The 1st Panzer Division (General Kirchner)*, in the centre, took the route Wallendorf, Martelange, Neufchâteau, Bertrix, Bouillon, Sedan (North).
>
> *The 2nd Panzer Division (General Veiel)*, on the right, took the route Vianden, Tintange, Libramont, Meuse River (between Flize and Sedan).
>
> *The 10th Panzer Division (General Schaal)*, on the left, took the route Eschternach, Redingen, Florenville, Bellefontaine, Meuse River (south of Sedan).

The 1st Panzer Division was followed by the Corps's artillery, Guderian's staff and the anti-aircraft unit. It had been assigned the leading role in the attack. The 10th Panzer Division, on its left, was followed by the Gross-Deutschland motorized regiment.

[1] The Grand Duchess had left her residence at dawn.

At 5.30 a.m. the central column drove into Martelange, the right-hand column into Strainchamps and the left-hand column into Habay-la-Neuve. Guderian had told them outright that their objective was the Channel. 'No one had any faith in the success of our operation,' he writes, 'apart from Hitler, Manstein and myself.'

These compact and slow-moving formations would have offered a magnificent target for aerial attack. But since the Germans had absolute mastery of the sky, the French air force was quite unable to keep track of them, calculate their strength and alert the High Command — let alone bomb them.

At 5.32 a.m. the 7th Panzer Division under General Rommel crossed the Belgian frontier thirty miles south of Liège.

The foreign ministers of Belgium and the Netherlands unsealed the secret instructions that had been sent to them in anticipation of this emergency. They read that they were immediately to demand assistance from France and Britain.

The Dutch and Belgian representatives in Paris immediately called on Prime Minister Reynaud and General Gamelin. The French High Command at once gave orders for:

(a) General Mittelhauser to get in touch with the Dutch High Command and inaugurate the activities of the French Military Mission under General Lascroux;

(b) General Champon to report to Belgian G.H.Q. and determine the structure of Allied Command with King Leopold.

At 5.35 a.m. the bulk of the Wehrmacht attacked along the whole of the Western Front. One hundred and thirty-five divisions, including ten armoured and eighty crack divisions, moved against Holland, Belgium and France.

The forces of the Reich were disposed as follows:

1. *In the north, from the sea to Aix-la-Chapelle:*

Army Group B (von Bock)
18th Army (General von Küchler), facing Holland with 1 armoured division (9th Panzer Division). 6th Army (General von Reichenau), facing Belgium west of the Meuse, with 3 standard army corps and the 16th Armoured Corps (General Hoeppner) consisting of 2 divisions (3rd and 4th Panzer Divisions).
2 air fleets (Generals Kesselring and Sperrle).

2. *In the centre, from Aix-la-Chapelle to Trèves:*

4th Army (General von Kluge) between Namur and Givet with 3 standard army corps and the 39th Armoured Corps (General Schmidt) consisting of 2 divisions (5th and 7th Panzer Divisions), the latter under General Rommel.

Army Group A (von Rundstedt)	Von Kleist's Armoured Group	The 41st Armoured Corps (General Reinhardt), consisting of 2 divisions (6th and 8th Panzer Divisions.) The 19th Armoured Corps (General Guderian) consisting of 3 divisions (1st, 2nd and 3rd Panzer Divisions). 1 motorized corps (General von Wietersheim) consisting of 3 divisions. 1 air fleet supplementary to the armoured group.

12th Army (General List), covering army facing south: no armour.

16th Army (General Busch), covering army facing south: no armour. 2 other air fleets.

3. *In the south, from the Maginot Line to the Swiss frontier:*

1st Army (General von Witzleben) facing the Maginot Line: no armour.

Army Group C (Ritter von Leeb)	7th Army (General Dollmann) along the Rhine: no armour. 1 air fleet.

Everything was apportioned in advance to give more strength to the attack; the German G.H.Q. had held in reserve only one armoured division (the 11th) and one motorized brigade.

The mission allotted to these German forces was to 'break through the enemy's frontier positions from the Moselle to the North Sea; occupy Holland; continue as far as Anvers and the line of the Dyle; capture Liège with the massive attacking forces on the left wing; reach the Meuse and force their way across the river between Namur and Carignan, near Sedan, by bringing to bear the whole weight of the available armoured and motorized divisions; finally, thrust onwards to the sea, bearing on the river system of the Aisne and the Somme.'

General von Manstein was on leave in Liegnitz (Silesia) when the launching of the offensive was announced on the radio. He writes:

Needless to say, all my thoughts and my most ardent wishes were with our units advancing through the Ardennes. Would they succeed in crossing Luxembourg and smashing the Belgian fortifications on either side of Bastogne before powerful French forces beat them to it? Would our armour manage to cross the Meuse at the first attempt and press on with their advance so that they could start encircling the enemy armies operating in the north?

It will come as no surprise to anybody if I say that I did not exactly entertain friendly feelings for those who had relegated me so far to the rear at the very moment when the plan for which I had fought so long and so stubbornly was being carried out in the west.[1]

Confronting the German armies, one hundred and thirty-four French, British and Belgian divisions prepared themselves for the onslaught. The Allied forces were disposed as follows:

1. In the north-west, from the sea to Longwy:

	7th Army (General Giraud) between the coast and Lille.
1st Group of Armies (Billotte)	The British Expeditionary Force (Lord Gort) in the region of Lille.
	1st Army (General Blanchard) facing Belgium.
	9th Army (General Corap) facing the Ardennes.
	2nd Army (General Huntziger) facing the Arlon Gap.

2. In the centre, from Longwy to Sélestat in Alsace:

	3rd Army (General Condé) in the region of Metz.
2nd Group of Armies (Prételat)	4th Army (General Réquin) facing the Saar.
	5th Army (General Bourret) in the region of Strasbourg.

3. In the east, from Sélestat to the Belfort Gap:

	8th Army (General Garchery) covering the Belfort Gap.
3rd Group of Armies (Besson)	6th Army (General Touchon) behind Belfort, held in reserve against a German invasion through Switzerland.

Three possibilities were open to the Allied Command:

1. To await the German onslaught on our northern frontiers;

---

[1] That very evening Manstein received orders to transfer the headquarters of the 38th Corps from Stettin to Brunswick. This first stage of the journey westwards brought him closer to the battlefield.

2. To move forward along the Escaut;
3. To move forward to the Dyle and resist along a front stretching from Anvers to Givet and passing through Louvain, Gembloux and Namur.

The third, worked out at the Arras conference on November 23rd, 1939 (despite objections from General Georges), had been approved by the French and British governments. It would enable support to be given to the twenty-two Belgian and ten Dutch divisions fighting on the side of the Allies. On the other hand, it would entail a delay of five — some people even said eight or ten — days, while our units moved into line and organized their fighting positions.

But this, despite its drawbacks, was the solution for which General Gamelin plumped. He notified General Georges of this decision at 6.30 a.m.[1]

In response to the C.-in-C.'s 'Personal and Secret Instruction No. 9'[2] thirty-three French and British divisions immediately pivoted on Givet and moved forward towards the Dyle. General Prioux's Cavalry Corps composed of the 2nd and 3rd Light Mechanized Divisions, whose mission was to slow down the German offensive ahead of the Dyle within the quadrilateral Maestricht–Liège–Namur–Anvers, crossed the Franco-Belgian frontier at 7.30 a.m. On the left of the Allied line-up Giraud's 7th Army sped towards Anvers and Breda. After landing at Flushing, in Holland, the 60th and 68th Divisions occupied the islands of Walcheren and Beveland, covering the mouth of the Escaut. 'This was far from being an attacking manoeuvre,' remarks General Gauché. 'The French army was leaving its frontier position (which it had fortified somewhat during the previous eight months) to take up another on Belgian territory (which it believed equally fortified). The operation was only attempted because the Command hoped to have time to carry it out without being seriously harassed by the enemy.'

The C.-in-C. issued the following order of the day:

The attack that we have been expecting since last October was launched this morning. Germany is waging a struggle to the death

---

[1] The 'Dyle Manoeuvre' had been laid down in every detail in the Generalissimo's 'Personal and Secret Instruction No. 9', dated 7.40 p.m., March 20th, 1940. On the morning of May 10th the Instruction was carried out mechanically, without any modification apart from the movement of the left wing towards Breda.
[2] The full text of the Personal and Secret Note No. 9 will be found in Roton, *Années cruciales*, p. 135.

MAY 10TH

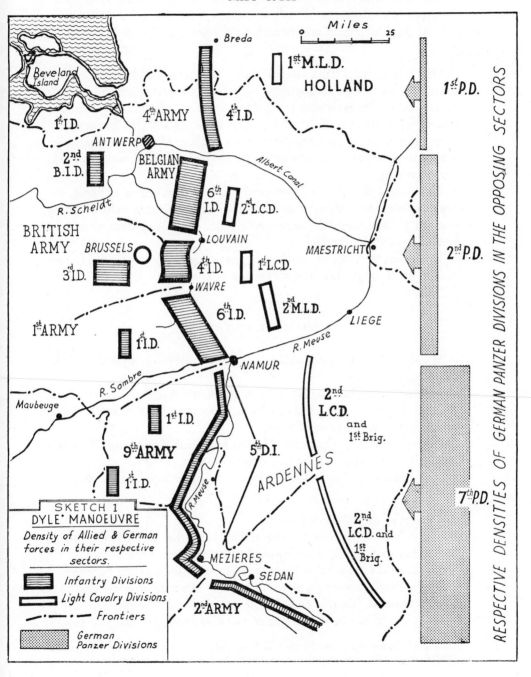

Miles 0 — 25

Breda

1st M.L.D.
HOLLAND

1st P.D.

Beveland Island

4th ARMY

4th I.D.

1st I.D.

ANTWERP

BELGIAN ARMY

2nd B.I.D.

R. Scheldt

Albert Canal

6th I.D.

2nd L.C.D.

2nd P.D.

MAESTRICHT

BRITISH ARMY

BRUSSELS

LOUVAIN

3rd I.D.

4th I.D.

1st L.C.D.

WAVRE

6th I.D.

2nd M.L.D.

LIEGE

1st ARMY

1st I.D.

R. Sombre

R. Meuse

NAMUR

Maubeuge

1st I.D.

2nd L.C.D.
and 1st Brig.

9th ARMY

5th D.I.

ARDENNES

7th P.D.

1st I.D.

R. Meuse

2nd L.C.D. and 1st Brig.

SKETCH 1
DYLE MANOEUVRE

Density of Allied & German forces in their respective sectors.

	Infantry Divisions
	Light Cavalry Divisions
-·-·-	Frontiers
	German Panzer Divisions

MEZIERES

SEDAN

2nd ARMY

RESPECTIVE DENSITIES OF GERMAN PANZER DIVISIONS IN THE OPPOSING SECTORS

against us. The watchwords for France and all her allies are: courage, energy, confidence.

As Marshal Pétain said twenty-four years ago: '*Nous les aurons.*'

GAMELIN

Meanwhile, the French Staff Officers who reached the selected line during the morning found nothing apart from Cointet defences.[1] 'On the actual site of the resistance point there were no trenches, no defensive structures, no fixed auxiliary defences, no anti-tank barriers. It was just an open plain, a sitting duck for the enemy's armour. Here in the Gembloux area, where the French Command wished to make its stand, no earthworks had been dug.'

By evening the French Command knew that, taken as a whole, the Dyle position was unorganized. Unless General Prioux held out long enough to win them the necessary respite, the Allied units would be unable to establish themselves.

But it was too late now to alter the prearranged plan. 'This was Gamelin's hour of judgment,' writes Pertinax.

POLITICAL SITUATION

Winston Churchill succeeded Neville Chamberlain as head of the British government.

After tendering his resignation the night before Paul Reynaud remained in office. He enlarged his Cabinet by incorporating Louis Marin and Jean Ybarnegaray as Ministers of State.

General Gamelin, whom the Premier had wanted to dismiss the night before, was 'provisionally' retained as C.-in-C.

Hitler broadcast the following speech to his troops and the German nation:

Soldiers of the Western Front!

The hour has struck for the crucial battle for the future of the German nation. For three hundred years the aim of the French and British rulers has been to prevent the consolidation of the European continent and, above all, to keep Germany in a state of weakness and powerlessness. To this end, France has declared war on Germany thirty-one times in the course of two centuries. For decades past,

---

[1] These defences, introduced by the French general of that name, consisted of a series of trestles connected by coils of barbed wire and preceded by anti-tank minefields.

the aim of the policy pursued by Britain's rulers has been to prevent Germany from unifying and to deny the Reich the resources essential for keeping eighty million men alive. Britain and France have pursued this policy whatever form of government was in power in Germany. It was the German people who were aimed at.

Under cover of a gigantic diversionary manoeuvre in south-eastern Europe, Britain and France seek to advance through Holland and Belgium to the Ruhr Basin.

Soldiers of the Western Front, your hour has come. The battle that is beginning today will decide the fate of the German nation for the next thousand years. Do your duty! The blessings of the German people go with you.

Hitler later revealed the true nature of his feelings to those about him. 'I did not sleep a wink during the night of May 9th–May 10th,' he said. 'Principally I was kept awake by anxiety over the weather. I was overcome with rage when I saw dawn break fifteen minutes earlier than I was assured it would. Yet I knew that it had to be thus! At 7 a.m. came the news: "Eben-Emaël has been silenced!" Then: "We hold one of the Meuse bridges ... "

'It was wonderful the way everything turned out according to plan! When the news came through that the enemy were moving forward along the whole front I could have wept for joy: they had fallen into the trap. It was vital that they should believe that we were sticking to the old Schlieffen Plan, and they *had* believed it!

'Several times in the course of the night I went to the operations room to pore over the relief maps. How lovely Felsennest was! The birds in the morning, the view of the road up which the columns were advancing, the squadrons of planes overhead. There, I was sure that everything would go right for me!'

Paul Reynaud told the French people of the German offensive in these terms:

Three free nations — Holland, Belgium and Luxembourg — were invaded last night by the German army. They have called the Allied armies to their assistance.

Between seven and eight o'clock this morning our soldiers, the soldiers of freedom, crossed the frontier.

The age-old battlefield of the Flanders plain is well-known to the people of our country. And confronting us, rushing at us, is the age-old invader.

Free men and women the world over will be breathlessly watching the drama ahead ...

France stands calm and strong. It is time to fall in. You already know that all parties have joined forces within the government. In this hour in which the best, the youngest, the liveliest, the strongest of our countrymen are about to risk their lives in solemn battle, one grave thought dwells in every house, every country cottage, every billet. One common thought raises us all above ourselves. Everyone is preparing to do his duty.

The French army has drawn its sword: France is gathering herself.

Yet behind this surface optimism the Premier could not conceal the secret apprehension that gnawed at him. 'I am worried,' he confessed to Paul Baudouin. 'Now we shall see what Gamelin is made of.'

In the evening, at the Gare de l'Est, the inquisitive watched the arrival of the first refugee train. 'It came slowly to a halt along the platform,' writes Fabre-Luce. 'People were amazed to see nobody get out. Exhausted from their sudden uprooting, from the danger and the journey, the poor devils only gradually recovered from their torpor ... The children's drawn faces made them look like old men and women, and their grandparents, jolted into their dotage, gave way like children ... '

MAY 11TH

Von Küchler's army thrust onwards through Holland. Huge bombing attacks were launched and battalions of paratroops fell in clusters from the sky. Encircled from the south, Rotterdam became a nightmare.

Giraud's 7th Army, which had hastened towards Breda to lend support to the Netherlands forces, ran slap into the 9th Panzer Division, which had forestalled it. The Luftwaffe intervened *en masse*, swooping to the attack with bombs and machine-guns. The 25th Division was flattened. The mobile sections of the 1st Light Mechanized Division turned about. As for the tanks, they had been unable to keep up with the army. They were being conveyed by rail and had not yet reached Anvers. In these conditions it was impossible to make contact with the Dutch army. As Bardies writes: 'We did not have the means to attack the German forces and free Rotterdam in a terrain so interlaced with canals and wide rivers.'

Twenty-four hours after the launching of the attack, the shape of the first German manoeuvre was clear: the initial objective of the Wehrmacht lay in forcing the Liège hinge. 'Yesterday's operations were astonishingly successful,' General Jodl recorded in his notebook. 'The armoured units of von Reichenau's army, supported by Kesselring's 2nd Air Fleet, have swept into the breach thus formed, threatening the entire Albert Canal position from the rear.'

Right at the start of the battle the bridges at Maestricht, Vroenhoven, Weldwezelt and Briegden had fallen intact into the enemy's hands.

The rapid advance on Rotterdam of von Küchler's armour had not allowed the Netherlands forces to make a stand on the Peel. They fell back towards the centre of Holland.

This withdrawal exposed the left flank of the Belgian army, which was already threatened in the centre by von Reichenau's armour. The Belgian forces were thus compelled to pull back towards Tongres — a retreat that widened the breach in the Belgian line of defence. The Germans rushed in and sped across the Albert Canal, using the undamaged part of the Maestricht–Liège road.

On the left their advance was hampered by the fort of Eben-Emaël, the beleaguerment of which had begun in the early hours of the battle.

During the night of May 10th–11th a detachment of engineers equipped with hollow-charge mines and linked by radio with parachutists installed on the turret of the fort had crossed the surrounding moat in rubber dinghies.

At 5 a.m. the final attack was made with grenades and flame-throwers. At 12.30 p.m. the fort surrendered. The garrison had lost two hundred out of a thousand men.[1]

At noon General Georges addressed the following telegram to Air Marshal Barratt, who was in command of the British Air Force in France, and to General Têtu, General Vuillemin's representative:

> In view of the seizure by German detachments of the bridges over the Albert Canal south-east of Maestricht, I demand instant intervention by the British and French air forces to slow down the progress of the German columns which might use these crossing points in order to effect a breach in the Belgian line. This operation is to be kept going so long as the threat continues.

But in vain did the bombers, with fighter protection, try to demolish the bridges and destroy the enemy columns emerging from them. They swooped down to 1,500 feet to improve their aim. German A.A. fire was fierce: one bomber was shot down; all of them were hit; next day only one could take the air; the others had to be repaired or scrapped. From the outset it was obvious that our air strength was no match for the enemy's.

At about 1 p.m. General Prioux's two mechanized divisions, deployed in front of Gembloux, found themselves battling in earnest against the two Panzer divisions belonging to von Reichenau's army. The enemy was able to call on a powerful air force, whereas Allied aerial defence was nil. Brave as they were, our units, fighting in small groups, could not long withstand the onslaught of the German armour.

On noting the French inferiority in mechanized strength, General Prioux grew uneasy. His mission, with the Belgian covering army, lay in gaining the 1st Army sufficient time to reach the Dyle and take up its positions; he judged that it was going to be hard for him to do so. At 3 p.m. he addressed the following message to General Billotte, commander of the 1st Group of Armies:

> In the absence of fighter forces it is impossible to guarantee that a

---

[1] The plan for capturing Eben-Emaël, including the use of hollow-charge mines, had been worked out by Hitler himself.

fierce thrust by the enemy will not speedily reach a point in the position to be covered.

While these operations were going on in Holland and Belgium, what was happening in the Ardennes?

Von Kleist's Armoured Group, which had crossed the minefields along the Belgian frontier during the night, had had no difficulty in throwing the 5th Light Cavalry Division and the 1st French Cavalry Brigade back on to the Semois. The decisive hour of the break-through was nearing.

At the same time Rommel dashed off this note to his wife:

> Today, for the first time since the start of the attack, I have a moment to draw breath and write. Everything is wonderful so far. I have gained a lead over my neighbours. I am quite hoarse from shouting and giving orders. I have had barely three hours' sleep ... Apart from that, I feel fine.

Later in the day, on his own initiative, General Gamelin altered the structure of the Allied High Command.

He delegated his powers to General Georges, Commander-in-Chief in the north-eastern theatre. General Georges in turn subdelegated his powers to General Billotte, commanding the 1st Group of Armies in the zone from which the French, British and Belgian forces were to operate.

This double delegation of powers had been accepted — not without objections — by the British. But it was not yet known whether the King of the Belgians would accept this formula, for it would make him subordinate to the general holding third rank in the French military hierarchy. Now, Leopold III was both a sovereign and the Commander-in-Chief of his army.

* * *

I. *Insufficient unity in the French High Command*

Under French law the political and military direction of the war was the government's responsibility. The execution of the government's directives was ensured by the 'War Committee'.

There was no single, permanent and responsible command. There were three Commanders-in-Chief: General Gamelin (land forces), General Vuillemin (air forces) and Admiral Darlan (sea forces) had to supervise operations by their respective commands quite independently in all theatres.

The idea of placing all available resources under the control of one man was envisaged only as a remote possibility. And he — General Gamelin, as it turned out — had merely vague and ill-defined rights of 'co-ordination', rights conferred by a delegation of the War Committee. His authority over the air force was limited: he was simply entitled to submit 'direct requests' to General Vuillemin. He had practically no authority over the naval forces commanded by Admiral Darlan.

Finally, he had a deputy at his side: General Georges, who exercised the functions of 'Commander-in-Chief of the north-eastern theatre'. But these functions, like the responsibilities that stemmed from them, remained confused and entangled with those of the Commander-in-Chief.

This incoherent and pointlessly complicated system led to:

(1) an excessive dispersion of headquarters;
(2) arbitrary allocation of powers and duties;
(3) considerable loss of time in the transmission of orders;
(4) lack of synchronization in their execution;
(5) a dangerous diffusion of authority.

So that in the most critical hours of the war — on May 14th and May 23rd, for instance — the French army would be literally leaderless, as a result of having too many leaders.

II. *Insufficient unity in the Inter-Allied High Command*

The lack of co-ordination between the three French services was even more pronounced in the inter-allied sphere.

The Belgian army came under the authority of King Leopold III, who so far would agree to comply only with the personal directives of General Gamelin.

As to the B.E.F., under General Lord Gort, agreement had been reached with the British High Command that it should comply with General Gamelin's instructions but not be subject to the orders of a general officer of lower rank, even if he were the commander of a Group of Armies.

III. *Insufficient armoured units*

To the 2,800 or so tanks of the Wehrmacht the French, according to M. Daladier, could oppose some 2,600. Even allowing for these figures, the power and effectiveness of French armoured units could not be compared with those of the German Panzer divisions, for the following reasons:

a. *Their tardy formation.* At the outbreak of war the tanks were scattered among twenty-five infantry support battalions (forty, including obsolete equipment) distributed over the whole front.

The first two French armoured divisions did not see the light of day till January 16th, 1940. The first was adequately trained and equipped by May 10th. The second still suffered from grave deficiencies. The third was not ready by May 10th. The formation of the fourth had scarcely begun. Its tanks were flung into the fray straight from the factory, without being run in.

b. *Their composition.* The French armoured division consisted of 169 tanks (including 18 on-the-spot spares), whereas the German Panzer division comprised, on average, 280 endless-track armoured vehicles, 200 of which were tanks (including 72 on-the-spot spares).

c. *The technical inferiority of their vehicles.* It might be true that some types were equal in armament, if not superior, to their German counterparts; but in general French tanks were slower. While the Germans had gone all out for mobility, the French had put the emphasis on power.

Their armour-plating was less strong, thickness for thickness, not (as has been claimed) because it was cast instead of being laminated — which is of minor importance — but because it was produced from unsuitable, low-grade phosphoric iron ore from Lorraine, whereas the Germans had used magnetic ore from Sweden and Czechoslovakia.

Their wireless equipment was inferior. Their petrol tanks did not hold so much, which restricted their range and independence. And just as they were dispersed among too many disparate units, so they were built in too many different designs with maximum speeds varying from 12 to 28 m.p.h.

IV. *Insufficient anti-tank weapons*

France's anti-tank equipment was inadequate both quantitatively and qualitatively. On September 1st, 1939, she had 3,800 25-mm. guns and 300 47-mm. guns. On May 10th, 1940, though she had consigned 300 25-mm. guns to Britain and 400 to Turkey, she had 5,000 of these and 1,200 47-mm. guns. But the personnel allotted to them had not yet mastered their use. And the 25-mm. gun had proved too light to be effective against tanks.

V. *Insufficient air strength*

'We went into battle,' declares General Weygand, 'with 450 fighters and 60-odd bombers, of which barely 30 were of recent design. All the rest were obsolete and so slow that they could attack only at night. They were up against 1,500 fighters (500 of them twin-engined) and 3,500 bombers.'

On May 10th the British air strength in France comprised 80 fighters and 150 bombers, shared by Lord Gort's Air Component and Air Marshal Barratt's Advanced Air Striking Force.[1]

To this numerical factor were added two others that still further accentuated German air superiority:

1. The presence, on the German side, of dive-bombers (Stukas) which were accurate in their aim and which were especially demoralizing to the French fighting man in that he was not prepared for this form of attack.
2. The perfect synchronization of the Luftwaffe and German armour, whose action on the ground it preceded, accompanied and reinforced.

Yet despite all these disadvantages French troops frequently did wonders ...

POLITICAL SITUATION

Alarmed by the bad news reaching him from the front, Paul Reynaud telephoned Daladier.

'We are emerging from our suit of armour!' he told him. 'I mean: from the fortified position along our frontiers, to go naked when we are inferior both in strength and equipment. We are exposing our naked bodies to the blows of the German army!'

'What would you have us do?' the Minister of National Defence answered laconically. 'Gamelin is in command. He is putting his plan into operation.'

In Washington, during a speech to the Eighth American Scientific Congress, President Roosevelt declared that he would do all he could to keep America out of the war.

---

[1] At this time Britain had a total of some 600-700 fighters and about 1,000 bombers.

MAY 12TH

MILITARY SITUATION

The situation in Holland was swiftly deteriorating. The Dutch army, already sorely tested, withdrew into the 'central bastion' covering the three main cities: The Hague, Amsterdam and Rotterdam.[1] Cornered against the sea, it was cut off from the Franco-Belgian forces and notably from Giràud's Army.

As a result of the German thrust towards Moerdyck, the French 7th Army was exposed on its right flank. General Giraud decided that his vanguard had ventured too far northwards and that it should be pulled back to the line Berg-op-Zoom–Lierre. This meant the final abandonment of his mission (the recapture of Rotterdam and the support of the Netherlands forces).

Massive German infantry forces crossed the Albert Canal at Vroenhoven. The Liège hinge was forced. The Belgian front was likewise broken in the area of Tongres.

The Belgians fell back on to the line Anvers–Louvain with the intention of basing their defence on Namur.

At 4 p.m. General Guderian drove to the fighting-line and urged his units on. 'Keep going! Keep going!' he shouted. 'Don't stop!' The French cavalry, which could muster only a dozen tanks in this sector, was swept off the roads. It took refuge in the woods and could do little to impede the enemy's advance. It had inflicted as much damage as it could beyond the Meuse; but this damage did not have much effect, the German engineers being very skilled at re-riveting.

In the evening, from Dinant to Sedan, the enemy was either level with the Meuse or within easy reach of it and was clashing with the French infantry. Throughout the night German motorized columns roared towards the battle with all their lights showing.

POLITICAL SITUATION

An inter-allied military conference was held in the château at Casteau, near Mons, which housed the Belgian G.H.Q. Those taking part were M.

[1] In pursuance of a plan adopted by the Dutch General Staff on February 20th, 1940.

Daladier, Minister of National Defence, the King of the Belgians, General Georges, General Pownall (representing Lord Gort) and General Billotte, commander of the 1st Group of Armies.

M. Daladier asked King Leopold if he would be so good as to 'align the conduct of Belgian army operations with the instructions that would be communicated to him by the Commander-in-Chief of the Allied armies'.

Leopold III replied that 'such a suggestion tallied entirely with his own feelings' and that he 'accepted it wholeheartedly'. From then on the Belgian army was merely a component part of the Allied front line.

For his part, General Pownall confirmed that the British High Command had agreed that delegation of powers be assigned by General Georges to General Billotte to 'ensure the co-ordination of the Allied armies in Belgium'.

MAY 13TH

Rotterdam was in chaos. The whole city was ablaze. The sky was blotted out by huge clouds of smoke which restricted visibility.

General Student, commander of the German airborne troops, was slowed down in his advance by the fires and debris obstructing the outskirts of the city. Several times he asked that the Luftwaffe should bomb the pockets of resistance and the bridges, where his paratroops were being held up.

By noon he was badly wounded and gave up his appeals. But though immobilized, he still received the city's surrender. All communication with the German G.H.Q. being cut off, he gave orders for fires to be lighted on the island in the Maas to call off the air attack that he had just summoned. These fires were the signal arranged between him and General Kesselring, to let the air crews know that the city had surrendered.

While this was going on down below, the bomber formations summoned by Student had taken off. When they were about ten miles from Rotterdam they split up into two groups. The left-hand group spotted the fires on the island and turned back. The right-hand group failed to see them on account of the poor visibility and severely bombed the town after its surrender.

With the surrender of Rotterdam the German High Command regarded operations in Holland as being virtually at an end.

Giraud's 7th Army, occupying the line Berg-op-Zoom–Turnhout Canal, was again seriously exposed. At 12.15 p.m., to stem the enemy's advance in this sector, General Gamelin sent the following message to General Lelong, French military attaché in London, and to the British Mission:

The advanced guard of our army on the left, which had been thrusting towards Breda, was unable to make a stand as a result of the intervention of a German armoured division, which makes it difficult for us to embark on an action against the bridges between Breda and

85

Dordrecht (20 kilometres south of Rotterdam). I think it would now be as well for the R.A.F. to attack these bridges and, if possible, destroy them.

At the same time Air Marshal Barratt, commander of the Advanced Air Striking Force, finding his resources inadequate, asked for five extra fighter squadrons to be flown out from England. His request was backed by Lord Gort and General Gamelin. The reinforcements were granted. But they were absurdly small — just a few dozen planes, when it was essential to throw every available aircraft into the battle.

The original plan had required Allied forces to establish themselves along the line of the Dyle by May 15th. On May 11th General Billotte had stipulated that they should be there twenty-four hours sooner. The manoeuvre, hastily carried out, was completed in the course of May 13th. A series of forced marches — some of them at the expense of artillery, which could not keep up — brought one unit after another into position during the day. The 1st Moroccan Division likewise took its place in the line that day, but the men were exhausted. In the last stage of their journey they had covered over forty miles. Contrary to expectation, the Luftwaffe made little attempt to impede these movements.

They were none too soon; for at 3.30 p.m. the general commanding the 3rd Light Mechanized Division — which had gone on ahead — reported that the withdrawal of his forces was urgent in view of the pressure of the enemy attack. At this point, though still fighting to slow down the enemy's advance (especially in the St Trond area), General Prioux's Cavalry Corps was falling back on to the 1st Army's outposts. Subjected to dive-bombing and hustled by the enemy's armour, the Cavalry Corps reached the Cointet defences (gaps had been made to let it through). Unfortunately the placing of the gaps had not been communicated to the corps commanders in sufficient detail. Many units did not manage to find them. They were trapped in the barbed wire of their own defences. A number of them were simultaneously decimated by the Panzers' fire and the explosion of Allied anti-tank mines.

When the Germans later reached this defensive position it was daylight. They had no great difficulty in finding the gaps and they negotiated them without much loss.

Thus, after the Belgian troops and the Cavalry Corps, the 1st Army was going to bear the brunt of the attack; and this time it would have to be borne 'without any thought of withdrawal'. Its objective, as laid down in Personal and Secret Instruction No. 9 (dated March 20th, 1940), was

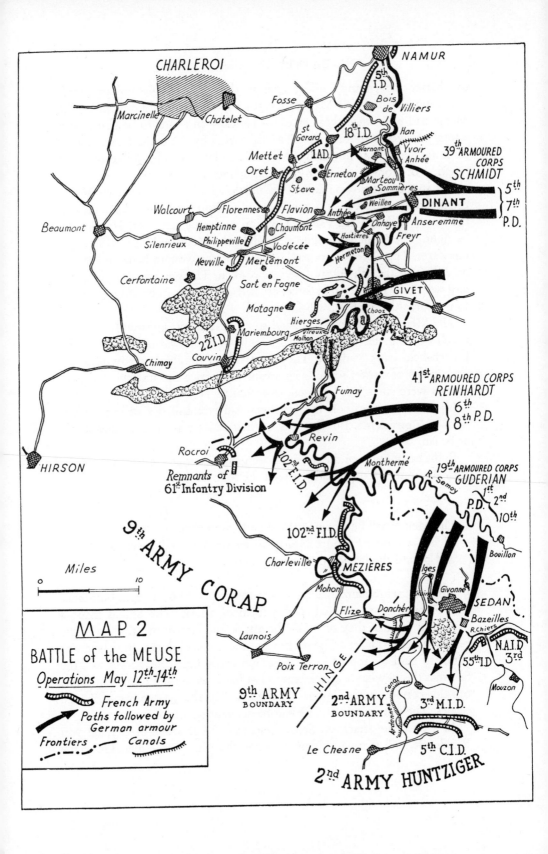

to 'shatter the enemy's effort against the Wavre – Namur position'.

During the night of May 12th–13th the German columns lining the Meuse had positioned themselves for attack — an attack to be made with a total of seven armoured divisions supported by the combined action of three air fleets. This powerful bludgeon stroke was to be delivered at the junction of Corap's 9th Army and Huntziger's 2nd Army.

The initial thrust was made in the north. At 1 a.m. the Germans hurled themselves at the river. The 7th Panzer Division, under Rommel, crossed the water with the 5th Panzer Division under General von Hartlieb on its right. The French battalion defending the Meuse at Houx was caught unawares. The German troops clambered up the western bank and settled in. A link in the 9th Army line was broken. The gap grew larger as the day went on. The German forces crossed the Meuse in unending streams to reinforce the established bridge-head.

The Meuse was likewise crossed south of Dinant, apparently without much fighting. Here again, small groups of men swarmed across to the French-held bank at dawn. They used rubber dinghies or rowing-boats or bundles of straw; some even swam. In a trice the nucleus defensive groups were encircled, besieged, overcome.

In the early afternoon the Germans had established a strong bridge-head in Monthermé. But the bulk of their effort was made farther south, at Sedan.

In the early hours of the morning General Guderian, commander of the 19th Armoured Corps, had received the following order:

H.Q., A Group

The Meuse will be stormed between Monthermé and Sedan by von Kleist's armoured group. Nearly all air strength will be engaged. It will pound the French defences for eight hours.

Normal preliminary shelling was indeed replaced by violent bombing. The French were not used to this form of attack. The Stukas made a diabolical noise as they dived to the attack and almost literally *placed* the bombs on their targets. The soldier had the impression that the plane was about to land on top of him. What especially taxed his nerves was the fact that this new-style attack was to last from noon till 4 p.m. 'Throughout this period,' notes Colonel de Bardies, 'the sky was empty of French planes. The soldier felt that he had been abandoned.'

At 4 p.m. the attack on Sedan began in the presence of General von Rundstedt. The German infantry crossed the Meuse on either side of the town. It succeeded in gaining footholds on the other bank, at Glaire and north of Bazeilles.

The French 55th and 71st Divisions, which bore the brunt of the attack, were B-class units made up of elderly reservists without much training and in poor physical shape. They did not have half the intended number (itself inadequate) of anti-tank weapons. Besides, they were spread out along broad fronts, each about ten miles wide. Disposed in depth, they had few men posted along the Meuse and the tallness of the banks made it impossible for more than a third of the guns to cover the river.

In the late afternoon the position of the 55th Division in front of Sedan had completely stove in.

General Guderian, who had crossed the Meuse in a dinghy, established that the first line of defence was pierced and that his own losses were slight. So he launched his tanks.

At 8 p.m. the Germans held a bridge-head nearly three miles broad and four miles deep. Light armoured units and anti-tank artillery, which had crossed the Meuse on rafts, advanced freely towards Rethel. Then, after clearing the Bar valley, the Germans swarmed up behind the detachments of Corap's Army that were defending the Meuse south of Mézières.

It was in the Sapogne area, at the hinge of the 9th and 2nd Armies, that the situation was most critical. Artillery formation, attacked unexpectedly, began to fall back with supply lorries.

At 9 p.m. the extreme left flank of Huntziger's Army likewise gave ground. The breach made by the Germans was growing dangerously large. The entire disposition of forces thought out by General Gamelin was in peril. 'By the evening of May 13th,' writes Pertinax, 'it was impossible to shut one's eyes to the fact that the house of cards had been undermined and was about to fall flat on the table.'

POLITICAL SITUATION

Queen Wilhelmina of the Netherlands decided to leave the Hague–Amsterdam redoubt. She asked the British government to send fighters to help her defend her country. London refused them, and instead sent a destroyer to help her leave Holland.

The Queen went aboard and asked to be taken to Flushing. The British captain replied that it was impossible and that there was nothing for it but to sail for an English port. In the end the Queen gave way.

That evening the Queen addressed the following proclamation to the Dutch people:

> Our heart goes out towards our compatriots, who in our beloved country will have to pass through hard times. In due course, however, with God's help, the Netherlands will regain their European territory.

In Rome Mussolini told Count Ciano: 'A few months ago I said the Allies had let victory slip from their grasp. Today I say they have lost the war. We have no time to lose. Before the month is out I shall enter the lists.'

MAY 14TH

MILITARY SITUATION

On learning that Giraud's Army had been ordered to withdraw, King Leopold realized that the Belgian army was going to be faced with an appalling dilemma. Either it must fall back towards France with the Anglo-French forces or — if the Germans fully exploited their break-through at Sedan — it would be driven back to the sea with a small group of Allied forces and compelled to surrender like Holland.

Prioux's Cavalry Corps had ended its withdrawal at the rear of the fighting line. Having suffered heavy losses in the course of the past few days, it had to be reconstituted.

The main units of the 1st Army had now made contact, but in highly unfavourable conditions. After their long march they had scarcely formed up. They were still without part of their artillery. It was in this precarious state that the army was fiercely and simultaneously attacked by tanks and dive-bombers.

But it was in the sectors held by the 9th and 2nd Armies that the situation was most disquieting. The attack launched on the Meuse the day before was reaching its zenith. The German pocket north of Dinant was growing. In the shelter of the bridge-heads previously established the bulk of the German armour now began to press forward. This huge mass of steel crossed the Meuse by means of a bridge put up at Gaulier by the German Engineering Corps.

Alerted by General Gamelin, who singled out the crossings at Sedan and Dinant as priority targets, the French air force now intervened force-fully. 'The tragedy was,' writes Colonel de Bardies, 'that it was too weak and consisted mainly of out-of-date planes. Yet there was still only one bridge in service at the time. The air force attacked it all day long ... We lost more than 40 planes.'

The British Advanced Air Striking Force (the strength of which had just been raised to 250 planes at Air Marshal Barratt's request) took part in the raid and suffered heavy losses. Six Fairey Battles attacked the German pontoneers; none returned. Not far away 60 British bombers raided some enemy columns that had crossed the Meuse; 35 failed to return. A harsh lesson, which the British were never to forget.

On the ground, meanwhile, Corap's ravaged army scarcely even *looked* like a disciplined force. The Luftwaffe pitched into the command posts; it scoured the roads, bombed the intersections, made it impossible for reinforcements to be brought up, disorganized communications. The withdrawal very soon acquired the appearance of a rout. The infantry shunned open country. The artillery was paralysed; most of the horses had been machine-gunned from the air; the guns were immobilized and could not be trained. Lorries heaped with men of all services scurried from the front.

At noon the 1st Armoured Division, which on May 12th had been transported by train to a point east of Charleroi, was ordered to stand by to go into action in the Dinant area. 'It took them a long time to reach their positions,' writes Bardies, 'for the roads were cluttered with fleeing troops and civilians ... It took the armoured division seven hours to cover twenty miles. It was short of petrol. It would be unable to fight that day. Its commander halted it.'

The 3rd Armoured Division, which arrived shortly afterwards in the zone held by Huntziger's Army, would likewise be unfit for action on May 14th. The 5th Light Cavalry Division, which had already suffered badly in the Ardennes, was annihilated.

Touchon's 6th Army, summoned to the rescue round about midday, did not get there in time. The day was over before its forward units could join battle.

In the evening the defence of the Bar had caved in. To retain a coherent army, General Huntziger had to fall back. But he was hesitant as to which direction to take. By retiring, he risked exposing either the Paris area or the northern flank of the Maginot Line. He telephoned Supreme Headquarters for instructions. He received no answer.

A few hours later General Georges, whom he had again approached, told him: 'Do the best you can.'

At this, the Commander of the 2nd Army withdrew westwards to the Chesne and the Stonne hills, while keeping his right flank, which would form a pivot, hinged to the Maginot Line.

General Huntziger having opened one leaf of the door to avoid being swept away, General Corap — after resisting on the first line — now opened the other.

At 1.30 a.m., following a telephone conversation with General Billotte, General Corap decided to abandon the entire stretch of the Meuse north of Sedan and make a stand along the line Rocroi–Signy l'Abbaye–Omont;

in other words he was moving back to the prearranged second position. 'Now this,' writes Bardies, 'existed only on paper. It was completely unmanned; the army corps that was going to pull back on the right of Corap's army — the 41st Corps — was a fortress unit, quite unable to manoeuvre. In short, the order could not be carried out.'

To the ten-mile gap that the Germans achieved at the expense of Huntziger's 2nd Army was now added a breach some thirty miles wide in the sector held till now by Corap's 9th Army. Seven of the Wehrmacht's ten Panzer divisions struck out towards the Channel ports via Péronne and Cambrai, with Rommel's 7th Panzer Division at their head.

This was the start of the 'German pocket' which was to cut the Allied forces in two. From then on their units fighting in Flanders were threatened with encirclement. The order for a general withdrawal should have been given at once. But the French High Command obviously did not grasp the intentions of the German General Staff. It underestimated the strategic significance of events on the Meuse front; in fact, it was not sufficiently informed of them. The 1st Group of Armies was not ordered back for another forty-eight hours, and by then it was too late to save them from the trap closing about them.

'It is no exaggeration to say that we lost the war that day,' writes Kammerer.

MAY 15TH

In Holland, General Winckelmann had capitulated. The whole Dutch army was taken prisoner with its leaders. Only the forces in Zeeland, under Admiral van der Stadt, were ordered to fight on beside the French.

The surrender of Holland compelled the 7th Army to hasten its withdrawal.

Receiving M. Pierlot, head of the Belgian government, at his G.H.Q. in Breendonck, King Leopold III led him to a map, pointed to the French coast lining the Straits of Dover and said: 'The Germans will be there within a week.'

When M. Pierlot suggested that in that case the Belgian army ought to retreat westwards and southwards, the King replied: 'No, not southwards — northwards.'

In Flanders the German 6th Army, supported by two air fleets under Kesselring and von Sperrle, tore into attack against the Allied forces. These consisted of the sixteen French divisions of Blanchard's 1st Army. Statistically the Germans were outnumbered two to one. But they had powerful air support, whereas Blanchard's was non-existent. Their armour was united in balanced divisions, backed by reconnaissance and magnificently equipped with anti-tank guns; they were linked by radio and acting in co-ordination with their aircraft. Their technical superiority was considerable. Above all, they were borne along by their tremendous fighting spirit.

The 1st Moroccan Division bore the brunt of the attack, on the Gembloux plain. The Allied front was dented. But after a momentary disarray the German thrust was contained. The armour had not managed to pierce the French lines.

Along the Meuse, on the other hand, the break-through was complete and the debacle that had started the day before was gradually taking final shape.

The success of the break-through was so complete that the German General Staff could scarcely believe their good fortune. An unexpected stiffening in French resistance round Stonne made them uneasy and prompted General von Rundstedt to issue the following order: 'Advancing beyond bridge-heads forbidden.' Blind with rage, Guderian blazed up at this 'disastrous' order.[1] He exploded, subjected Group Headquarters to vehement protests and finally won his case.

'Subsequently,' he was to write in his memoirs, 'I received no orders extending beyond the creation of bridge-heads on the left bank of the Meuse ... The High Command was principally concerned with slowing down my advance.'

A veritable race ensued between the various Panzer divisions. 'At about 9 a.m.,' writes Rommel, 'the tanks started moving forward. After a brief engagement with enemy tanks near Flavion, the Panzer Regiment advanced in column to Philippeville. On the way it passed numerous guns and vehicles belonging to a French unit whose men threw themselves flat at our approach. No doubt they had previously suffered badly from our dive-bombing.'

Progressing at about forty miles an hour the 7th Panzer Division successively passed through Seuzeille, Cerfontaine and Froidchapelle.

What were the French armoured units doing at the time?

The 1st Tank Division under General Bruneau advanced westwards of the Anthée–Dinant road. At 9 a.m. the 1st Semi-Brigade was already engaged. The struggle continued in deadly earnest till 5.30 p.m. When the 28th Battalion received the order to fall back to the line Florennes–Mettet it had only seven tanks left.[2] General Bruneau tried to regroup his decimated forces in the area of Solre-le-Château. His communications were so weak that he had to abandon the attempt. He then ordered the general retreat of his armour to Beaumont. But the Panzers had outflanked the French units and held many of the points through which they had to pass. A further twenty-eight tanks were destroyed in the course of this retreat. By the evening of May 15th nothing was left of the 1st Armoured Division. 'It found itself up against the two Panzer divisions that had crossed the Meuse at Dinant,' records Bardies. 'It fought bravely, though outnumbered two to one. It was sacrificed in the hope of stemming a rout, sacrificed entirely in vain, for the rout went on.'

The 2nd Armoured Division under General Bruché had been ordered at 12.15 p.m. on May 13th to head for Fourmies so as to attack towards Houx. But when its constituent elements reached Châlons station at 8 p.m.

---

[1] 'At heart,' writes the commander of the 19th Armoured Corps, 'Rundstedt and Halder had no confidence in the penetrating power of tanks.'
[2] This is the action to which Rommel refers above.

the traffic-control officer was unable to provide even one of the twenty-nine lifts of trucks needed for its conveyance.

On the morning of May 14th, General Bruché called at the 1st Army's provisional H.Q. in Valenciennes. There he learned that the order directing the 2nd Armoured Division to counter-attack towards Houx had been rescinded and that the division was to reassemble north of Charleroi, where it would relieve the 1st Armoured Division ('assigned to another mission').

But the 2nd Armoured Division never went to Charleroi.

[*Orders and counter-orders issued under misapprehension of the situation led to the loss of more than half the strength of this division.* — Ed.]

The 3rd Armoured Division was still considered unfit for service on May 10th. Some of the engines were not run-in. It still lacked armoured supply vans, light armoured cars and other essential equipment. It was hurried towards Sedan, but mechanically the High Command was asking too much of it. Paralysed by the faulty workmanship of its caterpillars, it too was to be attacked and destroyed in successive stages without in any way influencing the course of events.

Von Kleist later stated that its counter-attacks did not endanger the German advance in any way, despite subsequent claims. 'Guderian dealt with them without bothering me, and I did not hear about them till the day after.'

There remained one last group of tanks, which were hurried to the Sissonne area and baptized the 4th Armoured Division. Its leader, Colonel de Gaulle, was summoned to G.H.Q. for his instructions. 'These were communicated to me by the Chief of Staff,' writes de Gaulle. 'They were wide. "The High Command," General Doumenc told me, "wishes to establish a defensive front along the Aisne and the Ailette which will bar the way to Paris. The 6th Army under General Touchon, made up of units mustered in the East, will deploy there. With your division, which will operate alone in the Laon area, you must gain enough time for them to take up their positions." '[1]

While the 4th Armoured Division prepared to carry out the mission entrusted to it, other units that had been unable to take up their positions during May 14th entered the cauldron. It was in these conditions that General Touchon strove to plug the gap with the 6th Army. His main orders were to resist at all cost along the line Rocroi–Lêprou-les-Vallées–Signy l'Abbaye–Poix-Terron: the second line of defence.

---

[1] It will not escape notice that the role assigned by the French High Command to its last remaining armoured formation was still not an attacking one. This was a *delaying action* to enable Touchon's Army to re-establish a continuous front between the Aisne and the Ailette.

'The tragedy was,' writes Colonel de Bardies, 'that we did not know to which units this order applied. Those fleeing from the first line of defence were in no condition to carry it out. We needed organized units from behind the front. But of all the reinforcements announced by G.H.Q. only the 1st Battalion, 152nd Infantry, was in position. At about 12.30 p.m. it ran into a column of 200 tanks near Poix-Terron. It was held up and encircled; at nightfall it finally managed to disengage after losing all its 25-mm. guns and a third of its men but destroying some twenty tanks ... '

With the consent of G.H.Q. General Touchon decided to remuster his forces along the Aisne.[1]

General Corap was relieved of his command. He was replaced by General Giraud, recalled from Anvers. The troops of the 7th Army were to follow; they were to reconstitute the 9th, which was practically annihilated.

Meanwhile Guderian's and Reinhardt's Panzer divisions continued their thrust towards the sea. At 8 p.m. they were near Montcornet, twenty-two miles from Laon. As the crow flies, the breach in the flank of the French armies now measured forty-four miles. It stretched from Maubeuge to Château-Porcien. And now there was nothing left to stem the advance of the German columns.

'Looking back towards the east from a hilltop,' writes Rommel, 'I observed innumerable columns of dust rising as far as the eye could see in the gathering darkness, encouraging signs that the advance of our armour into conquered territory had begun.'

General Gamelin was overwhelmed by the reports reaching him from all sectors of the front. At 8.30 p.m., from his G.H.Q. in Vincennes, he telephoned M. Daladier, the Minister of National Defence, to inform him of the gravity of the situation.

POLITICAL SITUATION

M. Daladier received the C.-in-C.'s telephone call in his office in the Rue Saint-Dominique.

'Up to this point,' writes Pertinax, 'he [General Gamelin] seems to have cherished the illusion that everything could be "patched up". Suddenly his eyes were opened.'

Mr William Bullitt witnessed the scene. The United States ambassador

---

[1] 'Apparently General Touchon thought the Germans were using only slender forces and saw Sedan as a minor incident to be set right,' records Colonel de Bardies. 'He too had failed to grasp the enemy's intention.'

arrived at the War Ministry at 7.45 p.m. Daladier had only just got back from a meeting of the War Committee. The ex-Premier was confident about the way the battle was going. Gamelin had set his mind at rest. But then the telephone rang. The C.-in-C. was calling from the keep at Vincennes. Daladier listened impassively.

Suddenly he shouted: 'No! What you are saying cannot be true! You are mistaken! It cannot be true!'

Gamelin had just informed him that a German armoured column, having smashed everything in its path, was cruising along between Rethel and Laon. The news took Daladier's breath away. Somehow he found the strength to shout: 'You must attack at once!'

'Attack!' replied Gamelin. 'What with? I have no reserves left.'

Lengthy explanations followed. They ended in the General's saying: 'I have only a single corps between Laon and Paris.'

Daladier's face was becoming more and more contorted. He seemed to grow smaller before Mr Bullitt's eyes.

The ominous discussion finished with this exchange: 'So it means the destruction of the French army?'

'Yes, it means the destruction of the French army!'

At the same hour Churchill sent Roosevelt a cable which, writes Robert E. Sherwood, 'was full of dark forebodings for the German conquest of Europe with "astonishing swiftness". He contemplated the possibility of heavy bombing of Britain and of paratroop attacks. He predicted that Mussolini would burst into the war to collect his share of the "loot of civilization" ... He asked the President to proclaim a state of "non-belligerency" for the United States, which would mean supplying all kinds of aid but no armed action.'

What was the position of the United States government at the time? Langer states that in this moment of crisis the possibility of America's coming directly to the aid of her friends was extremely limited. Both public opinion and feeling within Congress were still rigidly isolationist, and the government's activities were severely hampered by the laws of neutrality formulated during the past few years. Supplying France with military aid was therefore out of the question.

Daladier and General Gamelin decided to wire Churchill for more intensive support from the Royal Air Force.

'The British Prime Minister ... promised to try to send more fighter planes to the continent,' states Langer. 'But nothing came of the project, for an overwhelming majority of the [British] War Cabinet voted it down.'

'Everything,' writes Colonel de Bardies, 'seemed to point to the fact that Britain's leaders, realizing that this first battle — and possibly the whole battle of France — was lost, feared for England's security and did not intend to expend their air strength on any pretext.'

That day Paul Reynaud spoke of Marshal Pétain for the first time.

'Oh, if only the Marshal were here!' he said to Paul Baudouin.

Without delay he sent for General Pujo and asked him to catch the Sud-Express that very night and fetch the Marshal from Madrid.

MAY 16TH

MILITARY SITUATION

Overnight General Gamelin decided to order the general withdrawal of French forces in Belgium. But whereas, if the situation were to be effectively remedied, this withdrawal should have been swift and wholesale, the Command was content with half-measures; so that in fact it was executed too slowly and on too small a scale for its aim to be fully achieved.

Lord Gort, who favoured the idea of the withdrawal, sent his government several telegrams on the subject. From these it emerged that:

1. He was to 'solicit' this order from General Billotte on the morning of May 16th.
2. The beginning of the withdrawal to the Escaut was fixed for the night of May 16th–17th. It was to be carried out in three stages and completed on the night of May 18th–19th.

General Billotte further stipulated that the intervening halts might be extended.

In pursuance of this order the Belgian army abandoned the Anvers–Louvain position which it had expected to defend.

The 1st Army followed the general movement and fell back on to Brussels and the Charleroi Canal.

Though necessary, this withdrawal disturbed the unity of the alliance in Belgium. The British, and Lord Gort in particular, regarded this 'breaking-off' as inadequate. On the other hand, the King of the Belgians carried it out reluctantly, for it meant handing his capital over to the Germans.

The 9th Army, now become Giraud's Army, continued its retreat between the Sambre and the Meuse.

General Gamelin repeated his appeal for British air reinforcements. That morning he sent the following telegram to General Lelong:

No. 529 Cab/D.N.   May 16th, 1940
            For Mr Winston Churchill

I venture to reiterate request for immediate dispatch of ten fighter squadrons.

Situation very serious. Naturally these ten squadrons would be based along the Lower Seine, where they are safe and whence it will be easy for you to get them back.

GAMELIN

The one favourable aspect of the situation was the regrouping of Hunt-ziger's 2nd Army in the Stonne area. And the German thrust in the neighbourhood of Laon was reported to be slowing down. Was there a chance of stopping the advance of the enemy columns and 'stabilizing' the front? The hope, briefly cherished, was soon gone.

For towards nightfall a German detachment approaching from the east succeeded in crossing the fortified position in the area south of Solre. At about 10 p.m. it reached the Solre–Avesnes road. It passed through the encampment of regrouped elements of the 18th Division, without bothering them too much, and sprang a surprise on an artillery group that was bivouacking along the Semousies road. Towards midnight it halted on the outskirts of Avesnes, with all its lights extinguished, seized some lone officers who were going by, veered westwards till it reached the Landrecies road and finally entered Avesnes with plenty of light and clatter as though it had in fact come from Landrecies.

This dramatic intrusion added considerably to the confusion south of the Sambre next morning.

The raid on Avesnes was, indeed, one of the most spectacular and effective of Rommel's deeds. Here is his account of it:

The light was fading. In the growing dusk farms were blazing here and there, towards Clairfayts and farther westward. I gave orders for an immediate penetration of the fortified zone and as much progress as possible towards Avesnes.

The moon had risen, so that for the time being we could not count on real darkness ... The long line of tanks drove through the line of fortifications and towards the first houses ... In the moonlight we could pick out the men of the 7th Motor-cycle Battalion who were advancing on foot beside us ... Already we were 500, then 1,000, then 2,000, then 3,000 metres inside the fortified zone. Amid the deafening roar of our engines and the rumble of our caterpillars it was impossible to make out whether the enemy was firing.

Soon we reached the first houses of Solre-le-Château. The inhabitants were rudely awakened by the rumble of our tanks, the clatter of the caterpillars, the roar of the engines. Soldiers were camping beside the road, army vehicles were parked in the farmyards and in some places on the road itself. With a look of terror on their faces civilians and soldiers piled into ditches and trenches and flattened themselves beside hedges ... We drove past long lines of carts abandoned by refugees who had fled in panic into the fields lining the road. We cruised on towards our objective (Avesnes). At frequent intervals I would take a quick look at the map with a shaded torch and send a radio message to Divisional H.Q., to give them our position and let them know that everything was going well ...

Suddenly we saw a flash from a hillock about 300 yards away and to the right of the road. Presumably a gun, well concealed in a concrete shelter, was firing at the flank of the 25th Panzer division ... I ordered the regiment to increase speed and fire salvos right and left as it cleared this second line of defence.

Firing began at once. All our shells were tracers and the regiment showered the countryside with light as it cleared the second line. We were quickly clear of the danger zone ... There was utter confusion among the French ...

We went through Semousies. It was the same story: soldiers and civilians fleeing on either side of the road ... In Avesnes itself, which had been shelled by our artillery shortly beforehand, the whole population stood packed between guns and vehicles on either side of the road before our advancing column. Everything pointed to the fact that the town was occupied by a sizeable French force.

We had reached our objective and that was the main thing. But the enemy in Avesnes (there must have been a battalion of tanks at least) profited from the gaps that had opened in the procession of Panzers. Heavy French tanks lost no time in sealing off the road running through the town. The street fighting became fiercer and fiercer. The battle in Avesnes lasted till 4 a.m. Finally the powerful enemy tanks were knocked out. The battle ended in the first light of dawn.

Meanwhile, in the sector between the Serre and the Aisne, the crews of Guderian's Armoured Corps were weary from their uninterrupted exertions during the past six days and ammunition was beginning to run out. But French resistance gave the impression of weakening. Guderian writes:

In the market-place in Montcornet were gathered several hundred French prisoners belonging to various units. Their eyes betrayed their surprise at seeing us. A company of enemy tanks trying to enter the town from the south-west was taken prisoner. It belonged to Colonel de Gaulle's division, which was reported to be in the area north of Laon. I set up my command post in the little village of Soizé, to the east of Montcornet.

Still farther south, in the Sissonne area, the French retreat went on, turning into more and more of a rout. Between the forces now commanded by General Giraud and the remnants of the 53rd Infantry Division there was a vast open space where the Germans were masters.

Throughout the day the exodus of civilian populations intensified. Already millions of refugees were on the roads.

They fled, accelerating their cars, pushing their hand-carts, bombed and machine-gunned by the German air force. In their scattered houses they had enjoyed relative safety. They preferred to congregate in long columns exposed to the enemy's fire. Their flight was suicide.[1]

The 1st Armoured Division was all but destroyed. Was the 2nd at last to be brought into action?
[*The splitting-up of this division and the irreconcilable orders issued to it prevented it from aiding General de Gaulle's attack at Montcornet. — Ed.*]

With members of his Staff, Colonel de Gaulle did some reconnoitring east of the Sissonne Canal. His findings were appalling. All the roads from the north were packed with pitiable convoys of refugees. There were also a number of unarmed soldiers. Overtaken in their flight by enemy mechanized detachments, they had been ordered to throw down their rifles and head south so as not to clutter the roads. De Gaulle writes:

At the sight of that distracted throng and those troops in headlong flight, and on hearing of that contemptuous piece of insolence on the part of the enemy, I was filled with indescribable fury. Oh, it was really too stupid! The war was off to an unspeakably bad start. So it was essential to go on. There was world enough and time.[2] If I lived I would fight, wherever I had to, so long as I had to, till the enemy was defeated and the national taint expunged. What I was able to do later I resolved upon that day.

During the night it was learned at General Gamelin's G.H.Q. that the 61st Division, which had been fighting along the Meuse, was falling back on Compiègne. This news caused consternation in Vincennes.

---

1 Fabre-Luce: *Journal de la France, mars 1939-juillet 1940.*
2 This reads like wisdom after the event. It is unlikely that de Gaulle had these thoughts at the time. But there is no reason to question the sincerity of his indignation.

THE BATTLE IN THE NORTH

POLITICAL SITUATION

M. Pierlot, the Belgian Prime Minister, M. Spaak, the Minister of Foreign Affairs, and General Denis, the Minister of National Defence, left Brussels — according to Admiral Keyes 'after urging the French and British' ambassadors to precede them, so as to justify their own flight'.

In the early hours of the morning Paul Reynaud, recalled from Louveciennes, heard General Gamelin confirm on the telephone to M. Daladier that 'the Germans may be in Paris tonight'.

At 10 a.m. General Héring, Military Governor of Paris, after being informed by G.H.Q. of the size of the breach that had opened in the front, wrote to the Premier:

> In the present circumstances I think it wise to suggest, so as to avoid any disorder, that you should prescribe the evacuation of the government ... the Chamber of Deputies and the Senate to the prearranged areas of withdrawal.[1]

At 11 a.m. Paul Reynaud called a meeting of some members of his government, the leaders of the Senate and Chamber, General Héring, M. Langeron (the Prefect of Police) and a number of other important people who happened to be available. They did not disguise their panic. Some of the opinions voiced were quite extraordinarily wild. It was even suggested that shallow-draught warships might sail up the Seine and defend Paris.

Transference of the seat of government to Tours was ordered and the departure fixed for 4 p.m.

Paul Reynaud was visibly alarmed. Immediately after the meeting, on his own initiative, he addressed the following telegram to General Weygand in Beirut:

> The gravity of the military situation on the Western Front is increasing. I request you return to Paris without delay. Make necessary arrangements for handing over your duties to officer of your choice. Desirable your departure be kept secret.

Then he sent Churchill the following SOS:

Last evening we lost the battle.
The way to Paris lies open.
Send all the troops and planes you can.

[1] Overnight General Gamelin had taken a few steps to strengthen the capital's defence. Forty squads of *Gardes mobiles*, withdrawn from the armies, were placed at the Military Governor's disposal; three anti-aircraft units (equipped with 1932-vintage 75-mm. guns) which had been due to leave for the front that day were left in the Paris area. Paltry measures.

In the meantime, a strange scene was occurring at the Ministry of Foreign Affairs.

'On this fine day,' writes Alfred Fabre-Luce, 'passers-by down on the quays were amazed to see a low cloud raining scraps of charred paper. It was the *auto-da-fé* of the Quai d'Orsay. Ton after ton of documents was being tipped, out of all the office windows, into a blazing fire in the centre of the courtyard. Projected pacts, dreamed-of partitions and secret engagements thus returned to their natural element: smoke. In Warsaw and Oslo the Wehrmacht had reaped a rich harvest. With these warnings in mind, the Quai sought to avert the publication of a new White Paper. (It was to appear all the same: at Charité-sur-Loire the Germans were to seize an army train containing copies of the destroyed documents.) This conflagration set imaginations working. Everyone was looking into his or her conscience and feeling wary of the retribution soon to be dealt out by the enemy, whose arrival would break in upon the petty corruptions of the Republic.'

'The third floor,' adds Roger Peyrefitte, an eye-witness of the scene, 'where the most important departments were situated, was also that of the most active defenestration. From there one could see the garden of the Minister's residence. On the veranda Paul Reynaud and Mandel looked on with livid faces as the attendants sprinkled petrol on the documents heaped on the lawn and stoked the fire with gardening tools.'

And Pertinax tells us: 'The impatience of Reynaud and his entourage was so great that, when the fire did not burn quickly enough for their liking, they thought of having some of the papers dumped in the Seine.'

At about 3.30 p.m. Paul Reynaud addressed the Chamber of Deputies:

Hitler means to win the war in two months. If he fails he is doomed, and he knows it ... The period we are about to pass through may have nothing in common with the one we have just passed through. We shall be called upon to take steps that only yesterday would have seemed revolutionary. Perhaps we shall have to change both methods and men ... (*Loud cheers.*)

Edouard Herriot presided at the meeting and ended it with the words:

France is alive to the grandeur and tragedy of this ordeal. She will live up to her past and her destiny ... No doubt the Chamber will wish to assign to its leader the responsibility of summoning it when the government has something to communicate. (*Widespread approval.*)

'We were far from the principle of uninterrupted sessions!' remarked

Louis-Dominique Girard. Beneath its innocuous exterior, M. Herriot's closing sentence was of capital importance, though its full significance did not become clear till several weeks later.

Meanwhile Mr Winston Churchill, alarmed by M. Daladier's appeal for help the night before and by M. Reynaud's message at about 12.30 p.m., flew into Paris.

At 5.20 p.m. an Anglo-French meeting was held at the Quai d'Orsay. It was attended by Winston Churchill, General Sir John Dill,[1] M. Paul Reynaud, Daladier and General Gamelin. The discussion was very lively. M. Roland de Margerie records:

Mr Winston Churchill began by stating that he had been none too clear how things stood on hearing that the government was thinking of leaving Paris.

General Gamelin then outlined the situation of our armies and stressed the seriousness of the bulge that the Germans had managed to create in our front ...

M. Paul Reynaud pointed out that the German tanks, followed by lorry-loads of infantry, had rushed into this gap and were now fanning out in three directions ...

In reply to a question from Mr Winston Churchill, the General [Gamelin] made it clear that at the far north of the line the French army that had advanced into the Low Countries ... had now fallen back towards the Escaut.

Mr Winston Churchill then declared that he could not understand how a withdrawal involving the abandonment of Brussels and Louvain could have been contemplated: as he saw it, the Anglo-Belgian armies in Brabant were well-placed to launch a vigorous counter-attack against the flank of the German armies advancing on Laon ...

M. Daladier firmly opposed this view; the French army had nothing left with which to cover Paris, and in these circumstances it was essential to fall back to the Sambre to avoid being left completely in the air.

[1] From then onwards there were to be two conflicting views within the British Cabinet and the Imperial General Staff. Winston Churchill and General Ironside were for continuing operations on the continent to the bitter end. Sir John Dill (Ironside's deputy) and Lord Gort advocated a policy of husbanding Britain's resources and withdrawing to the U.K. in anticipation of a long war. Their outlook was shared by several members of the Cabinet, especially by Mr Eden, Secretary of State for War, and Lord Halifax, Secretary of State for Foreign Affairs.
Slowly but surely the second view won the day. Mr Churchill came round to it, and on May 24th Sir John Dill replaced General Ironside as Chief of Imperial General Staff.

The Prime Minister, on the other hand, thought this was the time to stand firm ...

Mr Churchill was loath to take quite so serious a view of the threat constituted by the tanks. Unless they were backed by sizeable infantry units, they represented only a limited force ... He refused to see the spectacular raid by the German tanks as a real invasion.

'It is, though,' countered M. Daladier. ' ... The presence of the Anglo-French-Belgian armies in northern Belgium is now quite pointless.'

'On the contrary,' insisted Mr Churchill, 'this is the time for thrusting in that direction, not for retreating.'

General Gamelin appositely pointed out that it was Lord Gort himself who desired the withdrawal.

General Sir John Dill disclosed that he had been on the telephone to Lord Gort during the day ... The British general did indeed think it best to retire towards the canal behind the city of Brussels (the Lys Canal).

General Gamelin felt that this would have the advantage of shortening the front, and he added that it was very important for us that the British army should spread out more, so as to occupy a front corresponding to that held by the French army ...

Mr Churchill still could not understand the need for the withdrawal in Brabant. He had always been told that by directing their armies towards Amsterdam the Allies were gaining the support of the Belgian army and saving about twenty divisions. In his view it was better to make a stand, even though they might have to reduce strength in the north to reinforce the armies in the south.

General Gamelin stated that four divisions had already been drawn from reserves in the north and that there was no hope of finding more in the same area.

Mr Churchill was still doubtful as to whether they would be doing the right thing by abandoning Louvain. To which General Gamelin replied that the main thing was to arrest the Paris bulge ... It was to arrest this bulge that the French government had so persistently asked for the support of the Royal Air Force.

Mr Winston Churchill then explained at length that he could not weaken the defence of the British Isles and refused to modify the strategy of the R.A.F.

British fighter squadrons had gone into action near Sedan, he declared. It had to be admitted that out of 67 planes 36 had failed to return. Now, the bridges across the Meuse could be quickly rebuilt ... On the other hand, such sacrifices were justified if it were a case of attacking essential targets, the destruction of which affected or threatened the German war potential. Thus, the R.A.F. had attacked Germany within the Ruhr, with definite results. Now, of the 112 planes that had taken part in this night-time operation only two had failed to return. This was the type of operation that paid. The R.A.F. was going to continue along these lines.

During the morning, he went on, four additional squadrons ... must have reached the French front. That made eight in all — say 108 planes ... This was an impressive array, and one that must obtain results. But it was impossible to expect planes to fight tanks. Tanks could only be fought on the ground and by infantry.

Churchill was strongly critical of the French ministers, considering them 'incomprehensibly demoralized'.

In the evening a private reception was held at M. Paul Reynaud's residence. Mr Churchill and M. Daladier were invited. An eye-witness (Pertinax) has painted a striking picture of the scene:

The [French] Premier and the Minister of National Defence sat facing one another in the study in the Place du Palais Bourbon: Daladier crushed, bowed down with grief; Reynaud silent and with his head erect, like some small broken piece of machinery. The British Prime Minister walked to and fro, upbraiding them: 'You must not lose heart! Did you ever suppose we should achieve victory except after dire set-backs?' ...

To put new heart into his companions Churchill read out the telegram that he had sent to London after the meeting earlier in the day. In it he had tried to give some impression of the situation in France, even alluding to the archives burning in the garden of the Quai d'Orsay.

Mr Churchill then announced that the R.A.F. was willing to place ten extra squadrons at the High Command's disposal.

M. Reynaud thanked him warmly for this good news.

While this meeting was going on behind closed doors, the French national radio broadcast the following address by Paul Reynaud:

The absurdest rumours have been put about. It has been said that the government intends to leave Paris: that is false. The government is, and will remain, in Paris.

It has been said that the enemy was using new and unanswerable weapons, whereas our airmen are covering themselves with glory, whereas our heavy tanks outclass the German tanks of the same category.

It has been said that the enemy was in Rheims. It has even been said that he was in Meaux, whereas he has merely managed to form a broad pocket, south of the Meuse, that our gallant troops are striving to fill in.

We filled in plenty in 1918, as those of you who fought in the last war will not have forgotten!

In Washington President Roosevelt told Congress that he knew how anxious its members were that the United States should not be dragged into the armed conflict which was sweeping through Europe. He said that he would devote all his energies to warding off the danger of such an occurrence.

MAY 17TH

In the far north, squadrons of destroyers under the command of Admiral Platon completed the evacuation of the two cruelly decimated regiments occupying the island of Walcheren and Zuid Beveland, at the mouth of the Escaut.

The British Expeditionary Force withdrew to the line of the Senne. The 1st Army fell back from the Charleroi Canal to the frontier position.

The units of von Reichenau's 6th Army entered Brussels and forced the French frontier position south of Maubeuge. They reached the Mormal Forest and debouched on to the rear lines of communication of the 1st Army, whose right wing was completely exposed.

The order to fall back had come too late. Lord Gort, as Colonel de Bardies comments, 'had good cause to be concerned'.

Since the previous morning the 7th Panzer Division had advanced fifty miles, as a result of its bold tactics during the night. It reached the Sambre and crossed it without any difficulty.

On the Laon–Montcornet axis the 4th French Armoured Division (some of its forward elements had been at grips with Guderian's vanguard since the day before) prepared to stem the advance of the German 19th Armoured Corps. Lieutenant Galimand has painted a harrowing picture of the confusion in which France's best formations had been thrown into action:

> The first tank battalions arrived during the night of May 16th–17th. The 46th Battalion of the 6th Semi-Brigade, originally intended for service with light tanks, had just been transformed into a battalion equipped with heavy 'B' tanks. It had never executed a tactical manoeuvre and had been allowed only one practice spell with the 75-mm. gun ... Heroism and audacity made up for ignorance and unpreparedness. The tanks fought their way into Lislet and Montcornet. But there was no infantry to hold the positions taken by the armour, and the Stukas were in action again. De Gaulle gave the order to regroup west of the line Chivres–Sissonne.

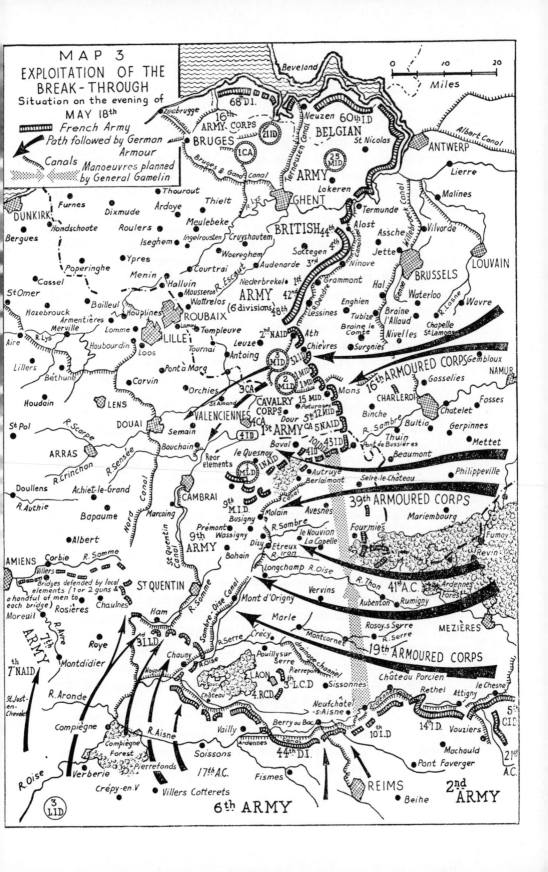

MAP 3
EXPLOITATION OF THE
BREAK-THROUGH
Situation on the evening of
MAY 18th
▬▬ French Army
◀━ Path followed by German
        Armour
░░ Canals
▒▒ Manoeuvres planned
        by General Gamelin

By a strange trick of fate Hitler was to bring about what de Gaulle and his 4th Armoured Division had failed to achieve.

On the morning of May 17th the Führer drove to von Rundstedt's headquarters. He recommended the commander of the A Group of Armies to pay the greatest attention to his left flank, which he considered dangerously exposed to a French counter-attack.

General von Kleist sped to Guderian's command post. He blamed him for his temerity.

'You have infringed the orders of the High Command,' he told him. 'They limited your mission to crossing the Meuse and establishing bridge-heads on the left bank of the river. Why did you exceed them?'

White with rage, Guderian protested and demanded to be relieved forthwith of his command. General von Kleist was stunned for a moment, but eventually agreed. Just as Guderian was preparing to hand over to the divisional commander appointed to succeed him, General List arrived. The commander of the 12th Army was amazed by this quarrel and asked what had caused it. He then revoked von Kleist's decision, asked Guderian to remain in command of the 19th Armoured Corps, and authorized the Panzers — pending better orders — to carry out 'fighting reconnaissance' missions (*Kampfaufklärungen*).

This was just what General Guderian wanted. He climbed back into his tank and ordered his units forward.

The first obstacle now confronting them was the Oise Valley. But once again the problem was not nearly as grave as had been anticipated. The tanks of the French 2nd Armoured Division, stationed at the approaches to the bridges, held up the enemy's armour for only half a day. Already Generals Hartlieb and Rommel, commanding the 5th and 7th Panzer Divisions, had pierced the canal linking the Oise to the Sambre.

Only a powerful air force would have been capable of halting the progress of the German armour. But where was it? In the course of the meeting in Paris the night before Churchill had promised to send another ten squadrons to the continent. But he had refused to abandon long-distance raids over the Reich itself, and hedged when asked to confine all R.A.F. operations to the fighting line and the area immediately behind it. Yet that would have been the only way to influence the course of the battle.

Disappointed by the British Prime Minister's obstinacy, General Gamelin sent him another telegram:

May 17th, 1940
For Mr Winston Churchill, on his arrival in London
Giraud's army has been under attack since morning, south of

Maubeuge. The fighting is very fierce. The consequences may be considerable, not only for France but for Britain. This line of attack is a particular threat to the communications of the British army. Once again I call for R.A.F. participation in the battle, in every form. In particular, the laying of magnetic mines in the Meuse would do much to hamper enemy reinforcements and supplies.

GAMELIN

'As from that day,' writes Kammerer, 'General Gamelin regarded the situation as lost. He told Paul Reynaud that from now on they must face the possibility of an armistice.'

POLITICAL SITUATION

In the morning a Cabinet meeting was held in Paris. Paul Reynaud had now firmly made up his mind to dispense with General Gamelin, but was not immediately successful in 'procuring his head'. Daladier continued to defend the C.-in-C. The meeting, like the stormy one on May 9th, broke up without any decision being taken.

In Washington President Roosevelt had a long conversation during the evening with Lord Lothian, the British ambassador. Deeply moved by the dramatic turn of events during the last few days, the President expressed anxiety as to the fate of the Royal Navy in the event of Britain's defeat. He expressed 'the desire to see His Majesty's Government place its fleet in the shelter of American ports'.

Lord Lothian, greatly taken aback by this American 'suggestion', lost no time in reporting it to the British Prime Minister.

MAY 18TH

Once again the Germans caught the French High Command napping with a lightning attack. In the north they crossed the Sambre and ominous infiltrations were reported in the Mormal Forest. Farther south they broadly outflanked Wassigny, where General Giraud had his headquarters. By evening the situation was again very confused. The morning's hopes were dashed. St Quentin and Péronne fell to the Wehrmacht.

General Gamelin ordered several units stationed in the Maginot Line to head north-westwards in order to strengthen the French positions along the Aisne and in the Argonne. To prevent the French High Command from effecting this manoeuvre on too large a scale and to compel it to maintain its strength in the fortified sector, the German 1st Army under von Witzleben launched a number of local attacks.

Air Marshal Barratt's Advanced Air Striking Force left Rheims for Central France and started evacuating its units to England.

Marshal Pétain arrived from Madrid during the morning. Accompanied by MM. Paul Reynaud and Daladier, he drove to La Ferté-sous-Jouarre for a talk with General Georges and later — at 6 p.m. — to Vincennes to confer with General Gamelin. Technical discussions apart, all that he said to Gamelin was: 'I pity you with all my heart.'

POLITICAL SITUATION

On his return from Vincennes, M. Reynaud asked Marshal Pétain to join the government as Deputy Premier. The Marshal agreed.

In the evening M. Reynaud took advantage of Marshal Pétain's appointment to reshape his Cabinet. He himself took over National Defence. M. Daladier was moved from National Defence to Foreign Affairs. M. Mandel was moved from the Colonies to the Interior.

During his trip to Paris two days earlier, Churchill had accomplished the impossible feat of boosting Reynaud's and Daladier's morale. But he had returned to London more alarmed than he had shown by the position of the French armies.

On May 17th he had addressed a long note to Mr Chamberlain, now Lord President, in which he had asked him to examine 'the consequences of the withdrawal of the French government from Paris or the fall of that city, *as well as the problems which would arise if it were necessary to withdraw the B.E.F. from France …*'

The same day a plan by the War Minister, Mr Anthony Eden, for the formation of Local Defence Volunteers, was 'energetically pressed'. The phrase is Churchill's. He adds: 'All over the country, in every town and village, bands of determined men came together armed with shot-guns, sporting rifles, clubs and spears.' For the War Office had emptied its depots to equip the divisions of the B.E.F. and was unable to supply them with anything better.

MAY 19TH

Round about midnight General Billotte drove to Lord Gort's headquarters. Afterwards, in his official report, Gort wrote: 'He ... told me of the measures which were being taken to restore the situation on the front of the French 9th Army, though clearly he had little hope that they would be effective ... In my opinion there was an imminent danger of the forces in the north-eastern area ... being irretrievably cut off from the main French forces in the south.'

Three plans thereupon occurred to the British general:

1. *Holding the line of the Escaut*, or in any case, the frontier defences and a line running southwards from them. But this presupposed that the gap had been plugged by successful counter-attacks from north and south simultaneously.
2. *Falling back to the Somme.* 'This plan,' commented Gort, 'had the attraction that we should be falling back on our lines of communication ... It would obviously be unwelcome to the Belgians, who would be faced with the alternatives of withdrawing with us and abandoning Belgian soil, fighting on a perimeter of their own or seeking an armistice ... It is doubtful whether ... there would have been sufficient time for the troops in the north to conform.'
3. *Withdrawing to the Channel ports*, making use of the various canals and holding a defensive perimeter long enough for the B.E.F. to embark, preferably in concert with the French and the Belgians.

'I realized that this course was in theory a last alternative,' continued Gort, 'as it would involve the departure of the B.E.F. from the theatre of war at a time when the French might need all the support which Britain could give them. It involved the virtual certainty that ... it would be necessary to abandon all the heavier guns and much of the transport and equipment. Nevertheless, I felt that in the circumstances *there might be no other course open to me.*'

At 3.30 p.m. Lord Gort telephoned his views to the Director of

Military Operations at the War Office. He gave him to understand that unless things unexpectedly took a turn for the better it would be necessary to consider evacuating the B.E.F. In anticipation of this eventuality Lord Gort ordered the Air Component to return to Britain. The R.A.F. now had only one auxiliary landing field in France — at Merville, twenty miles west of Lille.

The night of May 18th–19th, therefore, marked the crucial moment when the British High Command started thinking in terms of a separate strategy that might mean breaking with its French and Belgian allies. It will be noted that this decision was *prior* to the Belgian King's capitulation and to General Weygand's assumption of the role of Commander-in-Chief.

Meanwhile the French High Command had been struck — like Hitler — by the exposed position of the German Panzer divisions. The Wehrmacht's armoured divisions extended westwards like an outstretched finger for 125 miles. The rapidity of their advance had put the forward units out of step with the motorized infantry columns.

General Gamelin considered that it ought to be possible to 'cut the finger off' before it was too late. He drove to General Georges's headquarters in La Ferté-sous-Jouarre to outline the manoeuvre that he advocated. But he tells us that he found the Commander-in-Chief of the north-eastern front very agitated and so depressed that he judged him incapable of taking the helm in such dramatic circumstances. General Gamelin drew up his Personal and Secret Instruction No. 12, the text of which was as follows:

> *No.* 1012 — *CAB/F.T.*   *May 19th, 9.45 a.m.*
> *Without wishing to intervene in the conduct of the battle in progress, which is within the jurisdiction of the Commander-in-Chief of the north-eastern front ...* I consider that at the present time:
>
> 1. There are grounds ... for continuing the line of our Eastern armies and the covering of Paris farther westwards and for maintaining the link with the 1st Group of Armies.
> 2. So far as the 1st Group of Armies is concerned, rather than allow it to be encircled we must play a really bold game: on the one hand by opening the way to the Somme, if need be; on the other by flinging specially mobile forces against the rear of the German Panzer divisions and the motorized infantry divisions following them ...
> 3. With all available resources we must prepare an offensive by the

2nd Army, in conjunction with the right flank of the 6th, in the direction of the bridges at Mézières.

4. Participation in the battle must now be the aim of the entire French and British air strength. The fighters' main task is to retain control of the sky along the front held by the 1st Group of Armies and, as far as possible, to protect our movements behind the lines.

—The bombers are to attend to the columns advancing westwards, by attacking them from the rear and stemming their progress. Special attention is to be given to the group of Panzer divisions.

— Subsequently, and at the appropriate time, they are to stand by to support the action of the 2nd Army.

— Between times, they are to drop river-mines on the Meuse bridges.

5. It is all a question of time.

M. GAMELIN

[*It might almost be claimed that the first ten words of the Generalissimo's Instruction is the gem of the work.* — Ed.]

POLITICAL SITUATION

The Cabinet, reshuffled the night before, met in Paris and considered appointing Weygand Commander-in-Chief in place of General Gamelin.

At 7.30 p.m. Paul Reynaud received General Weygand in the Rue Saint-Dominique and informed him of his desire to see him take over command of the French army.

After a momentary silence Weygand told the Premier: 'I accept the heavy responsibility that you are asking me to assume. I shall do what I can, but I do not guarantee success'.

General Weygand then asked that his powers as C.-in-C. should be wider than those of his predecessor and that the French diplomatic service should do its utmost to keep Italy out of the war.

M. Paul Reynaud shook the General's hand with emotion. He thanked him for his 'courageous decision, which France would value to the full'.

Then the Premier addressed the following letter to General Gamelin, who received it at about 8.45 p.m.:

I have the honour of bringing to your notice two decrees that have just been signed by the President of the Republic. I send you the

MAY 19TH

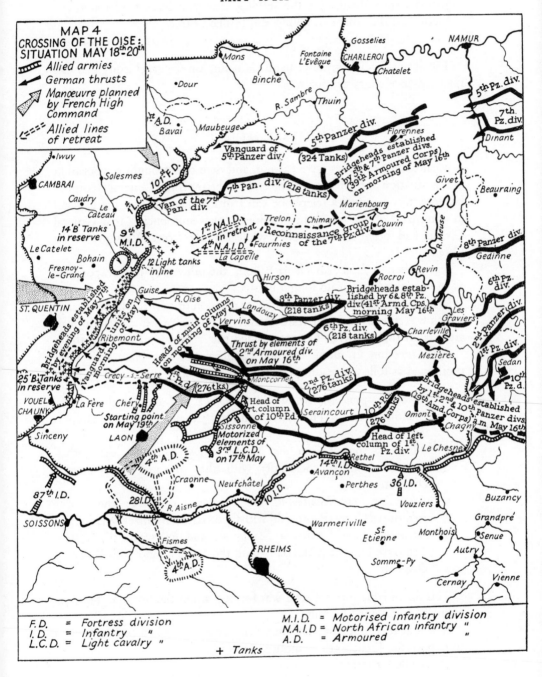

MAP 4
CROSSING OF THE OISE:
SITUATION MAY 18th-20th

🟦🟦🟦 Allied armies
➡ German thrusts
➡ Manœuvre planned
by French High
Command
⤙⤙⤙ Allied lines
of retreat

F.D. = Fortress division
I.D. = Infantry "
L.C.D. = Light cavalry "

M.I.D. = Motorised infantry division
N.A.I.D = North African infantry "
A.D. = Armoured "

+ Tanks

government's thanks for the services that you have rendered the
country in the course of a long and brilliant career.

PAUL REYNAUD

'I shall not dwell,' writes General Gamelin, 'on the cruel irony that this
final sentence contained for me.'

MILITARY SITUATION

Meanwhile the hours were passing, and each one brought a worsening
in the situation at the front. At the end of the morning General Georges's
headquarters received a telephone call from Amiens. It was the General
in command of the 9th Army engineer corps announcing that General
Giraud had been taken prisoner while driving from Wassigny to Le
Catelet.

'From then on,' records Henri Bidou, 'the 9th Army just evaporated;
as an organized unit it no longer existed.'

With the exception of the 9th Panzer division of von Küchler's Army,
which was still advancing towards Anvers, the whole German armour had
arrived on time at what has been called the 'rendezvous of May 19th'.

After meeting up along the line Cambrai–Péronne–Ham they were
positioned as follows, reading from north to south:

1. *Advancing from Maestricht via Gembloux and Binche:* the 16th
    Armoured Corps (Hoeppner) with the 3rd and 4th Panzer Divisions.

2. *Advancing from Dinant via Maubeuge and Solesmes:* the 39th
    Armoured Corps (Schmidt) with the 5th and 7th Panzer Divisions.

3. *Advancing from Monthermé via Vervins and Guise:* the 41st
    Armoured Corps (Reinhardt) with the 6th and 8th Panzer Divisions.

4. *Advancing from Sedan via Montcornet and Ribémont:* the 19th
    Armoured Corps (Guderian) with the 1st, 2nd and 10th Panzer Divisions.

This formidable mass of steel was forging along the Somme, between
Cambrai and Saint-Quentin.

It was at this moment that Guderian's armour clashed for the second
time with the French 4th Armoured Division.

De Gaulle writes:

120

The tanks had a series of objectives: Crécy, Mortiers and Pouilly. They were to get to the bridges and cut the enemy's path to La Fère. The artillery was with them ... We reached the Serre after chasing off various hostile forces that had infiltrated into the area. But north of the river the enemy was in position. He held the crossings in force and destroyed those of our tanks that tried to approach them. His heavy artillery came into play. In point of fact, we were at grips with the large German units pouring towards Saint-Quentin ...

And now came the Stukas! They were to bomb us till nightfall, deadly to the vehicles that could not leave the roads and to the artillery out in the open.

In the early afternoon General Georges ordered me to discontinue. The deployment of the 6th Army was completed and my division had at once to be put to other purposes ... I decided to retard the enemy for another twenty-four hours by regrouping the division around Vosges by nightfall, so that it would be ready to launch a flank attack if he tried to thrust onwards from Laon to Rheims or Soissons. The manoeuvre was carried out in an orderly fashion, even though the enemy was attempting to engage us at every point.

Guderian notes, on his side:

The threat to our left flank was slight. We were aware that the 4th Armoured Division, under Colonel de Gaulle, was in the vicinity: it had been making its presence felt since May 16th and had made its first appearance at Montcornet on May 17th. De Gaulle kept his appointments on the days that followed and, on May 19th, with a few isolated tanks, came within a mile and a half of my forward command post in Honon wood, which was quite unprotected except for some 2-cm. anti-aircraft guns. I was kept in suspense for some hours, till these unwelcome visitors turned about.[1]

By evening the German tanks were nearing Amiens, having covered nearly 50 miles at a stretch.

The situation confronting General Weygand could hardly have been graver. The French armies were worn out after nine days of uninterrupted fighting. Some of them — the 9th in particular — were already annihilated.

As for the large mechanized units, their present state was as follows:

[1] Guderian is mistaken. A glance at the map makes it quite clear that these tanks did not belong to the 4th Armoured Division, but to some other, unspecifiable unit.

Armoured divisions:

The 1st no longer existed.[1]

The 2nd had 20 'B' and 20 'Hotchkiss' tanks.[2]

The 3rd had only 15 'B' and 20 'Hotchkiss' tanks at its disposal.[3]

The 4th (Colonel de Gaulle's) had now only about 30 'B' tanks.

Weygand's first act as C.-in-C. was to suspend the execution of General Gamelin's 'Personal and Secret Instruction No. 12'. Before plunging into an operation on this scale he wanted to form a clearer idea of the situation at the front and establish personal contact with King Leopold, Lord Gort, General Billotte and General Blanchard.

---

[1] It had been flung, unsupported, into the counter-attack west of Namur on May 16th The enemy had surrounded it and destroyed it.

[2] Transported by rail to the Hirson area, its component units had been scattered to cover the approaches to the bridges over the Oise, where one by one they had fallen foul of the general chaos.

[3] On May 18th this force, which had only just been constituted, had been forthwith parcelled out among the battalions of an infantry division and engulfed bit by bit in an abortive counter-attack.

MAY 20TH

Alarmed by Lord Gort's telephone call to the War Office the night before, Britain's leaders took two important steps:

1. Without informing the French Admiralty, the British Admiralty made the first arrangements for evacuating the B.E.F. via Dunkirk.
2. Churchill, anxious to know how well-founded Gort's pessimism was, sent General Ironside over to see him.

Ironside reached Gort's Wahagnies H.Q. at 8.15 a.m. Gort wrote in his dispatch:

The Chief of the Imperial General Staff ... brought with him instructions from the Cabinet that the B.E.F. was to move southwards upon Amiens, attacking all enemy forces encountered, and to take station on the left of the French army. He [Ironside] was also to inform General Billotte and the Belgian Command, making it clear to the latter that their best chance was to move that night between the B.E.F. and the coast.

Similar information was to be given by the War Office to General Georges. During the day, however, it appeared that operations were actually being directed by General Weygand who later, on May 23rd, announced in a General Order that he was now Commander-in-Chief in all theatres of war ...

I put to him [Ironside] my view that withdrawal to the south-westwards, however desirable in principle, was not in the circumstances practicable.

In the first place, it would involve the disengagement of seven divisions which were at the time in close contact with the enemy on the Escaut and would be immediately followed up ... The B.E.F. would be obliged to disengage [these] seven divisions ... fighting a rearguard action, at the same time to attack south-westwards and finally to break through enemy forces on the Somme ...

Secondly, the administrative situation made it unlikely that sustained offensive operations could be undertaken. Communication with the bases was on the point of being interrupted ...

Lastly, though I was not in a position to judge, I had the impression that even if I had decided to attempt this manoeuvre, neither the French 1st Army nor the Belgians would have been in a position to conform.

Despite these pessimistic views, Gort told the C.I.G.S. that he was inclined, all the same, to launch a counter-attack south of Arras with two divisions — the 5th and the 50th.

'The C.I.G.S. agreed with this action and, accompanied by the C.G.S., he left for Lens to meet Generals Billotte and Blanchard.'

General Ironside met General Billotte in Lens. The latter approved Lord Gort's plan and stated that the French would support the attack with two 1st Army divisions. It could be launched simultaneously, from May 21st onwards.

General Weygand drove to G.H.Q. at Vincennes, where he had a conversation with General Gamelin. At about 8 a.m., without a word to his colleagues, the ex-C.-in-C. went away for ever.

Meanwhile, at this turning-point of the battle in which every hour was decisive, the tempo of events quickened.

The battle for Arras started at 1.40 a.m. At 6 a.m. Rommel reached Beaurains, two and a half miles south of Arras. But for several hours he was held up by French units that had cut into his lines of communication.

While this was going on, the Panzers of the 8th Panzer Division entered Cambrai and from there pushed on to Bapaume.

But the decisive action of the day went to Guderian's armour. By 2 p.m. it was on the outskirts of Abbeville. The town was captured and light detachments continued south to Aumale, while the 10th Panzer Division, in force, held the junction of the Avre and the Somme.

The gap between the French armies in the north and those in action along the Somme was 55 miles wide by the late afternoon.

At 8 p.m. Guderian's Panzers reached the coast, at Montreuil-sur-Mer.[1]

The bulk of von Kleist's armour forged on towards Calais and Boulogne, swinging inwards on the rear of the French 1st Army and the B.E.F. 'The object of the German manoeuvre was now quite plain,' writes Bardies.

[1] A forward battalion of the 2nd P.D. had already reached the Channel (at Noyelles) the night before.

'The break-through in the centre was to be followed by the envelopment of one wing — the stronger, solider left wing … And it certainly seemed that nothing, there and then, could impede its success.'

The Allied armies were well and truly cut in two, and not only by the Panzers but by infantry and artillery. A mass formation of Germans had interposed themselves between the left flank and the centre. All the Allied forces fighting in Belgium and Flanders were caught in a trap.

This mortal blow was to prompt Lord Gort to execute without delay the operation discussed in Lens by Generals Ironside and Billotte.

The attack on the left flank, which was so dreaded by the German High Command (and which General Gamelin had been planning to carry out at the time of his dismissal), had not been launched at the favourable moment. Now it was too late.

'Any anxiety on this score became superfluous,' writes General Blumen-tritt, General von Rundstedt's Chief of Staff. 'Nothing serious happened. The French remained on the defensive, confronting the 12th and 16th Armies. The crossing of the Meuse and the Franco-British advance into Belgium was the first miracle of this campaign. The immobility of the French in this sector was a second.'

'The Führer is wild with joy,' General Jodl writes in his diary. 'He sees victory and peace within his grasp.'

'Had I had as many motorized troops at my disposal then as I have now,' Hitler was to tell his intimates on October 17th, 1941, 'I could have started the southern offensive immediately and the French campaign would have been over in a fortnight.'

To avoid needless losses, Hitler called off the projected attack on the Maginot Line by von Leeb's Group of Armies.

The surviving tanks of the 2nd Armoured Division regrouped in the vicinity of Champlieu, where orders arrived for it to be reconstituted under the command of Colonel Perré.

POLITICAL SITUATION

That evening Reynaud, who was expecting Mussolini to declare war on France, sent for the United States ambassador and asked him to obtain American aid at all costs.

Churchill addressed a personal message to Mr Roosevelt about the latter's conversation with Lord Lothian, on May 17th, concerning the possibility of sending the Royal Navy to American ports:

With regard to the closing part of your talk with Lothian, our intention is, whatever happens, to fight on to the end in this island, and, provided we can get the help for which we ask, we hope to run them very close in the air battles in view of individual superiority. Members of the present Administration would [be] likely [to] go down during this process should it result adversely, but in no conceivable circumstances will we consent to surrender.

If members of the present Administration were finished and others came in to parley amid the ruins, you must not be blind to the fact that the sole remaining bargaining counter with Germany would be the Fleet, and if this country was left by the United States to its fate no one would have the right to blame those then responsible if they made the best terms they could for the surviving inhabitants.

Excuse me, Mr President, putting this nightmare bluntly. Evidently I could not answer for my successors, who in utter despair and helplessness might well have to accommodate themselves to the German will ...

MAY 21ST

MILITARY SITUATION

The Wehrmacht's official communiqué announced the previous day's successes in clarion tones: 'In the west, after a series of partial successes, the greatest offensive of all time has had its first strategic result: our forces have reached the sea.'

At Lord Gort's headquarters, preparations were made for the action decided on in Lens the day before.

At 12.30 p.m., the commander of the B.E.F. received a message from General Blanchard informing him that French forces would be unable to move till May 22nd or the night after, because the roads were so heavily blocked.

But Gort, who had prepared his action for May 21st and was fully alive to the importance of the time factor, decided to ignore the message and attack towards Arras at 2 p.m.

The action, commanded by General Franklyn, was carried out by the British 5th and 50th Divisions and 100 heavy and light tanks covered, on their western flank, by the 3rd Light Mechanized Division.

Here is Rommel's account of the battle of Arras:

While violent scraps were going on in the Tilloy–Beaurains–Agny sector, powerful armoured forces had swarmed out of Arras, subjecting us to heavy losses in men and equipment. The anti-tank guns that we speedily brought into action proved too light to be effective against the heavily armoured British tanks. Most of them were put out of action by the enemy artillery — likewise their crews. A large number of vehicles were set on fire. S.S. units in the vicinity (including the Death's-head Division) had to fall back under the weight of this attack. Finally the divisional artillery and some 88-mm. anti-aircraft guns managed to halt the enemy armour south of a line from Beaurains to Agny ...

'The losses suffered by the 7th Panzer Division in the course of the day,' states the Division's official history, 'were 89 killed, 116 wounded and 173 missing, or four times the losses suffered during the initial break-through and the early days of the invasion of France.'

The fighting ended at nightfall.

By 8 p.m. the armour of the 3rd Light Mechanized Division, which had captured Warlus and Gimencourt in the course of the afternoon, was spent. It had covered so many miles since May 10th that the worn caterpillars were beginning to break. At all events, this was the end of the line for them. Bardies comments: 'General Franklyn's attack could have maintained its impetus only had it been strengthened and supported by the French on the left.'

This operation was to be the only serious counter-attack launched by the encircled armies. It had extensive psychological consequences:

1. *On the British side:* It convinced Lord Gort once and for all that the only way out for the B.E.F. was to withdraw to Dunkirk, turning its back on any attempt to cut through to the south.
2. *On the German side:* It jolted the morale of the High Command to an extent quite out of proportion to its material results.

'Generals Kluge and Kleist were particularly disturbed,' writes Rommel. 'Kluge was in favour of delaying any resumption of the westward advance till the situation in the Arras sector had righted itself.'

At 3 p.m., after an extremely eventful journey, General Weygand drove into Ypres, where an important inter-Allied conference was to be held. Neither General Ironside (who had returned to London 24 hours earlier), nor Lord Gort, nor any representative of the R.A.F. was present.

The representatives waited for Gort for some time. Then, since time was pressing, they decided to start without him.

General Weygand outlined his plan of operations. It consisted of simultaneously striking southwards from around Cambrai and northwards from the Somme, so as to reknit the two branches of the battle-line somewhere near Bapaume.

This was the first suggestion of mounting a united counter-attack, in place of the small local counter-attacks so far attempted. Bardies writes:

That this effort was no longer to be centred on Sedan, as had previously been proposed, was due to the fact that General Weygand had estimated that German covering forces were now reinforced and solid in this sector and that it was too late to attack there. Furthermore, the action of the 1st Group of Armies would by that time have been too far from this attacking front to link up effectively with the action of the forces in the south.

Weygand examined the possibilities with King Leopold and General Billotte. The Belgians were to abandon the Escaut, which had become impossible to defend, and withdraw to the Yser where they would face eastwards as in 1914. While they were thus protecting the left of the line, along a 55-mile front bounded on the right by the Lys, the French and British would attack southwards, with eight divisions, along the Bapaume–Cambrai front. They would meet up with the French forces located south of the Somme, which would simultaneously attack northwards.

[*Here the plan was compromised by the unwillingness of the Belgians to leave their position on the plea that their troops were exhausted. All General Weygand could obtain was King Leopold's promise of a decision within twenty-four hours.* — Ed.]

The conference ended at 7 p.m.

After General Weygand's departure, King Leopold, General Billotte and General Fagalde discussed the problems arising from the withdrawal of the Belgian army. At present it was fighting between the Escaut and the Lys, its left wing still holding out between Gand and the sea. General Billotte pleaded in favour of the retirement to the Yser advocated by Weygand. The manoeuvre could be carried out by pivoting on Halluin. This withdrawal would have the additional advantage of reducing the 55-mile front currently held by the Belgian army to one of 30 miles. King Leopold finally agreed in principle. But the decision was not in black and white.

At about 9 p.m. Lord Gort at last reached Ypres, where he found the King of the Belgians, General Billotte and General Fagalde in conference. He apologized for not arriving earlier, blaming the congested roads.

General Weygand wanted to launch a heavy attack southwards so as to break through the encirclement of the units fighting in Flanders and enable them to pull back south of the Somme.

Lord Gort wanted to withdraw in a north-easterly direction, towards the Channel ports, so as to ensure the B.E.F.'s evacuation to England. But he refrained from saying so and his silences prompted this reproach from General Fagalde: 'You must do what has been agreed!'

In short: nothing positive came out of the Ypres conference.

Once again misfortune struck at the Allied High Command. General Billotte started back to his headquarters. When his car reached Locre it collided with a van. He was gravely injured and at once fell into a coma. He died on May 23rd without regaining consciousness.

For a day and a half there was to be *no overall command*. On May 23rd General Blanchard was to replace General Billotte as head of the 1st

Group of Armies, while General Prioux was to succeed Blanchard as commander of the 1st Army. The Cavalry Corps, previously under Prioux, was to be taken over by General Langlois.

The wavering caused by this accident was made even worse by the fact that the co-ordinating powers previously conferred on General Billotte *were not sought for General Blanchard.*

Lastly General Blanchard, who had not attended the Ypres conference, had only a hazy notion of General Weygand's plans.[1]

At the end of the Ypres conference, after General Weygand had gone, Lord Gort and Admiral Keyes discussed the difficult situation in which General Overstraeten was placed. Britain's envoy to King Leopold took the view that the plan to evacuate the B.E.F. via Dunkirk was tantamount to running out on the Belgian army, but he did not have the nerve to tell the King. He described the bitter feelings among the troops and at Belgian G.H.Q. Whereupon Gort, with a gesture of despondency, asked him: 'Do the Belgians really regard us as awful dirty dogs?'

Very late in the evening General Weygand returned to Paris. 'He had wasted precious hours,' writes Fabre-Luce, 'tracking down an absentee (Gort) and giving instructions to a man under sentence of death (Billotte).'

POLITICAL SITUATION

Paul Reynaud made a great speech before the Senate.

'The country is in danger,' he proclaimed. 'My first duty is to tell the Senate and the nation the truth.'

The Premier denounced the 'serious failures' of the 9th Army; he condemned General Corap and announced that 'these incredible mistakes will be severely punished'.

What was the situation when I arrived in the War Ministry the day before yesterday and was joined by Marshal Pétain and General Weygand? There was a breach of about 60 miles in our front. Pouring through this breach was a German army composed of armoured divisions followed by motorized divisions ...

Two days ago the armoured divisions had reached the line Le Quesnoy–Cambrai–Péronne and the Somme as far as Ham. During

---

[1] 'Blanchard lost valuable time in getting the hang of the plan that had been decided upon,' writes Bardies. 'He had to rely on the recollections of General Champon, who had gone to the conference with the King of the Belgians.' This state of affairs was scarcely calculated to increase Gort's confidence in the French High Command.

the past forty-eight hours the German advance has continued. At eight o'clock this morning the Command informed me that Arras and Amiens were occupied ...

In the midst of our country's misfortunes we can take pride in the thought that two of her sons, who would have been justified in resting on their laurels, have placed themselves at the nation's service in this tragic hour: Pétain and Weygand. (*Prolonged cheers.*)

Pétain, the victor of Verdun, the great soldier with the human touch, the man who knows how a French victory can come out of a cataclysm.

Weygand, Foch's man, who halted the German onslaught when the front was broken in 1918 and who was afterwards able to turn the tables and lead us to victory ... France cannot die.

For my part, if some day I were to be told that only a miracle could save France, that day I should say: 'I believe in the miracle, because I believe in France.'

But this stream of eloquence could not blind the soldiers at the front to the harsh realities confronting them. From the word go the French troops had been dramatically confronted with the evidence of their inferiority, and the events of the past week had merely added to the feeling. 'There were,' writes Fabre-Luce, 'no French planes above them, few French tanks around them, and behind them a vacuum — for the artillery had not even managed to take up its positions.'

MAY 22ND

As the days went by, the centre of activity shifted westwards and the landscapes acquired new shapes and colours. After the dark forest of the Ardennes and the green undulating hills of Hainaut and Laon, the eyes of the world were now upon the vast plains of Picardy and Flanders.

Two events had combined to make the situation almost irretrievable: the lack of liaison between Billotte and Blanchard, and the misunderstanding between Blanchard and Gort.

[*As regards the first, Billotte was mortally hurt before he could discuss the conference decisions with Blanchard. As regards the second, Gort attacked on May 21st, though he had learnt that the French could not do so, and Blanchard attacked on May 22nd, though he knew the British effort was over.* — Ed.]

In the morning the 25th Motorized Infantry Division attacked along the Auberchicourt–Cambrai axis. Smashing the resistance offered by the German 32nd Division, the 121st Motorized Infantry Regiment took Bantigny and reached the outskirts of Cambrai. But at 10 p.m. the 25th Motorized Infantry Division was ordered to fall back under cover of darkness and destroy the crossings of the Sensée and its canal.

While these disjointed operations were going on, the Germans were widening the gap that they had opened during the past few days. They debouched in Béthune and south of Saint-Omer. By the afternoon they were fighting to the south and east of Boulogne. Guderian reverted to his original plan and promptly swung the 1st Panzer Division round towards Dunkirk, neglecting Calais for the time being. A large number of infantry units, including an S.S. division, were busy in the Saint-Quentin area.

At 11 a.m. the Belgian High Command informed General Weygand that King Leopold had agreed that the Belgian army should move back to the Yser, after first halting along the Lys.

At noon an inter-Allied War Council opened in Vincennes. Eye-witnesses say that the meeting, held in General Weygand's office, was a dismal one. The British representatives were: Winston Churchill, 'looking dejected and serious', General Sir John Dill, Air Chief Marshal

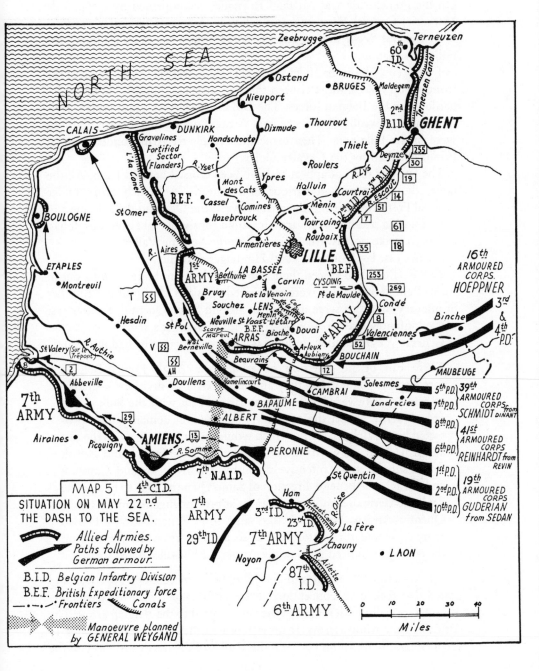

MAP 5

SITUATION ON MAY 22nd
THE DASH TO THE SEA.

Allied Armies.
Paths followed by
German armour.

B.I.D. Belgian Infantry Division
B.E.F. British Expeditionary Force
—·—·—· Frontiers ⌇⌇⌇ Canals

Manoeuvre planned
by GENERAL WEYGAND

Sir R. E. C. Peirse (the Vice-Chief of Air Staff) and General Lord Ismay. On the French side was M. Paul Reynaud, accompanied by Captain de Margerie, General Weygand and a few members of the latter's staff.

At General Weygand's request Colonel Simon began by outlining the military situation.

Two French divisions under General Fagalde were at the far north of the front, along the Escaut. Between these and the neighbourhood of Audenarde came the Belgian forces. The B.E.F. was farther south with 4 divisions, plus 3 divisions in reserve near Arras. Two further British divisions were in the Lille area. Then came the French 1st Army under General Prioux, flanked by the Cavalry Corps.

The Somme did not appear to have been crossed beyond Ham. All the same, the Germans had various bridge-heads. A French army under General Frère was skirting the area between the Oise and the Somme and concentrating steadily westwards. It would consist of eight divisions. It had orders to strike northwards so as to free the Somme Valley.

Farther east lay Touchon's and Huntziger's Armies.

The Germans had placed their armoured divisions at key-points out in front. Behind these units were motorized divisions. Apparently a number of infantry divisions were digging in around Saint-Quentin. Farther east massed infantry was already at grips with Huntziger's army.

General Weygand then outlined the manoeuvre that he had in mind.

There can be no question of asking the Anglo-French-Belgian forces still in the north — they amount to over 40 divisions — merely to retreat southwards in an attempt to join up with the bulk of the French army ... On the contrary, the situation demands that, protected by the Belgian army, which would cover them towards the east and if necessary towards the north, the available French and British forces should strike offensively southwards from around Cambrai and Arras in the general direction of Saint-Quentin, so as to take in the flank the German armoured divisions at present engaged in the Saint-Quentin–Amiens pocket. At the same time General Frère's French army ... would thrust northwards so as to increase the pressure on the enemy armoured units in the Amiens–Abbeville–Arras area ...

Mr Winston Churchill and Sir John Dill voiced their approval and stated that their own conception of the battle tallied with the Generalissimo's, especially with regard to the role allotted to the Belgian army. The British Prime Minister several times repeated that it was indispensable to 'reopen communications between the armies of the north and those of the south via Arras'. The battle was vital to the future of the war, for the supplying of the British forces via the Channel ports was becoming extremely hazardous.

Speaking for himself and the King of the Belgians, Weygand then lodged 'with equal firmness and precision' a demand that he considered fundamental.

'It is of vital importance to the success of the battle about to open,' he declared, 'that the R.A.F. should be fully engaged *in the theatre of operations* ... During the past few days it has been carrying out heavy raids against parts of Germany, especially the Ruhr, and has achieved considerable results by bombing enemy oil depots and refineries in Hamburg, Bremen and elsewhere. But in view of what is at stake, it is vital that the R.A.F. should provisionally, just for a few days, abandon its long-distance experiments so as to act constantly and immediately along the front itself or in the vicinity of the front. I therefore request that the R.A.F. be ordered to redouble its efforts in the area where the projected operations will occur.'

The British Vice-Chief of Air Staff replied that in present conditions R.A.F. Wellingtons could not attack in daylight and that, allowing for the outward and return journeys, the British fighters would have only enough fuel to keep them over the front line for twenty minutes. However, the bombers would harass the German lines of communication between the front and the Meuse, while the fighters, *based in England*, would fly over in relays.

The French Premier and the Commander-in-Chief informed Mr Churchill of the accident to General Billotte and of the changes in the command of the 1st Group of Armies. They assured him that General Blanchard and Lord Gort would be working 'hand in hand'.

In the course of the afternoon General Weygand had a further conversation with M. Paul Reynaud. A memorandum was drawn up, specifying the points established in the inter-Allied meeting.

Mr Churchill and the British delegation returned to London. The British Prime Minister took with him a summary of the projected plan of operations.

'All this was wonderful,' remarks Pertinax, 'and undeniably cohesive on paper. But it takes days and days to co-ordinate the workings of such a massive piece of machinery ... Some British officers stated that they had not found such-and-such a division in the position that Weygand had indicated ... By May 23rd the opportunity, slender as it might have been, had slipped by, and, try as he might, Weygand would never recapture it.

Every time he thought he was in a position to set the wheels in motion something would be missing, or fail, calling for a complete overhaul of the plan.'

On the same day the R.A.F. evacuated the airfield at Merville, its final base in France. All future operations, including Dunkirk, would be conducted from Britain.

At 10.30 p.m. Churchill summoned General Spears to the Admiralty. His brief visit to Vincennes and Paris had left him uneasy, and he thought it would be useful to strengthen the bonds between the French and British governments.

'I have decided,' he told Spears, 'to send you as my personal representative to Paul Reynaud. You will have the rank of a Major-General ... The situation is very grave.'

MAY 23RD

The manoeuvre conceived by Weygand between May 19th and May 21st was based on a military situation that no longer existed on May 23rd. While the Generalissimo had found himself obliged to go to the northern front in person and confer, first with the Belgians in the absence of the British, then with the British in the absence of the Belgians, precious time had been elapsing — time that the German forces had used to their advantage. The corridor to the sea was now crammed with German units, and what on May 20th had still been only a bold tank-attack, had become, forty-eight hours later, what Pertinax calls 'a solid-limbed army'. From north to south, the line-up had changed profoundly.

Under pressure from the enemy, the Belgians were forced to abandon Terneuzen and Gand. King Leopold's headquarters was informed by the French Command that it could no longer count on the bases of Gravelines, Dunkirk and Bourgbourg, which had become indispensable to the supplying of the French armies, and that it must make shift with Ostend and Nieuport. This decision finally drove the Belgian army northwards by compelling it to move closer to the bases without which it would be without food and ammunition. King Leopold was more sceptical than ever about the possibility of putting the Weygand plan into operation.

In the 1st Army sector, the enemy intensified his attacks between Béthune and Lens.

The British 5th and 50th Divisions, which had launched the attack in the Arras sector two days ago, were besieged along the Scarpe. They had already lost the majority of their tanks and were in no position to effect any further advance.

Meanwhile von Kleist's Panzer divisions were attacking the southern flank of the Allied forces between the sea and the Dieppe forest. Boulogne was threatened and soon to yield. ('Tanks notwithstanding, the attacker would have to use ladders to storm the ancient city walls, as in old prints,' records Massenon.) Calais was isolated. Other armoured units forged on to Lorette, Saint-Pol and the hills. Rommel skirted the western sectors of

Arras and closed in from behind on the British units still fighting in the town. Despite physical tiredness, the commander of the 7th Panzer Division was in the best of spirits. He rejoiced at the thought of what his units had accomplished. To his wife he wrote:

> This is triumph for my division. Everything is going well. Dinant, Philippeville, the piercing of the Maginot Line;[1] a forty-mile advance through France, overnight, to Le Cateau; then Cambrai, Arras, always far ahead of everyone else.

The outflanking of Arras from the west by Rommel's armour was extremely perplexing to Lord Gort. He was aware that his position was deteriorating hour by hour and he had but limited confidence in the success of the manoeuvre imposed on him by the French High Command. Churchill urged him to see General Blanchard. He did so. In his dispatch he wrote:

> I saw General Blanchard and proposed to him that to implement our part of the Weygand plan we should stage an attack southwards with two British divisions, one French division and the French Cavalry Corps. So far as we were concerned *the attack could not take place till May 26th at the earliest* ... I ... asked General Blanchard to enquire from G.H.Q. how such an operation could be synchronized with the attack from the line of the Somme which was *said to be* in process of preparation. I emphasized ... that the principal effort must come from the south and that the operation of the northern forces could be nothing more than a sortie.
>
> I never received any information from any source as to the exact location of our own or enemy forces on the far side of the gap; nor did I receive any details or timings of any proposed attack from that direction ...

From that moment Lord Gort, stung and disappointed, lost interest in the Weygand plan. *He decided to withdraw his forces northwards of Arras in the course of the night.* This move was the final blow to the C.-in-C.'s plans. What made it especially surprising to General Blanchard was that Lord Gort did not think it worth his while to warn him.[2]

---

[1] Rommel insists on applying the name 'Maginot Line' to what was merely its extension along the northern frontier of France: slender defences, hastily built and in no way comparable to the real Maginot Line.

[2] Perhaps this decision had been taken after General Blanchard's departure.

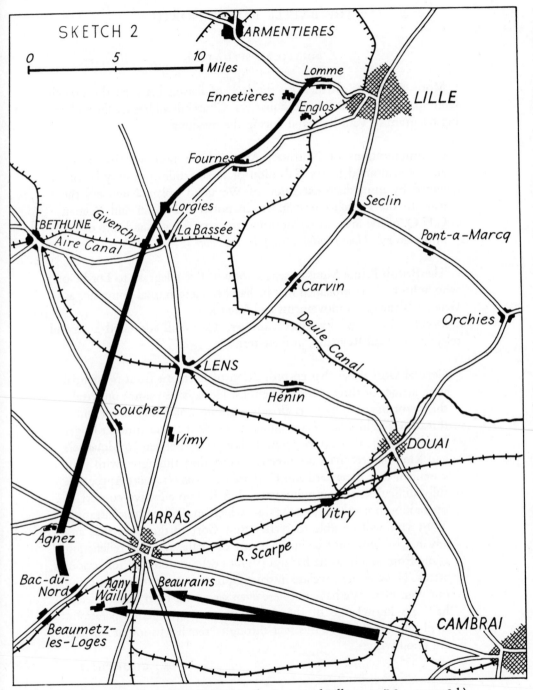

Progress of Rommel's division in the Arras and Lille areas (May 21st–28th)

THE BATTLE IN THE NORTH

More and more alarmed by the lack of liaison between the French Command and the B.E.F. headquarters, Churchill addressed the following telegram to Paul Reynaud during the morning:

Communications of Northern Armies have been cut by strong enemy armoured forces. Salvation of these armies can only be obtained by immediate execution of Weygand's plan. I demand the issue to the French commanders in north and south and Belgian G.H.Q. of the most stringent orders to carry this out and turn defeat into victory. *Time is vital as supplies are short.*

The British Prime Minister sent a copy of this telegram to Lord Gort, who in his reply complained that he had been left in total ignorance as to General Blanchard's movements and intentions.

Deeply concerned by Gort's answer, Churchill addressed a second telegram to Paul Reynaud, in these terms:

General Gort wires that co-ordination of northern front is essential with armies of three different nations. He says he cannot undertake this co-ordination, as he is already fighting north and south and is threatened on his lines of communications. At the same time Sir Roger Keyes tells me that up to 3 p.m. today (23rd) Belgian Headquarters and King had received no directive. How does this agree with your statement that Blanchard and Gort are *main dans la main*? Appreciate fully difficulties of communication, but feel no effective concert of operations in northern area, against which enemy are concentrating. Trust you will be able to rectify this. Gort further says that any advance by him must be in the nature of sortie, and that relief must come from south, as he has not (*repeat* not) ammunition for serious attack. Nevertheless, we are instructing him to persevere in carrying out your plan. We have not here even seen your own directive, and have no knowledge of the details of your northern operations. Will you kindly have this sent through French Mission at earliest? All good wishes.

W. CHURCHILL

'No wonder the Prime Minister exerted every ounce of will to get the

Weygand plan carried out,' writes General Spears. 'But he could do little beyond trying to infuse his own resolution into Reynaud, Weygand and Gort. Meanwhile the Weygand plan hung like a limp sail from the mast. Winston, like a new Aeolus, filled it momentarily with the power of his lungs, but the ship did not move.'

MAY 24TH

In the course of the night the British 5th and 50th Divisions evacuated Arras and withdrew to the Upper Deule Canal. Lord Gort ordered the blowing-up of bridges over the canal between Béthune and Pont-à-Vendin.

'The gap between the Northern Armies and those operating in the Somme area was previously about 19 miles,' declares General Weygand. 'I was hoping to reduce it considerably and even surmount it when, owing to the British retreat, the distance was increased from 19 to 44 miles.'

The Weygand plan was thereby made impracticable.

Since his visit to France, Sir John Dill shared Lord Gort's view: the salvation of the B.E.F. lay not in the break-out towards the south ordered by Weygand but in a withdrawal north-eastwards, allowing a swift evacuation to England via Dunkirk.

Meanwhile General Weygand, who knew nothing of the withdrawal ordered by Lord Gort, wired General Blanchard to put the preconceived plan vigorously into effect.

'Obtain close co-ordination of effort by Allied armies,' he told him. ' ... Salvation lies in the continuance of your attacking manoeuvre ... Am counting on the grim resolution of all concerned ... '

Surprised to learn of the British withdrawal towards the Deule and the abandonment of Arras, General Blanchard rushed to B.E.F. headquarters. Here he was received, not by Lord Gort (who was too busy), but by General Pownall, his Chief of Staff. 'Two solutions were considered,' General Blanchard wrote in his report:

(a) withdrawal to the Lys and occupation of a bridge-head covering Ostend and Dunkirk;

(b) resumption of the Arras–Bapaume attack, with the Belgians covering the operation on the Yser.

The second solution seemed preferable to General Blanchard, though he thought it would be very hard to put into practice.

Pending instructions from General Weygand, General Blanchard signed Instruction No. 40, confirming the order to carry out a counter-attack southwards and stipulating the conditions for its execution: two British divisions would have to take part in the attack.[1]

Meanwhile units of the 7th Army under General Robert Altmayer were attacking southwards towards Amiens. Their progress was halted about a hundred yards beyond the Bois Impérial.

Farther east, General Toussaint's 19th Infantry Division was launched against Péronne. It was to storm the Somme bridges and then thrust on-wards to Bapaume. It had the support of the 2nd Armoured Division, hastily regrouped under the command of Colonel Perré. Unfortunately the 2nd Armoured Division was now down to about 60 light and 10 heavy tanks.

[*The attack was launched with spirit, but the shortage of tanks, the strength of the resistance and the intervention of German aircraft, stopped dead two of the three assault columns. Only the third reached its first objective, Villers-Bretonneux. — Ed.*]

General von Reichenau's forces (comprising four, and later five, divisions, but not many tanks) struck solidly at the extreme right of the Belgian front, on either side of Courtrai, and broke through the lines after fierce exchanges.

The Belgian 9th and 10th Divisions intervened at once and for a time managed to plug the gap. The German bombers stepped up their attacks, pulverizing the lines, batteries, fighting posts, convoys and approaches with bombs and machine-guns. The Allied air forces provided very little relief. The arduous struggle continued. The Belgian right was thrust back to the line Roulers–Ypres.

Automatically, the British left was seriously threatened. Lord Gort warned General Blanchard of the difficult situation in which he was placed. He announced that he was going to be compelled to withdraw still farther northwards and demanded reinforcements. General Blanchard allotted him the 2nd Light Mechanized Division.

Rommel wrote to his wife:

I am on the outskirts of Béthune. In splendid form. On the go from morning till night.

At 4.15 p.m. General Weygand sent the following telegram to General Blanchard:

---

[1] General Blanchard signed this order as Commander of the 1st Army, for he had still not been officially advised of his appointment as Commander of the 1st Group of Armies (in place of General Billotte, who had died four days earlier).

1730.3/0 P.

You inform me of definite withdrawal to Upper Deule Canal carried out by the British during night of May 23rd–24th. If this withdrawal rules out preconceived plan, make every effort to form the widest possible bridge-head covering Dunkirk, indispensable for supplying battle.

'Thus,' records Colonel de Bardies, 'on the evening of May 24th General Weygand abandoned his plan.'

The Führer called an emergency meeting of his military advisers at his G.H.Q. in Charleville.

General von Brauchitsch suggested a large-scale armoured attack in the Vimy–Saint-Omer–Gravelines area. His intention was to bring severe pressure to bear on the Dunkirk pocket, cut off the retreating units of the 1st Group of Armies and finish them off. 'The greatest encirclement battle in history,' declared Keitel, 'must end in the annihilation of all the British, French and Belgian forces still fighting in Flanders.'

But Hitler rejected this, for it seemed to him to involve a needless waste of time. As he saw it, the fate of the Allied forces fighting in Flanders was already sealed. What did it matter if a few contingents escaped? They would have to abandon all their weapons and equipment.

Hitler sided with General von Rundstedt and decreed:

1. That the Panzer divisions should discontinue their advance north-eastwards. They should form up in the Saint-Quentin area, in preparation for the second phase of operations, timed to begin on May 31st.
2. That the task of ending the Battle of Flanders should be left entirely to the infantry and the Luftwaffe.

At the end of the meeting, to the amazement of everyone present, Hitler began to speak admiringly of the British Empire, the usefulness of its existence and the value of the civilization that Great Britain had introduced to the world. He compared the British Empire to the Roman Catholic Church, regarding them both as vital to general stability. 'He concluded by saying,' records Liddell Hart, 'that his aim was to make peace with Britain on a basis that she would regard as compatible with her honour to accept.'

The order to halt the advance of the armour was sent out to the corps commanders for execution. This unexpected order astounded the generals.

'Reinhardt's 41st Armoured Corps had already reached the line Aire–

Saint-Omer, twenty miles from Dunkirk,' claims General von Kleist. 'So the German armour was nearer the port than the bulk of the British forces.'

'I was right out in front, with the first tanks, near Bergues,' relates General Thoma. 'From there I could see everything that was going on in Dunkirk.'[1]

All the German generals were wondering just what could have prompted the Führer to issue this order.

Von Kleist questioned Hitler a few days later about his decision, pointing out that the Wehrmacht had wasted a unique opportunity by not occupying Dunkirk before the British escaped.

'Possibly,' replied Hitler, 'but I didn't want our tanks to get stuck in the Flanders mud.'[2]

To others, Hitler explained that the number of tanks that had been put out of action was so high that he wanted to know exactly what the situation was before he advanced any farther.

General Busch, unconvinced by this reasoning, considered that the Chancellor had something else in mind.

There have been countless arguments as to the real nature of Hitler's motives. After reading and comparing all the accounts so far published on this controversial point, it is impossible to draw any final conclusion.

'The Führer,' asserts General von Rundstedt, 'had counted on a speedy end to western operations ... He deliberately let the bulk of the B.E.F. escape, so as to make peace negotiations easier.'

'That is an absurd theory,' counters Guderian. 'It was by capturing the whole of Lord Gort's forces that we might have brought the British to terms. To leave them with the units that would enable them to raise and provide the backbone of further armies was, on the contrary, tantamount to urging them to go on with the war and to strengthening their resolve.'

'Goering had undertaken to settle Dunkirk's hash with planes alone,' claims General von Kleist.[3] 'He had begged Hitler to bestow the honour not on the army but on the Luftwaffe, thereby making the battle of Dunkirk a victory for the regime.'

---

[1] General Thoma is in error here. The Germans did not reach Bergues till after May 24th, nor can events in Dunkirk be seen from that town. But the psychological value of his statement is undiminished.

[2] It must be remembered that he had fought there as a common soldier in 1916–17 and had retained an 'appalling memory' of the experience.

[3] It was frequently said in German government circles that the army was 'royal' (having been created by Frederick II); that the navy was 'imperial' (having been created by Wilhelm II and Admiral Tirpitz); but that the air force was 'National Socialist', having been created since 1933, when the new regime came to power.

'There are no grounds for such an assumption,' retorts General Blumentritt. 'The Luftwaffe was mainly equipped with shrapnel bombs, which disintegrated, on impact, into a shower of small pieces and were very suitable for use against ground forces. At that time it did not have the penetrative delayed-action bombs which alone are capable of piercing the armour of warships. Hitler must have been aware of this, since Colonel Köller, Head of Operations of the 3rd Air Fleet, had personally reported the fact to the Army Group. It is hardly surprising, therefore, that in Rundstedt's headquarters the opinion swiftly spread that Hitler's order was dictated not solely by military considerations but by some secret political design.'

Only one thing is certain: Hitler halted the tanks and entrusted the end of the battle to the planes. By so doing, he and Goering gravely overestimated the Luftwaffe's powers of interception.

This decision was to have incalculable consequences. It was the German High Command's first serious strategic blunder since the start of hostilities, for it enabled the Allies to embark units from the Dunkirk trap that otherwise should not have escaped.

POLITICAL SITUATION

To the telegram that Churchill had sent him on the evening of May 23rd, Paul Reynaud sent the following reply *in the morning*:

May 24th, 1940

1. General Weygand explained to you, in my presence the day before yesterday, a plan of which you and the officers accompanying you entirely approved.

2. This plan was summarized by you in writing and General Weygand informed you he agreed with your summary.[1]

3. General Weygand is aware of all the difficulties of the situation but does not think any other solution possible ... Consequently Weygand this morning confirmed the order to carry out his plan.[2] The encircled armies must therefore make a desperate bid to join hands with the French forces which are marching from south to north in an attempt to debouch from the Somme and, in particular, from Amiens.[3]

[1] See p. 135.

[2] Allusion to the *first* telegram addressed to General Blanchard (No. 1721/3/OP) at 9.45 a.m.

[3] Allusion to the operations undertaken in Péronne and Amiens by units of the 7th Army.

4. It is urgent to supply Lord Gort's army via Dunkirk, which is protected by Fagalde's two divisions.

5. It is very desirable that you send troops to the harbours as you did yesterday to Calais.[1]

6. General Weygand has learned with surprise that, contrary to this plan, Arras was evacuated yesterday by the British.

7. General Weygand's liaison with the Belgian army is assured. He learnt yesterday evening that they repelled small incursions, and that their morale is excellent.[2]

8. Owing to the impossibility of communicating direct with Blanchard ... General Weygand is unable to answer you concerning the lack of liaison between Blanchard and Gort, but, as he is in direct communication with the Belgians, he is convinced his orders have reached Blanchard, and through him, Gort. The proof that co-operation exists between Blanchard and Gort can be adduced from the fact that, last night, a French division relieved a British one.

9. General Weygand has this moment learned of the evacuation of heavy British army equipment from Le Havre, which is profoundly disturbing to morale at the rear. He is surprised, as I am, not to have had previous warning of this.

10. You will, I am sure, agree with me that in this tragic hour a single command is more necessary than ever and that General Weygand's orders must be obeyed to the letter.

11. General Weygand is convinced that his plan can only succeed if the Belgian, Blanchard and Gort armies are animated by the grim determination to achieve the break-out which alone can save them.

At about 6 p.m., Paul Reynaud sent Churchill a second telegram, in these terms:

SECRET

May 24th, 1940

General Weygand now informs me that, according to a telegram from General Blanchard, contrary to the express orders confirmed this morning by General Weygand, the British army has decided

---

[1] At Vincennes, on May 22nd, Churchill had announced the disembarkment of two battalions of Guards, armed with 48 mobile anti-tank guns, to protect the Channel ports. But since then Boulogne had fallen and Calais had been cut off from the hinterland.

[2] This telegram was sent before von Reichenau launched his offensive in the Belgian sector. It refers to the situation as it stood on May 23rd.

upon and carried out a retreat of twenty-five miles towards the ports at a time when our troops moving up from the south were gaining ground towards the north to meet the Allied armies of the north.

This withdrawal has naturally obliged General Weygand to change all his arrangements. He finds himself compelled to give up his attempt to close the breach and re-establish a continuous front. There is no need to stress the seriousness of the possible consequences.

Paul Reynaud was visibly shattered by General Weygand's news of Lord Gort's retreat. He grumbled about the poor morale of the army and the civilian population, and even wondered whether it would not be wiser to put an end to hostilities. In a conversation with Baudouin at 10.30 p.m., he asked the following question:

'If Germany were to make reasonable peace proposals, would public opinion allow us to reject them?' But he added at once, without waiting for an answer: 'Since I have always advocated total war, I should resign if that were to happen.'

MAY 25TH

————— ◆◆◆◆ —————

During the night the Wehrmacht stormed Audenarde and advanced to the outskirts of Courtrai. It was on the Escaut and the Lys simultaneously.

In the 19th Armoured Corps's sector, the 1st Panzer Division lined the Aa Canal between Holque and the coast, while the 2nd dug in at Watten. At Saint-Omer a bridge-head was established by the 41st Armoured Corps. The fall of Calais was now just a matter of time.

At 2 a.m. General Blanchard was officially advised of his appointment as Commander of the 1st Group of Armies. His mission was to 'co-ordinate the activities of the Allied armies in the north'.

At the same time he received General Weygand's telegram, instructing him to organize as extensive a defensive perimeter as possible round Dunkirk 'in case it should become impossible to carry out the manoeuvre prescribed by the Commander-in-Chief'.

At about 4 a.m. M. Pierlot, the Belgian Prime Minister, accompanied by General Denis and Ministers Spaak and van der Poorten, arrived by plane at King Leopold's headquarters in Wynendaele. They demanded an audience. This was a last bid to persuade the King to leave Belgium and follow the Belgian government abroad.

The King received the ministers standing, as though to demonstrate his decision not to prolong the interview or be swayed by them.

'Within a short time,' he told them, 'possibly within a matter of days, it will be France's turn to give up the fight — for the unevenness of the conflicting forces leaves her with no hope of success. Once France is occupied, the two million fleeing Belgians who might still provide recruits for an army will return home. Only a tiny minority will remain abroad. The interior problem — that of occupied Belgium — will distinctly outweigh the exterior problem that may be posed by Belgian émigrés.'

'By remaining in Belgium,' the ministers replied, 'the King will be a symbol of inconsistency rather than unity. He will be conferring a political character on the capitulation and separating his cause from the Allies.'

'I shall protect my people,' said Leopold.

'Your Majesty has a mistaken view of the role he will be able to play,' replied M. Spaak. 'Under the German occupation he will be a Hacha or a deported person.'

'I have decided to stay,' repeated the King. 'I must share the fate of my people, whatever it may be. It is by remaining with them that I shall best be able to protect them. I have already said so in a letter that I am sending to the King of England today.'

King Leopold read out the letter that he was on the point of sending to the British Sovereign: 'Despite all the advice that I have received to the contrary, I feel that duty demands that I should remain among my people ... '

'It was a solemn moment,' writes Fabre-Luce. 'It was not yet light. Had they drawn back the blinds they could have seen the glow of burning towns in the night sky.' When he reached the end of the letter the King seemed eager to dismiss the ministers. But M. Spaak, exhausted after his journey, craved leave to sit down. He declared at once: 'I acknowledge once again that when the King has come to a decision, there is nothing to be done about it!'

The ministers wondered whether the King had foreseen all the consequences of his decision. They asked him:

'Will Your Majesty form a new government?'

The King looked surprised for a moment, then he replied: 'Naturally! I am not a dictator!'

Finally they asked him how much longer the Belgian army could hold out.

'Twenty-four hours at most,' he answered.[1]

The audience was over. The ministers took their leave of Leopold for ever.

Unwilling to assume responsibility for rescinding Weygand's orders for an offensive,[2] General Blanchard made one last attempt to persuade the British to abandon the idea of withdrawing to Dunkirk. The British demanded 24 hours to 'reflect and reconnoitre'. In fact their decision was already irrevocably taken.

After General Blanchard had left, Sir John Dill telegraphed to Mr Churchill, outlining the dangers now threatening the B.E.F. as a result of the breaching of the Belgian front. Far from entertaining any further

---

[1] In fact the Belgian army did not capitulate till May 28th — three days later.
[2] At this point General Blanchard had not yet received Weygand's second telegram, sent at 4.15 p.m.

thoughts of a southward offensive, Lord Gort was afraid that his last hope of reaching the coast might vanish unless the gap between the British left and the Belgian right were not swiftly stopped. He therefore decided to fall back to the line Ypres–Commines.

All the same, he was not opposed to the launching of the counter-attack proposed by Blanchard, so long as it were carried out by exclusively French units (i.e. with the three divisions and Cavalry Corps drawn from the 1st Army).

In reply to messages from Sir John Dill and Lord Gort, Mr Anthony Eden, the British War Minister, wired to the Commander of the B.E.F.:

> ... I have had information all of which goes to show that French offensive from Somme cannot be made in sufficient strength ... *Should this prove to be the case you will be faced with a situation in which the safety of the B.E.F. will predominate ...*

Lord Gort at once notified General Blanchard's headquarters that no British division would take any further part in the offensive.

But General Blanchard had gone to confer with King Leopold in Bruges and did not get the message till he returned.

In Vincennes General Weygand now realized that the strategic plan that he had devised on assuming command had hopelessly fallen through. Without wasting time on useless recriminations, the C.-in-C. immediately contemplated another manoeuvre.

He regarded the cleaving of his armies into two groups as irreparable. In these circumstances, the only solution was for them to fight with their backs to the sea, to form a perimeter round the coastal ports.

By gaining time in this manner General Weygand expected to be able to establish a defensive front, echeloned in depth, along a line stretching from south of the Somme to the Maginot Line and passing through Abbeville, Amiens, Laon and Rethel. There the French forces could wait resolutely for the enemy to embark on the second phase of his campaign. But for there to be time for this defence to be organized it was essential that the French, British and Belgian elements in the 1st Group of Armies should combine their efforts and make a stand for as long as possible.

General Weygand gave General Blanchard a free hand in ensuring the defence of the Dunkirk perimeter. At 7.25 p.m. he sent him a third telegram, worded as follows:

> You alone will remain judge of the decisions to be taken in order to save what can be saved — above all, the honour of the colours that are in your safekeeping.

At 10.30 p.m. General Blanchard returned to his headquarters. He found both Lord Gort's message and General Weygand's telegram waiting for him. The new commander of the 1st Group of Armies had therefore wasted the entire afternoon endeavouring to persuade, first British G.H.Q., then Belgian G.H.Q., to carry out a manoeuvre that would not now take place. Raging inwardly, he signed the order calling off the intended operation.

POLITICAL SITUATION

On reaching Paris, General Spears drove almost immediately to the War Ministry in the Rue Saint-Dominique, to pay his respects to Paul Reynaud. The Premier showed him Churchill's letter accrediting him.

Spears was then asked if he had seen Reynaud's last telegram to Churchill.

'Yes,' he replied, 'and his answer.'

'He then began to tell me,' writes Spears, 'how British generals always made for harbours.'

' "I know," I said. "I have just seen the ambassador, and he told me. But let us be serious," I went on. "If I am to do any good here, *Monsieur le Président et cher ami*, we should not theorize." ...

'I went on to say that it was natural perhaps to try to blame Gort for what seemed at the moment to be the failure of the break-through southwards. He was a foreigner. It was easy to say he was at fault. I did not know the exact situation, nor did anyone else ... '

Spears added that if Gort had fallen back it was because he had been compelled to do so.

> I then begged the *Président du Conseil* to set his face against recriminations, not to tolerate them. They were not only futile but very dangerous. They would evoke deadly rejoinders and engender very bad feeling ...
>
> 'If I might venture an opinion,' I concluded, 'it is that the only sensible thing we can do at the moment is to consider our common danger as calmly as we can, in complete harmony, and act together as brothers ... '

Reynaud nodded his head in approval. He got up once or twice, his small figure very erect, the shoulders of his black jacket thrown back, and walked up and down, his hands behind his back. Several times he stretched his neck and turned his head to one side as if putting on too high and too tight a collar; a characteristic gesture. His Chinese eyes, always so ready to emphasize his wit with a twinkle, did not smile, but his eyebrows, which were drawn high and shaped like open umbrellas, giving him an expression of unabating wakefulness and amused curiosity, shot several times half-way up his forehead, as if they had been half-closed, and lifted to avoid colliding with each other.

His attitude was one of undemonstrative cordiality and underlying understanding. He looked not in the least rattled. I said to myself as I had often done before: 'This is a likeable, gallant little man.'

He seemed to accept what I said, but I sensed a question in his mind which he hesitated to put, so, backing my guess, I said that Churchill was as firm as a rock and was not in the least dismayed. The only thing that would annoy him would be the bandying about of reproaches ...

It had been a friendly, if lively, talk, which Reynaud brought to an end by saying that General Weygand and other members of the War Committee were in his study, and would I come in and continue the discussion in their presence?

Spears agreed. In Reynaud's study he found Marshal Pétain, General Weygand, Admiral Darlan and M. Paul Baudouin.

After the usual exchange of greetings, Reynaud 'opened the discussion, giving me the lead to repeat what I had told him, but he stressed again particularly the difficulty in which General Weygand had been placed.'

Weygand later informed his colleagues that a Staff Officer had arrived from General Blanchard's headquarters. The officer's name was Commandant (Major) Fauvelle. Weygand asked that he should be heard. Spears writes:

Not for a moment had I thought that the others in that room, any more than myself, considered the war practically lost, although it had been obvious enough, even in London, that there was only one chance in a hundred of the entire Allied force in the north getting away. The idea of defeat, or even the shadow of such an idea, never crossed my mind, but, as Commandant Fauvelle told his story in fragments, revealing an appalling state of affairs, and as I realized that his catastrophic defeatism seemed to some extent at least to be accepted as the reflection of the real position, I felt cold fingers turning my heart to stone ... In my view nothing short of throwing Fauvelle out of the window would have been adequate.

'What was the situation when you left General Blanchard?' asked Reynaud.

'I believe in a very early capitulation,' replied Commandant Fauvelle.

'*Il ne s'agit pas de cela*,' said Reynaud and Weygand together.

Marshal Pétain did not say a word. He sat perfectly still, staring at the floor, as though overwhelmed by Commandant Fauvelle's appalling descriptions of the ordeals suffered by the French troops.

At 6.55 p.m. Paul Reynaud received the following telegram from Churchill:

> *May 25th*, 1940
>
> My telegram last night told you all we know over here, and we have still heard nothing from Lord Gort to contradict it. *But I must tell you that a Staff Officer has reported to the War Office confirming the withdrawal of the two divisions from the Arras region, which your telegram to me mentioned.* General Dill, who should be with Lord Gort, has been told to send a Staff Officer by air at the earliest moment. As soon as we know what has happened I will report fully ...

This telegram was irrefutable proof that Lord Gort had indeed started his withdrawal without informing the French High Command. But this question of procedure was very much a thing of the past.

At 7 p.m. a meeting of the War Committee was held in the Elysée Palace under the chairmanship of M. Albert Lebrun.

'Since May 25 all were agreed that defeat was inevitable,' writes William L. Langer. But nobody yet dared to express the thought.

General Weygand began by giving an account of operations from May 10th to the encirclement of the 1st Group of Armies in the north and in Belgium, 'where the situation has become very grave'.

'The 1st Group of Armies,' stated Weygand, 'is confronting the enemy to the east, the west and the south; the area that it occupies has become so constricted that it does not allow any considerable deployment of forces. I have no right to conceal from you that the situation may worsen rapidly.

'My last telegram to General Blanchard, sent this afternoon, gives him complete freedom of movement and commands that first and foremost he should preserve the honour of the flags entrusted to him. It is my duty to anticipate the worst ... '

To back up the C.-in-C.'s statements, Paul Reynaud read out the telegram that he had just received from Churchill. 'This telegram,' said the Premier, 'confirms the retreat of two British divisions from the Arras region.'

General Weygand resumed his summary and examined the situation along the rest of the front. The line held by French forces comprised the Maginot Line, the fortifications linking it to Montmédy, the Aisne, the Ailette, the Crozat Canal and the Somme, all the way to the sea. The High Command was currently massing all its remaining resources along this line, including the last of its reserves.

'A new line of defence, about a hundred and seventy-five miles long, is now being formed,' said the Generalissimo. 'What forces do we have at our disposal, to enable us to hold it?

'We are now left with 48 divisions. Adding 7 divisions recovered from the wreck of Corap's Army, 1 division taken from the Alpine Army and 3 divisions raised from our North African forces, the French army will number about sixty divisions in all.

'We are confronted by 130–150 German divisions, including 9 armoured divisions. So we are outnumbered three to one. Furthermore, our tank units are down by four-fifths. Our tank and bomber resources are bound to decline rapidly in the weeks ahead ...

'In which case, what are we to do? Aim at a shorter line. But what line? Three possibilities suggest themselves:

1. A line reaching from the sea to the Loire and covering Paris. *But this would mean abandoning the Maginot Line and its 150,000 men.*

2. A shorter line incorporating the Maginot Line. *But this would mean abandoning Paris.*

3. A transversal line formed by the Lower Seine, the Paris position, the Oise, the Nonette, the Marne, the Argonne, Verdun, Metz and the Maginot Line. After a battle along the present Somme–Aisne front, the army would have to regroup behind this position. In its favour is the fact that it covers Paris. *But we shall not have the requisite reserves to effect an orderly withdrawal, under pressure from the enemy, from the line Somme–Aisne to the line Lower Seine–Marne ...*

'So we must dismiss these three possibilities. In fact, France now has no choice. She is left with one, and only one, solution: to stand firm along the present Somme–Amiens position and there defend herself to the last ...'

M. Paul Reynaud expressed the view that France was going to have to negotiate with the Germans. But at what stage would it be best to begin peace talks? Before or after the fall of Paris? Before or after the destruction of the army?

'It is not certain,' he stated, 'that the enemy will grant us an immediate armistice.'

M. Paul Reynaud then fired a series of questions at General Weygand: 'What do you think the government's position would be if the French armies were to be scattered and destroyed, as you just visualized? What, in that event, would be the French government's bargaining powers if peace proposals were to be addressed to it? Would those bargaining powers not be greater before the destruction of the French armies?'

M. Campinchi, the Minister of Marine, raised the question of the Anglo-French agreement of March 28th and asked whether it did not make the conclusion of an armistice dependent upon prior British consent.

'True,' replied M. Albert Lebrun, 'we have signed an undertaking not to make a separate peace. Still, if Germany were to offer us comparatively favourable conditions, we must examine them very closely and think them over.'

General Weygand emphasized that he entirely understood the President's concern. The cessation of hostilities was an inter-Allied matter. But the drastic solution that he had visualized a while back — fighting till the last round of ammunition was spent, to save the nation's honour — was a grave decision that likewise could not be taken without consulting Britain.

The Premier declared that in view of the serious circumstances, these various questions must now be looked into with the British government. Was not Britain also threatened with the loss of her entire army? M. Reynaud believed that Britain would 'understand our anxieties'.

Then Marshal Pétain spoke. He pointed out that, in his opinion, the undertakings contracted between France and Britain could be taken literally only if there had been absolute reciprocity between the two signatories. Now, that was not the case. 'One nation's duty towards the other is proportionate to the aid that the other has given. At present Britain has flung only ten divisions into the fray.'

M. Campinchi agreed that peace talks must be started in the near future and that it was important to lay the need for them before the British. But he wondered whether M. Paul Reynaud, as signatory of the Anglo-French agreement of March 28th, was the right person for the task.

General Weygand, though unwilling to go into the question of personalities, was insistent that there should be immediate talks between the French and British governments, for an exchange of views concerning the near future.

But M. Reynaud — possibly struck by the weight of M. Campinchi's argument — seemed more guarded, all of a sudden, about the possibility of getting in touch with the British government. Churchill, he said, had expressed himself in favour of a life-and-death struggle, pending the active intervention of the United States.

M. Lebrun asked the Premier: 'In what form and how soon can France hope to receive effective aid from America?'

M. Paul Reynaud replied that he had put this question to Mr Bullitt more than a week before and asked him to place it before President Roosevelt. But so far he had received no answer.

Finally the War Committee decreed that the Premier should fly to London as soon as possible to alert Mr Churchill to the tragic dilemma facing the French government.

MAY 26TH

————◆◆◆◆————

The 'retrenched camp' to which the French, British and Belgians were falling back had a perimeter of just over 125 miles. This was an extremely small area for the number of units that had to be packed in.

The news from the Belgian front grew worse and worse. The German bulge round Courtrai was getting bigger. King Leopold was sending the British and French continual calls for help. General Blanchard was so alarmed that he ordered the 1st Army units to burn their colours.

General Blanchard then proceeded to King Leopold's H.Q. in Bruges. The two examined the means by which the Courtrai bulge might be overcome. But the Belgians had no reserves left. The King claimed that his troops were in no condition to launch another offensive. He demanded that the necessary counter-attack be carried out by British units in conjunction with the French 2nd Light Mechanized Division, which, having been sent to the front as a reserve the day before, was capable of intervening in the threatened sector. With this suggestion the meeting came to an end.

Following the Franco-Belgian meeting, General Michiels — King Leopold's Chief of Staff — sent a note to Lord Gort demanding instant support. He informed him that the Belgians 'can no longer check the thrust towards Ypres, since they lack the requisite forces; nor are they in a position to withdraw to the Yser, as stipulated, for such a manoeuvre would entail the destruction of their last remaining units.'

At almost the same moment Lord Gort received a message from Mr Anthony Eden, the War Minister, confirming that his chief concern should be to ensure the safety of the B.E.F., and adding:

> ... Only course open to you may be to fight your way back to west where all beaches and ports east of Gravelines will be used for embarkation. Navy will provide fleet of ships and small boats and R.A.F. would give full support ... Preliminary plans should be urgently prepared ...

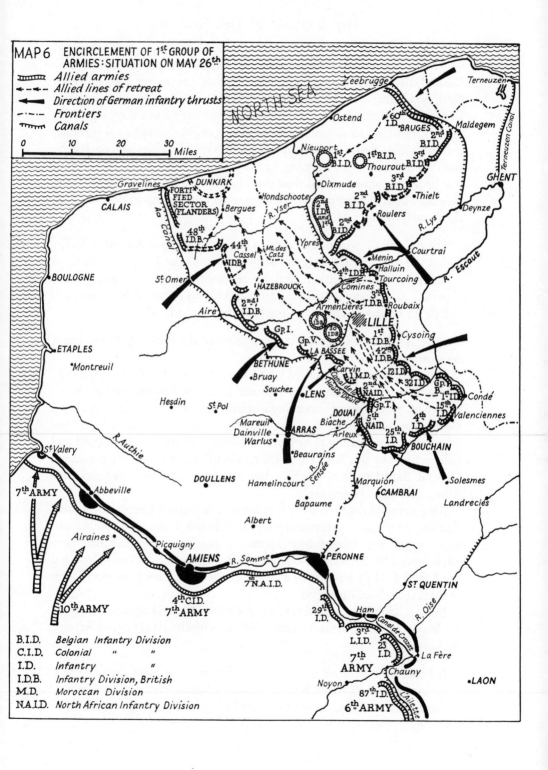

MAP 6 ENCIRCLEMENT OF 1ˢᵗ GROUP OF
ARMIES: SITUATION ON MAY 26ᵗʰ

▨▨▨▨	Allied armies
◄-·-·-	Allied lines of retreat
◄━━━	Direction of German infantry thrusts
-·-·-·	Frontiers
┬┬┬┬┬	Canals

0   10   20   30
Miles

B.I.D.   Belgian Infantry Division
C.I.D.   Colonial   "   "
I.D.   Infantry   "
I.D.B.   Infantry Division, British
M.D.   Moroccan Division
N.A.I.D. North African Infantry Division

NORTH SEA

Immediately after his visit to Bruges, General Blanchard called on Lord Gort. The latter had already given up the idea of defending the Lys. General Blanchard pointed out the extreme gravity of this decision. Gort stood firm. He did not intend deviating in the slightest from War Office Instructions (which he nevertheless refrained from showing to his visitor). His only aim, now, was to get out of Europe as fast as possible.

Meanwhile, things were happening quickly. The units of von Reichenau's 6th Army were stepping up their attacks. The Belgians' position was becoming more critical than ever. In the course of the afternoon the Belgian High Command sent a message to General Champon, head of the French Military Mission:

> The Belgian Command begs you to inform the Commander-in-Chief that the plight of the Belgian army is serious. The Belgian C.-in-C. means to go on fighting until his resources are entirely spent. At present the enemy is attacking from Eecloo to Menin. The limits of Belgian resistance are very close to being reached.

General Champon passed the message on to the French G.H.Q., but it remained unanswered.

At 6 p.m. General Blanchard paid a second visit to the Belgian G.H.Q., where his arrival was impatiently awaited. But the Commander of the 1st Group of Armies brought nothing but bad news. He announced that Lord Gort refused to launch a counter-attack against Courtrai and that the British were evacuating their frontier position on the Belgians' right and falling back to the line Ypres–Lille. To fill the vacuum thus created, General Blanchard had nothing but a light mechanized division consisting of a mere fifteen tanks.

King Leopold digested these statements and warned General Blanchard that his army was in great danger of annihilation. General Michiels stated that for the past twenty-four hours the Belgian Command had been advocating a British counter-offensive. After a good deal of shilly-shallying the British G.H.Q. now made it clear that the B.E.F. was in no position to undertake such an operation.

In Paris, after lunching with General Colson, General Spears was visited by Major Archdale, British Liaison Officer with the 1st Group of Armies. Spears records:

> If I had tried to imagine something that was the exact opposite of Commandant Fauvelle, here it was. Resolution, clarity of thought, utter determination, a spirit that banished all trace of fatigue from the

voice, if not from the appearance, of this officer who had left Gort yesterday in search of Georges and had had little sleep or food for many days ... he reflected the spirit of the army he had come from, full of fight, with a morale not dented or even scratched by defeat.

Archdale reported that, from the operational point of view, the most important factor was that there were no wireless communications whatsoever between the 1st Group of Armies. The French were forced to rely entirely on dispatch-riders. Co-ordination of operations had thereby become quite impossible.

Archdale said the atmosphere at British General Headquarters could hardly be better. It was one of complete resolution: there was no sign of frayed nerves, and the staff was barely ruffled. The only subject that raised the temperature perceptibly was that of liaison with the French and the non-receipt of orders. Whenever possible, officers slept for half an hour in the middle of the day. It was impossible to imagine a greater contrast than that between Blanchard's and Gort's headquarters. At the former there was an air of feverish but purposeless activity, work but no plans.

Archdale's information struck Spears as so interesting that he immediately took him to see Marshal Pétain. The latter received the two British officers in his room in the Boulevard des Invalides. General Bineau, the Marshal's Chief of Staff, was present.

Archdale faithfully repeated his account.

The Marshal asked him outright what he thought of General Blanchard. After some hesitation Archdale replied that Blanchard was very tired and not the man to inspire enthusiasm in an overstrained force. Yet the supreme need of the Northern Armies was to feel 'the grip of a commander, and confidence in him'.

Marshal Pétain questioned him about General Prioux, concerning whom Archdale waxed enthusiastic. He inspired confidence and would inspire confidence in the troops ... Pétain then asked if Prioux would enthuse the British also. I was as nettled as I was surprised at this and interjected that the British stood in no need of stimulants ...

The old Marshal said very sadly: 'It is then only the French who need encouragement.'

Even as this conversation was going on in Paris, Guderian was preparing to storm Calais, having encircled the town the day before. He called on the local British commander to surrender, but Brigadier Nicholson replied disdainfully: 'The answer is no, as it is the British army's duty to fight as well as it is the German's.'

But his resistance was short-lived, despite the desperate efforts of the French forces in the town. The handing-over of arms and surrender of troops was perfectly orderly.

After the fall of Calais the only ports still open to the Allies were Gravelines, Dunkirk and Ostend.

Guderian was already preparing to swoop on Dunkirk when he received a further order to halt, confirming that of May 24th. Once again the entire left wing of the German forces was categorically forbidden to cross the Aa.

The news took Guderian's breath away. What had been the point of creating a mechanized army if they were not going to use it at the vital moment? But this time he could only bow to the decision.

Farther east, the 39th Armoured Corps (comprising the 5th and 7th Panzer Divisions) had likewise been halted for the past forty-eight hours, near La Bassée. Rommel took advantage of the pause to overhaul his tanks and tot up the losses of the 7th Panzer Division. He wrote to his wife:

One or two days without fighting have done us a lot of good. All together the division has lost: 27 officers killed, 33 wounded and 1,500 men killed and wounded. That makes our losses about 12 per cent. There is unlikely to be any further fierce fighting, for we have given the enemy a thorough pasting.

That same day, Rommel was decorated, on the Führer's behalf, with the insignia of Knight of the Iron Cross.

Hitler now ordered the Luftwaffe to 'liquidate the Dunkirk pocket'. Field-Marshal Kesselring writes:

In view of the brilliant co-operation between Panzers and flyers that had characterized operations to date ... it seemed to me that the B.E.F. must capitulate within a matter of days. So I was particularly surprised to learn that my squadrons had been ordered to annihilate the remains of the B.E.F. almost without assistance from the army. The Commander-in-Chief of the Luftwaffe (Goering) must surely have received adequate warning of the effect that nearly three weeks of non-stop fighting had had on my airmen ... I reminded Goering that the new Spitfires had recently appeared on the scene, making our air operations difficult and costly — and in the end it was the Spitfires that allowed the British and French to evacuate the town by sea. Nevertheless, my warnings did not lead to any modification of our orders. Was this refusal to admit to a mistake due to stubbornness or weakness? Either way, our tired but gradually reinforced formations strained themselves to the limit to achieve the objective that had been assigned to them. Air Marshal Keller personally led his formations into battle and the number of sorties carried out by the exhausted crews was even higher than usual. The result, as might be expected, was that the Spitfires added appreciably to our losses. The bad weather was a further hindrance, making navigation even harder. No one who saw the mass of wrecks in the coastal waters and all the equipment scattered over the beaches, no one who heard at first hand the operational reports of our bomber, fighter and reconnaissance pilots could feel anything but the warmest admiration for the performance of our airmen, as for the incredible stamina, ingenuity and bravery of the British.

POLITICAL SITUATION

M. Pierlot and the Belgian ministers had taken advantage of their arrival in London to call on Mr Churchill and inform him of what they were already calling 'the King's defection'.

The British Prime Minister was deeply perturbed by this news. This was the first time that a European sovereign had preferred to share his people's trials rather than seek sanctuary in London. Would British prestige suffer? Through Lord Halifax, Churchill asked King George VI to advise King Leopold to leave Belgium.

Questioned on the telephone as to the advisability of such a step, Admiral Keyes replied that if the Belgian army were deprived of the King's leadership it would inevitably surrender sooner and the B.E.F. would be in danger. He did not think Churchill would be unduly impressed by the arguments of the Belgian ministers, who seemed to have only one idea in mind: the continuation of a political regime whose incompetence and lack of authority had been all too glaring during the previous fortnight.

As a result of the deliberations of the War Committee the night before, M. Paul Reynaud went to London with Colonel de Villelume and Captain Roland de Margerie, his *chef de cabinet*. As soon as he stepped off the plane at Croydon, the French Premier was driven to Downing Street, where he lunched *tête-à-tête* with Mr Churchill and Lord Halifax. They had just got back from a service of Intercession and Prayer in Westminster Abbey and were tense-faced. He made it clear to Churchill that 'in view of the wearing-down of our forces it would be wise, from now on, to bear in mind the possibility that France might be reduced to laying down her arms and seeking a solution through negotiations.' The possibility of Italy's declaring war was also raised.

In the afternoon the discussions were continued in the presence of General Ironside. Reynaud read out the note prepared by General Weygand, setting forth his views on the military situation.

Forewarned by General Spears of the grievances expressed in Paris against the British High Command, General Ironside rejected this note out of hand because 'it seemed to reproach Lord Gort for not complying with the Commander-in-Chief's instructions.' He repeated that the British army had been left without orders for several days.

The French Premier, 'not knowing where the truth lay', found himself quite unable to reply. He was afraid of causing a scene, so he left off reading Weygand's report. The argument ended abruptly.

At about 6.15 p.m. M. Paul Reynaud started back to Paris without any of the key questions that had prompted his trip to London having been asked, let alone resolved.

Immediately after his departure, the War Office sent the following telegram to Lord Gort:

> Prime Minister has had conversation with M. Reynaud this afternoon ... It will not be possible for French to deliver attack in the south in sufficient strength to enable them to effect junction with northern armies. In these circumstances no course open to you but to fall back upon the coast ... M. Reynaud communicating General Weygand and latter will no doubt issue orders in this sense forthwith ...

This telegram backed Lord Gort's plans; it also led him to believe that Reynaud and Weygand were in agreement with them, which was untrue.

Thereupon the Commander-in-Chief of the B.E.F. laid plans for the final withdrawal. 'He had already given instructions for the embarkation of a number of specialists,' records Bardies. 'He now ordered the withdrawal of all units not needed for rearguard actions.'

When he got back to the Rue Saint-Dominique, M. Reynaud found the following letter from Marshal Pétain lying on his desk:

The army is the country's material and moral rampart. The country's trust in it must be the subject of all your vigilance.

The army is *one* because it is founded upon discipline. The publicity given to the 'supersedings' of generals, *at a time when we are in dire peril*, hits the army, whether or not that is intended ...

If there has been dereliction of duty, there has also been magnificent leadership.

If blame can be apportioned, military leaders are not alone in having something to answer for ...

One has only to keep one's ears open to hear stories of generals committing suicide,[1] senior officers going over to the enemy, etc ...

The country's morale is not strengthened by the generals' attempts to pull the wool over people's eyes. On the contrary, the nation's verdict is one of treason and inadequate retributions ...

Thus the country is quite naturally forgetting its sins, those which we have all committed for twenty-two years: that predilection for a quiet life, that cessation of effort which, far more than individual lapses, have landed us where we are.

Yet we must confess our sins if we want to be saved.

The army must keep out of these controversies.

We must be implacable in stamping out weaknesses, wherever they stem from. But it is essential that our nation's affection and admiration for its army be preserved intact ...

From Washington, President Roosevelt sent the following message to Mr William Bullitt, the United States ambassador in Paris:

While we still hope the invasion will be checked, if the worst comes to the worst, we regard the retention of the French fleet as a force in being as vital to the reconstitution of France and of the French colonies and to the ultimate control of the Atlantic and other oceans and as a vital influence towards getting less harsh terms of peace. This means that the French fleet must not get caught bottled up in the Mediterranean ...

Finally, if the Germans hold out alluring offers to France based on surrender of the fleet, it should be remembered that these offers are

[1] It is a fact that General Corap had gone mad as a result of the charges that M. Reynaud had levelled against him in the Chamber of Deputies (on May 16th).

of no ultimate value and that the condition of France could be no worse, but in fact could be far stronger, if the fleet were removed as a whole to safe places.

[*The President also cabled to the United States ambassador in Rome, expressing his hope that the entry of Italy into the war might be avoided. He asked that he should be informed of the precise desires of Italy, which he would communicate to the British and French governments.* — Ed.]

In Rome Mussolini received Marshals Badoglio and Balbo at the Palazzo Venezia and informed them: 'I have sent Hitler a written statement, making it clear to him that I do not intend to stand idly by and that as from June 5th[1] I shall be in a position to declare war on France and England.'

Following this interview, the Duce received a letter from Hitler and a dispatch from Signor Alfieri, Italian ambassador in Berlin, giving an account of his discussion with Goering the day before.

'The latter raised the question of the date of our intervention,' writes Ciano, 'and suggested that we should attack when the Wehrmacht begins its all-out advance on Paris, after wiping out the Anglo-French-Belgian pocket [at Dunkirk]. The Duce agrees in principle.'

During the night the Belgian ministers arrived in Paris after making the journey from London. Most of their aides were already installed in the French capital.

---

[1] In fact this letter was not sent till May 30th (see p. 198).

MAY 27TH

At 3 a.m. Churchill sent the following message to Admiral Keyes:

Impart following to your friend [the King of the Belgians]. Presume
he knows that British and French are fighting their way to coast
between Gravelines and Ostend inclusive, and that we propose to
give fullest support from navy and air force during hazardous·
embarkation. What can we do for him? Certainly we cannot serve
Belgium's cause by being hemmed in and starved out ...

Then the British Prime Minister sent Lord Gort a telegram worded:

... It is now necessary to tell the Belgians[1] ... Your personal contact
with the King is desirable. Keyes will help. We are asking them to
sacrifice themselves for us ...

But both messages were to arrive too late. Leopold III did not have
time to consider them.

At 7 a.m. a military conference was held in Cassel to finalize plans for
joint measures likely to strengthen the defence of the Dunkirk perimeter.
Those present were General Koeltz, representing General Weygand,
General Fagalde, commander of the units guarding the bridge-head
perimeter, and Admiral Abrial, who commanded the maritime front
under the code-name 'Admiral North'. Lord Gort did not attend. He
was content to send General Sir Ronald Adam, entrusting him with the
task of organizing the bridge-head in collaboration with the French.

General Adam emphasized the need to avoid traffic congestion within
the perimeter. He told General Fagalde that he had decided to allow no
British transport north of the canal[2] apart from ambulances and vehicles
essential to tactics or supply. He asked General Fagalde to see that the
French did the same.

There was no agreement between the two commands on this point,

---

[1] Presumably of the re-embarkation of the B.E.F.
[2] The Colme Canal, which bounded the perimeter to the south-east.

because their aims were not identical, and General Adam was careful not to mention Lord Gort's latest telegram from the War Office.

Furthermore, the British government was pressing Lord Gort to lose no time. A further telegram arrived during the morning and was quite explicit:

> In case smallest doubt, your sole task now is to evacuate to England maximum of your forces possible.

General Spears records:

> I had become convinced that Weygand and the French generally were intent upon holding the country round the harbour and defending it as a beleaguered fortress. This was completely contrary to the British conception, and was absurd. The garrison would be reduced by starvation and lack of ammunition in a very short time. It would be a new Metz, with but two differences: the siege would be shorter and the responsible Bazaine would not be amongst the besieged.

These conflicting viewpoints were not dictated solely by different conceptions of strategy. They sprang from two irreconcilable psychological attitudes: that of a sea-faring race and that of a continental nation. And Spears writes elsewhere in his book:

> I suddenly realized with a clarity that had never before been vouchsafed me in all the long years I had worked with the French army, that to them the sea was much the same thing as an abyss of boiling pitch and brimstone, an insurmountable obstacle no army could venture over unless they were specially organized colonial expeditions endowed with incomprehensible powers ...
> To fall back to Dunkirk represented retiring into a fortress, which might be supplied by sea, but from which there was no retreat.

In an attempt to overcome this misconception on the part of the French, Spears explained that: 'behind the harbours lay God's own highway, the greatest, widest highway in the world, one that led everywhere; if the troops could get on to ships they would soon be in the line elsewhere.'

While the Cassel conference was going on, another Anglo-French meeting was being held in Dover. France was represented by Admirals Odend'hal and Leclerc and Post-Captain Auphan; Britain by Admirals Ramsay and Somerville. The purpose of the meeting was to work out how the evacuation was to be carried out. It was decided that the two nations should pool their shipping resources. Yet Vice-Admiral Ramsay,

Flag Officer Commanding Dover, and Admiral Abrial, commanding the northern sea front, retained sole responsibility, each within his respective zone.

Lord Gort and General Blanchard were unrepresented at this meeting. 'They were tardily and inaccurately informed,' writes Bardies. 'Later, therefore, they were unable to give their troops the orders that would certainly have avoided friction when the time came for them to embark.'

General Fagalde lost no time in organizing the defence of the landward side. The bridge-head had been divided into halves:

A Sector (outer): General Barthélemy. Front demarcated by Grave-lines, Watten, Cassel, Steenworde.
B Sector (inner): General Beaufrère. Front demarcated by the old Mardyck Canal, the Upper and Lower Colme Canals and the Franco-Belgian frontier position.

The German infantry units were making dangerous progress west of Hazebrouck and came within four and a half miles of Dunkirk, south-west of Bergues.

A nightmarish aerial attack (30,000 incendiary bombs were dropped) turned Dunkirk into an inferno.

Rommel, who had been reinforced with the tanks of the 5th Panzer Brigade, was on the move again. He was harassing the Franco-British forces falling back in the Lille area.

Without prior warning, British troops destroyed the telephone exchange in Lille itself. This played havoc with inter-Allied communications. Now there were only two lines open to London. Units completely lost touch with one another and the work of the intelligence service was brought to a standstill.

British troops had been pouring into Dunkirk since the day before. The task of evacuation was difficult under bombing. Only the outer harbour could be used. For a time it seemed that the port would be put completely out of action.

As has been stated, Lord Gort was not conversant with the decisions taken at the Dover conference. For one thing, he did not know that shipping resources had been pooled. Since his troops were first to reach the port and the only ships in sight were those the British had alerted before-hand, he wanted to embark his men at once.

The French protested.

Meanwhile disaster had struck at the Belgians. General von Reichenau had managed to effect three further break-throughs in their sector.

'The last of our reserves were in action,' writes General Michiels. 'We were left with only three weak regiments. Contact with the British was being maintained at our expense.'

The King decided that he had no choice but to capitulate.

At about 12.50 p.m., with the situation still worsening, he had a call put through to Lord Gort:[1]

> The King ... wishes you to know that his army is greatly disheartened. It has been incessantly engaged for four days and subjected to intense air bombardment which the R.A.F. have been unable to prevent. The knowledge that the Allied armies in this sector have been encircled and that the Germans have great superiority in the air has led his troops to believe that the position is almost hopeless ... He wishes you to realize that he will be obliged to surrender before a debacle follows ...

At 3.30 p.m. the King called together Admiral Keyes, General Champon and the members of the British and French military missions to the Belgian G.H.Q. He officially informed them that he intended asking for an armistice at midnight. The message was received in London at 5.45 p.m. It reached Paris at 7 p.m.

The King gave orders for an envoy to be sent to German G.H.Q. Anxious to 'do things properly', he notified General Champon of this decision and handed over control of the French 60th Division, which had been on loan to him.[2] General Champon managed to warn General Weygand by radio but was unable to get in touch with General Blanchard, whose command post had still not been located.

At 5 p.m. the Belgian envoy set out for the German 6th Army headquarters. He returned at 10 p.m. with the following answer: 'The Führer demands that the Belgian army lay down its arms unconditionally.'

At 12.20 a.m. a military surrender was signed by General von Reichenau, for the Wehrmacht, and General Desrousseaux, for the Belgian army.

At 1.30 a.m. notification of the German-Belgian armistice was telephoned to the French military mission. The latter had already left the Belgian G.H.Q. and moved to La Panne.

In London Sir John Dill was appointed Chief of General Staff in place

---

[1] By Admiral Sir Roger Keyes, who was in constant touch with King Leopold and his Staff.

[2] After being released by the Belgians the 60th Infantry Division was twice held up, first by General Champon and then by General Blanchard. On May 28th and 29th it was cut to pieces by the Germans along the Yser, between Nieuport and Dixmude. No more than 600 men were left by the time it reached Dunkirk on May 30th, headed by its commander General Teyssère.

of General Ironside, who was considered too much in favour of Anglo-French co-operation.

POLITICAL SITUATION

M. Paul Reynaud sent a message to President Roosevelt entreating the United States government to send France six destroyers and — still more important — 'clouds' of planes, of any type.

In Rome Count Ciano had two long conversations with M. François-Poncet, the French ambassador, and Mr Phillips, the United States ambassador.

The Italian Minister for Foreign Affairs writes:

The latter was to have given the Duce a message from Roosevelt, but he was not received ... Roosevelt was offering to mediate between us and the Allies. He would have been ready to accept personal responsibility for the carrying-out of any agreements that might have been reached, once the war was over. I told Phillips that Roosevelt was barking up the wrong tree ... With Mussolini it was not, fundamentally, a matter of getting this or that; *he wanted war* ...

The conversation with François-Poncet was likewise important, not for its result but as a pointer ... Leaving aside Corsica 'which was an integral part of France', he said we could make a deal over Tunisia, perhaps even over Algeria. I told him, as I had told Phillips, that it was too late ...

In Paris there was a Cabinet meeting in the Elysée Palace. In an atmosphere heavy with anxiety, M. Paul Reynaud announced the imminent capitulation of the Belgian army and vehemently condemned 'the unspeakable attitude of King Leopold'. The King, he said, had sent his envoy to the Germans without even consulting General Blanchard, to whom the Belgian army was responsible.

General Weygand announced that he had replied to General Champon's message in the following terms:

1. I am informing the government immediately.
2. Pending further orders I am instructing Blanchard to break with the Belgians.
3. Blanchard, in conjunction with General Gort, will take any emergency decisions likely to offset this act of desertion.

At M. Daladier's suggestion, the Cabinet then examined means of keeping Italy out of the war. M. François-Poncet's latest reports allowed them little hope of success.

The French government decided to inform Rome directly of the offers to which it was prepared to subscribe without having recourse to the mediation of a third party.

Following the meeting, M. Paul Reynaud told M. Pierlot and General Denis that King Leopold had sent an envoy to the Germans. 'The Allied command was not warned,' he asserted.

MAY 28TH

At about 9 a.m. a communication from the Belgian envoy, who was once again at General von Reichenau's headquarters, announced that the High Command of the Wehrmacht demanded free passage to the sea for the German columns.

The capitulation of the Belgian army dangerously exposed the left flank of the B.E.F. General Sir Alan Brooke hurried into the breach at the head of the British 2nd Corps and managed to re-establish a continuous line of fire between Ypres and Dixmude with the effective assistance of the French 2nd Light Mechanized Division. Meanwhile the French 60th Infantry Division, hurriedly pulled back, thanks to the lorries loaned by the Belgian army, formed a stop-gap between Dixmude and the sea.

While this fighting was going on to the left of the Anglo-French position, to the right (in the sector held by the British 44th Infantry Division) a heavy attack from the direction of Saint-Omer gave the Germans control of Cassel and the surrounding hills. They now held much the better terrain: the dry, bare, high plateau of Picardy. The Allies were defending the sodden Flanders plain.

Thus there was a bottle-neck between Cassel and Ypres; units of the B.E.F. and the French 1st Army still fighting in and to the south of Lille would have to squeeze through if they were to reach the sea.

In fact it was in the Lille sector that the biggest operation of the day took place. The 4th, 5th and 7th Panzer Divisions thrust out from the La Bassée area, seized the bridges over the Deule Canal and overnight completed the encirclement of the rear units of the 1st Army.

'The route followed by Colonel Rothenburg during the night of May 27th–28th,' writes Rommel, 'could be traced by the glow of the vehicles knocked out by his men. The Panzer division was leaving a trail of flames behind it.'

The British 5th and 50th Infantry Divisions fired every gun they had and for a time managed to contain the advance of Rommel's tanks. But the bottle-neck was tightening between Armentières and Halluin. The remains of the French 1st Army were going to have to negotiate this narrow defile.

Startled by this rapid worsening of the situation, the British decided to evacuate the line of the Lys and adopt that of Poperinghe–Ypres during the night of May 28th–29th.

On hearing this news, General Blanchard hurried to Lord Gort's command post in Hontekerque. Horrified, he explained to the commander of the B.E.F. that after the German capture of Cassel and the Flanders hills there was only one way out for the seven French divisions that had just reached Lille in their retreat from Valenciennes and Cambrai: it lay at the junction of the Anglo-French forces. The British retreat would enable the Germans to encircle the French units and force them to capitulate. General Prioux, who commanded them, declared that they were 'worn out and unable to move'.

To enable them to recover General Blanchard begged Lord Gort to postpone his withdrawal for twenty-four hours. Lord Gort refused. He said he had categorical orders from his government to subordinate everything to the safety of the B.E.F.

Lord Gort insisted that General Blanchard should order General Prioux back. He was convinced that any forces still south of the Poperinghe–Ypres line on the morning of May 29th would be irretrievably lost.

General Blanchard stuck to his view and asked Lord Gort the following question before going off to see General Prioux: 'Will the British forces pull back tonight *whatever the position of the French 1st Army along the Lys?*'

After a few seconds of silence General Pownall, Lord Gort's Chief of Staff, replied: '*Yes.*'[1]

Indignant at Gort's and Pownall's attitude, General Blanchard drove straight to the 1st Army command post to inform General Prioux of the decision taken by British H.Q. It would place the 1st Army in a tragic

---

[1] General Pownall's own record of the meeting, quoted by Churchill, gives a slightly different account of the facts. According to Pownall, no argument could prevail upon Blanchard to issue orders to withdraw to Dunkirk. 'He declared that evacuation from the beach was impossible. It was therefore idle to try — the chance wasn't worth the effort involved.'

Blanchard's attitude was described by Major Archdale as 'fantastic'. Blanchard, he said, hoped that the French units encircled in the north and those fighting farther south, in the Abbeville sector, would link up by worming their way towards each other along the coast.

General Swayne, Chief Liaison Officer to General Georges, recalls: 'The French would not embark their troops in ships, persisting that to do so would be to abandon France.' And General Spears writes: 'The four British divisions cut off, together with the 1st French Army around Lille, were able, thanks to the mechanical transport and their discipline, to fall back (as Churchill says) "with surprising rapidity, almost in a night", when Gort gave the order. Not so the French. They did not have the same advantages in transport, *but were in any case doomed*, for General Prioux, commanding the 1st Army, had decided not to withdraw that night (May 28th) and so lost his last opportunity of doing so.'

situation. With one accord Generals Blanchard and Prioux decided to pull back as much of it as was still mobile. Two columns were formed. Seven divisions stayed put, under General Molinié. They attempted a break-through. It failed.

Lord Gort complained of the jamming of the roads leading to Dunkirk and threw the blame on to the French, few of whom, he states in his dispatch, would abandon their vehicles unless compelled to do so at British Traffic Control posts.

General Blanchard stated: 'The roads are terribly cluttered and constantly flown over by German planes. On entering the bridge-head, the British are compelling the troops to abandon their heavy guns and motor vehicles.'

Yet the day was to be marked by an offensive effort on the part of the French, an attempt to force the Germans back from the large bridge-head that they had established south of the Somme, in the Abbeville sector.[1]

The operation was to be conducted by de Gaulle, with the hundred surviving tanks of the 4th Armoured Division. The broad Somme valley with its peat bogs and ditches was an impossible place for armour. So de Gaulle would attack the southern face, on the plateau, striking northwards to take the Camp de César (Hill 84) which commanded the bridges of Abbeville.

The orders reached the units at about 4 p.m. It was raining, there were breakdowns; the roads were cluttered, the crews weary from an overnight journey; delay followed delay. The preliminary bombardment had to be lengthened. Then the sky cleared and enemy reconnaissance planes got busy. The advantage of surprise was lost and it was much too late to reach the final target.

At nightfall, however, the 46th Battalion (with 13 'B' tanks), the 47th Battalion (with 19 'B' tanks) and the 44th Battalion (with about 50 'R35' tanks) gained ground and took a great many prisoners.

By 11 p.m. the Germans' main line of defence was appreciably dented.

Meanwhile Admiral Abrial set about organizing the perimeter from his command post in Bastion 32 at Dunkirk. 'Despite incessant bombardment,' writes Bidou, 'he supervised shipping movement, food supplies and the distribution of ammunition with his usual calm.'

In the west the perimeter was buttressed by the Mardyck fortress. Thereafter the line of defence extended to Bergues via the Louis fortress and followed the canals to Furnes and Nieuport. Within the perimeter, to the north, lay flooded ground. The area was a mile to three miles wide,

1 See sketch no. 3.

between Bergues and the region of Les Moères. Only the raised roads were free. North of the floods came another low-lying area and then the Dunkirk–Furnes Canal. Finally, there was a narrow strip of dunes bordering a large open beach that covered the whole breadth of the Allied positions and sloped gently down to the sea. There were no quays or jetties apart from those in Dunkirk itself, but along the shore, within about a mile of one another, were a number of seaside resorts: Coxyde, La Panne, Bray-les-Dunes, Malo-les-Bains.

Admiral Abrial was responsible neither to General Blanchard nor to General Weygand. He took orders only from Admiral Darlan, Commander-in-Chief of the French naval forces. At the start he had only a few local troops to defend the perimeter on the landward side. To these he added naval crews whose ships had been sunk. Finally he had 'under his authority' the land forces in the Boulogne–Calais–Dunkirk area, commanded by General Fagalde. Admiral Abrial likewise had at his disposal the French fleet in the Pas-de-Calais, under Admiral Landriau. This consisted of all the French ships already used in the Dunkirk area plus all available small craft in the Channel.

Thus the defence and supply of Dunkirk were to be carried out by all-French forces. Admiral Abrial expressed amazement to General Weygand at the lack of support he was receiving from the Royal Navy and the R.A.F.

On being informed of this situation General Weygand addressed the following message to the British authorities through General Lelong, French military attaché in London:

> *No. 565/Cab. D.N.*   *H.Q., May 28th,* 1940
> The Admiral commanding Dunkirk stresses the need for powerful air and naval cover to ensure the supply and partial evacuation of the forces fighting to defend the Dunkirk bridge-head. I have no doubt this need is realized by the British authorities ...

Meanwhile Admiral Darlan, who had heard M. Reynaud discuss the possibility of an armistice before the War Committee on May 25th,[1] rebelled at the idea that France might be induced to lay down arms after eighteen days of fighting, with her fleet still intact. After reflecting on the consequences that such an action might have for his warships, he sent Admiral Le Luc, Chief of Naval Staff, a confidential note written entirely in his own hand and faithfully mirroring his frame of mind at the time. Here is the text:

---

[1] See pp. 154-7.

176

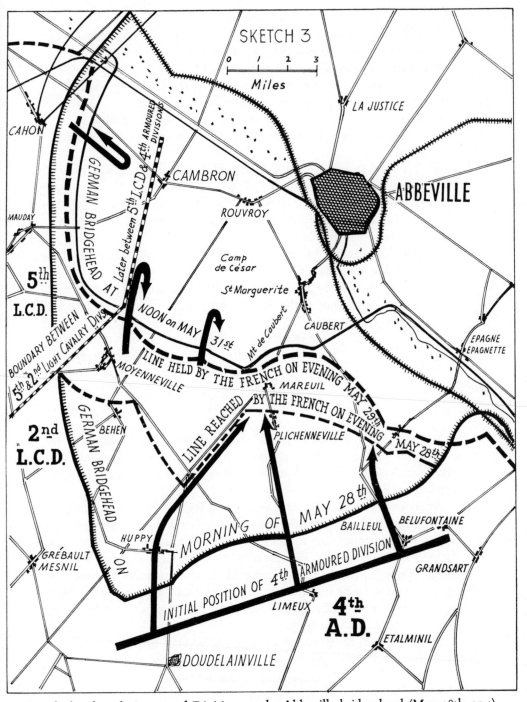

Attacks by the 4th Armoured Division on the Abbeville bridge-head (May 28th–31st)

Note to Admiral Le Luc

Should military events lead to an armistice with conditions imposed by the Germans, and should these conditions include the surrender of the fleet, *I do not intend to carry out this order.*

Consequently it would be advisable to give the following orders ... so that they can be passed on at the appropriate time:

1. If Italy is at war with us and not party to the armistice, all fighting ships will engage the Italian fleet or ports in mortal battle;

2. Those that survive the battle will take refuge in the most accessible *British*[1] port ... ;

3. If Italy is not at war or is party to the armistice, all fighting ships, aircraft and auxiliary or harbour craft will proceed to the most accessible British port;

4. All ships capable of crossing the Atlantic ... will endeavour to assemble at Halifax, Canada;

5. Ships would obey an order to return to France or to a port in enemy hands only if that order were headed with and followed by the words:

On behalf of Francis-Xavier.

F. D.

POLITICAL SITUATION

[*M. Charles-Roux, Secretary General of the Foreign Ministry, alarmed by the extent of the concessions to Italy projected by M. Daladier, protested against them. After consultation with M. Reynaud it was agreed to consult London before approaching Rome.* — Ed.]

At about 6 a.m. M. Reynaud sent for M. Pierlot, head of the Belgian government in Paris, to tell him that he considered himself compelled to make an immediate announcement to the French people about the Belgian army's surrender; that the news would cause bad feeling towards Belgians who had fled to France; that in the circumstances he could not answer for the safety of M. Pierlot's countrymen; and that the Belgian government must make its attitude clear and instantly condemn the King's unspeakable behaviour.

In other words M. Reynaud was demanding (and backing his demand with thinly veiled threats) that the Belgian Cabinet should associate itself

---

[1] Word underlined by Admiral Darlan.

with the condemnation that he himself was preparing. By throwing all the blame on the 'felon king', Reynaud meant to divert public anger from those who were really responsible for the collapse in Flanders.

Thereupon M. Pierlot drafted a statement beginning:

Belgians!
The King has opened negotiations with the enemy with a view to a cease-fire. This decision has been taken against the categorical and unanimous advice of the government. It does not bind the nation, since the King can exercise no power without his ministers. Belgium will be dumbfounded by the fateful news ...

But these terms seemed far too restrained to M. Reynaud. He altered them and handed M. Pierlot the following text:

The King has opened negotiations and *treated with the enemy* ... Belgium will be stupefied, but *the crime of one man cannot be imputed to the whole nation*. Our army has not deserved the fate that has befallen it ...

M. Pierlot agreed to this revision. He was only too glad to get out of proclaiming the King's dethronement, a national uprising and the adoption of the French constitution — all of which M. Reynaud had sought from him.

At 8.30 p.m., confident that the Belgian government would not contradict him, M. Paul Reynaud broadcast the following speech:

France can no longer count on the Belgian army. Since 4 a.m. the French and British armies have been fighting alone against the enemy in the north ...

It is this Belgian army which, at the height of the battle and without warning its British and French comrades-in-arms, has surrendered unconditionally on the orders of its King and opened the way to Dunkirk for the German divisions.

Eighteen days ago this same King sent us a call for help. We answered that call, in pursuit of a plan conceived by the Allied General Staffs last December.

And now, in the middle of the battle, King Leopold of the Belgians ... without warning General Blanchard, without a thought or word for the French or British troops who went to the aid of his country in response to his agonized appeal ... has laid down arms.

This is a deed without precedent in history.

The Belgian government tells me the King's decision was taken against the unanimous feelings of the responsible ministers ...

Young French generals, who have barely had time to take over from their predecessors, have covered themselves in glory. Our officers and our troops are a unity in which the nation has total confidence and which will tomorrow be the admiration of the world.

We knew that dark days would come. Come they have. France has been invaded a hundred times before and never beaten; let our courageous citizens in the north recall the fact ...

Our faith in victory is unshaken. The strength of every soldier, of every Frenchman, is increased tenfold. Misfortune has always made France greater. Never has she been more united than today.

We shall stand firm along the new line established by our great leader Weygand, in full agreement with Marshal Pétain, along the Somme and the Aisne. And because we have stood firm we shall win!

While the word 'treachery' spread through France like wildfire the Belgian government, meeting in their Paris embassy, released officers and officials from their oath of allegiance to the King, recorded that the latter was 'in the invader's power' and struck his name from the executory formula of decrees and judgments.

Admiral Keyes, head of the British military mission in Belgium, who had returned to London overnight, protested vigorously against MM. Reynaud's and Pierlot's condemnations of the King of the Belgians.

In the course of the afternoon Mr Churchill informed the House of Commons of the Belgian surrender. Far more restrained than his French colleague, he 'had no intention of suggesting to the House that we should attempt, at this moment, to pass judgment upon the action of the King of the Belgians in his capacity as Commander-in-Chief of the Belgian army', which had fought very bravely.

Mr Duff Cooper, the Minister of Information, aligned himself with Churchill's statement and declared on the B.B.C.:

The Belgian army have fought bravely, they have suffered heavily, they have yielded only before overwhelming odds. This is no time for criticism or recriminations.

On learning of the tenor of Churchill's and Duff Cooper's statements in London, Reynaud was both surprised and hurt. He immediately summoned General Spears.

'It was obvious that Reynaud was very upset indeed,' writes Spears. 'It was unavoidable that he should lean on the British in his struggle against the defeatists. If we, by implication, dissociated ourselves from the line he was taking, his position would be weakened, perhaps fatally so.'

Reynaud then questioned Spears about another statement in Duff Cooper's broadcast. It ran:

If anybody says to you: 'The French have let us down', you ought to reply: 'Either you are a paid agent of Germany, or you are an unpaid one doing German propaganda for nothing.'

'Does that mean,' Reynaud asked, 'that the French are being criticized in England?'

'Of course it does!' replied Spears. 'Not the French people. The British ... believe the French to be brave and are not criticizing them ... What they do blame is the French Command. They are fully alive to its failure. In fact, the more they admire the French troops, the less possible do they find it to understand what has occurred. There is a very natural feeling of perturbation and anger at discovering that our own forces have been placed under what appear to be such incompetent generals.'

Returning to Churchill's speech, Reynaud asked Spears what reasons could have led the Prime Minister to speak so moderately of King Leopold's defection. Spears replied that in his opinion Churchill's restraint was due to Admiral Keyes's declarations.

Reynaud immediately sent Churchill a wire saying:

At all costs stop Admiral Keyes from defending King Leopold.

Then he picked up his telephone and asked Frossard, his Minister of Information, to ensure that the French newspapers made no mention of Admiral Keyes's remarks or Duff Cooper's speech.

At 8 p.m. General Spears dined with M. Georges Mandel and M. Pierlot at the Ministry of the Interior. Marshal Pétain, General Weygand, M. Daladier, M. de Monzie, M. Serruys, President Lebrun and others were torn to pieces in the course of the meal. But none was more abused than King Leopold, of whom Mandel spoke sarcastically and contemptuously.

'His [Mandel's] own attitude was admirable,' writes Spears. 'Unfussed and unshaken ... The attitude of the French public towards the Belgian refugees and residents was discussed. If the men were not called up, the French reaction might be one of violent hostility; but had the Belgian ministers power to issue decrees?'

Mandel said there were at least 400,000 Belgian men in France: an acceptable legal formula would have to be found, and the Belgian government should then forthwith place all Belgians of military age at the disposal of the French military authorities.

After Pierlot's departure Mandel took advantage of the fact that he was alone with Spears to draw his attention to the equivocal attitude of Pétain and Weygand. The two men clearly inspired no confidence in him.

On leaving the Ministry of the Interior General Spears put through a long telephone call to London in the hope of getting Churchill to 'align' himself with Reynaud's position with regard to King Leopold's 'treachery'. 'I was not entirely successful,' he writes. It was easier for the head of government in a republic to brand a king a traitor than for the Prime Minister of a constitutional monarchy.

But side by side with the Belgian defection, another problem was bothering the Western powers: the increasing danger of Italy's entering the war.

Rightly concerned by the news reaching him from Rome, Mr Bullitt addressed the following telegram to President Roosevelt:

> I believe as strongly as I have ever believed anything that you will be unable to protect the United States from German attack unless you have the co-operation of the French and British fleets. I believe that one of the surest ways to obtain such co-operation would be by sending our Atlantic fleet to the Mediterranean.

Mr Bullitt also asked Mr Roosevelt, on M. Reynaud's behalf, to rush an American cruiser to Bordeaux to ship all French and Belgian gold reserves to the United States.

In the evening came Mr Churchill's reply to the draft of the French note concerning possible offers to Italy which had been conveyed to him during the day by M. Corbin, the French ambassador in London:

> ... We are convinced that at this moment ... it would be impossible for Signor Mussolini to put forward proposals for a conference with any success. I may remind you also that the President of the U.S.A. has received a wholly negative reply to the proposal which we jointly asked him to make, and that no response has been made to the approach which Lord Halifax made to the Italian ambassador here last Saturday.
>
> Therefore, without excluding the possibility of an approach to Signor Mussolini at some time, we cannot feel that this would be the right moment, and I am bound to add that in my opinion the

effect on the morale of our people, which is now firm and resolute, would be extremely dangerous. You yourself can best judge what would be the effect in France.

You will ask, then, how is the situation to be improved? ... Our success must depend first on our unity, then on our courage and endurance.

This very firm statement of the British view put an end to the scheme.

Reynaud comments in his memoirs: 'I considered that I had sacrificed enough to the suggestions of those who favoured placating Italy.'

In Rome, Count Ciano received Sir Percy Loraine, the British ambassador, who had called to discuss the question of the blockade and complain of the interruption in Anglo-Italian negotiations.

Ciano said there was no point in further talks: 'We are on the eve of entering the war. The Duce is in a hurry, for he is convinced that from now on things will happen fast and he means to stake a claim to part of the booty.'

Ciano went on to say that even if France were to offer Italy Tunisia, Algeria and Morocco, Mussolini would decline her proposals. The Duce's mind had been made up since May 8th.

MAY 29TH

At about 9 a.m. a telegram from General Blanchard reached French G.H.Q. in Vincennes. The Commander of the 1st Group of Armies informed General Weygand that despite his protestations Lord Gort had decided to take the withdrawal of his army to Dunkirk entirely into his own hands, with the result that the flank of the French 1st Army would find itself utterly exposed.

General Weygand at once telephoned M. Baudouin and asked the Cabinet to protest to the War Office.

In the course of the morning the Germans entered Gravelines and captured Les Cats hill, which dominated the entire Flemish plain. The French units operating in the area were encircled. The bulk of the 1st Army, including the 4th and 5th Corps, was unable to cross the Lys and reach Dunkirk. Its commander, General Prioux, had remained at his post throughout the retreat — in the rearguard, with the general commanding the 4th Corps. Both men, together with their staffs, were taken prisoner by a German armoured detachment at Steenwerck, on the Lys.

The rest of the troops were still putting up a desperate fight in the Lille area. Their fine stand immobilized the greater part of von Reichenau's army and was to gain extra time for the units moving into Dunkirk harbour.

In the Abbeville sector General de Gaulle had returned to the attack at 4 a.m. His remaining tanks crossed the Rouen–Abbeville highway. They held up two successive German counter-attacks from the direction of Mont-Caubert. The 4th Battalion of Chasseurs thrust onwards to Villers wood and Bienfay, while the 3rd Cuirassiers and the 1st Battalion of the 7th Dragoons reached the top of the hills overlooking the Somme.

By evening the French had taken a number of prisoners and the German units had suffered badly. But no substantial inroads had been made in their positions, whereas the 4th Armoured Division was literally worn out. Yet its commander was to ask it to make a further effort next day.

Lord Gort decided that the embarking operations were not going quickly enough. He complained to Admiral Abrial. The commander of the maritime front and the leader of the B.E.F. obviously did not understand each other. Afterwards Lord Gort wrote: 'Admiral Abrial had apparently received no orders from his government that the whole of the British troops were to be embarked and he professed great surprise when he heard of my intentions ...'

Deeply dissatisfied, Lord Gort drove to Dunkirk harbour so that he could personally direct the embarkation of the B.E.F. Some French troops had heard in Enguinegate the day before that British ships would take as many French as English soldiers. They therefore stood by, ready to board the vessels.

Visibly exasperated by the confusion all round him, Lord Gort categorically refused to accept them.[1] The French insisted. Determined to obey their leader's instructions to the letter, some British sailors were throwing French soldiers back into the sea.

Lord Gort informed the War Office of the incident. In the end he allocated two ships to the French.

A few hours later London sent him orders to embark British and French in equal proportions.

The situation was deteriorating rapidly. Dunkirk was now under fire from the German artillery, which was adding to the devastation already caused by the Luftwaffe.

Three hundred French warships and merchant ships took part in the evacuation. The 2nd Destroyer Flotilla lost all its vessels, including the gallant *Sirocco*.[2] The little mine-sweepers had possibly the hardest task of all. As swiftly as the Luftwaffe laid mines, the sweepers blew them up, with bombs falling and machine-guns chattering twenty yards away. More than fifteen failed to return.

The evacuation was screened from attacks by surface craft by light British ships and two French destroyers, the *Epervier* and the *Léopard*, which were too heavy to go to Dunkirk.

Lord Gort sent out an urgent call for help from the R.A.F. He got it. The Spitfires managed to hold off some of the enemy attacks. In the event, embarkations were never halted. But from now on they took place only at night, daily operations being too suicidal.

Enemy pressure grew hourly more intense. By evening the bridgehead was only fifteen miles wide and ten miles deep and it was being pounded constantly by the German artillery.

1 In his favour it must be remembered that the decisions taken at the Dover conference had not been passed on to him. The British were as bad at liaison as the French.
2 With her went down the colours of the 92nd Infantry Regiment, which the colonel had smuggled out of the outskirts of Lille, where his units were encircled.

Hitler called a meeting of the Commanders-in-Chief of the right wing of the German armies. Kesselring writes:

> He spoke with measured gravity, mentioning his fears of a powerful flanking attack by the bulk of the French forces, which would necessitate a speedy regrouping of our mechanized units. He drew a sober picture of the situation. We left the meeting with easy minds and with the feeling that he had devoted a great deal of care to the preparation of the operations ahead and that he was anticipating difficulties that we ourselves, enlightened by our own experience of the French and by our own military showings, did not expect in such measure.

Even before the fate of Dunkirk was sealed, even before Lille had fallen — for the remnants of the 1st Army were still making a stand in the town — Hitler was preparing for the second phase of the battle.

POLITICAL SITUATION

On May 26th M. Paul Reynaud had gone to London for talks with Mr Churchill. Since then he had given the French High Command no indication of the results of his trip. This silence worried General Weygand. He had accepted his responsibilities: he wanted the government to do the same. With this end in view he sent the following note to the Premier and Marshal Pétain.

For the Prime Minister
The resolve to defend ourselves to the bitter end along the present position, and the order forbidding all subordinate officers to look back, do not obviate the Commander-in-Chief's duty to examine, in view of the gravity of the situation, every hypothesis ...

In view of the enormous disproportion in strength and resources between attack and defence (the latter partly improvised in the course of the battle), it is possible that, despite the heroic effort of all, the positions currently being defended may be seriously dented.

If that were to happen the power of penetration and exploitation that the enemy derives from his armoured units and air force might swiftly enable him to reach the country's nerve-centres. In particular the French army might be powerless to halt a thrust against the Paris area, in which a considerable part of our war industry is concentrated. In that event France would be in no position to carry on a fight ensuring a co-ordinated defence of her territory.

In the great battles of the last war it was always possible to 'fill in' pockets made by attacks because armies had no organ of exploitation comparable to the tank-plane combination. In the course of the war of 1870 it was possible for the National Defence government, once the armies in the field had been annihilated, to reconstitute armies that were able to keep resistance going for five months and so save national honour. Today, even if France had — as she has not — the necessary weapons, clothing and equipment at her disposal, the enemy would not allow her time to organize [armies] and instruct them in the use of modern war machines.

The Commander-in-Chief acquainted the government with the military situation in the course of the meeting of the War Committee on May 25th. Since that date our armies on the left have strengthened their positions along the Aisne and the Somme. But the defection of the Belgian army is precipitating in the north the decision that will leave the German armoured divisions free to act against our line of defence ... [1]

The importance to be attached to victorious resistance along this line is so great that no effort should be spared to reinforce it. The need is pressing. That is why the Commander-in-Chief considers it necessary that the British government, informed of the situation, should be invited to lend the defence of our lines all the assistance in its power, to wit:

— 2 or 3 divisions formed in England,
— tank, anti-tank gun and anti-aircraft units,
— the assistance of planes based in England.[2]

Again, it seems just as necessary that the British government should know that there may come a point where, against her will, France will find herself unable to continue a militarily effective struggle to protect her soil.

This point would be marked by the final breaching of the positions along which the French armies have been ordered to fight without thought of withdrawal.

WEYGAND

On receiving this note, Marshal Pétain replied to General Weygand:

[1] In fact, as a result of the decision taken by Hitler on May 25th, the Panzer divisions were already freed. But General Weygand did not yet know this.

[2] 'In my note of May 29th,' General Weygand was to declare at Marshal Pétain's trial, 'I asked for British assistance to be accorded us as fully as possible and suggested that it should be along lines that I considered both reasonable and capable of swift realization.'

Paris, May 29th, 1940

My dear Weygand,

I can see nothing to add to your note for the moment, but it seems to me that it would be right to inform the British government as soon as possible and invite it to Paris.

Croyez, etc. ...

PH. PÉTAIN

M. Paul Reynaud comments that Pétain, like Weygand, 'avoided *writing* the word "armistice" '. Reynaud is forgetting that at this same meeting of the War Committee it was he who first uttered the word.[1] But since his visit to London on May 26th he had turned a deaf ear whenever this burning question was raised. So in his reply to General Weygand he deliberately side-stepped the issue:

I have informed the British government, through its ambassador, that the following points emerge from the note you sent me this morning:

1. In compliance with the general instructions given by the government you have decided to fight without thought of withdrawal along the line of defence decided by you and stretching from Abbeville to Switzerland.

2. If the positions currently defended along this line were to be seriously dented, France would be in no position to continue a struggle ensuring a co-ordinated defence of her territory.

3. In view of the decisive importance for the Allies of resistance along this line the French government entreats the British government to accede to the requests made in your note.

The fact that, in the considered hypothesis, the whole territory of the nation could no longer be defended does not necessarily mean that we could end hostilities in conditions compatible with the honour and vital interest of France.

So, since in the considered hypothesis the enemy would be likely to make rapid thrusts throughout the length and breadth of the country, I ask you to be so kind as to look into the possibility of fortifying a national redoubt round a naval harbour enabling us to use the freedom of the seas and, in particular, to communicate with our allies. This national redoubt would have to be planned and supplied like a real fortress. It would comprise the Brittany peninsula ...

PAUL REYNAUD

[1] See p. 156.

This was the Premier's first allusion in writing to the 'Breton redoubt' and to the possible continuation of the war from North Africa. His ideas on the subject seemed still pretty vague, for on the evening of May 23rd — barely a week earlier — he had suggested bringing the Algerian and Tunisian divisions to France and had told Baudouin that they must not hesitate to *'strip Africa bare for the home country'*. Substantial levies had already been made there. Now, in a complete volte-face, Reynaud was talking about calling up two whole classes — in other words, half a million men — and sending them to Morocco to be trained and equipped.

Paul Reynaud was displeased to find that General Spears's intervention had not prompted London to change its tune on the subject of King Leopold. He sent for Sir Ronald Campbell, British ambassador in Paris, and asked him to convey to his government a note from L.-O. Frossard, French Minister of Information, protesting against Churchill's speech in the House of Commons the day before. The British ambassador forwarded this note to London.

After the British ambassador's departure, the Premier had a long talk with the United States ambassador. Adopting the very words that Reynaud had used to him, Mr Bullitt cabled President Roosevelt:

It is now or never for the United States. If you can send your Atlantic fleet to Tangier and inform Mussolini that you are doing so after the fleet has started, he will not dare to strike. Otherwise he will strike, and in a very few months you will face a joint attack by Germany, Italy and Japan alone.

In Rome Mussolini assembled the Chiefs of Staff of the Italian armed forces in his study in the Palazzo Venezia and informed them officially of his decision to enter the war on a date still to be determined, but on or after June 5th.

'The motives that have led me to take this grave decision,' he told his listeners, 'are as follows:

'1. Whatever we do, we cannot avoid war.

'2. We cannot wage it with the Allies.

'3. We can only wage it with Germany.

'Only the date remains to be fixed. That is the thorniest problem which we have to solve, for it is dictated by the very rhythm of the war.

'After the speedy occupation of Norway and the annexation of Denmark,' explained the Duce, 'I thought I would time our entry for early September. Now, in view of the fact that Holland is captured, Belgium has capitulated, France is invaded and the general situation is now quite clear, I consider that it would be appropriate for us to declare war any day from June 5th onwards ...

'Besides, I regard the Allies' fate as virtually sealed. In the letter that Hitler sent me yesterday and that I have already read to Marshal Badoglio, the Führer told me: "Germany has mobilized 220 divisions; 10 are in Norway, 15 in Poland, 25 or 30 must be regarded as engaged; that leaves 165 intact divisions for Germany to throw into battle whenever she thinks fit, against 70 or 80 French divisions – for the support of the British divisions cannot be counted on. Furthermore, the superiority of the German air force to the French air force is overwhelming. Less so to the R.A.F., though the Luftwaffe is incontestably superior." '

Mussolini finished reading the letter, then asked: 'Can anything be done to alter that? No ... I am inclined to wonder whether the French resistance [along the Somme and the Aisne] will not have been crushed by the time we intervene.

'France can hope for nothing before 1942, and by then she will have gone under completely.

'If we delay another fortnight or another month our military situation will be unchanged, whereas by intervening at once we shall not give Germany the impression of joining in when the job is done ...

'All this may weigh very heavily when peace is signed.'

'The Italian High Command came into being at 11 a.m. this morning in the Palazzo Venezia,' wrote Count Ciano. 'The Duce will be assisted by Badoglio, Graziani, Priccolo and Cavagnari. I have seldom seen Mussolini so happy. He has realized his lifelong dream of becoming his country's military leader in time of war.'

MAY 30TH

━━━━◆•◆•◆━━━━

MILITARY SITUATION

Overnight the British 4th Division reached Nieuport. It was incorporated in a combined Franco-British corps that had orders to defend the sector stretching from Bergues to Les Moères, to the south-east of the entrenched camp.

The dramatic situation of the troops encircled in Dunkirk aroused the keenest apprehension in the heart of the British Cabinet. Most ministers feared the B.E.F. might be lost in its entirety. In the early hours of the morning Mr Anthony Eden sent secret instructions to Lord Gort *authorizing him to capitulate 'when in his judgment ... no further proportionate damage could be inflicted on the enemy'.*

The evacuation of British troops continued throughout the day, thanks to the joint efforts of the French and British navies. The latter had mobilized all available ships and small craft. The R.A.F. played a vigorous part in the battle, striving ceaselessly to drive off the waves of German bombers attacking the moles and beaches.

General Lelong, head of the French military mission in London, informed General Georges that two British divisions were to remain in France and would be reinforced as soon as possible. The same went for the R.A.F.

In reply to this message, General Weygand sent General Lelong the following telegram:

No. 1272/3, *F.T.*   *May 30th,* 1940

The Commander-in-Chief thanks the British Command for this display of solidarity, but thinks he should draw the attention of the Chiefs of Staff to the situation of the British air force remaining in France.

At the present time only three fighter squadrons are left on our soil; all the others have returned to Britain. Now, once the Battle of Flanders is over the latter will be unable to play a profitable part in the new battle, which may open along the Somme, Champagne or the Meuse front.

The whole weight of the battle will be borne by the French army, which will suffer terribly.

The Commander-in-Chief earnestly requests the British High Command to be so good as to consider the gravity of this situation and to take measures to ensure that, from now on, a large portion of the R.A.F., especially fighters, *should be based in France in anticipation of the coming battle.*

But the British government did not share these views.

In the Abbeville sector the 4th Armoured Division renewed its effort of the previous day. The target prescribed by de Gaulle was Caubert, to enfilade the ridge and the Camp de César. But the Germans had received reinforcements during the night, and despite the magnificent persistence of the French troops this third day of the attack was marked by a series of heavy set-backs.[1]

POLITICAL SITUATION

Before 4 a.m. General Spears was summoned to the British embassy, where an urgent personal telegram from Churchill awaited him. He was to show it to Reynaud at once. It made the following points, among others:

1. We have evacuated nearly 50,000 from Dunkirk and beaches, and hope another 30,000 tonight.
2. We wish French troops to share in evacuation to fullest possible extent.
3. As soon as we have reorganized our evacuated troops, and prepared forces necessary to safeguard our life against threatened and perhaps imminent invasion, we shall build up a new B.E.F. from Saint-Nazaire.
4. I am bringing Regulars from India and Palestine; Australians and Canadians are arriving soon.
5. At present we are removing equipment south of Amiens beyond what is needed for five divisions. But this is only to get into order and meet impending shock, and we shall shortly send you new scheme for reinforcement of our troops in France.
6. I send this in all comradeship.

After several hours of fruitless searching, Spears learned that Reynaud

[1] See sketch on p. 177.

had spent the night in his private flat. The Premier had been doing his physical exercises and wore a kimono.

Spears passed on the message that he had just received from Churchill, but its contents 'evidently gave Reynaud neither satisfaction nor solace'. He was like a bear with a sore head.

He said sourly, almost sarcastically, that he was very glad Churchill had emphasized that the French would be evacuated in equal numbers with the British. If this were not so, French opinion would be *déchaînée* against England. I answered that ... it was only Winston's strong hand that prevented British opinion being *déchaînée* against the French Command and the French generally.

We looked at each other steadily for a moment after this. When Reynaud broke the silence he said, in a tone I had never heard him use when talking of Churchill, a tone whose impatience was emphasized by a shrug of annoyance, that his resentment was as deep as was his incomprehension of the Prime Minister's attitude towards the King of the Belgians ...

Then for a moment Reynaud allowed me a horrifying glimpse of the abysmal inefficiency of the French military machine. He himself must have felt like a blind man groping across a glacier full of crevasses. It seemed that the disorganization was such that the Staff declared there were neither the weapons to arm nor the uniforms to clothe the young classes.

When I thought of the immense depots in France, the vast stores of weapons, I was dumbfounded. The millions of rifles used in the last war had not been destroyed, they were in France somewhere, but where? No one knew. Was there no end to the rot?

As I was leaving, Reynaud said that it was imperative we should send over every man we could lay hands on; even the men from Dunkirk should be put straight into boats and returned to France; but I pointed out that on reflection he would surely see such a panic measure was not the way to achieve effective resistance.

At 10.30 a.m. there was a meeting of the War Committee in the Rue Saint-Dominique. Present on the French side were M. Reynaud, Marshal Pétain, General Weygand, Admiral Darlan and Paul Baudouin; on the British, Sir Ronald Campbell and General Spears.[1]

General Weygand began by reporting on the military situation.

[1] It is noticeable that no French observer attended meetings of the War Cabinet, the British equivalent of the *Comité de Guerre*.

'The decisive battle,' he declared, 'is being engaged at odds of three to one against the French. Any troops whatsoever Mr Churchill can send would be immensely valuable. I am particularly short of infantry and am engaging partly trained troops.'

Supported by Reynaud, the Commander-in-Chief begged that even those men who had escaped from Dunkirk should be immediately shipped back to the Somme front.

At this General Spears repeated what he had said to Reynaud earlier. Such a measure would only make confusion worse confounded. Neither the War Office nor the British government could possibly consent to what would be literally throwing away men without the least chance of their affecting the issue in the smallest degree ... All the soldiers returning from Dunkirk must be sorted, regrouped, reorganized and rearmed. Only after that could they be sent back to France. To act in any other way would be both self-deception and a crime.

General Weygand finally sided with this view.

'The situation,' he said, 'is so serious that I beg any units of the B.E.F. with any cohesion should be transhipped back to France immediately. Their presence would have a magical effect on the armies on the Somme.'

While the War Committee was talking in Paris, part of the Belgian parliament was meeting in Limoges.

The ministers, arriving one by one, found themselves up against a shrieking mob that had invaded the hall and stairway of the municipal theatre. They were cheered, but with these words: 'Long live the Belgian Republic!' The cry was a warning: it would be turned against them if they were foolhardy enough to defend the King. To be on the safe side, M. Bétoulle, receiving them in his capacity as mayor of Limoges, delivered a pointed speech of welcome in which he made quite plain to them what their feelings ought to be. 'The King,' he said, 'has betrayed not only his Allies but his people as well.'

M. van Cauwelaert, the leader of the Chamber, charged his sovereign (not wishing to be left out of things) with having 'broken cleanly with military honour, delivered his throne into the enemy's hands and surrendered the army at a time when the outcome of the battle was still undecided'.

M. Spaak declared that the reason put forward by the King for staying in Belgium and sharing the fate of his troops was 'mad, stupid, worse still: criminal'.

When M. Pierlot's turn came, he spoke of 'dishonour'.

Finally M. Gillon, leader of the Senate, read out a resolution beginning:

'The senators and representatives now in France are unanimous in stigmatizing the capitulation initiated by Leopold III, for which he bears exclusive responsibility before history.'

This resolution, which in conclusion merely stated 'the impossibility of Leopold III's reigning, struck the Assembly as inadequate.

In the lobbies there was talk of not only deposing the King but banishing the dynasty. One leading light of the Belgian aristocracy was already seeking a successor to Leopold from another House. 'What about the Grand Duchess of Luxembourg? She behaved well. Or her husband? Or her son?' Thus spoke courtiers who, only a month before, had been currying favour at Laeken.

Finally the resolution was amended. In the revised text the impossibility of Leopold's continuing to reign was considered not merely 'juridical' but 'moral'. By adopting this formula M. Pierlot avoided being outbid by those who demanded the King's dethronement.

At the same hour, in the Château de Laeken, Leopold III received Mr Cudahy, the United States ambassador, who had requested a final audience before returning to America. 'Three weeks earlier,' writes Fabre-Luce, 'the two men had been sitting in the same room. Since then the sun had shone without a break and the red rhododendrons had not had time to wither. Everything was the same, but everything was different.'

Afterwards the ambassador said that he had never seen a more poignant expression of sadness on a human face. It was as though the cruel spectacle of the past twenty days had left a permanent scar. Yet there was no sign of weakness in his behaviour. His eyes shone with the same unshakeable honesty and he retained his proud military bearing, so characteristic of his personality.

In Washington Mr Cordell Hull, Secretary of State at the White House, sent a reply to Mr Bullitt's dispatches of May 28th and 29th. In his memoirs, Cordell Hull recalls that, after discussing the ambassador's messages with the President:

... I cabled Bullitt on May 30th Mr Roosevelt's decision that it was absolutely impossible to consider sending the fleet to the Mediterranean. The presence of our fleet in the Pacific at this time we considered to be a very practical contribution to the maintenance of peace in that ocean. The British government appreciated the importance of this contribution, and we assumed the French government did too. The warships we had in the Atlantic were required for patrol duty or for special service in South and Central American waters ...

The presence of an American fleet at this time in the Mediterranean, I added, would result in very serious risks. It would be impossible to base the fleet on any ports in or near the Mediterranean should Italy enter the war. And unless we sent a fleet sufficiently large to be effective, the impression created would be just the opposite of what we wanted.

In Paris several members of the Cabinet — including Anatole de Monzie, Minister of Public Works, Ybarnegaray and Chautemps — were stung to learn that the note prepared by M. Daladier on the night of May 27th had not been sent to Rome, for fear of antagonizing the British government. They were fully aware that this delay was due to the obstructionism of M. Charles-Roux, Permanent Under-Secretary to the Ministry of Foreign Affairs;[1] but they would not accept the idea that French policy should be determined by a civil servant — however senior — who was not a member of the government.

Taking the view that France should do everything in her power to keep Mussolini out of the war, they pressed M. Daladier, Minister for Foreign Affairs, to go ahead.

Early in the morning M. Daladier sent M. Paul Reynaud a new draft note suggesting negotiations between France and Italy but not making any specific offers. His covering letter ran:

Minister for Foreign Affairs to Monsieur Paul Reynaud, Prime Minister

The military situation, already causing anxiety before the capitulation of the Belgian army, has worsened since the defection of King Leopold ... The end of operations in Flanders will release 30 infantry divisions and all the German army's armoured divisions ...

Again, information reveals that Signor Mussolini is more and more resolved to seek satisfaction of his territorial aims in war ...

In these circumstances I consider that the government of the Republic would be seriously failing in its responsibilities if it neglected the possibility, however slender, of keeping Italy out of the war ...

In the absence of any objection on your side, I therefore propose to hand the attached note to the Italian ambassador today ...

ED. DALADIER

[1] Roland de Margerie told General Spears that Charles-Roux was strongly opposed to the attempts being made by Daladier and others to buy off Italy. 'He [Charles-Roux], resisting a fresh onslaught, had refused to sign a draft telegram on the subject and threatened to resign and appeal to the President of the Republic if the project was persisted in. Margerie said he hoped and believed Churchill's stand on the Italian question had put a stop to action which could only add humiliation to defeat.'

The gist of the note was as follows:

We wish to state:

1. That there is no incompatibility between France and Italy stemming from the difference in the two countries' internal forms of government;

2. That we are prepared to consider any measures likely to give strength and continuance to this mutual independence of the two forms of government;

3. That we are likewise prepared to examine here and now all the Mediterranean questions affecting Italy's development;

4. That, in the development of such negotiations to general ends, France, determined to go back on neither her alliance nor her undertakings, would back any steps towards the establishment of a new statute of Mediterranean collaboration;

5. That, in order to reach a lasting security agreement rather than a particular and precarious settlement, we wish to adopt the method of direct negotiation between the interested parties.

On receiving this draft M. Paul Reynaud summoned M. Charles-Roux to the Rue Saint-Dominique.

Charles-Roux records:

The Premier handed me a document, asking me if I were familiar with it. I replied that I was not ... The note told Italy of France's preparedness to examine with her all Mediterranean questions and to stand by any useful solutions. But it was rather too inclined to promise things that it was not in our power to implement. Thus I pointed out that we had no control over Malta and Gibraltar ... Then there was the question of whether it was to be communicated to London before being handed to the Italian ambassador. M. Paul Reynaud called Marshal Pétain and General Weygand to witness that in present circumstances it was impossible to do anything which would separate us from England. The two military leaders expressed their agreement.

So the word 'back'[1] was replaced by the word 'welcome', which left our ally *hors de cause*. And the British government was to be consulted in advance.

M. de Monzie's account of what followed runs thus:

3 *p.m.*: I learned of further shilly-shallying. Campbell[2] came round to

---

[1] In paragraph 4 of the note.
[2] Sir Ronald Campbell, British ambassador in Paris.

examine the document, which was already watered down as far as it could be. No allusion, now, to the projected conference of September 5th, 1939.[1] That would be dangerous! A two-nation conference was practically a prelude to a four-nation conference! The danger being exclusively one of peace — O shameful irony! — minds must not be faced with such dreadful prospects. In another paragraph, mention was made of France's backing steps that would enable Italy to guarantee her maritime freedom. 'Back' was replaced by 'welcome'. I immediately railed against Gibraltar, that outworn rock which, having ceased to obstruct communications, was now obstructing negotiations.

4 p.m.: Campbell refused to give clearance to the text. He looked anything but pleased and wanted to submit it to his government — for which he demanded a two-hour stay of events.

6 p.m.: London's permission was at long last obtained.[2]

The British government, apprised of this second note, replied that it had no objections but did not wish to be associated with it: it was entirely the French government's responsibility.[3]

'Thus,' Charles-Roux emphasizes, 'even if the step had no effect, at least it could do no harm.'

In Rome Mussolini sent a message to Hitler, officially informing him of his intention to enter the war. The Duce wrote:

Once again I thank you for the message that you sent me. I was particularly interested by the information you gave about the fighting efficiency of the troops in the various armies engaged ...

I have put off answering for several days because I wanted to tell you of my decision to enter the conflict on June 5th. If, to co-ordinate my movements better with yours, you consider that I should delay the gesture a day or two, let me know. But the Italian people are unquestionably impatient to take up arms on the side of the German people ...

---

[1] The original draft alluded to the four-nation conference suggested by Mussolini at the beginning of September 1939. The initial text had been worded by MM. de Monzie and Serruys. It had been approved by M. Chautemps.

[2] M. de Monzie mistakenly writes '6 p.m.' and '8 p.m.'. We have corrected these times, going by the statements of M. Charles-Roux.

[3] Spears comments: 'It is evident the British government felt certain this note would yield no result, but did not wish to refuse any action which the French government, in its desperate straits, thought might help them.'

MAY 30TH

In anticipation of your answer I ask you to accept, Führer, the expression of my comradely friendship.

MUSSOLINI

'The decision is taken,' Count Ciano wrote in his diary. 'The die is cast. This morning Mussolini handed me the message informing Hitler of our entry into the war.'

MAY 31ST

By now the whole of Dunkirk town was an inferno. The harbour and its approaches were a tragic sight.

The embarking of British troops was in full swing. While the piers were still in use, the troops were marched as far out as possible, so that ships could be loaded along the whole length of the pier.

But soon embarkation in the docks became impracticable, for the sluice-gates were destroyed and the water was full of wreckage. In the face of the losses occasioned by these dramatic conditions the British Command decided to embark its men from the beaches east of the town. The boats picked them up by anchoring as close as possible to the shore, and the men waded out till they were up to their waists in water.

In the end the destroyers did not even anchor, and the men were picked up in a matter of moments, absolutely anyhow. The beaches were black with the poor devils, who were quite unprotected and continuously machine-gunned by Luftwaffe fighters swooping low over the beaches. 'There were innumerable tragedies,' writes Kammerer. 'All our light destroyers, apart from the very smallest, ended their days there' — including the *Bourrasque* which sank in sight of Ostend. Of the 800 men who had embarked in her, only 300 could be saved.

The French Cavalry Corps, comprising all three light mechanized divisions, regrouped at Malo-les-Bains and began to embark, without equipment or heavy guns, under ceaseless attack from the Luftwaffe and the German 105-mm. batteries.

The task of evacuation was still further complicated by the fact that the Germans were installing coastal batteries on either side of the town. These compelled the Allied ships to sail directly over the sandbanks, which was possible only at certain hours because of the tide.

The British Cabinet had decided that the Commander of the B.E.F. should return to England when the size of the force remaining on land was reduced to three divisions. This condition now being fulfilled, Lord Gort went to Bastion 32 to take his leave of Admiral Abrial and General Fagalde.

'My government has recalled me to London,' he told them, 'but I am leaving General Alexander behind with three British divisions which will act under your orders for the defence of the bridge-head.'

Gort confirmed this decision in writing. General Fagalde at once established a plan of defence incorporating the three British divisions.

In the afternoon Alexander arrived at Bastion 32 with two British generals. A meeting took place, attended by Admiral Abrial, Admiral Leclerc, General Altmayer, General Fagalde and the head of his *troisième bureau*, Commandant Lehr. Fagalde informed Alexander of what Lord Gort had told him that morning and outlined his plan of defence.

'Unfortunately that is quite impracticable,' said Alexander. 'I have to re-embark for England tonight with my three divisions.'

'But Lord Gort has placed you under my orders!' replied Fagalde.

'Lord Gort is now at sea,' said Alexander. 'I alone am responsible for the British troops still in France. If we remain here another twenty-four hours we shall all be taken prisoner. Consequently I have decided to re-embark without delay.'

This statement stunned the French. Abrial and Fagalde strove to get Alexander to go back on his decision, but in vain.

'All I can do,' he said, 'is delay my embarkation till tomorrow, June 1st. But I can go no further.'

At their insistence Alexander agreed to telephone London.

He returned a few hours later. In the meantime Admiral Abrial had received a telegram from Paris informing him that in the course of a meeting of the Supreme War Council held that day in the Rue Saint Dominique it had been decided:

1. that British and French embarkations were to be carried out *pari-passu*;
2. that the British would form the final rearguard.

Admiral Abrial showed this dispatch to Alexander.

'Had my Prime Minister been here instead of in Paris,' declared Alexander, 'he would never have subscribed to these conditions.' And he added: 'I have been in touch with Mr Anthony Eden. He has ordered me to co-operate with the French forces in the fullest measure compatible with the security of the British troops. I consider their existence seriously threatened and I am sticking to my decision to embark tomorrow, June 1st.'

Abrial and Fagalde did their utmost to get him to reverse this terrible decision. He would not budge. Exasperated, Fagalde could not restrain himself from telling General Alexander what he thought of his behaviour.

One of the British generals accompanying Alexander turned to Fagalde and said quietly: 'It isn't too good, is it?'

'No,' Fagalde replied in English, 'it isn't good at all.'

All this time the remnants of the 1st Army were continuing to fight heroically in the Lille area, holding up seven German divisions. They were in an abysmal position. Ammunition was running out and the wounded had to be evacuated to the hospitals in Lille, which were already in German hands.

At 3 p.m. General von Reichenau sent a message calling for the surrender of the French troops; he paid tribute to their heroism and said that he was prepared to accord them the honours of war.

At the council of war in Charleville on May 24th Hitler had timed the launching of the second phase of the offensive for May 31st.

But the date had to be put back six days to enable the Panzer divisions, which had fought without respite since May 10th, to replenish and repair their equipment.

Despite this delay there was unusual activity in front of the French lines between Saint-Quentin and the mouth of the Somme. Anxious that the French should not be caught napping again, as they had been at Sedan on May 14th, General Weygand ordered a series of reconnaissances and small-scale local actions. Colonel de Bardies writes:

> Each division was visited by an officer from Army H.Q., Army Group H.Q. and G.H.Q., who made sure that proper anti-tank measures had been taken.

It was within the framework of these instructions that the 2nd Armoured Division, regrouped south-east of Roye, moved forward into the area east of Poix to attack the bridge-head that the Germans had formed round Abbeville; the repeated attacks of the 4th Armoured Division on May 28th, 29th and 30th had not managed to destroy it.

But the 2nd Armoured Division had suffered heavily since its action against the Somme bridges. On the night of May 24th–25th it had won back and destroyed the bridges at Epenancourt, Pargny and Béthencourt.[1] On the night of May 25th–26th it had stormed the bridge at Saint-Christ and likewise destroyed it. After which, relieved by companies of the 117th and 41st Infantry Regiments respectively, the tanks had fallen back to Morchain and Marchélepot.

---

[1] This was the first time in French military history that tank formations had attacked in the middle of the night (assisted, it is true, by brilliant moonlight). The results were excellent, and after first protesting against this violation of the rules the High Command congratulated the battalions that had launched these attacks.

A few days' rest would have enabled the division to overhaul its vehicles. Alas! Before it had time to get its breath back it was subjected to a series of marches and counter-marches in support of a scattered and exhausted infantry. These comings and goings had cost the division dearly. It had covered nearly 125 miles, with paltry results. The crews had not slept for three days and nights. Officially the division had 196 tanks at its disposal, but in fact only 132 were in use. Over fifty had broken down ...

POLITICAL SITUATION

In Rome Ciano wrote:

Alfieri telephoned to say that he had handed the message to Hitler. The Führer was very pleased with it: more — enthusiastic. But he decided to wait till he had conferred with his generals before letting us know whether the chosen date suits him.

I submitted to the Duce the draft of the communiqué announcing the declaration of war. He approved it, but advised me to discuss it with the King, who was very touchy on the subject since, under the terms of the constitution, declaring war was his prerogative.

Daladier handed a note to Guariglia last evening. It states quite clearly that they are ready to do anything to avoid war. But Mussolini refuses to consider the note and has decided not even to reply to it.

In Paris the Supreme War Council met in the War Ministry at 2 p.m. Churchill was accompanied by Mr Clement Attlee, leader of the Labour Party, Sir John Dill, Chief of the Imperial General Staff, and General Spears.

M. Paul Baudouin writes: 'The threat of the imminent collapse of France hung over this meeting, which was heartrending.'

Churchill spoke first. He thought the Council would be very happy to hear that the latest news from Dunkirk (it was timed twelve noon that day) was that 165,000 men, including 10,000 wounded, had been evacuated.

'But how many French?' Weygand asked querulously. 'The French are being left behind!'

'The Prime Minister looked at him for a moment,' says Spears. 'The light had died out of his face, his fingers were playing a tune on the edge of the table; out came his lower lip as if he were going to retort, and I expected one of those sentences that hit like a blow, but his expression changed again ... A wave of deep emotion swept from his heart to his eyes, where tears appeared not for the only time that afternoon: "We are companions in misfortune," he said, "there is nothing to be gained from recrimination over our common miseries."

'The note he had struck was so true, went so deep, that a stillness fell over the room ... '

Then, in a different tone, Churchill raised the question of Narvik. He suggested that the area should be evacuated at once. Béthouart's Division — comprising one Polish regiment, one half-brigade of Foreign Legion troops and one half-brigade of Chasseurs Alpins — amounted to about 16,000 men. Then there was the British Brigade. This force was immobilizing a large number of cruisers and destroyers, which the Admiralty might need urgently elsewhere. By withdrawing the force the Allies would recover a hundred anti-aircraft guns. The Royal Navy would provide transport. The King of Norway had been invited to spend the rest of the war in London.

Reynaud agreed to this evacuation. He requested that the troops and anti-aircraft guns be shipped to France: they would be extremely useful on the Aisne and Somme fronts. And the destroyers released from their duties in Norwegian waters should, he said, be used to strengthen the Allied naval units in the Mediterranean.

Churchill's reply was that he could give no undertaking in the matter. Britain was urgently in need of troops and A.A. guns. The infantry would have to be regrouped on its return from Norway and reorganized on the Clyde. And the ships that were made available would be used to protect British territorial waters.

'But it is vital that these troops should be sent to the Somme!' objected Reynaud.

Churchill refused to be swayed. His intransigence brought this discussion on Narvik to a close. The Supreme Council then turned to Dunkirk.

Churchill repeated the figures: 165,000 men, including 15,000 French, had been embarked.

M. Reynaud drew attention to the lack of proportion between these numbers. He pointed out that of the 220,000 British encircled in Dunkirk 150,000 had been taken off, whereas of the 200,000 French only 15,000 had been rescued by May 31st. Something must be done to increase the proportion of the French to the British.

Churchill agreed. He then read out a letter from Gort to Weygand indicating:

1. That Gort would hold on as long as possible to cover the embarkation of the troops;
2. That it was essential to press on with the evacuation at all speed;
3. That the French Command should issue specific orders in this sense.

Weygand said this programme met with his approval. He emphasized the vital role of Admiral Abrial, who was, he claimed, responsible for the whole of the evacuation. Backed by Reynaud, he asked that everything possible should be done to embark also the eight French divisions that were farthest from the coast. These troops were still fighting desperately in the Lille area, caught in a vice-like grip by von Reichenau's army on one side and List's on the other.

'Dunkirk must not be abandoned,' he said, 'till our divisions in the south are finished.'

Churchill replied that in his view these units could not hold out for more than forty-eight hours and that only the four French divisions already within the Dunkirk perimeter could be saved.

He said he was deeply concerned that the French should have no grounds for complaint that the British had given priority to their own men. The proof of their determination that the French should be treated absolutely fairly was that today, May 31st, had been laid down as a French day: today the French had absolute priority over the British.

Churchill's imperious voice now dominated the proceedings.

'There are,' he said, 'four French divisions in the Dunkirk perimeter: General Fagalde's two divisions and the two very reduced ones of General de la Laurencie. Also three British divisions. The three British will stand and allow the French to escape ... That and the sea transport will be the British contribution to offset the heavy French losses which must now be faced.'

General Weygand said that he hoped the embarkation would not be brought to an end even after the four divisions had been evacuated. The operation must continue till there was no hope of saving any French troops outside the perimeter.

'There is,' replied Sir John Dill, 'but little chance of the troops south of the Mount Kemmel line escaping.'

'It will not be possible to keep Dunkirk open very much longer,' Churchill said. 'Forty-eight hours perhaps, if we are fortunate. The risk to our shipping and the losses are too great to be long endured. The enemy's shore batteries now compel our ships to follow a longer and more exposed route ... We have had to give a hard order to General Gort: unwounded men must have precedence over the wounded as so many more can be moved; the country's imperative need is for men with whom to reconstitute fresh divisions without loss of time.

'We hope in a day or two to be able to enlist the help of the United States to succour the wounded we shall have left behind. Our army will have lost everything but its rifles, everything the men do not actually carry. We shall have lost 1,000 guns, which is extremely serious; there are not more than 500 guns in England today. We have lost thousands of lorries.

'The loss of guns is most grave and presents a terrible danger in the event of an attempted German invasion. Should a small German force, well equipped with artillery, land in England, it could not be opposed by a force of equivalent strength ... '

Churchill fell silent, as though already imagining the details of this appalling struggle. Then Reynaud spoke. He said the evacuation was a triumph for the British navy and air force. The fight put up by the R.A.F. against tremendous odds was nothing short of heroic. He wished to thank the Prime Minister for his generous proposal that British divisions should play a part in defending the perimeter. But it must not be forgotten, he added, returning to a topic that was clearly preying on his mind, that the fearful danger our troops were running at Dunkirk, and the loss of many French divisions which had jeopardized the safety of France, were directly attributable to the defection of King Leopold. It was time London woke up to the fact.

Reynaud then asked Britain to promise France the full support of her air force. He hoped that as soon as the Dunkirk operation was over the full strength of the R.A.F. would be made available on the new front. He did not believe the Germans would attack Great Britain till the French had been liquidated. Also, it was imperative that all troops recovered from Dunkirk should be sent back to France as soon as they were re-equipped. This was a question of days, not of weeks. The Germans were not going to delay their attack till the Allies had fortified the lines of the Somme and the Aisne.

Churchill replied that he was not authorized by his government to promise the support of the R.A.F. When Reynaud insisted he said he would think the matter over. He would do everything in his power to help France, but the French government must not cherish illusions as to the scale of the air support it could expect from Britain.

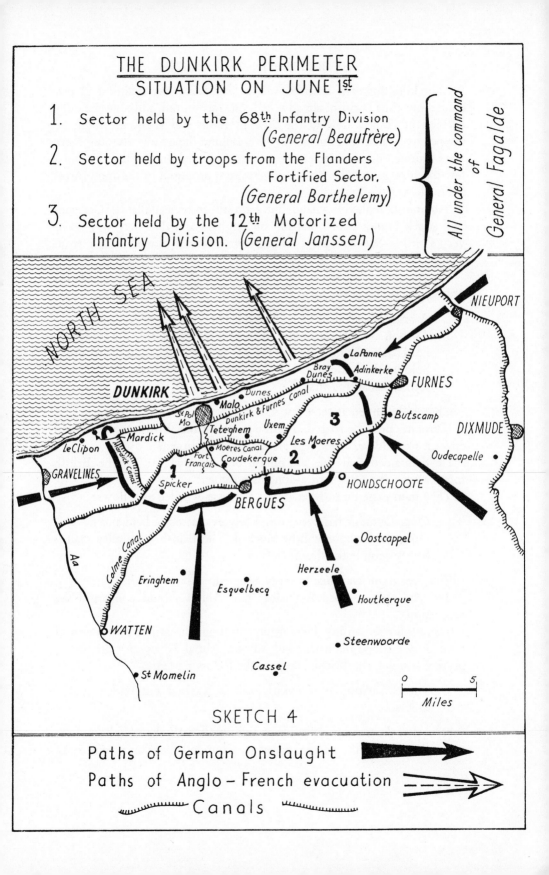

THE DUNKIRK PERIMETER
SITUATION ON JUNE 1st

1. Sector held by the 68th Infantry Division (*General Beaufrère*)

2. Sector held by troops from the Flanders Fortified Sector. (*General Barthelemy*)

3. Sector held by the 12th Motorized Infantry Division. (*General Janssen*)

All under the command of *General Fagalde*

NORTH SEA

NIEUPORT

La Panne

Bray Dunes

Adinkerke

FURNES

DUNKIRK

Dunes

Malo

Dunkirk & Furnes Canal

Butscamp

DIXMUDE

St Pol Mo

Teteghem

Uxem

3

Mardick

Les Moeres

Oudecapelle

le Clipon

Moeres Canal

Coudekerque

2

Mardick Canal

Fort Français

1

GRAVELINES

Spicker

BERGUES

HONDSCHOOTE

Colme Canal

Oostcappel

Aa

Eringhem

Herzeele

Esquelbecq

Houtkerque

WATTEN

Steenwoorde

St Momelin

Cassel

0   5
Miles

SKETCH 4

Paths of German Onslaught

Paths of Anglo-French evacuation

Canals

Churchill's forecasts with regard to land forces were almost as discouraging. The British already had one armoured and one infantry division in France. One of the three divisions still in Britain might be shipped over: he could not say for sure. Behind these three divisions there were fourteen in training, but they were equipped only with rifles and a few machine-guns. The British government proposed to summon forces from all over the Empire.

'No doubt,' replied Reynaud, 'but I am still convinced that the Germans will attack France before starting on England and that they will do so very shortly. We too are recalling our overseas troops — even from Tunisia, despite the Italian threat.'

At last they were ready to begin a communiqué. Admiral Darlan produced a draft, in the form of a telegram to Admiral Abrial:

1. A bridge-head shall be held round Dunkirk ...
2. As soon as you are convinced that no troops outside the bridge-head can make their way to the points of embarkation the troops holding the bridge-head shall withdraw and embark, the British forces embarking first ...

Churchill jumped at these last words.

'Certainly not!' he roared. 'I refuse to accept that British troops should embark first! *Nong! Partage! — bras-dessus, bras-dessous!*'

He demanded that the last phrase be amended to: ' ... the British forces acting as a rearguard as long as possible.'

They then passed on to Paragraph 3. It was worded as follows:

3. Once Dunkirk has been completely evacuated of land and naval units, the harbour will be blocked. The British Admiralty shall be responsible for this operation ...

This paragraph was unanimously adopted.

'Do you agree,' asked Reynaud, 'that Abrial should command the evacuation?'

There followed an involved argument about the respective powers of Lord Gort, General Blanchard and Admiral Abrial. Finally, for the sake of peace and quiet, the British accepted the following text:

4. The evacuation of Dunkirk will be carried out under your orders.

Now that the main topic had been fully dealt with, the members of the Council turned to the general situation. Churchill made an inventory of the immense forces Great Britain was mobilizing the world over. The French, says Spears, were only listening with polite attention.

'Then suddenly his voice changed and the atmosphere of the conference was transformed. It was as if the great wings of Rude's Angel leading youth to victory were beating in the room, changing the air, filling it with sound ...'

Churchill was saying that France and Britain must maintain the closest, the most trustful, the most complete unity. Every effort must be made to keep up the public spirit. Whatever the issue of the battle in France, the British government and people would go on to the bitter end, however great the hardship, however immeasurable the sacrifices. His voice had assumed a tone and volume which compelled absolute attention, and I thought that Danton, whose statue was not far away, must have spoken with such a voice and with similar eloquence when the Revolutionary Tribunal paled lest the torrent and fury of his words should be heard through the closed windows and unleash the waiting mob.

'The peoples of France and Britain were not born to slavery,' he said, 'nor can they endure it ... I am absolutely convinced,' the words were rolling on like waves, symmetrical and formidable, crashing on to our consciousness, 'that we have only to fight on to conquer. If Germany defeated either ally or both, she would give no mercy. We should be reduced to the status of slaves for ever. Even if one of us is struck down, the other must not abandon the struggle. Should one of the comrades fall in the battle, the other must not put down his arms until his wounded friend is on his feet again.

'We shall carry on with the war if every building in France and Great Britain is destroyed. The British government is prepared to wage war from the New World if through some disaster England herself is laid waste. The British people will fight on until the New World reconquers the Old. Better far that the last of the English should fall fighting and *finis* be written to our history than to linger on as vassals and slaves.'

Everyone in that room was deeply moved, carried away by the emotion that surged from Winston Churchill in great torrents. It was not necessary to understand his words to seize his meaning. The interpreters were silent, it never occurred to them to translate the sentences as they poured from him, hot and passionately sincere. When they did translate, even the pale echo of the original words was formidable, as is a great storm passing from sight and hearing beyond a mountain range. I was spellbound. I did not hear the Prime Minister often in the Commons during the war as I was away so much, but I cannot believe that any speech he ever made there carried more force or conviction. It was a pity it fell on such barren soil.

JUNE 1ST

The remnants of the 1st Army, which had been fighting in the Lille area, surrendered after running out of ammunition. At 9 a.m. two battalions, drawn from all the units that had taken part in the battle, marched past General Wegner in the main square of Lille. A German detachment presented arms.

General de Gaulle, summoned by General Weygand, drove to French G.H.Q. in the château at Montry.

The Commander-in-Chief congratulated him on his fine leadership of the 4th Armoured Division at Montcornet and Abbeville.

Then the two generals turned their minds to the second phase of the battle, which seemed imminent.

'Any day now I shall be attacked along the Somme and the Aisne,' said Weygand. 'I shall be saddled with twice as many German divisions as we ourselves have. ... *If* things don't happen in too much of a rush, *if* I have time to remuster the French forces that escape from Dunkirk and *if* the British army returns to share in the fight and the R.A.F. is prepared to pull its weight in Europe, we still have a chance. Otherwise ... !'

General Weygand concluded his exposé with a wave of the hand that was fully indicative of his helplessness. General de Gaulle recalls that he left G.H.Q. 'with a heavy heart'. One can well believe him.

M. Reynaud summoned General Spears and told him, for Churchill's immediate information, that the French Secret Service had just received news that the Germans would attack across the Somme between June 3rd and June 5th, in the direction of Amiens–Paris and Rheims–Paris.

He then announced that at the moment nine German Panzer divisions were almost entirely withdrawn from the fighting for overhaul. This great mass of armour, while temporarily immobilized, would be a sitting target for air attacks. He asked that the R.A.F. should intervene without delay at points that would be indicated by General Georges.

General Spears telephoned London and passed on this request to General Ismay. The latter told him that tension was mounting between Admiral Abrial and the British Command in Dunkirk.

A few hours later Churchill sent Paul Reynaud the following telegram:

Crisis in evacuation now reached. Five fighter squadrons, acting almost continuously, is the most we can do. but six ships, several filled with troops, sunk by bombing this morning. Artillery fire menacing only practicable channel. Enemy closing in on reduced bridge-head. By trying to hold on till tomorrow we may lose all ... Situation cannot be fully judged by Admiral Abrial in the fortress, nor by you, nor by us here. We have therefore ordered General Alexander, commanding British sector of bridge-head, to judge, in consultation with Admiral Abrial, whether to try to stay over tomorrow or not. Trust you will agree.

'And, pray, what do you think General Alexander's decision will be?' Reynaud asked acidly.

Spears, who had delivered the message, said he could not be certain, but he would not be surprised if Alexander decided to close the harbour some time during the night.

'I note,' said Reynaud icily, 'that the decision to have a united command only lasted twenty-four hours.'

At 4 p.m. Sir Ronald Campbell, British ambassador in Paris, called on M. Reynaud and delivered a telephoned message from Churchill, confirming the previous one.

It is hardly possible that embarkation can be prolonged beyond daylight tomorrow. It is therefore desirable that the operation should come to an end tonight. Up to date 225,000 men have been embarked ... [1]

A little later in the day General Spears informed the French Premier that General Alexander had decided to stop embarkation on the night of June 1st–2nd.

Meanwhile, the evacuation of Dunkirk was continuing in increasingly dramatic conditions. Enemy pressure was intensifying hourly. The sky, streaked by the flashes of exploding bombs, was blacked out by the thick spiral curls of smoke rising from town and harbour. Spitfires and Stukas spun round and round in this apocalyptic setting. The constant drone of their engines was drowned by the shrill whistle of bombs and the roar of the German coastal batteries, which held the town's approaches trapped in their crossfire.

In the midst of this inferno, Admirals Abrial and Platon (the latter had

[1] Of these 225,000 only 18,000 were French.

been appointed governor of Dunkirk) were doing all that was humanly possible to ensure the movement of troops through the town and direct the escaping columns to the beaches that were least exposed to the enemy's fire.

At 6 p.m., when all units not taken prisoner were within the perimeter and the embarkation of the Cavalry Corps was complete, General Blanchard sailed for Dover aboard the *Bouclier*. Other passengers were General Langlois, commander of the Cavalry Corps, and his staff.

Commandant Marchal remained in Dunkirk with a group of some twenty tanks, to share in the last-ditch stand.

At midnight, in accordance with the instructions that he had received from the War Office, General Alexander ordered the last remaining British units to withdraw into the harbour and embark with all possible speed.

Afterwards he toured the beaches and harbour in a motor boat to see that no British elements were left ashore. Then he himself embarked in a British sloop.

POLITICAL SITUATION

Rome was the scene of feverish political activity. President Roosevelt had instructed the United States ambassador to lodge a further, and more pressing, appeal to the Italian government to stay out of the war. On behalf of the Duce, Count Ciano told Mr Phillips: 'America has no more at stake in the Mediterranean than Italy in the Caribbean. So Roosevelt will get nowhere. On the contrary, he will do well to remember that his pressure is only strengthening Mussolini's purpose.'

M. François-Poncet made a last attempt to institute discussions on the basis of M. Daladier's note. 'He realized from my answers,' writes Ciano, 'that the time for cherishing hopes and illusions was past: Mussolini had set his mind on the sword.' François-Poncet did not press for a direct reply.

JUNE 2ND

MILITARY SITUATION

All British troops had now embarked, including the 20,000 who had formed the rearguard under General Alexander.

But there were still thirty or forty thousand French soldiers in Dunkirk. The beaches were covered with them. The scene was appalling in other respects. The town, devastated and in ruins, was burning from end to end.

The position was aggravated by the fact that, now that the British troops had departed, thanks to the concerted efforts of the French and British navies, both the R.N. and the R.A.F. were keeping out of the way.

Since the sky over Dunkirk was no longer protected against the waves of German bombers, the French Command was forced to suspend daylight operations so as to cut down losses. General Janssen, commander of the 12th Motorized Infantry Division, which was guarding the eastern side of the perimeter, was killed when a bomb fell on his command post.

General Weygand sent the following telegram to General Lelong for transmission to the British High Command:

> Admiral North has telegraphed this morning that, excluding the 25,000 defending the Dunkirk bridge-head, there remain about 22,000 other French. All the British will have left by this evening. Since we may hope to evacuate 22,000 men tonight, the 25,000 defenders will still be left tomorrow morning. Consequently Admiral North has declared that he is remaining in Dunkirk and postponing the blocking of the harbour. He asks for full British sea and air support tomorrow (Monday) to evacuate the 25,000 fighting men who, by holding on, will have enabled the last British contingents to sail. You will insist forcibly, in the name of the Commander-in-Chief, that Admiral North's request be met, and you will stress that the two armies' community of interests demands that the French rearguard should not be sacrificed.

Admiral Darlan protested strongly to the British Admiralty about 'the way in which it seems to have lost interest in the outcome of the Battle of Dunkirk now that the British contingents are safe'.

And General Fagalde wrote that once the British evacuation was completed, no British planes were seen in the sky over Dunkirk.

POLITICAL SITUATION

At 10.30 a.m. the War Committee met in M. Reynaud's room.

Admiral Darlan began by stressing the flagrant lack of proportion that still existed between the number of French and the number of British troops evacuated. But he acknowledged that this difference was partly due to a basic misunderstanding. The French took the view that Dunkirk could still be defended, whereas the British were bent on hurrying the evacuation, leaving the French with the task of defending the place.

'This,' observes Baudouin, 'was painfully at variance with Mr Winston Churchill's declaration at the Supreme War Council meeting on May 31st, insisting that the British be accorded the honour of forming the rearguard.'

[*A distressing discussion followed between Weygand and Spears on the subject of the use of British ships to withdraw small contingents of British troops from Dieppe, Havre and Cherbourg. Why withdraw them if it were the intention to send others? Spears promised to question the War Office on this matter.* — Ed.]

When this argument was over Reynaud drew up the following telegram for Churchill, at the request of the Commander-in-Chief:

... With regard to the army, General Weygand draws attention to the fact that the B.E.F. was to have been expanded during the current period to 14 divisions ...

With regard to the air force, we need the support both of bombers and fighters.

We earnestly request that the British bomber force should provide, before and during the battle about to be engaged, action at least as powerful as that which it has provided in the battle in the north ...

The effectiveness of British co-operation, both on land and in the air, will largely depend on the speed with which it is provided ...

Late in the day Paul Reynaud received a telegram from General Noguès, Commander-in-Chief of French forces in North Africa, concerning his plan to conscript two classes in France and send them to Algeria and Morocco for training.

[*Reynaud learnt from General Noguès that there could be no question of his taking 500,000 recruits for training, owing to shortage of accommodation, clothing and arms — as well as doctors at the period of maximum heat, which young recruits could hardly stand. The most he could accept would be 20,000, clothed, armed and equipped. Reynaud was angered by this message. — Ed.]*

In Rome the King of Italy had consented to the declaring of war. Mussolini sent the following message to Hitler:

Rome, June 2nd, 1940

Führer,

I thank you cordially for your message in reply to the one I sent you through Ambassador Alfieri. The victorious conclusion of the stupendous battle of Flanders has aroused the enthusiasm of the whole Italian people, and mine with it.

With regard to Italy's intervention in the conflict, I fully appreciate the advisability of postponing it, to enable your air force to destroy the French air force first ... My programme is as follows: On Monday, June 10th, repeat June 10th, declare war. Begin hostilities at dawn on June 11th. ...

MUSSOLINI

'I *must* declare war,' the Duce told Filippo Anfuso[1] that day. 'I can't just sit back and watch the fight. When the war is over and victory comes I shall be left empty-handed!'

---

[1] Count Ciano's *chef de cabinet*.

JUNE 3RD

―――――◆••◆―――――

MILITARY SITUATION

French evacuation operations reached their height on the night of June 2nd–3rd.

But at the very time when the Battle of Dunkirk was nearing its close, when the only French forces remaining within the perimeter were elements of the 16th Corps under General Fagalde and when the first German units were appearing on the outskirts of the town, a new Anglo-French incident occurred. Feelings ran high.

Some British ships had returned to Dunkirk in search of French survivors. Fierce enemy bombardment had prevented them from coming close to the beach, so they had anchored some distance out while the French troops tried desperately to reach them.

The ships grew tired of waiting and sailed. The troops' disappointment may be imagined.

On returning to London the crews of these vessels complained that they had spent hours waiting in vain: the French troops had not turned up at the rendezvous.

This news spread through the town like wildfire, prompting outbursts against the French who were accused of exposing the British crews to attack for nothing.

Churchill telephoned Spears to convey his annoyance. He declared that he would be sending no more ships to Dunkirk.

Spears managed to calm him, however. He made it clear that stopping evacuations would give rise to a storm of recriminations in Paris: there was no point in making things worse. The Prime Minister finally gave in. It was no doubt thanks to General Spears that a last fraction of the rearguard (22,000 men) were ultimately saved.

At midnight the 12th Mechanized Division covering the front was ordered to break off and fall back on to the town.

POLITICAL SITUATION

Late in the afternoon Mandel asked Spears to call and see him at the Ministry of the Interior. He complained of the British attitude to the King of the Belgians, which rankled with him as it did with Reynaud. A number of Belgian aristocrats were loudly defending the King's action, he said. Loyalty was no doubt a fine thing, but there were hundreds of thousands of Belgians in France. Many of them were being enrolled in labour units. If they gained the impression that the King's surrender was justified, they would no doubt feel there was a good deal to be said for following his example.

Mandel then gave Spears a list of 'suspects'. Laval, he said, was by far the most dangerous. He was clever and unscrupulous. Flandin came next. But neither he nor Laval was dangerous so long as the government remained in Paris. If the government left and those two stayed behind, one or the other or both might attempt to form a new government. The answer was simple: *whatever happened, they were not to stay behind.*

Then there was Bonnet, but he did not count.

Spears assured Mandel that he would do everything in his power to win Churchill over to the French Cabinet's views, particularly with regard to King Leopold.

Not wishing to aggravate Anglo-French tension, Churchill sent the following message to Paul Reynaud late in the afternoon:

We are coming back for your men tonight. Please ensure that all facilities are used promptly ...

Paul Reynaud replied:

Thank you for giving orders to send ships to save the rearguard, which has played a decisive role in the evacuation. I am giving instructions to Weygand and Darlan to take advantage of these facilities with the minimum loss of time, insofar as the fighting permits.

MILITARY SITUATION

During the night of June 3rd–4th a supreme effort was made to embark a further 50,000 men. These were to be the final evacuations.

At about 10 p.m. Admiral Abrial, General Fagalde (commander of the 16th Army Corps) and a number of other senior officers went aboard a small, fast motor vessel. Admiral Abrial had decided to leave the port only after the evacuation was completed. Thus from 10 p.m. till 2 a.m. the motor vessel patrolled the various harbour basins and the surrounding beaches. Steering was difficult. The night was inky dark. Lights were strictly forbidden. German fighters were circling the harbour all the time.

'From time to time,' General Fagalde tells us, 'a black, voluminous mass would emerge from the darkness a few feet ahead of the launch and head straight for us. It was one of the last steamers entering the harbour and searching for the quay that had been assigned to her. The launch would narrowly miss her and continue her tour.'

Finally, at about 2 a.m., the harbour and beaches were silent. The evacuation was over. After checking that the breakwaters had been blown up and the harbour rendered useless, Admiral Abrial ordered the young ensign steering the launch to head for Dover.

JUNE 4TH

The 12th Infantry Division reached Dunkirk at 5 a.m. Its progress was badly hindered by the debris. It was daybreak by the time it reached the eastern mole. A handful of officers and a few men tried to escape inland. Others – about 150 – climbed aboard the lifeboats of sunken ships. These desperate bids were seldom successful.

'Dunkirk has fallen,' wrote Admiral Darlan in his notebook. 'The two navies have made superhuman efforts and achieved the impossible. If this massive evacuation has succeeded, it is thanks to the tenacity of Abrial and Platon.'

The German High Command published a recapitulatory communiqué covering the principal events since the start of the offensive:

> The great battle of Flanders and Artois is over. It will go down in military history as the greatest annihilating battle of all time.
>
> When, on the morning of May 10th, the Wehrmacht began the decisive battle in the west, the Führer and Supreme Commander had assigned as its strategic targets the breaching of the fortified positions along the frontier south of Namur and the creation of preliminary conditions permitting the destruction of the French and British armies operating north of the Aisne and the Somme.
>
> At the same time it had orders to take rapid possession of Holland and thus eliminate the territory providing bases for British land and air operations against the northern flank of the German army.
>
> On June 4th the Wehrmacht can announce to its Supreme Commander that this stupendous task is accomplished ... The first phase of this campaign is over. This considerable success has been achieved thanks to the exemplary performance of the Luftwaffe. For the full gallantry and momentum of our army on the ground could be fully deployed only within the area protected by our air force ...
>
> The full extent of our victory in Holland, Belgium and northern France can be gauged by the enemy's losses and the volume of booty captured. French, British, Belgian and Dutch losses in terms of

prisoners are in the region of 1,200,000 men. To these must be added the figure, not yet known, of dead, drowned and wounded. The arms and equipment of some 75 to 80 divisions, with their light and heavy guns, their tanks and all other kinds of vehicles, have been destroyed or captured. Between May 10th and June 3rd the Luftwaffe shot down 1,841 enemy machines, 1,142 of them in aerial combat and 699 with A.A. guns. Some 1,600 or 1,700 machines, at least, were destroyed on the ground.

Likewise at sea, the efforts to save the B.E.F. with warships and merchant ships have cost the enemy dearly.

Sunk by bomber attacks were: 5 cruisers, 7 destroyers, 3 submarines and 9 other warships, plus 66 merchant and transport ships ...

In addition, hit by bombs and partially destroyed were: 10 cruisers, 24 destroyers, 3 small destroyers and 22 other warships, as well as 117 merchantmen and troopships.

Sunk by the audacious action of light naval forces were: 6 destroyers, 2 submarines, 1 transport ship, 1 auxiliary cruiser and 1 unidentified warship.

By comparison with these figures and in view of the scale of our success, the Wehrmacht's losses seem trivial:

10,252 dead	
8,463 missing	Officers, N.C.O.s and men
42,523 wounded	

Between May 10th and June 3rd the Luftwaffe lost 432 machines. The German navy operating off the coasts of Holland, Belgium and northern France has not suffered the loss of a single vessel ... Germany commands the whole southern and eastern coastline of the North Sea and the Channel. Since our adversaries persist in refusing peace, the fight will continue till they are utterly destroyed.

The British had succeeded in repatriating 215,000 out of some 250,000 men.

The French had managed to save, at most, 125,000 out of 380,000 men.

'We were hoping to capture the whole of the British army,' Field-Marshal Keitel was to declare later, 'but the forces at our disposal in Abbeville were inadequate and those on their way from the east did not intervene swiftly enough, with the result that a gap was left for the enemy to slip through.'[1]

[1] Kesselring writes: 'We were quite unaware in 1940 that the number of British and French who escaped was over 300,000, the figure given today. Even 100,000 would have struck us as greatly exaggerated.'

Field-Marshal Keitel, Commander-in-Chief of the German armed forces, paid tribute to the way in which the evacuation of Allied troops was carried out. 'The evacuation of Dunkirk was an astounding success,' he declared. 'Up to two thousand men were taken aboard a single destroyer ... Never in my life have I seen a greater accumulation of weapons, vehicles, fuel, etc. than at Dunkirk.'

But although the Germans had allowed some of the Allied forces fighting in Flanders to escape, the French, British and Belgians suffered cruel losses.

These losses amounted to:

> 22 Belgian army divisions (out of 22)
> 9 B.E.F. divisions (out of 10)
> 24 French infantry divisions (out of 67)
> 2 light cavalry divisions (out of 5)
> 3 light mechanized divisions (out of 3)
> 1 armoured division (out of 4)

— say 61 divisions out of 124, in other words 50 per cent of the total Allied effectives.

At Pétain's trial General Weygand stated: 'Three-quarters, if not four-fifths, of our most modern equipment was captured. Our units in the north were the best armed. *They were our spear-head. The best of the French army was captured.*'

'Thus was *finis* written on the Belgian expedition,' Paul Reynaud concludes laconically. 'That expedition had been undertaken against my wishes, and it would be childish to blind oneself to the fact that, in British eyes, the French High Command was to blame for it.'

From then on, France could count only on her own reduced forces.

In the east, from Longuyon to the Swiss border, she now had 17 divisions — either fortress troops or older conscripts — to support the fortified area and deal with a possible invasion through Switzerland. It was no longer possible to get hold of a single man from Lorraine or Alsace or the Alps.

Between Longuyon and the sea, to halt more than 100 enemy divisions, all of them flushed with victory, General Weygand had altogether (including the troops recently trained, recalled or conscripted from Africa):

> 43 infantry divisions
> 3 armoured divisions
> 3 cavalry divisions

'But,' asks Bidou, 'could the word "division" still honestly be applied to them? Of the 43 infantry divisions ten or a dozen were termed "light divisions" and consisted of two regiments instead of three, while others were still being formed: the 2nd Armoured Division had only 86 tanks and the 3rd 50. As for the three light cavalry divisions, they had only 40 light armoured cars between the three of them.'

Such were the forces with which General Weygand went into a battle on which the fate of the country depended.

POLITICAL SITUATION

In the course of the afternoon Winston Churchill made a great speech in the House of Commons. After summarizing operations since the start of the campaign he said:

When a week ago today I asked the House to fix this afternoon as the occasion for a statement I feared it would be my hard lot to announce the greatest military disaster in our long history. I thought — and some good judges agreed with me — that perhaps 20,000 or 30,000 men might be re-embarked. But it certainly seemed that the whole of the French 1st Army and the whole of the British Expeditionary Force north of the Amiens–Abbeville gap would be broken up in the open field or else would have to capitulate for lack of food and ammunition ...

Speaking of the Belgian capitulation, he declared:

Suddenly, without any prior consultation, with the least possible notice, without the advice of his Ministers, and upon his own personal act, he [the King] sent a plenipotentiary to the German Command, surrendered his army, and exposed our flank and means of retreat.

Then, paying tribute to the heroic efforts of the Royal Navy and the Royal Air Force, Mr Churchill stated that, despite almost insurmountable difficulties:

The Navy, using nearly 1,000 ships of all kinds, took over 335,000 men, French and British, out of the jaws of death and shame back to their native land and to the tasks which lie immediately before them.

We must be careful not to assign to this deliverance the attributes of a victory. Wars are not won by evacuations ...

This was a great trial of strength between the British and the German air forces. Can you conceive a greater object for the power of Germany in the air than to make evacuation from these beaches impossible and to sink all the ships which were displayed, almost to the number of a thousand, in the waters outside?

... Nevertheless, our thankfulness at the escape of our army, and of many men whose loved ones have passed through an agonizing week, must not blind us to the fact that what has happened in France and Belgium is a colossal military disaster ...

The British Empire with the French Republic, linked together in their cause and in their need, will defend to the death their native soil, aiding each other like good comrades to the utmost of their strength ...

We shall not flag or fail. We shall go on to the end. We shall fight in France, we shall fight on the seas and oceans, we shall fight with growing confidence and growing strength in the air. We shall defend our island whatever the cost may be. We shall fight on the beaches, we shall fight on the landing-grounds, in the fields, in the streets, and in the hills: we shall never surrender; and even if, which I do not for a moment believe, this island or a large part of it were subjugated and starving, then our Empire beyond the seas, armed and guarded by the British fleet, would carry on the struggle, until, in God's good time, the New World, with all its power and might, steps forth to the rescue and the liberation of the Old.

'For the first time,' writes Fabre-Luce, 'Churchill was publicly envisaging the possibility of Germany's conquering the whole of Europe. If that were to happen, Britain would continue the fight from her empire. He had mentally accepted this exigency already. His thoughts dwelt beyond the seas. He was like the sailor buffeted by the storm, battling on from the top deck of the ship, then from a lifeboat, then from a raft, never giving up. He did not bow his head at this terrible prospect. He even thought of it with a kind of exaltation, as though it were the sublime consummation of his adventurous career.'

Astonished by the vehemence of Churchill's condemnation of the King of the Belgians — so different from the moderate tone that he had adopted in his speech on May 28th — some M.P.s asked him, after the adjournment, why he had altered his view. Referring to the concerted representations of Reynaud, Frossard and Mandel, he admitted that the French government had expressed surprise that his earlier speech should have been in such sharp contrast to Reynaud's own public assessment of the Belgian surrender.

Admiral Sir Roger Keyes was highly indignant when told of this answer. He wrote and asked Churchill whether he really thought this a worthy declaration in view of Leopold's reiterated requests that the B.E.F. should be instructed to take action to prevent the Belgian army's being outflanked from the right — requests with which Churchill had felt unable to comply. Furthermore, London had been warned as early as May 20th that the King would be forced to capitulate if the British and Belgian armies were split up. King Leopold had regarded their separation as inevitable if the British persisted in their attacks southward, and — added Keyes — both Churchill and Ironside had shared this view. Keyes said that he hoped Churchill would not allow these slanderous attacks on the King to continue unchecked, merely for the sake of bolstering French morale.

At the same time, M. Paul Reynaud sent a new appeal to President Roosevelt, asking him for 'planes, clouds of planes'.

Marshal Pétain had a long talk with Mr Bullitt, the United States ambassador. He told him that the British had not sent over any planes since the evacuation of Dunkirk. They had left only one division behind on French soil, he said, and they claimed that they were unable to send any more.

Altogether, the blow to the Allies of their defeat in the North was not confined to the number of men lost or the volume of equipment destroyed. From now on, Britain and France were to drift farther and farther apart. For Britain, Dunkirk marked the 'end of the beginning'; for France, the 'beginning of the end'.

SECOND PHASE

THE BATTLE OF FRANCE

(June 4th–June 25th)

JUNE 4TH

———•◆•◆•———

MILITARY SITUATION

While the remains of Dunkirk were smouldering, while the motor launch containing Admirals Abrial and Platon was drawing away towards the horizon, while the first German units were reaching the moles and while General Beaufrère, with Lieutenant de May de Termont, was on his way to Malo-Centre to inform General von Kranz of the town's surrender, there were signs on both sides of the fighting line that preparations were being made for the second phase of the campaign – the Battle of France.

Indeed, for the past twenty-four hours reports by French air crews had indicated that the Wehrmacht was redistributing its forces for a new attack.

'At the end of operations in the north,' writes General Kesselring, 'came a period of regrouping southwards ... No one who saw from the air, as I did, von Kleist's and Guderian's armour veering round towards the Somme and the Aisne, after striking towards the Channel, could stifle a feeling of pride at the flexibility and skill of the German Command and fighting-fitness of the troops.'

As the giant German war-machine swung round, Rommel was ordered to the new fighting positions without delay. He wrote to his wife:

> We are on the move again. The six days' rest we have just taken have done us a world of good and enabled us to bring our equipment more or less up to the mark.[1]
>
> The new advance will not be very arduous. The sooner we get on with it, the better. The country hereabouts has been almost untouched by the war. Everything has happened so quickly!

The French had not been idle, either. Aiming to avoid a repetition of the break-through at Dinant and Sedan, General Weygand had conceived a defence echeloned in depth. As early as May 25th he had sent out a general order to the troops in these terms:

[1] The reader may recall that the 7th Panzer Division had been rested on May 31st (see p. 202).

1. The battle on which the fate of the country depends will be fought, without thought of withdrawal, from the position that we now occupy. All officers, from army commanders to platoon commanders, must be filled with the grim desire to stand and fight to the death. If commanders set an example their troops will stand firm, and they will be justified in compelling obedience from them, if need be.

2. To be sure of stopping the enemy, we must show constant aggressiveness. If the enemy reveals offensive intentions in any sector, we must reply with swift and savage counter-preparations. If the enemy succeeds in establishing in our front one of those bridge-heads that he uses for pouring in tanks and then switching to an armoured attack, we must — however minute this bridge-head — instantly force the enemy back to his own lines by crushing him with artillery and aerial fire and counter-attacking. We must meet infiltration with infiltration ... This applies as much to divisions as to regiments, battalions and companies.

3. The whole area behind the principal line is to be organized as deeply as possible into a *quadrillage* ['chequer-board'] of resistance centres, especially along the main-roads ...

4. Military police are to block the rear of the divisional zones.

5. Every day divisional generals must see their colonels, colonels their battalion commanders, battalion commanders their companies, captains and lieutenants their sections and men.

Activity. Solidarity. Resolution.

WEYGAND

Since then, there had been a constant flow of minutes and instructions at all levels. They were inspired by three main principles:

1. Quadrillage

Plane-tank co-ordination having proved itself a powerful weapon for achieving and exploiting a break-through, General Weygand ordered the construction, in considerable depth, of staggered strong-points capable of being defended on all sides. The artillery would be enclosed in them and the enemy, after forcing the lines, compelled to negotiate them. Commanders of Military Districts throughout the war zone were instructed to ring the villages with barricades and install small garrisons of troops or volunteers in them. They were further recommended to erect anti-tank obstacles strewn with mines and covered by machine-guns. What about units fighting in the open country? They, if they felt that they were surrounded, would adhere to the same principle. In other words, they would not attempt to fall back — which would be disastrous — but would set up a hedgehog defence and form 'breakwaters of resistance'.

2. Entrenchment of units

Enemy tanks would come rumbling forward, firing in all directions. If the defender did not let himself be driven back, the enemy desisted and tried elsewhere. So if they were to be masters of the situation, the French must not suffer losses, either when attacked by planes or when attacked by tanks. The solution was to be deeply entrenched. It was therefore laid down in the most imperative terms that, over the whole area of the battle-field, from forward limits to rear limits, all troops should take cover in deep dug-outs and keep their eyes and ears open, in readiness to pounce.

3. Aggressiveness in defence

Far from allowing the enemy freedom to manoeuvre, the French must everywhere worry him, harass him, keep him under the threat of artillery and aerial bombardment, speedily mount attacks at every level, attempt to cross rivers, infiltrate on all sides.

Every fighting man in France, whatever his rank, was aware that the nation was on the brink of one of the direst hours in her history. Gone was the apathy that had characterized the days leading up to the German offensive of May 10th! This time France was not going to be caught napping: officers and men alike were steeling themselves for the onslaught. But judicious as they were, the High Command's minutes and instructions could not produce men and armaments from a top hat. And even if they could, would there have been time to make proper use of them?

General Weygand's main concern was to screen Paris and keep the enemy's armour away from the barren regions of Champagne, whence it would threaten France's eastern armies with encirclement. He devoted his maximum resources to these two objectives. But having done this, he was afraid of having insufficient forces to obstruct the Abbeville–Rouen route effectively. His mind was so much on this part of the front that a few days earlier he had sent a series of orders to General Georges to emphasize the importance of the Somme sector:

The Commander-in-Chief cannot stress too vigorously all that is to be gained ... from our controlling the whole stretch of the Lower Somme.

Consequently every attempt must be made to dislodge the enemy from the south of the river, seize crossings and establish bridge-heads ...

An immediate crossing to the left bank of the river by German armoured divisions would, if these instructions are not adhered to, enable the enemy to achieve a break-through, affording him possession of outlets from which it would become impossible to dislodge him.

Our resistance along the Somme would thus be compromised and our break-out made impossible.

WEYGAND

General Georges was in full agreement with the Commander-in-Chief as to the threat of the three bridge-heads that the Germans held at the southern end of the Somme (at Péronne, Amiens and Abbeville). He was convinced of the need to reduce them, starting with the most dangerous: the one at Abbeville. So he ordered General Altmayer to dislodge them at any price, employing units of the 10th Army, including the British 51st Division under General Fortune and the 2nd Armoured Division under Colonel Perré.

A similar operation had already been attempted on May 28th–30th by General de Gaulle's 4th Armoured Division. In vain. After a series of costly attacks its remnants had had to be rested in the vicinity of Marseille-en-Beauvaisis. Would this new attempt be more successful than the last?

Probably it would have been, had it been mounted with adequate strength. Unfortunately there was a shortage of men and equipment, and an even more telling shortage of time. The French had to act very, very quickly if they were not to be forestalled by an enemy offensive ...

Sorely tested by the marches and counter-marches inflicted on it in the course of the past week, the 2nd Armoured Division could have done with a few days' rest. Its crews were worn out. It could muster only 133 tanks.

But General Altmayer, 10th Army commander, and General Delestraint, Inspector General of Tanks,[1] took the view that there was not a minute to be lost and that the operation should be launched at the earliest possible moment. Consequently they decided that the attack should start at dawn on June 4th and be made by the following units:

51st Highland Division (British);[2]

[1] General Delestraint had just been made commanding officer of the Armoured Group whose task it was to co-ordinate the thrusts of the 2nd and 6th Armoured Divisions. (The 1st Armoured Division, hurriedly reconstituted, was to join them a few days later.)

[2] This division was holding the defensive front, and three of its battalions were to take part in the attack: two from the 152nd Highland Brigade (4th Battalion Cameron Highlanders and 4th Battalion Seaforth Highlanders), and one from the 153rd Highland Brigade (1st Battalion Gordon Highlanders).

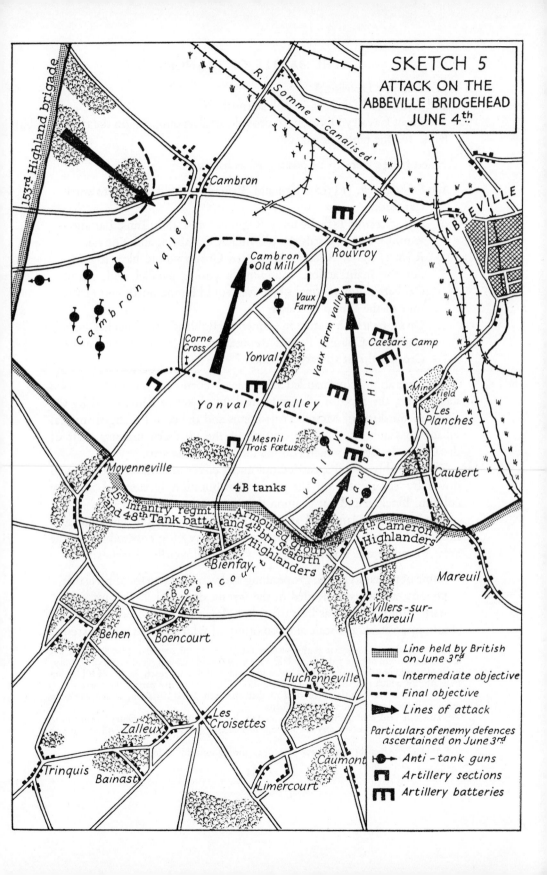

SKETCH 5
ATTACK ON THE
ABBEVILLE BRIDGEHEAD
JUNE 4th

153rd Highland brigade

R. Somme - 'canalised'

Cambron

ABBEVILLE

Cambron valley

Cambron
Old Mill

Rouvroy

Vaux
Farm

Vaux Farm valley

Caesar's Camp

Corne
Cross

Yonval

Mine
field

Les
Planches

Yonval valley

Mesnil
Trois Fœtus

Caubert Hill

Caubert

Moyenneville

4 B tanks

5th Infantry regmt.
and 48th Tank batt.

Armoured group
and 4th btn. Seaforth
Highlanders

4th Cameron
Highlanders

Bienfay

Mareuil

Boencour

Villers-sur-
Mareuil

Behen

Boencourt

Huchenneville

Zalleux

Les
Croisettes

Caumont

Trinquis

Bainast

Limercourt

Line held by British on June 3rd	
Intermediate objective	
Final objective	
Lines of attack	

Particulars of enemy defences
ascertained on June 3rd

Anti - tank guns

Artillery sections

Artillery batteries

31st Infantry Division;[1]

2nd Armoured Division (at full strength);[2]

2nd Light Cavalry Division (to provide artillery support, on the right flank, for the tanks' advance).

Allied forces were to be positioned as follows:

1. *On the left:* 153rd Highland Brigade would attack towards Cambron.
2. *Left of centre:* 15th Infantry Regiment and 48th Tank Battalion would thrust towards the old mill at Cambron and Yonval.
3. *Right of centre:* Roche's Armoured Group would have to carry out the main action, following a course parallel with Mont Caubert ridge. Its final objective would be the north end of the spur of the Camp de César.
4. *On the right:* 4th Battalion Cameron Highlanders, which had been placed at Colonel Perré's disposal, would support the Roche Group's thrust towards Caubert.[3]

The operation, commanded by General Fortune,[4] was to be in two stages: first, the capture of an intermediate objective demarcated by the northern outskirts of Mesnil-Trois-Fœtus and the road leading from that village to Caubert; then the capture of the northern military crest of the Camp de César, which commanded the whole area.

The assembly of units, carried out under cover of darkness, was slowed down by congestion on the roads. Ammunition lorries and infantry columns blocked and cut in upon the divisions' movements.

The attack was launched at 3.30 a.m., after a brief but intensive preliminary bombardment. But at daybreak a heavy fog covered the whole area. Visibility was down to twenty yards. Colonel Perré writes:

> Some of the tanks had to grope along and were held up for appreciable periods; a few even headed in the wrong direction ... The infantry started moving forward on time, but after a few hundred yards ran into opposition, the scale and proximity of which caught it unawares.

[1] It attacked with only one regiment (the 15th); its second regiment (the 81st) did not arrive till the night of June 3rd–4th, and the very most it could do was act in a reserve capacity; its third regiment (the 94th) was held up on the roads and did not reach the Bresle till late on June 4th, by which time there was no possibility of its playing any part in the operation.

[2] For the purpose of this offensive it recalled the 40th Tank Battalion, which had been temporarily on loan to the 1st Army Corps.

[3] The 40th Tank Battalion advanced behind the left flank of the 15th Infantry Regiment, so that it could counter-attack any enemy unit debouching from the Moyenneville–Cambron valley.

[4] Anglo-French co-operation was exemplary throughout this action.

The artillery observation posts were blinded by the fog and the batteries adhered imperturbably to their timetable, unable to make the adjustments for which these incidents called; some forty minutes after the start of operations they lengthened their range in pursuance of orders — abandoning all direct support, as it were, when such support was still needed.

Yet despite this set-back the units advanced with admirable grit. Mesnil-Trois-Fœtus, Villers wood, Yonval and Vaux farm were captured one by one. Soon the intermediate objective was reached. It was even exceeded ...

But the Germans resisted fiercely. They too realized the importance of the Abbeville bridge-head. Small groups of heavily armed machine-gunners fought from deep, narrow trenches terminating in an underground redoubt. When one group was knocked out by tank-fire, another instantly leapt into its place and kept up the defence.

At 7.10 a.m. the first word of alarm came from Colonel Roche: 'At 7.30 a.m. the tanks will have only another half-hour's fuel and it is impossible to refuel them in their present positions. It is urgent that the ground we have won should be occupied by infantry.'

Yet, fearing that the infantry might be left in the air if the tanks withdrew, Colonel Perré ordered the refuelling to be carried out on the spot. This meant a hold-up in operations. And the losses were severe. Of the 73 tanks that had actually taken part in the fighting, the enemy had destroyed 27; 6 others had broken down on the battle-field and been put out of action by their crews. To these figures must be added 28 vehicles which were no longer in any condition to fight. And the rest were on their last legs.

In these circumstances Colonel Perré considered a frontal attack on the Mont Caubert–Camp de César spur, which was thick with minefields and anti-tank guns, impracticable. He wrote to General Fortune: 'Resuming the attack with diminished resources, in the form previously attempted, can only lead to further failure. Re-engaging the 2nd Armoured Division immediately would mean wrecking it for a long time to come. It is for the Command to decide whether it attaches such value to the Abbeville bridge-head. If so, the division could attack tomorrow.'

General Fortune likewise took the view that the attack should restart with ampler resources — especially when he learned, during the evening, that the infantry was starting to show signs of fatigue. The company (part of the 17th Battalion of Chasseurs) that had captured Mesnil-Trois-Fœtus was dislodged; the 15th Infantry Regiment was for no apparent reason falling back on its starting base; and the Scots, who had reached the intermediate objective, were beating a fighting retreat to Villers wood and Bienfay ...

It was dark by now. Within a few hours dawn would be breaking. Such a lot could happen between now and then ... Wisdom surely demanded that the attack should not be remounted for at least three days.

But who could say whether, tomorrow even, it would not be too late?

JUNE 5TH

MILITARY SITUATION

The Allies' worst fears were realized: from Péronne to the sea, an avalanche of fire and steel came hurtling towards them.

At midnight Hitler recorded a proclamation to the German people ending in these words:

> I further order the ringing of bells for three days. May their ringing accompany the prayers which the German people will continue to offer for their sons, for this morning the German divisions and air units have been assigned new tasks in the fight for the freedom and future of our people.
>
> The Führer's Supreme Headquarters,
> ADOLF HITLER

At 1 a.m. the Wehrmacht High Command issued the following communiqué:

> The second great offensive is being launched today. It will be carried out with new and very powerful forces, including many plane and tank units that have not yet been used in battle.

These were the new German positions:

1. *From the mouth of the Somme to south of Laon:*

4th Army (General von Kluge), from the mouth of the Somme to Amiens, with Hoth's Armoured Corps of 2 divisions:

    5th Panzer Division ⎫ at Abbeville
    7th Panzer Division ⎭

Army Group B (von Bock)   6th Army (General von Reichenau), from Amiens to the Oise, with von Kleist's Armoured Group of 4 divisions:

    9th Panzer Division ⎫ at Amiens
    10th Panzer Division ⎭

237

$$
\left.\begin{array}{l}\text{3rd Panzer Division}\\\text{4th Panzer Division}\end{array}\right\}\text{ at Péronne}
$$

9th Army (General Strauss), newly formed,[1] from the Oise, south of Laon, to the Aisne.

Withdrawn: 18th Army (General von Küchler).[2]

2. *From east of Laon to Montmédy:*

2nd Army (General von Weichs), from the Chemin des Dames to Rethel.[3]

12th Army (General List), from Rethel to the left bank of the Meuse, with Guderian's Armoured Group of 4 divisions:

Army Group A (von Rundstedt)

$$
\left.\begin{array}{l}\text{1st Panzer Division}\\\text{2nd Panzer Division}\\\text{6th Panzer Division}\\\text{8th Panzer Division}\end{array}\right\}\begin{array}{l}\text{in reserve, along the}\\\text{Aisne, facing the hills}\\\text{of Champagne}\end{array}
$$

16th Army (General Busch), from the right bank of the Meuse to Montmédy.

3. *From Montmédy to the Belfort Gap:*

1st Army (General von Witzleben), from Montmédy to the Rhine.

Army Group C (Ritter von Leeb)

7th Army (General Dollmann), along the Rhine to the Swiss frontier.

Between the Channel and the Meuse the German High Command had massed 104 fully-manned standard divisions.

It was with the six Panzer divisions of Army Group B (two to each of the bridge-heads that they had established on the left bank of the Somme) that the Germans were going to strive to smash the Allied lines.

To withstand the German onslaught and hold a line of 275 miles covering the heart and nerve-centres of France, General Weygand had only some forty divisions,[4] plus the remains of three armoured divisions. This is how the French forces were disposed:

---

[1] This was one of the large new units, as yet unused in battle, alluded to in the official German communiqué.

[2] On and after June 8th von Küchler's army would take up its position between the sectors held by the 4th and 6th Armies respectively.

[3] Not yet used on the Western Front.

[4] The French High Command was expecting to add a further eight by June 12th. These were: the 82nd and 85th (from Africa), the 53rd and 59th (reconstituted), the 235th, 238th and 241st (newly formed) and the 7th Light Mechanized Division (likewise newly formed).

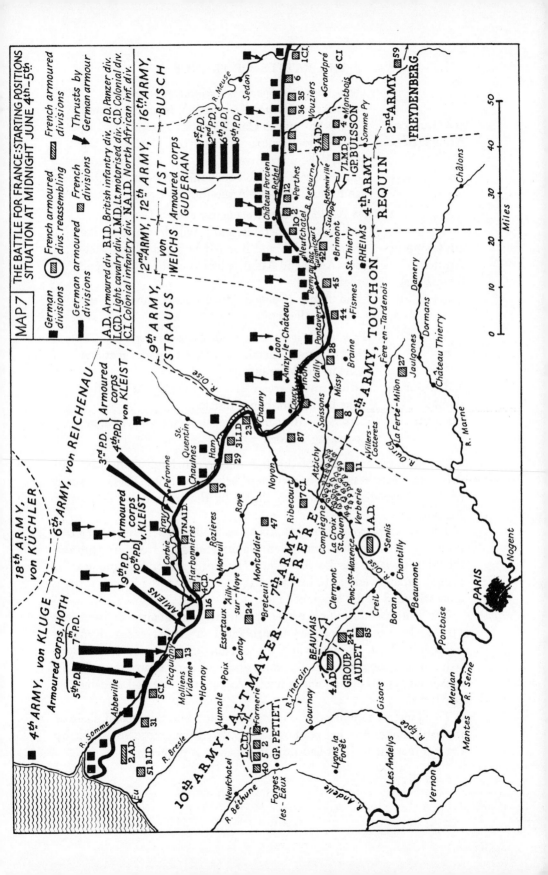

MAP 7 THE BATTLE FOR FRANCE: STARTING POSITIONS
SITUATION AT MIDNIGHT JUNE 4th–5th

■ German divisions
■ German armoured divisions
— Thrusts by German armour
◎ French armoured divs. reassembling
▨ French divisions
▨ French armoured divisions

A.D. Armoured div. B.I.D. British infantry div. P.D. Panzer div.
L.C.D. Light cavalry div. L.M.D. Lt.motorised div. C.D. Colonial div.
C.I. Colonial infantry div. N.A.I.D. North African inf. div.

1. *From the mouth of the Somme to Neufchâtel-sur-Aisne:*

3rd Group of
Armies (Besson)

10th Army (General Altmayer), from the mouth of the Somme to Corbie (east of Amiens).

7th Army (General Frère), from Corbie to the Oise Valley, inclusive.

6th Army (General Touchon), between the Oise and Neufchâtel-sur-Aisne (east of Berry-au-Bac).

2. *From Neufchâtel-sur-Aisne to east of the Meuse:*

4th Group of
Armies
(Huntziger)

4th Army (General Réquin), withdrawn from the Maginot Line and inserted between Neufchâtel-sur–Aisne and Attigny, blocking the Champagne region.

2nd Army (General Freydenberg), covering the Meuse Valley.

3. *From the Maginot Line to the Swiss frontier:*

2nd Group of
Armies
(Prételat)

3rd Army (General Condé), facing the fortified line in the Metz district.

5th Army (General Bourret), facing the fortified line in the Strasbourg district.

8th Army (General Laure) along the Upper Rhine, covering Belfort.

To offset the weakness of this line the French High Command had striven to create 'resistance breakwaters' behind the front. These consisted of three *groupements de manœuvre* shared by the 3rd and 4th Groups of Armies.

Two of these *groupements de manœuvre*, under Pétiet and Audet respectively, were to deal with enemy units emerging from Amiens and thrusting towards the Lower Seine. The third, under Buisson, was to counter-attack westwards, in Champagne, to protect the French fortress units stationed in the Maginot Line.

The British contribution was insignificant: one infantry division (the 51st, under General Fortune) incorporated in Altmayer's 10th Army fighting in front of Abbeville; the remains of an armoured division, reduced to 3,000 men and 180 tanks, under General Evans; three R.A.F. squadrons (35–40 planes) and a few A.A. batteries that had remained in Le Havre.

To all intents and purposes, France was going into this second phase of the battle alone. And her position was rendered even more vulnerable by the fact that she had not had time to organize it properly.

Yet for all the gravity of the situation, General Weygand did not intend to lose heart. To boost the troops' morale, he issued the following Order of the Day:

Officers, N.C.O.s and soldiers of the French army!

The battle of France has started. The order is to defend our positions without thought of withdrawal.

Let the thought of our country, wounded by the invader, inspire in you the unshakeable resolve to stand firm.

Hold on to the soil of France, look only forward!

The fate of our country, the preservation of its freedoms and the future of our sons depend on your tenacity.

Army G.H.Q.,
WEYGAND

At 4 a.m. the German offensive opened with fierce artillery and aerial bombardments along the whole front between the sea and the junction of the Ailette and the Aisne.

On the ground the German attack began with an initial thrust in the sector south of Péronne. It was delivered by the following elements of Reichenau's 6th Army:

11th *Army Corps*, which, with two divisions in line (the 87th in the west and the 44th in the east) and one in reserve, lined the Somme Canal from Sailly-le-Sec to south of Bray and later held the western portion of the Péronne bridge-head;

33rd *Division*, deployed along the eastern front of the bridge-head and the Somme, in the Cizancourt–Pargny area;

94th *Division*, confronting the right wing of the French 29th Infantry Division.

Immediately after the attack (at about 3.30 p.m.) Hoeppner's 16th Armoured Corps poured into the bridge-head. This Corps would now assume the main effort along the path Assevillers–Roye–Ressous-sur-Matz. It would consist of the 3rd Panzer Division (General Stumpf) with 320 tanks; the 4th Panzer Division (General Stever) with 324 tanks; and the SS-V Motorized Infantry Division.

The 640-or-so tanks engaged in this sector were massed along a six-kilometre front: 100 tanks to the kilometre, exactly the density advocated by Eimannsberger and Guderian for an attack on a defended position. Behind the centre of this army an Army Corps of three infantry divisions was stationed in reserve.

Confronted by these impressive forces, the French lines were held by the following units:

On the right, the 29th Infantry Division
(General Gérodias), holding a 15-kilometre front along the Somme, from Canizy to the north-westerly ridge at Briost.
On the left, the 19th Infantry Division
(General Lenclud), occupying an 11-kilometre front from Saint-Christ bridge to Foucancourt.

These two large units, which were to bear the brunt of the attack, were flanked:

On the right, by the 3rd Light Infantry Division, covered by the Somme and with its command post in Crisolles;
On the left, by the 7th North African Infantry Division (General Barré), with its command post in Hangest-en-Santerre.[1]

The German plan was to smash the French position by means of a single rush along the axis Assevillers–Omiécourt–Route Nationale 17, the 16th Armoured Corps advancing in bulk to Route Nationale 337, then to Route Nationale 334. This main thrust would be flanked and extended by the surrounding infantry divisions. The first wave moved forward both in line and in V formations, with the tanks either at fifty-yard intervals or in column of route. Each battalion of tanks was followed by a group of motor-cyclists and truck-borne fusiliers, together with a detachment of sappers. A third wave was made up of tank units that had apparently been drawn from the columns on either wing.

Between 9.30 a.m. and 10 a.m., after a renewed artillery barrage, the German infantry launched a mass attack along the whole bridge-head front, while the French began heavy firing in front of the main line of resistance.

At noon the French position seemed far more favourable than might have been expected. After eight hours of determined effort, the German infantry had made no deep penetration in our lines. It had merely managed to quell or encircle a few advanced posts. The 'defence in depth' advocated by Weygand was yielding excellent results.

But what had become meanwhile of the German armoured columns? 'Making use of the terrain, slipping through the gaps,' writes General

---

[1] The 7th North African Infantry Division had been raised (from French garrisons in North Africa) between February 15th and March 15th, 1940.

Perré, 'they had given a wide berth to the strong-points of the front line, limiting themselves to occasionally detaching one or two sections to explore the outskirts of a village and neutralize it or lend a hand to the infantry, but never tarrying.'

Throughout the morning the quadrilateral Omiécourt–Marchélepot–Licourt–Curchy was overrun in every direction by detachments of Panzers.

By noon the bulk of the German armour was six miles ahead of its infantry. It was out of range of its artillery and cut off from its supplies.

'Our tanks were greeted with truly hellish gunfire,' writes Captain von Jungenfeld of the 1st Battalion of the 4th Panzer Division. 'In a trice the first of them, caught in the cross-fire, were in flames. The position was far from heartening ... Now it was up to our artillery to deal with the French; their defence was really very strong, and we had very little ammunition for the guns on our tanks. It was exactly noon — 11 a.m., French time. A long day still lay ahead of us, and there was no telling how much longer the enemy's blocking fire would keep us from our supply lines ... '

But despite the delicacy of their situation, the Panzers had achieved considerable results. Communications were completely disorganized behind the French lines. Command posts were isolated. The greater part of the French artillery was neutralized or restricted to defending itself against the tanks. Replenishment of ammunition had become impossible. The French position looked sound at first glance, but it was deeply undermined by the ant-like activities of the Panzers. A dangerous situation, and one that was to exact an ever-increasing toll in the course of the afternoon.

Hoth's Armoured Corps, comprising the 5th and 7th Panzer Divisions under Generals Rommel and Hartlieb, had likewise switched to attack at Flixecourt and within the Abbeville bridge-head.

At about 4.15 p.m. Rommel drove to an observation post and watched the start of the attack. 'The preliminary barrage,' he writes, 'began on the dot and was an incredible sight. The flashes of bursting shells streaked the sky from one end of the horizon to the other.' An hour later the whole Somme front was ablaze.

At 9.35 a.m. French G.H.Q. was notified that the British were beginning to withdraw some of the anti-aircraft defences from Le Havre. Weygand immediately telephoned Paul Reynaud and asked him to 'beg the British Command to abandon this project and, broadly speaking, to maintain in Le Havre the anti-aircraft batteries as well as the barrage balloons that it had installed there'.

At 9.45 a.m. General Weygand voiced his dissatisfaction in the following note to the French Prime Minister:

> The Commander-in-Chief is obliged to point out that appeals to the British government have continued to no avail.
>
> We are being subjected to the German attack without having benefited from any further assistance from Britain. Neither fighter-planes, nor new divisions.
>
> WEYGAND[1]

Rommel then drove to the point at which the 2nd Battalion of the 6th Regiment of Fusiliers was to cross the river. There he learned that the railway bridge and road bridge had fallen into his pioneers' hands intact. Part of the engineering battalion was already at work removing the rails and sleepers on the railway bridge to enable the division to use it for all its vehicles.

All this time Altmayer's 10th Army and Frère's 7th Army were bearing the full weight of the battle.

The early attack south of Péronne, Amiens and Abbeville spread all the way to the sea in the afternoon.

At noon the 5th and 7th Panzer Divisions, now beyond Hangest, were ordered to continue their advance without interruption. Rommel immediately laid plans to this end.

'I was able to give all my orders by word of mouth,' he writes, 'without disturbance from the artillery fire still intermittently spraying our position. At 4 p.m. precisely the tanks rolled. The various sections acted in perfect co-ordination, almost as though it were a peacetime manoeuvre.'

The French colonial troops, entrenched in the small woods covering the southern slopes of Hills 116 and 104, fought desperately; but the German tanks blasted the woods so savagely as they passed that there was no stopping them. Rommel continues:

> Firing and fighting without pause, my tanks advanced on both sides of Le Quesnoy and came out on to the vast bare plain that stretches to the south. They forged on through the fields, where the corn was already tall. All the enemy detachments hiding in them were destroyed or forced back. A large number of prisoners were brought in. Many of them appeared to be drunk. The majority were coloured

[1] For some days past, alarmed by France's military weakness, General Weygand had constantly stressed the need to increase British participation. 'At the time,' writes Paul Reynaud, 'I often found myself wondering whether the insistence with which — at Weygand's request — I appealed to our ally for help was not excessive.'

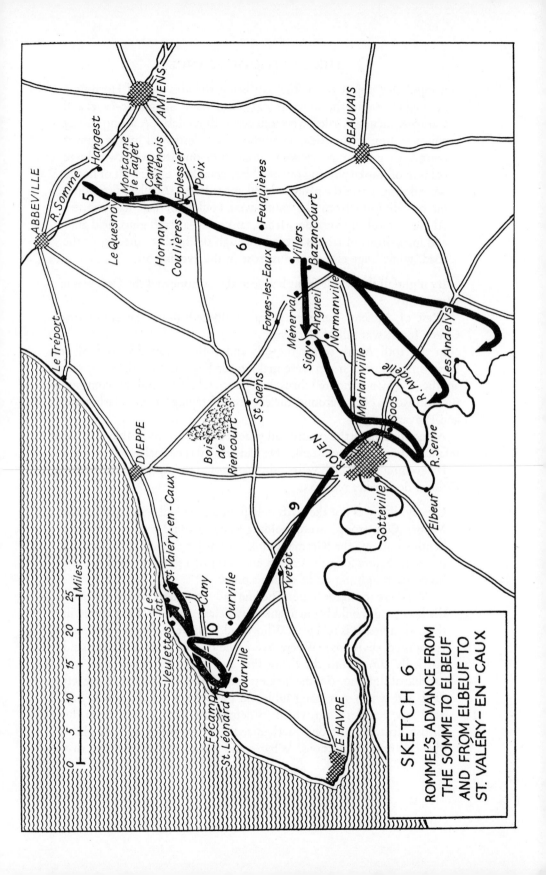

SKETCH 6

ROMMEL'S ADVANCE FROM
THE SOMME TO ELBEUF
AND FROM ELBEUF TO
ST. VALÉRY–EN–CAUX

troops. Our objective for the day being the area east of Hornoy, I decided to resume the attack at 7.25 p.m., via Montagne-le-Fayel and Camp-Amiénois. Orders were sent out without delay. A strong enemy concentration in the Riencourt woods was destroyed by the Panzer regiment's gunfire as we went along. On our left we saw a huge column of smoke pouring out of a blazing tank-wagon; a lot of horses were fleeing across the plain, saddled and riderless. Artillery fire falling on our division from the south-west could not halt its progress. Along a broad and very deep front, tanks, anti-aircraft guns, field guns and lorry-loads of troops surged through the fields to the east of the road, while huge clouds of dust rose in the evening air.

By nightfall the whole front between the Somme and the Oise was in a state of flux.

West of Amiens, the enemy had infiltrated along the entire front. Coucy forest was full of Germans.

In the 10th Army sector the 9th and 10th Panzer divisions of von Kleist's Armoured Group were making for Poix. In the 7th Army sector another German armoured thrust had passed Chaulnes and was continuing towards Roye. Near Péronne, the enemy was trying to seize Harbonnières and Proyart.

Along the Ailette the enemy had attacked with a considerable volume of infantry, though without tanks. He had crossed the canal at several points.

By evening the French were losing control of the stretch of the Somme. Colonel de Bardies remarks:

Clearly, this was not the swift collapse that we had witnessed on the Meuse. Our troops were holding their ground ... But we were hemmed about; the [German] tanks got as far as our armies' second position; before long the French line was just a series of small strongholds, each fighting on its own account.

Was there room for hope? The line had not faltered, but tomorrow the bombing would begin again. Any beleaguered post is captured in the end, unless it is relieved. Who would relieve us? Fresh divisions? Armoured divisions? Where were they? The French Command hurriedly threw into the firing line every unit in France that was capable of fighting. But the luckless 10th Army, which was on the left flank and which was being subjected to the brunt of the attack, had very few vehicles with which to defend the gaps — apart from the British armour, just one mechanized cavalry group and the three old-style cavalry divisions. What could horse-soldiers do? Die, that was all. In addition, however, there were the remnants of the 2nd Armoured Division — which was now down to fifty tanks, including five B-type vehicles.

The figures given by General Perré are slightly higher: sixty-seven light tanks, six B-type tanks. Either way, this was a very slender force to set against the seventeen-hundred odd Panzers that the Germans had lined up along the Somme front. The odds were hopelessly uneven.

POLITICAL SITUATION

The War Committee met in the French Premier's room at 10.30 a.m. General Weygand began by announcing gravely that the German attack, inaugurating the second phase of the battle, had been launched at dawn; it was still too early for results to be known. He read out the notes that he had recently sent to all area commanders and heads of units concerning *quadrillage* and defence in depth. He also revealed the imperative instructions that General Georges had sent to the Commanders of the Groups of Armies, defining the missions of the units under their command:

The mission of the 3rd Group of Armies (General Besson) will be to bar the enemy's direct way to Paris via the Oise Valley, at the same time safeguarding its left wing by holding the Somme crossings *without thought of withdrawal*.
The mission of the 2nd Group of Armies (General Prételat) will be:

1. to hold, *till its resources are exhausted*, the hinge between the Maginot Line and the Aisne, the 2nd Army at all costs maintaining its link with the 6th Army;
2. to hold out, *without thought of withdrawal*, along the Maginot Line and the Rhine.

As for the 4th Group of Armies (General Huntziger), it was to maintain its links with the 2nd on the right and the 3rd on the left by holding on unshakeably along the Aisne and denying the enemy access to the Champagne region.

A weighty silence followed General Weygand's words.
Then M. Paul Reynaud informed Marshal Pétain that he had decided to reshuffle his Cabinet, and offered him the post of Minister for Foreign Affairs. The Marshal declined, objecting that he was not qualified for the job, and asked General Weygand for his opinion in the matter.

'The Marshal's great prestige,' declared the General, 'must remain one of the pillars of our army's morale.'

Reynaud did not press the point.

He and General Weygand then discussed the very grave prospects facing the country.

'It is certain,' Reynaud declared, 'that the government will be unable to negotiate with the Germans, whether they refuse or put forward dishonouring — and therefore unacceptable — conditions.'

'If the worst comes to the worst,' observed Weygand, 'if the battle is clearly lost, the truly courageous thing would be to negotiate with the enemy.'

'My views are unchanged,' replied the Premier. 'I am convinced that no peace, no armistice, will be acceptable.'

There followed a rather lively argument about a question tabled by a deputy concerning the collapse of the 9th Army on the Meuse. The Premier considered this question 'natural'. But Marshal Pétain and General Weygand were far from sharing his opinion. Finally, for the sake of peace and quiet, M. Reynaud admitted the untimeliness of such a question.

Following the meeting of the War Committee, in reply to a long note from the British Premier outlining the reasons that prevented Britain from sending France more substantial military aid, M. Paul Reynaud handed the following memorandum to General Spears and asked him to transmit it to Churchill without delay:

June 5th, 1940

1. *British Divisions*

General Weygand's opinion is that, unless he has the means of supplying the battle, there is the greatest risk of its being lost. The dispatch of the British divisions must therefore be speeded up.

The first division will not embark, so you tell me, for another seven days.

But eight days will elapse between its landing and its employment at the front.

There is a risk that this first division itself will arrive too late.[1]

My conclusion is that, in view of the fresh factor of this morning's offensive, the dispatch of the British divisions should be accelerated to the maximum.

[1] Indeed. According to Reynaud's calculations it could play no part till June 21st. The armistice was signed on June 23rd.

2. *Fighters*

You indicate that because of the heavy losses suffered by British fighter-planes you can at present only replenish the three squadrons now in France.

You are therefore rejecting the request formulated on June 3rd … to send to France:

1. *Immediately* ten fighter squadrons;
2. As soon as possible, ten other squadrons (these twenty squadrons representing half the fighter force based in England).

I cannot believe that your decision will stand in the face of the fresh factor of this morning's offensive.[1] … If the British air fighter force does not lend our army the support asked for by General Vuillemin, it is to be feared that the battle will be lost and Paris occupied by the enemy.

3. *Bomber Force*

Thank you for your statement, which gives us complete satisfaction.

The French government has full confidence in the spirit of total solidarity of the British government and its leader.

Insisting further on the need for closer co-ordination between air and ground units, Paul Reynaud suggested to the British government that it would be advantageous to subordinate the combined air forces of the two countries to a single command — in the event, to General Weygand.

In the evening General Spears brought the British government's reply. This stated that:

1. Unity of command of the bomber forces was possible — under a British air force officer.
2. Unity of command was not practicable in respect of fighter forces.

What Spears did *not* tell the French Premier was that Churchill was on the point of losing patience, overtaxed by the continual demands of the French. Weygand's claim to the role of commanding the British units struck him as inconceivable. 'A well-organized air force was something they [the French] had no conception of,' comments Spears. 'No pains had been taken to study ours … '

[1] The withdrawal of the R.A.F. was understandable while it was still not known whether, after Dunkirk, Germany would attack Britain first. The launching of the new offensive proved that the O.K.W.'s aim was to defeat France first. So Britain was in no immediate peril.

General Spears also handed Reynaud a private message from Churchill. It was rather sharp in tone:

Private and Personal

1. Your comments will be examined by the General Staff, who have orders to send the two divisions as soon as possible.

    Permit me to observe that your divisions picked out of Dunkirk are not to enter the line for a month. We are trying to send one of our seasoned divisions in a fortnight.

2. Fighter aircraft. General Vuillemin's demand was altogether unreasonable and his letter has made the worst possible impression on everyone here ...

During the night Paul Reynaud reshuffled his Cabinet. This was the second reshuffle since he took office.[1]

Its aim was to exclude Daladier and de Monzie, whom he considered too much in favour of peace talks with Italy and advocates of a more independent policy with regard to Britain. 'The reshuffle of June 5th–6th did not awaken a favourable response in every quarter,' writes Kammerer. 'Bergery, for one, declared in the lobby that the Prime Minister was giving more thought to Britain than to France.'

[1] The composition of the new French government was as follows:

MINISTERS:

Premier, National Defence and Foreign Affairs: Paul Reynaud.
Deputy Premier and Minister of State: Marshal Pétain.
Ministers of State: Camille Chautemps, Louis Marin, Jean Ybarnegaray.
Interior: Georges Mandel.
Finance: Yves Bouthillier.
Munitions: Raoul Dautry.
Air: Laurent-Eynac.
Navy: Campinchi.
Justice: Albert Sérol.
Information: Jean Prouvost.
National Education: Yvon Delbos.
Labour: Charles Pomaret.
Communications: Jules Jullien.
Public Works and Transport: Frossard.
Health: Georges Pernot.
Pensions: Albert Rivière.
Food: Henri Queuille.
Colonies: Louis Rollin.
Commerce and Industry: Albert Chichery.
Blockade: Georges Monnet.

Under-Secretaries of State:
Presidency of the Council, Foreign Affairs, Secretaryship of the War Cabinet and the War Committee: Paul Baudouin.
National Defence and War: General de Gaulle.
Public Works: Février.
Vice-Presidency of the Council: Robert Schuman.
Aircraft Production: Colonel Mény.

Round about midnight Paul Reynaud had a telephone call from President Roosevelt, who assured him of his fullest sympathy and promised to help the Allies as much as ever he could. The President concluded by saying that he would go as far as the law would permit, and even a little further. But he did not tell M. Reynaud what he had told Mr Cordell Hull, namely that he was beginning to find the French Premier's calls for help 'irritating'.

In Rome Count Ciano recorded in his *Political Diary*:

The Germans have attacked the line of the Somme. No information is available at the moment, but everyone is convinced that they will cross it swiftly enough. French morale has not yet recovered and their defensive organization is bound to be incomplete. Is this the decisive battle?

The Duce, who was planning to attack France right at the start, has decided to bombard the British ports in the Mediterranean and play a waiting game with regard to France.

General Weygand, for his part, wrote: 'Italy's entry into the war seemed daily more imminent.'

JUNE 6TH

At daybreak the German attack was resumed, with repeated air and tank attacks. The French were finding it harder and harder to maintain ammunition supplies.

Along the Ailette, at Coucy and Anizy-le-Château, the 7th and 28th Divisions put up fierce resistance but suffered heavy losses. Gradually the defence gave way. The enemy thrust on in the direction of Soissons and Vailly. The position having worsened in the afternoon, General Touchon decided to pull his forces back to the Aisne in the course of the night.

On the far left, in the 10th Army sector, there were early reports of faltering. Despite the High Command's categorical orders to 'hold on without thought of withdrawal', the British 51st Divsion under General Fortune fell back on to the Bresle under pressure from the enemy. The French 31st Division, which was holding the waterways of Abbeville on its right, was caught up in the withdrawal.[1] Orders were sent to General Altmayer to do everything to re-establish the position along the Bresle. Pétiet's *groupement de manœuvre* was placed at his disposal. It made a vigorous intervention in the Poix area, but was unsuccessful in freeing the encircled strong-points. In the evening the Army Commander wanted to engage the remains of the 5th Cavalry Division in the same area, but did not manage to bring it up in time. So he was compelled to deploy the reserves in second position.

It was in the centre, in the sector held by Frère's 7th Army, that the situation was at its worst, as a result of the faltering of the 6th Army along the Ailette. In front of Péronne, where the 3rd and 4th Panzer Divisions were operating, the enemy — reported to be nearing Roye the day before — had enlarged the pocket stretching towards Ham and Harbonnières. French bombers made three attempts to upset these formations, but they met with little success. The 1st Armoured Division, now reduced to one battalion of 'B' tanks and one battalion of 'R.35' tanks, tried to intervene.

---

[1] Withdrawal to the Bresle had been sanctioned by General Altmayer and the sectors of the two divisions had been fixed. — Ed.

Having no air support, it suffered heavy attacks by enemy dive-bombers. At 11 a.m. the armoured division pulled back, having lost half its total strength.

At 6 p.m. the Commander-in-Chief sent his congratulations to the 6th, 7th and 10th Armies on the fine bearing of the troops and asked them to resist with the same obstinacy along the second position. 'The battle is only just beginning,' he said. 'We must not lose a minute in organizing, perfecting, encouraging.'

Yet by the evening of June 6th, the 3rd Group of Armies was falling back along the whole front. The 10th Army was withdrawing to the Bresle, the 7th towards Davenescourt and Ribécourt, the 6th towards the Aisne between Attichy and Vailly. Nothing was yet lost: the battle would have to be continued in depth. But there were no reserves. The second position was unfortified.

'Thus,' writes General Weygand, 'at the end of the second day the enemy was forcing us to conduct the battle quite differently from the way we had planned. The system of defence as originally laid down consisted of holding on along the Somme–Aisne line by means of unlimited resistance from strong-points that were to go on fighting even if overrun or encircled.'

POLITICAL SITUATION

At 10.30 a.m. the War Committee met in M. Reynaud's room. It was attended by Reynaud, Pétain, Weygand, Darlan, Baudouin and Spears. Vuillemin was absent.

Paul Reynaud seemed in excellent spirits. President Lebrun had ratified the ministerial reshuffle. Daladier was out of the government. President Roosevelt had telephoned during the night. All these factors seemed to have restored his self-confidence.

But when General Weygand spoke it was obvious that he had seen Churchill's messages of the day before and that he was strongly dissatisfied with them.

[*Generals Weygand and Spears debated hotly the withdrawal of the British 51st Division, both of them being ignorant of the full facts.* – Ed.]

Reynaud then raised the question of British air support. Weygand saw this as an opportunity to give free rein to his dissatisfaction:

'What is happening in the air now is but a repetition of what happened in the north when the British refused to attack Arras. I support and endorse every word that General Vuillemin has written! Mr Churchill may think General Vuillemin's demands unreasonable. Perhaps if he saw the condition of our army he would think we were unreasonable to go on fighting ... '

'*Mon Général,*' interjected Spears, 'we have not got pet objectives of our own, we are trying to strike where it hurts most. Again this is not my business, but have you indicated to Air Marshal Barratt the targets you have in mind, or the reconnaissances you require?'

General Weygand was compelled to admit, to the utter amazement of all those present, that he had never once seen Air Marshal Barratt since the start of operations. Turning to Reynaud, Spears asked if he might suggest that General Weygand should meet Air Marshal Barratt as soon as possible: he would be delighted to arrange it.

[*Again bitter exchanges followed between Weygand and Spears, regarding British support in the air.* — Ed.]

Spears then turned to Reynaud, who was visibly bored by this dispute, and said he would send him a note in writing on the subject. He returned to Churchill's last messages and read them over again.

'Can nothing more be done?' asked Reynaud. 'It is very little in view of so desperate a situation. Are its full implications fully grasped in London? ... What will a large fighter force avail you in England if France is beaten to her knees? There can be no limit to human effort if it is a question of living or dying, and that is the truth staring us in the face since the decisive battle was started yesterday.'

Weygand said with sincere emotion: 'Please tell your Prime Minister that if he could see the condition of the men and the divisions we are throwing into the battle, he would then perhaps not hesitate to engage fighter squadrons, however imperfectly organized. We are forming the Dunkirk troops into divisions as best we can, but these will have only six battalions instead of nine. They are miserably equipped and are very poor in artillery. There is, however, no choice. We are in mortal peril!'

Spears promised to give Churchill his message word for word.

Reynaud then asked Weygand about the possibility of defending a 'national redoubt' in Brittany.

'I could not guarantee its defence,' replied Weygand. 'Not even for a short time.'

'In that case,' said Reynaud, 'if we are refused a peace compatible with the honour and vital interests of France, we shall continue the war from North Africa.'

General Weygand pointed out that this new conception of operations raised a problem that he would have to refer to General Noguès. M. Reynaud agreed to a telegram being sent to the Commander-in-Chief of French Forces in North Africa. General Weygand drew attention to the fact that these forces were extremely slender: seven divisions, composed in the main of native troops. No modern equipment. No tanks. No A.A.

'Agreed,' replied Reynaud. 'But North Africa will not be attacked by the Germans — only the Italians.'

Marshal Pétain remarked that if the present battle were lost they would have no choice but to negotiate with the enemy.

'If we are offered acceptable conditions,' amended Paul Reynaud.

The meeting rose and Reynaud walked to the door with Spears.

'You know I have complete confidence in Churchill,' he said, shaking him warmly by the hand.

On leaving the War Committee, General Spears set about organizing a meeting between General Weygand and Air Marshal Barratt. Then, immediately after lunch, he returned to the Rue Saint-Dominique with the British ambassador, Sir Ronald Campbell, and handed the following letter to the French Premier:

Private and Confidential
June 6th, 1940

My dear Président,

With reference to what General Weygand said this morning, there are some points I should like to develop ...

There is a real difference of outlook between the French and the British air forces ... The French air force is naturally considered an adjunct to the army. It is just another weapon in the hands of the Commander-in-Chief. With us this conception only applies to a section of the air force — that attached to the army. The remainder — that is, by far the greater part of our air force — has a strategy, a policy and a point of view of its own.

It is inevitable that an air force with this point of view must fear being bound to a Command whose outlook is so different from its own.

I am bound to say that if General Weygand presses his point, that the role of our government and of our air force should consist solely in making available and handing over to him the maximum number of our air forces, to be employed by him without query or question according to his conception of the use of air power, I fear that we shall be faced with the worst kind of trouble ...

What is evidently required is that General Weygand's very real needs and requirements in the air should be translated into British air terms and mentality by somebody standing beside him. And it is also evident, as I said this morning, that the situation expounded by one of our own air officers would be more readily understood and appreciated by our own Command than were requests for support put forward — as was obviously the case yesterday — in a way that was ill-understood and led to misapprehension in England.

Yours very sincerely,

E. L. SPEARS

Spears took advantage of the fact that he was alone with Reynaud and the British ambassador to encourage the head of the French government to continue the war from North Africa if the defence of Metropolitan France proved impossible.

Reynaud spoke of the steps that he was taking to defend Paris. With regard to North Africa, he complained of General Noguès's guardedness, and read out the latter's telegram of June 2nd insisting that he could take only 20,000 recruits.

Reynaud said he was determined to send over at least half a class at once — say 120,000 men. The French General Staff said they could transport only 20,000 men a month, so he was sending General de Gaulle to London to ask if the British navy could help. This visit would also provide the new Under-Secretary for War with an excellent opportunity of meeting the British leaders.

After this discussion General Spears went to Marshal Pétain's office in the Boulevard des Invalides. Churchill's envoy was alarmed by the Marshal's allusion, at the meeting of the War Committee that morning, to the possible need to negotiate with the Germans.

But the Marshal remained impenetrable. He greeted Spears most courteously, but was not anxious to confide in him. He led him over to a map and pointed to the line along which the battle was raging: 'Abbeville to Rethel. That is well over 200 kilometres, and the Germans are attacking or may attack at any moment anywhere along that line. Nor is there anything to prevent their attacking elsewhere if they choose. They have certainly not got less than 10 Panzer and 120 infantry divisions. Against what?'

The Marshal paused for a moment, then continued: 'Sixty of ours, one of yours. And in what condition, I ask you? You cannot even help us in the air ... In all our battles in the last war there was time; if caught unawares, by making a great effort, and maybe by sacrificing ground, in a short time we collected troops to close the breach and, presently, to counter-attack. This time there are no reserves, *vous m'entendez*, no reserves at all. It is hopeless — *c'est sans espoir …*'

The Marshal went on to say that the country had been rotted by politics. 'The people can no longer discern the face of France through the veil that politicians have thrown over it. As you know, a matricide is led to the guillotine with a veil over his face. It is that sort of veil, but it is over the face of the mother. The murderer has thrown his veil over his mother's face.'

Suddenly he changed the subject.

'This appointment of de Gaulle is not going to help matters,' he said. 'Do you know him?'

'No,' replied Spears, 'but I thought he was highly spoken of. Has he not done very well in command of the armoured division at Abbeville?'

'He thinks he knows all about the mechanics of warfare. His vanity leads him to think the art of war has no secrets for him. He might have invented it. I know all about him. He was once on my staff and wrote a book, or at least I told him how to do so. I gave him the outline and corrected it, in fact annotated it in my own hand. When he published it he did not even acknowledge my contribution …'

All this had little connection with the purpose of Spears's visit.

'Do you not consider it regrettable, *Monsieur le Maréchal*,' he asked, 'that at our morning meetings General Weygand so persistently attributes the worst motives to the British and is so rude about them?'

But this was a topic that the Marshal was unwilling to discuss with a third party. He shut up like a clam, listening to Spears in silence as he led him towards the door.

'As I stood with him in the hall,' writes Spears, 'after having failed so signally to elicit any reaction on the subject of Weygand, I spoke of Britain's attitude to the war, and he listened patiently as I asked him to realize that the British were in deadly earnest when they said they intended to fight the war to its bitter end … "If France should ever side with the Germans, which I cannot conceive, not only would she lose her honour, but she will never recover physically. She would be bound to a Germany on whose windpipe our thumbs will soon be closing … "

'I then developed the theme that so long as we held together, did not break the link uniting us, our joint victory would one day compensate us for all we were losing today or might lose tomorrow.

' "It is possible that one day, and for a while, France may be driven to fight back from Africa, as we may be to fight back from Canada and the remainder of the Empire." '

But the Marshal maintained a lofty silence.

At the end of this discussion Spears returned to the British embassy, where he found an urgent telegram from Churchill:

It said that the embarkation of the 52nd Division had been accelerated to the utmost. It was starting next day (June 7th) and, to gain time, two harbours were being used. The whole division should be in France by June 13th. To provide support more rapidly than could be done by sending a Dunkirk re-formed division, the Canadians were being sent over on June 11th. A third division would follow as soon as possible if the French could provide artillery. I was to find out about this and inform London ...

Spears immediately took this message round to Reynaud, who was clearly delighted with it.

'*Ce brave Churchill! vraiment c'est un brave type!*'

'He is always better than his word,' said Spears.

'*C'est vrai, non vraiment, c'est très bien,*' Reynaud kept saying.

'You see,' Spears went on, 'he is throwing everything he possibly can into the battle. From what I can make out, there will be no troops left in England when the Canadians leave save the Dunkirk men who have not yet been sorted out or rearmed. We could hardly do more for Kent, were it invaded, than we are doing for you.'

Reynaud then read out the note that he had just received from General Weygand:

1. General Weygand received today General Pownall, General Gort's Chief of Staff, who informed him of the arrival of the 52nd Division ...

   As soon as possible after the landing of the first division there will arrive a second, followed by a third. As soon as there are four British divisions in France, Lord Gort will reassume command of the B.E.F.

   This is an excellent programme, and it will be even better if it is pressed forward, in view of the grave circumstances created by the new German attacks which are extending every day.

2. General Weygand has today seen Air Marshal Barratt. He has satisfied himself, and has ascertained from Generals Georges, Besson and Têtu (representing General Vuillemin at General Georges's headquarters), that perfect liaison exists between Britain and France, by making most effective use of the British

aviation placed at the disposal of our front, in accordance with French plans.

From now on the *total British bomber strength* based in France and in Great Britain is acting in support of our battle.

As for the fighter force, nothing is as yet finally settled, as the British government has not yet made a decision (information at 5 p.m.). Air Marshal Barratt explained the difficulties to be sur-mounted. General Weygand asked him to consider the dramatic circumstances under which we are fighting this battle and to plead our cause in London.

To sum up, the British government is giving us aviation, and it will be well employed.

WEYGAND

'The atmosphere,' remarks General Spears, 'was now relatively cheer-ful.'

On leaving the Rue Saint-Dominique Churchill's personal envoy called at the Ministry of the Interior for a talk with Georges Mandel. He des-cribed his interview with the Marshal (which brought some ironical remarks from the Minister) and informed him that he intended going to London next day.

'Be careful,' said Mandel, 'and do not be away long. I know what I'm talking about. Events are moving very fast.'

At 7.45 p.m. Reynaud broadcast the following speech:

In the past fortnight I have made two speeches. Each time I brought you bad news. On May 21st I said in the Senate: 'The Germans are in Amiens.' On May 28th I told you: 'The King of the Belgians has betrayed us; the way to Dunkirk lies open.'

Today, at an hour that is still grave, I am here to give you ground for hope. Not words, but facts ...

Today we are witnessing the Battle of France. This is an all-out attack, preceded by a proclamation by Hitler to his troops. Everything is now being flung into the battle — planes and armoured divisions — in a further attempt to infiltrate, and then smash, our front. The whole world is following this battle's progress with bated breath, for the fighting of June 1940 will, as Hitler has said, determine its fate for hundreds of years.

What risk do we run? That of seeing a reign of oppression estab-lished within and beyond the confines of Europe, a reign under which men of non-Germanic blood will be allotted the role of mere slaves ...

This dream of German hegemony is going to find a stumbling block in French resistance, for the France that is standing up to Hitler today is not the France of between the wars. It is another France, just as the Britain fighting Hitler is no longer the Britain of these past twenty years ...

Our prime duty is to acknowledge our own faults. In their successive governments and in the outlook of the man in the street, the democracies have long lacked clearsightedness and boldness. Notions of patriotism and military worth have been too much neglected. Let us admit it once and for all, and so close this chapter in our history, and toil with the grim energy of men whose eyes have at last been opened.

In Rome Ciano wrote:

Not much news of the Battle of the Somme. Now that they are clinging to their soil, the French are fighting with their traditional courage, even if they have lost practically all hope. The reshuffle of Reynaud's Cabinet has been interpreted here as a sign of political collapse.

JUNE 7TH

At dawn the first position of the 'Weygand Line' was pierced from end to end, and the situation was to deteriorate hourly throughout the day.

On the right of the sector held by the 3rd Group of Armies, Touchon's 6th Army had fallen back behind the Aisne, though it still held the crossing at Attichy. Frère's 7th Army had fallen back to the Davenescourt–Moreuil stretch of the Avre. The 19th Division, which had been subjected to the onslaught of the Panzer divisions south of Péronne, had gone. The battle was raging all along the front.

The situation grew rapidly worse in the 10th Army sector, which was on the left wing of the Allied line. The army's second position was broken at Poix before any counter-attack could be launched. A breach some 15 miles broad opened in the French lines between Hornoy and Conty. A huge mass of German armour poured through it, heading for Formerie[1] and Forges-les-Eaux: this was Hoth's Armoured Corps, comprising the 5th and 7th Panzer Divisions.

The French High Command sought to stem their advance by filling in the breach. 'And then,' writes Colonel de Bardies, 'came disaster. The 17th Infantry Division was being brought up in lorries, to reinforce the front; but owing to an error in the transmission of orders the vehicles were unloading too far north. Suddenly the German armour was upon the lines of lorries that covered the road, twenty men to a lorry. Chaos. Panic. The riflemen hurriedly got into line, soldiers were running in all directions, the battered, overturned lorries were in flames. No deployment was possible. Infantry and artillery alike scattered and faded in the countryside. Half the infantry and nearly all the artillery fell into German hands ... '

Rommel dashed off this note to his wife:

Your birthday has been a day of real victory. We have well and truly bestirred ourselves. The enemy is showing more and more frequent signs of disintegration. We are all very well. I have been sleeping like a log.

[1] Site of the 10th Army H.Q.

By midnight the armoured vehicles of the 7th Panzer Division, which had covered some 25 miles during the day, were within 22 miles of Rouen. Forges-les-Eaux and Neufchâtel-sur-Béthune lay behind them.

General Besson, commander of the 3rd Group of Armies, had by now flung all his reserves into the battle. Seeing the enemy's exploitative manoeuvre towards the Lower Seine take shape, he came to the conclusion that the position was extremely serious. And indeed, this sudden German thrust in the direction of Rouen and Les Andelys constituted a grave threat to the left wing of the Allied armies. There was every danger of its jeopardizing the re-establishment of Besson's forces along this cross-valley, were the Germans to smash through the defensive shields hastily formed by the Seine bridges.

Late in the day the French air force reported that a large column of enemy tanks was moving south-westwards along the Amiens–Poix road and that considerable infantry and artillery forces were advancing on Molliens-Vidame.

By evening Altmayer's 10th Army was split in two. During the night of June 7th–8th the Command ordered withdrawal to the Seine and the fortified area round Paris. The battle of the Lower Somme was lost.

To strengthen the Lower Seine line and the Paris advanced posts, two further divisions were transferred to the 3rd Group of Armies. The 57th Division, taken from Laure's 8th Army, was moved to the rear of Frère's 7th Army, covering the Paris position. The 48th Division, from Africa, was placed in the hands of General Héring, Governor of Paris, for the defence of the Seine around Meulan and the Oise around Pontoise.

The 100,000 or so men who had got out of Dunkirk, via England, had been conveyed during the past few days to the area between Caen and the Seine. Units from 17 different divisions were hopelessly intermingled. The troops were in terrible shape. None of them was armed (everything had been abandoned at Dunkirk to make more room on the ships) and many of them were only half-clad.

Yet the situation was too serious for the High Command not to try to make use of them. General Georges gave orders for them to be regrouped: an army corps of four divisions was to be drawn from them. But this was a large undertaking, involving time as well as hard work. Now, units of the German 4th Army were already beginning to line the Seine south-east of Rouen. They were less than sixty miles away, and within three days the van of the 5th Panzer Division would be bearing down upon Le Mans and Laval ...

In an attempt to slow down the German advance, if not to halt it, the

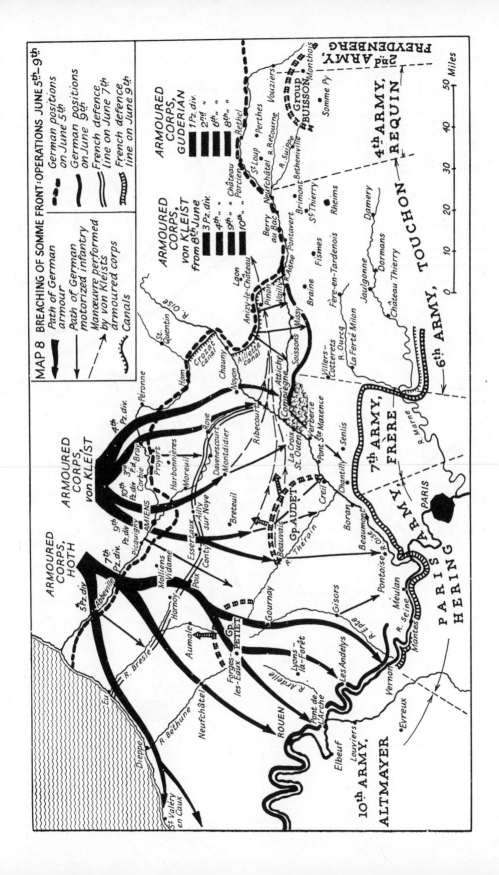

MAP 8   BREACHING OF SOMME FRONT: OPERATIONS JUNE 5th–9th

German positions on June 5th
German positions on June 9th
French defence line on June 7th
French defence line on June 9th

Path of German armour
Path of German motorized infantry
Manœuvre performed by von Kleists armoured corps
Canals

ARMOURED CORPS, von KLEIST from 8th June
3 Pz.div.
4th "
9th "
10th "

ARMOURED CORPS, GUDERIAN
1 Pz.div.
2nd "
6th "
8th "

ARMOURED CORPS, HOTH

ARMOURED CORPS, von KLEIST

2nd ARMY, FREYDENBERG

Group BUISSON

4th ARMY, REQUIN

6th ARMY, TOUCHON

7th ARMY, FRÈRE

PARIS ARMY, HERING

10th ARMY, ALTMAYER

Gp. AUDET

Gp. PETIET

Monthois
Somme Py
Perthes
St. Loup
Vouziers
Rethel
R. Retourne
R. Suippe
Neufchâtel
Bethéniville
Brimont
Château Porcien
Rheims
St. Thiery
Fismes
Damery
Dormans
Château Thierry
Jaulgonne
Fère-en-Tardenois
R. Ourcq
La Ferté Milon
Villers-Cotterets
Berry au Bac
Aisne Pontavert
Braine
Wissy
Soissons
Pinon
Vailly
Anizy-le-Château
Laon
Attichy
Aillette Canal
Compiègne
Crozat Canal
Chauny
Noyon
Ham
Péronne
St. Quentin
R. Oise
La Croix St. Ouen
Verberie
Pont Ste. Maxence
Senlis
Chantilly
Boran
Creil
Therain
Beaumont
Gournay
Beauvais
Breteuil
R. Noye
Conty
Essertaux
Ailly sur Noye
Contoire
Montdidier
Davenescourt
Ribecourt
Roye
Harbonnières
Proyart
Bray
Corbie
Amiens
Picquigny
Molliens Vidame
Hornoy
Poix
Gournay
Forges-les-Eaux
Lyons-la-Forêt
Aumale
Neufchâtel
R. Béthune
R. Bresle
Eu
Dieppe
St. Valéry en Caux
Abbeville
Rouen
Elbeuf
Louviers
Pont de l'Arche
Les Andelys
R. Ardelle
Vernon
Mantes
R. Seine
Meulan
Pontoise
Gisors
R. Epte
Evreux
Paris
R. Marne

3rd Pz.div.
10th "
1 d.Bray
9th div.
4th div.
7th Pz.div.
5 Pz.div.

0   10   20   30   40   50 Miles

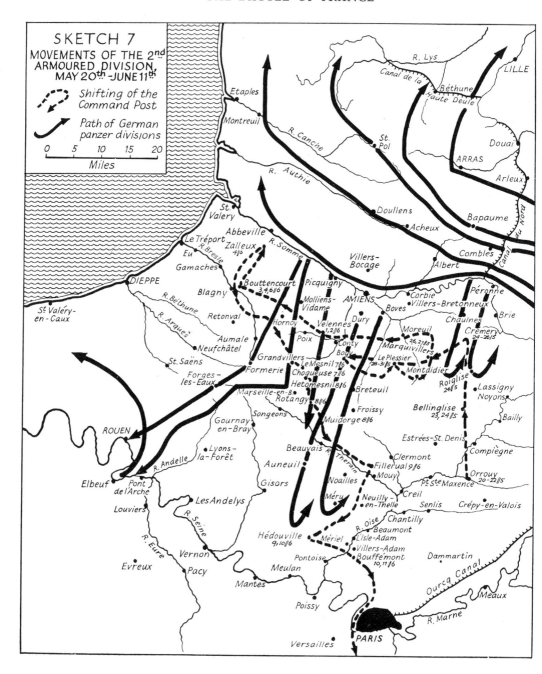

SKETCH 7
MOVEMENTS OF THE 2nd
ARMOURED DIVISION,
MAY 20th – JUNE 11th

Shifting of the
Command Post

Path of German
panzer divisions

0   5   10   15   20
Miles

officers and men of the French light mechanized divisions, brought back from Dunkirk via Southampton and Brest, were hastily regrouped in the Rambouillet area. They received new equipment, straight from the factory; and thus two small-scale divisions were formed.

POLITICAL SITUATION

In the early hours of the morning M. Paul Reynaud sent for General Spears and asked if Churchill would have any objection to his giving the Army and Foreign Affairs Commissions of the Senate, which he was to meet in joint session that afternoon, the exact figures of Allied forces engaged on June 6th. His idea was to show the senators how important a part the British were playing in the battle, especially in the air, and thus counteract the strong criticism that the French were levelling at their Allies.

The normally imperturbable Spears was astounded. 'In no country in the world,' he writes, 'would people not have been critical of an ally bearing so small a part of the common suffering and loss, but the French give way more readily than other nations to the temptation to criticize their friends.'

Spears put through an urgent call to London and informed General Ismay of Reynaud's intentions. Ismay declared without hesitation that, whatever happened, the French Premier must be stopped from putting them into practice; he would refer the matter to Churchill at once.

At the War Committee meeting at 10.30 a.m. General Weygand outlined the previous day's events to his Prime Minister, dwelling particularly on what had happened in the 10th Army sector. He again drew particular attention to General Fortune's withdrawal, of which he had received a detailed report.

At about 12.30 p.m. General Spears again called on M. Reynaud. He had received 'a most immediate telegram from Ismay saying that the Prime Minister strongly objected to any information being given concerning the forces engaged that day and the day before'.

'Nevertheless,' records Spears, 'so that Reynaud should be made aware of the scale of our efforts, I might tell him for his personal information that 144 British fighters had been engaged on June 6th, and that an even larger force would be operating today, June 7th.'

In the course of the afternoon M. Reynaud addressed the Army and Foreign Affairs Commissions of the Senate. Deferring to Churchill's wishes, he gave no indication of the size of the forces engaged in the battle and confined himself to giving the senators a brief picture of the operations.

At about 6 p.m. Mr Churchill sent a further message to M. Paul Reynaud, dwelling on the increased activity of the R.A.F. and promising the support of nine fighter squadrons. It ended as follows:

I am advising the War Office of your complaints concerning General Fortune. He has had to hold an extended front and has suffered very heavy losses.

Shortly afterwards General Spears left for London aboard Mr Churchill's personal Flamingo, which had been sent to Boucq aerodrome for him. Before he left, M. Reynaud had asked him to tell Churchill that he (Reynaud) and Mandel were almost alone in their hope of being able to continue the struggle.

When General Spears returned to France the government had left Paris.

In Rome the British ambassador, Sir Percy Loraine, called to take his leave of the Italian Minister for Foreign Affairs. 'He is sad,' wrote Ciano, 'and is fully alive to the gravity of the hour for his country. But he speaks, with imperturbable firmness, of fighting to the finish and he confirms his faith in victory "because the British are not accustomed to being beaten". Personally he is much taken up with his journey home and anxious as to what will become of a foal that he has to leave behind in Italy.'

JUNE 8TH

The advance of Hoth's Armoured Corps was speeding up. At 11 a.m. a powerful column of tanks reached Gournay. Thus the farthermost reaches of the gap, from Neufchâtel-sur-Béthune to Gournay via Forges-les-Eaux, were in enemy hands for a breadth of 25 miles.

This advance made the split in the 10th Army final. The western portion (comprising the 9th Army Corps under General Ihler and the British 51st Division under General Fortune) was retreating southwards in the hope of reaching a port from which they could re-embark. These forces were to continue fighting for another few days.

The eastern portion (consisting of the 10th Corps, reinforced by the 25th which had only just reached the front) was beating a fighting retreat north of Beauvais.

In the course of this retreat the 10th Army Corps and the 13th Infantry Division, hotly pursued by the 2nd Motorized Division of Hoth's Armoured Corps and by General von Manstein's 38th Army Corps, were threatened with total destruction. They were to be saved purely and simply by the forceful intervention of the French 2nd Armoured Division.

After breaking off action against the Abbeville bridge-head during the night of June 5th–6th, the latter had moved south of Poix, to the Grand-villers–Hétomesnil–Crèvecœur area. There, along a front six miles wide and two and a half miles deep, it had set up a staggered defence line. Mixed detachments were posted at crossroads to slow down the enemy's advance and enable French units to escape destruction. It was during this action, one of the toughest in which the 2nd Armoured Division had been engaged, that Commandant Masséna, Prince d'Essling, was gravely wounded, at the head of his tank battalion.

In the 6th Army sector (General Touchon) the situation had likewise worsened considerably. During the night the enemy had succeeded in crossing the Aisne at Missy, 6 miles up river from Soissons. That morning he crossed it at Pommiers, 3 miles down river from the same town. Soissons was therefore overrun on both sides. In the afternoon the two pincer movements connected. The Germans controlled a twenty-five-mile stretch of the Aisne on either side of Soissons. By early evening there was a continuous, if shallow, German bridge-head between Vailly and Vic.

Thus the 3rd Group of Armies was broken on both wings by the dual German advance upon Rouen and Soissons. The 7th Army, forming a shield along the Crozat Canal and the Ailette, was in trouble. On the left it was outflanked by the German columns that had reached Roye; on the right by enemy infiltrations in the Saint-Gobain forest. Both were trying to close the ring behind the French divisions holding this sector (the 29th and 23rd Infantry Divisions and the 3rd Light Infantry Division). Bardies writes:

> The encircled strong-points resisted stoutly ... But they were left unsupplied and unrelieved, and in the end they had to yield ... Gradually the breaches made by the armour widened, outflanking the near-by defences, which had resisted at first, and enabling them to be encircled and then destroyed. Stage by stage the front was collapsing. It was essential that such forces as were still free should be rapidly pulled back.

In these circumstances the French High Command considered that it had no choice but to order the general withdrawal of the 3rd Group of Armies. The order was given that evening. The headquarters of the 10th Army was moved south of the Seine to Vaucresson (near Saint-Cloud), so that it could assume command of fresh formations.

General Georges's Personal and Secret Instruction No. 113 laid down for the whole Group of Armies the manoeuvre to which they were to conform and the line along which they were to re-establish themselves:

> The *left* will stand firm along the Lower Seine.
>
> The *centre* will cling to the 'Paris Defence Position' — a semi-circular line forming a shield in front of the capital, passing through Pontoise, Beaumont, Chantilly and Senlis, and supported by the Oise and the Nonette.
>
> The *right* will halt the Germans who have crossed the Aisne, along the Ourcq whose upper reaches run from east to west.
>
> The new front of the 3rd Group of Armies will then be the following (from left to right):
>
> 1. *From the mouth of the Seine to Vernon:*
>   The 10th Army (General Altmayer), reconstituted with fresh troops.

2. *From Vernon to Boran-sur-Oise:*
   The Paris Army (General Héring), consisting of several divisions, the remains of Audet's *groupement de manœuvre* and the right-hand portion of the 10th Army.

3. *From Boran-sur-Oise to the junction of the Ourcq and the Marne:*
   The 7th Army (General Frère), replenished with reinforcements.

4. *East of the Ourcq, in the direction of the Champagne area:*
   The 6th Army (General Touchon).

It was at this point that Rommel carried out one of his most dashing manoeuvres. At 6 a.m. he had suggested to the Army Corps H.Q. that his forces should make a mock attack on Rouen, then turn off and seize the bridges over the Seine at Elbeuf. Headquarters had agreed and the tanks had moved forward at 10.30 a.m. The Andelle had been crossed at noon, and at 2 p.m. Sigy had been captured by means of an attack from the west. At about 8 p.m. a company of Panzers had been dispatched along the road to Rouen to seize the cross-roads five miles east of the town. Then came the astonishing night attack on Elbeuf. Rommel describes it:

The darkness made it hard for us to follow the route with our inadequate maps. The din we made driving through the villages woke people and had them rushing into the streets to cheer us — for they thought we were British! We passed a French anti-aircraft battery; there was still a light in the look-out post and the sentry presented arms to us. At Les Anthieux we headed south and reached the Seine at midnight.

Our brakes shrieked and roared on the bends. A light shone here and there on the other bank; there were others at various points along the railway running through the Seine valley. There was no sign of enemy troops and everything seemed to favour the success of our raid on the Seine bridges, which were now only about ten miles away ...

In Elbeuf itself our vehicles became jammed in the narrow streets of the district north of the Seine. The task-forces were late in arriving and could not begin their mission on time.

Thinking that all was not lost, I ordered the battalion commander to launch his attack on the two bridges forthwith. Under cover of darkness I myself approached one of them. There were civilians in the streets; the cross-roads were blocked with sand-bags.

The first task-force finally moved in. It was nearly 3 a.m. But the task-force did not reach the bridge, for the French blew it up before our men had covered a hundred yards. A few minutes later the same happened with the second bridge. There was a series of heavy explosions, far and near, from west to east.

I was extremely annoyed at this set-back. I had not the slightest idea where the bulk of my division was. I therefore decided that we should withdraw from the narrow pocket into which we had ventured. The troops pulled out without a moment's delay. Luckily the Seine valley was bathed in mist and we had nothing to fear from the enemy artillery on the opposite bank.

Rommel's attempt to capture the Elbeuf bridges and von Hartlieb's attack on Rouen had been thwarted. The French engineers had blown them up in time. But these bold incursions still had one immediate result: three British fighter squadrons that had been refuelling at Rouen airfield decided to pull out and return to England. They never operated in this sector again.

POLITICAL SITUATION

Alarmed by the sudden unfavourable turn of events in the Lower Seine area, M. Paul Reynaud wrote to Mr Winston Churchill asking him — yet again — to step up British military aid to France. His message was worded as follows:

Rouen and Le Havre are directly threatened and, with them, the supply route to Paris and to half the army. Thank you for your effort, but the situation demands an even stronger one. For one thing, the fighter squadrons should be based in France so that they can give of their best …

The nine fighter squadrons that you are good enough to promise us amount to only a quarter of the thirty-nine fighter squadrons that, according to your statements at the last meeting of the Supreme War Council, you had at your disposal on May 31st.

It is my duty to ask that you, like us, should throw all your forces into the battle.

PAUL REYNAUD

But once more Churchill evaded the question:

We are giving you all the support we can in this great battle, short of ruining the capacity of this country to continue the war. We have suffered in today's air fighting very heavy and disproportionate losses, but we shall carry on tomorrow.

W. CHURCHILL

Sensing that this exchange of notes would not produce the desired effect, the French Premier decided to hasten General de Gaulle's departure to London in the hope that he would succeed in modifying Mr Churchill's attitude, especially with regard to the role of the R.A.F.

Before leaving for England General de Gaulle drove to General Weygand's headquarters in the Château de Montry. He was keen to call on the Commander-in-Chief in his new role as Under-Secretary of State for War. A week had elapsed since his previous visit (on June 1st), a week in which there had been developments enough to fill several months.

'You see!' Weygand said to him. 'I was right when I told you the Germans would lose no time in attacking along the Somme! They certainly *have* attacked! They have crossed the river. I cannot stop them.'

'All right,' answered de Gaulle, 'so they have crossed the Somme. And then?'

'And then? It will be the Seine and the Marne ... '

'Yes. And then?'

'And then? It will be all over!'

'What!' cried de Gaulle. 'All over? What about the world? What about the Empire?'

General Weygand laughed despairingly.

While this quarrel was going on in the military sphere, differences of opinion were beginning to show in government circles. Some ministers still supported the idea of fighting to the end; others were more in favour of signing a peace treaty. The discussion led M. Camille Chautemps, the Deputy Premier, to confess to M. Baudouin that he now saw little hope of a successful outcome to the fighting.

'We must put an end to it,' he said. 'It is pointless and we must prevent the spread of destruction throughout the country. Marshal Pétain understands the position best.'

In Italy general mobilization was in full swing. The country was now fully prepared for war. Ciano records:

Mussolini read me the text of the speech that he is to deliver at 6 p.m. on Monday, when the whole nation will have been told to listen in. It is an appeal to the people, phrased in his most classical style and briefly setting forth the reasons for our intervention.

271

JUNE 9TH

Von Bock's Group was now advancing four armies abreast: the 4th Army (von Kluge), the 18th Army (von Küchler), the 6th Army (von Reichenau) and the 9th Army (Strauss), supported by the 5th and 7th Panzer Divisions of Hoth's Armoured Corps. Fully exploiting its successes of the day before, it was beginning a dual manoeuvre to outflank Paris:

(*a*)   westwards, towards the Lower Seine;
(*b*)   eastwards, towards the Marne in the region of Château-Thierry.

In the early morning Hoth's Armoured Corps reached Rouen; farther up river von Manstein's Army Corps was in sight of Les Andelys and Vernon, and sweeping towards the latter.

The western portion of Altmayer's 10th Army was withdrawing as swiftly as possible towards Yvetot and the Lower Seine. Rommel was ordered to thrust towards the coast so as to bar the way to Le Havre and encircle these units.

The eastern portion of the 10th Army managed to re-establish itself along the lower reaches of the Oise, where it would amalgamate with Héring's Army.

Farther east things were going particularly badly with Frère's 7th Army, which was pulling back to the Oise between Compiègne and Chantilly. The river had to be crossed in very difficult conditions. Things went fairly smoothly during the morning, but at 6 p.m. Sainte-Maxence bridge was bombed and blown up. At 8 p.m. Verberie bridge was likewise blown up, before any units had crossed it. This left only the suspension bridge at Lacroix-Saint-Ouen, which was jammed with convoys, the railway bridge and a foot-bridge at Pont-Sainte-Maxence.

By late evening the French were under ever-increasing pressure along the river. Losses were severe. The 1st and 24th Army Corps had to abandon much of their equipment on the west bank. By the time they reached the east bank their numbers were substantially reduced.

But, however important these incidents might be, the main event of

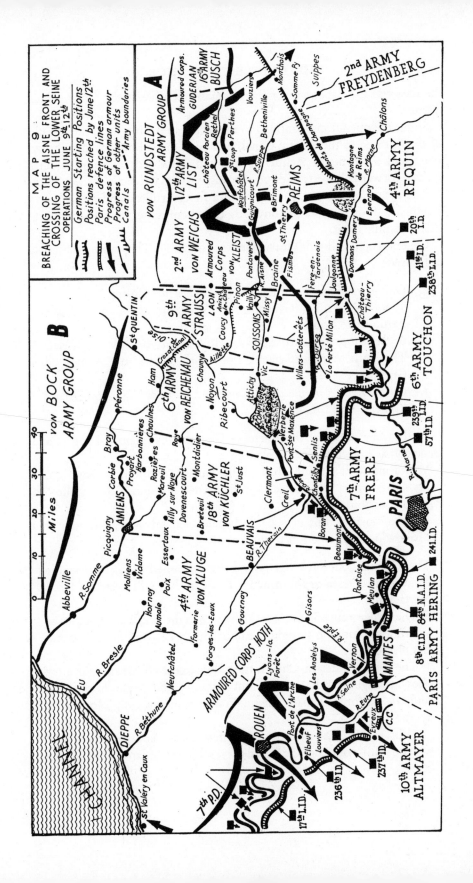

MAP 9

BREACHING OF THE AISNE FRONT AND
CROSSING OF THE LOWER SEINE
OPERATIONS JUNE 9th-12th

German Starting Positions
Positions reached by June 12th
Paris defence lines
Progress of German armour
Progress of other units
Canals
Army boundaries

the day was the expansion of the German offensive in the Champagne district.

So far the operations, confined to the sector stretching from the mouth of the Somme to the Ailette Canal, had been carried out exclusively by von Bock's Group of Armies. Now von Rundstedt's Group in turn moved forward all the way down the Aisne to the left bank of the Meuse.

The action began at 3.30 a.m. with a fierce artillery and aerial bombardment. From 5.30 a.m. onwards the enemy was attacking along a hundred-mile front.

General von Rundstedt's forces were considerable. They were positioned as follows:

1. *On the left, from east of Laon to Neufchâtel-sur-Aisne:*
   The 2nd Army (General von Weichs) with von Kleist's Armoured Group.

2. *In the centre, from Neufchâtel-sur-Aisne to the Aisne–Meuse Canal:*
   The 12th Army (General List) with Guderian's Armoured Group.

3. *On the right, from the Aisne Canal to Montmédy:* The 16th Army (General von Busch).

At the very outset of this offensive Guderian had named Langres and Besançon as objectives for his armour.

Von Rundstedt's troops had eight Panzer divisions — about 2,000 tanks — to support their attack on the French positions held by the 6th Army (Touchon) and the 4th Army (Réquin).

On the morning this new battle began, General Weygand addressed the following proclamation to his troops:

The German offensive has now been unleashed along the whole front, from the sea to Montmédy. Tomorrow it will stretch as far as Switzerland.

The order remains for every man to fight without thought of withdrawal, looking straight ahead of him, wherever the Command has placed him.

The Commander-in-Chief is fully alive to the efforts and gallantry shown, magnificently and without pause, by the armies in the field and the air force. I thank them. France demands even more from them.

Officers, N.C.O.s and men, the safety of our country requires of you not only your courage but all the resolution, initiative and fighting spirit of which I know you are capable. The enemy will soon reach the end of his effort. We are on the last stretch. Hold on!

But the enemy, attacking with fresh troops, lost no time in crossing the Aisne and forming bridge-heads on the south bank. His main effort was directed against Château-Porcien and by afternoon he was within easy reach of Saint-Loup. Farther westwards he succeeded in establishing bridge-heads at Guignicourt and Pontavert. The Germans were gaining ground particularly rapidly in the Soissons sector.

That evening G.H.Q. left La Ferté-sous-Jouarre for Briare. In view of the worsening situation General Weygand sent the following note to M. Reynaud:

> Should the Prime Minister have decided, in principle, on evacuating the authorities from Paris, it is the Commander-in-Chief's duty to inform him that in view of the military situation he considers it advisable to proceed with this evacuation, though not in the case of ministers whose presence in the capital till the last moment the Prime Minister may regard as indispensable.
>
> WEYGAND

POLITICAL SITUATION

Early in the morning a plane took General de Gaulle to London. It was Sunday. The British capital looked calm, indifferent almost. The streets and parks with their placid pedestrians, the long queues outside the cinemas, the streams of cars, the liveried commissionaires in the doorways of clubs and hotels: these were not part of the wartime world. It was strikingly obvious that the bulk of the population was oblivious to the gravity of events in France: it was all happening too quickly for them. Clearly, the British still regarded the Channel as a very broad stretch of sea.

De Gaulle was received by Churchill at 10 Downing Street. It was the first time the pair had met. De Gaulle writes:

> The impression that he made on me strengthened my conviction that under such a fighter Great Britain would certainly not falter. Mr Churchill struck me as being up to the toughest task, so long as it were a grand one. The assurance of his judgment, the breadth of his culture, the knowledge that he had of most of the topics, nations and men involved, in fine his passion for the problems associated with

war, were amply displayed. Above all, he was by his very nature built for acting, risking and playing the part in a very forthright and unreserved manner. Such were my first impressions.

What followed merely confirmed them by revealing, in addition, Mr Churchill's peculiar eloquence and the use he knew how to make of it. Whatever his audience — a crowd, an assembly, a council, even a solitary companion — the original, poetic and moving flow of his ideas, arguments and sentiments gained him an almost infallible ascendancy in the dramatic climate in which the poor world was gasping. As an experienced politician, he employed this angelic and diabolical gift alike to stir the sluggish English dough and to fire the imaginations of foreigners. The very humour with which he flavoured his words and gestures and the way in which he used charm at one moment and anger at another made one aware of the degree to which he was master of the terrible game in which he was engaged ...

De Gaulle began by delivering the message with which Reynaud had entrusted him, namely that the French government was determined to go on fighting whatever happened — from its Empire, if need be. Churchill showed great satisfaction with the news.

Then the Under-Secretary of State for War broached the problem of British air support:

Since the evacuation of the British army at Dunkirk, the Royal Air Force had been making only an episodic contribution to the battle. Furthermore, with the exception of a fighter group that was still sharing the fortunes of our own air force,[1] the British squadrons, being based in Great Britain, were too far away to benefit a front that was constantly shifting southwards. My pressing demand that at least part of Britain's air support should be moved to the airfields south of the Loire met with a categorical refusal from Mr Churchill.

Churchill categorically refused to provide France with the support of the bulk of the British air force, thus revealing that he no longer believed in the possibility of a military recovery in Europe.

De Gaulle let the matter drop, telling the Prime Minister that he was quite right to hold on to his air forces: Great Britain could take no other decision.

[1] De Gaulle is here referring to the squadrons that had been refuelling in Rouen and that had been recalled to Britain the day before.

De Gaulle and Churchill then moved on to the problem of land forces. The Prime Minister promised to send over a Canadian division and to keep the 51st in France, together with the remnants of the Mechanized Brigade, which was still fighting.[1] But he stated that he could not give even an approximate indication of when the B.E.F., which had just escaped destruction in Belgium, would be capable of returning to the battle.

'Thus,' writes de Gaulle, 'unified strategy by London and Paris was practically at an end.'

After this interview he went to the War Office, where he had a talk with Anthony Eden. Then he successively saw A. V. Alexander, the First Lord of the Admiralty, Sir Archibald Sinclair, the Air Minister, and General Sir John Dill, Chief of the Imperial General Staff. To these he outlined the plan that M. Reynaud had asked him to prepare in collaboration with Colonel de Villelume, whereby 500,000 men would be shipped to North Africa, explaining that France needed the Royal Navy's support in the operation. But the heads of the British Admiralty were very guarded.

In the evening de Gaulle flew back to France. He landed at Le Bourget, which had just been bombed again.

In Rome it was considered that the German advance would settle the battle once and for all.

M. François-Poncet, the French ambassador, called to take his leave of the Italian Minister for Foreign Affairs. 'He is sad and depressed,' wrote Ciano. 'Personally he would favour a separate peace, but he does not know what his government's intentions are.'

Between 9 and 10 p.m. there was a Cabinet meeting in the Elysée Palace. General Weygand had been summoned to it.

The Commander-in-Chief outlined the military situation. He explained that the Germans had reached the Somme below Paris and that a new and powerful offensive had just been launched in the Champagne region. Thus the capital was immediately threatened from west, east and north. Paul Reynaud then reported on the political situation in the light of the latest telegrams from M. François-Poncet. The Cabinet was flabbergasted to learn that Italy's entry into the war was now only a matter of hours away.

In closing, M. Paul Reynaud hinted that the government should prepare to leave Paris. It was planned that the evacuation was to be carried out in two phases. But M. Yvon Delbos, whose name figured among those

---

[1] These units were to be evacuated from Le Havre on June 12th and 13th, so that they should not be taken prisoner by Rommel's Panzer Division.

to leave in the first phase, protested. There could be no question, he said, of dividing ministers into two categories. Those who were to go on ahead feared that charges of cowardice might be levelled against them. Those who were to stay behind were afraid that they might be suspected of wishing to bargain with the enemy.

The argument became embroiled. When President Lebrun brought the meeting to a close, agreement had still not been reached.

JUNE 10TH

————— ✦✦✦ —————

In compliance with orders received the night before, the 7th Panzer Division got ready to strike towards the Channel.

At 5 a.m. Rommel wrote to his wife:

Soon we shall reach the sea between the Somme and the Seine. I am in excellent shape, though always on the go. Our successes are extraordinary and it seems inevitable that the other side will crack soon. We had never imagined that the war in the west would turn out like this.

At 7.30 a.m. Rommel drove to Barentin, the rallying-point for his division. At 9.30 a.m., after refuelling, it moved towards Yvetot.[1] Rommel writes:

At 10.30 a.m., when the Panzer regiment came in sight of Yvetot, I launched the reconnaissance battalion against the cross-roads two miles west of Ourville, the regiment following close behind along the same road. I posted my signals team immediately behind the first tanks. All the other units in the division were ordered by radio to advance rapidly. There were now two columns moving along the road, occasionally abreast, the tanks on the left and the reconnaissance battalion on the right. Wherever the lie of the land permitted, the tanks drove along beside the road. The entire division was heading for the sea at an average speed of 25–40 m.p.h.

Shortly afterwards the division ran into the rearguard of the French 31st Division, due to embark at Fécamp that afternoon. There was a sprinkling of British among them. This column was soon broken ... Accompanied by my signals team, I set out ahead of the regiment via Les Petites Dalles (ten miles east of Fécamp and six miles west of Veulettes), heading for the coast.

The sight of the sea, lined with cliffs on either side, enraptured us — as did the thought of reaching the French coast-line. We dismounted

1 See sketch on p. 245.

and walked across the shingly beach to the water's edge till the waves were breaking over our boots. Several dispatch-riders in long raincoats walked on in this way till the water came up to their knees. I had to call them back. Behind us Colonel Rothenburg, arriving in his staff car, drove down the bank and on as far as the water. We had fulfilled our mission and barred the enemy's way to Le Havre and Fécamp.

In the afternoon the division captured Fécamp, after silencing the coastal batteries and shelling some Allied warships that were lying offshore: several of them were hit. The armoured division then drove down the coast towards Tourville, arriving there at 10 p.m. Then Rommel returned to Veulettes, where he had set up his divisional headquarters. He got back there at 3 a.m., having covered sixty miles since leaving Barentin.

But however spectacular this dash, it was by no means the most dramatic event of the day. For the battle's centre of gravity no longer lay in the Lower Seine area, but in Champagne, where von Rundstedt's Army Group had returned to the attack, with even greater intensity, at 6.30 a.m.

In the early hours an extremely powerful Panzer force belonging to Guderian's Armoured Group poured out of the Château-Porcien–Rethel front and swept beyond the Retourne, while another column, setting out from the Attigny area, lost no time in reaching Vouziers. In the Champagne plain, devoid of natural obstacles, the tanks manoeuvred at will and it seemed as though nothing could now impede their advance.

Meanwhile Buisson's Group, consisting of the 3rd Armoured Division, the 7th Light Mechanized Division and the 3rd Mechanized Infantry Division, was ordered to counter-attack towards Château-Porcien, on the flank of the enemy pocket. The 3rd Armoured Division and the 7th Light Mechanized Division had moved up overnight. But the 3rd Motorized Infantry Division had been left a long way behind, for it was having to cover the distance on foot. It was to arrive too late to play any part in the counter-attack.

In the morning the tank units — heavily reduced in strength, especially now that the 3rd Armoured Division had donated a battalion of tanks to the 7th Light Mechanized Division — mustered at their starting base and vainly marked time in anticipation of the preliminary bombardment. This did not take place. The surprise element was lost, for in the meantime the units had been spotted by the Luftwaffe. The Germans thus had time to set up a formidable anti-tank defence and to advance a powerful force of heavy tanks beyond the Retourne.

When the attack was finally launched in the afternoon, the fighting was very fierce, costly on both sides but hopelessly unequal. After an initial success the French units were beaten back and dispersed. 'Here, as at Dinant and Sedan,' writes General Roton, 'our large mechanized units were not given the opportunity to make full use of their shock-potential.'

While these operations were going on in the 4th Army Sector, Touchon's 6th Army was also in a critical position. The Ourcq front, held by exhausted divisions, had been forced by a massive tank attack, and the enemy spear-head had reached the Marne at Château-Thierry and Jaulgonne. This advance had compelled the 6th Army to disengage.

Disengagement of the 6th Army meant withdrawal for the 4th, which was left very much 'in the air' south of the Aisne. The French High Command was thereby faced with a really intricate problem. To resolve it, General Georges placed the 6th Army under the orders of the No. 4 Group of Armies (Huntziger). In his Personal and Secret Instruction No. 115 he specified the manoeuvre with which the two armies were to link up:

> The 6th Army will block the Fismes–Rheims road as long as possible to allow the left of the 4th Army to dig in along the Saint-Thierry–Brimont range (in front of Rheims).
>
> On the Marne, the 4th Group of Armies will have to re-establish itself with its left flank at Damery bridge.

POLITICAL SITUATION

Loyal to his principle of 'asking the maximum from the troops but being frank with the government', General Weygand sent a further note to M. Reynaud:

VERY SECRET

No. 1501 — 3rd B/FT.   *June 10th, 1940, 10 a.m.*

The note addressed to the Prime Minister on May 29th made clear to the government the conditions in which the anticipated battle was going to be fought.

This battle began on June 5th. Our armies are fighting heroically. They are inflicting considerable losses on the enemy. But our shortage of divisions leaves no room for reliefs. Fatigue, lack of sleep and losses are diminishing their power of resistance.

On the morning of the sixth day of battle I have to record that the enemy's attacks are forcing more and more substantial withdrawals upon us. Every day the enemy is extending his offensive farther eastwards. Thanks to the number of fresh units at his disposal, he can give even more scope to his ventures, which already extend along a front reaching from the Channel to the Argonne.

At one point along this front German armoured units have succeeded, by swiftly exploiting a partial success, in splitting the forces of our left-hand army into two and seriously threatening the Lower Seine.

Our armies are re-establishing themselves along the front Lower Seine–Paris security position–Marne, the last line along which we can hope to offer effective resistance.

I concluded my note of May 29th by pointing out that 'there might come a time whereafter, for all her determination, France would find herself unable to continue a militarily effective struggle to protect her soil.' I added that 'this moment would be marked by the decisive break-through of the defence positions along which the French armies have been ordered to fight without thought of retreat.'

I am far from having lost all hope of halting the enemy, as the order I issued yesterday shows. Our armies are fighting and their movements are still co-ordinated.

But the events of the past two days of battle make it my duty to warn the Prime Minister that the final breaking of our lines of defence may occur at any moment.

Should the enemy manage to seize the Lower Seine crossings and outflank the Paris area from the south; should he succeed in making another deep armoured thrust in the Champagne region; or should our divisions, tired out and diminished by losses, be powerless, under the pressure of an enemy three times stronger, to re-establish themselves solidly along the line Lower Seine–Paris position–Marne: then our armies would go on fighting till their supplies and strength were exhausted. But their disruption would be merely a matter of time.

WEYGAND

At 10.30 a.m. the War Committee met at the War Ministry in the Rue Saint-Dominique. It was attended by M. Paul Reynaud, the three service ministers, Louis Marin, Camille Chautemps, Georges Mandel, Georges Monnet, the Under-Secretaries of State and M. Paul Baudouin. General de Gaulle was present for the first time.

Commenting on the note that he had just delivered to the Premier, General Weygand expressed the fear that Paris might be outflanked from the west and south.

Reynaud pointed out that the note drew no positive conclusions. In reply to this, Paul Baudouin suggested that if the Marshal were present he would insist that conditions for an armistice should be looked into without delay, first with Britain and then with Germany.

'The situation is deteriorating day by day,' said Baudouin.

'If the situation is deteriorating, it is because we are allowing it to deteriorate,' declared General de Gaulle, stung by the reading of General Weygand's note.

'What suggestion have you to offer?' countered General Weygand.

'It isn't for me to offer any suggestions,' answered de Gaulle.

'Then tell these gentlemen about your trip to London,' Reynaud suggested, to smooth things over.

De Gaulle then revealed that he had seen Churchill, but that the British categorically refused to strip their island of fighter cover by basing their planes in France. As for land forces, they were willing to maintain those that were still in Europe; but they would send no more 'till they could be supported by the French air force'. This amounted to saying that it was impossible to set a date on such a move.

This statement, as may be imagined, did little to comfort the ministers present. Someone expressed anxiety about the fate of the capital. Reynaud replied that the threat to Paris was becoming greater all the time. There could now be no doubt as to the government's need to retire to Tours. Last night's Cabinet meeting had been unable to agree on a plan of evacuation. The Premier suggested that another meeting be held that afternoon to determine the circumstances of the departure. The suggestion was adopted unanimously and the War Committee adjourned.

At 4 p.m. M. François-Poncet rang M. Reynaud from Rome to inform him that Italy had declared war on France and Great Britain.

'I saw M. François-Poncet first,' wrote Ciano. 'He endeavoured to hide his emotion. I said to him: "You have probably realized why I have sent for you." He replied: "I am not very bright, but this time I have." But he smiled only momentarily. After listening to the declaration of war he replied: "This is stabbing a man who is already down ... "

'Sir Percy Loraine was more calm and collected. He listened to my communication without batting an eyelid or losing colour. He confined himself to making a note of the exact wording that I had used, and asked whether he was to regard it as notice of intention or as the real declaration of war. On receiving confirmation that it was the declaration itself, he took his leave in a courteous and dignified manner ... '

Shortly afterwards, Mussolini delivered the following speech from the balcony of the Palazzo Venezia:

Fighters of the land, the sea and the air, Blackshirts of the Legions and the Revolution, men and women of Italy, the Empire and the kingdom of Albania: Listen!

The hour marked out by destiny is sounding in the sky of our country: the hour of irrevocable decisions.

The declaration of war has already been notified to the ambassadors of Great Britain and France.

We are entering the lists against the plutocratic and reactionary democracies of the West which have hindered the advance and often threatened the very existence of the Italian people.

... Today we are determined to face all the risks and sacrifices of war. A nation is not truly great if it does not regard its undertakings as sacred and if it recoils from those supreme trials that decide the course of history.

If we are taking up arms, it is to settle — after settling the problem of land frontiers — the problem of sea frontiers.

We mean to shake off the territorial and military shackles strangling us in our sea, for a race of 45,000,000 is not truly free if it has not the freedom of the oceans.

This titanic struggle is only a phase in the logical development of our revolution. It is the struggle of the poor large races against the exploiters who are fiercely holding on to all the wealth and gold in the world.

It is the struggle of the fecund and poor races against the sterile races of the west. It is the perennial struggle of two currents of thought.

Now that the die is cast and that we have burnt our boats, I solemnly declare that Italy has no intention of dragging other races — her neighbours on land or sea — into the conflict. Let Switzerland, Yugoslavia, Greece, Turkey and Egypt take note of my words. It rests with them, and solely with them, whether or not these words are strictly borne out by events.

Italians! At a memorable meeting — in Berlin — I said that, according to the laws of Fascist morality, when one has a friend one stands by him to the end.

That is what we have done. And that is what we are going to do with Germany, her people and her victorious armies.

... We have only one watchword. It is clear-cut and binds everyone from the Alps to the Indian Ocean: *conquer*.

And conquer we shall, to procure at last a long period of peace with justice for Italy, Europe and the world.

People of Italy, to arms! Show your tenacity, your courage and your worth!

At the same hour the Spanish government decided to move its armed forces into Tangier, thus bringing the international administration of the zone to an end.

King Haakon and his government left Norway, which was now completely overrun, and sought refuge in London.

At 5 p.m. there was a final Cabinet meeting in the Elysée Palace. This time there were no arguments: all ministers were in favour of leaving.

As soon as the meeting was over, M. Reynaud returned to the Rue Saint-Dominique. Almost at once the United States ambassador, Mr Bullitt, was ushered in. Had America at last made up her mind to intervene? Alas, no. Mr Bullitt was merely calling to say goodbye. He would not be accompanying the government in its exodus; he was staying in Paris to protect American nationals and property.

Clearly disappointed, M. Reynaud handed him the following note for President Roosevelt:

Mr President,

For six days and six nights our divisions have been fighting, without an hour's respite, against an army overwhelmingly superior in numbers and equipment. Today the enemy is almost at the gates of Paris.

We shall fight in front of Paris, we shall fight at the rear of Paris, we shall ensconce ourselves in one of our provinces and, if we are driven out of it, we shall go to North Africa and, if need be, to our American possessions.

Part of the government has already left Paris. I myself am on the point of joining the armies. It will be to intensify the struggle with all our remaining forces, not to abandon it ...

Even as I write to you, another dictatorship has struck France in the back. A further frontier is threatened. A naval war is about to start.

You responded generously to the appeal that I sent across the

Atlantic some days ago. Today, June 10th, 1940, it is my duty to ask you for further and still more substantial assistance ...

I am confident in the solidarity of the American people in this vital struggle that the Allies are waging, not only for their own safety but for the safety of American democracy.

PAUL REYNAUD

At 7.30 p.m. M. Reynaud broadcast the following speech to the French people:

We are in the sixth day of the greatest battle in history. The conflagration started along the Somme. It has spread to the Meuse ... Nothing will weaken our will to fight for our land and our liberty.

The trials ahead of us are severe; we are ready for them; our heads will not be bowed.

Signor Mussolini has chosen this moment to declare war on us. How can this action be judged? France has nothing to say. The world looking on will judge ...

In the course of her long and glorious history, France has been through worse trials. At such times she has always astonished the world. France cannot die!

At about 8 p.m. (French time) President Roosevelt, addressing the University of Virginia in Charlottesville, declared:

On this tenth day of June 1940 the hand that held the dagger has stuck it into the back of his neighbour.

On this tenth day of June 1940 ... we send forward our prayers and our hopes to those beyond the seas who are maintaining with magnificent valour their battle for freedom.

But time was passing. The hour fixed for the government's departure was drawing near.

Finally the ministers drove off. For all their attempts to keep up appearances, their nocturnal departure looked very like a bolt. In the last-minute confusion nobody informed General Héring, Military Governor of Paris, of this important decision.

At 11 p.m. an official communiqué broadcast over the radio informed the population:

The government is compelled to leave the capital for imperative military reasons. The Prime Minister is on his way to the armies.

This laconic announcement was prefaced and followed by the French Radio's new call-sign: '*Aux armes, citoyens!*'

Before midnight the ministerial convoys drove out of Paris through the Porte de Châtillon. The car containing M. Reynaud and General de Gaulle left at midnight. It reached Orléans at daybreak after a slow and arduous journey down the cluttered highway.

As soon as the ministers had gone, the population of Paris came streaming after them. De Gaulle recalls that:

Cars buffeted each other amid the oaths of tyro drivers. The villages were already 'fortified', retiring into their shells like towns in the Middle Ages. In front of the anti-tank wall, lined with ancient carts and broken-down cars, drivers and passengers were asked for their papers. A stationary line of fugitives stretched far into the distance. But suddenly a convoy of luxurious, white-tyred American cars came sweeping along the road, with militiamen on the running-boards and motor-cyclists surrounding the procession: it was the Corps Diplomatique on its way to the châteaux of Touraine.

JUNE 11TH

While the convoy of ministerial cars drove towards the Loire, which it was to reach in the early hours of the morning, General Héring, the Military Governor of Paris, summoned the Prefects of the Seine and of Police to notify them that they were now under his command, and to inform them that 'the capital will be defended to the last'.

But General Héring's task was too much for one man. It entailed:

1. Commanding the Paris Army, which consisted in the main of units from the 7th and 10th Armies, though to these had now been added a few units that had not yet been employed in battle and that formed a shield north of the capital, stretching from Pontoise to the Ourcq and passing through Creil and La Ferté-Milon;

2. Maintaining law and order within the capital, and the defence of the city proper.

So he dispatched General de Lanurien to General Weygand's G.H.Q. in Briare, to point out that he 'could not devote himself to the organization and command of an improvised army, which might have to pull out at any moment and whose left flank was seriously threatened, and at the same time retain responsibility for the military government of Paris'.

Along the Channel coast, north of the mouth of the Seine, events were taking a disastrous turn.

The western portion of Altmayer's 10th Army, whose southward retreat had been cut off by the swift thrust of Rommel's armour the day before, now had its back to the sea. The Allied forces in this area, under General Ihler, commander of the 9th Army Corps, consisted of elements of the British 51st Division (General Fortune), the 31st and 41st Alpine Infantry Divisions, remnants of the 2nd and 5th Light Cavalry Divisions and part of the 13th Battalion of Chasseurs Alpins, which had been flung into the Battle of France immediately upon its return from Namsos in Norway. Of the 60,000-odd men encircled, only about 20,000 (most of them forward elements of the British 51st Division) were to reach freedom via Le Havre or the ferries across the Lower Seine.[1]

Round about noon the 7th Panzer Division set out from Veulettes with the Panzer Regiment and part of the 6th Fusiliers, and started northwards up the coast towards Saint-Valery-en-Caux. It ran into fairly stiff British resistance near Le Tôt.[2]

Dieppe harbour, which had become useless, had been abandoned without a fight during the hours of darkness. Admiral James, C.-in-C. Portsmouth, and Admiral Platon, commander of the Normandy sectors, were striving to organize a naval evacuation from Saint-Valery-en-Caux.

Here, the units that General Ihler had taken over were forming a square with their backs to the sea, the British in line facing west, the French facing south and east.

But this evacuation was thwarted by the heavy mist, the highly unfavourable geography of the place and the fact that Rommel had very swiftly managed to install heavy guns upon the cliffs; they were battering Saint-Valery harbour and the beaches.

From the cliff-tops, whence his artillery was unleashing all its fury, Rommel had a clear view of the situation in and around Saint-Valery. He could see the British troops moving about among the harbour installations; others, equipped with guns and vehicles, were in the northern part of the town.

The intensive bombardment continued throughout the afternoon. Towards evening Rommel sent truce-bearers, suggesting a surrender timed for 9 p.m. General Ihler refused.

While these disorganized 10th Army units were thus fighting every inch of ground with their backs to the sea, a meeting was being held in the Château du Muguet, General Weygand's residence, six miles from Briare, where G.H.Q. was now being installed. The Commander-in-Chief was examining the position with General Georges.

The news that had reached him during the night and in the early morning was very grave.

In the west the Germans had crossed the Seine at several points, including Elbeuf, Saint-Pierre du Vauvray, Les Andelys and Vernon. The slender barrier that the High Command had tried to form along the Lower Seine was pierced through and through: it had held for less than twenty-four hours.

[1] Having reached Le Havre by a series of forced marches, these elements of General Fortune's division (two motorized brigades) finally sailed for England on the night of June 12th–13th.
[2] See sketch on p. 245.

East of Paris the situation was no less alarming. The German columns that had reached the Ourcq on June 9th were now on the banks of the Marne between Château-Thierry and Jaulgonne. The encirclement of Paris was taking shape.

But the position was most critical of all in the Champagne region. While von Rundstedt's forces were continuing to exert intense pressure along the whole of the 4th Army front and against the left of the 2nd Army, a great mass of tanks, belonging to von Kleist's Armoured Group, had poured towards Rheims. Simultaneously another column, proceeding through Braisne and Fismes, was approaching the town from the west. Caught in this pincer movement, Rheims fell a few hours later.

Still farther east the 1st, 2nd, 6th and 8th Panzer Divisions, as well as the 29th and 20th Motorized Infantry Divisions composing Guderian's Armoured Group, were advancing along a front reaching from the Marne, near Épernay, to the Argonne. This was the start of an exploiting manoeuvre on the grand scale, aimed at the encirclement of the French units in the fortified sector.[1]

To hold the new positions between the sea and Longuyon the French were now left with the equivalent of about thirty standard divisions — *half the number put into line at the start of the battle on June 5th.* And there was no possibility of relief: all reserves had been thrown in.

So much for General Georges's schemes for keeping German armour out of the Champagne region. Secret and Personal Instruction No. 115 had been outstripped by events before ever it could be put into operation.

Generals Weygand and Georges took the view that there were only two possible solutions:

1. Either cling to the fortified position, so long as resources allowed, and pull back the forces round the Montmédy bridge-head, thus forming a pivot on which to manoeuvre;
2. Or else abandon the fortified position and attempt a unified retreat covering the heart of the country.

The advantage of the first solution was that it conserved to the very last a front solidly buttressed by the fortifications of the Maginot Line; but it abandoned almost the whole country to the enemy and left the army with no prospect other than that of capitulating in the east, in the Vosges, or along the Swiss frontier.

The second solution, difficult to put into practice, could only lead to the Allied lines being cut into small pieces. But it afforded a certain

[1] See map no. 10 p. 337.

amount of hope that the bulk of our forces might not have to capitulate.

It was the second solution that was finally adopted. The plan for the manoeuvre, laid down in Personal and Secret Instruction No. 1444/F.T.3, aimed to guarantee the protection of the heart of the country for as long as possible while the required withdrawal was going on, and at the same time to maintain the armies' cohesion.

The Instruction stipulated that if the Lower Seine–Paris position–Marne line were broken, the armies would fall back along the general routes given below:

> *3rd Group of Armies (General Besson):*
> 10th Army: Rouen–Argentan.
> Paris Army: Orléans.
> 7th Army: Paris–Orléans.
> *4th Group of Armies (General Huntziger):*
> 6th Army ⎫
> 4th Army ⎬ Châlons-sur-Marne, Troyes, Nevers.
> 2nd Army ⎭
> *2nd Group of Armies (General Prételat):*
> 3rd Army ⎫
> 5th Army ⎬ Sarrebourg, Épinal, Dijon.
> 8th Army ⎭

'The High Command was not blind to the fact that it would be very hard to maintain contact between the armies during the manoeuvre,' writes Roton. 'It might be possible for the forces in the centre, firmly linked at the outset along the Paris position, to retain cohesion, but the same could not be said for the 10th Army, whose mission would take it farther and farther from the general line of withdrawal.

'For the armies on the right, which would have to compete in speed with the enemy thrust that had started in the Champagne region and was moving south-eastwards, the difficulties would be even greater.'

So General Weygand, alive to the many problems posed by a retreat carried out in such conditions, gave General Georges strict orders to put Personal and Secret Instruction No. 1444 into effect only on receipt of a further communication.

This would become necessary soon enough. For in the evening a weighty mass of armour belonging to Guderian's Group crossed the Suippe at Bétheniville.

This hammer-blow, aimed almost at the centre of its position, compelled the whole of the 4th Group of Armies to retreat southwards. General

Huntziger ordered his army commanders to do everything in their power to dig in along the following line:

6th Army (*Touchon*): along the Marne, from the Ourcq to Damery.
4th Army (*Réquin*): along the line Montagne de Reims–Monts de Champagne–Somme-Py–Monthois.
2nd Army (*Freydenberg*): along the line Grandpré–Dun-sur-Meuse.

Nothing to report on the Alpine front. The R.A.F. carried out a sortie over northern Italy and bombed Turin.

POLITICAL SITUATION

The government temporarily installed itself in Tours and its environs, including Langeais, Azay-le-Rideau, Cangé, Ligueuil and Chissey.
[*Learning that Mr Churchill was coming to take part in a meeting of the Supreme War Council, M. Reynaud believed, falsely, that he had been invited by Weygand. Deeply angered, he asked Huntziger if he would take over from Weygand. Huntziger refused. Churchill was actually coming of his own accord.* — Ed.]
While General de Gaulle was calling on General Huntziger, M. Reynaud, Marshal Pétain and General Weygand were meeting in the Commander-in-Chief's command post in the manor-house at Vaugereau, near Briare.

At 2.15 p.m. General de Lanurien was announced. He brought a message from General Héring concerning the organization of the defence of Paris.

The French Premier and the Marshal took a stroll in the garden. The Commander-in-Chief digested the latest news brought from Paris by General de Lanurien, comparing it with what General Georges had told him about the general situation.

The Germans had crossed the Seine in force below Paris; they were progressing very swiftly along the Marne. Paris would therefore shortly be threatened with double envelopment. To defend Paris in these circumstances would be an empty gesture. It would in no way affect the outcome of operations, but would inflict irreparable losses upon the city, both in human lives and in historical treasures.

After giving long thought to the matter, General Weygand decided to take two important steps:

1. He agreed that General Héring's responsibilities were too onerous and officially transferred some of them to General Dentz. Henceforth General Héring would command the *Paris Army* and go wherever fate took it, while General Dentz, commanding the *Paris Area*, would stay put up to and including the moment when the Germans might enter the city.
2. He decided to declare Paris an 'open city'.

As a result, no demolitions were to be effected and the retreating units were to by-pass the city. Starting from the Nonette, which marked the limit of the Paris position, two successive lines of withdrawal were laid down:

1. Écouen, Gonesse, Aulnay-sous-Bois;
2. Rambouillet Forest, Chevreuse, Juvisy.

The Generalissimo went out into the garden and told the Prime Minister and the Marshal of the decisions that he had just taken. Both remained impassive, voicing — according to Weygand — 'neither objections nor approbations'.

Much has subsequently been written about this decision of the Commander-in-Chief's. 'Abandoning Paris without a fight,' says Pertinax, 'was quite unprecedented. In 1870–1 the war had continued in the provinces only as a result of the capital's heroic resistance. But was Paris to be martyred? So that more French forces might have time to rally in North Africa, were the French to endure the destruction of monuments, memories and stones that to them were the incarnation of their country?' Yes, according to some. But 'General Weygand did not share this view. He settled the matter without consulting anyone.'

Weygand himself has written:

I was led to act as I did by motives that would brook no denial. The fighting at the gates of the capital in 1814 and the siege of 1870 had left no traces save the demolition or burning of a few buildings in the centre or on the outskirts. But in view of the weapons of destruction in use in the last war, fighting on the fringes and in the heart of the town would cause complete havoc. I should not have hesitated to demand the cruellest sacrifices from the Parisians' resolution ... had I thought that such sacrifices might be of any military use; that was not the case. It was primarily to my decision that Paris owes the fact that she has conserved her beauty intact.

293

These decisions were passed to General de Lanurien at about 3 p.m., but General Héring did not hear of them till the following day.

At about 4 p.m. M. Reynaud, Marshal Pétain, General Weygand and General Georges drove to the Château du Muguet, where the Supreme War Council was due to meet.

Identifying himself with General de Gaulle's theories, M. Reynaud raised the question of the 'Breton redoubt'.

'Instead of retreating southwards,' he asked, 'would it not be wiser to muster our forces in the Brittany peninsula, like a hand extended to England and America?'

But the military leaders (this was the first that Georges, at least, had heard of the scheme) saw basic flaws in the idea. Where was France to find enough men to establish a 100-mile front sealing off the enemy when her armies, without the smallest reserves, were already fighting in positions that were stretched to breaking-point? How were her troops, massed in Brittany, to be supplied with food, guns and ammunition?

General Weygand severely criticized these 'airy notions', and defended his plan for a general withdrawal. M. Reynaud remained undecided. He accepted Weygand's view in principle, yet he did not give up the idea of a Breton redoubt. How wonderful it would be if the two could be reconciled!

A confused, fruitless argument followed. Reynaud declared irritably that the military problem was insoluble because it was overshadowed by a political problem of international dimensions: the problem of the agreements binding France to Britain.

'The British government is not aware of our true situation,' said the Prime Minister, 'so we must fight on.'

'It soon will be!' retorted the Commander-in-Chief.

And indeed, Mr Churchill and his advisers were about to land at Briare. The Premier had left London at 2.30 p.m. He was flying over in his personal Flamingo, escorted by a dozen Hurricanes. With him were Anthony Eden, General Sir John Dill, Chief of the Imperial General Staff, General Ismay, General Lund, General Spears and Captain Berkeley, General Ismay's interpreter.

Shortly before leaving, Churchill had called a Cabinet meeting in the course of which Air Marshal Dowding, Commander-in-Chief Fighter Command, had warned ministers that if any more fighter squadrons were sent to France he would not guarantee the security of the British Isles.

The Flamingo and its escort landed at Briare airfield at about 7 p.m.

The French colonel who met them and was to escort them to the Château du Muguet looked very mournful. But Churchill was all smiles.

As soon as they reached the château the British party were shown into the dining-room. Awaiting them were Paul Reynaud, Marshal Pétain, General Weygand, Captain de Margerie, Colonel de Villelume and General de Gaulle, who had just got back from Arcis-sur-Aube.

It was the first time Spears had seen the former commander of the 4th Armoured Division, and he was instantly impressed by his appearance:

A strange-looking man, enormously tall; sitting at the table he dominated everyone else by his height, as he had done when walking into the room. No chin, a long, drooping, elephantine nose over a closely-cut moustache, a shadow over a small mouth whose thick lips tended to protrude as if in a pout before speaking ... That afternoon he had a look of confidence and self-possession which was very appealing. He had, I thought, brought it from Abbeville, where he had fought a successful tank action (the only one). Fresh air had given his sallow skin a healthy colour. His cheeks were almost pink ... I perceived that afternoon what was perhaps the real de Gaulle, or maybe that part of him which might have prevailed had he remained a soldier, straight, direct, even rather brutal.

Reynaud invited Mr Churchill to open the discussion.

The question was, said the latter, how best to carry on with the struggle. His own impression was that as soon as the front was stabilized in France the Germans would turn on England. He hoped so for two reasons. It would give France relief and enable the British to take a fuller and more equal share in the struggle; but above all it would give the R.A.F. the opportunity of smashing the German air power, as he was sure it was capable of doing. A Canadian division was landing at Cherbourg that night. A second division would land about June 20th. If the French army could hold out for a year — till the spring of 1941 — it would once again have 20 to 25 British divisions at its disposal.

Reynaud thanked him for this information, but had difficulty in hiding his irritation at the glaring unawareness of the situation revealed by Churchill's remarks. He then asked the Commander-in-Chief to report on military operations.

General Weygand began by pointing out that the entire strength of the French army had been engaged in the battle ever since May 10th.

'Now,' he continued, 'we do not have a single battalion to call on. On the left-hand side of the front, from Abbeville and Amiens to Rheims, our armies have been fighting for over six days without a moment's rest. At night they try to dig in along new positions. For the past forty-eight hours the attack has been extended eastwards to the Meuse ... The fierceness of the attacks, carried out with a numerical superiority of three to one, has compelled us to pull back to what the Command had considered to be the final lines of defence ... Yesterday's reports make it clear that, in the armies that have been fighting since the start of the battle, the men are literally exhausted, fighting by day, marching at night and dropping with fatigue the moment they reach their new positions. I am bound to admit that all reserves have been used up along the whole of this position. *We are balanced on a razor's edge, not knowing which way we may fall from one moment to another ...*'

The General could not guarantee that the lines would even hold tomorrow. He read out a dispatch that had arrived at 3 p.m. from the Group of Armies covering the area between Rheims and the sea:

... The density of the units is so weak that they now offer merely a thin screen against the enemy's advance. Some divisions are down to three or even two battalions. There are no reserves behind the fighting line. Nothing could illustrate the situation better than the following picture: along the Seine an 85-mile sector is being held by five divisions, two of which consist of only two regiments, plus the remains of the 3rd Light Mechanized Division. Along the Oise two sound infantry divisions, backed by three exhausted divisions, are holding a 20-mile sector. Along the Oise and the Ourcq (a 35-mile sector) there are five infantry divisions, only one of them really up to the mark, backed by the 4th Light Mechanized Division, which has been thrown into battle even though the engines of its vehicles have not been run in. Along the Ourcq and the Marne a 27-mile front is being held by a single two-regiment division and part of the 52nd Division ... Every unit in the French army is fighting unflinchingly. The outcome is in the lap of the gods.

Weygand said he could play no further part in the battle as Commander-in-Chief, since he had no reserves to call on. In conclusion he emphasized that the French army, true to its quality, was not weakening in the slightest; but it was heavily outnumbered in men and equipment.

Mr Eden and Mr Churchill intervened almost in the same breath to remind him that a Canadian division was due to land that night with 72 guns.

'*Messieurs, messieurs!*' Weygand implored them. 'We must face up to the situation that confronts us and bear in mind the conditions in which the battle is being waged! No doubt a number of points along the front have not yet been attacked; but in addition to the operations now in progress, we must expect a German offensive north of Basle, a crossing of the Rhine and a thrust towards Belfort ... So far we still have a balanced, if worn, disposition. If the general disposition is dislocated and split up, it would become impossible to continue a co-ordinated defence of France. Any other statement would conflict with the truth.'

Then, after a pause, he added almost in a whisper: 'If you consider it might help our cause I am ready to stand down ... '

'There is no question of that!' exclaimed Reynaud, waving the suggestion aside.

During the Commander-in-Chief's report, Churchill's gaze had several times rested on de Gaulle. The latter had been listening to Weygand quite imperturbably, smoking one cigarette after another. Not a muscle of his face had moved. Spears writes that Churchill was searching for something he had failed to find in the other French faces, adding: 'The fact that he returned several times to a study of de Gaulle made me think he had detected in him the thing he was looking for.'

Weygand then suggested that, for its further enlightenment, the Council should summon General Georges. Having heard nothing of the discussion, the latter would be able to give his opinion without being influenced by the Generalissimo's exposé.

An officer was sent to fetch General Georges from his headquarters. The Commander-in-Chief of the north-eastern theatre looked ghastly when he entered the room. The picture he drew of the situation fully bore out General Weygand's remarks.

' ... Some divisions are divisions in name only,' he said, 'consisting merely of an infantry regiment and a few guns. No reinforcements are available. But a considerable effort has been made to form further divisions from men undergoing training or returning to the front after recovering from wounds, and these have been used to strengthen the line. Yet the French army is now just a thin screen made up of weak units and tired men with no reserves behind them. *We are literally poised on a tightrope*, for if a powerful enemy thrust occurs at any point whatever, we do not have the resources to meet it. So we are at the mercy of chance.'

General Georges then drew attention to the fact that a German thrust was building up against Châlons and the Argonne, and that the danger was just as great as in the west, for lack of units.

Churchill broke in to remind the meeting of the movement of the British 52nd Division to the Le Mans area[1] and the imminent landing of the Canadian division with strong artillery support. He said he would later be able to send a third and a fourth division, but he must retain a small force in Britain to repel a possible German invasion.

General Georges pointed out that the French armies were now out-numbered three to one, that their losses in armaments had been severe and that the Germans' numerical superiority was increasing daily.

Churchill expressed regret that the British army could not play a bigger part in the Battle of France. It could not be blamed for this. Britain had come out of the Battle of Belgium almost literally stripped, and was now doing everything she could to send maximum reinforcements to France.

M. Reynaud said that German numerical superiority was now greater than ever, since the Allied armies had lost a third of their numbers.

'Never,' commented General Weygand, 'not even during the Battle of Verdun, were major French units so dislocated.'

And Marshal Pétain recalled that at Verdun French divisions had been relieved every three days.

M. Reynaud summed up the situation by emphasizing that the enemy were at the gates of Paris, that the Seine and the Marne had been crossed and that the troops were utterly exhausted. Only the day before, he had been talking to an officer who had spent five sleepless nights in a row. The officer had told him that the Luftwaffe had constantly shown such over-whelming superiority that the infantry got the feeling that it was entirely undefended.

'The only immediate assistance Britain can give us,' said Reynaud, 'is that of her air force.'

The discussion sharpened at once. Mr Churchill reminded his listeners that the British Command was daily doing its utmost to throw more planes into the battle. Between six and eight fighter squadrons flew back and forth from England each day. Then there were Air Marshal Barratt's forces: six bomber and five fighter squadrons.

The British Prime Minister promised that as soon as he got back to London he would see whether this position could be improved. Britain's hesitancy in the matter was dictated not by selfishness, but by the profound conviction that if her fighter defence was broken down she would be unable to continue the war.

Reynaud replied, according to Spears, that 'nothing was less desirable

---

[1] This unit, still being formed, was commanded by Brigadier-General Sir John Laurie. It was subject to the orders of the Commander of the French 10th Army.

than the break-up of the British air force except that of the western front'.

For his part, General Georges declared that there could be no comparison between the effectiveness of squadrons flying over from England and that of units stationed in France. Reynaud supported this, remarking that in the arrival of more planes from Britain lay the only likelihood of tilting the balance.

Mr Churchill replied that Britain's resistance in the air was the consideration most likely to bring the United States into the war, and that it was essential to preserve intact the instrument upon which America's armed intervention might depend.

'No doubt history will say the Battle of France was lost through lack of aircraft,' remarked Reynaud.

'And through lack of tanks,' returned Churchill, 'and through the enemy's numerical superiority.'

'The depressing effect on morale caused by German air superiority, especially by their dive-bombers, must also be taken into account,' said Reynaud.

Mr Eden pointed out that the British could not help in that respect. Possessing no such machines, they could not inflict similar punishment on the Germans.

'Yes, but fighter-planes can drive the bombers off,' replied Reynaud.

Infantry, said Churchill, always felt they were unprotected from the air. Arriving back in England from Dunkirk, British troops had booed the R.A.F. pilots to whose efforts they owed their safety. The men in the line never saw a plane.

M. Reynaud returned to the question of the performance of British fighter-planes, which would, he said, be far superior, if the squadrons were stationed in France. Weygand begged that every available fighter should be sent over to 'play their part in the battle that will seal the fate of both nations'.

'No!' roared Churchill. 'That isn't true!' There was a wider horizon, he said, a vaster field to be considered. Today it was the Battle of France, tomorrow it would be the Battle of Britain; everything that was lost today could be retrieved tomorrow.

'He looked very fierce,' records Spears, 'and it was quite evident that nothing would make him surrender the last air defence of Britain ... There was obvious relief amongst the English, who had been watching him intently and perhaps with some fear that French eloquence and the magnitude of the French disaster, which had so obviously awakened his deepest sympathy, might cause him to give way.'

'We are ever grateful but ever thirsting for more,' said Reynaud.

'We are in desperate straits,' said Weygand, 'which is why any assistance that might be accorded us is truly indispensable. The heads of government and the generals have met to see what exactly would happen in the event of the armies' being dislocated ... Were our present line to be broken, there would be no hope of re-establishing it, since there is nothing behind it. Once this defensive battle is lost I see no way of preventing the total invasion of France, in view of the power and penetration of the German Panzer divisions. If anyone can see a way of achieving victory, let him be appointed! I shall serve him with the same devotion that I am shown by all my colleagues. But if we must think in terms of the total occupation of the country, one is driven to wonder how France could carry on with the war!'

Mr Churchill then asked whether it would not be possible to establish an Atlantic bridge-head — in Brittany, for example.

'I am having the question looked into,' said Reynaud. 'General René Altmayer is studying it on the spot ... '

General Weygand was surprised to hear this and repeated his earlier objections to the scheme. He said the problem presented two difficulties, the first strategic, the other concerning supplies. It was hard to make a last-ditch stand at Point A and at the same time withdraw troops to Point B. Also, 70 per cent of the armies' needs were supplied from the Paris region. Brittany certainly offered the advantage of open communications with Great Britain, but it had neither fortifications nor resources. Everything should be done to hold it, but he did not think it could be long defended, especially since the Luftwaffe would make life very hard for the occupants of such a small area.

But, suggested Churchill (calling Weygand to witness), they could still defend Paris! It was a huge town; they could fight on the outskirts, they could fight in the heart of the city; they could fight in the main squares, in the side-streets, on the corner of every block and at every cross-roads! They could defend it quarter by quarter, street by street, house by house!

His voice swelled, his words flashed, his sentences came tumbling out. 'And,' writes Spears, 'the pageant of history, the lurid glow of burning cities, some as beautiful as Paris, collapsing on garrisons who refused to accept defeat, arose before our eyes. The French perceptibly froze at this.'[1]

---

[1] Churchill's remarks, said Spears, 'led all the French to sit back in their chairs with the tension of a motorist pressing hard on the brakes, save de Gaulle and de Margerie, who was completely absorbed in his work of translating'.

'What you are now saying is meaningless,' replied General Weygand. 'Reducing Paris to ashes will in no way affect the final result.'

Churchill then suggested that if co-ordinated warfare were to become impossible, the French could still carry on guerrilla warfare in various parts of the country. It would harass the enemy and scatter his forces, as France's forces were themselves now scattered, and it might weaken his position a good deal. Perhaps this was the way of gaining the few months' respite that the Allies needed while they were waiting for America to come into the war.

'Oh no!' protested Marshal Pétain. 'The whole country would be destroyed! By the time the United States has made up her mind, guerrilla warfare will have reduced France to ashes!'

'Our towns would certainly have a bad time of it,' said Reynaud.

Mr Churchill emphasized that the alternative was no less appalling. No doubt, he said, it was easy to speak as he was speaking when one represented a country that had not yet suffered and that did not know the horrible pressure now brought to bear on France. But Great Britain would have to be crushed before she resigned the struggle. Should the French army find itself compelled to give up, Britain would fight on in the hope of Hitler's being ruined by his very victories. With her air force and her fleet, the British Empire would be able to hold out for years and subject Europe to the tightest blockade.

But what, in such circumstances, would become of the French fleet? These were nightmarish questions, said Churchill. Whatever happened, Britain would fight on. If she were invaded, if she were to experience all the horrors of war on her own soil, it would make a great impression in the United States ... The war would soon become a war of continents.

'It is possible,' he continued, 'that the Nazis may dominate Europe, but it will be a Europe in revolt, and in the end it is certain that a regime whose victories are in the main due to its machines will collapse. Machines will one day beat machines.'

The meeting ended at 9.30 p.m.

Subsequently Mr Churchill spent a few moments talking privately to General Georges. He asked the General whether the situation was quite as black as it had been painted. He was told that it was.

'The French army's capacity for resistance is running out,' said the General. 'Before long, the signing of an honourable armistice will be the only way out.'

At 10 p.m. the British and French representatives at the Supreme War Council meeting sat down to dinner in the Château du Muguet. During the meal Mr Churchill, trying to be friendly, turned to Marshal Pétain and said:

'Think back! We went through difficult times in 1918 but we got over them. We shall get over these in the same way!'

'In 1918,' the Marshal replied rather coldly, 'I gave you forty divisions to save the British army. Where are the forty British divisions that we would need to save ourselves today?'

Churchill started at this unexpected reply. He turned to de Gaulle, who was sitting next to him, and spoke to him, and him alone, for the rest of the meal. In his *Mémoires* de Gaulle writes: 'Our talk strengthened my confidence in his determination. He himself probably took away the impression that de Gaulle, though empty-handed, was no less resolute.'

'Presently,' recalls Churchill, 'when we left the dinner table and sat with some coffee and brandy, M. Reynaud told me that Marshal Pétain had informed him that it would be necessary for France to seek an armistice and that he had written a paper upon the subject which he wished him to read. "He has not," said Reynaud, "handed it to me yet. He is still ashamed to do it."

'He ought also to have been ashamed to support even tacitly Weygand's demand for our last twenty-five squadrons of fighters, when he had made up his mind that all was lost and that France should give in. Thus we all went unhappily to bed in this disordered château or in the military train a few miles away ...'

JUNE 12TH

———◆•◆•◆———

Trapped against the Channel coast, General Ihler's troops had fought all night under shelling from the German batteries up on the cliffs surrounding Saint-Valery-en-Caux.

At 6.30 a.m. Rommel drove to those sectors along the front where the Chasseurs Alpins had made several attempts to break through. As he drove through the fields he could see his own formations firmly entrenched on all sides.

By noon Saint-Valery was in flames. The German armour came rumbling into the town. The tanks advanced slowly, yard by yard, their guns pointing eastwards, past the lines of vehicles parked on one side of the harbour. Fires were raging on the far side of the town. Military equipment, including a large number of lorries, was piling up on the quays.

The British were surrendering in increasing numbers.

'The town hall and many of the houses round it had been burnt out or were still burning,' wrote Rommel. 'The barricades that the French had erected with guns and lorries had likewise felt the weight of our gun-fire. British and French troops were now pouring into the market place from all sides. There they were formed into columns and promptly marched westwards. Our infantry cleaned up the town, street by street, house by house.'

General Ihler was taken prisoner. He asked to speak to the German commander, and stated that he was prepared to capitulate on behalf of his troops since they had used up all their ammunition.

The German artillery was ordered to cease fire. In the next few hours a dozen generals, including four divisional commanders, were taken prisoner and brought before Rommel. Among them were General Fortune and the commanders of four French divisions. 'We were particularly surprised at the phlegmatic manner in which the British officers accepted their fate,' wrote Rommel. 'The General [Fortune] and his staff officers walked laughingly back and forth outside the house where they had been assembled ... '

Twelve thousand men, including eight thousand British, were driven off in the vehicles of the 7th Panzer Division alone. The total number of prisoners captured at Saint-Valery is put at 46,000. Equipment seized amounted to 58 tanks, 56 guns, 17 anti-aircraft guns, 22 anti-tank guns, 368 machine guns, 3,550 rifles and 1,133 lorries.

At about 8 p.m. Rommel returned to his headquarters in the château at Auberville. That evening he wrote to his wife:

> The battle is over here. One corps commander and four divisional commanders reported to me in Saint-Valery market place. They had been compelled to surrender by my division. Wonderful moments!

It must be pointed out, however, that this success was not wholly due to the activities of the 7th Panzer Division. Rommel had received considerable assistance from the 2nd Motorized Infantry Division in the south and from General von Hartlieb's 5th Panzer Division in the south. Von Hartlieb had attacked in the direction of Veules-les-Roses.

Meanwhile the 5th Panzer Division, forming part of Hoth's Armoured Corps, had progressed beyond Évreux and was now surging towards Dreux and Chartres. Altmayer's 10th Army was all but annihilated and the move to outflank Paris from the south was taking shape.

In the east von Kleist's Panzer divisions were streaming towards Saint-Dizier and Troyes. The troops of von Rundstedt's Army Group had crossed the Marne at Château-Thierry and Châlons, after swamping the Allied defence in the Champagne hills. All French units stationed in and around the fortified sector were threatened with encirclement.

General Weygand therefore instructed General Georges to carry out the order for general withdrawal issued the day before. Details of its execution were set out in General Georges's *Plan de manœuvre* No. 2026 3/OP. The armies were to pull back to the general line Caen–Alençon–Loire (between Tours and Briare)–Le Morvan–Côte d'Or–Dôle–Champagnole–Les Rousses. Under the formidable weight of the whole German army, now surging southwards with little but the Loire to halt its progress, no other solution was possible. The whole front was broken, from the Channel to the Meuse. Only one thing mattered any more: to salvage whatever could be salvaged.

'The orders were straight out of a text-book,' writes Bardies. 'They provided for a withdrawal along five successive lines of retreat – R1, R2, R3, R4, R5 – to be conducted academically with coherent forces and sound communications, the protection of the left flank being assured by mere "mobile holding forces".' This was all very well on paper, but the reality of the battlefield was very different. 'It was a difficult — I would even say a hopeless — undertaking,' General Georges was to declare later. 'Four hundred thousand, possibly five hundred thousand, harassed, weary, unarmed men: that was all that France's might now amounted to.'

Furthermore, General Weygand was very late in deciding on this manoeuvre. Bardies writes:

> The Group of Armies holding the Maginot Line was still intact when it received the order to withdraw at 3 p.m. on June 12th. It was made up of three fine armies — the 3rd (Condé), the 5th (Bourret) and the 8th (Laure) — all full of go and simply longing to fight. But the Group was in a difficult position, for it now formed a pronounced salient within the German lines ... More than a salient, in fact: a horseshoe. The 8th was outflanked from the east; the 3rd and 5th, on the horseshoe bend, were outflanked from the north, north-east and north-west ... Furthermore, if the fifteen or so field units fighting in the sector at the time were capable of manoeuvring, the fortress units were unprepared for a withdrawal. The commander of the Group of Armies was therefore anxious to have as much time as possible to effect the withdrawal and would have preferred to begin it earlier. He had frequently pressed the point with the Commander-in-Chief.
>
> By the time the battle was lost and General Weygand finally ordered the withdrawal, it was too late for the Group to break free: Guderian's armour was already pouring towards Langres.

At the same time as he ordered General Georges to carry out Personal and Secret Instruction No. 1444, General Weygand sent General Héring confirmation of his decision to declare Paris an 'open city' and informed him of the lines of withdrawal that he had determined the day before.[1]

General Héring immediately handed over his responsibilities as military governor of Paris to General Dentz, who assumed them as from 6 p.m. General de Gaulle had left for Rennes at dawn — after a very short night's sleep in the Château du Muguet — to deal with the organization of the 'Breton redoubt'. Steering his way through the columns of refugees heading southwards to the Loire, he somehow covered the 220 miles from Briare to Rennes, where he arrived at about 10 a.m.

[*General de Gaulle described in detail the plans for this enterprise. To hold a front*

[1] See p. 293. 'What General de Lanurien can have got up to that day I do not know,' writes General Weygand. 'On the morning of June 12th General Héring had to ask me for orders that he should have received the night before.' No doubt the delay was due to the crowding of the roads, which made the journey to Paris almost impossible.

of more than 90 miles there would be available three skeleton divisions and some odds and ends. The scheme did not even take account of the time needed for the projected concrete works to dry.—Ed.]

At 6 p.m. or thereabouts, General de Gaulle drove from the headquarters of the 10th Military District to the château at Beauvais, where he and General Colson spent some time working on the plan for shipping young conscripts to North Africa. De Gaulle was not to be deterred by General Noguès's objections or the British Admiralty's refusal to loan France the necessary tonnage.[1]

'Frankly,' writes de Gaulle, 'the scenes that I had witnessed the day before[2] and the isolation in which I was now placed made me fear that defeatism had gained too strong a hold and that the plan would never be put into operation. Yet I was determined to do everything in my power to get the government to adopt it and impose it on the High Command.'

Without delay de Gaulle asked the French Admiralty to examine the problem of shipping 900,000 men and 100,000 tons of equipment from Bordeaux to Casablanca *within forty-five days.*

The French Naval Staff was flabbergasted by these figures. Admiral Darlan writes:

These 900,000 men did not even belong to large units already in formation. They consisted of Poles, new conscripts, transit personnel and technicians. The operation would have required two hundred merchant ships — many more than were docked in the unoccupied home ports and in North Africa. The Admiralty therefore had to assemble, and then refuel, all this shipping. At the same time, both men and equipment had to be taken to Bordeaux by rail. This last problem was by no means the simplest, since the railway lines running from north to south were either cut by the invasion or congested. We did not even know that a large proportion of the 900,000 in question had already fallen into enemy hands.

The naval chiefs fell to wondering 'what master-mind could have dreamed up such a fantastic plan'.

On the Alpine front there was still nothing to report. As a reprisal for the R.A.F.'s bombing of Turin the day before, the Italian air force carried out a series of raids on Toulon, Hyères, Saint-Raphaël, Calvi, Bastia and

---

[1] The British naval authorities had just been told to stand by to evacuate all remaining British elements in France. The Lords of the Admiralty obviously preferred to devote their ships to repatriating their own countrymen rather than transporting French troops to North Africa.

[2] At the Supreme War Council in Briare.

Bizerta. At Toulon and along the coast the formation of the attacking planes was broken by anti-aircraft fire before the bombing began. The Italians' aim was inaccurate and little damage was done.

POLITICAL SITUATION

All was calm in the Château du Muguet, where Churchill had spent the night. Two officers on General Weygand's Staff were breakfasting in the conference room. Suddenly the door burst open.

An apparition which they said resembled an angry Japanese genie, in long, flowing red silk kimono over other similar but white garments, girdled with a white belt of like material, stood there, sparse hair on end, and said with every sign of anger: '*Uh ay ma bain?*'

It was Churchill, who found that the château's facilities left much to be desired. The French officers were dumbfounded. It took them several moments to recover. 'But as usual,' adds Spears, 'he made his meaning perfectly clear even in French, and his needs were attended to.'

It was nearly 8 a.m. when he came downstairs. He was greeted by the British contingent, which had been joined by Air Marshal Barratt and Colonel Woodall. M. Reynaud was awaiting him in the conference room, together with General Weygand, Admiral Darlan, General Vuillemin and General Koeltz. General Georges was absent. Marshal Pétain had sent his excuses.

General Weygand briefly repeated the exposé that he had given the day before, adding items of news that had come in during the night.

Then M. Reynaud returned to the question of aviation. Air Marshal Barratt stated that at the moment he had only 50 to 60 fighters and 70 to 80 bombers fit for operations. Moreover, his bombers were all Battles, better suited for night than for day work.

'What we need,' insisted Reynaud, 'is nine squadrons of fighters based in France.'

Barratt dismissed this out of hand. The project would require additional transport and additional aerodromes. This argument put an end to the discussion of British air support, and Air Marshal Barratt and Colonel Woodall left the meeting.

Churchill again raised the question of the 'Breton redoubt' and the defence of Paris; but the force had gone out of his remarks and the French listened politely but without much attention.

Finally the meeting broke up, without achieving any tangible result. Paul Baudouin afterwards commented that France was asking her ally for only one thing — planes; and these Mr Churchill refused to send, taking the view that it was not for him to sanction sacrifices in support of the faltering French army.

As he was leaving the meeting Churchill took Admiral Darlan aside and said to him: 'Darlan, I hope you will never surrender the fleet.'

'There is no question of doing so,' answered the Admiral. 'It would be contrary to our naval traditions and honour. We shall never hand over to Germany or Italy. Orders to scuttle will be given in the event of danger.'

'If only the United States could hear our appeals,' said Reynaud, 'and understand, before it is too late, how greatly we stand in need of their help!'

Then Churchill turned back to the others and declared solemnly, stressing every word: 'We are in the closest touch with the United States and will continue to impress on their government the gravity of the situation and the urgency of our needs, but there is a matter the importance of which overshadows all others, and which I must put to you. Should there be a fundamental change in the situation I must request you, before coming to a final decision which may govern French action in the second phase of the war, to let the British government know at once. They will come over immediately to meet the French government at any convenient place which you choose to indicate, to discuss the new circumstances with you.'

General Spears records that when he heard these words it dawned on him for the first time that 'we were within sight of a cross-roads at which the destinies of the two nations might divide.'

Churchill sat deep in meditation throughout the flight home. Finally his thoughts resolved themselves into a definite opinion. Since a cessation of hostilities on the French front was now a distinct possibility, he decided that 'we must now concentrate our main efforts on the defence of our Island.'

General Spears returned to the hall of the château, where he had a long talk with General Georges who had just arrived from his command post. Georges did not disguise the fact that the end was near and that the army's powers of resistance were nearly exhausted:

The scenes he conjured up became as living as if I had witnessed them myself; they took shape in my mind as the continuation of events I had myself witnessed in the last war ... But Georges described battle scenes worse than anything I had witnessed. The shooting from the air of all horse transport, the concentrated effort of the remnants of a whole division to man-haul three or four guns by night to a new position, the attempt to dig-in in readiness for the battle that must last the whole long June day, and so the next night and the night after that ...

Soon Marshal Pétain arrived. He seemed to be in the grip of some deep emotion, for he had much more to say for himself than usual.

He told Spears that it was 'murder to keep the army fighting on in present conditions'.

'An armistice is inevitable,' he said, 'and it is sheer pusillanimity to shirk the issue. Whilst ministers hesitate and think of their reputations, soldiers are being killed and the land of France is being ruined. We must pay now, and pay dearly, for the anarchy we have indulged in for so long. Where now are the deputies who sought popularity by voting against any measure of rearmament? And the *Front Populaire*, where are its leaders now that the poor deluded chaps who went about with clenched fists have nothing but clenched fists to shake at the German tanks?'

'But *Monsieur le Maréchal*,' Spears objected. '... You know we shall fight on. You must fight on in Africa or elsewhere until we have developed our strength and we can make a *retour offensif* together.'

'Africa?' said Pétain. 'What is the use of sending recruits to Africa, as Reynaud wishes? There are no rifles there to arm them with. In any case, the disorganization of the Ministry of War is such that they could never get the men to the harbours, still less to the sea, and — if they could — Italian submarines would undoubtedly drown them.'

Spears continued obstinately: 'You cannot leave us to fight on alone in what will still be our common struggle.'

'You have left us to fight alone,' said Pétain, and there was an edge of subdued anger to his words.

A few moments later the Marshal said that as France could not continue the struggle, wisdom dictated that England too should seek peace, for she certainly could not carry on alone. 'You have no army,' he went on. 'What could you achieve where the French army has failed?'

'But you heard the Prime Minister?' asked Spears.

'Words are very fine,' answered Pétain, 'but you cannot beat Hitler with words. You are cruelly mistaken if you think you can hold out alone for more than a month!'

Then, in the tone — writes Spears — of putting someone in his place for being insufferably presumptuous, he added: 'It is sheer folly to suppose that you will succeed where the French army has failed.'

At 7.45 p.m. a Cabinet meeting was held in the Château de Cange on the outskirts of Tours. M. Albert Lebrun presided.

M. Reynaud arrived with the intention of urging the government to retire to Quimper, within the Breton redoubt, pending a further move to London or North Africa.

General Weygand arrived with the no less fixed intention of asking the government to conclude an armistice. He had wanted to broach the subject at the Supreme War Council meeting the evening before. Reynaud had stopped him, pointing out that this was the government's concern, not the Commander-in-Chief's. Weygand had given way, so as not to make a scene in front of the British. This time he was determined to speak his mind whether others liked it or not.

So the two conflicting lines of thought were to be brought violently into conflict. 'It was a painfully embroiled meeting,' records Baudouin. 'Minds clashed and never achieved harmony.'

When asked for his opinions on the military situation General Weygand reminded ministers of his notes of May 29th and June 10th and deplored the fact that his warnings had gone unheeded. Only a cease-fire, he asserted, could now save the country from utter disorder.

'We can no longer put off seeking an armistice,' he declared. 'Seek one now while there is still time, while our forces still have a certain cohesion. It is a question of keeping order among the civilians, as well as among the troops. Do not forget that five or six million civilians have been pouring southwards for weeks past. The Belgians set off the people in the north, the people in the north set off those in the Ile-de-France and Normandy, and the people in central France followed suit; and so now there are five or six million of them pouring southwards in terrible chaos, starting to mingle with the troops, with nothing to eat or drink.

'I do not enjoy telling you these things, Messieurs! Remember that it was I who in Rethondes, on November 11th, 1918, read out the conditions imposed on Germany by Marshal Foch, in the name of the victorious Allies. This is the most bitter moment in my life. It is time for another armistice. It is our turn to seek one from the enemy. I could order the armies to fight to the finish in a hopeless cause. It would be easy for me to give that order. But I must listen to the voice of duty. Today France can inquire into the conditions for an armistice without blushing. I can proudly say that I have fought a battle on the Somme that has shown the French army in its true colours again. It has saved its honour in the eyes of the world, and to come to terms will now be no disgrace for it.'

But only Marshal Pétain and two other ministers supported him. M. Reynaud and several members of the government registered their disapproval in what amounted to full-length speeches. M. Reynaud dwelt on the irrevocable nature of the agreements that he had signed with Britain on France's behalf. He stressed the compulsion to stand by an undertaking.

'France,' he repeated, 'can neither conclude a separate peace nor open negotiations with a view to an armistice without Britain's consent. To act in any other way would be to forfeit our honour.'

Knowing that every hour brought further needless death and destruction, Weygand spoke out fiercely against this view:

'Honour, *messieurs?*' he cried. 'There is far more honour in those who are fighting than in those who are merely sitting back and watching!'

The atmosphere was growing increasingly stormy.

'What will the Anglo-Saxon world think if we act in this way?' asked M. Reynaud. 'France is an Empire; if France is lost, the Empire will save her. Her sea and air forces will fight side by side with the British. The United States will send tanks and planes. The government must retire to the Breton redoubt and from there direct the battle in association with the British government. If it cannot stay there, it will move to North Africa or even Central Africa and await the assistance that will bring victory.'

'M. Paul Reynaud's decision seemed unshakeable,' wrote Baudouin in his memoirs. 'In my opinion it led to the material prostration of France, the capture of all our armies and the massacre of civilians on the roads.'

Against M. Reynaud's schemes and the rhetoric of some of the ministers, General Weygand set the exhaustion of the troops who had been fighting without respite or relief ever since the start of the offensive, pulverized by bombing that the French air force was absolutely powerless to prevent; the decimated divisions, which were now reduced to a handful of battalions; the artillery regiments, down to a few guns ...

And against them he also set the impossibility of holding out in the Breton redoubt which, he emphasized, existed only in the Premier's imagination and had as yet no forces capable of defending it.

But nothing, it seemed, could induce a change of heart in Reynaud and his supporters. 'There were continuing floods of eloquence on the same theme,' writes Weygand. 'No concern for the men who were fighting. It was a nauseating spectacle.'

The Generalissimo concluded his argument with the words: 'Unless an armistice is sought without delay, chaos will take hold of the armies, as it has already taken hold of the civilian population in the towns and on the roads. If that happens there will be no point in an armistice, for the harm will have been done. The French armies have been ordered to continue the battle. Rest assured that what is left of them will fight on till the point of total annihilation has been reached.'

The government had reached deadlock. What now? M. Chautemps suggested a compromise. Since some solution must clearly be found, and since Churchill, only that morning, had requested that the French should let the British government know at once before coming to a final decision, *why not ask him to attend a Cabinet meeting* and make him realize the prospect that now faced France?

After a good deal of argument this solution was finally adopted by the Cabinet, which required Reynaud to act along these lines. He agreed, and promised to telephone Churchill and ask him to come to Tours next day.

'As I left the meeting,' states Paul Reynaud, 'I reflected that the words which Mr Churchill's natural generosity and very strong affection for France had prompted him to speak (at the Supreme War Council meeting in Briare) might encourage some members of my government to pronounce in favour of an armistice. Marshal Pétain and General Weygand had heard them. So I decided *to have a private word with the British Premier first.*'

'It was 11 p.m. when the ministers separated,' writes Bouthillier. 'Dusk had slowly overtaken the Loire valley. In the pale June darkness each returned to his lodgings. And strange lodgings they were! By some singular quirk of organization the members of the government had been allotted separate accommodation all over the countryside, from one end of the province to the other. On leaving the meeting, each minister vanished into some vast château or manor-house, there to shelter his alarms.'

'I reached the Château de Chissay round about midnight,' M. Paul Reynaud tells us, for his part. 'There I found M. Bouthillier, Minister of Finance, General de Gaulle and my associates. The general, just back from Brittany where he had seen General René Altmayer, told me about the Breton redoubt while I ate a hasty meal.'

'Naturally I favoured Quimper,' writes de Gaulle. '*Not that I had any illusions as to the chances of holding out in Brittany*, but if the government retired to Quimper it would be bound to put to sea sooner or later ... Once on board ship, the ministers would in all probability make for Africa, either directly or stopping off in England. At all events, Quimper was a move towards forceful decisions.'

In Rome Mussolini addressed the following telegram to Hitler:

Thank you for the telegram that you sent me after I took the decision to enter the fray. I need hardly say that I shall conduct the war with extreme vigour.

With regard to the exchange of troops in token of our comradeship, I suggest that you send me fifty anti-aircraft batteries, together with their crews and ammunition. I consider that these batteries will be sufficient to improve the anti-aircraft defences of the principal industrial centres of Piedmont and Liguria. For my part, I can send you an armoured division that is ready and can leave as soon as the general agreement is concluded. Please tell me whether you agree to my proposal, in which case the Staffs will submit to you the plan for its application.

As a reprisal for the first bombing of Turin by the British, which cost us fourteen civilian dead and thirty civilian wounded, I have ordered a massive bombing of southern France.

So far as raw materials are concerned, the experts' report will show you that my demands are modest and that you will receive useful compensations in exchange.

Should there be a pause in operations, I think it would be useful for us to meet.

I shall keep you informed of the development and progress of our operations.

Accept, Führer, my comradely sentiments.

MUSSOLINI

JUNE 13TH

MILITARY SITUATION

The Paris Army was ordered to withdraw to the Loire.

The 2nd Armoured Division, which had by-passed the city on its western side the night before — while its commander, making his way through the deserted centre, was thinking of bearing away the coffin of the Unknown Warrior with his last tanks — was now heading through Verrières woods for Arpajon and Chamarande, where it was to regroup.[1]

General Héring gave instructions for the following notice to be affixed to the walls of the capital:

> General Héring, having been called away to command an army, is placing the military government in the hands of General Dentz. Paris is declared an open city. Every step has been taken to ensure, in all circumstances, the safety and provisioning of the inhabitants.

In the afternoon the Germans reached Pantin and Aubervilliers.

West of Paris, in the sector held by the remains of the 10th Army, a disquieting breach, some ten miles wide, had opened in the French line between Évreux and Pacy-sur-Eure. There was a risk that the gap would widen in the days ahead, for the two armies on the left had been ordered to centre their withdrawals on different points: The Paris Army was to centre on Orléans, whereas the 10th Army, *which had received direct instructions from M. Reynaud to bar the way to the Breton redoubt*, was to centre first on Argentan and then on Rennes.

East of Paris, the enemy was building up round Montmirail. Towards noon the air force reported a considerable concentration of armoured and motorized vehicles in the area. The attack on the 6th Army occurred in the afternoon. Late in the day the Germans reached the Upper Seine at Romilly.

On the 4th Army front the 2nd Panzer Division, fully exploiting its success of the day before, thrust on towards Vitry-le-François and Saint-Dizier. The road to Dijon lay open for Guderian's armour.

[1] See sketch-map on p. 264.

This bold thrust, paving the way for an encirclement of the left wing of the 2nd Group of Armies, alarmed General Georges. He drew General Prételat's attention to the need to hasten his vacation of the Maginot Line and effect his withdrawal as swiftly as possible.

Lieutenant-General Sir Alan Brooke arrived in Cherbourg to assume overall command of the 52nd Division, which had landed during the night, and of the other British formations still dotted about France.

The *Eastern Prince*, the first American ship to bring arms to Europe, left Gravesend harbour.[1] Edward R. Stettinius writes:

... The arms we sent in June of 1940 were only a stop-gap. But they went to men who almost literally had no arms at all, in the most critical hour of Britain's history since the Spanish Armada sailed into the English Channel. ...

Besides the guns, we also tried to send some planes we had in service. They were not the 'clouds of planes' for which Premier Reynaud of France desperately imagined might be sent when he made his last appeal for aid to the President on June 13th. America had no 'clouds of planes' to send in June of 1940. But the navy agreed to release 50 of its Curtiss-Wright SBC-4 dive bombers, and the army 93 of its Northrop A-17-A light attack bombers. These also were traded in to the manufacturers for later-type planes then in produc-tion[2] and resold to the British and French as the rifles had been.

Most of the planes were flown to Halifax, where the French air-craft carrier *Béarn* was waiting.[3]

POLITICAL SITUATION

At Marshal Pétain's trial, General Weygand was to declare:

Before we can gain full insight, the obscurities of June 13th will have to be illumined. Before we may know how the honour of France was preserved, it is essential that complete light be shed on them. Personally I am not capable of shedding it. But since I have such full insight into my own and Marshal

---

[1] It did not reach Britain till June 23rd, the day after the armistice was signed.

[2] In *The White House Papers of Harry L. Hopkins*, Robert E. Sherwood states that this deal, which benefited the United States' army and navy, came about as the result of 'some subtle and possibly questionable legal shenanigans worked out by Henry Morgenthau's lawyers in the Treasury Department'.

[3] They were never to reach Europe.

Pétain's actions and none in other matters, I ask that, after I have shed light on what I did, light be shed on what others did.

June 13th, 1940, was indeed a crucial day in the history of the period. It is important to examine it very closely and overlook nothing that may help the light to break through.

Early in the morning General de Gaulle drove to the Château de Chissay, M. Reynaud's residence. After a long discussion the latter decided, despite the general's arguments in favour of withdrawing to Quimper, to transfer the seat of government to Bordeaux.

'This,' writes de Gaulle, 'only made me more determined to demand, at the very least, the signing of an order instructing the Commander-in-Chief to plan and prepare the shipments to Africa ... '

M. Reynaud drew up a note to General Weygand, specifying what the government now expected of him. General de Gaulle made a number of emendations. Here is the final text:

June 13th, 1940

In the event of the 'final breaking of our lines of defence' you indicated in your note of June 10th that our armies, separated by this break-through, would go on fighting 'till their supplies and strength were exhausted'.

The aim and result of this sacrifice would clearly be to save the nation's honour, in keeping with the highest traditions of the French army.

I am not surprised that you should contemplate it.

But I think that, in that eventuality, rather than risk the destruction, on the spot and in a hopeless fight, of the fragments of the French army, it would be advisable to try and obtain a positive result from the prolonging of our resistance.

In this respect it seems to me that two courses are open to us, both vitally important from the point of view of continuing the war.

The first course would lead to our armies covering the very heart of the country for as long as possible, linking up with those of our forces that are defending the Alpine border.

The second course would lead to our establishing and defending a national redoubt in Brittany. I am glad that I have obtained your agreement on this point.[1]

Such a redoubt — lying close to England, which would send us

---

[1] This was untrue. General Weygand had always steadfastly opposed the idea. In taking steps to put it into practice he was merely obeying orders.

troops and supplies (and her air force might assist in its defence) —
would enable us to maintain, to the Allies' advantage, a bridge-
head on the continent for as long as possible ...

Even if we were to fail, even if we were to be torn bodily from the
heart of the country and the Brittany peninsula, we should have
shown our people and the world that we had fought to the last to
continue bearing arms on French soil. We should still be able to move
to our Empire and organize means of fighting by making use of the
freedom of the seas.

Round about noon, M. Jeanneney, leader of the Senate, and M. Herriot,
leader of the Chamber of Deputies, arrived at Chissay to inquire into the
situation. The former, writes de Gaulle, 'showed resolute bearing in the
midst of the confusion and made one think of Clemenceau, whose close
collaborator he had been in 1917 and 1918.[1] The latter, affable and fluent,
gave eloquent expression to the manifold emotions at work within him.'
Both urged the Premier to act vigorously and defy the 'capitulards'.
Both said they were prepared to accompany the government to Algiers.
M. Reynaud had only to say the word ...

M. Lebrun and the members of the government decided to meet at the
Château de Cangé (M. Lebrun's residence) at 3 p.m. to receive Mr
Churchill, who had announced his intention of flying over again.

Meanwhile, as a result of Reynaud's telephone call the night before,
Churchill was on his way back to France. With him were Lord Halifax,
the Foreign Secretary, Lord Beaverbrook, Minister of Aircraft Production, Sir Alexander Cadogan, Permanent Under-Secretary of State for
Foreign Affairs, General Ismay and Captain Berkeley. They landed at
Tours aerodrome, not far from Cangé, at 1 p.m. There was nobody to
welcome them. M. Reynaud, who was unable to leave Chissay, had
sent Paul Baudouin to meet them; but his car had broken down.

Extremely put out, Churchill and his party drove to the Grand Hotel
in Tours, where they ate a very poor lunch. Baudouin joined them when

[1] 'One of the best things about France,' writes General Spears, ' ... is that, in spite of the
buffoons and charlatans so apt to steal the political limelight, the solid middle and intellectual
classes assert themselves by placing power in hands such as those of Jeanneney. And in doing
so they have the approval of the whole country, for the French have a fundamental, ineradi-
cable respect for wisdom, science, age and that moral rectitude which people like to know
exists although they may seldom feel inclined to practise it themselves. He [Jeanneney] was
typical of the *haute bourgeoisie*, a meaningless term in England where its counterpart does not
exist. I cannot imagine an older member of that class relaxed, or having a good time, or clad
otherwise than in sombre town clothes with very stiff collars, simply because I have never seen
one who did not answer this description, or who did not move about amidst heavy, sombre
furniture.'

they were halfway through the meal. Churchill asked him to describe what had happened in French government circles since he had left Briare at 10.30 a.m. the day before.

'In response to his request,' writes Baudouin, 'I outlined General Weygand's exposé at the Cabinet meeting the night before. I described the somewhat confused mood of the meeting.

'Mr Churchill stated that he was not surprised that the general had suggested an armistice, for since the Briare talks he had known that the French army had reached the end of its resistance.'

After lunch M. Baudouin accompanied Mr Churchill and the British ministers to the Prefecture. There, instead of being driven to Cangé, they were shown to a small room on the first floor that served as the Prefect's office. M. Mandel, the Minister of the Interior, had taken it over for the time being and was on the point of beginning lunch. Churchill records in his memoirs:

> This faithful former secretary of Clemenceau, and a bearer forward of his life's message, seemed in the best of spirits. He was energy and defiance personified. His luncheon, an attractive chicken, was uneaten on the tray before him. He was a ray of sunshine. He had a telephone in each hand, through which he was constantly giving orders and decisions.

M. Reynaud then arrived, followed a few minutes later by General Spears. Churchill took Spears aside and asked him what was going on. Spears swiftly brought him up to date with the situation. Baudouin, he said, was now 'doing his damnedest to persuade Reynaud to throw up the sponge'. Churchill replied that he had gathered as much: Baudouin had ruined an already inadequate meal by seasoning it with an outpouring of oily defeatism.

It was now 3.30 p.m. The conference was about to begin. Having finished his lunch, M. Mandel left the room, carrying his tray, and Reynaud replaced him at the desk.

·M. Reynaud was first to speak. Though he personally was opposed to an armistice, he knew that a section of his government did not rule out this solution, and that the arguments in favour of a cease-fire were daily acquiring more weight. So, in compliance with the instructions that he had received from the Cabinet the night before, he laid the question before his British colleague with extreme clarity.

After depicting the plight of the French army, sacrificed as the vanguard of the democracies, and the desperate nature of the battle now being fought on French soil, M. Reynaud asked: 'Does not Great Britain consider that France can say, "My sacrifice is so great that I am asking you to allow me to sign an armistice," while maintaining the solidarity implicit in our agreements?'

Mr Churchill was deeply moved. Tears shone in his eyes. After some moments he slowly answered, weighing every word:

'We realize the position you are in. We shall offer no recriminations in case of such an event. Come what may, Great Britain will restore France in all her power and dignity, whatever her attitude may have been after her defeat.

'However,' Churchill continued after some reflection, 'it would be advisable to make a final appeal to President Roosevelt before coming to such a grave decision. Our conduct will then be determined by the tenor of his reply.'

'The declaration that Mr Winston Churchill has just made is deeply moving,' replied Reynaud, 'and I am considerably touched by it. The French government will therefore telegraph to Mr Roosevelt indicating the changes that have occurred in the situation and telling him the truth: the French army, the advance guard of democracy, has been destroyed holding the first line. Will the bulk of the democratic forces follow? The United States is involved, as well as Great Britain. If America does not intervene, or intervenes too late, Hitler's fight against the democracies will be the fight of the Horatii against the Curiatii ... I very much hope that Mr Winston Churchill can identify himself with my message and let the President know that it is *his* message too, Great Britain's as well as France's. And, speaking for myself, I am anxious to thank him for his words.'

Churchill said he thought they could leave it at that for the time being. If Mr Roosevelt advised fighting on, they would be faced with a new factor, in the light of which they would have to reconsider the situation. But there were a number of questions that the French and British governments should examine together. For, whatever else happened, the war would go on and become grimmer all the time. They were fast approaching a complete blockade, and the Nazis would seize everything that would ease their supply situation. The Allies must not shrink from these appalling prospects. If the Allies fought on with success, if they could see the winter through, the struggle would then develop with full fury. France would not escape the consequences of the coming duel between Britain and Germany, and it was to be feared that events might give rise to Anglo-French antagonism. All these problems required thorough examination.

'What causes me most concern,' replied Paul Reynaud, 'is the likelihood, should the war go on, of Britain's indirectly inflicting suffering on the French people. It would be an unspeakable catastrophe if Britain and France were to part company. I shall believe, till my dying day, that there can be no separate independence for the two countries. That is why, even if Mr Roosevelt is unable to give us counsel or hope ... I should like at least to avoid any lasting antagonism between France and England ... '

'We shall have to consider the whole position after the receipt of the American answer,' said Churchill. ' ... It can be expected within twenty-four hours. For the moment, the only move open to us is to put the situation to the American President, with the greatest frankness. As I said earlier, if that answer is unfavourable and if you then announce your intention of suing for a separate peace, we shall have a host of problems to look into.'

He then suggested a short adjournment so that he might confer with his colleagues. He led Halifax, Beaverbrook, Cadogan and Ismay down into the garden of the Prefecture.

Meanwhile, Reynaud and Baudouin went into the next room to join the leaders of the two Assemblies, MM. Jeanneney and Herriot, and M. Mandel.

Jeanneney and Herriot were crestfallen. They fiercely reproached Reynaud; they found it intolerable that he should have given the British to understand that France might one day decide on a separate armistice.

Mandel exclaimed indignantly: 'I want to see Churchill at once; it is unthinkable that matters be left as they stand!'

Meanwhile General de Gaulle had arrived, highly displeased at having been left out of the discussion. He had not been notified till the early afternoon. Thereupon he had rushed over from Beauvais, 'fully alive to the alarming possibilities of this unexpected meeting' of which Reynaud, with whom he had spent part of the morning, had not thought proper to inform him. When he got to Tours he found the courtyard and corridors of the Prefecture filled to overflowing with politicians, government officials and journalists who had gathered in the hope of picking up news, and who resembled 'the tumultuous chorus of a tragedy nearing its end'. He strode into the Prefect's office without waiting to be invited.

The conference resumed at once.

Churchill said that nothing in the discussion that he had just had with his colleagues had led any of them to change his views. They saw how France was placed. They realized that her ministers felt they had their backs to the wall. Britain's friendship for her was undiminished. Whatever happened, France could rest assured that Britain would not withdraw from the fight. She would fight on to the end, no matter how, no matter where, even if France left her to fight alone.[1]

'We think that President Roosevelt should be approached without delay,' he added. 'We are returning to England this evening and will send him an appeal that will be identical with yours.'

M. Reynaud noted this statement and warmly thanked the British ministers for it.

In closing, Churchill asked Reynaud to arrange for the 400 German pilots shot down and taken prisoner in the course of the battle to be sent to England. Reynaud agreed to this request and gave immediate instructions for it to be dealt with.

'At no point,' Baudouin emphasizes, 'was there any mention of the French fleet ... '[2] And Reynaud, in his memoirs, bears out this assertion.

The meeting ended at 5.20 p.m. Mr Churchill went into the adjoining room and spent about ten minutes talking to MM. Jeanneney and Herriot.

General de Gaulle made use of these moments to buttonhole General Spears and ask him if it were true that Churchill had said Britain 'would understand if France concluded an armistice and a separate peace'? It would be most unfortunate if he had, for it would give the defeatists the right to say: 'What is the good of fighting on when even the British do not expect us to?' Also, it would weaken the position of those who were not prepared to let France break her undertakings to Britain. De Gaulle added that Baudouin was putting it about that France was now released from her promise.

General Spears said this was quite wrong. Churchill had used the words 'Je comprends' in the sense of 'I understand what you say', not in the sense of 'I agree'.

The British ministers started their journey back to England. Aghast at Churchill's compréhension, de Gaulle returned to Beauvais with the determination to resign as Under-Secretary of State. Mandel was furious. He got into the car that was to drive Reynaud to Cangé, where the entire Cabinet had been waiting since 3 p.m.

While all this had been going on in Tours, France's ministers had been cooling their heels at Cangé. General Weygand had joined them. A faint drizzle moistened the trees in the park and cast a veil of melancholy over the horizon. M. Reynaud arrived shortly before 6 p.m., accompanied by M. Mandel. A Cabinet meeting was immediately held under the

[1] De Gaulle writes in his *Mémoires*: 'Turning to the prospect of an armistice between French and Germans, a prospect which I had supposed would make him flare up, he [Churchill] evinced, on the contrary, a compassionate understanding.'
[2] The official minutes contain no reference to the matter.

chairmanship of M. Lebrun. The ministers were all longing to hear what the Prime Minister had to report.

Weygand records that Reynaud 'opened the meeting by stating that he had seen Mr Churchill, that the latter was on his way back to London, and that he had told Mr Winston Churchill that the French government *had decided not to conclude an armistice but to continue hostilities*'.

His listeners were dumbfounded. First M. Bouthillier and then M. Chautemps pointed out in 'mild, carefully chosen but crystal-clear terms' that Reynaud had failed to carry out his promise to get Churchill to address the Cabinet, and that, worse still, he had told Churchill that the government had decided to go on with the war, *whereas the government had stated the night before that it had come to no decision.*

'M. Paul Reynaud was extremely embarrassed,' writes Weygand. 'He said that he had no control over the British Prime Minister's movements and that Mr Churchill had been in a hurry to get back to England; but concerning the other matter he offered no reply.'

Paul Baudouin writes that he was 'amazed to hear the Prime Minister ... state that he had merely informed Mr Churchill of the French government's decision not to follow General Weygand's advice'.

The discussion that followed was even more confused and exasperating than the one the night before. Mandel, says Baudouin, 'held silently aloof, a pillar of contempt, his cold eye discerning with amusement, in all his colleagues, a fear and mediocrity beyond even his ample expectations'.

Reynaud announced that he was going to send a final appeal to President Roosevelt, demanding that the United States should enter the war at once, and that they must await his answer before coming to a decision.

'That is a mere gesture,' said Weygand. 'Battles are won with men and equipment, not with gestures!'

Reynaud defended himself inch by inch and caused further acrimony by letting slip a remark about 'the military not wanting to fight'.

This really put Weygand's back up.

'It is painful,' he exclaimed, 'to see a government apparently quite unresponsive to the efforts of an army that is being torn to shreds by shelling and bombing that it cannot return ... !'

Again M. Lebrun strove to calm the two sides. But at this point Lieutenant-Colonel Chapuis, of the President's military staff, entered the conference room to inform the Commander-in-Chief of a telephone call that he had just received from his aide-de-camp, Captain Gasser.

The latter had learned from General Dentz that forward elements of the German army now held Pantin and that the enemy would enter

Paris next day. While on the line to Paris, Captain Gasser had found himself talking to a duty officer at the Ministry of Marine. This officer had told him that a communist government had been set up in Paris, that Thorez was to install himself at the Elysée that night and that the police and the Republican Guard had been disarmed by the mob.

Greatly alarmed by this news, Weygand immediately passed it on to the Cabinet. The meeting had been suspended for a time, in an attempt to secure confirmation. M. Mandel put through a call to M. Langeron, the Prefect of Police. The Prefect was still at his post. He was able to assure Mandel that all was calm in Paris and that there were no reports of a communist uprising.

Meanwhile, General Weygand was telephoning General Dentz, who confirmed that the Germans were likely to enter the city next day, but assured the Commander-in-Chief that there were no signs of unrest in the capital; on the contrary, a silence of death hung over the city.

'People should check their information before they communicate it to the government!' Mandel said curtly, adding a number of scathing remarks about the bungling behaviour of professional soldiers who tried to dabble in politics.

The incident being closed, the meeting was re-opened.

General Weygand reiterated his demand that hostilities be brought to an end as swiftly as possible.

'And I,' countered M. Reynaud, 'repeat that we must await President Roosevelt's answer.'

'Let us at least make use of the interval,' suggested Weygand, '... to safeguard the French fleet by sending it to North African ports. In my view, all such measures should be taken before embarking on armistice negotiations with the enemy.'

'What is the point of seeking an armistice,' replied M. Campinchi, 'if the government is determined not to hand over the fleet? That is a condition the Germans are bound to impose.'

Almost in the same breath MM. Monnet and Rio affirmed: 'Negotiating an armistice will inevitably lead to placing the fleet at Germany's disposal; and that will mean forfeiting our honour.'

At this, General Weygand flew into a rage again: 'There is no question of that! There can never be any question of handing over any part of our war-fleet! I should be the first to reject the armistice if that condition were imposed by Germany!'

'The matter is my responsibility,' said Admiral Darlan, 'and I have already given formal undertakings on the subject.'

'How the war is to be conducted rests with the government,' said Weygand, 'but as Commander-in-Chief it is important that I should know which way to turn. I hear that the government intends to retire to Bordeaux. Are we to continue work on the Breton redoubt, which was originally intended as a means of allowing the Cabinet to continue the war in association with the British government?'

To rule out any misunderstanding, General Weygand then returned to what seemed to him the heart of the matter.

'Whatever happens,' he declared, 'our armies will go on fighting. They will strive to halt the enemy along the main invasion routes and to screen the nation's nerve-centres. But the government must realize that in deciding to continue the struggle it is asking the troops to fight beyond their resources and imposing fresh sufferings and sacrifices on the nation. It is for the government, now, to address the country and the army — to make them understand the reasons for these demands and to imbue them with sufficient fervour to bear them.

'Personally I have told the army as much as I could. It has answered my appeal and I pay tribute to its bravery. Now it is for the government to make its voice heard. But if its voice *is* to be heard, it must display a courage equal to that which it is demanding from the men in the field.

'Last night I told the Cabinet that France no longer had the resources to fight on in the hope of defending such soil as was still free. Most of the ministers who spoke expressed their resolve to continue the battle. Of course, I too could display verbal courage of the same order. From the châteaux in which my headquarters are installed I could play the hero in front of the government and ... strike a pose that would win favour with the Cabinet. But not with the troops, and certainly not with my conscience ...'

Several ministers protested, whereupon Weygand exploded: 'I have already told the Prime Minister: "The government should have stayed in Paris. The Roman Senate did no less when the barbarians entered Rome."[1] Since Paris has been abandoned, ministers should at least have the courage to remain in France, come what may. In the first place because it is only on that condition that the people of France will accept the sacrifices that are being demanded of them ...'

'But is it not an even crueller fate for these ministers to abandon their native soil?' objected President Lebrun.

[1] 'I really did say that,' Weygand writes in his memoirs, 'but I admit that I was wrong. It would have been a mistake for the government to place itself in enemy hands in such a manner. Moreover, by the time I made that remark the government had been away from Paris for three whole days.'

'Nobody will see it in that light,' answered Weygand. 'The general opinion will be that, while they continue to allow our countrymen to be killed, bombarded, burnt and otherwise afflicted, all without hope of resistance, they have carefully found a safe nook for themselves in Africa or elsewhere. In the second place, do they really imagine that the Germans would not follow them? And what control do they suppose that they would continue to exercise over France? How long would they remain out of the country? Long enough for American factories to turn out the planes and tanks that would enable the Allies to win it back?'

'Two or three years,' chimed in M. Dautry, the Minister of Munitions.

The Commander-in-Chief left a few moments later, but his departure did not bring the discussion to a close. The atmosphere was electrically charged.

Suddenly Marshal Pétain rose to his feet. There was immediate silence. Was he going to walk out too? No. Emerging from his long silence, he drew a sheet of paper from his pocket and slowly read out the following statement:

We all acknowledge that the military situation is today very serious. It is such that unless the French government seeks an armistice there is a danger that the troops, no longer listening to their leaders, will give way to a panic that would render the army incapable of carrying out the smallest manoeuvre.

We must carefully examine what would be the consequences of continuing the struggle. Even if one accepts the idea of our being enabled to fight on by the establishment of a national redoubt, one has to admit that the defence of such a redoubt could not be organized by French units that have been put to rout, but only by fresh British units.

But even if this redoubt could be organized in a coastal area, my opinion is that it would not constitute a guarantee of security and would lead to the temptation to abandon such an insecure refuge.

Now, it is impossible for the government to abandon French soil without fleeing, without deserting. Whatever happens, it is the government's duty to remain in the country, on pain of no longer being recognized as such. To deprive France of her natural defenders, in a period of general confusion, is to deliver her into the enemy's hands. It is to kill the spirit of France and so make it impossible for her to revive.

We must stay here and await the resurgence of France, rather than expect it from a conquest of our land by Allied arms, undertaken in unforeseeable conditions at an unforeseeable time.

I am therefore against abandoning French soil and for accepting the suffering that will be inflicted on our country and on her sons. The revival of France will be the fruit of this suffering.

So the question of the moment is not whether the government shall seek an armistice, but whether it shall consent to leave Metropolitan France.

For myself, I declare that — outside the government, if need be — I shall refuse to leave Metropolitan France. I shall remain among the French people, to share their hardships and their sorrows.

To my mind, an armistice is essential to France's survival.

The tone of this statement was in striking contrast to that of the discussion that had preceded it. But it was not this that struck President Lebrun: what amazed him most was the singular manner in which the statement was delivered. 'In all my twenty years of attending Cabinet meetings,' he was to say at the Marshal's trial, 'that was the first time I ever saw a minister read out a prepared speech.'

Reynaud, for his part, was particularly startled by the veiled threat contained in the peroration: 'Outside the government, if need be, I shall refuse to leave Metropolitan France.' If the government moved to Africa, did the Marshal really contemplate staying behind? And if he remained in France with General Weygand, was it not because they intended making a deal with the enemy? At this unexpected prospect the ground seemed to open under the Prime Minister's feet. The Marshal's statement threatened to undermine his plan for withdrawing to North Africa.

'What you are suggesting is contrary to the honour of France!' he snapped; and in his memoirs he adds: 'Never in our history, probably, had a Marshal of France elicited such a remark.'

But it was getting late. The evening was drawing on. M. Reynaud felt he was losing ground. What was to be done?

Suddenly a series of explosions rattled the windows. War was approaching and making its presence felt. The Germans were bombing Tours aerodrome. This reminder of reality had its effect on everyone present.[1] The government voted unanimously in favour of moving to Bordeaux.

Anxious to avoid a split in the Cabinet M. Reynaud suggested that it would be better to wait till then before asking for a vote of confidence and

---

[1] 'It was like a summons bidding us be on our way,' President Lebrun remarked at Pétain's trial.

instituting, if necessary, a ministerial reshuffle. Besides, he still had one last trump up his sleeve: the possibility of an American intervention. The meeting thus ended without any decision having been taken.

Meanwhile General Spears was having a private talk with Mandel in the Prefecture at Tours. The Minister of the Interior was sitting at the Prefect's desk, 'cold and precise as usual'. He told his visitor how disappointed some of his colleagues had been at not seeing Churchill: they had accused Reynaud of tricking them, reminding him of his promise to invite Churchill to confer with them. Spears asked him whether Reynaud had really made such a promise. 'He certainly did,' said Mandel.

'But he never gave Churchill the least indication of this,' exclaimed Spears, feeling that something disastrous had occurred. 'Why did *you* not tell Churchill? *You* knew.'

'As you are aware, I was not present at the Supreme Council meeting,' answered Mandel coldly. 'I naturally thought the two Prime Ministers had discussed the matter and that it had been found that Churchill could not spare the time ... '

Spears had the impression that something irreparable might have happened that day. 'I was so depressed,' he writes, 'that I carried on the rest of the conversation rather perfunctorily, putting my questions with no great zest.'

The Minister of the Interior went on to assess the various members of the government, dividing them into two groups: '*les mous*', the soft, and '*les durs*', the tough. Of the *mous*, Chautemps was particularly dangerous. 'In that wonderful voice of his,' said Mandel, 'he depicts the misery of the refugees in their cars. He always ends by giving a heart-rending account of the poor old grandmother in the back seat weighted down with babies and a cage full of canaries. The old lady he elects to tell us about always has *très mal au ventre* — a bad pain in her inside. The account invariably affects our colleagues deeply.' Spears comments:

I left Mandel more impressed by him than ever. His detachment and objectivity in all this confusion were indeed astonishing. A very curious man. One side of his mind was watching the antics of his colleagues with ironical amusement ... The other side ... was watching events through those eyes that were like thimbles full of sea water, behind which lay the cold alertness of a barracuda always ready to pounce with startling rapidity on anything that passed within its vision. If it was possible to be fond of a fish, I should have been fond of Mandel. For he was like a fish, if you could imagine one with the straight damp locks of black hair hanging like seaweed over its gills. I expected him to pounce on the defeatists at any moment. But the opportunity did not come in time, or perhaps the fear that his religion might weaken his authority held him back.

No sooner had Spears gone than Mandel had a visit from General de Gaulle, who disclosed both his horror at Churchill's conciliatory attitude and his wish to resign from the government. The Minister of the Interior strongly discouraged him from doing so.

'Mandel spoke with a gravity and determination that impressed me deeply,' writes de Gaulle. 'He was as convinced as I was that France's independence could only be preserved by continuing the war ... "Who knows?" he said finally. "We may yet persuade the government to move to Algiers ... Great tasks lie ahead of you, General! ... Think only of what has to be done for France, and bear in mind that your present post may, in certain circumstances, make things easier for you." I must admit that this line of argument persuaded me to delay my resignation.'

It was as well de Gaulle followed Mandel's advice, for France was to need him almost at once.

Mandel's next visitor was Paul Reynaud. The two men had a long, frank talk together, safe in the knowledge that they could not be over-heard. Subsequently Reynaud decided to send General de Gaulle to London on a double mission:

1. *Officially* he was to obtain sufficient tonnage for surviving French forces to be shipped to North Africa;
2. *Unofficially* he was to resume contact with Churchill, get him to go back on the too 'understanding' statements that he had made in the course of the afternoon and urge him to lend Reynaud more active support in his stand against those members of his government who favoured a cease-fire.

In 1946, when he voluntarily gave evidence before the National Assembly's Committee of Inquiry into events in France between 1933 and 1945, M. Reynaud declared: 'I do not mind admitting that, being opposed to an armistice, I campaigned for the authorization given by the British to be withdrawn.'

JUNE 14TH

MILITARY SITUATION

Early in the morning the regiments of von Küchler's 18th Army entered Paris and marched along the Champs-Elysées.

Le Havre had fallen. General Rommel wrote to his wife:

> Went into Le Havre and inspected the town. It all went off without bloodshed. At present we are shelling seaborne targets with our long-range guns. Have already set a troopship on fire today.

At 8 a.m. Lieutenant-General Sir Alan Brooke, who had been placed in command of all British units still in France, called at General Weygand's G.H.Q. in Briare to find out what use was likely to be made of his forces.

General Weygand outlined the position of the French armies, which had disintegrated into four widely separated groups and were now incapable of organized resistance. He then spoke of the defence of Brittany — 'an operation resulting from a decision taken by the Allied governments'.[1]

Afterwards, General Weygand and Sir Alan Brooke drove to General Georges's headquarters. General Georges did not conceal the fact that he considered the projected Breton redoubt unworkable with the forces at his disposal — notably the 10th Army, now only a ghost of its former self. The idea of defending Brittany with the aid of 'a dozen divisions gradually built up by the War Ministry from officers and men returning from Belgium and from equipment dispatched from arsenals in the west and south' seemed 'romantic' to General Weygand. He asserted that this plan had been adopted 'without consulting the High Command'. But since the Allied governments had decided to put it into effect, the Commander-in-Chief had to carry out their orders.[2] In view of the fact that such British formations as were available were scattered about in the Le Mans and

---

[1] An allusion to Paul Reynaud's letter to General Weygand the night before (see p. 316).

[2] 'Neither General Weygand nor General Georges made any secret of their lack of enthusiasm for the projected "Breton redoubt" ... ,' writes General Roton. 'But our military leaders were men of discipline; it was therefore "within the framework of the decision taken by the French and British governments to organize a redoubt in Brittany" that the co-operation of the British troops was envisaged.'

Saint-Nazaire areas, the simplest plan was to group them in the vicinity of Rennes, where they could participate in the defence of the Breton bastion.

Under the impression that His Majesty's Government had endorsed the plan, General Brooke signed the following note jointly with Generals Weygand and Georges:

> *G.H.Q., North-East Front*   *June 14th, 1940, 10.30 a.m.*
> General Brooke, commanding the British Expeditionary Force, got in touch on the morning of June 14th with General Weygand, commanding all the theatres of operations, and General Georges, commanding the N.E. Front, to determine how the British troops in France should be employed.
>
> Under the arrangements agreed to by the French and British governments to organize a redoubt in Brittany, the following decisions were taken:
>
> 1. That the British troops now disembarking (the Brooke Corps, the last of the 52nd Division, and the Canadian division) should be concentrated at Rennes.
> 2. That the British troops engaged with the 10th Army (Evans Division, Beauman Division, and the 52nd Division less those elements not yet disembarked) should continue in their present task under the orders of the General Commanding the 10th Army ...

The French military leaders were hoping that this document would render them secure from any further misunderstandings of the kind that had arisen between Lord Gort and General Blanchard at the time of the Battle of Arras.

But doubts assailed General Brooke when he got back to his headquarters in Le Mans. He telephoned Sir John Dill, Chief of the Imperial General Staff, and explained the situation to him. In his dispatch Brooke wrote:

> I asked whether the Brittany scheme had H.M. Government's approval and told him that both Generals Weygand and Georges appeared to consider it impracticable with the force available. The C.I.G.S. informed me that he knew nothing of the Brittany scheme but said he would refer the matter to the Prime Minister.
>
> I told the C.I.G.S. that, in view of the general state of disintegration which was beginning to spread in the French army, I considered that all further movement of troops and material to France should be stopped and that arrangements should be started for the

evacuation of the B.E.F. from all available ports. The C.I.G.S. informed me that orders had been issued to stop the dispatch of further troops and material to France.

An hour later the C.I.G.S. telephoned to say that the Prime Minister knew nothing of the Brittany plan ... As H.M. Government had not been consulted with regard to the Brittany scheme, and the withdrawal of the B.E.F. had been approved, I requested the C.I.G.S. to inform General Weygand ...

The C.I.G.S. telephoned me again at 8.15 p.m. and said that it was most important that everything should be done to ensure good relations between ourselves and the French and to avoid, in every possible way, giving them the impression that the B.E.F. was deserting them. I replied that I would most certainly see that this was done, that I was moving no troops engaged with the 10th Army ...

Soon afterwards Brooke spoke to Churchill, who recalls in his memoirs: 'On the night of June 14, as I was thought to be obdurate, he [General Brooke] rang me up on a telephone line which by luck and effort was open, and pressed [his] view upon me. I could hear quite well, and after ten minutes I was convinced that he was right and we must go. Orders were given accordingly. He was released from French command.'

General Brooke's own account continues: 'The Prime Minister agreed to my proposal ... Moves to ports of embarkation were therefore continued.

'At 10.35 p.m. I spoke to the C.I.G.S. and told him of the Prime Minister's approval for evacuation. The C.I.G.S. informed me that I was no longer under the orders of General Weygand ...'

Simultaneously Air Marshal Barratt limited the number of British fighter-planes authorized to take part in operations in France to eighty.

In the west a fierce attack by von Kluge's Army drove the remains of the 10th Army back to the Risle. The Panzers of Hoth's Armoured Corps were streaming towards Caen, Argentan and Alençon.

In the centre the withdrawal of the Paris Army and the 7th Army was made extremely difficult by the increasing hordes of refugees cluttering the roads.

Between Paris and the Meuse the German advance was speeding up. The 3rd, 4th, 9th and 10th Panzer Divisions of von Kleist's Armoured Group had crossed the Seine at two points and were in Troyes and Sens. The left-hand column was surging towards Clamecy, via Joigny, and the right-hand column towards Monthard, via Châtillon-sur-Seine.

At this point the German 3rd Group of Armies (von Leeb), hitherto playing a waiting game, went into action. As General Weygand had foreseen, the battle now extended all the way to the Swiss border.

In the course of the day Prételat's 2nd Group of Armies, in the Saar fortified sector, was attacked by three fresh infantry divisions enjoying air and artillery support.

To escape the pincer-movement that was starting to entrap them, the Allied armies in the east would have to outstrip the German armour heading for Belfort and Besançon. Unfortunately the orders to withdraw, given on the afternoon of June 12th, arrived too late. The Allied units were unable to start back in time to forestall the movements of the Wehrmacht.

Nevertheless, desperate efforts were made to avoid encirclement. The 3rd Army (Condé) hurriedly pulled back its front to the northern outskirts of Metz, in conjunction with the 2nd Army (Freydenberg), which was trying to hold out in Verdun. The 5th Army (Bourret) likewise pulled back. The task of the 8th Army (Laure), which formed a pivot founded on the Vosges mountains and the Belfort fortress, was to cover the withdrawals of the 5th and 3rd Armies, which had to strike much farther southwards if they were to break out.

So General Laure did not hasten his departure. But when he heard that the Germans were in Chaumont he grew alarmed at the danger that might threaten his line of retreat, and ordered the formation of an anti-tank barrier along the Saône and the Est Canal, between Auxonne and Épinal. 'Unfortunately,' notes General Roton, 'this screen was to remain very precarious on account of the scantiness of our resources.'

A wholly successful aero-naval operation was launched on Genoa by the 3rd French Squadron, consisting of four 10,000-ton cruisers — the *Foch*, the *Algérie*, the *Dupleix*, and the *Colbert* — and four flotillas of light cruisers.

At the end of the bombardment the squadron returned to Toulon. The light cruiser *Albatros* was the only vessel to suffer any damage. She was hit at close range by a 152-mm. shell from a coastal battery, but was able to reach harbour.

POLITICAL SITUATION

In the early hours of the morning M. Reynaud drew up a final appeal to President Roosevelt. Here is the text:

Thank you for publishing in America the message that I sent you on June 10th.

I told you then that for six days and six nights our troops had been fighting without an hour's respite, outnumbered by three to one and with only a fifth of the enemy's resources.

Four days of bloody fighting have come and gone since then. Our army is now cut into several fragments. Our divisions are decimated. In some cases generals are commanding mere battalions. The Reichswehr [*sic*] has just entered Paris. We are going to attempt to pull back our exhausted forces in order to engage in further fighting. It is doubtful whether, being at grips with the enemy, who is constantly replenishing his troops, they can succeed in this.

In the most tragic hour of her history, France is faced with a choice.

Is she to go on sacrificing her youth in a hopeless struggle?

Is her government to leave her soil to avoid falling into enemy hands and to be able to continue the fight at sea and from North Africa? ...

Or is France to ask Hitler for his armistice conditions?

We can choose the first course, that of resistance, only if a possibility of victory shows in the distance, only if a light shines at the end of the tunnel.

Now, in the present situation, despite the weakening of the enemy's forces due to the sacrifice of the French army, the defeat of our loyal ally, Britain, if left to fight with her own forces alone, seems possible, if not probable.

Consequently, France can only continue the struggle if American intervention turns the tables by making the victory of the Allies certain.

The only chance of saving the French nation, the advance guard of the democracies, and hence of saving Britain, at whose side France will then be able to remain with her powerful fleet, lies in throwing the weight of American power into the balance this very day.

This is likewise the only chance of preventing Hitler from attacking America after destroying first France and then Britain, thus renewing Horatius's fight against the three Curiatii.

I know that declaring war does not depend on you alone.

But I tell you now, at this grave hour in your history, as in ours, that unless you can give France firmly to understand, in the hours ahead, that the United States will enter the war in the very near future, the destiny of the world will change ...

PAUL REYNAUD

A few hours later Mr Drexel Biddle, Washington's new ambassador to the French government,[1] called on Paul Reynaud. He was told that an immediate declaration of war by the United States was the only hope for Britain and France, if the latter was to continue the fight from North Africa. He was also told that the French army was torn to shreds and that M. Reynaud had had the greatest difficulty in persuading the Cabinet to fight on.

In the cable that he sent to the White House immediately afterwards Mr Biddle said it was quite clear that unless the United States took some positive step in the next forty-eight hours, the French government would consider that it had no alternative but to surrender.

Yves Bouthillier writes:

> While, on the fighting fronts, fleeing civilians became entangled with the troops continuing the battle, the ministers reached Bordeaux via the ancient provinces of Poitou and Saintonge.
>
> Parthenay, Saint-Maixent, Saint-Jean-d'Angely and Saintes were the stages in this trying journey through a region that was untouched by war but overflowing with refugees.
>
> It was still quite light when the official cars drove over the Gironde bridges and made their way through packed streets to the Prefecture and the hotel in which accommodation had been prepared. Both buildings were scenes of indescribable bustle. The invisible bonds that the city's guardian spirit mysteriously weaves in the shadows to turn a mass of human beings into a society, were slackening already. We had reached the stage where the civilian population, feeling that it was no longer either governed or safeguarded, was seized by a strange vertigo; the stage where people, aghast at the spectacle of a State disintegrating, were ready to give way to despair.'

That evening General de Gaulle ate a hasty meal in the Hotel Splendide with his aide-de-camp, Lieutenant Geoffroy de Courcel. Marshal Pétain was sitting a few tables away from them.

The General walked silently over to pay his respects. The Marshal shook hands with him, without uttering a word. The two men were never to see each other again.

A few moments later General de Gaulle got into his car and headed for Rennes, on his way to England.

Meanwhile General Weygand was on his way to Bordeaux. Late in the

[1] In place of Mr Bullitt, who had stayed in Paris to ensure the protection of the embassy and the American colony.

afternoon he had received a note from Marshal Pétain, informing him of what had happened at the Cabinet meeting after his departure the day before:[1]

> The Cabinet decided last evening not to come to a decision about asking Germany for an armistice till a telegram had been sent to Mr Roosevelt ... asking him to declare war on Germany.
>
> The Marshal considers that the latest possible time at which a decision can be taken is noon on Saturday.
>
> This will mean holding a Cabinet meeting in Bordeaux late tomorrow morning.[2]
>
> General Weygand's attendance is necessary.
>
> The Commander-in-Chief will have to be in Bordeaux — at M. Baudouin's residence, 58 Rue Saint Genès, telephone number 868-20 — by 10.30 a.m.

The urgency of this message impelled General Weygand to drive to Bordeaux during the night. Not wishing to do so without the Prime Minister's agreement, however, he telephoned M. Reynaud late that evening and told him about the Marshal's message.

'You will always be welcome at Cabinet meetings,' said M. Reynaud.

Speaking of these events eleven years later,[3] he stated: 'I told General Weygand, "If you have any technical information to give, you can come." For I did not preside at meetings of the Council of Ministers, despite my title,[4] and I had told President Lebrun that I considered it inadmissible that General Weygand should launch into appraisals at Cabinet meetings as he had at Cangé.'

---

[1] This note had been delivered to Vaugereau at 5 p.m. by Commandant Minart, an officer serving on the Marshal's staff.

[2] In other words, the following day — June 15th.

[3] Before the National Assembly's Committee of Inquiry in 1951. M. Reynaud added that General Weygand had not told him where he and the Marshal had arranged to meet, 'for he was not open'.

[4] *Président du Conseil.*

JUNE 15TH

At 8.45 a.m. General Georges received the following message from General Sir John Dill, Chief of the Imperial General Staff, with the request that it should be passed on to General Weygand:

> Due to the present situation and the difficulty in communications, General Brooke can no longer hope to receive orders from the French Supreme Command.
>
> I have informed him that he need no longer consider himself under the orders of the Supreme Command, but that he ought to continue co-operation with French troops operating in his vicinity.
>
> I am taking your agreement as given from now.

This telegram finally put an end to Anglo-French military collaboration. As a result, those elements of the Canadian division that had reached the area of concentration headed back to Brest, there to re-embark without having fired a shot; the pioneer groups were evacuated via Saint-Malo, and various signals units headed for the coast. General Brooke's staff was reduced to four officers and two secretaries.

Lieutenant-General J. H. Marshall-Cornwall assumed command of 'Normanforce'. On learning that the French 10th Army was beginning a general withdrawal towards Brittany, he ordered 'Normanforce' to proceed to Cherbourg by a series of forced marches.

During the morning General Georges called his subordinates together in Briare: General Besson, commander of the 3rd Group of Armies, General Huntziger, commander of the 4th Group of Armies, and all the commanders of the armies in the centre.

These officers examined the situation. It struck them as desperate. The Wehrmacht was advancing along three main paths. In the west it was striking downwards towards the mouth of the Loire; in the east it was heading for Lyons and the Rhône valley. In the north-east the encirclement of the 2nd Group of Armies was under way.

It was becoming impossible to meet the enemy's probes with front or

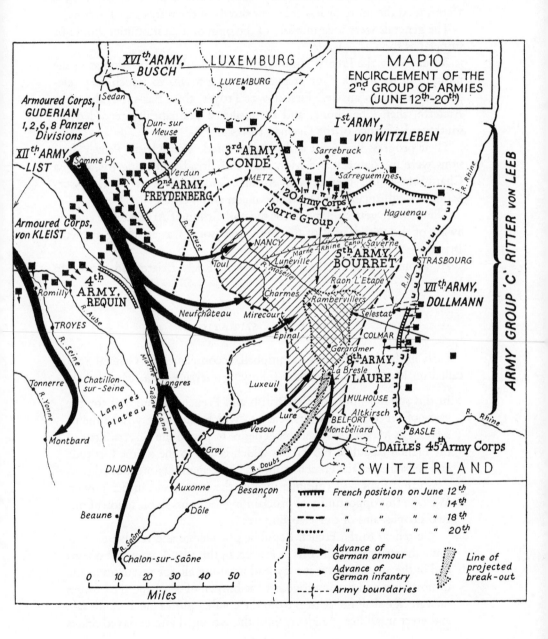

JUNE 15TH

MAP 10
ENCIRCLEMENT OF THE
2nd GROUP OF ARMIES
(JUNE 12th–20th)

even, quite often, with units of much size. All recoverable resources in the various sectors were organized into holding-forces and positioned along the rivers at points where the enemy would be compelled to cross; to these were added the more or less coherent shreds of the retreating divisions.

The generals were unanimously of the opinion that hostilities should be stopped as soon as possible.

All day long the French High Command sought information as to the position of its armies. One after another the towns to which they telephoned ceased to answer. First it was Troyes, then Bar-sur-Aube, then Auxerre, then Chaumont; and their silence dramatically recorded the southward advance of the German forces.

Their progress was swift and uninterrupted. Von Kleist's Panzer divisions were in Clamecy and Montbard and already thrusting towards La Charité-sur-Loire, Nevers and Autun. Guderian's were in Gray-sur-Saône and advancing on Dijon, Besançon and Vesoul.

Things were getting difficult for the 2nd Group of Armies. The enemy, aware of the withdrawal of the Rhine garrisons, was attacking at Neuf-Brisach.

At about 5 p.m. General Georges's staff left Briare and retired to Vichy.

POLITICAL SITUATION

Early in the day Sir Ronald Campbell, accompanied by General Spears, called on M. Reynaud with the following message from Mr Churchill:

> In this solemn hour for the British and French nations and for the cause of Freedom and Democracy to which they have vowed themselves, His Majesty's Government desire to pay to the Government of the French Republic the tribute which is due to the heroic fortitude and constancy of the French armies in battle against enormous odds ...
>
> Great Britain will continue to give the utmost aid in her power. We take this opportunity of proclaiming the indissoluble union of our two peoples and of our two Empires ...
>
> We renew to the French Republic our pledge and resolve to continue the struggle at all costs in France, in this island, upon the oceans and in the air, wherever it may lead us, using all our resources to the utmost limit and sharing together the burden of repairing the ravages of war. We shall never turn from the conflict until France stands safe and erect in all her grandeur, until the wronged and enslaved States

and peoples have been liberated, and until civilization is freed from the nightmare of Nazidom. That this day will dawn we are more sure than ever. It may dawn sooner than we have the right to expect.

Simultaneously Mr Mackenzie King, Prime Minister of Canada, Mr Menzies, Prime Minister of Australia, and Mr Frazer, Prime Minister of New Zealand, sent M. Reynaud what he has subsequently called 'telegrams of encouragement, equally lofty in inspiration, urging him to fight on to the end in the defence of a sacred cause'.

Although the French Premier was 'deeply touched by these tokens of sympathy from the ends of the earth', Sir Ronald Campbell and General Spears sensed the extent of his nervousness and preoccupation.

'Everything,' he kept saying, 'depends on Roosevelt's answer to my last telegram.'

But Spears's reaction was that Reynaud 'knew these hopes were an illusion which served no other purpose than to postpone decision'.

Now the outlook grew blacker than ever. Scarcely had Spears and Campbell left the room than Reynaud received a communication from General Georges's headquarters. The Commander-in-Chief of the North-Eastern Theatre informed him of the steps taken by Sir Alan Brooke to withdraw British forces.

M. Reynaud was amazed at this new 'pull-out', so at odds with the declarations that he had just received from the British Prime Minister and the Dominion leaders. He asked London what motives there could possibly be for this retreat. His only reply was a brief telegram from Churchill saying that General Brooke had informed the Chief of the Imperial General Staff (Sir John Dill) that Weygand had told him French resistance had ceased. Churchill added that, in the circumstances, he was sure Reynaud would agree that the Allied cause would best be served by suspending the landing of further British forces in France till the position became clearer.

Obviously this was yet another misunderstanding. When Sir Alan Brooke had called at G.H.Q. in Briare the day before, General Weygand had told him that French resistance 'would not last much longer'. He had not told him that it 'had ceased'. The Commander-in-Chief protested hotly when he heard how his words had been twisted. It seemed to him that these constant 'misunderstandings', coming one upon another, were hard to explain …

Next came Admiral Darlan. The Premier had sent for him the night before, through General de Gaulle. He was extremely put out.

'M. Paul Reynaud,' writes the Admiral, 'casually indicated that the period of forty-five days suggested by General de Gaulle [for the shipment of 900,000 men to North Africa] was now reduced to ten!

' "*Monsieur le President*," I answered, "it is physically impossible to call together, in the space of ten days, two hundred ships that are today scattered about the oceans of the world. But I have ten troop-ships in Bordeaux harbour. Each of them can carry 3,000. So 30,000 will leave tonight if they are ready to embark." '

M. Reynaud then told him that he did not know where the men intended for Africa were, or even how they were to reach Bordeaux.

'In that case,' said the Admiral, 'how can you ask me to evacuate 900,000 men in ten days?'

Darlan strode out of the Prime Minister's office, furious at having his time wasted by an entirely nonsensical project.

At this point Reynaud received a report from M. de Saint-Quentin, French ambassador in Washington. It left little room for hope of an armed intervention by the United States. The ambassador stated:

I backed your telegram in the most forceful terms. Mr Sumner Welles assured me that the United States government was determined to go as far as it could on the Allies' behalf short of entering the war, for neither Congress nor public opinion would follow it that far. In the event of war, the President would have against him not only the Republicans, but also the top unions and a number of dissident Democrats, who would be only too happy at finding grounds for a favourable attack.

Mr Cordell Hull, Secretary of State at the White House, took the view that by sending his last telegram Reynaud had carried out the intention with which he had been toying since May 18th: he had covered himself by appealing to America to come into the war, knowing that unless she did so, the defeat of France was inevitable.

M. Reynaud had scarcely had time to digest this report when he received a further call from Sir Ronald Campbell.

The ambassador was concerned at the wave of anti-British feeling current in certain circles in France. He considered this quite unjustified, for Britain had constantly done everything in her power to help France, even going so far as to stifle the very real grievances that His Majesty's Government might have voiced against her ally. Sir Ronald said he hoped the French Premier would do everything he could to stamp out this attitude, which would make a deplorable impression if it became known in London.

'That is why,' the ambassador added, 'the British government is alarmed at the idea that M. Paul Reynaud might be induced to relinquish office. His Majesty's Government is likewise afraid of the French fleet's falling into enemy hands.'

The Premier set Sir Ronald's mind at rest on this last point: France would never hand her warships over to the Germans.

[*The next visitor was M. Zaleski, the Polish Foreign Minister, who had taken refuge in France with General Sikorski. He urged M. Reynaud to fight on. He then visited M. Mandel and asked him why he did not carry out a* coup d'état. *Mandel said he would have done so if he had not been a Jew.* — Ed.]

Just before lunch MM. Jeanneney and Herriot paid a joint call on M. Reynaud. The Premier expressed his alarm at the increasingly rapid advance of the German armies. He also revealed his annoyance with the High Command, which was 'very disobedient to its government's instructions'.

'Perhaps another government than mine will resign itself to signing an armistice,' he burst out. 'For my part I am determined never to lay down arms.'

The leaders of the two Assemblies guessed that serious dissensions were beginning to show in the heart of the Cabinet. This only made them more emphatic in encouraging M. Reynaud to stick to his guns.

As the hours went by, Bordeaux became more and more crowded — not only with refugees, but with deputies and senators flocking to the temporary seat of government in ever-increasing numbers. Among them were — to name but a few — Auriol, Bergery, Paul Boncour, Ramadier, Vincent Badie and Charles Reibel. Some had been summoned by the Minister of the Interior — Pierre Laval, for instance, who had moved into Adrien Marquet's rooms in the *mairie*. Others, like Léon Blum, had been sent for by their friends.

Cliques began to form, backing or rejecting this or that solution and bound by temperament, interests or creed. Surely this was the moment to summon both Assemblies and invite the representatives of the people to give their views on these grave problems?

But summoned they were not. 'MM. Herriot and Jeanneney deliberately refrained from convoking Parliament,' writes Louis-Dominique Girard. M. Reynaud writes in his memoirs: 'Had I been able to call the Chamber together, I should have consulted it ... ' Constitutionally, indeed, Parliament alone was empowered to take the final decision. Since the Cabinet was divided as to the advisability of leaving France or staying put, it was for the people's representatives to express, by vote, their view of how the national interest could best be served.

Assemblies had sat in Bordeaux before now. There was a quorum of members present. So what explanation can there be for the failure of MM. Jeanneney and Herriot to call them together? Previous commentators consider that there were two main reasons for their attitude.

On May 16th M. Herriot had closed the last Paris meeting of the Chamber of Deputies with the words: 'No doubt the Chamber will wish to assign to its leader the responsibility of summoning it when the government has something to communicate.'

Thereby, without any vote being taken, he had implicitly extended to Paul Reynaud and his government the plenary powers accorded to Daladier under the law of November 30th, 1939. This has been regarded, not unreasonably, as parliamentary juggling. All the same, it provided a legitimate basis for M. Reynaud's methods of government.

That was the first reason. But the second was probably more cogent. 'It was,' writes Girard, 'that none of the heads of the Third Republic intended to implicate the parliamentary system in the most dramatic decision in our national history.'

Not that they were concerned with placating some distant future. Nobody in Bordeaux that day knew what lay ahead. The fact was, most members could sense the disrepute into which they had fallen in the eyes of the nation. The idea of going to Africa appealed strongly to many of them. But they wondered how their departure would be interpreted by the electors. They therefore preferred to leave the responsibility of deciding to others. This was an hour when everyone should have been prepared to face up to his responsibilities, but many senators and deputies preferred to say nothing, only to claim afterwards that their wishes had been ignored.

There were some, however, who did not see the matter in this light. M. Vincent Auriol sought out M. Herriot. After explaining that, for his part, 'his duty as mayor was to remain in the midst of those under his jurisdiction and not leave his fellow-citizens to face the invader alone,' he asked him point-blank: 'Aren't you and Jeanneney going to call an emergency meeting of the nation's representatives?'

M. Herriot stared at him in open-eyed amazement.

'What on earth for?' he exclaimed, throwing up his hands. 'What a spectacle *that* would be for the nation!'

At 2.30 p.m. Admiral Darlan, M. Bouthillier and Paul Baudouin had met in the Grand Hotel, where Marshal Pétain was staying. Shortly afterwards, General Weygand arrived. He had had a long and arduous journey. His train had taken sixteen hours to get from Briare to Bordeaux. He apologized for his irritability at the Cabinet meeting two days before and promised to be better-tempered in future.

Paul Baudouin then disclosed the true tenor of the discussions in Tours. He revealed to his four companions that Mr Churchill had stated that he 'understood the painful need to seek an armistice that was about to confront France'.[1]

Light began to be shed on the imbroglio of June 13th. Darlan, Weygand and Bouthillier were dumbfounded on learning the truth. The Marshal was more and more inclined to resign from the government, 'so that he should no longer be a party to the massacre of our troops'.

After this meeting, which ended at about 3.15 p.m., General Weygand went to see M. Reynaud, who had asked him to call in the early afternoon.

M. Reynaud told the Commander-in-Chief of his anxieties.

'Since we must stop fighting,' he said, 'the best solution is a military capitulation, binding only the army but leaving the government freedom of movement.'

General Weygand bridled at this suggestion.

'I refuse,' he replied indignantly, 'and I shall always refuse, whatever may happen, to bespatter our colours with this shame!'

'So far as I am concerned,' said Reynaud, 'I shall not surrender. You must obtain a cease-fire, like the Dutch Commander-in-Chief, and then, when the fighting has stopped and the moment is ripe, leave for North Africa — not with a haste that would suggest panic, but in time to avoid falling into enemy hands.'

Weygand thereupon begged leave to point out that there could be no comparison between the position of a monarch such as the Queen of the Netherlands and that of 'the head of one of those ephemeral governments, of which the Third Republic has already seen more than a hundred in the seventy years of its existence'. Once the Prime Minister had gone, he would be replaced and forgotten. The government could not leave France!

'*L'Algérie, c'est trois départements français!*' observed Reynaud.

'*Ce n'est pas la même chose!*' replied Weygand, refusing to budge from his position.

The discussion ended in utter discord.

'The conclusion that I drew from this meeting,' declares Reynaud, 'was

---

[1] Baudouin: *Neuf mois au gouvernement.*

that I would relieve General Weygand of his command that very day, after the Cabinet meeting.'

The Cabinet meeting was held in the Bordeaux Prefecture at 4 p.m. President Lebrun took the chair.

Admiral Darlan began by reporting on the naval operations in the Mediterranean the day before. Then General Weygand analysed the military situation. More emphatically than ever he stated that it was deteriorating hour by hour and that an armistice must be urgently sought.

General Lafont, commander of the 18th District, asked to be admitted. He brought a message from General Georges announcing that the situation had grown even worse since that morning. 'As things stand,' he wrote, 'a political decision is urgently called for.'

Then Darlan and Weygand withdrew at President Lebrun's invitation.

M. Reynaud read out the telegram that Churchill had sent earlier in the day. Once again he expressed the view that France's honour required her to remain at war.

It was M. Chautemps's turn to speak. He appealed to his colleagues' humanity. He drew a really tragic picture of the military situation and asked the government to think of the troops, who were just sitting ducks for the enemy.

Reynaud replied that 'if the Command considered there was no choice he was prepared to order it to cease fire, as the Dutch Command had done, which had not prevented the government of that country from going to London and remaining at war'. A number of ministers backed this suggestion.

'Nobody,' continued Reynaud, 'is better qualified than Marshal Pétain to go and tell General Weygand, who is waiting in the next room, that this solution in no way conflicts with the army's honour.'

Marshal Pétain acceded to this wish. He left the Cabinet room and returned a quarter of an hour later with the news that General Weygand adhered entirely to his original view that 'a capitulation of the kind envisaged by M. Reynaud would be a dishonour for the army'.[1]

M. Reynaud repeated that he personally was determined to hold out till the end.

'You want to hold out till the end?' one of the ministers interjected. 'But you *are* at the end!'

To 'overcome the deadlock to which Reynaud's weakness had brought the government' M. Chautemps suggested a compromise.

[1] Subsequently neither Pétain nor Weygand had any recollection of this conversation. Bouthillier confirms it. It certainly seems to have taken place.

'You are asking us to leave France,' he said, turning to Reynaud. 'It is an unprecedented action and you, like us, are aware of its extreme gravity. We do not refuse. But if the government is prepared to follow you to North Africa, it must be protected from adverse public opinion. I am convinced that the Germans' conditions for an armistice will be unacceptable; but we must prove it, and to prove it we must ask what they are. Once this proof has been offered, the French people will realize that the government had no choice but to leave France, and all the ministers will follow you to North Africa.

'Let us therefore ask the Germans what their conditions would be. And, so that we do not fail in our undertakings, let us inform the British government that we are taking this step.[1] Mr Churchill, who has on various occasions shown us so much understanding and sympathy, would surely not withhold his consent.'

This suggestion, which Léon Blum was later to describe as a *coup de théâtre*, took Reynaud completely by surprise. He was fully aware that to ask the Germans for their conditions was almost certainly to pave the way for negotiations. He defended himself vigorously and stated that it was out of the question. But he saw that a whole section of the Cabinet favoured the suggestion. 'The Pétain-Weygand clique,' he writes in his memoirs, 'was joining hands with the Chautemps clique.'

Five years later, at Marshal Pétain's trial, he declared that he sensed this so strongly that he took a sheet of paper and drew a line down the middle. 'On the right I entered the names of those who spoke for the Chautemps suggestion, on the left the names of those who took my line. There were thirteen names on the right, for the Chautemps suggestion, and six on the left, for mine.'

At this, Reynaud turned to the President of the Republic and said: 'I have no choice but to hand in my government's resignation!'

President Lebrun protested strongly.

'If you go,' he said, rising to his feet, 'I go too!'

Later he admitted that this may have been a purely instinctive reaction; for if others were free to leave office, he was not.

M. Reynaud wrestled with his conscience. 'Those were perhaps the gravest moments in my political life,' he tells us. 'I said to myself: "If I persist in my resignation, President Lebrun will presumably choose Camille Chautemps. That will mean an armistice for certain." If, on the other hand,

1 It was not a question of seeking an armistice, Chautemps emphasizes, but of asking the Germans to name the conditions under which *an armistice might be possible*. If these conditions proved unacceptable, the matter would be settled. If perchance they were acceptable, the government would *then* approach the British for their consent.

I agree, specifying that it is in the name of the majority (for I cannot personally forfeit my honour in the eyes of the heads of the British government, who are my friends, by passing myself off as the author of the armistice proposal), when I appear before this same Cabinet tomorrow I shall say: "By getting me to seek the authorization of the British government,[1] you implicitly acknowledged yesterday that it [that authorization]·was necessary; *you do not have it*; therefore we must fight on."' '

Much to M. Lebrun's relief, M. Reynaud therefore decided not to resign yet.

The President declared the meeting closed at 7.55 p.m.

M. Reynaud walked into the adjoining room, which contained General Weygand and several other persons whom the government had summoned in case they should be needed for consultation.

The Premier went straight up to the Commander-in-Chief and said baldly: 'General, as we agreed earlier, you are going to seek the surrender of the army.'

General Weygand thought he must be dreaming.

'I have never agreed to anything of the kind!' he cried. 'Nothing will compel me to perform an action of which I thoroughly disapprove!'

'Not even if I give you a written order to cover you?' asked Reynaud.

'Not even then! No human force can make me sign the surrender of an army that has fought as ours has! ... '

'Calm down, calm down!' said Reynaud. 'I must have misunderstood you.'

These final words were too much for Weygand.

'Certainly not!' he cried. 'I shall not calm down, nor shall I hold back what I have to say! The government can dismiss me if it likes, but never shall I agree to such an outrage! Never shall I inflict such ignominy upon our colours! You were mistaken, *Monsieur le Président*, if when you summoned me from such a distance to take over the command, you supposed that you found in me a man who was ready to stoop to any task! The cessation of hostilities, like the decision to go to war, is the government's business.[2] Let it show itself capable of facing up to its responsibilities!'

'Don't worry, it will!' said Reynaud, walking out of the room. For he was convinced that there was nothing to be gained from further exchanges.

---

[1] Oh no! Chautemps did not say that the government should seek the *authorization* of the British government. He said that it should ask the Germans for their conditions and simultaneously *inform* the British that it was taking this step. The two things are not the same.

[2] M. Reynaud had curtly pointed this out to him in front of Mr Churchill at the Supreme War Council meeting in Briare on June 11th.

In his memoirs Weygand writes: 'Matters could not be left as they stood ... I went into the room where the Cabinet meeting had just been held, meaning to put the President of the Republic in the picture: he was talking to MM. Bouthillier and Mandel. When I attempted to relate what had just happened he refused to listen unless the Premier were present. I was about to leave, wondering what was the best way of making myself understood, when the latter, alerted by my aide-de-camp, walked back into the room ... '

'Do you take me for a child?' Weygand asked President Lebrun. 'Was *this* what I was recalled from Beirut for — to walk into a trap? I have been involved in the nation's affairs for too long not to know how far everyone is to blame for the present tragedy ... '

'Kindly be quiet!' replied M. Lebrun. 'The acrimony of your remarks is really too much ... '

'You may remember that in 1933, when I was in command of the army, I protested to you, as supreme chief of the armed forces, about certain steps that the government took against my advice and that ran counter to the interests of national defence! Even then you refused to listen to me!'

'Those were trivial questions,' replied M. Lebrun.

'Trivial? On the contrary. Serious matters were at stake: the gradual pensioning-off of five thousand officers, under the terms of a Finance Bill, and the refusal to vote several hundred millions for rearmament ... '

'That is past history,' said M. Lebrun. 'The problems facing us today are on a vastly different scale.'

'Say what you like: no one can force me into a discreditable action that I refuse to carry out.'

Disgusted by the government's shilly-shallying, and by discussions that dragged on and on without resulting in any decision, General Weygand returned to his headquarters. He did not attend either of the Cabinet meetings that were held next day.

So the idea of military surrender was dropped. Did Reynaud relieve General Weygand of his command, as he had thought of doing before the Cabinet meeting? No.

When asked, in later years, what led him to change his mind, he replied: 'To break with Pétain and Weygand at that moment would have delivered a fatal blow to the country's morale.'

At about 9 p.m. M. Reynaud summoned Sir Ronald Campbell, the British ambassador, and General Spears.

As he entered the office, Spears could not help noticing how tired the

Prime Minister seemed. 'Reynaud looked pale,' he writes; 'washed-out would be the right description ... '

Reynaud began by describing his taxing fight against the pro-armistice faction in his government. He told his visitors of General Weygand's refusal to surrender and of Chautemps's compromise suggestion.

Then he picked up his pen and drafted the following telegram for the head of the British government:

> At the meeting of the Cabinet this afternoon it was held that at a moment when the enemy is on the point of occupying the entire country, which will mean inflicting cruel privations and suffering on the French nation, the departure of the government would be considered by the people as desertion.
>
> This might give rise to violent reactions on the part of the public unless it had been established that the peace conditions imposed by Herr Hitler and Signor Mussolini were unacceptable as being contrary to the vital and honourable interests of France.
>
> The Cabinet does not doubt that these conditions will in any event be unacceptable, but has decided that it is indispensable that this should be proved beyond doubt. If this course is not adopted the government will break up, as many of its members would in that case refuse to leave the soil of France.
>
> With a view to ascertaining German and Italian conditions, the Cabinet decided to seek leave of the British government to enquire through the United States government what armistice terms would be offered to France by the German and Italian governments.
>
> The Prime Minister is authorized,[1] if the British government will agree to the French government's taking this step, to declare to the British government that the surrender of the French fleet to Germany would be held to be an unacceptable condition.
>
> Should the British government withhold its consent to this step, it seems likely, in view of the opinions expressed at the Cabinet meeting, that the Prime Minister would have no alternative but to resign.

General Spears was about to protest at the last paragraph when an official entered the room and handed Reynaud a paper. 'As he read it,' writes Spears, 'he grew still paler, his face contracted, his eyes became just slits ... ' It was Roosevelt's reply to his last message of June 14th.

[1] It is as though the idea of 'authorization' had become a real obsession to the author of this document.

'Our appeal has failed,' he said tonelessly, 'the Americans will not declare war.'

He handed the telegram to Campbell and Spears, who read:

Confidential   *Washington, June 15th, 11 a.m.*

I am sending you this answer to your message of yesterday, which, I am sure you realize, has been the object on our part of the most serious and friendly examination.

Allow me, in the first place, to reiterate to you the expression of the ever-increasing admiration with which the American people and its government pay tribute to the brilliant courage displayed by the French armies on French soil in their resistance to the invader. I must also repeat in the most solemn terms that, neglecting no possible effort under present conditions, the government of the United States has allowed the Allied armies to order in this country, during the last few weeks, aeroplanes, artillery and ammunition of all kinds, and that, so long as the Allied governments pursue their resistance, it will redouble its efforts in the same sense. I think it possible to say that, with each passing week, an ever-increasing amount of war material will be placed at the disposal of the Allied armies.

In conformity with its policy of non-recognition of the acquisition of gains achieved by force of arms, the government of the United States will refuse to recognize the validity of any attempt of a nature to impair the independence of France and its territorial integrity.

In these hours, so heart-rending for the French people and for yourself, I assure you of my deepest sympathy, and I can furthermore assure you that, so long as the French nation continues to defend its liberty, and in so doing the cause of democratic institutions in the world, it can rely upon receiving from the United States in ever-increasing quantities material and supplies of all kinds.

I know you will understand that these declarations imply no military commitments. Congress alone can undertake such engagements.

F. D. ROOSEVELT

While Campbell and Spears were perusing this fateful document, M. Reynaud had returned to his message to Churchill, not to admit defeat — which would have been wholly out of character — but to add the following postscript:

It was agreed (in Tours) last Thursday, at your suggestion, that the question of authorizing a request for an armistice would be reconsidered if President Roosevelt's reply was negative.

This eventuality having materialized, I think the question must now be put afresh.

Then he handed the complete text to the British ambassador with the words: 'Kindly transmit this to Mr Winston Churchill as quickly as possible. Make it clear to him that the decision was not taken by me personally but by the Cabinet, under the chairmanship of M. Albert Lebrun. It is essential that I get an answer, telephoned if possible, early tomorrow morning.'

'That doesn't give us much time,' said Sir Ronald.

'Just think how the members of the Cabinet who favour an armistice are going to cash in on the American reply!' returned Reynaud. 'I should like to be able to face them … tomorrow morning with a British answer that will offset it.'

Spears writes: 'The blow [of Roosevelt's telegram] had not been the less painful for being expected. He bore it well.'

After Sir Ronald Campbell's and General Spears's departure — round about midnight — M. Reynaud received a call from Mr Drexel Biddle, the United States ambassador. The Premier did not conceal his profound disappointment at America's attitude. Since there was no further hope of her making an armed intervention it would be hard not to sound the Germans for their armistice conditions.

Mr Biddle expressed astonishment, whereupon M. Reynaud launched into a detailed explanation of the 'compromise' that M. Chautemps had suggested at the last Cabinet meeting.

More than ever surprised, Mr Biddle then asked Paul Reynaud how he could have given his consent to such a risky enterprise. Once the French government had started on the downward slope, where would it stop?

M. Reynaud waved the ambassador's fears aside: this was the one way of showing the French people the severity of the German conditions and thus justifying the government's flight to Africa and England. He only hoped the conditions would not be too moderate.

After leaving Reynaud, Sir Ronald Campbell and General Spears called on Mandel. They told him the gist of Roosevelt's telegram, of which he knew nothing. The Minister of the Interior took the bad news with unshakeable serenity, remaining as cold, dispassionate and objective as ever. In return, he gave them a full account of the Cabinet meeting, telling them of Weygand's carefully-staged introduction of General

Lafont with an alarming message from General Georges, and dwelling particularly on Chautemps's 'compromise' proposal, of which he spoke in the most scathing terms.

In conclusion, Mandel asked his visitors to persuade Churchill to be firmer than ever with France. The British government must refuse to release France from her obligations: any suggestion of sympathy, or even 'understanding', would only encourage the waverers.

Spears and the ambassador then returned to their hotel, where the General put through a telephone call to Churchill. He told him practically word for word what Mandel had said and asked if there were any possibility of his meeting Reynaud next day. Churchill said he would think it over.

Spears and Campbell then composed a lengthy telegram to the British Prime Minister. This was coded and dispatched at 1.20 a.m. and reached its destination at 4 a.m. (on June 16th).

Before retiring for the night, Campbell and Spears decided to do everything in their power to stop the French government from asking the Germans for their armistice conditions.

In his account of these events Spears writes:

> The telephone conversations we had had with London, guarded hints for the most part, had left us with the impression that the government's view coincided with the advice we had been tendering, which was that a stiff attitude would yield far better results than an over-sympathetic one. We had by now had ample opportunity to realize that sympathy tended to be translated into condonation, and concessions to be taken as proof that we were following the same path as France. Our last conversation with Mandel had reinforced this point of view. It was a relief to find, from a Foreign Office telephone call to Campbell two or three hours after he had gone to bed, that opinion in London was hardening in this sense.

Meanwhile General de Gaulle had not been idle. After leaving Bordeaux by road the night before, he had reached Rennes early that morning, where he spoke in turn to General René Altmayer, General Guitry, commander of the Military District, and M. Jouany, Prefect of Ille-et-Vilaine.

He began by inquiring what progress had been made with the constructional work for which he had given orders on June 12th. He learned that General Altmayer had personally reconnoitred the whole length of the line Couesnon–Vilaine. It had been divided into five sectors assigned to commanders-designate of the rank of general or above. Although these officers had been given control of a number of depots, lack of equipment and materials had restricted their operations to felling trees, cutting trenches and driving in piles alongside approach roads. The public works concerns contacted by M. Borie had still not received either technicians or material from the Maginot Line, and were merely making preparations to take on refugees. The engineers were beginning to study plans for blockhouses, but none was under construction; they were inadequately staffed to mine the roads and bridges, and they had no explosives. Malestroit's Belgian division had given notice that it could provide a labour force of only 3,000 men, but even these were incapable of covering long distances on foot, because their boots and shoes were so worn. The infantry depots had only a small number of Lebel rifles; the N.C.O. and officer-cadet training centres at Fontenay-le-Comte and Coëtquidan were the only places where there were any up-to-date machine-guns or automatic rifles. The artillery depots had nothing but worn-out practice guns, and the tank depot in Vannes was empty apart from some old 1918-model Renault FTs. To attempt an effective defence of the line Couesnon-Vilaine, the French would have needed fourteen divisions plentifully equipped with anti-tank and anti-aircraft weapons. And the German armoured divisions were within three days of reaching the area ...

This report did nothing to alter General de Gaulle's plans. He promised the additional support of a 3rd Polish Infantry Division, now being formed in Coëtquidan;[1] he gave instructions for as many foot-battalions as could be raised in the two military districts to be placed at the disposal of General Robert Altmayer, Commander of the 10th Army; he sanctioned a number of detailed measures taken by General Guitry and enjoined him to hold out at any cost with the forces at his disposal.

General de Gaulle can have had little faith in the effectiveness of these orders. From the military point of view the Breton redoubt was indefensible, and from the political point of view there was now no question of moving the government to Brittany: it had already installed itself in Bordeaux ...

Nevertheless, the Under-Secretary of State for War left without changing any of his previous orders. He got into his car and told his driver to head for Brest along the Route Nationale which, near Morlaix, runs within a few miles of Carantec, where his family had been sheltering since May 25th.

[1] This force was still undergoing training. It was so poorly equipped that there was only one rifle to every ten men.

He reached Brest at 4 p.m. and drove to the Port-Admiral's office, where he met Admiral Traub[1] and Admiral de Laborde, C.-in-C. Western Theatre, Naval Operations. That morning the latter had received a telegram from Admiral Darlan, worded as follows:

General de Gaulle, Under-Secretary of State, will reach Brest by road at 4 p.m. this afternoon. Place a high-speed vessel at his disposal to take him to Plymouth, where it will remain subject to his orders. Ask C.-in-C. Western Approaches (Admiral Sir Dunbar Nasmith) to place a car at his disposal, on arrival, to drive him to London, where he is to be delivered this evening.

Beside himself with rage, de Gaulle roundly abused Marshal Pétain and General Weygand, openly accusing them of treason. For a moment the Admiral wondered whether he should not place him under arrest for insubordination. But if de Gaulle was his junior in the service hierarchy, he was his senior in the political hierarchy, since he was a member of the government. Consequently Admiral de Laborde confined himself to cutting the conversation short. Instead of seeing him off personally, he had an orderly escort the general to the gang-plank of honour in the naval dockyard.

At about 4.30 p.m. de Gaulle went aboard the light cruiser *Milan*. This extremely modern vessel, capable of forty-five knots, immediately set sail for Plymouth. Also aboard was a party of chemists led by General Lemoine. They were taking a stock of heavy water to Britain, M. Dautry having ordered that it should not fall into German hands.

The general was withdrawn and thoughtful for a time. Suddenly he asked the ship's captain: 'Would you be prepared to fight under British colours?'

'A French officer fights only under the French flag!' replied the captain.

After a brief pause the Under-Secretary of State said gloomily: 'Do you think it is any fun being General de Gaulle today?'

The *Milan* docked at Plymouth at about 10 p.m. General de Gaulle stepped straight into the car that was waiting for him and drove off towards London, where he arrived at daybreak.

In Rome Mussolini received Herr von Mackensen, German ambassador, who brought Hitler's reply to the Duce's message of June 12th. Politely but firmly the Chancellor rejected any idea of Italian participation in the Wehrmacht's operations in France. Mussolini was deeply mortified. If

[1] The Port-Admiral.

the Italian divisions wished to set foot in France, they were going to have to do so under their own steam.

Mussolini immediately sent for Badoglio and asked him to time the attack on the French frontier for June 18th.

Badoglio objected that there were two obstacles to the operation. The first was technical: it would take Italy's defensive forces twenty-five days to gear themselves to an offensive. The second was moral: the French army was crumbling and Germany needed no assistance whatever to complete her victory.

After some moments' silence Mussolini replied: '*Signor maresciallo*, as Chief of General Staff you are entitled to advise me on military topics, but not on political topics. Responsibility for those rests entirely with me. If we merely look on while France collapses, we shall have no right to demand our share in the booty. If I do not demand Savoy, which is French, I must have Nice, Corsica and Tunisia. As for mounting the attack ... let me tell you that in view of the position in which the French army is placed, there is no need to waste all those days in moving up artillery. Moreover, I shall give orders personally to the Chiefs of Army Staff.'

JUNE 16TH

————◆◆◆◆————

In the course of the day the 7th Panzer Division advanced, via Évreux, all the way from the Seine to the vicinity of Laigle.

In compliance with orders received from the Chief of the Imperial General Staff, Sir Alan Brooke completed the embarkation of all remaining British units in France, including those elements that had been incorporated in the 10th Army.[1] By the end of the day 47,000 men and 250 vehicles of all kinds had been evacuated to England.

The enemy thrust was accentuating all along the front. In the west the remains of the 10th Army withdrew beyond the Dives. Fighting continued along the line Argentan–Mortagne. What was left of the French armies retreated towards Rennes. Thanks to the activities of the Cavalry Corps partially re-formed on return from Dunkirk,[2] the withdrawal could be effected without the units' being overtaken and encircled by enemy tanks. In order to maintain a link with the Paris Army, the Cavalry Corps was ordered to hold out as long as possible along the line Chartres–Châteaudun–Blois.

On the right, the bulk of the 6th and 7th Armies regrouped behind the Loire – the 6th, greatly diminished, between Decize and Gien; the 7th between Gien and Orléans. The Paris Army had taken its time: most of it was still in the Châteaudun area. For the second day running the Germans bombed all the bridges over the Loire, causing heavy losses to the columns of refugees and troops massed at the crossing-points.

In the afternoon the 8th Army Chief of Staff telephoned to General Georges: 'Enemy bombardment of the Loire bridges remains very fierce. Innumerable convoys of refugees. All this conspires to make the situation truly tragic. We have been making superhuman efforts ... '

Meanwhile what had become of the 2nd Armoured Division?

On leaving Chamarande on June 13th – its stay in the town had lasted

[1] Bardies comments: 'It should be noted that the British entertained no thoughts of preserving a bridge-head in France. Could they have done so? Possibly in Dunkirk and Calais a few days earlier, but certainly not in Brittany.'

[2] See p. 265.

only a few hours — the division had been ordered to cover the retreat of the Paris Army, in conjunction with the Cavalry Corps and the remains of the 4th Armoured Division. Its mission was to do all that it could to impede the German advance through the Beauce area, by carrying out a series of delaying actions along a line running through Étampes, Oinville-Saint-Liphard, Toury and the forest of Orléans.

Round about noon on June 16th the division, which was fighting a rearguard action in the Angerville–Méréville–Sermaize area, encountered fierce opposition at Boisseaux and Léouville. The position worsened in the early afternoon. It was learned that Pithiviers had fallen into the hands of the Germans, and that the latter had moved detachments forward as far as Châtillon-le-Roi and launched motorized elements along the main road from Pithiviers to Orléans.

It became clear that the 2nd Armoured Battalion was being methodically outflanked in the east and that its encirclement was imminent. A hasty retreat was called for, especially since fuel was running out and no fresh supplies could be expected. Any delay would mean that the division would have to give up the struggle north of the Loire ...

Then came two items of news that were even more alarming. The first, brought in by a liaison officer at about 5 p.m., announced that fighting was already in progress on the outskirts of Orléans and that enemy units were patrolling the area to the south of where the division stood, thus cutting off its line of retreat. The second, received at 5.30 p.m., was an order from General Besson, Commander of the 3rd Group of Armies, for the tanks of the 2nd Armoured Battalion to withdraw to Bourges as swiftly as possible.[1]

There could be no question of making a detour to the west, for fuel supplies were too low. There was only one way out for the division. As soon as darkness fell it must strike directly southwards, smashing its way through any obstacles it might encounter.

Two columns were immediately formed:

1. *The western column*, under Colonel Roche, would cross the Loire at Jargeau;[2]
2. *The eastern column*, under Commandant Mahuet, would force its way across the river at Châteauneuf.[3]

---

[1] This order was dated 9 a.m., June 16th. This shows just how difficult communications had become.
[2] It was made up of the 48th Tank Battalion, a company of the 17th B.C.P., the headquarters staff and signals company, the two 105 groups, and Service Corps elements. Its retreat was covered by Aubert's Group.
[3] It was made up of the 40th Tank Battalion, the 17th B.C.P. (less one company) and the engineers. Girier's Group formed the rearguard.

But by nightfall the confusion on the northern bank of the Loire was indescribable. The roads were lined with burnt-out cars and skeletal frames of blasted lorries. Here and there a tank lay still smouldering in a field. In the midst of this chaos, hundreds of thousands of refugees were darting forward, rushing back or going round in circles, some dumb with horror, others screaming in panic. In pitch darkness the exhausted regiments strove to find a way through this throng, consisting mainly of women and children. Nobody knew where our units were, or where the Germans were, with the result that hundreds of our batteries, imagining that they were encircled, were inadvertently opening fire on our own troops.[1] And to add to the nightmare Italian planes, newcomers to the battle, intensified their raids on the bridges, particularly at La Charité and Gien.

So it was not without difficulty that the Roche column progressed towards the river, shearing its way through enemy advance parties and tumbling into a German ambush at Chilleurs. Fearing capture, the 40th Tank Battalion and Girier's Group decided to branch westwards. They finally reached the Mer bridge and crossed it in the small hours.

Meanwhile, the Mahuet column met with enemy fire almost throughout its journey. After being attacked at Rebrechien it sped through Loury and finally reached Jargeau, where it was unable to cross the river till next morning. Thereafter these various groups converged on La Ferté-Saint-Aubin, the rallying-point that had been assigned to them.[2]

But if the throng of refugees choking the bridges impeded the withdrawal of the French army, it also slowed down the enemy's advance, which was going much faster in other sectors of the front — especially in the area between the Loire and the Saône.

The mass of Guderian's armour, which had occupied Langres the day before, split up on leaving the town and followed the roads leading to Dijon and the Saône crossings.

Besançon fell during the evening. The Germans took several thousand prisoners and captured thirty tanks in the town. The position of the 2nd Group of Armies was becoming very critical. It was outflanked to the south and attacked from the east, in Alsace, where the enemy was threatening Colmar and Sélestat; and now it was subjected to an attack in the north, at Gros-Tenquin, where French fortifications were at their weakest. The fortress units made a fine stand, but the line was broken. The enemy thrust on towards Château-Salins and Sarrebourg.

---

[1] This happened on several occasions, especially at Guignonville, Toury and Les Aubrais.
[2] Apart from the 40th Tank Battalion and Girier's Group, which were stranded by lack of fuel in the Boulogne woods (south of Chambord).

In fact, the Germans were starting to invest on all fronts. During the morning General Prétélat reported on the new situation: 'My left flank is under the orders of General Freydenberg. I do not know whether the Germans are in Dijon, but General Pagézy, the local commander, has fallen back to Chalon-sur-Saône. Dôle is not occupied, but Besançon is. This is all part of the enemy's encirclement drive. I have authorized General Laure's attempt to save what he can from the Belfort fortress.'

That same day General Laure decided to hack his way south-westwards towards Belfort, before the enemy cut his last remaining lines of communication.

The disengagement drive towards Besançon was to be carried out by General Daille with the 45th Army Corps, comprising the 67th Division, the Polish 2nd Division, the 2nd Brigade of Spahis, the two artillery groups of the 13th Corps, a heavy artillery regiment and a battalion of the 12th Fortress Infantry Regiment.

When news reached General Laure of the forcing of the Saône barrier, he decided to route his withdrawal via the south bank of the Doubs.

The fate of the 3rd, 5th and 8th Armies now hung entirely on the success of this break-out.

POLITICAL SITUATION

M. Reynaud spent the early part of the morning impatiently awaiting Churchill's reply to his telegram. But when 10 a.m. came and there was still no word, he decided he could wait no longer. He therefore asked the leaders of the two Assemblies, MM. Jeanneney and Herriot, to call on him at the Prefecture. He reminded them that the constitution required him to consult them before moving the seat of government and asked them to approve its transference to North Africa. The leaders agreed. M. Reynaud asked them to confirm their attitude before the Cabinet.

The Cabinet met at 11 a.m. and the leaders of the two Chambers were brought in. Speaking for himself and M. Herriot, M. Jeanneney repeated his approval of the plan to move the government to North Africa. He added that, in their view, this move was likely to lead to the continuation of the war. M. Reynaud thanked the two leaders on the government's behalf. Whereupon MM. Jeanneney and Herriot withdrew.

As soon as they had gone the President of the Republic came in and took the chair. The Cabinet got down to business.

M. Reynaud began by reading out President Roosevelt's reply to his appeal of June 14th. M. Lebrun records that the words of the President's telegram had 'a profoundly depressing effect on the Cabinet'.

'The reply was very sympathetic, very kind, very compassionate, very obliging,' said Charles-Roux at the Marshal's trial. 'It made specific allusions to material aid. On the question of hostilities, it briefly but explicitly reserved Congress's right to decide ... So the reply was kind, it was comforting. But it cannot be said to have contributed anything new to the situation.'

No one could have expressed himself in choicer terms.

M. Chautemps then asked the Premier to inform his colleagues of the result of the representations that the previous night's Cabinet had instructed him to make to the British government.

'Nothing is settled yet,' M. Reynaud answered defiantly. 'I am still waiting for Mr Churchill's answer to the questions I put to him last evening through Sir Ronald Campbell. But what I *can* tell you is that the British Cabinet has never ratified its leader's conciliatory statements ...'

At this, Marshal Pétain rose to his feet.

'I can no longer remain in the government,' he said. 'Our armies are disintegrating more and more as time goes by. The inevitable solution has been put off all too long. I have no wish to be associated with this delay, for which the whole of France is paying.'

These words brought utter dismay to the meeting. Everyone sensed that in these tragic hours the French were turning more and more to the Marshal. If he resigned, the government would fall. As he made to leave the room President Lebrun burst out: 'Oh no! You are not going to do *that* to us now!'

The majority of the ministers present begged the Marshal to remain in office and continue to 'afford the government the benefit of his prestige'. The Marshal gave in but refused to sit down again.

Returning to the Anglo-French agreement of March 28th and to the representations that he had been instructed to make to the British government, M. Reynaud pointed out that 'when you have approached your ally on such a serious matter — that of releasing you from your word — etiquette demands that you should at least wait for his reply.'

'When will you have it?' asked the Marshal.

'I think I shall be in a position to communicate it to the Cabinet in the course of the afternoon. Please be patient till then, *Monsieur le Maréchal*.'

'Very well,' said Pétain. 'I shall stay. But only on condition that you hurry up and come to a decision.'

General Weygand had preferred not to attend the Cabinet meeting.

But he had had several talks with Senator Reibel about the pitiful plight of the French army.

'Within a matter of days, or even a matter of hours,' he had told him, 'they will be cut to ribbons. Is it humane, is it reasonable, to treat the French army in this way ... ? If the government leaves, what will be left of France and the French people? Will the latter accept such an act of desertion ... ? Is it not likely that in the midst of ruin, destitution and death, with the army completely destroyed, the nation will fall into the hands of small local governments through a kind of nation-wide communization? ... Make the President of the Republic and the ministers realize that things cannot go on as they are without the deadliest perils for France ... And, whatever you do, act quickly, quickly, quickly!'

M. Reibel hurried round to the Prefecture and described Weygand's fears to the President of the Republic.

'Ah, my dear Senator!' replied M. Lebrun. 'What a curious situation! It is the military — Pétain and Weygand — who want to end the war, and civilians — Paul Reynaud, Louis Marin and Mandel — who want to continue it!'

But the President was more deeply moved than he was prepared to let on.

In London, where General de Gaulle had arrived in the middle of the night, grave news was expected. M. Corbin, French ambassador, and M. Jean Monnet, leader of the Economic Mission, paid the general a very early call at the Hyde Park Hotel.

'We do not yet know what the British reply will be this morning,' said M. Corbin. 'We think they are going to agree, subject to certain guarantees concerning the fleet. So the end is near. Especially as the Cabinet is to meet in Bordeaux some time today and the meeting shows every likelihood of being decisive.'

He and M. Monnet went on to explain that it had occurred to them that some kind of *coup de théâtre*, introducing an entirely new element into the situation, would be likely to boost morale and at least strengthen M. Paul Reynaud's resolve to move the government to Algiers. They had therefore prepared with Sir Robert Vansittart, Permanent Secretary at the Foreign Office, what seemed a remarkable plan whereby London would formally propose to the Bordeaux government a union between France and Britain.[1] The two nations would announce the fusion of their govern-

[1] Louis-Dominique Girard writes: 'The birth of this scheme, arising at a moment when it was least expected and in the indescribable crisis atmosphere that prevailed in the provisional capital of France, deserves examination.

'The declaration germinated in the mind of M. Jean Monnet, leader of the French Economic

ments and the pooling of their resources and losses — in short, the complete merging of their destinies. Faced with such a proposal in such circumstances, France's ministers might be prepared to hold out. But the scheme had still to be adopted by the British government.[1]

'You are the only person who can get Mr Churchill to agree to it,' de Gaulle was told. 'You are due to have luncheon with him shortly. That will be a golden opportunity, provided you approve of the idea.'

He thought the plan over. Its 'grandness' of conception had an immediate appeal for him. No doubt putting it into practice would raise certain difficulties. But so what? It would comfort M. Reynaud in this hour of extreme crisis and strengthen his appeal to the French government to stand firm.

De Gaulle was invited to lunch at the Carlton Club. Churchill was accompanied by MM. Corbin and Monnet and Major Morton, his private secretary. Right at the start of the conversation, Churchill spoke of his fears concerning the fate of the French fleet.

'Whatever happens,' de Gaulle told him, 'it will not be handed over voluntarily. Pétain himself would not consent to that. Besides, the fleet is Darlan's fief. A feudal lord does not surrender his fief. But to be sure that the enemy never lays hands on our ships, we must remain at war. I must say your attitude in Tours came as a disagreeable surprise to me. You seemed to set little store by our alliance. Your resignedness is playing into the hands of those people at home who are in favour of capitulating. "You can see we are driven to it," they are saying, "the British themselves are giving their consent." Oh no! You must do something quite different from that to bolster us up in the terrible crisis that confronts us.'

Mr Churchill seemed shaken by this argument, and spent several moments in whispered consultation with Major Morton.

---

[1] 'I was not the prime mover,' Churchill writes in his memoirs. 'I first heard of a definite plan at a luncheon at the Carlton Club on June 15th, at which were present Lord Halifax, M. Corbin, Sir Robert Vansittart and one or two others. It was evident that there had been considerable discussion beforehand ... Vansittart and Desmond Morton had met M. Monnet and M. Pleven ... and been joined by General de Gaulle ... '

Delegation in London. Actually it was not the product of his imagination but the distortion of various other schemes that were under examination. These had been worked out by the members of private organizations that had been invited (in November 1939) to prepare the plan for a concerted peace which France and Great Britain would have to "sell" to the world after their joint victory over Germany ... From *federation* to *union* was only a step. M. Jean Monnet, very familiar with these preliminary studies, did not hesitate to take it in the panicky atmosphere of London after Dunkirk. Anxious to prevent an armistice, M. Jean Monnet and General de Gaulle lost no time in drawing up a text from which they expected truly miraculous results.'

De Gaulle then broached the subject of the projected Franco-British Union.

'Lord Halifax has already mentioned it to me,' said Churchill, 'but it is an enormous undertaking.'

In his memoirs Churchill recalls that his first reaction was unfavourable. But General de Gaulle was insistent, and after some discussion the Prime Minister came round to his way of thinking. He immediately summoned the British Cabinet. De Gaulle and Corbin drove with him to Downing Street and waited in an adjoining room while the ministers debated the issue.

In Bordeaux, Sir Ronald Campbell had received the following telegram from Lord Halifax shortly before lunch:

London, June 16th, 12.35 p.m.

Please give M. Reynaud the following message, which has been approved by the Cabinet:

Our agreement forbidding separate negotiations, whether for armistice or peace, was made with the French Republic, and not with any particular French administration or statesman. It therefore involves the honour of France.

Nevertheless, provided, but only provided, that the French fleet is sailed forthwith for British harbours pending negotiations, His Majesty's Government give their full consent to an enquiry by the French government to ascertain the terms of an armistice for France. His Majesty's Government, being resolved to continue the war, wholly exclude themselves from all part in the above-mentioned enquiry concerning an armistice.

General Spears was very perturbed by this message and told the ambassador so. He writes:

I felt it a mistake to do anything in the nature of releasing the French from their agreement. The door once opened would never be closed again ... There was another aspect to this message. Might not the French, especially the navy, feel insulted by the peremptory condition that they should sail forthwith to British harbours? Would this not be taken as proof of distrust or at least lack of confidence (which it was) and afford them a pretext for refusing any proposal aimed at achieving the same result which we might subsequently make?

'After all,' I argued, 'we are in the last resort dependent on the decision of the French themselves, and if they get it into their heads that we wish to hold their fleet as hostage, the outcry concerning the honour of the flag raised yesterday by Weygand may be renewed with greater stridency by Darlan today.'

The ambassador drew his attention to the fact that the British Cabinet had known of Mandel's point of view before sending this telegram and had still approved it. He (Sir Ronald Campbell) must therefore carry out his instructions and hand the message to M. Reynaud.

Fearing a violent French reaction to the clause concerning the navy, Spears suggested that they should first sound M. Jeanneney, 'in whose loyalty and courage we placed complete faith'. So Campbell and Spears called on the leader of the Senate.

M. Jeanneney was fully alive to the importance of the question. But he declined to give any opinion. Having exhausted all the arguments that seemed likely to pierce his reserve, Campbell and Spears had no choice but to call on M. Reynaud and hand him the British government's telegram.

M. Reynaud pulled a face as he read it. But not for the reasons that Campbell and Spears had anticipated. Its wording was the very opposite of what he had expected. He had counted on a categorical veto from Churchill, not a conditional authorization. He did not intend that France should break her alliance, nor did he wish those members of his government who favoured an armistice to use this message to strengthen their position. He therefore decided to reject the British proposal.

'What a very silly thing to do,' he said, 'to ask that the French fleet should go to British harbours when it is in fact at this very moment protecting Algeria and the Western Mediterranean ... This suggestion means offering all French North African harbours to the Italian fleet as targets!'

Returning to his first impression, Spears now felt definitely that Churchill's message was a mistake and that London had opened a dangerous door to the defeatists.

The French Premier was anxious to secure the retraction of the telegram. But how? There was only one way out: he must see Churchill as soon as possible. A further meeting was arranged between the two heads of government. It was to be held next day, June 17th, in Concarneau. Spears writes:

As we were about to leave, Reynaud said somewhat peevishly, addressing the ceiling, that he understood he had been described to London as being rather soft — *mou*. The meeting with Churchill would give him an opportunity to show him that he had been misinformed. This was a dig at me, and I realized Mandel had been using me as a goad to his leader. If it could help I did not mind, however much I liked Reynaud personally.

Campbell and Spears left the Prime Minister's office at 2.30 p.m. He was sorely perplexed ...

But from then on, events were to proceed apace. At about 3.30 p.m. Reynaud received a telephone call from Downing Street. It was from General de Gaulle. There were rumours in London that the French government was on the point of resigning. De Gaulle begged the Premier to do nothing of the kind.

'What would you have me do?' replied Reynaud. 'My position gets more difficult every hour. The British themselves are going out of their way to open the door to negotiations.'

'Sit tight!' urged de Gaulle. 'Before the end of the afternoon I hope to be able to send you a very important communication on behalf of the British government. It will be a real *coup de théâtre*.'

'All right,' said Reynaud. 'But hurry! I shall have to receive it in time for the Cabinet meeting at 5 p.m.'

At 3.55 p.m. Sir Ronald Campbell received a second telegram from the Foreign Office. It was worded as follows:

London, June 16th, 2.45 p.m.

You should inform M. Reynaud as follows:

We expect to be consulted as soon as any armistice terms are received. This is necessary not merely in virtue of treaty forbidding separate peace or armistice, but also in view of vital consequences of any armistice to ourselves, having regard especially to the fact that British troops are fighting with French army.[1]

You should impress on French government that in stipulating for removal of French fleet to British ports we have in mind French interests as well as our own, and are convinced that it will strengthen the hands of the French government in any armistice discussions if they can show that the French navy is out of reach of the German forces. As regards the French air force, we assume that every effort will be made to fly it to North Africa, unless indeed the French government would prefer to send it to this country ...

---

[1] This is untrue. The last British troops had pulled out 24 hours before. This also gives the lie to the statement attributed to General Brooke, according to which 'all French resistance had ceased' (see p. 339).

At 4.10 p.m. Sir Ronald Campbell and General Spears delivered this telegram to Reynaud in his office.

If anything, this further message made things worse. It rendered the French Premier's position still more precarious, for it confirmed the fact that the British Cabinet was prepared to sanction an armistice on condition that the French fleet sailed for British ports.

M. Reynaud raised the same objections as before: it was impossible to withdraw French naval forces from the Mediterranean. But the British spokesmen maintained that it *must* be withdrawn — 'for we saw clearly,' writes Spears, 'that London expected us somehow to get the French fleet out of the clutches of the Germans.'

In London the British Cabinet was nearing the end of its discussions, which had lasted for two hours. General de Gaulle and M. Corbin were still waiting in the adjoining room. From time to time one or other of the British ministers would come out and consult them on a point of detail.

Suddenly the door opened and all the British ministers filed in, with Mr Churchill at their head. 'We agree!' they cried. And indeed, the approved draft differed only slightly from the text that the Frenchmen had submitted.

'The General read it [the draft Declaration of Union],' writes Churchill, 'with an air of unwonted enthusiasm and, as soon as contact with Bordeaux could be obtained, began to telephone it to M. Reynaud.'

The time was 4.30 p.m.

In Bordeaux Reynaud, Campbell and Spears were still engaged in their bitter-sweet discussion of the telegrams from the Foreign Office. Suddenly the telephone rang. Reynaud lifted the receiver. A moment later his whole expression brightened.

'One moment,' he said, 'I must take this down.'

Grasping a sheet of foolscap that was lying on the table, he began to write, repeating each word as he recorded it.

' ... Listening, I became transfixed with amazement,' records Spears. ' ... Reynaud was taking down in French, from de Gaulle's dictation in London, the text of the Declaration of Union proposed by the British government. On he wrote in a frightful scrawl, getting more excited as the message unfolded ...

'Finally Reynaud stopped writing and said into the telephone: "Does he agree to this? Did Churchill give you this personally?"

' "Yes," said de Gaulle. "It is the decision of the British government. The Cabinet is going to resume its deliberations. The text has been approved, all but a few words that are still liable to alteration; but those are merely points of detail. You will probably be called on to become leader of the first Joint War Cabinet."

'A pause followed these words: de Gaulle was handing the receiver to Churchill.

'"Hullo?" said the British Prime Minister. "Reynaud? De Gaulle is right. Our proposal may have tremendous consequences. You must sit tight!"

'"All right," said Reynaud. "Anyway, we are due to meet tomorrow."

'"That is so," replied Churchill. "Till then! In Concarneau."'

Reynaud put the receiver down. 'He was transfigured with joy,' writes Spears. '... He was happy with a great happiness in the belief that France would now remain in the war ... The sense of the generosity of the offer was overwhelming, the sincerity of the gesture completely convincing.'

Here is the text of the proclamation:

At this most fateful moment in the history of the modern world the governments of the United Kingdom and the French Republic make this declaration of indissoluble union and unyielding resolution in their common defence of justice and freedom against subjection to a system which reduces mankind to a life of robots and slaves.

The two governments declare that France and Britain shall no longer be two nations, but one Franco-British Union.

The constitution of the Union will provide for joint organs of defence, foreign, financial and economic policies.

Every citizen of France will enjoy immediately citizenship of Great Britain; every British subject will become a citizen of France.

Both countries will share responsibility for the repair of the devastation of war, wherever it occurs in their territories, and the resources of both shall be equally, and as one, applied to that purpose.

During the war there shall be a single War Cabinet, and all the forces of Britain and France, whether on land, sea or in the air, will be placed under its direction. It will govern from wherever it best can. The two Parliaments will be formally associated. The nations of the British Empire are already forming new armies. France will keep her available forces in the field, on the sea and in the air. The Union appeals to the United States to fortify the economic resources of the Allies, and to bring her powerful material aid to the common cause.

The Union will concentrate its whole energy against the power of the enemy, no matter where the battle may be.

And thus we shall conquer.

'This must be typed at once so that you can have it for the Cabinet meeting,' said Spears, and gathering Reynaud's script he dashed off to the adjoining secretaries' room.

There he found Paul Reynaud's friend, Comtesse Hélène de Portes.

'As I handed a secretary the paper,' writes Spears, 'she stepped behind him and read over his shoulder, holding his arm to prevent his turning the pages too fast for her to read them. It was difficult to tell from her expression whether rage or amazement prevailed. But both feelings were apparent. As she went on delaying the secretary to read herself, I told him curtly the message must be typed without a moment's delay.'

When Spears returned to Reynaud's office, the Premier's exultation 'had if anything increased'.

'I shall die defending these proposals,' he exclaimed.

But it would soon be 5 p.m. From the adjoining room could already be heard the voices of ministers gathering for the Cabinet meeting.

On returning to the British consulate, Sir Ronald Campbell found another telegram from the Foreign Office, instructing him to suspend all action and to cancel the two telegrams concerning the French fleet sent at 12.35 p.m. and 2.45 p.m. These had been superseded by the Declaration of Union.

But was there still time to inform Reynaud? Spears and Campbell leapt into a car and tore round to the Prefecture to retrieve the two telegrams from Paul Reynaud and tell him that there was no need for him to give any further thought to them.[1]

The Premier was obviously pleased with the new message. It would allow him to omit mention of the two earlier ones to his colleagues: *thus he would be the only minister to know of them.*

Meanwhile the *Primauguet* left Le Verdon, carrying part of the Bank of France's gold reserves to Dakar.

M. Reynaud had suggested some time earlier that American ships should convey the nation's gold to safety.[2] But the French Admiralty had protested, insisting that the task was wholly its responsibility.

At 5.15 p.m. the Cabinet met under President Lebrun. M. Reynaud began by informing his colleagues of the 'negative result of the representations to the British government with which the majority had entrusted him the day before'. He confined himself to remarking briefly that 'its

[1] Concerning this incident, Churchill writes: 'A messenger was ... sent [to Reynaud] to say that the two earlier messages should be considered as "cancelled". "Suspended" would have been a better word ... '

This decision had presumably been taken by Churchill during his lunch at the Carlton Club, and resulted from his whispered consultation with his private secretary (see p. 361).

[2] The rush for the spoils was beginning. Each nation was angling for the security that best suited her interests. Britain wanted the fleet, the United States wanted gold.

consent was first given conditionally, then withdrawn.' But he did not say what the condition had been. He merely read out the opening of the first British communication:

> Our agreement forbidding separate negotiations, whether for armistice or peace, was made with the French Republic, and not with any particular administration or statesman. It therefore involves the honour of France.

Thus the Cabinet was kept in ignorance, not only of the tenor of the two telegrams but of their very existence.

At this point several ministers made to protest, but M. Reynaud cut them short: 'I now have a communication of the highest importance to make to you,' he announced in ringing tones.

He then read out the text of the Franco-British Declaration of Union. He went on to say that he was to meet Churchill in Concarneau next day to discuss how the Declaration should be put into effect. Most of the ministers reacted with utter amazement. M. Chautemps at once declared that he 'did not want France to become a Dominion'. Several others, including M. Ybarnegaray, allied themselves with his protest.

Paul Baudouin writes: 'I remember how stunned nearly all the ministers were when M. Reynaud informed them of this proposal ... It in no way satisfied our expectations. It did not loosen the stranglehold on the country ... '

Coming at such a time, the British offer prompted more alarm than reassurance. Many ministers saw it as a take-over bid rather than a projected amalgamation. 'While Metropolitan France, deprived of a government, was subjected to German domination,' writes Louis-Dominique Girard, 'the French Empire itself would be made subordinate to a British government that might lose it by continuing the war or barter it in any future negotiation with the Reich.'

But what would be left of France, stripped of her fleet, her Empire and her gold, and with her civilian population delivered into the invader's hands?

'I detected a unanimous feeling of disapproval round about me,' writes Weygand concerning the Declaration of Union. 'Instantly it was borne in upon me that it could not be otherwise, for the circumstances of material inferiority in which her sacrifice to the Allied cause had landed France would have placed her, in the event of acceptance, in a state of vassalage impossible to conceive of.'

At that moment an usher entered the conference room and handed M.

Reynaud a note that had been hastily scribbled by Madame de Portes.

'I hope,' she had written, 'that you are not going to play at being Isabella of Bavaria!'

Suddenly the door opened and General Lafont walked in. His appearances had become almost ritual. He handed the President of the Republic a further message from General Georges. M. Lebrun immediately read it to his colleagues:

> 5 p.m. Situation worse still. In the east, northern outskirts Dijon and Saône front reached by enemy. In the centre, numerous armoured columns heading for La Charité threaten encirclement No. 3 Group of Armies. Forest of Fontainebleau occupied. Supply situation for troops and retreating civilians serious. Manoeuvring difficult on account of road-jamming and bombing of railways and bridges. Vital you make decision.
>
> *Signed:* GEORGES

This message was a forceful reminder of the present: while these ministerial wranglings dragged on, the war was continuing.

'That is an appalling picture of the army's position!' said President Lebrun. He was deeply moved.

'It is quite impossible for us to leave France without asking the enemy to make his conditions known,' said M. Chautemps.

Most of the ministers supported him. The discussion grew heated.

M. Mandel said tartly: 'There are some people here who want to fight and others who don't!'

'No!' returned M. Chautemps. 'There are some Frenchmen driven to despair by their country's plight and trying to find a way out ... Anyway, I don't need lessons from you!'

The atmosphere was becoming stormier and stormier. Disagreement was on the point of degenerating into a quarrel.

'France's honour is at stake!' cried M. Reynaud. 'You cannot tamper with the agreement of March 28th!'

Several ministers protested against such a one-sided conception of the Anglo-French agreement. Then M. Baudouin spoke. He told the President of the Republic and the whole government of Winston Churchill's statements in Tours, in the course of the discussion that he had attended. M. Reynaud denied them vehemently: they did not, he said, tally with his own recollections.

The feelings of most members of the Cabinet were later pithily expressed by M. Lebrun (at Pétain's trial):

Though he may still wave a sheet of paper to remind us of the obligations there set forth, from the moment one of the signatories of an agreement such as that of March 28th withholds part of his forces for his own defence (like the British Empire), instead of risking them in the common fight, he no longer has the moral authority to say: 'I cannot release you from your undertaking.'

This was the view that emerged from the opinions voiced by most ministers. M. Reynaud sensed that he was losing ground and that the majority of the government was no longer behind him.

'I then stated,' writes Reynaud, 'that in those circumstances the government would meet at 10 p.m. to tender its resignation.'

The meeting broke up at 7.30 p.m.

At 7.45 p.m. Sir Ronald Campbell and General Spears walked into the hall of the Prefecture. They were met by Roland de Margerie, who told them flatly: 'The Prime Minister is going to tell you that he is to resign.'

'What's that? What did you say?' exclaimed Spears. He had been elated by the arrival of the Declaration of Union, and de Margerie's words brought him down to earth with a bump.

'The Prime Minister is going to tell you that he is to resign,' Margerie repeated in the same tone, showing them into a room that was not the one where Reynaud generally received them.

'So this was the end,' writes Spears. 'Reynaud was beaten, he had not made the grade; France was leaving us to fight alone ... It was like stabbing a friend bent over you in grief and affection.'

When Reynaud appeared, Spears asked him what effect the Declaration of Union had had on the Cabinet. Reynaud shrugged helplessly and told him of their fears that France would become a British Dominion.

'Was the Cabinet informed that Churchill proposes to meet you tomorrow and may already have started?'

'Yes,' answered Reynaud, 'but it made no difference ... '

'Have you actually resigned?' asked Spears after a few moments.

'Not yet. But I intend doing so at the next Cabinet meeting, at 10 p.m.'

Spears and Campbell decided that they had no choice but to send an urgent message to Churchill, telling him to hold up his journey.

In London the War Cabinet sat till 6 p.m. Then Mr Churchill dined. Afterwards he made final arrangements for his journey to France. With him he took Sir Archibald Sinclair, leader of the Liberal Party, Mr Attlee, leader of the Labour Party, the three Chiefs of Staff and various important officers and officials. He got to Waterloo at about 8 p.m. A special train was waiting for him and his party. He writes:

We could reach Southampton in two hours, and a night of steaming at thirty knots in the cruiser would bring us to the rendezvous by noon on June 17. We had taken our seats in the train. My wife had come to see me off. There was an odd delay in starting. Evidently some hitch had occurred. Presently my private secretary arrived from Downing Street breathless with the following message from Campbell at Bordeaux:

'Ministerial crisis has opened ... Hope to have news by midnight. Meanwhile meeting arranged for tomorrow impossible.'

On this I returned to Downing Street with a heavy heart.

Now that Paul Reynaud had ceased to be Prime Minister, it was as though there were no French government at all.

Having informed Churchill of the situation, Spears and Campbell called on Mandel to sound him for his views on this latest turn in the crisis. They found him in a cold rage.

'*Il n'y a rien à faire avec ces gens-là!*' he said. 'I called Chautemps a coward, and so did Rio. When there were protests I distributed the same diploma to his supporters, but it was no use ... No, Reynaud has lost all authority.'

Then, after a pause, he added sadly: 'You should have held France to her signature. Churchill has been too nice. His kindness, his chivalry and loyalty may sometimes be a fault; they have been in this case.'

Campbell and Spears left Mandel to his anger and went off in search of M. Jeanneney. They begged him to use all his influence with President Lebrun to persuade him either to refuse Reynaud's resignation or to entrust the latter with the formation of the new government. But the leader of the Senate answered very evasively.

'What about Mandel?' suggested Spears. 'Couldn't he be entrusted with the formation of the new government?'

M. Jeanneney preferred not to give an opinion.

At 9 p.m. President Lebrun summoned Reynaud, Jeanneney and Herriot to his office. It had been suggested at the Cabinet meeting, he said, that the Germans should be sounded for their armistice conditions — the argument being that the enemy's demands were bound to be so exorbitant that the whole French nation would favour their rejection. M. Jeanneney discerningly drew attention to the danger that the army would then be hamstrung.

M. Lebrun asked M. Reynaud if he were prepared to remain in office if it entailed carrying out the policy advocated by the majority of ministers.

'That is impossible,' answered M. Reynaud. 'If an armistice is sought, it will not be by me.'

'Then who, tomorrow?' asked M. Lebrun.

'Paul Reynaud!' replied M. Jeanneney.

M. Herriot's answer was more cautious: 'That is your concern,' he said.

At 10 p.m. came the third Cabinet meeting of the day. M. Reynaud officially announced his government's resignation. The ensuing silence was interpreted by President Lebrun as 'a clear enough indication of the wishes of the majority'.[1]

Turning to M. Reynaud, M. Lebrun asked him for the second time: 'I want you to remain in office. Are you prepared to carry out the policy advocated by the majority?'

Again M. Reynaud refused.

'That I cannot do,' he said. 'If you want that policy carried out, apply to Marshal Pétain.'[2]

In later years he was to explain: 'I said "Marshal Pétain" because I had made him admit in front of the Cabinet that it would be a dastardly crime for us to hand over our fleet to Germany so that she could stab our ally in the back ...

'I said to myself: "In Germany's eyes, France is beaten and it is a question of beating Britain as soon as possible; she needs the assistance of the French fleet, so she will ask for it in the armistice. Since Marshal Pétain cannot give it to her, after what I have made him admit in front of the Cabinet, I shall take over the reins again and perhaps we shall continue the war." '

By 11 p.m. the President was growing really concerned: it was essential that the nation should have a government next day, 'for unless it did, the distressed souls I saw wherever I went would have the added care of saying: "France hasn't even a government now!" '

So, as Reynaud walked out, accompanied by Mandel, Louis Marin, Rio and Campinchi, M. Lebrun drew Marshal Pétain aside and said: 'Are you willing to form a government?'

The Marshal instantly produced a list from his dispatch-case, handed it to the President and answered: 'Here it is!'

[1] At the Marshal's trial M. Lebrun said: 'There was no Chamber of Deputies, there was nothing left at all. In a word: I couldn't help being impressed by the majority that had built up within the Cabinet. The President of the Republic is an arbiter. I would arbitrate in accordance with the vote that had just been expressed.'

[2] General Weygand writes: 'M. Reynaud was thus putting into execution the programme suggested at the War Committee meeting on May 25th — that of getting another government to take the decision.' (See p. 156.)

The speed of the Marshal's response has subsequently been interpreted as evidence of a conspiracy, but at the time it made quite a different impression on the President.

'I was unused to such speed,' he writes in his memoirs. 'I recalled, not without bitterness, the agonizing formations of governments over which I had presided during my stay at the Elysée Palace.' And at the Marshal's trial he admitted that he had experienced a certain relief: 'France had a government. The announcement could be promulgated in the *Journal Officiel* next day.'

At this point M. Charles-Roux raised an objection. On hearing that the Marshal was thinking of giving Pierre Laval the Foreign Ministry, he spoke out strongly against the appointment and threatened to resign as permanent secretary at the Quai d'Orsay.

'I knew,' he explains, 'that M. Pierre Laval had what I shall call a personal quarrel with Britain dating from 1935. I was afraid that he might turn his personal quarrel into a national quarrel for France.'

President Lebrun likewise objected.

'M. Laval as Minister for Foreign Affairs?' he said to the Marshal. 'That is impossible. Our relations with the British are none too good. Don't make them worse.'

At which stage M. Laval arrived. With him was M. Adrien Marquet, the mayor of Bordeaux, whom the Marshal was thinking of making Minister of the Interior. Pétain suggested that Laval should be content with the Ministry of Justice. Laval declined and stalked out. M. Marquet took his side and refused the Interior. He left the room shouting: 'Have they gone mad?'

The Marshal did not press them. He appointed Baudouin in place of Laval and Pomaret in place of Marquet.

At about 11.30 p.m. the decrees were signed by the President of the Republic, and the Marshal's first Cabinet was finally formed. It was composed as follows:

Deputy Premier: M. Camille Chautemps.
National Defence: General Weygand.
War: General Colson.
Air: General Pujo.
Marine: Admiral Darlan.
Justice: M. Frémicourt.
Interior: M. Pomaret.
Foreign Affairs: M. Paul Baudouin.

Finance and Commerce: M. Bouthillier.

Colonies: M. Albert Rivière.

National Education: M. Albert Rivaud.

Public Works: M. Frossard.

Agriculture and Food: M. Chichery.

Labour: M. Février.[1]

Ex-servicemen and Families: M. Ybarnegaray.

Under-Secretary of State to the Presidency of the Council: M. Raphaël Alibert.

Under-Secretary of State for Refugees: M. Robert Schuman.

Sir Ronald Campbell and General Spears had reached the Prefecture at about 10.30 p.m. The building looked dark and deserted. Inside, the hall was dimly lit on account of black-out precautions. The crowd that had collected outside was beginning to disperse, and the oppressive silence inside was in dramatic contrast to the earlier noise and bustle. It was in this forlorn and unlit setting that the Reynaud administration had crumbled. It was like being in a theatre after the fall of the curtain: the footlights were out, the players gone.

Spears walked through the hall. 'Passing by a large column I was startled to see a tall figure flat against it, shrouded in its shadow. It called me by name in a loud whisper. I stopped and looked up at de Gaulle.'

De Gaulle had landed in Bordeaux at 9.30 p.m., convinced that his proposal had been enthusiastically accepted and that it had enabled Paul Reynaud to remain in the saddle. By now he knew the worst. Coming immediately after the cheerful mood prevailing in Downing Street, the pessimism of the Rue Vital-Carles had been a great shock to him. He was plainly overwrought.

'I must speak to you,' he said, 'it is extremely urgent.'

'But I can't now,' answered Spears. 'The ambassador and I are just going in to see the Premier.'

'You must,' de Gaulle insisted. 'I have very good reason to believe Weygand intends to arrest me.'

'We shan't be long, I think,' said Spears. 'If you stay exactly where you are till we come out, it should be all right ... '

Spears and Campbell were then shown into the room where Reynaud had last received them — *not* the office set aside for the Prime Minister.

They had expected Reynaud to look crushed; but he was relaxed, if

---

[1] MM. Février and Rivière, members of the *Section française de l'Internationale ouvrière* party, were entering the government on the express instruction of Léon Blum, following a meeting between Blum, Albert Sérol, Georges Monnet and Fernand Audeguil.

more reserved than usual. 'He was going through a necessary formality,' observes Spears, 'a producer giving an account of the last disastrous performance of a play to its backers.' In carefully worded sentences he explained that he had just handed his resignation to President Lebrun; that the Council was still in session; that Marshal Pétain had been asked to form the new government; and that Jeanneney and Herriot had decided that the Marshal must be allowed to try his luck. Finally, he gave his assessment of the various members of the new team. Having laid down the too onerous burden of power, he was reviewing events purely as a by-stander, as though he were in the lobby of the Chamber.

'The ambassador and I stared at Reynaud,' writes Spears. ' ... All words were useless now. I searched my mind to think of anything that was worth saying or doing and found nothing, only a growing realization that there were two worlds in that room and Reynaud had left ours ... There is not much one can say to a departing soul.'

Suddenly the ex-Premier remembered that he had planned to meet Churchill in Concarneau next day. He asked what time the Prime Minister would be arriving.

'I shall be glad to talk things over with him,' he said.

This was too much for Spears. 'The idea that the Prime Minister should risk his invaluable life and others our nation could not spare, that at such a moment the direction of the war might be suspended for what in fact would have been a chat with Reynaud was more than I could bear ... '

'Tomorrow,' he said, 'there will be another government and you will no longer speak for anyone. The meeting has been cancelled.'

The ambassador gestured wearily to Spears, to indicate that the conversation had gone on long enough. The British representatives took their leave, bitterly disappointed by this last interview.

They walked back across the hall. De Gaulle was still there, with his back to the same column. Waiting had made him tenser than ever. He looked very pale. He repeated in a whisper that he had good reason to believe Weygand meant to have him arrested. He understood there was a British warship in the river. He wished to return to England as soon as possible.

Spears and the ambassador conferred rapidly in an undertone. This was hardly the place for such a discussion. Sir Ronald suggested that the three of them should meet at his private residence.

A few minutes later, therefore, Campbell, Spears and de Gaulle were alone together in a room in the Hotel Montré. They decided that, to avoid arrest, de Gaulle should spend the night aboard the cruiser *Berkeley*.

He would fly to London next morning in the plane that Churchill had put at his disposal. Spears rang the Prime Minister for his approval.

While this secret discussion was going on in the Hotel Montré, President Lebrun's staff was drafting an official communiqué. As soon as it was finished it was given to the Press:

> In the present grave situation the Cabinet, acting on the suggestion of M. Paul Reynaud, has decided that the leadership of France should be entrusted to a man of high standing enjoying the respect of the whole nation.
>
> In consequence M. Paul Reynaud has handed in the Cabinet's resignation to the President of the Republic. M. Lebrun has accepted this resignation, paying tribute to the patriotism that prompted it, and has immediately appealed to Marshal Pétain, who has agreed to form the new administration.
>
> The President of the Republic has thanked Marshal Pétain who, by assuming the heaviest responsibility that has ever weighed on a French statesman, is displaying still further proof of his devotion to our country.

At about 1 a.m. General Spears called on Mandel and told him that he and de Gaulle would be leaving for England in a few hours. He begged the Minister of the Interior to board the plane with them. He had already asked Reynaud to go, he said, but the ex-Premier had refused.

'There must,' insisted Spears, 'be an authorized French voice, not pledged to surrender, to guide the French Empire.'

At that moment Béatrice Bretty put her head round the door and said: 'The trunks are packed, Georges.'

But Mandel was unwilling to leave Bordeaux.

'I shall not go tomorrow,' he told Spears. 'It would look as if I was afraid, as if I was running away. Wednesday, perhaps.'

'It may be too late,' said Spears. Then, seeing that Mandel was not to be swayed, 'I hope to see you in London soon, very soon ... '

Meanwhile the new government had met under the chairmanship of M. Albert Lebrun. General Weygand attended as Minister for National Defence. He came armed with the very latest news of the military situation. The encirclement of the 2nd Group of Armies was now complete. Any substantial regrouping along the Loire seemed quite out of the question. The British had evacuated the last of their units. America had made it clear that she could not supply any direct military aid.

There was therefore no choice but to 'ask Germany for her armistice conditions', acting along the lines advocated by M. Chautemps.

This resolution was adopted without more ado, for on this issue ministers were undivided. It only remained for them to agree on the choice of mediator. Someone proposed Switzerland. The Marshal suggested Spain, where he enjoyed considerable prestige. This solution won the Cabinet's approval.

The meeting ended at midnight.

At 1 a.m. (it was now June 17th) the Marshal sent for Señor de Lequerica, the Spanish ambassador.

When Señor de Lequerica reached the Rue Vital-Carles, he was at once shown to the office of M. Paul Baudouin, the new Minister for Foreign Affairs. Also present was M. Charles-Roux, the Permanent Under-Secretary. The interview was a short one. M. Baudouin handed the ambassador a note in which the Spanish government was asked to inform the German government through diplomatic channels that the French government had requested it to 'find out on what conditions Chancellor Hitler would be prepared to end operations and conclude an armistice'.

A few moments later M. Baudouin received the United States ambassador. He told Mr Biddle that the French army was completely crushed and that it was vital that the present massacre be stopped. To ask Germany for her conditions was not to accept them. If they proved incompatible with the honour and dignity of France, they would be made public. The impossibility of accepting them would then be obvious to the French people. This would give them the courage to fight on.

M. Baudouin categorically assured Mr Biddle that the French fleet would never be handed over to Germany.

M. Baudouin likewise received Sir Ronald Campbell and explained the appalling series of circumstances that had forced France to take this step.

———•◦◦◦•———

On the extreme left the main thrust came from Rommel's 7th Panzer Division. The Führer had entrusted its commander with a special mission: to capture Cherbourg as quickly as possible in order to prevent the last British units, now falling back in the Cotentin peninsula, from reaching the port and embarking. This meant a race between the German armour and General Marshall-Cornwall's 'Normanforce'.[1]

The British troops had started for the coast at midnight on June 16th and were hurrying along the two roads leading to Cherbourg: the one on the left, which runs through Coutances and La Haye-du-Puits, and the one on the right, which runs through Saint-Lô, Carentan and Valognes. But they were slowed down by columns of French soldiers and refugees.

The 7th Panzer Division, which was in the vicinity of Laigle, started moving forward at dawn. Its orders were to reach the Nonnant–Sées road and then make straight for Cherbourg, smashing its way through every obstacle that it encountered. By this time German air reconnaissance crews had reported seeing warships and transport vessels at Cherbourg. It seemed likely that the evacuation had already started.

By 1 p.m. the division was near Boucé, and by midnight it had covered more than 150 miles, pausing only in Flers to refuel. But it was still 25 miles from Cherbourg. And by then the British units were in the port. They had driven 200 miles in twenty-four hours.

In Laval, principal town of the department of Mayenne, the civilian and military authorities were faced with difficulties typical of these crisis days. The town had been made the evacuation centre for the entire population of Aisne. The normal population of Laval was 28,000. Now it had to shelter an additional 80,000.

In addition, 400,000 who had come from Laon, Saint-Quentin, Vervins, Soissons and Château-Thierry were strewn along the road between Paris and Quimper. They were lost in the flood of refugees from fifteen other départements. There could be no question of regrouping them, aiding them

[1] See sketch on p. 391.

or even advising them. Food was running short. An epidemic of dysentery had broken out, particularly among the women and children packed in the cellars.

In Rennes, likewise packed with refugees, 2,000 were killed and 900 injured by an intensive air-raid.

In Brest a number of cruisers forestalled the arrival of the Panzer divisions by sailing for Dakar with the remaining gold reserves of the Bank of France.

In Saint-Nazaire work on the uncompleted *Jean-Bart* was vigorously stepped up in an attempt to save the 35,000-ton battleship from falling into German hands.

In the centre the German columns that had crossed the Loire at La Charité[1] and Nevers were threatening Touchon's and Frère's decimated armies from the rear. On the right the enemy was striking boldly southwards through the Saône and Rhône valleys in a bid to cut off the Alpine Army. Guderian's Panzers had reached Pontarlier and Montbéliard. The units that made up the 39th and 41st Armoured Corps were close to physical exhaustion, but they were spurred on by a commander who was determined to forge ahead.

Within a week the Panzers had advanced from Charleville to the Swiss border. When Guderian triumphantly telephoned Hitler with the news that he had entered Pontarlier, the Führer told him he must be wrong — surely he meant Pontailler-sur-Saône?

Then Guderian ordered a general 'left-wheel' towards Belfort and the Meuse, in order to mop up resistance in the Jura hills and attack the Maginot Line from the rear. By 9 a.m. General Prételat was telephoning from Bourg to announce that he was cut off from Belfort. Was he to rejoin his troops? General Georges pressed him to make every effort to get through by plane, since his presence would put fresh vigour into the fighting.

All over France, the roads were a sorry sight. The long lines of cars and lorries moved more and more slowly, like an outflow of lava cooling and setting. Petrol was running out. Another few gallons and that would be the end. Vehicles that had been brought to a standstill were being tipped off the roads to make room for those that were still on the move — for the time being.

But if the cars could be halted, panic could not. 'The roads were silent now,' writes Fabre-Luce, 'but they were still packed with men of military

---

1 At La Charité the Germans seized a goods van that was standing neglected on a siding. It contained all the secret documents of the French General Staff. The Wilhelmstrasse published them a few weeks later, in the form of a White Paper.

age afraid of being captured, soldiers trying to make their way home, Polish or Spanish workers freed by the Ministry of Munitions.'

At 9.30 p.m. General Sir Alan Brooke left Saint-Nazaire aboard the armed trawler *Cambridgeshire*.

ARMISTICE NEGOTIATIONS

The gist of Paul Baudouin's 1 a.m. conversation with Señor de Lequerica had been telephoned to Madrid. It reached the Wilhelmstrasse at 3 a.m. From there it was sent by special wire to Hitler in Sedan.

The Führer at once got in touch with Mussolini, informing him of the French request for an armistice and suggesting talks in Munich.

POLITICAL SITUATION

At 7 a.m., the time on which they had agreed the night before, General Spears sat waiting for de Gaulle in the hall of the Hotel Montré. The time moved round to 7.30 a.m., and still no sign of him. Spears began to fear that he really had been arrested by Weygand, for he had not spent the night on board the *Berkeley*. At the last moment they had been unable to get in touch with the captain of the ship, which was moored at Le Verdon.

At last de Gaulle and his aide-de-camp arrived. 'They had brought quite a lot of luggage,' writes Spears, 'which was stowed away in my car; and then, at de Gaulle's request, a curious little comedy was played ... The stratagem consisted in conveying the impression that he was quietly driving about Bordeaux on his lawful occasions ... We drove to the two separate buildings where what there was of the Ministry of War was lodged, and de Gaulle, without leaving the car ... told officials whom he sent for at both places to make a series of appointments for him ... at specific times later in the morning.'

When they reached Mérianac aerodrome they agreed that de Gaulle should behave as though he had come to see Spears off and that Spears should haul him aboard at the last moment. The luggage was put aboard. Spears climbed into the cabin. The engines started up. Suddenly Spears reached out his hand as though in a last farewell and pulled de Gaulle into the plane. The door slammed shut. The plane took off, climbed and vanished over the horizon -- to the open-mouthed amazement of the chauffeur who had driven them to the aerodrome.

'We flew over La Rochelle and Rochefort,' writes de Gaulle. 'Ships were burning in the harbours,[1] set on fire by German planes. We went over Paimpont, where my mother was lying dangerously ill. The forest was a mass of smoke from the blazing ammunition depots.'

The plane landed at Jersey to refuel. The day was chilly. While the mechanics were filling the tanks, de Gaulle and Spears went into the canteen. De Gaulle ordered a coffee.

' ... Taking a sip,' writes Spears, 'he said — in a voice which indicated that without implying criticism he must nevertheless proclaim the truth — that this was tea and he had asked for coffee. It was his first introduction to the tepid liquid which, in England, passes for either one or the other.

'His martyrdom had begun.'

While de Gaulle was flying to England a strange scene was being enacted in Washington. On his own initiative Colonel Jacquin, head of the French Purchasing Commission in the United States, sold all existing French contracts to the British. These included contracts with armament manufacturers worth billions of francs. Edward R. Stettinius comments:

> For the French ... much was at stake. The government which had appointed them was gone. All on their own, they were about to dispose of all the war assets of France in the United States ... By 3.30 a.m. on June 17th the transfer was complete.

In Bordeaux the political day got off to a late start, for the members of the new Cabinet had worked till 3 a.m.

Before going to the Cabinet meeting, M. Baudouin awoke to the fact that in the extreme confusion that had marked the last moments of the Reynaud government France had neglected to seek an armistice with the Italians. To repair this omission, the Minister for Foreign Affairs sent for the Papal Nuncio, Mgr Valerio Valeri, and at 9.45 a.m. handed him the following note:

> The French government led by Marshal Pétain requests the Holy See to be so kind as to draw the Italian government's attention as swiftly as possible to the note for the German government that was last night handed to the Spanish ambassador to France.
>
> It likewise begs the Holy See to inform the Italian government of its desire to join in seeking the bases of a lasting peace between the two countries.

---

[1] Including the *Champlain*, which was packed with British troops. 'Hundreds of tiny figures could be seen in the water,' writes Spears.

When the Cabinet meeting opened, M. Baudouin told his colleagues about his series of interviews with Señor de Lequerica, Sir Ronald Campbell and Mr Drexel Biddle. He likewise informed them of the note that he had just handed to Mgr Valerio Valeri.

The Marshal shut himself away in the Prefecture to write the appeal that he was to address to the French people. At about 12.15 p.m. the radio technicians installed microphones, and at 12.30 p.m. he sat down at a modest whitewood table and gravely read these words into a microphone:

Frenchmen!

Answering the call of the President of the Republic, I am from today assuming control of the government of France. Certain of the affection of our wonderful army, fighting with a heroism worthy of its long military traditions against an enemy superior in numbers and equipment; certain that by its magnificent stand it has fulfilled its duties to our Allies; certain of the support of the ex-servicemen whom it has been my honour to command, I bestow myself on France to palliate her misfortune.

In these painful hours my thoughts are with the unfortunate refugees suffering dire hardship on the roads. I send them my sympathy and concern. It is with a heavy heart that today I tell you we must stop the fighting.

Last night I communicated with the enemy, asking him whether he is prepared to join us in seeking ways — honourably, as between soldiers after the fray — of putting an end to hostilities.

Let all Frenchmen rally round my government in this time of tribulation, subduing their fears and hearkening only to their faith in our country's destiny.

The French listened to his words with deep emotion. All over the country, in the towns and on the roads, the cry went up: 'It's over! It's over! The nightmare is over!'

The news swept through France. Crowds of refugees congregated round public buildings to cheer the Marshal. People stood on their doorsteps, weeping, while a flood of fervour and gratitude surged out to the illustrious old man who had, by assuming power, assumed far more — the grief of the entire nation ...

The announcement prompted instant official reaction on the other side of the Atlantic. The Marshal had barely finished speaking before Mr Roosevelt sent for Mr Morgenthau, Secretary of the Treasury, and ordered him to freeze all French property in the United States.

He then urged the Senate to adopt a resolution asserting that it would recognize no transference of territories belonging to the western hemisphere between non-American powers. This was aimed at France's American possessions — particularly those in the West Indies.

Finally, he summoned Mr Cordell Hull and told him to deal with the question of the French fleet without delay. Mr Cordell Hull therefore sent Mr Biddle a telegram instructing him to seek an immediate interview with Admiral Darlan. He was to inform the Admiral that unless it took steps to prevent the fleet from falling into enemy hands, the French government would be pursuing a policy detrimental to the preservation of the French Empire and to the chance of restoring France's independence; it would also permanently forfeit the friendship of the United States.

Britain was not slow in following the American example. At 4.45 p.m. Sir Ronald Campbell called on M. Charles-Roux and gave him the texts of the two telegrams that he had shown to M. Reynaud the day before. The Permanent Under-Secretary for Foreign Affairs was flabbergasted. At Marshal Pétain's trial he declared: 'Sir Ronald Campbell brought me two telegrams that had been handed to Paul Reynaud the day before and then withdrawn. I had never seen them before. M. Paul Baudouin had not seen them either, on June 17th, and could not understand why they had shuttled back and forth between the British ambassador and our government. We therefore decided to ask M. Paul Reynaud and Sir Ronald Campbell to enlighten us next day.'

General Spears had driven to Downing Street and contacted Sir Robert Vansittart and Churchill. What had been his motives in bringing de Gaulle to London? Later he was to outline them to his wife in terms that left no room for doubt:

France was going to be cut off, he said, from all the outside world, and subjected from now on to relentless propaganda, and that propaganda would be directed to the purpose of bringing the French in against us. Such an idea appeared unthinkable now, but the war might last a very long time, and the people of France would know nothing about it save what the Germans chose to tell them. We would be obliged, moreover, eventually to bombard French towns. If the German propaganda were successful and the French as a nation took up arms against us, then we might lose the war. One thing and only one thing would counteract German influence — the fact that a French force was fighting with us.

Presumably these were the views that he expressed to Churchill and

Vansittart. But the latter did not immediately share them. He thought it unwise to add to Anglo-French tension while the French government still held a trump card — her fleet — and could severely damage Britain's cause, either by using it herself or by handing it over to the Germans.

Spears argued that de Gaulle was really only the forerunner of a Reynaud-Mandel government, which would shortly be arriving in London. Why not make use of him in the meantime?

Vansittart objected that the Republican regime was utterly discredited in France. Would it not be better to take advantage of the way things stood and try to set up a constitutional monarchy in its place?

Spears retorted that if Britain took that line she could say goodbye to the idea of getting Reynaud and Mandel to come to London. Britain, he said, had everything to gain from France's remaining a republic.

'The first thing to do was to hoist the colours,' writes de Gaulle. 'The radio was there for that. On the afternoon of June 17th I disclosed my intentions to Mr Winston Churchill. What could I, a castaway on Britain's shores, have done without his help? He gave it at once and as a first step placed the B.B.C. at my disposal.'

On learning of the Marshal's broadcast appeal, de Gaulle decided to reply next day, June 18th.

Churchill himself spoke without delay. He recorded the following address, to be broadcast at 9 p.m.:

> The news from France is very bad, and I grieve for the gallant French people, who have fallen into this terrible misfortune. Nothing will alter our feelings towards them, or our faith that the genius of France will rise again ... What has happened in France makes no difference to British faith and purpose ...

His tone, it will be noticed, was deliberately restrained.

If Spears still expected to see Mandel in London he was to be disappointed, for the ex-Minister of the Interior had been arrested in Bordeaux while lunching in the Chapon Fin. His constant secret meetings and his flow of sarcasm at the Marshal's expense had led the government to suppose that he was preparing a *coup*, in association with General Bührer, Chief of Staff of the colonial troops. A group of deputies, including M. Herriot, called on M. Lebrun to protest: had parliamentary immunity been abolished, they asked?

When news of Mandel's arrest reached the Marshal he gave orders for his immediate release. But this was not enough for Mandel. He demanded a written apology. The Marshal complied. The terms of the letter did not satisfy Mandel. He compelled the Marshal to rephrase it at his dictation, in the presence of MM. Pomaret and Frossard.

All the same, Mandel had experienced some anxious moments.

Meanwhile there were more serious problems to be solved. The Marshal's midday broadcast had been generally interpreted as an immediate 'cease-fire'. This had led to fatal vacillation among the troops. They did not know whether or not to fire at the advancing German columns. During the afternoon General Georges informed General Weygand that whole regiments had stopped fighting.

The Commander-in-Chief hurriedly rectified this mistake by enjoining all army commanders to fight on.

The confusion arose from the fact that the Marshal had said: 'We must stop the fighting.' Baudouin had the evening newspapers alter this sentence to: 'We must *try* to stop the fighting.'

Finally, the Minister for Foreign Affairs dispelled any lingering doubts in a broadcast at 9.30 p.m.:

The French government has decided to ask Germany for her conditions. It goes without saying that she will accept none that conflicts with her honour or dignity. France could not consent to clauses involving the end of all spiritual freedom for her people ...

Our exhausted troops have been unable to compensate for the tanks, guns and planes that we lacked. Even without the threat of Italian invasion, we were only 40 million against 80 million ...

That is why the government led by Marshal Pétain has had to ask the enemy what his peace conditions would be. But, for all that, it has not abandoned the struggle or laid down arms. As Marshal Pétain said this morning, the country is prepared to seek ways, in honour, of putting an end to hostilities. It is not prepared, and never will be prepared, to accept dishonouring conditions, to forsake the spiritual freedom of our people, to betray the spirit of France.

If the French can only preserve these spiritual values that they prize more than life, they will agree to any individual sacrifices. But if they are forced to choose between existence and honour, their choice is made, and by their total sacrifice they will preserve the spirit of France and all that it implies to the world.

For all its grandiloquence, Baudouin's speech did not produce the desired effect. It worried his listeners; they wondered what further sacrifices were to be demanded of them ... Something, they thought, must be holding up the armistice. But what? Unaware of the slowness of diplomatic procedure, they had been hoping that everything would be settled that very evening. Now they resigned themselves to the idea that their troubles were not over yet ...

The leaders of the two Assemblies were even more worried. Their acceptance of Pétain's government had been lukewarm. They distrusted the Marshal and were keeping a close watch on him, subjecting his every word and every action to a rigid scrutiny. There was one passage in M. Baudouin's broadcast that disturbed them considerably: his reference to 'peace conditions'. At 10.30 p.m. they obtained an interview with President Lebrun and handed him the following protest, written by M. Herriot:

> At a time when events are moving so swiftly that they are in danger of outpacing us, we wish to repeat that nothing would induce us to accept, as compatible with the honour of France, a separate peace breaking our undertakings to Great Britain and Poland, seriously compromising our relations with the United States, ruining our reputation in the eyes of the world (especially with races that have thrown in their lot with us) and, indeed, strengthening our enemies' hand against our Allies by the surrender or even the disappearance of our fleet.

Thus the two leaders remained firm and watchful to the very end.

But round about midnight M. Herriot received a telephone call from Lyons town hall. He learned that the Germans were nearing the town and that it might be bombarded at any moment. His heart sank. He rushed to the Marshal's residence, got him out of bed and begged him to urge General Weygand to declare Lyons an 'open town' without delay, so as to avoid 'needless death and destruction'.

This was a really grave decision, for the Lyons salient covered the Alpine army. If Lyons were declared an open town and offered no resistance, the Wehrmacht would be free to pour into the Rhône valley and attack all the troops manning the Italian border from the rear.

'It was as a result of this step,' M. Herriot records with a hint of smugness, 'that the decision was taken to declare all centres of more than 20,000 inhabitants "open towns" ' — a measure that made the continuance of the war practically impossible.'

General Roton writes:

> During the night a telegram from the government reached headquarters of the north-eastern sector declaring any centre of more

than 20,000 inhabitants an 'open town'. Such centres were to be defended only from the outside ... No obstruction or demolition was allowed. General Georges fiercely protested against this decision, which would seriously hamper the defence of the rivers, since it was precisely those towns of more than 20,000 inhabitants that afforded the main crossing-points. In many places it was going to lead to friction between the local civil authorities, who wished to prevent fighting on the edges of their towns, and the military command, whose mission was to halt or impede the enemy's advance.

The problem was aggravated by the fact that most townships south of the Loire were crowded with refugees and that mayors sought to apply the government's decision, not in accordance with the normal population of towns, but in accordance with the number of people present on June 17th.

JUNE 18TH

MILITARY SITUATION

In the course of June 17th the troops had received two conflicting orders. On the one hand they were not to fight in centres of more than 20,000 inhabitants; on the other, they were not to *stop* fighting anywhere else till the armistice was signed. These instructions were hard to reconcile and did not make for unity of defence. Yet, almost everywhere, they were scrupulously observed.

In the west the battle for Cherbourg was beginning.[1] General J. H. Marshall-Cornwall, commander of the British forces, gives the following account:

> In order to protect the embarkation at Cherbourg, I had asked for a fresh battalion of the 52nd Division to be left to occupy a covering position some 20 miles to the south. This, combined with the 5 French battalions of the Cherbourg garrison, ought to have provided ample security, and I had hoped to continue the embarkation until the 21st in order to remove all the stores and mechanized vehicles. The enemy, however, again upset our calculations by the speed with which he followed up our rapid withdrawal. At 9 a.m. on the 18th, a column of 60 lorries, carrying motorized German infantry, reached the covering position near Saint-Sauveur. Finding resistance there, they turned west to the sector held by French troops, and succeeded in penetrating the position by the coast road. The French made little attempt to resist, and I had to make the decision at 11.30 to complete the evacuation by 3 p.m. The covering battalion (5th Bn. K.O.S.B.) was withdrawn between 12 noon and 3 p.m. and the last boat left at 4 p.m. All weapons were removed, except one 3.7-inch A.A. gun, which broke down and was rendered unserviceable, and one static Bofors gun which could not be removed in the time. Two anti-tank guns also had to be abandoned during the withdrawal. When the last troopship left, the Germans had penetrated to within 3 miles of the harbour.

[1] See sketch on p. 391.

And here is Rommel's description:

At dawn the Commander of the 7th Panzer Division drove to the positions held the night before, outside Denneville, 25 miles south of Cherbourg. The attack was launched at 8 a.m. in the face of gunfire from a handful of French sailors ... The battery was not silenced till 10 a.m., after two hours' intensive shelling by the division's artillery and A.A. guns. Whereupon the division continued on its way to Cherbourg, via Barneville and Les Pieux — but more slowly this time.

At 9 p.m. the Germans launched their attack on Querqueville.

Examining the spot and its surroundings, my scout had discovered a position from which we could observe the naval harbour from within a mile and a quarter. As day broke we picked out the defensive works on the quays and breakwaters, and the harbour itself, where only a few small vessels were now at anchor. Otherwise the roadstead was empty: the British had presumably left ...

Farther south the other units of Hoth's Armoured Corps had had no difficulty in breaking through the very thin line sealing off the Brittany peninsula. They swept onwards to Rennes, where they captured several generals, including René Altmayer. The only forces to escape capture were the 3rd Army Corps and the Cavalry Corps, which now amalgamated under General de la Laurencie. These withdrew to the Lower Loire, digging in on the left of the Paris Army under General Héring.

Along the Loire the enemy had established a further bridge-head at Briare and now lined the river from Gien to Digoin. Farther east, forward elements of von Kleist's Armoured Group had encircled Moulins and were heading for Vichy and Roanne, after occupying the industrial centre of Le Creusot. General Besson, Commander of the 3rd Group of Armies, was alarmed by this growing threat from the rear and gave orders for the withdrawal to the Cher to be begun that night.

In the Rhône valley the German motorized divisions were beyond Macon. Now they were advancing rapidly on Lyons.

Still farther east the 1st Panzer division was storming Belfort. Guderian personally led the attack against those forts that refused to surrender, capturing them one by one. Meanwhile, on his left, the 2nd, 6th and 8th Panzer Divisions crossed the Meuse from north to south, between Remiremont and Charmes.

Thus the situation was at its most critical in the triangle held by the 2nd

Group of Armies. The French units were packed tight in an area bordered to the north, by Château-Salins, the Sarrebourg Canal, the Vosges passes (these were being bitterly defended) and the Upper Moselle as far as Épinal. Three corps belonging to Condé's 3rd Army that had been ordered to fight their way out southwards were trapped between the Épinal–Toul reach of the Moselle and the Neufchâteau–Void reach of the Meuse. South of this sector the units entrusted to General Daille likewise failed to break free. The encirclement of the 2nd Group of Armies was now complete. There could be no hope of escape.

Activity in and round the sea-ports was growing ever more intensive. The following Admiralty order was put into effect:

To All Authorities

5025/5026

Premier reminds all servicemen that no armistice has yet been concluded and that it is their duty to continue resisting to the utmost.

No warship must fall into enemy hands intact. In case of need, the rallying point for any warship or aircraft is North Africa.

Any warship or aircraft having difficulty in getting there and in danger of falling into enemy hands is to be destroyed or scuttled on orders from higher authority.

These instructions were carried out with perfect discipline.

In Brest the 35,000-ton battleship *Richelieu*, which had just completed its trials, put to sea under Captain Marzin. It was preceded and followed by eighty vessels, the force being commanded by Admiral Moreau.

In Saint-Nazaire the battleship *Jean-Bart* was still unfinished. Post-Captain Ronarc'h successfully urged the shipbuilders to put every ounce of energy into their work.

Now that all possible precautions had been taken, the remaining units either scuttled or fled. Sloops and patrol-ships unable to head out to sea were scuttled at Lorient on June 19th, after the heroic defence of the port by Admiral de Penfentenyo; and the same thing happened at La Pallice on June 22nd and at Le Verdon on June 24th. In other words, vessels were scuttled just as soon as German forces reached the outskirts of these ports.

The French Mediterranean Fleet was in a less vulnerable position. All the same, the commander of the Toulon Squadron, Vice-Admiral Duplat, issued strict instructions as to when and how vessels were to be scuttled.

In these circumstances, was it fair for Churchill to write eight years later

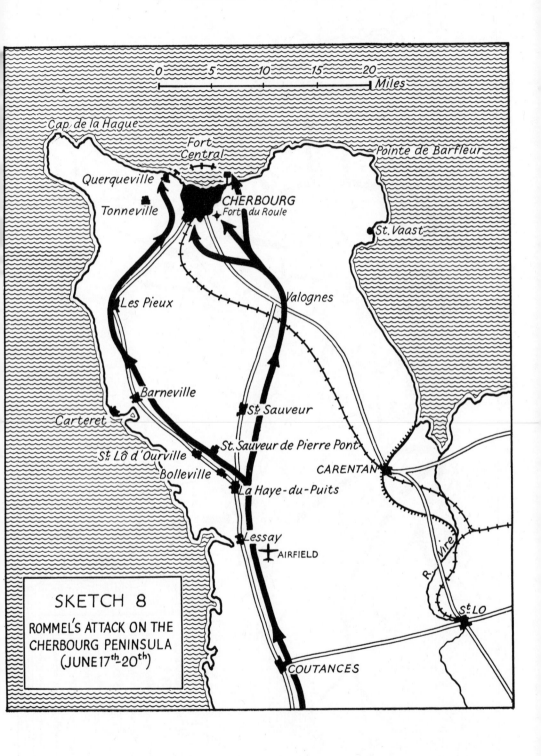

0   5   10   15   20
Miles

Cap de la Hague

Fort Central

Pointe de Barfleur

Querqueville

CHERBOURG
Fort du Roule

Tonneville

St. Vaast

Les Pieux

Valognes

Barneville

Carteret

St. Sauveur

St. Sauveur de Pierre Pont

CARENTAN

St. Lô d'Ourville

Bolleville

La Haye-du-Puits

Lessay

AIRFIELD

R. Vire

St. LO

COUTANCES

SKETCH 8

ROMMEL'S ATTACK ON THE
CHERBOURG PENINSULA
(JUNE 17th-20th)

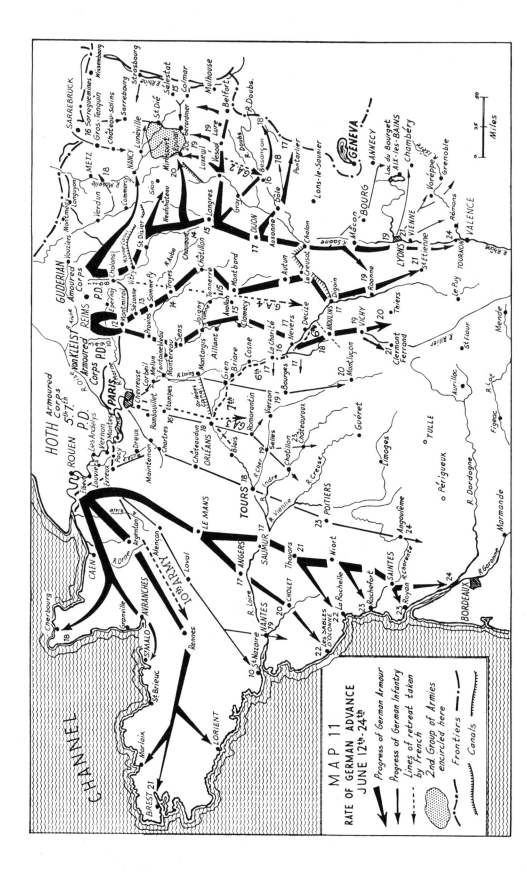

MAP 11

RATE OF GERMAN ADVANCE
JUNE 12th–24th

Progress of German Armour
Progress of German Infantry
Lines of retreat taken by French
2nd Group of Armies encircled here
Frontiers
Canals

that in those tragic days no French warship stirred? 'History is there to answer that *not a single undamaged unit* of the French fleet was captured in our Atlantic ports,' writes Varillon.

And that was not all. For once the ships had been scuttled, the harbour installations were likewise destroyed. In Cherbourg, the arsenal was blown up. In Brest, Lorient and La Rochelle, oil reservoirs, magazines, ammunition dumps, workshops, office-blocks, quays, docks — all were ablaze, sending up thunderous roars and blotting out the sky with giant plumes of smoke.

The work of demolition was carried so far that local civilians grew alarmed. What was the point of blowing up bridges, scuttling ships and wrecking fleets of lorries when, in a matter of days, France would be in desperate need of these things? Mayors and deputies began to rail against the inflexibility of military orders, which were a permanent danger to their towns. In these closing days of the battle, a struggle developed — not between the army and the enemy, but between municipalities and service headquarters, the former seeking to save as much as they could, the latter intent on complying rigidly with their instructions to take all possible steps to impede the enemy's advance.

ARMISTICE NEGOTIATIONS

During the night Hitler had left his Charleville H.Q. by special train with Ribbentrop and members of his military and civil staffs.

After some hours the train was stopped at a small wayside station in the Black Forest. This break in the journey had been arranged by ambassador Hewel, a member of Ribbentrop's staff, who had flown from Berlin with a written note from the Spanish government officially confirming the French request for an armistice. Hitler, together with Ribbentrop and several officers, got out of the train and went to meet ambassador Hewel. The latter beamed as he handed the Führer the Spanish government's note. After he had read it, Hitler gave free rein to his joy, performing a brief dance on the platform at which his coach had stopped.

Ambassador Abetz has described how pained he was by newsreel shots of this scene. 'The Führer's movements and bearing,' he writes, 'seemed to me ill-suited to the gravity of the moment. I thought then of Frederick II, whom Hitler so much admired, and who, at the end of the Seven Years War, sat listening to a Bach chorale in the solitude of a Berlin church instead of attending the victory march-past.'

Then Hitler, Ribbentrop and their party got back into the train and continued on their way to Munich.

Count Ciano wrote in his diary:

> The Germans lining the railway track gave us a very warm welcome. In Munich, at the Prince Charles Palace, we met Hitler and Ribbentrop. The Duce and the Führer retired for private discussions, leaving Ribbentrop and me alone. I found Ribbentrop transformed: calm, level-headed, favouring peace. He stated at once that it would be advisable to offer the French moderate armistice conditions, especially with regard to the navy, so that the French fleet should not join the British. Ribbentrop's words gave me the feeling that the *Stimmung* towards Britain had changed: if London wanted war, it would be total war, absolute and pitiless. Yet Hitler made numerous reservations concerning the advisability of destroying the British Empire, which even today he regarded as an important factor in maintaining world balance. I asked Ribbentrop point-blank: 'Which would you prefer, the continuation of the war, or peace?' Without a moment's hesitation he answered: 'Peace.' He also alluded to vague contacts between London and Berlin, via Sweden. I spoke of our demands on France ... But Ribbentrop was unwilling to carry the discussion too far, for he still did not know what exactly Hitler's views were on the subject.

Meanwhile, Hitler was telling Mussolini that it would be politically inept to occupy the whole of France: it would only encourage the French to set up a government in Britain or elsewhere. He went on:

> It is better to allow the existence of a French government *in France*. That is why Germany will not occupy France beyond the Loire, apart from a coastal strip along the Atlantic, adjoining Spain, and another strip in the east, along the Swiss border.
>
> So far as the fleet is concerned, the best thing would be for France to scuttle it; the worst, for it to unite with the British naval forces. In view of the considerable number of France's smaller warships, the united Franco-British fleets would be able to organize large convoys. That would mean that Great Britain would be able to keep herself supplied without difficulty and to transport (from the mother country, Canada, India, etc.) sizeable armed forces to many places (from Egypt to Portugal), thereby maintaining or creating a whole series of subsidiary theatres of war. This would lead to a long war and the impossibility of striking a decisive blow against the enemy ...

In these circumstances it would be unwise to ask the French for the outright surrender of the fleet. France would not agree, and against the very small probability of seeing the French sink their fleet, we should risk the far greater probability of seeing them send their naval forces to England.

Consequently, our best plan is to ask them to assemble their fleet in a way that would make it impossible for it to be either moved or scattered — either in French ports under our control, or in neutral ports (preferably Spanish).

Furthermore, it seems wise to leave France the hope of getting her fleet back at the time of the peace treaty ...

The discussion was continued between Hitler, Mussolini, the Ministers for Foreign Affairs and the representatives of the two armies — Marshal Keitel and General Roatta. Ciano wrote:

The conditions for an armistice with France were decided in principle. With regard to the fleet, Mussolini took a much tougher line than Hitler, whose main concern was that the French navy should not go over to the British. His desire to conclude a peace as swiftly as possible was obvious from every word he said. Hitler was like the gambler who has broken the bank: he wanted to leave the table and risk no more ... Mussolini was obviously put out. He was conscious of playing second fiddle.

Mussolini and Hitler then discussed how the signing of the armistice should be conducted. The Duce pointed out that the Italian government had as yet received no official request for an armistice. He took the view that the two armistices should be simultaneous. Consequently the Germans sent the following communication to the French government:

The Reich government is prepared to inform the French government of its conditions for a cessation of hostilities. It recommends that the French government should send plenipotentiaries for this purpose. The Reich government will indicate when and where these plenipotentiaries can be received as soon as their names have been communicated to it.

The Reich government points out that the agreement to end hostilities can be discussed only if the French government also contacts the Italian government through the Spanish government.[1]

[1] Apparently the Italian government had as yet received no intimation of M. Baudouin's interview with the Papal Nuncio (see p. 381).

THE BATTLE OF FRANCE

At 10.30 a.m. Marshal Pétain asked the Spanish ambassador, Señor de Lequerica, to call on him in the Rue Vital-Carles. He asked him whether he had received any answer from the German government. The ambassador replied that there was still no word. The Marshal showed disappointment, concern even. The delay seemed ominous and put him in an awkward situation. Germany's silence strengthened the hand of those who were still hoping to go to Algiers.

At 11 a.m. the Cabinet met in the Prefecture. M. Lebrun presided.

As he was crossing the hall to attend the meeting, Admiral Darlan was buttonholed by Mr Drexel Biddle who handed him the text of the note that Mr Cordell Hull had sent the day before.[1]

Broadly speaking, the Cabinet regarded the fleet as a trump card to be retained at all costs, either as a weapon, if France had to fight on, or as a means of exerting pressure if peace talks were opened with the Axis Powers. It must certainly not be handed over to Germany: on that point everyone was agreed. But nor must it be sent to British harbours. The general view in France at the time was that Britain would not hold out for long.

After closely examining the question, the French government unanimously adopted the *solemn and irrevocable* decision 'not to let the fleet fall into enemy hands in any circumstances. If its surrender were included in the armistice conditions they would be rejected out of hand, *however grave the consequences of such a refusal.*'

This decision was immediately wired to M. Corbin, French ambassador in London, for official communication to the British government.

Then, without waiting for the end of the Cabinet meeting, M. Baudouin passed on the news to the United States ambassador. As a result of this interview, Mr Biddle cabled to Cordell Hull that 'he [Baudouin] wished to assure me in the name of the government in the most solemn manner that the French fleet would never be surrendered to the enemy: *La question ne se pose pas* ... '[2]

M. Baudouin gave the same assurance to Sir Ronald Campbell.

Encountering Sir Ronald on his way from the Cabinet meeting, Admiral Darlan confirmed that if an emergency arose the fleet would sail for the ports of a powerful friend.

---

[1] See p. 383.
[2] In French in Mr Biddle's cable.

After the meeting the Marshal invited M. Reynaud to call on him, and in M. Baudouin's presence asked him to accept the post of ambassador to Washington. M. Reynaud began by declining the offer. The armistice conditions were not yet known, and no doubt he was still hoping they would be unacceptable. If they were, the Pétain administration would be short-lived.

'When you appealed to me I answered "Present!"' the Marshal said with a trace of bitterness. ' ... If I appeal to you now, it is because France needs your help. You cannot withhold it from her at a time like this.'

Finally M. Reynaud agreed. He asked only that his appointment should not take effect till the armistice conditions became known.

The Marshal gladly agreed. But, anxious to speed the ex-Premier's departure, he instructed him to draw up a written notice of the appointment for submission to President Lebrun. That same evening he cabled Washington for President Roosevelt's approval.

Mr Drexel Biddle was delighted at the appointment. He told M. Reynaud that he was certain to achieve a good deal, for his stock was very high in the United States.

After a meeting of Belgian ministers, M. Pierlot sent the following telegram to M. Alberto Palacios Costa, Argentinian minister in Berne:

The Belgian government in Bordeaux requests the Argentinian legation in Switzerland personally to acquaint Belgium's minister in Switzerland with the position that it expects to adopt upon the cessation of hostilities in France, so that he may inform Brussels:

The government will state:
1. that it came to France to continue the war side by side with its guarantors;
2. that the French army has stopped fighting;
3. that, under these circumstances, Belgians in France must avoid any action hostile to the Germans;
4. that the fate of Belgian officers and men must be identical with that of French officers and men;
5. that the population and refugees will have to carry out scrupulously the instructions that are given to them;
6. that the government will resign as soon as the fate of the Belgian troops and refugees in France is determined, in order to facilitate the likely peace negotiations between Germany and Belgium.

But France did not only have Britain, the United States and Belgium to consider: there was her Empire too, where the disastrous news from

Europe was causing an ever-increasing stir. The populations of the overseas possessions had been stunned by the Marshal's midday broadcast the day before. Misled by the false optimism and rigid censorship of the Press, people could hardly believe their ears when they heard the hero of Verdun tell them that France was going to have to give up the fight. Justifiably, his words produced the same reaction of shock in Dakar as in Morocco, in Tunis as in Syria, in the West Indies as in Indo-China.

M. Peyrouton, Resident-General in Tunisia, was especially alarmed: the territory for which he was responsible bordered Italian Tripolitania, and its population included a high percentage of Italian immigrants. So he was one of the first to speak out:

Tunisians, Frenchmen, friends of France residing in Tunisia!

Grave events have occurred since we last spoke together. A new government led by Marshal Pétain, the most taintless figure of modern times, has felt driven to inquire into the conditions under which the likelihood of bloodshed respecting neither women nor children might be honourably terminated.

One day soon, ravaged France may have to lay down arms. Our soldiers will have paid with their blood for the short-sightedness and blundering of recent years. France retains her honour. And her Empire. Sixty million men and huge territories freed of ancient yokes by our civilizing genius. Sixty million men to whom the supporters of colonial expansion — and today, more than ever, I am proud to number myself among them — brought ... peace, justice and health. Conscious of what it owes us and of what its fate would be were it to fall to the barbarians in the days ahead, that Empire is taking a stand that displays both its courage and its gratitude. We take off our hats to it.

We in this bastion of North Africa, this backbone of the Empire, must not be disheartened; united under His Highness the Bey and our civil and military leaders, we must leave despondency to the cowards ...

Each of us must bear in mind that the most insidious attempts will be made to undermine morale. Our enemy needs to lie in order to triumph. Let us not play into his hands. Nothing is over. But we are paying the price.

For too long we have selfishly lived on words and dreams: a state of affairs that suited all of us and even profited some. The future is in the hands of decent men solely inspired by patriotism. They are legion but dare not declare themselves. Let them show themselves, let them assert themselves. They will save Tunisia and her crucified mother, Eternal France.

This broadcast earned M. Peyrouton a good deal of commendation, including telegrams from M. Puaux, Syrian High Commissioner, M. de Coppet, Governor-General of Madagascar, M. Boisson, Governor-General of French West Africa, and M. Brunot, French Commissioner in the Cameroons.

In more or less identical terms these men expressed their determination to go on fighting. The armistice, they said, should bind only Metropolitan France. They offered to combine under General Noguès, Resident-General of Morocco and Commander-in-Chief of the North African theatre.

The latter sent the following message to the government:

All troops, together with the French and Moslem populations of North Africa, beg me, with moving representations, to ask the government respectfully to continue the fight and defend North African soil.

The natives in particular, who — so they declare — are prepared to serve with us to the last man, would not understand how we could conceivably relinquish their territory without joining with them in trying to hold on to it, when in 1939, as in 1914, they replied en masse to our appeal that they should come and fight side by side with us in France ...

It is with respectful but ardent insistence, therefore, that I ask the government, in the name of our country's most vital interests, to come and continue the fight, or allow it to be continued, in North Africa ... It is the only way for France to retain her Moslem Empire. There, later, she will find new and alert forces that will play an essential part in her future.

To allow North Africa to defend itself is to begin to get France back on her feet.

In Bordeaux there was utter chaos. Senators and deputies were short of news and exhausted from their appalling journey. For information, they went to the building that housed the leaders of the Assemblies and the various parliamentary treasurers. They soon split into two camps: one in favour of the government's leaving for North Africa, the other advocating its remaining in France.

Prominent among the former were — in addition to MM. Daladier,

Mandel and Reynaud — ex-ministers Campinchi, Rio, Laurent-Eynac, Dautry, Rollin and Delbos, together with the leaders of the two Assemblies, MM. Jeanneney and Herriot.

The chief exponents of the view that the government must not leave Metropolitan France were MM. Pierre Laval and Adrien Marquet. They were backed by MM. Portmann, Piétri, Cayrel, Georges Bonnet, Charles Reibel, Gaston Bergery, Thellier, Lafaye, Scapini, Briquet, Rauzy, Lhévéder, d'Auddifred-Pasquier, des Rotours, Baroux, Émile Perrin, Dommange and several others.

MM. Jeanneney and Herriot, who were urging the Cabinet to leave, were afraid that the majority would vote against them. So they persisted in calling no meeting of the two Assemblies. Left to their own devices, members held impromptu meetings, forming groups that fairly represented their views. Members who wanted the government to leave would meet unofficially in the two leaders' ante-rooms and in a classroom of an elementary school in the Rue Anatole France, where M. Barthe, Questor of the Chamber, had provisionally set up office. Those who wanted it to stay would rally round MM. Laval and Marquet in the committee room of Bordeaux town hall. That morning, between seventy and eighty senators gathered in M. Barthe's office in the Rue Anatole France.

At 12.30 p.m. President Lebrun called together Marshal Pétain, M. Jeanneney and M. Herriot. Again the main talking-point was whether the government should remain in France or go to North Africa.

MM. Jeanneney and Herriot were strongly in favour of leaving. The Marshal was against.

'You know that I have decided to stay in France come what may,' he said.

MM. Jeanneney and Herriot pressed the point. The Marshal would not be swayed. No decision was taken.

In the afternoon the leaders of the Assemblies again called on M. Lebrun. They had thought of an ingenious way of skirting the Marshal's resistance: since some ministers wanted to go to Africa and others did not, why not split the government in two? The Marshal, exercising a kind of regency, would remain in France with General Weygand and the military, together with two or three ministers, including Pomaret (Interior) and Frossard (Public Works), while the President of the Republic, the leaders of the Assemblies, Vice-Premier Chautemps and all other ministers would leave. So that the government could continue to function, the Marshal's powers would be delegated to M. Chautemps. M. Herriot writes:

We were adhering to the idea of not allowing the State to be taken prisoner in the person of the President of the Republic.

M. Albert Lebrun stated that he agreed with us but was at odds with the Marshal, who was unwilling to leave France. He advised us to go and see him. It would be better, we said, if the Marshal were gracious enough to come and confer with us.

At 5 p.m. there was a further meeting at the Prefecture. Present were M. Lebrun, the Marshal, MM. Jeanneney and Herriot and M. Alibert, Under-Secretary of State at the Prime Minister's Office.

The leaders of the Assemblies again told the Marshal that 'it was the government's duty not to let itself be captured.' The Marshal stuck to his guns and confirmed his intention of staying among his compatriots to share their sufferings and exert, on their behalf, the influence that he knew he had over the Germans.

M. Herriot then pointed out that harmony could be reached by splitting the government in two. President Lebrun backed this suggestion: he too was in favour of leaving. He was expecting to drive to Perpignan next day and set sail for North Africa. He asked the Marshal to give his agreement. The Marshal repeated that he was not going to leave France.

'I consider myself in duty bound to go to Algeria,' insisted M. Lebrun, 'and since you do not wish to accompany me I shall form another government there.'

'What value and authority will it have?' asked the Marshal.

'We shall achieve important ends,' replied M. Lebrun. 'For one thing, we shall be able to appoint ambassadors ... '

MM. Jeanneney and Herriot pointed out that in any case it would be the only legitimate government.

The Marshal was well aware of how little ice this government would cut — legitimate or not — with people in Metropolitan France. This endless wrangling was beginning to irritate him. These people made themselves out to be so important, but they had neither the authority to end the war nor the resources to continue it! If they wanted to go, let them go ...

In the end, therefore, though determined to remain in France, he accepted the idea of dividing the government. 'If it can be done,' he said, 'I'm willing.' He would delegate his powers to the Deputy Premier, Chautemps, who would take with him such ministers as he chose.

'M. Jeanneney and I considered the matter settled by this formal agreement,' writes M. Herriot. 'We were to withdraw to North Africa. National sovereignty had been preserved.'

Dignity, perhaps, had been less well preserved. But in view of the way things stood ...

Responsibility for transporting the ministers and members of parliament rested with Admiral Darlan, who announced that the liner *Massilia* — armed but carrying a civilian crew — was available for the purpose. She was already under steam, at the mouth of the Gironde.

Meanwhile M. Laval had been informed of the meeting in the Prefecture and of the Marshal's agreement to the idea of dividing the government. He hurried round to the Marshal's office. Foreseeing the long-term consequences of such a decision, he reminded Pétain of how ill-starred the splitting of the National Defence government had proved in 1870, and argued that a two-part government was bound to break up. He was horrified by President Lebrun's suggestion that a new Cabinet should be formed in Algiers, one from which the Marshal would be excluded. The hero of Verdun was wrong to believe that the Algiers Cabinet would have no authority: it was himself who would be stripped of power. To put this scheme into effect would be to sanction the legitimate government's escape. The Marshal would be deprived of the Seals of France and incompetent, not only in practice but in law, to govern a nation running wild in the presence of an enemy who was bent on occupying the whole of it.

Laval went on to emphasize that, once it was in Algiers, the government was bound to be subjected to British influence or even British pressure, to say nothing of the uninformed opinion prevailing in France's North African possessions.

'As a result of all this,' he concluded, 'the armistice might fall through, whatever conditions are attached to its offer. And that would mean continuing the war in conditions that would bring frightful consequences for the whole country. Why are you destroying in a moment all the efforts that you have made in the past few days to put an end to the sufferings of the French people?'

M. Laval's remarks perturbed the Marshal deeply. The political game was not an easy one ...

The B.B.C. broadcast Churchill's 3 p.m. speech in the Commons. [*This great oration, one of the most famous in English history and particularly remembered by the words 'their finest hour' in the final sentence, is so familiar to British readers that it seems unnecessary to print it again.* — Ed.]

General de Gaulle, for his part, had worked out the address on which he had decided at the time of his meeting with Spears and Churchill the previous day. He had written out the text and submitted it for their approval. Shortly before 6 p.m. he and Lieutenant de Courcel went to the studio that the B.B.C. had placed at his disposal. He made the following appeal:

> The leaders who have for many years headed the French armies have formed a government.
>
> That government, alleging the defeat of our armies, has opened negotiations with the enemy to put an end to the fighting.
>
> True, we have been, and still are, swamped by the enemy's mechanized strength both on land and in the air ...
>
> But has the last word been spoken? Must hope vanish? Is our defeat final? No.
>
> For France is not alone. She is not alone — she is not alone ...
>
> She has a vast Empire behind her. She can unite with the British Empire, which controls the seas and is fighting on. Like Britain, she can call on the huge industrial resources of the United States.
>
> This war is not confined to the luckless soil of our country. This war has not been settled by the Battle of France. This war is a world war. For all our mistakes, all our delays, all our sufferings, there are plenty of resources in the world to enable us to crush our enemies one day. Though shattered with mechanized strength today, tomorrow we shall win with greater mechanized strength. The fate of the world depends on it.

After a long pause, he added:

> I, General de Gaulle, now in London, call on French officers and men who are on British soil, or may find themselves on British soil, with or without their weapons, and on engineers and skilled munition-workers who are on British soil, or may find themselves on British soil, to get in touch with me.
>
> Whatever happens, the flame of resistance must not and will not be extinguished.
>
> Tomorrow, as today, I shall be broadcasting from London.

Later, in his memoirs, de Gaulle was to write: 'As these words passed my lips I felt a life come to an end within me: the life that I had led within the framework of a secure France and an indissoluble army. At the age of forty-nine I was embarking on an adventure, like a man flung out on a limb by fate.'

Jean Marin and Jean Oberlé immediately placed themselves at his disposal, offering to fight on at his side by broadcasting on his behalf.

'In launching this appeal to the French people,' de Gaulle told Oberlé later, 'I was hoping that many of them would be able to come to England; I was hoping that a large number of ships would come too; I was hoping that it would have a telling effect on the French mind. As I saw it, the fact that I had been a member of the government till Pétain's arrival on the scene might weigh in my favour politically.'

But the appeal fell flat. The only reaction of the ruling circles in Bordeaux was to instruct General Colson to send a wire to the French ambassador in London:

No. 10,978 D   *June 18th*, 1940
War Minister to Military Attaché, London: Tell General de Gaulle he is now subject to Commander-in-Chief again and is to return without delay.

Signed: COLSON

In Munich, telegrams of congratulation were pouring into the Führer's headquarters.

Herr von Schulenberg, German ambassador to the Soviet Union, telegraphed from Moscow:

M. Molotov expressed the Soviet government's warmest congratulations on the magnificent success of the German armed forces. Molotov informed me of the Soviet action undertaken against the Baltic States. He added that the time had come to put an end to the intrigues whereby Britain and France tried to sow discord and mistrust between Germany and the Soviet Union in the Baltic States.

Herr Stahmer, German ambassador to Japan, cabled from Tokyo:

Mr Matsuoka, Minister for Foreign Affairs, expressed his and the Japanese government's satisfaction at our brilliant feat of arms. He begged me to convey to you the congratulations of H.M. the Emperor, who sees our victory as the consummation of Germany's traditional military virtues.

Herr von Stohrer, German ambassador in Spain, telegraphed from Madrid:

Señor Serrano Suñer has conveyed to me the congratulations of the Caudillo and the Spanish government, and has asked me to pass them on to you. The Madrid Cabinet considers that the victorious outcome of the war in the west opens up new prospects rich in promise for our two countries. The army leaders have been very favourably impressed by the new tactics employed by our High Command, and by the dash and valour of our troops.

At 1 p.m. the French naval base at Biscarosse reported the landing of a British flying-boat carrying Mr A. V. Alexander, First Lord of the Admiralty, and Sir Dudley Pound, First Sea Lord. The moment they reached Bordeaux they called on Admiral Darlan. Admiral Auphan, who was present at the lengthy discussion between the trio, recalls:

> The British were concerned about the fate of our fleet ... They imposed no conditions on the subject [of the armistice] and never once asked that our fleet should previously dock in British ports; but they sought reassurances as to the future of our ships.
> Admiral Darlan told them outright that if the armistice agreement (the clauses of which were not yet known) demanded the surrender of the fleet, as we ourselves had demanded in 1918, the French government had unanimously decided to reject the clause and, if need be, to abandon all idea of an armistice. He gave them an explicit promise that in no circumstances would our ships be placed at the Germans' disposal for use against them. Of his own accord he gave his word of honour (asking me to associate myself with it, so as to lend it more weight) that, whatever happened and whatever the circumstances, our warships would never be used by anyone but us: they would remain French or be destroyed. When the British took their leave they were moved, cordial and, to all appearances, satisfied.
> Such was the origin of the permanent orders to scuttle sent to all ships at that time.

JUNE 19TH

In Cherbourg the battle was entering its decisive phase. Shells rained on the naval harbour. Soon flames were spurting from the large area occupied by sheds and depots. Thick palls of smoke showed where the heaviest explosions had occurred. The fusilier regiment had been ordered to start occupying the town without waiting for the bombardment to end. When the entire harbour was hidden from view, Rommel concentrated his aim on the Querqueville Fortress, hoping this would encourage the garrison to surrender.

Meanwhile, M. Vaur and his deputy were making representations to the military authorities. At about 2 p.m. Vice-Admiral Le Bigot, Port-Admiral of the 1st District and governor of Cherbourg, considered that his three main objectives had been achieved:

(a) Protection of the complete embarkation of British forces;
(b) Use of all available shipping for the evacuation of non-combatants;
(c) Destruction of all equipment of any possible use to the enemy.

Furthermore, the garrison was on the point of running out of ammunition. He therefore decided that there was nothing to prevent him from capitulating. He sent a delegation of naval officers to Rommel's command post in the Les Couplets redoubt. The formalities were soon concluded.

'I called on the garrison in each fort to hoist a white flag in token of surrender,' wrote Rommel, 'and then march off along the road from Cherbourg to Les Pieux. The N.C.O.s were to take charge of the column. The officers were to assemble at the Port-Admiral's office. All weapons were to be unloaded and stacked inside the forts.'

The official surrender took place in the Port-Admiral's office at 5 p.m.

'Thus ended the capitulation of Cherbourg,' noted Rommel. 'All accessible forts on dry land had in the meantime been occupied by our troops. The clearing-up of the town and forts began at once.'

Immediately after capturing Cherbourg, Rommel wrote to his wife:

June 20th, 1940

I don't know whether that is the right date; I've rather lost track of time these last few days.

The division carried out the attack on Cherbourg in a single thrust, covering a distance of 220 to 230 miles, and took the powerful fortress in spite of fierce resistance. There were a few bad moments for us, and to begin with the enemy outnumbered us by twenty or forty to one. In addition there were between twenty and thirty-five forts in fighting trim and a large number of isolated batteries.[1] However, by keeping on the move, we managed to comply with the Führer's special order that Cherbourg should be captured at the earliest possible moment.[2]

In Brittany the Panzers of Hoth's Armoured Corps were on the outskirts of Lorient and Morlaix. They were striking swiftly towards Brest, which they were to enter at 7 p.m.

In the Lower Loire sector, Nantes, earlier declared an open town, had not been defended. The Germans were establishing a bridge-head on the left bank of the river.

Sensing that there was not a moment to be lost, Commandant Ronarc'h decided to weigh anchor at 3 a.m. so that the *Jean-Bart* would be in the Loire channel at high tide.

[*Thrice attacked from the air in the Channel, and once hit by a bomb which failed to pierce the steel deck, the battleship got out, fuelled at sea — having sailed with empty tanks to diminish her draught — repaired a dangerous breakdown and finally reached Casablanca. This was a magnificent performance by the crew of an unfinished ship. — Ed.*]

In Saumur, where the Germans had been marking time for forty-eight hours, there were violent clashes. The young cadets at the Cavalry School, still under instruction prior to being sent to the firing line, did not mean to allow the establishment to be captured without a fight. They had heard on the radio, two days before, that France would soon have to lay down arms. 'The words coursed through us like fire-water,' one of them wrote later. 'We had made up our minds to fight all the same, while the armistice was unsigned, purely for the sake of honour.

'At the prompting of a keen officer, Colonel Michon, the school — comprising 2,200 men — was to defend the Loire from Montsoreau bridge

---

[1] Rommel is exaggerating somewhat.

[2] This is not strictly true. The object of the operation had been to prevent 'Normanforce' from embarking. In fact, all the British had escaped. Once again the Germans had allowed their quarry to get away.

to Gennes bridge, a front of fifteen miles. It was armed only with training weapons ... But every one of those youngsters was filled with firm resolve and manly courage.'

For two whole days (June 19th–20th) they fought with the frenzy of despairing youth; for two whole days they held the German forces on the Saumur bridges. Then ammunition ran out and their stand was broken. The flow of Panzers finally cleared the Loire.

Within the Loire loop the Germans reached the Cher at Vierzon and Romorantin. Another column entered Bourges. Farther eastwards, after vainly attempting to blast out the holding-force at Moulins, the German columns took Vichy and Roanne and continued their advance towards Saint-Étienne.

In the Saône valley the German forces outflanked Lyons from the west. By afternoon, light elements were thrusting their way into the southern end of the town.

In Lorraine and the Vosges mountains the Eastern Group of Armies was attacked along the line of the passes and confronted by powerful tank thrusts towards Lure and Luxeuil. The French made a fine stand, but they were running short of ammunition.

Meanwhile, to escape the double threat of encirclement resulting from the forcing of the Lower Loire and from the Germans' deep encroachment via the Upper Loire and the Allier, the French High Command instructed its armies to continue their retreat southwards, making use of the Vienne, the Charente and the Dordogne.

In the afternoon the Luftwaffe bombed Poitiers just as the café radios were relaying these words of M. Pomaret's: 'Listen carefully! I assure you that you are quite safe!'

The railway station was flattened. Two trains packed with refugees had been standing at the platforms. As a result of unforgivable negligence they had been halted beside an ammunition train. The ammunition train blew up. The death-roll was enormous.

The Luftwaffe also bombed Bordeaux during the night, killing sixty-three and wounding eighty. This raid caused grave disturbance among the civilian population.

ARMISTICE NEGOTIATIONS

At 6.25 a.m. the French government received the German communication asking for a list of members of the French delegation.

At 7 a.m. Marshal Pétain summoned General Weygand, Admiral Darlan, M. Baudouin, M. Alibert and M. Charles-Roux to his private residence to determine its composition. The first thing to be decided was: who was going to lead it? Baudouin said to General Weygand: 'Why don't you go and receive the German conditions yourself?'

General Weygand replied that he was ready for any sacrifice, but recalled that in 1918 the Germans had not sent their Army C.-in-C. to Rethondes. The matter was gone into, and it was decided that General Weygand was indeed too high-placed for the task. General Huntziger,[1] commander of the 4th Group of Armies, was selected instead. It was thought that a diplomat should accompany him, and M. Charles-Roux put forward the name of M. Noël, former ambassador in Warsaw. After some discussion, M. Charles-Roux himself was also chosen. The rest of the delegation was to be made up by Rear-Admiral Le Luc, Deputy-Chief of Naval Staff, General Parisot and General of Air Force Bergeret.

This list of names was immediately handed to Señor de Lequerica for communication to the German government. M. Baudouin also gave him the following note for the Italian government:

July 19th, 7 a.m.

The French government requests the Spanish government to inform the Italian government that it is prepared to join with it in considering a cessation of hostilities. It was in this spirit that two mornings ago the French government sent the Holy See, for conveyance to the Italian government, a copy of its note to the German government.

The French government was hoping, in fact, that negotiations with the Reich and with Italy could take place simultaneously. In Munich Mussolini, too, was demanding that the German and Italian armistice delegations should be amalgamated. Hitler was opposed to the idea. He had agreed that the two armistices should *take effect* simultaneously, but he wished them to be *negotiated and signed* separately.

Ciano wrote: 'The Duce thinks that he can see a psychological reason for this, Hitler presumably being unwilling for the French to meet the Germans and the Italians on the same terms.'

Early that morning the Italian delegation left Munich for Rome. On his return to the Palazzo Venezia, Mussolini reflected that the Italian-German agreement that the two armistices should take effect simultaneously

---

[1] His command post was now in Châtel-Guyon. He immediately set out on the road to Bordeaux, without knowing why he had been sent for.

afforded him several days' breathing space. He decided to turn them to account by launching an immediate offensive in the Alps.

'When Badoglio was told of this plan, he roundly condemned it,' wrote Ciano. 'But the Duce insisted. Then I spoke to him myself. I consider it not only inglorious, but dangerous from the point of view of morale, to pounce on an army that is already beaten ... '

Impressed by the appositeness of these remarks, Mussolini stated that he would confine the attack to two small sectors: one near the Swiss frontier, the other in the south, along the coast.

Hastily summoned from Châtel-Guyon, General Huntziger reached Bordeaux in the late afternoon. Colonel Bourget recalls that the general gave a start when he learned the nature of his mission. ' ... His pale blue eyes shone with intense emotion and despair. Who could understand his feelings better than General Weygand?'

When the time came for Huntziger to leave, the two generals stood in the doorway for some moments. Their handshake was prolonged.

POLITICAL SITUATION

After determining the composition of the French armistice delegation, the Marshal attended a Cabinet meeting at 9 a.m. M. Baudouin informed his colleagues of the German communication that had arrived shortly beforehand and of the composition of the French delegation, to which they gave their approval.

The Cabinet then turned to the question that obsessed every minister in the room: should they, or should they not, sail to North Africa? Most of them, especially M. Chautemps, took the view that the government must in no circumstances be taken prisoner. In view of the speed of the German advance, it was unwise to remain in Bordeaux a day longer.

This view was adopted, but there was hesitation as to where the government should pause on its way to the Mediterranean. Toulouse was too near. Nîmes was too exposed, in view of the German advance in the Rhône valley. Port-Vendres was too small, and was crowded with refugees. At Chautemps's suggestion, M. Pomaret suggested Perpignan, which was finally decided upon. President Lebrun made no attempt to conceal his eagerness to be out of Bordeaux.

Preparations for the move were started at once.

But at that juncture two planes arrived from London. The first brought MM. Monnet and Pleven, who were hoping to persuade M. Herriot to go to England. The second brought Lord Lloyd, Churchill's Colonial Secretary. He drove straight to the British ambassador's residence, where he found Sir Ronald Campbell and Mr Alexander.

The ambassador took his two visitors to call on M. Baudouin, then on MM. Jeanneney and Herriot and finally on President Lebrun. Lloyd and Alexander again raised the question of the fleet: what steps had the French government taken to ensure that its warships would not fall into enemy hands?

The Minister for Foreign Affairs gave them the most explicit assurances:

> I informed them of the measures taken to prevent its [the fleet's] ever falling into our enemies' hands and being used by them. I gave them my word of honour that irrevocable orders had been given to this effect. They declared themselves satisfied with my statements.

M. Baudouin's next visitors were MM. Leca and Devaux, former *chefs de cabinet* to M. Reynaud. They advised him that the latter had now firmly made up his mind to go to Washington as French ambassador. 'But it is important that you should ask him again,' they told Baudouin.

MM. Leca and Devaux were in favour of his leaving at once. They had talked him into taking them with him as financial attachés.

With the Marshal's approval M. Baudouin drove to the Hotel Splendide to see M. Reynaud. The ex-Premier told him that he 'had not yet come to a final decision, though he was very tempted to accept the post'. He asked Baudouin to get the President of the Republic to sign the document appointing him ambassador, on the understanding that the appointment should not be gazetted 'till his acceptance became final'.

M. Bouthillier immediately signed the decrees appointing MM. Leca and Devaux attachés to the French Financial Delegation to the United States. But M. Lebrun refused, pending further orders, to sign M. Reynaud's own decree of appointment. He made no secret of his hostility to the idea of the ex-Premier's leaving the country while the armistice conditions were still unknown. He wanted to keep him up his sleeve in case France had to fight on.

Meanwhile, Sir Ronald Campbell had decided that Lord Lloyd's and Mr Alexander's representations had been inadequate. At 10 p.m. Marshal Pétain received the British ambassador, who was accompanied by Lord Lloyd and Mr Alexander. M. Baudouin and Admiral Darlan were present. The Admiral solemnly renewed the pledges regarding the fleet that he had given the day before. The Marshal solemnly confirmed them. At the end of the interview Baudouin advised Sir Ronald Campbell that the Cabinet was to meet at 9 a.m. next day to discuss the question of leaving Bordeaux.

At about 11 p.m., before getting into his car, Lord Lloyd took Baudouin's arm and led him into the park surrounding the Marshal's residence.

'It was so dark that we walked slap into the sentries,' writes Baudouin. 'Lord Lloyd became very insistent. He pressed me to join the group of ministers who were sailing for North Africa next day. He assured me that I could personally count on Britain's friendship.

' "I and other members of the British Cabinet," he announced, "will come and confer with you and your colleagues as soon as you reach Morocco or Algeria. Morocco would be better, on account of the Italians." '

Baudouin did not reply. Thereupon Lord Lloyd stopped suddenly and, leaning closer to his companion, said: 'You must understand that France's interests and Britain's are intertwined. You will be rewarded!'

'It's marvellous to assert with such conviction that for serving Britain one will reap rewards in the next world,' returned Baudouin.

At 6 p.m. General de Gaulle broadcast a second appeal on the B.B.C.:

... In view of the confusion in Frenchmen's minds, *in view of the liquefaction of a government now subservient to the enemy*, in view of the impossibility of setting our administration in motion, I, General de Gaulle, French soldier and leader, am conscious of speaking in the name of France.

In the name of France I formally declare as follows:

It is the absolute duty of any Frenchman who still bears arms to continue resistance. Laying down arms, evacuating a military position or agreeing to place any portion of French soil under enemy control would be a crime against the nation.

At this present hour I am speaking first and foremost for French North Africa, for intact North Africa.

The Italian armistice is merely a crude trap.

In Clauzel's, Bugeaud's, Lyautey's and Noguès's Africa, honour demands a strict refusal to comply with enemy conditions ...

De Gaulle was not the only one with his eyes on the Empire. The British government had beaten him to it. During the day the British consuls in Tunis, Algiers and Rabat called on, respectively, M. Peyrouton, Resident-General in Tunisia, M. Le Beau, Governor-General in Algeria, and General Noguès, Resident-General in Morocco. They urged the French officials to break away from the Bordeaux government, emphasizing that they would derive considerable political and financial advantages from so doing. Similar pressure was brought to bear on M. Boisson, Governor-General in Dakar, and on M. Puaux, High Commissioner in the Levant. But these overtures were cold-shouldered. France's representatives were not to be bribed. They refused to yield to British approaches 'before they had had a chance to see how things were going to turn out'.

In Bordeaux a serious view was now being taken of General de Gaulle's absence without leave. At General Weygand's orders, General Colson asked London to confirm receipt of his previous telegram (June 18th).

But at this point a new and totally unexpected crisis arose, making the Marshal's task more complicated than ever. It seemed that in addition to all her other tribulations, France might now have to face a war with Japan in the Far East. That, at least, was the impression given by the Tokyo government's ultimatum to General Catroux, Governor-General of Indo-China, demanding:

1. The closing of the China border to lorries carrying petrol and trains carrying war materials;
2. The supervision of the China border by Japanese officials;
3. The acceptance of these measures within twenty-four hours, the reply to be handed to the Japanese High Command by midnight on June 20th.

In his telegram conveying these demands to General Catroux, M. Arsène Henry added: 'In the immediate acceptance of this ultimatum lies the possibility, though not the certainty, of saving Indo-China.'

JUNE 20TH

In the course of the day the enemy succeeded in crossing the Loire, both east of Tours and at Saumur. Along the Cher he broke through at Selles and pushed southwards, scattering the left wing of the 5th Army: four French divisions vanished almost without trace. Farther east, the Germans entered Montluçon, Riom and Thiers.

But in places the French were still resisting fiercely in an attempt to slow down the enemy's advance. These were acts of individual bravery, desperate sacrifices that could do nothing to alter the course of events. For nothing could now stave off the final debacle, so fast approaching, nor the withdrawal southwards of France's dislocated units, hopelessly entangled in the panic-stricken flow of refugees. Some formations had been in the front line since May 10th; they had been fighting, without respite or hope of relief, since the start of the battle. The men were exhausted: though anxious to fight on to the last, they were collapsing at the road-sides.

At one point during the day, some civilians saw a car bearing the tricolour flag draw up beside a group of prostrate soldiers. A general got out. He was elderly, rather short, and haggard with strain and lack of sleep. He walked over to the men and said: 'Bear it just a little longer! March just a little farther!'

Those who heard him say that he spoke very gently, very like a father talking to his children. It was General Weygand.

In the evening the remains of General Daille's 45th Corps, after two days of fierce fighting in the Lomont area, crossed into Switzerland and were interned. They had been faced with vastly superior armour and had resisted till food and ammunition gave out.

At 1.30 p.m.[1] Admiral Darlan sent the following message to all senior naval officers:

June 20th, 1940

1. The Admiral of the Fleet believes that he may be able to retain command of naval forces and is taking steps to ensure as much.

[1] Even before the armistice delegation had left Bordeaux.

2. In the event of the Admiral of the Fleet's being unable to exercise his command freely, naval forces would become subject to the orders of Admiral de Laborde, then of Admiral Esteva, then of Admiral Abrial, and next of Admiral Gensoul.

3. All these general officers, or those who might be called upon to succeed them, will have to comply with the following general orders:

(*a*) Fight fiercely to the last until a true French government, independent of the enemy, gives orders to the contrary;

(*b*) Disobey any other government;

(*c*) Whatever orders are received, never surrender a warship to the enemy intact.

Admiral of the Fleet

DARLAN

ARMISTICE NEGOTIATIONS

At 5 a.m. the German government wired the French government, direct, to say that the composition of the delegation was acceptable and that its itinerary would be fixed in a later communication. At 11.45 a.m. a second message arrived, worded as follows:

The High Command of the Wehrmacht will expect the French armistice delegation in the course of June 20th, from 5 p.m. onwards, German Summer Time, at the Loire bridge near Tours.

A cease-fire will be ordered within a sector stretching ten kilometres on either side of the Poitiers–Tours road and along the Loire, between Tours and Blois.

The time at which the French delegation is due to reach the Loire bridge is to be communicated to the High Command of the Wehrmacht.

At 2.30 p.m. the delegation left Bordeaux. In the first car, which bore the tricolour flag denoting the presence of the commander of a Group of Armies, sat General Huntziger and M. Léon Noël. The roads were heavily congested. All the way to Angoulême, and even beyond, the cars had to fight their way through the crowds surging southwards. On foot, on cycles and in lorries, thousands of men, mostly unarmed and of various ranks and units, mingled in the flight from the front. They formed a sorry spectacle, and one that confirmed the delegates' fears as to the state of much of the army.

After Poitiers, the delegation proceeded along one of the army's strategic highways. It was practically empty. The villages and farms were abandoned. The light was fading. As it neared Tours the convoy passed a few men still at their posts. They were young officers and N.C.O.s belonging to a cavalry division and waiting, gun in hand, behind flimsy barricades, for the enemy to appear. Artillery fire could be heard in the distance; it came from the east, somewhere near the Sologne. There was a giant blaze in the direction of Tours. Away to the west, a dimmer glow. There were no other indications of a battle. True, hostilities had been suspended, since 5 p.m., along a ten-kilometre front.

The cars drew up in the outskirts of Tours. It was about 10 p.m. The delegation was very late. One of the main districts of the town was ablaze. The Town Clerk and Chief of Police came out to meet the delegation and conduct them to the German outposts, for the city itself had not yet been occupied.

The cars drove along the Loire with their lights full on. Then the motor-cycle escort stopped and dismounted, and the car containing the two chief delegates drove on slowly towards the German lines. A dark figure appeared in the middle of the road: it was a German army sergeant. He examined the delegation's credentials. A light armoured car appeared from out of the shadows. It was to lead the Frenchmen to their destination.

They crossed the Loire at Vendôme, using a pontoon bridge. In Vendôme itself — the town was packed with German troops — they were met by General von Tippelskirch, who announced that he was to be attached to them throughout their mission. He also told them that they were going to have to drive farther towards Chartres (they still did not know where they were being taken).

They cruised on in darkness, through the southward-streaming German columns. 'They were like an irresistible flood,' writes Léon Noël. 'Convoy followed convoy. The cars drove through Chartres without stopping ... Day broke. In the early hours of that fine summer morning [this was June 21st] the refugees — mostly on foot, but occasionally on carts or cycles — were heading northwards again. Dirty and exhausted, they had failed to escape the invasion and were trying to make their way home.

'The enemy troops provided a striking contrast with this jetsam ... Young and sturdy, the men had the relaxed look of well-fed soldiers leaving their barracks to take part in manoeuvres. Their uniforms were impeccable, their equipment splendid ... '

416

After leaving Chartres, the convoy headed for the Fontainebleau road, via Villacoublay. It entered Paris by the Porte d'Orléans.

'In the capital, which had been occupied for a week, there were very few people about. The Swastika flew from the Palais Bourbon, the Quai d'Orsay, the Hotel Crillon, the Ministry of Marine and, in the distance, the Eiffel Tower.'

At 7.30 a.m. the convoy at last drew up outside the Hotel Royal Monceau in the Avenue Hoche. German sentries stood on guard. The French delegation, worn-out after seventeen hours on the road, were to be allowed a short rest.

POLITICAL SITUATION

The Cabinet met at 10 a.m. President Lebrun announced that he had made up his mind to leave in the course of the day. But there was renewed uncertainty among ministers. The line taken by some was that, though the speed of the German advance certainly made it essential for them to leave Bordeaux, it did not follow that they should sail to North Africa. M. Chautemps suggested a compromise: the government should move to Perpignan, as agreed. This solution was adopted. The departure was timed for 2.30 p.m.

Soon afterwards M. Pierre Laval called on Marshal Pétain. He had heard that the Marshal was thinking of sending Paul Reynaud and two of his colleagues to Washington. The news was causing him considerable alarm, for he viewed these appointments as serious political blunders.

'But why?' asked the Marshal. 'M. Reynaud's presence in Washington can only help our country. It will clear up misunderstandings that have arisen in the United States during the past few days with regard to my government's activities.'

'How,' replied M. Laval, 'can you fail to realize the interpretation that is bound to be placed on this journey? M. Reynaud has made every effort to get Mr Roosevelt to declare war on Germany. And this is the moment you choose for such a gesture — when our delegates are sitting across the table from the German authorities, asking them for their armistice terms! I must confess I cannot understand you ... Why are you bent on undoing with one hand what you are so arduously striving to do with the other?'

Whereupon the senator for the Seine stalked out, leaving the Marshal to ponder on an aspect of the question that had not previously occurred to him.

Meanwhile, the Ministry of the Interior and the fiscal departments of the two Assemblies were making preparations for moving the seat of government. M. Didkowsky, head of the Sûreté, received instructions to prepare accommodation in Perpignan. He requisitioned the Grand Hotel, turning out the Duke and Duchess of Windsor, who had been staying there.

The members of the Assemblies were to follow the government. Herriot sent for MM. Perfetti and Barthe, treasurers of the Chamber, and instructed them to inform the deputies.

At 11 a.m. the nation's representatives met in a disused classroom in the Rue Anatole France. The session was a noisy one. At 11.45 a.m. M. Perfetti arrived and announced that 'the Cabinet had just decided on the corporate bodies' immediate departure with the government, and that MM. Léon Blum and Jeanneney were already on their way to Port-Vendres.' The deputies present decided to pack their bags and follow suit.

But it was all a mistake. Round about noon M. Herriot rang M. Barthe to inform him that only the government would sail from Port-Vendres. The deputies and senators would sail from Le Verdon, aboard the *Massilia*.

The Marshal remained imperturbable. The others could do what they liked: he had no intention of leaving. He made this quite clear in the speech that he broadcast at 12.30 p.m.

People of France!

I have asked our enemies to put an end to hostilities. Yesterday, Wednesday, the government selected the plenipotentiaries who are entrusted with receiving their conditions.

I took this decision, a hard one for a soldier, because the military situation demanded it. We had hoped to make a stand along the Somme–Aisne line. General Weygand had regrouped our forces. His name alone presaged victory. Yet the line gave way and enemy pressure compelled our troops to fall back.

By June 13th it became inevitable that we should seek an armistice. This defeat has surprised you ... We shall learn from the battles we have lost. Since victory [in 1918] the spirit of enjoyment has overshadowed the spirit of sacrifice. People have taken more than they have given. They have wanted an easy time; today they are faced with calamity.

I was with you in the glorious days. *As head of the government I am, and shall remain, with you in the dark days. Stand by me.* The fight is still the same. It is for France, her soil and her sons.

Meanwhile, the time of the government's intended departure was drawing near. President Lebrun was preparing to leave Bordeaux and join M. Jeanneney in Port-Vendres (M. Herriot having already installed his luggage aboard the *Massilia*), when a telephone call informed him that the Marshal had called another Cabinet meeting.

M. Lebrun was considerably taken aback. He rang M. Alibert. The Under-Secretary of State at the Prime Minister's office confirmed the news.

'But I can't delay,' groaned M. Lebrun. 'My car is waiting for me. I want to get to Port-Vendres. A light cruiser will take me to Algeria ... '

The silence that greeted these remarks alarmed him.

'What am I to do?' he asked.

'The Cabinet is to meet in a few moments,' replied M. Alibert. 'Wait till then.'

M. Lebrun hesitated, then allowed himself to be swayed. He put through a call to M. Jeanneney, but the latter was already on his way to Perpignan. Word finally reached him in Toulouse. Amazed, he ordered his chauffeur to turn the car round and hurry back to Bordeaux.

The anti-Algiers faction had gained a few hours.

The Cabinet met at 2.30 p.m. The Marshal informed his ministers that the armistice delegation had just left. It was to meet the Germans in Tours at 7 p.m. He hoped to have news from it that evening and asked the government to postpone its departure till then. The ministers agreed. Only M. Chautemps seemed dissatisfied.

In the course of the afternoon the senators adopted the following motion:

The senators here present have unanimously decided not to sail in the *Massilia* but to go to Perpignan, where the government is. They consider that if the government were not to leave France, they would be in the peculiar situation of crossing the sea while decisions were being taken.

While all this was going on, President Lebrun was still cooling his heels in the Prefecture. He no longer knew what to make of the position. M. Alibert had advised him to wait till the end of the Cabinet meeting, but surely it must be over by now? Was light going to be shed at last?

At last M. Chautemps arrived. The President asked him what was happening. The Vice-Premier told him that the armistice delegation was on its way to Tours, where it was to meet the Germans that evening.

At that moment the Marshal walked into the room, followed by M. Alibert. The Marshal sat down without saying a word.

'*Monsieur le Président de la République*,' Chautemps was saying to Lebrun. 'I should like to repeat your instructions to ensure that I have not mistaken them. I am to leave for Algiers immediately and there assume control of the government. I shall call senators and deputies together — those, at least, who have been able to follow us out — and we shall take any measures that will assist the continuance of the war from the Empire. Marshal Pétain is remaining on French soil to ensure, through his personal prestige, the fullest possible protection of persons and property. You, *Monsieur le Président de la République*, are going to join us without delay. Are we agreed?'

'Entirely agreed, my dear Prime Minister,' replied M. Lebrun. 'My luggage is packed.'

The Marshal simply bowed his head.

So everything was settled. Departure was imminent. The participants of the scene were on the point of rising when M. Alibert said suddenly: '*Monsieur le Président de la République*, I have very important news for you. I learned it only as we were on our way here and have not yet had time to inform Marshal Pétain. But I feel it is likely to influence your decision. *It is untrue that the Germans have crossed the Loire.*[1] On the contrary: the High Command tells us that our troops are resisting stoutly and that the river-line has not been broken at any point.'

'That certainly *is* important!' said the Marshal.

M. Lebrun was clearly put out.

'Do you not feel, *Monsieur le Président de la République*,' Alibert pursued, 'that it would be advisable to postpone any final decision till tomorrow morning?'

'It would certainly be wiser,' the Marshal emphasized.

'Very well,' said M. Lebrun, making an effort. 'But this is the last time. I shall remain ready to leave. Let me see dispatches as they come in …'

M. Chautemps was dumbfounded. M. Alibert stood up. The Marshal followed suit, and the pair left the President's office.

The anti-Algiers faction had scored again.

But it was 5.30 p.m. The coach for Le Verdon, where the *Massilia* was anchored, was on its way out of Bordeaux with those senators and deputies who had been unable to find alternative means of transport. M. Herriot, preferring not to be separated from M. Jeanneney, had his luggage brought ashore. Paul Boncour likewise decided to remain behind.

The *Massilia*'s departure was delayed for a number of reasons. In the first place the crew refused to put to sea. Next, they violently displayed

[1] Subsequently M. Alibert did not hesitate to admit that he told a lie that day.

their hostility to certain members of parliament whom they accused or abandoning France.[1] Jean Zay, still in uniform, was set upon. His képi was sent flying across the deck.

'The panicky flight from Bordeaux was such an appalling spectacle,' M. Reynaud later wrote in his memoirs, 'that I decided to remain there till the last minute, leaving only when the government did so.'

But not all members of the Assemblies had gone aboard the *Massilia*. There were some who thought it their duty to remain in France and who were prepared to respond to the Marshal's broadcast appeal, which they felt had been addressed as much to them as to the French people.

Some sixty of them went to Bordeaux town hall to express their feelings to M. Laval. The latter sensed that it was touch-and-go whether the government would remain in Bordeaux. He suggested that a delegation should call on the Marshal and show him that his appeal had not been in vain. The suggestion was approved and M. Laval went to see the Prime Minister, accompanied by MM. Portmann, Piétri, Georges Bonnet, Bergery and Scapini. The Marshal received them with obvious satisfaction: their support was a promising indication of the way others felt.

In the Prefecture M. Lebrun was growing restless again. He had been assured that the German forces might reach Bordeaux at any moment. How could such information be reconciled with what M. Alibert had just told him?

He telephoned the Marshal and asked if he had received any news from the armistice delegation.

'No,' replied the Marshal. 'I have still heard nothing from General Huntziger.'

'Really, this is too bad!' exclaimed the President. 'It is impossible to deliberate under threat of enemy invasion. We have waited too long as it is. I'm leaving tonight.'

The Marshal strove to calm him: they would soon hear now, he insisted.

M. Lebrun hung up without disclosing his intentions.

It was 11 p.m. The anti-Algiers faction decided that they must intervene. If the government left Bordeaux there would be no armistice, and the whole of France would be overrun by the Wehrmacht ...

M. Alibert took some of the Marshal's personal writing-paper and dictated an order to every minister, directing him to remain in his residence till 8 a.m. next day, pending further instructions, and not on any account to leave the town before receiving them. M. Alibert then set the Marshal's stamp on the orders and signed them.

[1] She finally sailed at 1.30 p.m. next day.

The faction had gained another night; but it was an exhausting business, waiting for the German armistice terms, and the situation was growing steadily more entangled.

Meanwhile in London events had taken an unexpected turn. Early in the day General Lelong had replied to the telegrams that General Colson had sent him on June 18th and 19th:

No. 1092   London, June 20th, 1940, 6.35 a.m.
French military attaché to War Minister, Bordeaux
General de Gaulle has received order contained in telegram No. 10,978 D. This order has been repeated.

At 6 p.m. Churchill addressed a secret session of the House of Commons. After reviewing events since May 10th, he turned to the position in France. Here are the notes that he had made for this part of his speech:

> B.E.F. a fine Army. Only 10 Divisions.
> Without proper Armoured Divisions.
> Well-equipped, but placed in a hopeless
> strategic situation.
> Much to be thankful for.
> Melancholy position of the French Govt.
> We have to make the best of them.
> No criticisms, no recriminations.
> We cannot afford it, in public.
> Pétain. Reynaud, Darlan.
> 5 precious days largely wasted.
> Surprise if mercy shown by Germany.
> The French fleet. The French Empire.
> Our policy.
> Urge them to continue but all depends
> upon the battle of Britain.

That evening General de Gaulle felt his courage faltering. He called on General Lelong and asked him to inform Bordeaux that he was prepared to return to France. But the British refused to provide him with any means of transport.

During the day the situation in Indo-China had worsened considerably. The Japanese ultimatum expired at midnight. Since the British and Americans were urging France to resist and displaying so much interest in the fate of her Empire, now — if ever — was the time for them to support their words with action by joining forces with her.

Thus it was with impatience that General Catroux awaited the response to the appeals that he had made, the night before, to London and Washington.

The replies came in the course of the evening. Lord Halifax, Britain's Foreign Secretary, suggested that General Catroux would share His Majesty's Government's view that it was obviously in the interests of Indo-China and of the British Empire to avoid being dragged into hostilities in the Far East. There were, he said, reasons for supposing that Japan's present intentions towards Indo-China might be limited to such measures as she considered necessary to putting an end to the war with China.

Mr Cordell Hull, Secretary of State at the White House, said that the United States was at present in no position to provide Indo-China with any support. He advised General Catroux — off the record, of course — to give way to Japan's demands in order to gain time. This view was confirmed by M. de Saint-Quentin, French ambassador in Washington.

Thus in the East, as in the West, France was left to fend for herself. General Catroux could see no alternative to informing the Japanese government that he 'had decided to meet its demands'. At midnight, when the time-limit expired, General Catroux ordered the frontier to be closed.

JUNE 21ST

After the capture of Cherbourg, the 7th Panzer Division was ordered to Rennes, there to play its part in the final operations in Brittany.

Rommel wrote to his wife:

> *Rennes, June 21st,* 1940
>
> Reached here without difficulty. The war has become practically a lightning Tour de France. Within a few days it will be over for good. The local people are relieved to see everything happening so peacefully.

Morlaix and Lorient fell during the day. In Brest, Hoth's armour had been relieved by standard infantry units. The town was a scene of desolation. The harbour was empty. Ships that had been unable to put to sea had been scuttled. The dockyard was a heap of rubble.

By evening the whole of Brittany was occupied.

But the main event of the day, from the point of view of military operations, was the launching of a fierce offensive in the Alps. At dawn, nineteen of the thirty-two Italian divisions massed in the sector stormed the French positions.

The French High Command had drawn so heavily on the Alpine Army in the past few weeks that it was down to skeleton size. France's defences in the area took the form of three fortified sectors:

1. *In the north:* the fortified sector of Savoy;
2. *In the centre:* the fortified sector of Dauphiné;
3. *In the south:* the fortified sector of the Alpes-Maritimes.

These were manned by fortress units and by three Class 'B' divisions: the 64th, 65th and 66th Infantry Divisions.

The French were in a difficult position from the very first, for even as the Italians attacked from the east the Germans were sweeping down the Rhône valley to take them from the rear. General Olry responded swiftly and decisively by splitting his forces into two groups. The first, facing

MAP 12

DISTRIBUTION OF
OPPOSING FORCES
ON THE ALPINE FRONT
JUNE 21ST 1940

ITALIAN ATTACKS
PATH OF GERMAN
ADVANCE

LAUSANNE

Bourg

St.Claude

R. Saône

R. Ain

R. Rhône

GENEVA
R.D.S.

Bonneville

R. Avre

Annecy
R.D.S.

4th
ARMY

LYONS

8th C.I.D. on 10th JUNE

2nd C.I.D on 12th JUNE

Albertville
S.F.S.

Chambéry

R. Isère

R. Arc

S.F.S
&
66th I.D.

Lanslebourg

1st A.I.D.
101st M.D.

2nd A.I.D.
ALPINE
CORPS

5th A.I.D.

GRENOBLE

14th A.C.

St.Jean de Maurienne

66th I.D.

59th I.D.
53rd, 11th & 9th I.D.

Elements of
7th I.D.
10th I.D.
24th I.D.
41st I.D.
51st I.D.
133rd
102nd M.D.
1st C.D.

Uriage
14th A.C.

R. Romanche

1st & 2nd I.D.
A.I.D.
26th I.D

★ 1st A.C.

7th
ARMY
in reserve

VALENCE
G.H.Q. ALPINE ARMY

Die

Briançon

A.I.D.

4th A.C.

★?

R. Drac

F.D.S.
&
64th
I.D.

8th I.D.

R. Drôme

Gap
F.D.S.

Embrun
64th I.D.

R. Ubaye

2nd A.C.

36th I.D.
33rd I.D.
16th I.D.
4th I.D.

4 A.I.D.
201 I.D.

1st
ARMY

3rd A.C.

R. Ayques

R. Durance

Digne

R. Tinée

A.I.D.

3rd I.D.

15th A.C.

Orange

65th I.D.

32nd I.D.

6th
I.D.

Forcalquier

R. Var

Levens

85th I.D.

St. Pons

F.S.A.M.

Avignon

R. Durance

R. Verdon

15th A.C.

Vence
15th A.C.

F.S.A.M.

22nd I.D.

44th I.D.

5th I.D.

Aix-en-Provence

2nd C.I.D.

Draguignan

MARSEILLES

Toulon

MEDITERRANEAN SEA

north-westwards, would meet the German advance; the second, facing south-eastwards, would deal with the Italians.

The latter were exerting pressure all along the line. In the north twelve battalions tried to capture Bourg-Saint-Maurice, advancing via the Seigne pass, the Petit Saint-Bernard, and the Mont pass, but they managed only to surround a small fortified post near the Petit Saint-Bernard pass, and even that they could not take. Yet the French positions were held by only four battalions and forty-four guns.

In Maurienne the Italians attacked in force. Their objective was Modane, which they strove to reach by way of the Mont-Cenis, Sollières, Belle-combe and Clapier passes.

At 5.30 a.m. more than a thousand shells landed on the La Turra fort, but it continued to resist stoutly. But farther south some French recon-naissance groups were outflanked by two battalions and driven back from Le Planey to the La Tuille dam.

In Briançon there was an artillery duel between the Italian fort at Chaberton and a battery of French 280s. Within hours Chaberton was compelled to cease fire, every gun having been put out of action.

At the end of the day the Italians were being held all along the line, except on the Le Queyras headland where they had managed to encircle the village of Abriès.

In the evening, to counteract the possible consequences of German thrusts on either side of the Massif Central, the French High Command ordered the 16th and 19th Districts to form defence groups to cover Toulouse from the east and Bordeaux from the north.

POLITICAL SITUATION

At 7 a.m. the British Military Attaché brought M. Baudouin a letter from Sir Ronald Campbell. It registered the ambassador's surprise that he had not been informed of the armistice terms. Baudouin replied that though there was every excuse for edginess, it ought not to exceed cer-tain bounds. He requested the attaché to tell the ambassador that the French government had as yet received no word from its delegation.

Shortly afterwards there was a telephone call from Captain Gasser, one of General Weygand's staff officers. He announced that the delegates had reached Tours just before midnight, crossed the lines at about 4 a.m. and were apparently being taken to Paris.

At 9 a.m. the Cabinet met to examine the situation. Having no further information, the Minister for the Colonies read out a long cable from General Catroux informing the government of events in Indo-China. Failing to appreciate the colony's exposed position, the government showed considerable irritation with the general's decisions.

Marshal Pétain and General Weygand then turned to the question of Morocco. Deeply perturbed by General Noguès's message of June 18th, they had wired instructions for him to come to Bordeaux. The Resident-General's arguments showed that he did not properly grasp France's position. Only by direct contact would he gain the right impression. But General Noguès had replied that he could not leave Morocco without risking grave consequences.

General Weygand replied in the following terms:

The government understands your reasons for staying at your post. Kindly give straight answers to the following questions:

What, in your opinion, given the almost complete impossibility of our reinforcing you or sending you further ammunition, are:

(a) the chances of prolonged resistance in Algeria, Tunisia and Morocco, taking into account a possible intervention by the Axis powers via the Spanish Riff;

(b) the chances and effectiveness of land and air offensives based on Tunisia ... ?

At 11 a.m. a substantial group of senators and deputies met in the civic reading-room. After brief deliberation, all but three of them voted in favour of sending delegations to MM. Jeanneney and Herriot to protest against the 'intolerable pressure that they were bringing to bear on the President of the Republic to get him to go to Algiers'. But these delegations had no effect on the leaders of the two Assemblies.

It was therefore decided that another delegation, led by M. Laval, should call on President Lebrun himself.

At 1.30 p.m. the *Massilia* finally sailed from Le Verdon. There were no further incidents. Of the two-hundred-odd members of Parliament in Bordeaux, she was carrying only eighteen deputies and one senator to Casablanca.

In the early afternoon M. Laval and his colleagues went to the Prefecture and asked to speak to the President. Among the delegation were MM. Marquet, Piétri, Georges Bonnet, Portmann, Gérente, Bergery, Rauzy, Landry, Barthe, Dommange and Crutel.

Previously alerted by telephone, M. Lebrun stood waiting with his back to the window. His face was ravaged by grief and fatigue. He motioned to his visitors to sit, then did so himself. He made an obvious effort to keep calm, while his visitors, who chose to remain on their feet, were all talking and gesticulating at once.

M. Laval spoke in a loud metallic voice.

'More than a hundred senators and deputies have just met,' he said. 'They have appointed a delegation which I am instructed to present to you ...'

He paused, then continued:

'Why are we here?

'To discuss your plan to leave France.

'To protest against that plan.

'To beg you not to carry it out!'

M. Lebrun said nothing. M. Laval added forcefully: 'You cannot, you must not leave! We will not agree to the government's using these almost fraudulent means to go to Africa and continue a fight that is clearly hopeless.'

M. Lebrun was stunned, but he recovered sufficiently to say: 'The position is not as simple as that ... The matter does not rest with me alone. The government has discussed it. It will discuss it further ... Some may go, others may stay.'

Laval interrupted him with an impatient wave of the hand.

'Don't you realize,' he asked, 'that if the head of state, ministers and leaders of the Assemblies leave France, the ministers who stay behind will not have the necessary authority to speak for our country? But there is more to it than that. By taking away the State Seals, the President of the Republic will be taking away the government of France: he will be the sole master of policy. Now, if any policy stands condemned by events it is the Reynaud-Churchill policy ... Only two men — General Weygand and Marshal Pétain — are competent to say whether the war can be continued ...'

'But how on earth,' asked M. Lebrun, 'could the government of France remain autonomous and free when exposed to the risk of capture in territory held by the enemy? ...'

At that point M. René Dommange spoke up.

'*Monsieur le Président*,' he said, 'it is your government that would no longer be free and autonomous after abandoning forty million Frenchmen on their own soil in the midst of battle. Those abandoned people would themselves constitute the true government of France. It is we who would form it, for we shall never leave France ...'

M. Lebrun made no reply. The delegates were silent. Then M. Laval continued, more vehemently than ever: 'If you leave this land of France, you will never set foot on it again. Yes, once it becomes known that you chose to leave in the hour of our country's greatest distress, one word will be on everyone's lips: defection. Perhaps even a worse one: treason.'

Laval took a step towards Lebrun, clenching his fist to hammer out the final words on the presidential desk: 'Your duty, *Monsieur le Président*, is to follow the Marshal's example ... You have the right to leave if you want. But you must do so only as a private individual. Hand in your resignation ... '

Bending towards the President, the ex-Premier launched this final appeal: 'Do not listen to the counsel of those who have led our country into the abyss ... Oh, why have you followed it for so long?'

'The Constitution made it my duty to do so,' replied M. Lebrun. 'I have consulted the leaders of the two Assemblies, MM. Herriot and Jeanneney ... '

'Oh, Jeanneney!' Laval burst out. 'I hate that man for all the harm he has done to France!'

He spoke with such violence that the Undersecretary of the Prime Minister's office, who was standing outside the door (listening, no doubt), wondered whether the President was being attacked.

'Monsieur Laval,' said Lebrun, 'the louder you speak the less well I can hear you. Do please lower your voice!'

With these words the conversation came to an end. One by one, the senators and deputies stepped dejectedly forward to take their leave of M. Lebrun. M. Laval alone made straight for the door. Whereupon the Head of State went after him and clasped both his hands with sincere emotion.

After dinner M. Baudouin called on the Marshal with M. Bouthillier. He informed the Prime Minister that M. Reynaud had sent word that he did not intend to be captured by German troops and that he wanted to be sent to Washington without delay. Unless he was made ambassador very soon he would go to Madrid.

'M. Paul Reynaud has called on me in person,' returned the Marshal. 'He asked me to appoint him without further delay. But I am not so sure that I shall give him the post now. It is too late or too early. I am wondering whether it would be wise, at the very moment when our plenipotentiaries are face to face with the German plenipotentiaries, to send out an ambassador who might make people think we are making a last bid to drag the United States into a war against Germany ... '

At 1.30 p.m., still escorted by General von Tippelskirch, the French delegation left the Hotel Royal Monceau for Compiègne. On the outskirts of the forest a group of officials appeared. The cars slowed down, then stopped. They were in Rethondes.

The Frenchmen passed the monument to the 1918 armistice. A large Nazi flag was draped over it. Followed by his colleagues, General Huntziger walked past the black-uniformed S.S. guards of the Leibstandarte Adolf Hitler. The guards presented arms. The Frenchmen saluted the colour.

The railway carriage in which Foch had signed the armistice in 1918 stood within a few yards of them. In the background, dominating the clearing and in no way concealed, rose the Marshal's statue.

Hitler was there. The delegates could see him through the carriage window. He was sitting and seemed lost in thought. An aide-de-camp informed him that the French delegation had arrived. The officer came out again at once and invited the Frenchmen into the coach.

Inside, the Chancellor, Goering, Hess, Grand-Admiral Raeder, Ribbentrop, General Keitel (the Commander-in-Chief) and other generals rose and extended their arms in salute. Raeder and Goering saluted with their batons, afterwards laying them on the table.

The Führer motioned to the delegates to sit. General Huntziger took the chair directly facing him.

Without a word, Hitler signalled to General Keitel to open the proceedings. The General read out the following statement on his leader's behalf:

Trusting in the assurances given to the German Reich by President Wilson and confirmed by the Allied powers, the German armed forces laid down their arms in November 1918. Thus ended a war which neither the German people nor its government had desired and in which, despite their overwhelming superiority, our adversaries had succeeded in decisively beating neither the German navy nor air force.

Yet the German armistice commission had no sooner arrived than the solemn pledges were broken. Thus did November 11th, 1918, inaugurate, in this railway carriage, the sufferings of the German people. Everything that could be inflicted on a race, by way of dishonour, humiliation and moral and material suffering, had its beginning here. Perjury and breach of promise were heaped upon a race whose only weakness, after more than four years of heroic resistance, was to lend credence to the pledges of the democratic leaders.

On September 3rd, 1939, twenty-five years after the opening of hostilities in the world war, France and Britain again, without the slightest cause, declared war on Germany. Arms have given their verdict. France is beaten. The French government has requested the German government to announce terms for an armistice.

The fact that the forest of Compiègne has been chosen for the handing-over of those conditions is explained by the determination to efface once and for all, by an act of reparative justice, a memory that was a far from glorious page in the history of France and that was felt by the German people to be the greatest dishonour of all time.

France has collapsed after resisting heroically and being beaten in an uninterrupted series of bloody battles. That is why Germany has no intention of giving the armistice terms and negotiations a flavour that would humiliate a gallant adversary.

The aim of the German demands is:

1. To prevent a resumption of fighting;
2. To provide Germany with the guarantees required for the enforced pursuit of the war against Britain;
3. To create the conditions necessary for the establishment of a fresh peace, the main object of which will be the reparation of the wrongs inflicted by force on the German Reich.

Keitel then read out the text of the armistice terms, clearly articulating every word.

At 3.30 p.m. the German Chancellor handed each of the French delegates a copy of the text. Then he rose and extended his right arm in salute, looking the Frenchmen straight in the eye. He left the carriage with his retinue to the strains of *Deutschland über Alles*.

The head of the French delegation handed General Keitel the credentials empowering him to 'take cognizance of the armistice terms and peace terms'.

Keitel was amazed at this wording.

'Are you or are you not empowered to accept the agreement?' he asked curtly.

'After taking cognizance of it,' answered Huntziger, 'I shall have, in any case, to seek instructions from my government.'

'But you are termed "plenipotentiaries"!' retorted Keitel, more taken aback than ever.

M. Léon Noël intervened to observe that the German delegates had been allowed the same latitude in 1918, though they had likewise been termed 'plenipotentiaries'.

Keitel did not press the point. He announced that the meeting would resume as soon as the delegation had studied the text and that the French would be allowed to ask for clarification of details.

Before withdrawing, General Huntziger asked in what circumstances the armistice with the Italians would be discussed.

'Article 23 deals with that,' Keitel answered curtly. 'It stipulates that the Franco-German agreement will come into force as soon as the French government has come to terms with the Italian government on the question of the cessation of hostilities.'

So there were to be no joint negotiations with Germany and Italy! The French delegation was crestfallen by this unexpected decision. The outlook was indeed alarming, for if Italy's claims turned out to be excessive, France would be faced with the choice of accepting them as they stood or continuing the war against both countries, for the Franco-German armistice would be null and void ...

General Huntziger indicated that the French government was anxious to receive assurances that it would be allowed to deliberate freely and to communicate with its delegates without hindrance. The general therefore sought permission to wire Bordeaux immediately and inform the French government — who still did not know where the delegation was — that contact had been made with the German leaders. He likewise asked that the Wehrmacht should suspend its advance towards Bordeaux.

General Keitel categorically refused the use of wireless telegraphy. If the delegation wished to send a message to its government, the German High Command would transmit it in clear.

The French delegates then asked for a plane to be put at their disposal so that a member of their party could fly to Bordeaux. Again General Keitel refused. As for halting the Wehrmacht's advance, the German Commander-in-Chief declared that 'the two delegations were meeting for the purpose of ending hostilities; while the agreement was still unsigned, operations could not be interrupted, even locally.'

'France's position is such,' he concluded, 'that it is vitally important for her that the armistice should be concluded as swiftly as possible.'

The French delegates then withdrew to the tent that had been erected for them, there to examine the armistice terms article by article.

The terms were worded as follows:

1. The French government orders the cessation of hostilities against
    the German Reich on French soil, in French protectorates and
    mandates and on the seas. It orders that French troops already
    encircled by German troops shall immediately lay down arms.
2. With a view to safeguarding the interests of the German Reich,
    French territory north and west of the line drawn on the attached
    map will be occupied by German troops. Where areas of occupied
    territory are not yet in the control of German troops, their
    occupation will be effected immediately after the conclusion of
    the present agreement.
3. In the occupied areas of France, the German Reich enjoys all the
    rights of an occupying power. The French government under-
    takes to facilitate the implementation of these rights in every
    possible way, with the assistance of the French administration.
    The French government will immediately call upon all authorities
    and all French administrative services in the occupied zone to
    comply with the regulations of the German military authorities
    and to collaborate properly with the latter.

    The French government is free to function anywhere in the
    unoccupied zone or, if it so wishes, to move to Paris. In the latter
    event, the German government undertakes to accord all neces-
    sary facilities to the government and its main administrative
    departments so that it shall be capable of administering occupied
    and unoccupied zones from Paris.
4. French armed forces on land, at sea and in the air are to be de-
    mobilized and disarmed within a period yet to be determined.
    Exempt from these obligations are such units as are needed for
    the preservation of internal order. Their strength and armament
    will be determined by Germany and Italy respectively.

    The French armed forces stationed in areas to be occupied by
    Germany will be speedily recalled to the unoccupied zone and
    there demobilized. Before being recalled to the unoccupied
    zone, such troops will lay down their arms and equipment where-
    ever they happen to be when the present agreement comes into
    force. They will be responsible for the orderly handing-over
    of equipment and arms to the German troops.
5. As a guarantee of the strict observance of these armistice terms,
    Germany may demand the surrender, in good condition, of all

heavy guns, tanks, anti-tank devices, military aircraft, anti-aircraft guns, small-arms, and all transport facilities and ammunition belonging to units of the French army engaged against Germany and not, at the time when the present agreement comes into force, in the zone to be occupied by Germany. The German armistice commission will decide the scale of such surrenders.

6. Arms, ammunition and war materials of any kind remaining in unoccupied French territory — where these have not been left at the disposal of the French government for arming authorized French units — are to be stored or placed in security under German or Italian control respectively. The German High Command reserves the right to take all necessary steps to this effect, to prevent wrongful use of this material. The manufacture of further war material in unoccupied territory is to cease at once.

7. All land and coastal fortifications, with their arms, ammunition and equipment, together with stores and installations of all kinds within the areas to be occupied, are to be surrendered in good condition. Also to be handed over are the plans of these fortifications, likewise the plans of those already captured by German troops. All details as to the placing of mines, mine-fields, delayed-action fuses, chemical barriers, etc., are to be handed to the German High Command. Such obstacles are to be removed by French forces on demand by the German authorities.

8. The French war fleet — with the exception of that portion which is left at the disposal of the French government to safeguard its interests in its colonial empire — will be assembled in harbours to be determined and demobilized and disarmed under the control of Germany or Italy respectively.

The selection of these harbours will be based on the ships' home ports in peacetime. The German government solemnly declares to the French government that during the war it does not intend to use for its own purposes the French war fleet stationed in ports under German control, apart from units needed for coast-guarding and mine-sweeping.

It further declares, solemnly and categorically, that it does not intend to stake any claims to the French fleet on concluding the peace. Apart from that portion of the French war fleet, to be determined, which will be assigned to the task of protecting French interests in the colonial empire, all warships outside French territorial waters are to be recalled to France.

9. The French High Command is to provide the German High Command with full details of all mines laid by France, of all booms in harbours or off coasts and of defensive and protective military installations.

   The sweeping of mine-fields is to be carried out by French units, where the German High Command so demands.

10. The French government undertakes not to engage in any hostile activity against the German Reich in the future, either with any portion of its remaining armed forces or in any other way.

    The French government will likewise prevent members of the French armed forces from leaving French soil and see that no arms, equipment, ships, planes, etc., are shipped to Britain or abroad.

    The French government will prohibit French nationals from fighting against Germany in the service of nations with which Germany is still at war. French nationals who do not comply with this order will be treated as insurgents by the German forces.

11. French merchant vessels of every kind, including coastal and harbour craft, will not be allowed to leave port till further orders. The resumption of commercial traffic is subject to prior approval by the German or Italian governments respectively.

    French merchant vessels absent from French harbours will be recalled to France by the French government or, if that is impossible, directed to neutral harbours.

    All German merchant vessels now held in French ports will be returned in good condition if so requested.

12. Orders will be issued at once forbidding the take-off of all planes on French soil. Any plane taking off without the previous consent of the German Command will be considered an enemy plane by the German air force and treated as such.

    Air force aerodromes and ground installations in the unoccupied zone will be placed under German or Italian control respectively. It may be required that they be put out of action. The French government is expected to place all foreign planes in the unoccupied zone at the disposal of the German authorities, or to prevent them from continuing on their way. Such planes are to be handed over to the German authorities.

13. The French government undertakes to ensure that, in the zone to be occupied by German forces, all military installations, establishments and stores are handed intact to the German forces.

Further, it is to ensure that harbours, industrial firms and naval dockyards remain in their present condition and are neither destroyed nor damaged in any way. The same applies to all means and channels of communication, including railways, roads and waterways, all telegraphic and telephonic networks and all navigational aids round the coasts. In addition the French government undertakes to carry out all necessary repairs when so ordered by the German High Command.

The French government will ensure that adequate skilled personnel, and a quantity of rolling-stock and other transport facilities corresponding with normal peace-time conditions, are available in the occupied zone.

14. All radio stations on French soil are to cease transmissions at once. Their resumption in the unoccupied zone will be subject to special regulations.

15. The French government undertakes to convey goods between the German Reich and Italy through the unoccupied zone, as and when required by the German government.

16. The French government will institute the return of the population to the occupied zone in collaboration with the appropriate German authorities.

17. The French government undertakes to prevent any transference of financial resources or reserves from the zone to be occupied by German forces to the unoccupied zone or abroad. Such resources and reserves may be disposed of only with the consent of the German government, on the understanding that the government of the Reich will bear in mind the needs of the inhabitants of the unoccupied zone.

18. The cost of maintaining the German forces of occupation on French soil will be borne by the French government.

19. All German prisoners of war and civilian prisoners, including those arrested and convicted for acts in favour of the German Reich, are to be handed over to the German forces without delay.

The French government is required to surrender, on demand, all German nationals indicated by the government of the Reich who are either in France or in French possessions, colonies, protectorates and mandates.

The French government undertakes to prevent the transference of German prisoners of war or civilian prisoners from

436

France to French possessions or foreign countries. In the case of prisoners already transferred from France, or of German prisoners of war unfit to be moved, accurate lists are to be presented, giving details of their whereabouts.

The German High Command will attend to German prisoners of war who are sick or wounded.

20. Members of the French armed forces who are prisoners of war of the German army will remain prisoners of war till peace is concluded.

21. A German Armistice Commission, acting on orders from the High Command, will regulate and control the execution of the armistice agreement.

The Armistice Commission is further called upon to ensure the concordance of this agreement with the Franco-Italian armistice agreement. The French government will send a delegation to the offices of the German Armistice Commission for the purpose of representing French interests and receiving orders for execution from the German Armistice Commission.

22. This armistice agreement will come into force as soon as the French government has likewise reached an agreement with the Italian government relating to the cessation of hostilities. The cessation of hostilities will take place six hours after the Italian government has informed the German government of the conclusion of this agreement.

The German government will wire news of this event to the French government.

23. The present armistice agreement is valid till the conclusion of the peace treaty. It may be instantly rescinded at any time by the German government if the French government does not fulfil the obligations assumed by it in the present agreement.

At 6 p.m. the French delegation returned to the railway carriage. This time General Keitel was absent. His place was taken by General Jodl.

General Huntziger began by protesting against the size of the suggested zone of occupation. But General Jodl broke in to remind him (though of this the French delegation was only too well aware) that military operations were still going on.

Referring to the Führer's declared intention of concluding an equitable peace with France, General Huntziger replied: 'We have been beaten by

Germany, but she has nothing to gain from dishonouring us or abasing us!'

'I can understand your feelings,' said General Jodl, 'but if the French delegation goes on raising considerations of that kind, we shall get no-where. I am not empowered to modify the text of the agreement: I am merely authorized to furnish explanations.'

France's two chief delegates then fired a whole series of questions, particularly concerning the extent, density and duration of the occupation, the future of Paris, the fate of the civilian population and the arrangements with regard to prisoners, etc.

Jodl was evasive, or said that the subject would have to be referred to General Keitel. Finally, faced with the insistence of the French, he flared up.

Speaking for Marshal Pétain, General Huntziger asked that France should be permitted to retain an army of a hundred and twenty to a hundred and thirty thousand men, excluding police and gendarmerie, 'to ensure maintenance of order in both zones'.

General Jodl did not reply.

General Huntziger and M. Léon Noël then insisted on being allowed to telephone Bordeaux. Jodl asked whether they were sure of being able to wind things up that evening.

'No,' answered General Huntziger. 'A further conversation will be necessary tomorrow morning, when we have been in touch with the government and been able to study the clauses of the agreement more closely.'

The French delegates' firmness prompted General Jodl to suspend proceedings again so that he could submit General Huntziger's request to General Keitel, together with the fundamental questions raised by the delegation.

Discussions were resumed half an hour later. This time General Keitel took the chair. In imperious tones he gave the following 'final' answers to the questions submitted:

No modification of the demarcation line could be considered, because of the requirements of the war against Britain.

If, however, instead of returning to Paris, the government chose to settle in some other town — Orléans, for example — certain adjustments might be made to the position of the 'green line'.

Germany herself will accept responsibility for maintaining order in the occupied zone; however, Germany agrees to France's retaining an army of 100,000 men, subject to Italy's consent.

With regard to Paris, the scale of [German] forces will be kept to the absolute minimum compatible with the requirements of the German military administration.

With regard to prisoners, in principle they are to remain in captivity till the signing of the peace treaty; but subsequent negotiations may result in the application of more liberal measures.

Finally, General Keitel gave the French delegation permission to telephone Bordeaux.

The French delegation again withdrew to its tent. At 8.15 p.m. General Huntziger and General Weygand were at last in touch. The latter anxiously asked the former where he was and what his overall impressions were.

'I am in a tent at Rethondes,' answered Huntziger, 'beside the railway carriage ... '

General Weygand could picture the scene only too well.

'My poor friend ... '

General Huntziger continued: 'The terms are harsh, but they contain nothing conflicting with honour.'

'What about the fleet?' asked Weygand.

'The Germans do not require it to be surrendered to them.'

'And the rest?'

'We have been handed a document comprising twenty-three articles. It constitutes a whole and may not be modified ... I'll read it to you ... '

'Please send us a copy of the armistice terms tonight ... One does not seal a country's fate with words dictated on the telephone. Remind them of Rethondes in 1918. They had seventy-two hours to sign, an aeroplane and a printed text.'

'I shall ask them,' answered Huntziger.

When the dictation was over, General Weygand telephoned the Marshal and informed him that the armistice terms had come in.

'What are they like?' asked the Marshal.

'Harsh but not dishonouring,' replied Weygand.

At 10.15 p.m. the Marshal called on the general with MM. Baudouin and Bouthillier. MM. Alibert, Charles-Roux and Admiral Darlan were there already. The Marshal notified the President of the Republic and called a Cabinet meeting for 1 a.m.

Shortly afterwards General Huntziger rang to say that the Germans had refused permission for General Parisot to fly back to Bordeaux. They required an answer by 11 a.m. next day (10 a.m. Bordeaux time).

The French delegation then started back for the Hotel Royal Monceau in Paris, reaching it at 2.30 a.m.

Meanwhile the articles of the Franco-German armistice had been communicated to the Italian government. Ciano wrote:

The ceremony chosen by Hitler for signing the armistice has greatly impressed the Duce. We have been studying the terms with Badoglio. They are moderate, and show that Hitler wishes to come to terms swiftly. In these circumstances Mussolini dare not demand the occupation of certain zones that interest us; it might result in negotiations being broken off and seriously compromise our relations with Berlin. The Duce will confine himself to demanding the demilitarization of a strip, thirty miles wide, along the Franco-Italian frontier, without prejudice to the claims he may make when peace comes.

Mussolini is deeply humiliated by the fact that our troops have not advanced an inch; they did not succeed in breaking through today and were stopped by the first French fort that returned their fire ... Mussolini blames the Italian people. 'What I lack is the right material. Even Michelangelo needed marble to carve his statues. Had he had only clay, he would have been a mere potter. A race that has been enslaved for sixteen centuries could not possibly become a race of conquerors within the space of a few years.'

Desperately anxious to improve Italy's military situation before the arrival of the Armistice Delegation, Mussolini asked the German High Command to drop paratroops behind the French units holding the Alpine passes. But the German High Command refused.

He then asked that the German armoured units driving down the Rhône valley should speed up their advance. To this the High Command agreed.

The order was dispatched to General von Rundstedt, but with the following rider: 'Do not hurry too much.'

JUNE 22ND

In the Vosges the ring had tightened round the French forces. With General Weygand's approval, General Georges instructed General Condé to hold out, whatever the cost. The prospect of an early armistice justified this last effort.

But by evening the situation was worse than ever. Having run out of food and ammunition, General Condé was authorized to seek a cease-fire on condition that he was accorded the honours of war. General List agreed to this. All France's eastern forces — some 500,000 men — were taken prisoner after fighting to the very last.

Little now remained of the French armed forces. The 10th Army, which had retreated from the Somme to Brittany, had been captured almost to a man. So, in the east, had the 3rd, 5th and 8th Armies, together with part of the 2nd.

In the Alps the Italians renewed their attacks along the whole front. As on the previous day, they were contained by the French outposts — except along the coast, where they made slight progress in the area east of Menton.

ARMISTICE NEGOTIATIONS

On examining the German proposals, General Weygand, Admiral Darlan and MM. Baudouin, Bouthillier, Alibert and Charles-Roux decided that France would have to seek a number of amendments, especially with regard to the articles dealing with the occupation of Paris, the surrender of air force equipment, and the home ports of warships. The latter could scarcely be disarmed in metropolitan ports held by the Germans.

At 1 a.m. the Cabinet met under M. Lebrun. General Weygand opening the proceedings began by reading out the text telephoned by General Huntziger. For all their harshness the articles of the agreement, taken as a whole, gave the French government a 'feeling of relief'.[1] True, France would be almost completely disarmed and her fortresses dismantled; yet at first glance the armistice proposals seemed to offer certain advantages: the surrender of the fleet was not demanded; France would retain an autonomous government and an independent administration; and she would have sufficient land and naval forces to maintain order at home and look after her Empire. Finally, there was no demand for military bases in her overseas territories.

MM. Chautemps, Frossard, Rivière and Février were not, however, in favour of accepting these conditions. M. Lebrun was hesitant. 'The Cabinet was undecided,' writes Baudouin in his memoirs.

'Had I thought we should come to this,' murmured Chautemps, 'I would never have taken office.'

Suddenly Admiral Darlan spoke out against the armistice.

'We must fight on,' he declared. 'I shall give orders for the fleet to bombard the Italian ports.'

There and then he sent the following message to the Admiralty for transmission to ships' captains:

1,655/02. 40.   *June 22nd*, 1940
I hereby stipulate that, since nothing has yet been settled, hostilities are to continue.

F. DARLAN

While the Cabinet debate continued, Sir Ronald Campbell, who had called to see if there were any news, was talking in another room with M. Charles-Roux. The British ambassador, normally so collected, was very on edge. On learning the nature of the German armistice conditions, he sent in a note to M. Baudouin at 1.30 a.m. In it he suggested that the French ministers could hardly fail to realize the insidious nature of the article concerning the fleet. The Germans, he said, could not be trusted: they always went back on their word. The Cabinet must forgive him for stating the obvious; his excuse lay in his deep concern.

M. Baudouin read the note to his colleagues. 'We understood it the more readily because we shared the British ambassador's fears,' he writes. 'We were all determined not to accept the article ... as it stood.'

At 3 a.m. the ministers agreed to adjourn till 8 a.m., by which time some of them would have been able to get together and work out the necessary amendments.

As the meeting broke up, Sir Ronald Campbell buttonholed M.

[1] The very words used by President Lebrun.

Baudouin and complained forcefully of the 'cavalier fashion in which the government was treating him'. The British government, he said, should not be unrepresented at a discussion in the course of which the French government was determining its attitude.

Baudouin was obviously nettled.

'The British government's representative may not attend the Cabinet's deliberations,' he retorted. 'If the British government cares to get the Germans to extend the short notice that they have served on the French government, I shall listen to your remarks with pleasure. But we have to give an answer by 9 a.m. ... '

But, anxious to avoid any step that might serve as an excuse for a rupture between the two governments, he handed Sir Ronald the copy of the armistice agreement that he had annotated during the Cabinet meeting.

At 3.30 a.m. the principal members of the government met informally to list the amendments sought from the German High Command. These related especially to four points:

1. *The Fleet*
Admiral Darlan, M. Baudouin and M. Charles-Roux asked that French ships should be disarmed in North African and West African ports and not in their pre-war home ports, for a large proportion of the fleet was based on Cherbourg, Brest or Lorient, which would lie in the occupied zone (*Art.* 8).

2. *The Air Force*
General Weygand asked that air force equipment should be 'stored' in the unoccupied zone, and not surrendered (*Art.* 5).

3. *Political Prisoners*
M. Charles-Roux strongly protested against this clause and asked that the second paragraph of Art. 19 should be deleted.

4. *Demarcation Line*
M. Charles-Roux asked that the demarcation line should curve farther northwards so as to leave Paris in the unoccupied zone.

At 8.30 a.m. Sir Ronald Campbell called on the Permanent Secretary for Foreign Affairs. He was extremely tense. M. Charles-Roux gave him a detailed explanation of the German terms and the amendments that the French government was seeking.

At 8.45 a.m. the Cabinet reassembled. 'The atmosphere was very different from the night before,' writes Baudouin. ' ... It was clear that a section of the Cabinet was now pinning its hopes for a hitch on the armistice with Italy.' And M. Lebrun recalls: 'The Cabinet considered that, harsh as they were, the armistice terms contained nothing dishonouring; it therefore started to examine the articles one by one.'

After going through the clauses of the agreement with a fine toothcomb, the ministers agreed that General Huntziger should sign, subject to the Germans' accepting the proposed amendments.

Once again they examined the possibility of continuing the war from France's African possessions. Her Governors- and Residents-General were clearly prepared to fight on. General Weygand showed his colleagues the telegrams from General Noguès, which were proof of this. But would it be physically possible for them to do so? North Africa was threatened on two sides: in Tunisia, by the Italians; in Morocco, by a German invasion via Spain and Gibraltar.

Furthermore, North Africa was now without the four fully trained and equipped divisions previously stationed there. They had been sent to the Alpine frontier, where they were brilliantly filling their defensive role. All that remained was a few 'mixed' – in other words, native – divisions which, in the event of an invasion, would have to face German steel more or less bare-handed. And the native troops, who could not stand up to aerial bombardment (especially Stuka attacks), would soon take to their heels.

The Cabinet ratified General Weygand's decision to send General Koeltz to Algiers, so that he could explain the situation in France to General Noguès and return with accurate data.

The amendments proposed by the French government were telephoned to General Huntziger in Rethondes.

At 11.5 a.m. the two delegations were again face to face in the railway carriage. Immediately, General Huntziger, who was afraid that the peace-talks with Italy might last several days, asked General Keitel whether steps had been taken to prevent Bordeaux from being occupied.

General Keitel replied that he was aware that Marshal Pétain had appealed to Hitler to suspend the German army's advance in that area, but he could not disclose the Führer's reaction while the French government had still not accepted the armistice agreement. Keitel's tone was as curt as it had been the day before. Like General Jodl, he was ever ready to hint at the compromises that might be worked out subsequently, but when the French delegates asked him to commit his remarks to paper he answered haughtily: 'The word of a German soldier is worth more than a scrap of paper.'

On the question of shifting the demarcation line, General Huntziger met with a categorical refusal.

He then broached the subject of the air force, suggesting that France's remaining aircraft should be stored in the free zone and not surrendered. General Bergeret supported him. On behalf of General Vuillemin he asked Keitel to make representations to Marshal Goering for the surrender of aircraft to be waived.

Keitel did not have the nerve to cold-shoulder this request, but before approaching Marshal Goering he exacted the promise that, while the talks were going on, French air-crews would not be allowed to fly their planes abroad, especially to Britain. The head of the French delegation gave him this assurance.

In the end, the following addition was made to Article 5:

> The surrender of military aircraft may be waived if all planes still in the possession of the French armed forces are disarmed and stored under German supervision.

They then turned to the amendment to Article 8, concerning the fleet. This was accepted after a rather heated argument, but the Germans refused to write it into the armistice agreement. Admiral Auphan states that the official German reply ran as follows:

> There is no need to insert the suggested alteration in the agreement. The Germans do not refuse to accept the proposal, but they consider it a practical measure, to be submitted to the Armistice Commission.

'In other words,' writes Auphan, 'for reasons of prestige and *amour-propre* that are readily understood, as victors they were unwilling to alter the original wording of their *Diktat*, but fundamentally they were acceding to the request of the French Admiralty.'

The proposed amendment to Article 19, relating to the surrender of certain political refugees, was rejected out of hand. Keitel flew into a rage the moment the question was raised, his steely grey eyes flashing as he spoke of 'those instigators of war, those inciters to hatred who, moreover, betrayed their own nation'. He made the retention of Article 19 a *sine qua non* condition for the continuance of talks, but stated that he would limit his demands to offenders who were of German nationality.

General Huntziger then turned to Article 22, which made the application of the Franco-German armistice dependent on the signing of the Franco-Italian armistice. He was particularly concerned about this clause, for he was afraid that Italy might enter wholly unjustifiable demands for everything that Germany had not already staked a claim to; that she might seek to occupy the whole of Metropolitan France south of the Loire, Corsica, Tunisia and other bits of the French Empire.

Keitel swore that he did not know what the Italian terms were.

'Italy has declared war on us,' said General Huntziger, 'but she has not waged it.[1] We do not need an armistice with Italy, because the armistice has coincided with her declaration of war ... This is a situation deeply resented by the French people.'

Abandoning his notes, he gradually yielded to emotion.

'If we are faced with unacceptable demands in Rome, the whole structure of our agreement will collapse. You will crush us, you will harm us still further. We shall bear it, but we shall not sign and we shall recover our freedom of action. Come what may, France considers honour preferable to life.' After a pause he added in a calmer voice: 'I respect the intention to soften some of the very harsh clauses of the agreement, an intention revealed in certain of General Keitel's statements. If the government orders me to sign, France will comply faithfully, acknowledging the fact that the war has gone against her ... But that will not happen if in Rome we meet with unjustifiable greed ... '

The wording of these remarks, and the tone in which they were made, clearly affected the German officers. General Keitel himself could not hide the fact that they had pricked his soldier's conscience.[2] He did not protest. All he said was: 'I am not qualified to answer you, any more than I am in a position to advise the Italians. All I can say is that the Italian delegation will be informed of our deliberations and agreement.'

The time-limit set by the German High Command had long since expired.

'We must settle matters,' said Keitel. 'It is for the French government to decide whether or not they want a cessation of hostilities or whether they prefer to waste precious time deliberating. It is entirely up to them. The Reich government and the German army, for their part, have no reason to desire the cessation of hostilities.'

At that moment he was handed Hitler's reply to Marshal Pétain's request. 'Provided the armistice agreement is signed in the course of the day,' he announced, 'the Führer is willing to exclude Bordeaux from military operations while France is negotiating with Italy.'

---

[1] It was forty-eight hours since General Huntziger had left Bordeaux. He was unaware that the Italians had launched an offensive in the Alps.

[2] Field-Marshal Keitel was later to confide to the author: 'At that moment General Huntziger genuinely moved me. That was exactly what I should have said had I been in his position. I did not know how to answer him.'

It was 4 p.m. The meeting was adjourned to enable General Huntziger to make one last telephone call to the French government and obtain final instructions: was he, or was he not, to sign the armistice agreement?

At 4.5 p.m. the French delegation informed Bordeaux of the results of its negotiations and of the improved position regarding military aircraft and the fleet.

Three-quarters of an hour went by. At 4.50 p.m. the telephone rang. Was this the end? Not yet.

General Weygand told General Huntziger: 'There is now only one point on which the French government would like assurance. It asks that the French government's requests and the German government's answers should be appended to the agreement so that official trace shall be kept of them ...'

But the French delegation felt that it had gone as far as it could in pressing the Germans to commit their replies to paper. To reopen the question might give rise to an incident quite different from the result hoped for by the Bordeaux government.

At that moment (6.34 p.m.) one of General Keitel's aides-de-camp handed General Huntziger the following letter from his superior:

General,

After waiting some five hours for a final decision as to whether the armistice agreement laid before you is, or is not, to be deemed concluded by the fact of your signature, I am setting 7.30 p.m. (German time) as the absolute time-limit for a final answer.

On expiry of this time-limit, I shall consider that negotiations have fallen through ...

Signed: KEITEL

There were only fifty-six minutes left.

But the French Cabinet appeared to have changed its mind, for immediately afterwards General Huntziger received the following order:

No. 43/DN. The French delegation is instructed to sign the armistice agreement with Germany.

Report execution of order.

The delegation will go to Rome, where their credentials have been sent by cable.

Confirmation of this order was immediately sent by teleprinter.

It was 6.42 p.m. The two delegations reassembled in the railway carriage for the signing ceremony.

447

'By order of my government,' said General Huntziger, 'I declare that the French government has decided to sign the armistice agreement that we have drawn up.'

Then he read out the following short statement:

'At the time of appending his signature at the foot of the armistice agreement, the head of the French delegation feels bound to make the following declaration: "Compelled by the fortune of war to abandon the fight in which she was engaged side by side with her Allies, France finds herself subjected to very harsh demands, in circumstances that underline their severity.

' "She is entitled to expect that, in the negotiations that lie ahead, Germany will display the kind of spirit that will allow two great neighbouring peoples to live and work in peace." '

After handing General Keitel a copy of this declaration General Huntziger added: 'General, you are a soldier, and you know how great an ordeal what I have just done is for a soldier. We of the French Army must never have to rue the action that I am about to perform.'

The German generals, too, were clearly moved. General Jodl had tears in his eyes.

General Keitel replied: 'It is honourable for the victor to honour the vanquished. I wish to pay tribute to the courage of the French soldier. I request a minute's silence to honour the memory of those who, on both sides, have laid down their lives for their countries.'

Everyone present stood and observed a minute's silence. General Keitel then signed the armistice agreement. General Huntziger followed suit. It was 6.50 p.m. The armistice was concluded.

The delegates rose and saluted each other. Keitel said he would like to have a private word with General Huntziger. The other delegates left the carriage.

'General,' said Keitel, 'as a soldier I can sense what you must have suffered. I wish to convey my great esteem for the way in which you have defended your country's interests to the very end, and to express my fullest sympathy as a soldier.'

The German general proffered his hand.

'Thank you, General,' Huntziger answered with great simplicity. 'Forgive me for being unable to say more.'

At 7.5 p.m. the French delegation got into their cars and returned to Paris, there to await the plane that was to take them to Rome.

At 9.30 p.m. the French government received notification that the German High Command had acceded to its request (made by Marshal

Pétain on the evening of June 20th) that Bordeaux should be excluded from the fighting area. News of this decision was publicly announced at once.

As soon as the French delegation had left, a detachment of German sappers went to the clearing at Rethondes and started dismantling the railway carriage, in compliance with the following order from the Führer:

After the completion of the ceremony in Compiègne I order that:

1. The historic carriage, the commemorative plaque and the monument celebrating the French victory are to be conveyed to Berlin.
2. The pedestal of the carriage and the rails and stones marking the site are to be destroyed.
3. The statue of Marshal Foch is to remain intact.

ADOLF HITLER

In Italy preparations were being made for the reception of the French delegation. 'Since there has been no fighting,' wrote Ciano, 'the Duce desires that there should not be the slightest pomp ... Mussolini would like to delay the signing as long as possible in the hope that Gambara ... will reach Nice. It would be a good thing. But shall we get there in time?'

POLITICAL SITUATION

In the early hours of the morning Sir Ronald Campbell had informed the British government of the contents of the armistice agreement, the draft version of which had been communicated to him by M. Charles-Roux.

At 11 a.m. Mr Winston Churchill broadcast a fierce attack on the French government:

His Majesty's Government have heard with grief and amazement that the terms dictated by the Germans have been accepted by the French government at Bordeaux. *They cannot feel that such or similar terms could have been submitted to by any French government which possessed freedom, independence and constitutional authority.* Such terms, if accepted by all Frenchmen, would place not only France but the French Empire at the mercy and in the power of the German and Italian dictators.

Not only would the French people be held down and forced to

work against their ally, not only would the soil of France be used with the approval of the Bordeaux government as the means of attacking their ally, but the whole resources of the French Empire and of the French navy would speedily pass into the hands of the adversary for the fulfilment of his purpose ...

When Great Britain is victorious she will, in spite of the action of the Bordeaux government, cherish the cause of the French people, and a British victory is the only possible hope for the restoration of the greatness of France and the freedom of its people. Brave men from other countries overrun by Nazi invasion are steadfastly fighting in the ranks of freedom. Accordingly, His Majesty's Government call upon all Frenchmen outside the power of the enemy to aid them in their task and thereby render its accomplishment more sure and more swift. They appeal to all Frenchmen, wherever they may be, to aid to the utmost of their strength the forces of liberation, which are enormous, and which, if faithfully and resolutely used, will assuredly prevail.

In the course of the day the British consuls in Rabat, Algiers and Tunis energetically renewed the representations that they had already made, on June 18th and 19th, to the Governor-General of Algeria and the two Residents-General. At the same time they offered the High Commissioners full military, naval and financial assistance if they wished to break with the French government.

For the past forty-eight hours de Gaulle had been kept out of the radio war. When M. Weil-Curiel was summoned back to France and asked de Gaulle what he ought to do, the general replied: 'You had better leave London for the time being, since you have been ordered to do so. I can do nothing for you. I am nothing yet.'

But now London was prepared to use any possible means to discredit the French government. The British authorities therefore granted General de Gaulle some of the facilities that they had grudged him the day before. To begin with, they allowed him to make use of the B.B.C. At 6 p.m he broadcast his third appeal to the French people:

A makeshift government, giving way to panic after seeking an armistice, now knows the enemy's conditions.

It follows from these terms that French land, sea and air forces will be entirely demobilized, that our arms will be surrendered, *that French territory will be wholly occupied* and that the French government will be under the domination of Germany and Italy ...

Now, many Frenchmen do not accept capitulation or slavery, for reasons known as honour, common sense and the good of the country.

I say honour, because France has undertaken to lay down arms only with the agreement of her allies. While her allies are fighting on, her government has no right to surrender to the enemy. The Polish government, the Norwegian government, the Belgian government, the Dutch government, the Luxembourg government, though driven from their soil, have seen their duty in this light.

I say common sense, because it is absurd to regard the fight as lost. True, we have suffered a heavy defeat ... But we still have a vast Empire, an intact fleet and plenty of gold. We still have allies whose resources are immense and who rule the seas. We still have the huge potentialities of American industry. The same fighting conditions that have caused us to be beaten by 5,000 planes and 6,000 tanks can tomorrow give us victory by 20,000 tanks and 20,000 planes.

I say the good of the country, because this war is not a Franco-German war to be decided by one battle; this war is a world war. No one can foresee whether the races that are neutral today will still be so tomorrow, and whether Germany's allies will always be her allies. If the forces of freedom were finally to triumph over those of slavery, what would be the fate of a France that had submitted to the enemy? Honour, common sense and the good of the country command all free Frenchmen to continue the fight wherever they are and however they can.

Churchill's speech and de Gaulle's claim that the whole of Metropolitan France was to be occupied caused a certain amount of alarm among the French people, especially since the armistice terms had not yet been made known to them. Intrigue manifested itself on the fringes of the government and in circles close to the President of the Republic. It aimed:

1. at creating a hitch at next day's Cabinet meeting, which would have to ratify the signing of the Rethondes agreement;
2. at trying to prevent its application by sabotaging the peace talks with Italy.

Marshal Pétain and General Weygand decided to fight back.

For a start General Colson, acting on orders from General Weygand, quashed de Gaulle's promotion to the rank of acting general.

Secondly, Marshal Pétain decided to bring MM. Laval and Marquet into his government. At first M. Lebrun refused: he was unwilling, he said, to antagonize the British government. The Marshal pointed out that as things stood there could be very little objection to M. Laval's joining the government, and that being tactful towards Britain would get France nowhere. On the contrary: the government's hand would be strengthened if he were made a minister, for he was an influential figure in parliamentary circles. In the end the President gave way.

In Algiers, where General Koeltz had just arrived, General Noguès summoned MM. Le Beau and Peyrouton so that they could converse with the government's envoy.

General Koeltz began by relating how things really stood in France. Then he asked General Noguès what was the exact total of the forces at his disposal. 'It emerged from this exchange of views,' writes Peyrouton, 'that our manpower had been drained by levies for the Belgian and Alpine fronts, that our equipment was out of date and that we had no ammunition and no capacity for manufacturing any.'

What, in these circumstances, could France possibly hope to achieve? General Koeltz asked General Noguès to write him a memorandum, summarizing the points that they had examined, so that he could hand it to the government in Bordeaux.

At 11.30 p.m. Sir Ronald Campbell knocked at the door of M. Baudouin's residence. The minister woke with a start, slipped on a dressing-gown and opened the door in person. Campbell announced that he was returning to London in compliance with orders from his government. Since Bordeaux harbour lay within the zone to be occupied by the Germans, the destroyer that was to take him to England could wait no longer.

Half an hour later the representatives of Canada and South Africa called on Baudouin and told him that they, too, were leaving France. This was an unexpected blow for the Minister for Foreign Affairs. They made it plain that they were not doing so at their own choice: they were yielding to heavy pressure from the British ambassador.

At dawn Sir Ronald Campbell left Bordeaux by road, taking with him the Canadian and South African ministers and the whole of the embassy staff.

On reaching Saint-Jean-de-Luz the diplomatic convoy boarded the cruiser *Galatea*, which sailed on the night of June 23rd–24th.

M. Baudouin writes: 'This brutal breaking-off of relations, at a time when their preservation was a mutual duty for the two countries, had not been ordered by the British government. In a telegram to the French government Lord Halifax stated that Sir Ronald Campbell's only instructions had been to avoid being taken prisoner.'

JUNE 23RD

————◆•••◆————

The Wehrmacht continued its southward thrust down the Atlantic coast. In the morning it reached Rochefort and Royan, poured into Poitiers and swept on towards Angoulême. Farther east it had left Issoudun and Châteauroux behind, but had not yet crossed the Creuse. In the upper Loire valley there was serious fighting in the area north-west of Saint-Étienne, at the Fouillouse dam.

General Georges once again drew the Commander-in-Chief's attention to the dire effects of the government's decision to declare all centres of more than 20,000 inhabitants 'open towns'. This decision was paralysing defence and leading to daily conflicts between combatants and the civilian population. General Olry, too, protested against the failure to destroy the bridges in Lyons, which had enabled the Germans to sweep rapidly down the Rhône valley.

'I cannot be expected to forfeit my honour by sacrificing my army,' he said.

Moreover, the arrival of German armour in the Gironde estuary presented the French High Command with yet another problem. With the consent of the German Command, the area round Bordeaux had been demilitarized in order to safeguard the independence of the French government. This entailed the risk of the enemy's swinging rapidly south-eastwards towards Marmande and Agen, thereby further compromising the withdrawal of what little remained of the 3rd Group of Armies.

A force of five German divisions tried to cross the Isère at Voreppe, where there is a bend in the river. The gap was defended by sailors using anti-tank batteries and by the gunners of the 2nd Group of the 104th Artillery Regiment under Major Azais de Vergeron. The Germans were driven back. Behind them they left artillery batteries, three heavy tanks and lines of vehicles. They had set fire to petrol stations beyond Voiron.

In the Alps the Italians again returned to the attack. Even though they had brought up considerable reinforcements they were no more successful than the day before.

453

Late in the day they managed to capture Menton, but were unable to fight their way out of the town on the other side, being caught in heavy fire from the French strong-point at Cap-Martin, which remained undamaged.

Admiral Darlan sent the following telegram to Admiral Godfroy, commander of Force X in Alexandria:

05123 *June 23rd*, 1940, 5 *p.m.*
If armistice agreement is signed between France, on the one side, and Germany and Italy, on the other, you will cease all operations or acts of hostility and assemble in a French port that I shall announce to you, provisionally Bizerta. Stop. Acknowledge receipt.

That same day Admiral Sir Andrew Cunningham, C.-in-C. Naval Forces in the Eastern Mediterranean, wrote to Admiral Godfroy (in French):

My heart is wrung with sympathy for your country, my dear Admiral, and if there is anything I can do to ease your position I hope you will ask me.

Admiral Godfroy was in a very delicate situation. His ships were based in Alexandria, a British port. He was under orders to, and constant surveillance by, a British admiral with whom he was on the friendliest terms. Yet not for one moment did he think of responding to General de Gaulle's appeals.

Meanwhile, the news from Britain was far from comforting. There was talk in London of seizing all French shipping (and shipping chartered by France) in British ports or at sea, and of completely blockading the French coasts.

At 9.10 a.m. Admiral Odend'hal, head of the naval mission in London, sent this wire to the French Admiralty:

No. 1321 *June 23rd,* 1940
British government still unfamiliar with wording of naval clauses signed. Fully familiar only with original German wording communicated by its ambassador. Is afraid of seeing our fleet, once disarmed, fall into enemy hands and used against it. Can you instruct me?[1]

At 3.30 p.m. the French Admiralty replied:

---

[1] This telegram confirms that Churchill had launched his attack the day before without knowing the final armistice conditions or the fate of the amendments sought by the French government.

No. 5147   *June 23rd,* 1940

All provisions accepted are conditioned by the fact that the French
fleet will definitely remain French, under the French flag, in French
ports, with French skeleton crews. Stop. These conditions do not
endanger British interests. Stop. On the other hand, the attitude of
the British authorities that you report can only be viewed as un-
friendly. Stop. Insist that measures contemplated are hastily called
off.

The first shipload of American arms reached England on board the
Eastern Prince.

Admiral Darlan gave orders for the *Béarn,* carrying about a hundred
American planes, to be diverted to the West Indies.

ARMISTICE NEGOTIATIONS

At 5.25 a.m. the French delegation drove to Le Bourget aerodrome,
where the Germans were setting up heavy anti-aircraft defences. Three
Junker aircraft stood waiting for them. At 8.25 a.m. they touched down
at Munich. They were due to fly on to Rome at 9.30 a.m., but their
departure was delayed till 11.30 a.m. to enable the Italian authorities to
make arrangements for a fighter escort beyond the Brenner Pass.

On landing at Littorio, the Frenchmen were taken, by a route by-
passing Rome, to the villa that had been assigned to them. It was the
Villa Manzoni, belonging to Italy's ex-ambassador to Paris. Weary from
their exertions, the delegates rested on the terrace for a time, among the
yew trees and the roses, in the golden sunlight of the late afternoon.

After this brief moment of relaxation they were driven, at 7.30 p.m., to
the Villa Incisa, on the Via Cassia, where the negotiations were to take
place. Peasants waved to them as they went along. A guard of honour
presented arms as the delegates' cars drew up and a number of high-
ranking officers and senior officials came forward to greet them.

A few moments after their arrival they were shown into the dining-
room, where the Italian delegates were already assembled. Mussolini had
decided against appearing in person. He was represented by his son-in-law,
Count Ciano, the Minister for Foreign Affairs, who was resplendently
attired. On his right sat Marshal Badoglio and General Priccolo, on his
left Admiral Cavagnari and General Roatta. Ciano writes:

Badoglio did not conceal his emotion. He was anxious to treat the

455

French delegates with great courtesy. Among them was Parisot, who is a personal friend of his. Heaven knows how often they have maligned the Germans together!

We rose to receive the French and greeted them with Roman-style salutes. They bowed their heads in reply. They behaved correctly, affecting neither disdain nor humility. Ambassador Noël alone was deadly pale.

In ringing tones, emphasizing the closing words, Count Ciano declared: 'The Duce of Fascist Italy, Head of the Government, Supreme Commander of the Italian Armed Forces in operation, has instructed Marshal Badoglio, Chief of the General Staff of the Armed Forces, to inform you of the terms of the armistice between Italy and France.'

Marshal Badoglio then handed each of the French delegates a copy of the Italian text and asked General Roatta to read out the French translation.

France's representatives felt an enormous wave of relief as they listened to the terms. For the occupation zone demanded by Italy was limited to the territory occupied by her troops at the time the agreement was signed.

The two sides shook hands warmly, as though the agreement were already concluded. General Huntziger was taken aback. 'The Fascist delegates seemed genuinely moved, somewhat contrite and possibly humiliated.' The entire proceedings had taken only twenty-five minutes.

The French plenipotentiaries then returned to the Villa Manzoni to examine the Italian terms more closely. They had been provided with a direct line to Bordeaux: a tactful gesture for which they were grateful.

General Huntziger telephoned General Weygand that night and told him of the Italian armistice terms.

POLITICAL SITUATION

At 11 a.m. the Cabinet met under M. Lebrun. MM. Laval and Marquet attended for the first time as Ministers of State.

The government took a final look at the articles of the Franco-German armistice agreement and ratified General Huntziger's signature.

The Minister for Foreign Affairs informed his colleagues of the unexpected departure of the British ambassador, together with the representatives of Canada and South Africa. He then told them of the attempts by the British consuls in Rabat and Tunis to urge General Noguès and M. Peyrouton to break with the French government. M. Pomaret, Minister of the Interior, announced that identical representations had been made to M. Le Beau, Governor-General of Algeria.

The government was unanimous in declaring these advances intolerable. General Weygand said that, in his view, de Gaulle was the chief offender. He added that he had quashed his promotion to the rank of acting general; but that in itself did not seem adequate. He should be cashiered for insubordination, since he had disregarded his superiors' instructions when they had ordered him back to France. The Minister of War, General Colson, confirmed this.

The Cabinet accordingly decided:

1. to strike Charles de Gaulle's name off the army list;
2. to recall its three consuls from Tunis, Rabat and Algiers.

M. Baudouin was told to wire instructions to this effect to M. Corbin, French ambassador in London. The ambassador was also to protest against Mr Churchill's offensive speech the day before. The meeting ended shortly before noon.

Immediately after luncheon M. Baudouin called on M. Reynaud to ask him what he thought of the decisions taken by the Cabinet. The ex-Premier now knew that the German conditions would be accepted and that there was no hope of his returning to office in the near future. He was therefore anxious to remain on the best possible terms with his successor.

He dissociated himself from General de Gaulle and deplored the speech that Mr Churchill had made the day before. He offered, of his own accord, to send the British Premier a personal message that would allay his fears and — if that were possible — 'clear up the misunderstanding that existed between the two governments'.

[*In fulfilment of the Cabinet's decisions, M. Baudouin sent a message to M. Corbin expressing 'astonishment' at the attitude of Mr Churchill. M. Corbin at once resigned. — Ed.*]

M. Jean Monnet, head of the economic delegation to Britain, who had paid a flying visit to Bordeaux on June 19th–20th, had been able to gauge on the spot the small response to General de Gaulle's appeals. Generally, they had fallen on deaf ears; otherwise, the most frequent reactions had been those of condemnation or hostility. He was widely accused of being in Britain's pay and openly criticized for his attacks on the Marshal. Only a tiny minority had been influenced by his remarks.

Back in Britain, M. Monnet sent the general the following letter, to put him on his guard against the error that he was falling into:

London, June 23rd, 1940

My dear General,

After meeting you I had a talk with Sir Alexander Cadogan and repeated to him what I had said to you and Brigadier Spears.

I consider that it would be a great mistake to form an organization in Britain that might be viewed in France as an authority set up abroad under the protection of Britain. I entirely share your desire to prevent France from giving up the fight, and I am convinced that the Bordeaux government should have sent to North Africa the Head of State, the leaders of the two Chambers and a number of members of the government who, along with General Noguès, would have made North Africa a bastion of French resistance ... If resistance can be organized in North Africa, I am sure that it will find an enormous echo in France and all her overseas colonies.

But the attempt at resuscitation cannot at present come from London. It would strike the French people ... as a movement protected by Britain, inspired by her own interests and, in consequence, doomed to a failure that would make subsequent efforts at recovery more difficult ...

JEAN MONNET

But General de Gaulle paid no heed to this advice.[1] He had convinced General Spears that an authority must be set up in opposition to the Marshal's government under the name of the 'French National Committee'. Churchill had given his consent to this scheme, in the belief that other leading figures would come over and take part.

In the course of a meeting held at 3 p.m. at the French lycée in London, General de Gaulle broadcast the news of the formation of this new organization.

That same afternoon the B.B.C broadcast these two statements by the British government:

First statement

The British government find that the terms of the armistice just signed, in contravention of agreements solemnly made between the Allied governments, reduce the Bordeaux government to a state of complete subjection to the enemy and deprive it of all liberty and of all right to represent free French citizens.

H.M. Government therefore now declare that they can no longer

---

[1] He could not have done so, even had he wished: the British had already prevented him from leaving England.

regard the Bordeaux government as the government of an independent country.

Second statement

H.M. Government have taken note of the proposal to form a provisional French National Committee fully representing independent French elements determined on the prosecution of the war in fulfilment of the international obligations of France.

H.M. Government declare that they will recognize such provisional French National Committee and will deal with them in all matters concerning the prosecution of the war so long as that Committee continues to represent all French elements resolved to fight the common enemy.

But some members of the British Cabinet were unenthusiastic about the formation of the French National Committee. Suppose France were to regard this action as an excuse for her to break the undertakings that she had given regarding the fleet? The damage done to Britain's cause would far outweigh any advantages that might derive from the activities of a few isolated Frenchmen. For what were the latter at the time but, to quote Lady Spears, 'a very small company of magnificent madmen'? 'Reason,' she adds, 'should have convinced them that they had no chance of succeeding.'

So Lord Halifax asked King George VI to send President Lebrun a personal telegram. It took the following form:

I learn with deep anxiety and dismay that Your Government under the cruel pressure of these tragic days contemplate sending the French fleet to French North African ports where it would be dismantled. This must in effect leave the French fleet where it would be in evident danger of falling into hostile hands.

I need not remind you, *Monsieur le Président*, should this occur, how great would be the danger involved to our common cause and I rely on the solemn and explicit assurances already given to My Government that in no circumstances would Your Government assent to any conditions that involved this consequence.

A strange message to send to a government whose legality was being contested!

While London talked of turning North Africa into an invincible bastion, the French Cabinet met at 5.15 p.m., under M. Lebrun, to hear the report of General Koeltz, back from his mission in Algiers. He read out a note from General Noguès.

[*General Noguès, though he suggested that if German and Italian forces entered Spain he should at once invade Spanish Morocco, indicated that if German troops reached this territory no prospect existed of holding French North Africa. — Ed.*]

The idea of resisting in North Africa had been just another pipe-dream, like the Breton redoubt.

In the evening Marshal Pétain broadcast the following speech:

Frenchmen!

The French government and people yesterday heard Mr Churchill's words with grieved astonishment.

We can understand the anguish that prompted them. Mr Churchill fears, for his own country, the afflictions that have fallen on ours. during the past month.

There are, however, no circumstances in which the French people can endure without protest lessons from a foreign minister ...

Our flag remains unstained. Our army has fought bravely and loyally ...

Nobody will succeed in dividing the people of France in her moment of agony.

France has not been sparing with her blood or her energies. She is conscious of having earned the respect of the world. And it is from herself, initially, that she expects salvation. Mr Churchill must realize this. Our faith in ourselves is unshaken. We are undergoing a harsh ordeal. We have surmounted others. We know that our country remains intact so long as her children's love for her endures. That love has never been more fervent.

The land of France is no less rich in promise than in glory.

Sometimes one of our peasants will find his field ravaged by hail. He does not despair of the harvest ahead. With the same faith he ploughs the same furrow for the future corn.

Does Mr Churchill think the people of France will refuse the whole country the love and faith that they accord to their smallest plot of land?

They are facing up to their present and the future.

As for the present, they are convinced that they are showing more greatness in admitting their defeat than in opposing it with idle talk and hollow schemes ...

460

JUNE 24TH

━━━━◆◦◦◉◦━━━━

Saint-Étienne was captured during the morning, the Fouillouse dam having yielded during the night after offering stiff resistance.

The enemy stepped up his efforts in the Rhône valley, where his forward units reached the outskirts of Tournon. Aix-les-Bains was captured. Communications along the northern Alpine front now appeared to be threatened. After failing to cross the Isère at Voreppe, the Germans were trying to cut their way through to Chambéry farther north-eastwards by storming the village of Les Échelles. This was defended by two companies, one belonging to the 25th Senegalese, the other to the 215th Infantry.

These two companies defended the approaches to the village with great skill, holding out all day though considerably outnumbered, and disputing every inch of ground. Late in the day the town was outflanked and the lines of retreat were blocked. Preceded by a bugler and displaying a sheet as a flag of truce, the mayor — M. Viard — went out to meet the Germans. With him were two local inhabitants, MM. de Vaulxerre and Vrigny.

Colonel von Marwitz was so impressed with the stand made by this handful of soldiers that he allowed them to fall back. At 8.20 p.m. the two French companies, still bearing arms, carried out an orderly evacuation of Les Échelles.

On the right bank of the Rhône the Germans reached Andance. The attack was launched in the early hours of the morning. This sector was held by a brigade of Spahis under Colonel Jouffrault. The 6th Algerian Spahis defended the outskirts of the town, while eight miles farther on the 4th Moroccan Spahis barred the road to Le Puy. This brigade went on fighting till nightfall, ceasing fire (at 10 p.m.) only when they were out of ammunition.

On the Alpine front the French positions were still intact on both northern and eastern flanks.

ARMISTICE NEGOTIATIONS

In Bordeaux the Cabinet met to examine the Italian armistice terms, which General Huntziger had telephoned from Rome during the night.

Its ·clauses followed those of the German agreement. Only three articles were different:

2. Italian forces will maintain their positions on the lines that they have reached in all theatres at the time the present armistice agreement comes into force, for its full duration.[1]

3. In Metropolitan France the zone between the lines referred to in Article 2 and a line 50 kilometres east as the crow flies shall be demilitarized for the duration of the armistice.

   In Tunisia the zone between the Libyan–Tunisian frontier and the line shown on the attached map will be demilitarized for the duration of the armistice.

   In Algeria, and in French African territories south of Algeria and bordering on Libya, a zone 200 kilometres wide adjoining the Libyan frontier will be demilitarized for as long as hostilities last between Italy and the British Empire and for the duration of the present armistice; the French coastal colony in Somaliland will be wholly demilitarized.

   Italy will have full and constant right, for the duration of the armistice, to use the port and harbour installations at Jibuti, together with the French section of the Jibuti–Addis-Ababa railway, for transport of any kind.

4. The zones to be demilitarized ... will be evacuated by French forces within ten days of the cessation of hostilities.

Article 13, relating to the French fleet, reproduced word for word Article 8 of the Franco-German armistice agreement.

'A kind of stupor,' writes Paul Baudouin, 'came over certain members of the Cabinet who, only the day before, had been insisting that Italy would demand occupation of the whole left bank of the Rhône and of the Mediterranean coast' — thus cutting off Metropolitan France from the Empire and depriving the unoccupied zone of all access to the sea. 'The President's bearing suggested keen disappointment. But no more than on previous days did he give frank expression to his feelings. He did not say a

---

[1] In other words, apart from Menton and the fringes of the Tarentaise and Maurienne valleys, no French territory would be occupied by Italy.

word against the armistice.' Yet he knew, as did the whole Cabinet, that accepting the Italian terms meant accepting the German terms.

After studying the former, the French ministers decided that it would be madness to reject them.

Admiral Godfroy, who was in Alexandria at the time and who thus cannot be accused of being swayed by panic, writes: 'The armistice terms maintained us in a territorial position that was, in some respects, *un-hoped-for* in comparison with what would quickly have happened otherwise.'

That is exactly what Marshal Pétain and General Weygand must have been thinking. So, subject to certain minor changes in the regulations concerning the zones that were to be demilitarized, the government notified General Huntziger of its provisional acceptance.

General Weygand then announced that he had received a personal communication from General Noguès, forwarding a telegram from General Mittelhauser — commander of the Middle East theatre — which was worded as follows:

Beirut, June 23rd, 10.30 p.m.
To General Noguès, C.-in-C. North African theatre
With the High Commissioner's agreement I have publicly advocated fighting on. I take it that an Imperial French government will be formed in North Africa, together with a Supreme Command of Empire forces. I should be grateful if you would keep me informed. It strikes me as urgent that someone should take over the conduct of the war and co-ordinate the conduct of military, naval and air operations in liaison with the British Command ...

General Noguès wrote that he had received similar messages from M. Boisson, Governor-General of French West Africa, from the Governor of French Equatorial Africa and from the High Commissioner in the Cameroons.

General Weygand firmly decided to try to tip the scales with the weight of his authority. He sent the following reply to the Commander-in-Chief of the North African theatre:

The date and time of the commencement of armistice will be instantly communicated to you ... The government appeals to your sense of duty, on which it knows it can count, to maintain the strictest discipline within our forces and, round about you, the spirit of harmony and confidence in the government.

The same message was sent to the military authorities in French West Africa and French Equatorial Africa and to General Mittelhauser, and to all Governors- and Residents-General.

Simultaneously M. Baudouin dispatched the following telegram to General Noguès, who was responsible to him as Resident-General in Morocco:

> It is clear from the telegrams that have come from you during the past few days that an understandable agitation has been spreading among the populations that you administer at the idea that the French government might abandon to foreign occupation, without a fight, all or part of the territories that we either own or protect.
>
> I can only assure you that such an idea is devoid of foundation ...

Finally, at 12.45 p.m. Admiral Darlan repeated and confirmed, in the following message, the orders to scuttle that he had already sent on June 20th to all port-admirals and commanders of warships:

> Armistice clauses will be separately notified in clear. Am taking advantage final communication that I can transmit in code to state my feelings on the subject:
>
> 1. Demobilized warships are to remain French, under French flag, with French reduced crews, in French metropolitan or colonial ports.
> 2. Secret precautions are to be taken for scuttling so that enemy or foreign power seizing a ship by force cannot use it.
> 3. If Armistice Commission responsible for interpreting text were to decide otherwise than in first paragraph, at time of execution of this new decision, warships, in the absence of further orders, would be either sailed to the United States or scuttled ...
> 4. Ships thus sheltering abroad are not to be used for operations against Germany or Italy without the order of the Commander-in-Chief French Naval Forces.
>
> XAVIER 377[1]

At 3.40 p.m. the French armistice delegation returned to the Villa Incisa, where negotiations proceeded under the chairmanship of Marshal Badoglio. The other Italian representatives were Admiral Cavagnari and Generals Priccolo and Roatta. Count Ciano did not attend this second meeting. 'Marshal Badoglio asked to be alone,' he wrote in his diary, 'so as not to give the impression of being under supervision. General Keitel had

---

[1] Admiral Darlan's code-name.

not been under supervision at Rethondes.' The Italians' desire to be conciliatory was obvious. Marshal Badoglio agreed to several modifications, some of them important.

Articles 3, 4 and 6 were all slightly reworded.

General Huntziger pointed out that the ten-day time-limit allotted for the demilitarization of certain areas was too short.

'I assure you,' answered Badoglio, 'that the Italian Armistice Commission's policy will always be to smooth out difficulties.'

'Nor will you find any ill will on our side,' said General Huntziger. 'If we sign, we shall comply.'

Articles 7 and 9 also came in for a few minor adjustments.[1]

With regard to aircraft, General Bergeret asked, as at Rethondes, that French planes should be stored under supervision rather than surrendered. His request was granted. So was Admiral le Luc's in respect of home ports: French ships were provisionally authorized to remain in North Africa.

'We have no intention of touching your ships either during or after hostilities,' said Marshal Badoglio.

The Marshal also waived the demand for the handing-over of political refugees.

At 5.30 p.m. General Huntziger informed Bordeaux that the French government's and delegation's suggestions had been accepted by the Italians, with only a few formal reservations.

At 7.10 p.m. the French delegation received the following message from General Weygand:

No. 61/D.N.
The French delegation led by General Huntziger is instructed to sign the armistice agreement with Italy. Report execution.

And so the two delegations came face to face for the last time, in the dining-room of the Villa Incisa.

General Huntziger began by thanking Marshal Badoglio for the manner in which he had presided over the discussions. He then read out the following statement:

'In the present infinitely painful circumstances the French delegation finds some consolation in the firm hope that the peace soon to come will allow France to carry out her work of reconstruction and renovation, and will provide a solid basis for the establishment of lasting relations between our two countries, in the interests of Europe and of civilization.'

[1] Concerning the military status of Syria and Somaliland.

Marshal Badoglio replied in these terms:

'The wishes that you have expressed are mine. I should be unable to address any other words to you. I hope France recovers. She is a great nation; she has a great history, and I am sure she will be able to safeguard her future. As one soldier to another, I can assure you that I hope so with all my heart.'

The agreement was signed by the heads of the two delegations at 7.15 p.m.

The moment the news reached him, Admiral Darlan sent the following telegram to Admiral Godfroy:

June 24th, 1940, 9.10 p.m.

Armistice signed. Assemble Beirut. Comply swiftly. Urgent.

Admiral Godfroy immediately informed Admiral Cunningham of the instructions that he had received. The British admiral replied immediately:

I deeply regret to have to tell you that I yesterday received orders not to allow your squadron to leave Alexandria. I ask you to regard this situation as inevitable in present circumstances.

I am afraid this order forbidding ships to sail must be applied to destroyers.

Admiral Godfroy informed the French Admiralty.

Thus even before the armistice had come into force the battleships *Duquesne, Tourville, Suffren, Duguay-Trouin* and the destroyers *Fortuné, Forbin* and *Basque* were held by the British in the roads off Alexandria, controlled by the flagship *Warspite,* the *Malaya,* the *Barham* and a squadron of six destroyers.

In Philadelphia the United States Republican Party, which was holding a conference, adopted a motion stating its determination not to let the nation take part in a foreign war.

POLITICAL SITUATION

In Bordeaux the government set about dissipating the heightening prejudices of Britain and America.

M. Lebrun sent the following message to King George VI in reply to the latter's telegram of the previous day:

In the midst of the cruel events that my country is experiencing, after exhausting the final possibilities of military resistance to the invasion, of which it has borne the brunt almost entirely with its own forces, I can only remind Your Majesty of the repeated assurances given by my government to the British government that the French war fleet will not be able to be used against Great Britain. I like to hope that those assurances are likely to keep Your Majesty's government to the path of friendship along which my country wishes to be able to persevere.

Marshal Pétain asked M. Reynaud to carry out his suggestion of sending a personal message to Mr Churchill asking him not to question the word of the French government. Consequently M. Reynaud telegraphed to the head of the British government:

I appeal to your friendship and to the trust that you have always shown in me. Nothing would delight Hitler more than a permanent political quarrel between our two countries. Your speech yesterday so affected me that I have discussed it with Marshal Pétain ... The stipulations of the armistice agreement [on the subject of the fleet] are admittedly liable to cause you concern. But I have just questioned Admiral Darlan on the subject, in the presence of Marshal Pétain. Darlan stated that when the terms relating to this measure are discussed before the armistice commission, steps will be taken to ensure that the enemy will *in no circumstances* be able to use our fleet against Britain ...

This should reassure you in the matter.

You were good enough to tell me ... that 'were a government other than mine to adopt a different policy and seek an armistice, not only would Britain waste no time in useless recriminations, but she would bear in mind the appalling sacrifices which France ... had taken upon herself; and that when victory finally came, France would be restored to all her power and dignity.'

Those words moved me profoundly.

I am sure that those feelings are still alive deep inside you.

Croyez à mon amitié,

PAUL REYNAUD

M. Roger Cambon, in charge of the London embassy since M. Corbin's resignation, went to the Foreign Office to demand the recall of the three British consuls (in Rabat, Algiers and Tunis) who had sought to persuade General Noguès, M. Le Beau and M. Peyrouton to disobey their government.

The official who received him said that he 'could not allow a foreign power to address criticisms, even indirect ones, at His Majesty's overseas representatives'. M. Cambon was then politely but firmly shown the door.

Now speaking on behalf of the 'National Committee' that he had founded the day before, General de Gaulle sent the following telegram to General Noguès:

London, June 24th, 1940

We inform you of the setting-up of a French National Committee to link all French resistance elements with each other and with the Allies. We ask you to figure personally in the composition of this Committee. All here consider that you should be head of French resistance. Accept the expression of our respect and hope.

For the National Committee in formation,

GENERAL DE GAULLE

At 6 p.m. he broadcast his fourth appeal to the French people:

This evening I shall merely say — for someone must — what shame and rebellion stir in the hearts of all true Frenchmen.

There is no point in going into the ins and outs of the Franco-German and Franco-Italian armistices. They boil down to this: *France and her people have been delivered to the enemy bound hand and foot.*

But though this capitulation may be written on paper, there are countless men, women, young people and children who do not bow to it, who will not accept it, who want nothing to do with it.

France is like a boxer felled by a terrible blow. She is out on her feet. But she knows, she senses that she is still full of profound and vigorous life ...

She knows, she senses that in her Empire, powerful resistance forces are at work to save her honour ...

She knows, she senses that she deserves better than the slavery accepted by the Bordeaux government.

It is essential to muster, wherever it can be done, as large a French force as possible ...

I, General de Gaulle, am undertaking this national task here in Britain.

I call upon all members of the French land, sea and air forces, I call upon French engineers and skilled munition workers who are on, or may reach, British soil, to rally to me.

I call upon the officers and men of the French land, sea and air

468

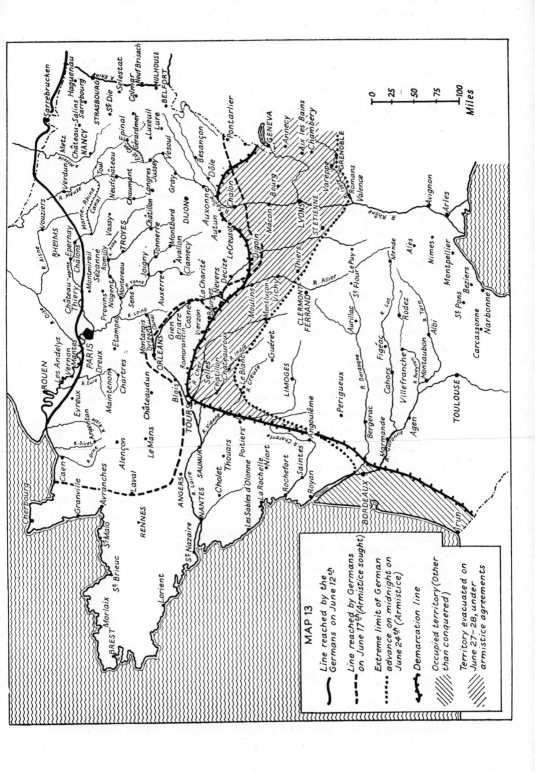

MAP 13

Line reached by the
Germans on June 12th

Line reached by Germans
on June 17th (Armistice sought)

Extreme limit of German
advance on midnight on
June 24th (Armistice)

Demarcation line

Occupied territory (Other
than conquered)

Territory evacuated on
June 27–28, under
armistice agreements

forces, wherever they may be at present, to get in touch with me ...
Long live Free France in honour and independence!

But the announcement of the formation of the 'French National Committee' had been greeted, in London, with a good deal of reserve. Morand says that General de Gaulle's claim that he was authorized to place all Frenchmen in Britain under his jurisdiction had caused widespread consternation among them, for they could picture themselves being forced to choose between being interned and joining a rebel group.

Kammerer writes: 'Many Frenchmen in London saw the formation of the Committee as an entirely private venture directed against the Bordeaux government — so much so that hesitations within the British Cabinet led Lord Halifax to forbid any further broadcast appeal by the "French National Committee".'

This was because the British government was still hoping to see a 'dissident' French government crystallize round such prominent figures as Daladier, Mandel, Reynaud or General Noguès. They were unwilling to associate themselves too early with the activities of General de Gaulle, lest they should ruin their chances of attracting a stronger team to Britain's side.

For was not such a team assembling even at that moment? After an uneventful crossing the *Massilia* anchored at Casablanca with the group of deputies and senators who had left Bordeaux on June 21st.

M. Mandel arrived in Morocco with the clear intention of forming a rival government, which he would head. Counting on the support of some of those who had made the crossing with him, he had prepared a proclamation.

But soon the cat was out of the bag. The head of the Havas agency had insisted on showing the proclamation to the censor before publishing it. The Residency was in an uproar. The proclamation was intercepted and M. Mandel was prevented from telephoning Rabat. For all the vehemence of his protestation, the ex-Minister of the Interior was asked to leave the Hotel Excelsior. He was put aboard the *Massilia* again and kept under close watch.

Meanwhile M. Daladier, too, had been trying to get in touch with General Noguès so as to win him over to the idea of setting up a government in Morocco. He was similarly unsuccessful.

MILITARY SITUATION

At 9 p.m. the French High Command received the message announcing the cessation of hostilities on all fronts. It was immediately communicated to subordinate authorities. The hour given for the cease-fire was 12.35 a.m., French Summer Time.

At 10 p.m. General Olry gave the following figures for the operations on the Alpine front:

Of the thirty-two divisions in the Italian army, nineteen were wholly or partly engaged against the outposts — and in a few cases the main elements — of our six divisions.

We were outnumbered seven to one in Tarentaise, four to one in Maurienne, three to one in Briançonnais, twelve to one in Queyras, nine to one in Ubaye, six to one in Tinée, seven to one in L'Aution and Sospel, and four to one in Menton.

Our adversary only made contact with, or approached, our main position in Tarentaise and near Menton. All our fortified advance posts held out, even when encircled ...

JUNE 25TH

MILITARY SITUATION

At 12.35 a.m. the bugles sounded the cease-fire all along the front. At 2 a.m. the Franco-German and Franco-Italian armistices came into force. The campaign was over.

In Germany the atmosphere was one of unlimited joy. At 8 a.m. Hitler broadcast the following speech to the German people:

> After fighting valiantly for six weeks our troops have brought the war in the west to an end against a courageous enemy. Their heroic deeds will go down in history as the most glorious victory of all time. We give thanks to the Lord for his benevolence.
>
> I order that flags be displayed throughout the Reich for ten days, and the pealing of bells for seven.
>
> ADOLF HITLER

In Italy the predominant feelings in ruling circles were bitterness and disappointment.

'The armistice terms have not yet been divulged,' wrote Count Ciano, 'but already rumours are flying about and causing obvious unrest. People were expecting an immediate and expense-free occupation. They assumed that all territories not conquered by force of arms would be made ours under the terms of this agreement. When the document is published, their disillusion will be greater still.'

In Britain the government issued the following communiqué:

> The signature of the armistice by the French government brings to an end the organized resistance of the French forces at home. In the French Colonial Empire, however, there are encouraging signs that a more robust spirit prevails ...
>
> His Majesty's Government are prepared to make the necessary financial arrangements to enable the French Colonial Empire to play its part. As stated by the Prime Minister, the British aim is the complete restoration of the metropolitan and oversea territory of France.

In France the atmosphere was generally one of withdrawn bereavement; but mingled with this was a feeling of intense relief.

POLITICAL SITUATION

With General Weygand's approval M. Baudouin sent the following telegram to General Noguès and all other civil and military leaders in France's Empire:

... Before the middle of the month of June it was apparent to the High Command and to the government, not only that the situation could not be saved, but that its progressive worsening ... would inevitably lead to the total occupation of the country, despite heroic resistance that continued even after it had become hopeless ...

The British government, having followed the course of military operations in France hour by hour, was ignorant of none of the many aspects of the situation that compelled us to seek an armistice and to justify our seeking it, even before the date when we resigned ourselves to doing so ...

The cessation of hostilities with Germany would have occurred in fact even if an armistice agreement had not brought it about in law.

The total occupation of the country by the Germans would have occurred if the armistice had not been concluded to limit it, in law and in fact, to a partial — though, alas, very extensive — occupation.

As for the armistice with Italy, that was rendered necessary by the fact that Germany decided to make the implementation of the Franco-German armistice dependent upon it.

In facing this tragic situation the government was not blind to the fact that the armistice terms were bound to be conditioned, according to my information, by the exhaustion of Metropolitan France's last potentialities of military resistance. But it concluded, after mature reflection and with full knowledge of the facts, that an armistice was the only way of limiting the sufferings that the nation is enduring ...

Indeed, the armistice with Germany makes no provisions with regard to our oversea possessions, and the armistice with Italy excludes any military occupation of any part of the said possessions ...

I was anxious to give you an accurate account of the circumstances that led us to stop fighting and I count on your patriotism to

473

maintain round about you the discipline, calm and loyalty whereby the ordeal from which our country must strive to emerge can be surmounted.

General Noguès's position — like that of many other high officials in the Empire — was as follows: though he personally would have been inclined to go on with the war, he was unwilling to commit any action that might split France into two camps.

Having informed France's Residents and Governors-General of the motives that had prompted the government's decisions, M. Baudouin disclosed the armistice terms to the Press, stating that they were 'harsh but in no way dishonouring'.

At about the same time Mr Churchill made a long speech in the House of Commons:

The House will feel profound sorrow at the fate of the great French nation and people, to whom we have been joined so long in war and peace, and whom we have regarded as trustees with ourselves for the progress of a liberal culture and tolerant civilization in Europe. There is no use or advantage in wasting strength and time upon hard words and reproaches. We hope that life and power will be given to us to rescue France from the ruin and bondage into which she has been cast by the might and fury of the enemy — and by other causes. We hope, however, that the French Empire, stretching all over the world, and still protected by sea-power, will continue the struggle at the side of its allies ...

We shall certainly aid, to the best of our ability and resources, any movement or any action by Frenchmen outside the power of the enemy, to work for the defeat of Nazi German barbarism and for the freedom and restoration of France. What our relations will be with the Bordeaux government I cannot tell ... We do not know whether we shall be allowed to have any British representative in the restricted region called 'Unoccupied France' ... but, relying upon the true genius of the French people, and their judgment upon what has happened, when they are allowed to know the facts, we shall endeavour to keep such contacts as are possible through the bars of their prison. Meanwhile we must look to our own salvation and effectual defence ... The safety of Great Britain and the British Empire is powerfully, though not decisively, affected by what happens to the French fleet. When it became clear that the defeat and subjugation of France was imminent and that her fine army, on which so many hopes were set, was reeling under the German flail, M. Reynaud, the courageous Prime Minister, asked me to come to Tours, which I did on June 13th, accompanied by the Foreign Secretary and the Minister for Aircraft Production, Lord Beaverbrook. I see that some accounts have been given of these conversations by the Bordeaux government which do not at all correspond with the facts ...

Although I knew how great French sufferings were, and that we had not so far endured equal trials or made an equal contribution in the field, I felt bound to say that I could not give consent ... [to France's negotiating for a separate armistice] ... We agreed that a further appeal should be made by M. Reynaud to the United States and that if the reply was not sufficient to enable M. Reynaud to go on fighting ... then we should meet again and take a decision in the light of the new factors.

On June 16th I received a message from M. Reynaud, who had then moved to Bordeaux, to say that the American response was not satisfactory, and requesting the formal release of France from her obligations under the Anglo-French agreement. The Cabinet was immediately convened, and we sent a message, of which I do not give the exact text, but I give the general substance — *Separate negotiations, whether for armistice or peace, depend upon an agreement made by Britain with the French Republic and not with any particular French administration or statesman. They therefore involve the honour of France. However, in view of all they have suffered, and of the forces evidently working upon them, and provided that the French fleet is dispatched to British ports and remains there while the negotiations are conducted, His Majesty's Government will give their consent to the French government asking what terms of armistice would be open to them ...*

The same evening, June 16th, when I was preparing, at M. Reynaud's invitation, to go to see him, and I was in fact in the train, I received news that he had been overthrown and that a new government under Marshal Pétain had been formed, which government had been formed for the prime purpose of seeking an armistice with Germany. In these circumstances we naturally did everything in our power to secure proper arrangements for the disposition of the French fleet. We reminded the new government that the condition indispensable to their release had not been complied with, the condition being that it should be sent to a British port. There was plenty of time to do it, and it would have made no difference to the negotiations: the terms could hardly have been more severe than they were ... Everything was, of course, fusing into collapse at that time, but many solemn assurances were given that the fleet would never be allowed to fall into German hands. It was therefore 'with grief and amazement', to quote the words of the government statement which we issued on Sunday, that I read Article 8 of the armistice terms.

This article, to which the French government have subscribed, says that the French fleet, excepting that part left free for the safeguarding of French interests in the Colonial Empire, shall be collected in ports to be specified and there demobilized and disarmed under German or Italian control. From this text it is clear that the French war vessels under this armistice pass into German and Italian control while fully armed ...

But barely had the British Prime Minister concluded his speech than he was handed a dispatch. It was from the British consul in Morocco, announcing M. Mandel's unexpected arrival in Casablanca and his intention of setting up a rival government there.

Churchill immediately summoned the Cabinet, for the news deserved close examination. The formation of a Mandel government in North Africa would be, in itself, a *coup de théâtre* capable of altering the whole course of events. But there was still better news: by a happy coincidence most of the French fleet was now in African ports. Far from representing a danger, it might perhaps be used in conjunction with the Royal Navy.

Such a stroke of luck would not occur twice. It must immediately be turned to account.

The British Cabinet considered that Mandel, a former Colonial Minister, was particularly well equipped to cause a rift between the Empire and Metropolitan France, and decided to send out two emissaries to support him in his bid. The men chosen for this delicate mission were Mr Duff Cooper, Minister of Information, and Lord Gort, who, after serving as commander of the B.E.F., had just been appointed Governor of Gibraltar. They immediately left for Rabat by flying-boat, landing in Le Bou-Regreg at 6 p.m.

They were met by General Dillon, British liaison officer to General Noguès. But strict orders had been sent to all aerodromes and ports that no British national should be allowed to land. As their flying-boat was not capable of returning at once, they were allowed, out of courtesy, to go to the British consulate while the ground-staff carried out their repairs. There Mr Duff Cooper and Lord Gort tried to telephone M. Mandel in Casablanca. But they were refused a line.

Mr Duff Cooper then went to the Residency to express his indignation. General Noguès was on his way to Algiers, so he was received by the Deputy-General, M. Morize.

M. Morize asked him to make no attempt to get in touch with M. Mandel in Casablanca or with General Noguès in Algiers. He explained that he had received strict orders to this effect and that, as a loyal administrator, he had no choice but to obey them.

'In any case,' he added, 'it will be impossible for you to meet M. Mandel: he has been arrested and is under surveillance.'

Deeply disappointed, the British emissaries started back to Gibraltar at dawn on June 26th.

The 'Casablanca Plot' had been short-lived.

At 3 p.m. the Cabinet had met in Bordeaux. The armistice was signed and the situation in France now seemed less confused; but at this point storm-clouds began to gather in other parts of the sky.

Admiral Darlan informed his colleagues of the messages that he had received from Admiral Godfroy during the night and of the blocking of Force X ordered by Admiral Cunningham.

The government decided to protest to London and authorized Admiral Darlan to send the following telegram to Admiral Godfroy:

No. 5163-64   *June 25th*, 1940

1. The government is protesting to British government against Admiralty decision inadmissible from any point of view, especially after repeated assurance by Marshal Pétain and myself of non-employment of French fleet against Great Britain.
2. Following [British] government's reply I shall send you instructions on course to follow ...

Graver still was the news from Indo-China. M. Rivière, Minister for the Colonies, reminded his colleagues of the events of the past few days.

On his own authority, General Catroux had decided to close the China border on June 20th. He had agreed to the establishment of a Japanese mission in Tongking, led by General Nishihara. Its purpose was to supervise frontier traffic and lay an embargo on all arms.

M. Rivière was extremely upset by this unauthorized move on the part of General Catroux. He regarded Japan's partial annexation of France's authority in Tongking as 'intolerable'. He considered that General Catroux should be relieved of his post. The Cabinet shared this view. But whom were they to appoint in his place? The position called for a shrewd administrator, and a man whose loyalties were not likely to be diverted ...

Admiral Darlan proposed Admiral Decoux, C.-in-C. French Naval Forces, Far East, who was at present at Saigon aboard the *Lamotte-Picquet*. The Cabinet adopted this suggestion, in the hope that a change of Governor-General might discourage the Japanese from making further encroachments.

'The situation in Indo-China could have rapidly become serious,' records Baudouin. 'Our military forces there were very weak.'

They were, indeed, practically non-existent, whereas Japan's might on land and sea was unimpaired.

But the central problem was still France, and it was to wounded but confident France that the Marshal addressed himself in his broadcast that evening:

Frenchmen,

I am addressing you today, Frenchmen of Metropolitan France and beyond the seas, to explain the motives for the two armistices that have been concluded — the first with Germany three days ago, the second with Italy yesterday.

The first thing one must stress is the profound delusions under which France and her Allies laboured as to Germany's real military strength and the effectiveness of the economic weapon: freedom of the seas, blockades, the resources at their disposal. A war can no more be won today than it could yesterday solely with gold and raw materials...

The Battle of Flanders ended with the capitulation of the Belgian army in the field and the encirclement of the British and French divisions. The latter fought bravely. They constituted the elite of our army; for all their gallantry, they were able to save part of their effectives only by abandoning their equipment.

A second battle was launched on the Aisne and the Somme. To hold this line sixty French divisions, without fortifications and almost without tanks, fought against a hundred and fifty German infantry and ten German armoured divisions. Within days the enemy had broken through our positions, divided our forces into four small groups and invaded most of the French homeland ...

By June 15th the enemy was crossing the Loire and pouring across the rest of France.

In the face of such an ordeal, armed resistance had to cease. The government was forced to come to one of two decisions: either to stay where it was, or to sail overseas. It considered the matter and resolved to stay in France so as to preserve the unity of our people and to represent them in consultation with the enemy. It considered that in such circumstances its duty was to obtain an acceptable armistice by appealing to the enemy's sense of honour and reason.

The armistice is concluded.

The fighting is over.

On this day of national mourning my thoughts are with the dead and all those whom the war has afflicted in heart and body.

Their sacrifice has kept the flag of France flying high and untarnished. They remain in our memories and in our hearts.

The terms to which we have had to subscribe are severe. A large area of our country is going to be occupied for a time ...

At least honour is saved. No one will use our planes or our fleet ...

You were prepared to fight on. I knew that. The war was lost in Metropolitan France. Was it to be prolonged in our colonies?

I should be unworthy to remain your leader had I agreed to shed French blood to prolong the dreams of a few Frenchmen who knew nothing of the conditions in which we were fighting. I was unwilling to place either my person or my hopes outside the soil of France.

My concern has been as much for our colonies as for Metropolitan France. The armistice safeguards the bonds that unite it with them. France is entitled to count on their loyalty.

It is to the future that we must now apply ourselves. A new order is beginning.

You will soon be home again. Some of you will have to rebuild that home.

You have suffered. You will suffer still more. Your lives will be hard. *I* shall not gull you with misleading words. I hate the lies that have brought you to so much harm.

The earth does not lie. It remains your refuge. It is your homeland itself. A field laid fallow is a portion of France dying. A fallow field resown is a portion of France coming to life again.

Do not hope for too much from the State. It can only give what it receives. Count for the present on yourselves, and for the future on the children in whom you have instilled a sense of duty ...

Our defeat sprang from our laxity. The spirit of enjoyment destroys what the spirit of sacrifice has built up.

The first thing I urge on you is an intellectual and moral recovery.

Frenchmen, you will achieve it, and you will see, I swear, a new France spring from your fervour.

This appeal profoundly moved the millions who listened to it. François Mauriac was quite overcome. A few days later he wrote:

Marshal Pétain's words on the evening of June 25th had an almost other-worldly ring to them. This was no human being talking to us; from the remotest depths of our History rose the cry of our great, humiliated nation. This old man was sent to us by the dead of Verdun and by the innumerable host of those who, for centuries, have been handing on that same torch which our feeble hands have just let fall.

THIRD PHASE

THE END OF A REGIME
(*June 26th–July 10th*)

JUNE 26TH

———◆◆◆———

Drum-rolls sounded in every village in France: it was the town crier.

'*Avis!*' he bellowed.

Doors were opened under a grey sky. Men, with their hands in their pockets, and women with anxious faces and heads covered, stood about in groups.

'*Today, June 26th,*' announced the crier, '*is a day of national mourning. At eleven o'clock everyone will gather at the war memorial ... A one-minute silence will unite in the nation's homage, the glorious dead of* 1914–1918 *and those, no less glorious, of* 1939–1940.'

The crier went on his way. The men and women dispersed without a word. They had a quarter of an hour to change into black — which, since they were peasants, meant their Sunday clothes.

MILITARY SITUATION

In pursuance of the armistice agreement, German motorized infantry units occupied Bayonne, Saint-Jean-de-Luz and Hendaye, together with the whole Atlantic coast from the Gironde to the Bidassoa.

Other units withdrew to the demarcation line, evacuating Château-roux, Montluçon, Clermont-Ferrand, Thiers, Vichy, Saint-Étienne, Roanne, Annonay, Vienne, Lyons, Grenoble and Mâcon.

Admiral Darlan addressed the following instructions to all members of the French navy:

No. 3158   *June 26th,* 1940, 8.7 *a.m.*

1. I am in possession of the clauses of the two signed armistices: none of them is dishonouring; our navy and air force must see the exceptional treatment accorded them as a tribute to their performance and an acknowledgment of their worth. Do not rely on the texts that are to appear simultaneously in the French and enemy Presses: they may be incomplete.

    Await receipt, from me, of complete texts and minutes of

discussions diminishing their severity on various points — minutes brought back by our delegates, including Vice-Admiral Le Luc.

2. Once and for all I repeat that we are keeping all our warships and all planes belonging to our naval air service, that the size of our service is not to be limited and that our enemies have solemnly undertaken not to touch our navy in the peace treaty. As losers, what more can we hope for? ...

In London Mr Hugh Dalton, Minister of Economic Warfare, stated that there could be no further question of sending supplies to France and that he had ordered the blockading of the French coasts.

That evening General de Gaulle broadcast his reply to Marshal Pétain's speech of the previous day:

Monsieur le Maréchal,

On the air, above the sea, a French soldier is about to speak to you.

Yesterday I heard your voice, which I know so well, and not without emotion I listened to what you were telling the French people in order to justify what you have done.

First you described the military inferiority that led to our defeat. Then you said that, faced with a situation that was considered hopeless, you assumed power so as to obtain an honourable armistice from our enemies.

Next you stated that, in view of the enemy's terms, there had been no other alternative but to stay in Bordeaux and accept them, or to reject them and go and continue the war from the Empire, and that you thought it your duty to stay in Bordeaux ...

Our military inferiority did indeed turn out to be terrible. But to what was this inferiority due?

It was due to a mistaken military plan. France has been crushed, not at all by the size of the German forces, not at all by their superior courage, but solely by the enemy's offensive and tactical mechanized power. Every serviceman knew it. If France did not have that mechanized power, if she had been given a purely defensive army, a static army, whose fault was that, *Monsieur le Maréchal?*

Did you, who directed our military organization after the 1914–1918 war, who were Commander-in-Chief till 1932, who were War Minister in 1935, who were the most eminent military figure in our country, ever support or seek or demand the indispensable reform of that mistaken plan? ...

And it is in the same tone, *Monsieur le Maréchal,* that you are urging

surrendered, plundered, subjugated France to resume her toil, to
recuperate, to recover. But in what atmosphere, by what means and
in the name of what do you expect her to recover under the German
jackboot and the Italian pump? ...

In his memoirs General de Gaulle writes: 'The almost total lack of
response from prominent Frenchmen certainly did not add to the prestige
of my enterprise. The fewer the prominent persons who came, the fewer
the prominent persons who wanted to come.'

For the most part, Frenchmen in Britain were far from keen to be
enrolled in the Gaullist organization. Béthouard's division was showing
impatience at the slowness of its repatriation. There was a stormy incident
in Liverpool where some French munition workers, whom the authorities
seemed intent on keeping in Britain, marched on the French consulate.
It took police cordons to stop them.

In Germany most people thought in terms of negotiation. Rundstedt,
Manstein, Brauchitsch and Kesselring were all convinced that the war was
nearing its end and that Britain would open peace talks in the near future.

Only Guderian and von Epp were sceptical. 'The German people were
overjoyed,' writes the former Commander of the 19th Armoured Corps,
'and Hitler was satisfied with the armistice that had just been signed. For
my part I was less enthusiastic ... '

Presumably Hitler was convinced that diplomacy would produce
better, and above all speedier, results than recourse to arms. His lack of
confidence in Italy's military worth and his desire to handle Britain with
kid gloves prompted him to accentuate the peace moves already begun in
Madrid and Stockholm.

The greatest obstacle lay in Churchill's unshakeable determination. But
reports suggested that his personal stock was falling and that his eviction
from the political arena was by no means out of the question.

But if the atmosphere in the west favoured a *détente*, things were very
different in the Far East. The Japanese government was becoming more
and more demanding.

In Indo-China General Catroux was greatly surprised by Bordeaux's
orders to resist the Japanese. He sent the following telegram to M.
Rivière, Minister for the Colonies:

I think you will more accurately appreciate the threat that Japan is
dangling over Indo-China by considering the fact that part of her
fleet is heading for the Tongkingese coast. This event will enable
you to grasp more clearly the loss of face that France's recent

capitulation has entailed in Asia, and to realize that the time for taking a tough line with the Japanese is past.

When one is beaten, when one has few planes and anti-aircraft guns and no submarines, one strives to protect one's property without having to fight, and one negotiates. That is what I have done.

You tell me that I should have consulted you and carried out the instructions in your last telegram. My answer is that I am 10,000 miles away from you, that you can do nothing for me and that I was subject to a very brief time-limit.

I acted on my own initiative. I shall do so again ...

MILITARY SITUATION

All over Europe there were signs of a *détente*.

In Germany and the occupied countries the Wehrmacht was demobilizing part of its forces. All infantry divisions formed in the autumn of 1939 were being sent home. In addition, a number of motorized units were returning to their peace-time stations within the Reich. These steps confirmed the German generals' impression that hostilities were nearing their end.

In Alexandria Admiral Cunningham came to a gentlemen's agreement with Admiral Godfroy with regard to Force X. The British admiral gave his word of honour that he would not try to seize the French ships anchored in the roads, in return for which the French admiral undertook not to put to sea without previously notifying his British colleague.

Admiral Godfroy immediately informed Admiral Darlan of this arrangement. Darlan was far from pleased. Under the terms of the Rethondes agreement all French ships, without exception, were to return to France. To agree to some of them remaining immobilized in Alexandria was to risk giving the Germans the impression that the French government was trying to shirk the armistice conditions — at the very moment when negotiations concerning the retention of the fleet in North Africa were about to open in Turin and Wiesbaden.

POLITICAL SITUATION

In all this wrangling over the fleet it was the naval officers who tried not to exacerbate matters and the politicians who were really intransigent. This contrast was perceptible not only in London but in Washington — as witness the attitude of the Secretary of State at the White House.

At 3 p.m. Mr Cordell Hull summoned M. de Saint-Quentin and sternly informed him that the United States was deeply concerned that France should not allow Germany to get control of the French fleet. The

United States, he said, had made no secret of the support that she had given France, and as a result she had incurred Germany's enmity. It would be most unfortunate if France were to provide Germany with a weapon that could be used against the United States — especially at a time when the French were saying that the U.S. Pacific fleet was of real value to France's considerable interests in the Far East.

True, Mr Cordell Hull also sent for Lord Lothian, the British ambassador, and told him that it was high time the British government placed the Royal Navy in the shelter of American ports.

Churchill's position was extremely delicate, and for all the indomitable optimism that he displayed in public he must have gone through many anxious moments when he was alone. The island's shield lay shattered and he had little else with which to defend the United Kingdom against the threat of invasion — just two or three regular divisions and a few Territorials. No plans had been made for evacuating overseas — his intention, in the event of disaster, being to 'die buried beneath the ruins of the capital'.

He could not bear the idea that his fellow-countrymen might refuse to follow his lead. Surely they must realize that it was their tradition to stand alone and that they had never done so in more splendid circumstances. But suppose the British people did not measure up to events? Suppose the House voted him down and compelled him to resign?

The old campaigner accepted the challenge. But if he were going to fight on, he must shake the British people out of their torpor, he must show them that this was no time to be dreaming of peace. He must capture their imagination by some spectacular and irrevocable action from which there could be no going back. He needed a success story.

The material for such a story was within his grasp: the French fleet. Since it refused to sail to British ports, since he could not secure it by getting the African colonies to break with Bordeaux, he would destroy it ...

JUNE 28TH

———— ◆•••◆ ————

POLITICAL SITUATION

In the early hours of the morning Churchill instructed the Admiralty to prepare Operation 'Catapult'. The British admirals were astounded by this decision, for it seemed to them to entail incalculable consequences for Britain.

Since the destruction of the French fleet was likely to produce unfavourable repercussions in Gaullist circles, it was thought advisable to bind the latter more firmly to the British government before launching the operation.

That evening a communiqué was issued, recognizing General de Gaulle as the leader of all Free Frenchmen, wherever they might be, who rallied to him in defence of the Allied cause.

M. Reynaud was involved in a terrible road accident while driving to Le Grès with Mme de Portes. In Sète she got him to take the wheel, thinking to distract him from his worries; but almost at once the car swung into one of the plane trees lining the road. Mme de Portes was killed instantly. M. Reynaud suffered head injuries and had to be rushed to a clinic in Montpellier.

JUNE 29TH

ARMISTICE NEGOTIATIONS

The French delegation to the Italian armistice commission settled down to talks in Turin. At 6.50 p.m. its leader, Admiral Duplat, had the following message telephoned to Bordeaux:

> With regard to the disarming of warships, the Italians agree to the allocation of ports suggested by the French Admiralty, subject to Germany's approval.

POLITICAL SITUATION

The period for which the Germans had undertaken to respect Bordeaux's neutrality expired on June 30th. Consequently the French government left the banks of the Gironde for Clermont-Ferrand.

Since his arrival in Bordeaux, M. Laval had become convinced that the Constitution would have to be revised. This undertaking struck him as the logical outcome of the tragedy that had just steeped France in blood. How could the regime responsible for the defeat outlive the disaster that it had been unable to prevent?

The idea was still in its infancy, and was put forward for the first time that morning at a Cabinet meeting attended by the Marshal, M. Alibert, M. Baudouin, M. Bouthillier and M. Laval himself. In the afternoon MM. Laval and Alibert further suggested calling the senators and deputies together as soon as possible and getting them to adopt a motion authorizing the Marshal to promulgate, in one or more acts, a new constitutional law.

Before the Marshal had time to give his approval M. Laval leaped into his car and drove to Royat, where he called on M. Lebrun. The President could see no objection to reshaping the Constitution: its failings had been brought home to him on many occasions.

An hour later Laval was back in Clermont.

'Well, you've got it,' he told the Marshal.

'Got what?'

'President Lebrun's consent,' he answered with a smile.

Though remaining impassive, the Marshal was stunned by the speed with which things were happening.

In Britain General de Gaulle continued his recruiting work. He went to Trentham Park, where the French units that had fought in Norway were encamped.

General Béthouard, who commanded the division, had arranged for the 'Leader of the Free French' to see every platoon. General de Gaulle was thus enabled to win over a large proportion of the two battalions of the 13th Demi-Brigade of the Foreign Legion, two hundred or so Chasseurs Alpins, two-thirds of a tank company, a few gunners, engineers and signallers and a number of staff and junior officers.

JUNE 30TH

MILITARY SITUATION

Mussolini drove to Lanslebourg, in Maurienne, to congratulate the Italian troops who had fought on the Alpine front. On the way down from the Mont-Cenis he noticed, on his left, a fort that had refused to surrender and was still flying the French colours. This was the La Turra fort, some 9,000 feet above sea-level. Its garrison, commanded by Sub-Lieutenants Prudhon and Chandesris, consisted of nine N.C.O.s and forty-one Chasseurs and gunners. Though encircled by several divisions, they had repulsed all enemy attacks for ten days.

Mussolini gave orders for them to be freed, with the honours of war.

ARMISTICE NEGOTIATIONS

The French delegation to the German armistice commission moved into the Hotel Rose in Wiesbaden.

General Huntziger immediately raised the question of the stationing of the fleet. He asked that *all* its bases should lie outside the German-occupied zone, thus ruling out the Atlantic ports of Cherbourg, Brest, Lorient and Saint-Nazaire. He pointed out that the Italians agreed with the proposed distribution and that the request, already made in Rethondes, had been virtually accepted by General Keitel.

After brief deliberation the Germans gave their consent.

This important piece of news was sent immediately to Admiral Odend'hal, for communication to the British Admiralty.

POLITICAL SITUATION

The German peace offensive went ahead. In the course of a private luncheon the Duke of Alba hinted to Lord Halifax that Hitler would be prepared to put an end to hostilities. Germany's demands would be limited to the restitution of the colonies taken from her by the Treaty of Versailles. There was only one condition: that Churchill should take a back seat.

The French government left Clermont-Ferrand for Vichy. Marshal Pétain and Pierre Laval made a detour via Royat in order to call on M. Lebrun. The Deputy Premier briefly outlined the 'constitutional bill' that he was working on.

'We'll look into that,' said M. Lebrun, who had thought things over since the day before and suddenly seemed less keen on the idea. 'Draw up the text and we'll talk about it ... '

Did he secretly hope that M. Laval was riding for a fall?

The Marshal could see little hope of the Chamber's adopting a 'constitutional bill'. But he let Laval carry on: he could always disown him if the plan fell through.

In Indo-China, General Catroux went to Hanoi to begin talks with the Japanese mission (headed by General Nishihara) concerning the execution of the demands contained in the ultimatum of June 19th. Realizing that he could count on no French, British or American aid, he arrived in Tongking convinced that the best line for him to follow was that of a Franco-Japanese rapprochement.

JULY 1ST

At 2.25 a.m. the British Admiralty cabled Gibraltar: 'Be prepared for "Catapult" July 3rd.'

Vice-Admiral Somerville cabled back:

After a talk with Holland and others Vice-Admiral Force H is impressed with their view that the use of force should be avoided at all costs. Holland considers offensive action on our part would alienate all French wherever they are.

To this the Admiralty replied at 6.20 p.m.:

Firm intention of H.M.G. that if French will not accept any of your alternatives they are to be destroyed.

In Plymouth, French warships were towed into the dockyard one by one. The *Paris* was berthed that evening. Admiral Cayol asked the British the reasons for this move. Dissatisfied with their explanations, he boarded each ship in turn and gave their captains the following instructions:

'Keep a party in permanent readiness to scuttle your vessels, and scuttle them if a foreign power makes slightest attempt to seize them.'

POLITICAL SITUATION

Tired of being thwarted in his recruiting efforts by France's official military and naval missions, whose task was to repatriate French soldiers and sailors, General de Gaulle asked the British government to put an end to this ambiguous situation. Since the British authorities had recognized him as 'leader of all French nationals in Britain', he reasoned that they should sever contact with organizations that refused to submit to his orders.

As a result, the heads of the various missions were summoned by the British ministers to whom they were accredited, and told that they must either leave the country or take service in Britain.

494

The bonds still uniting Britain and France were being broken one by one.

Relations between France and the United States, on the other hand, showed signs of improvement. Mr William Bullitt, who had stayed on in Paris when the Germans arrived, paid a fact-finding visit to the French government before returning to Washington. In turn he called on M. Lebrun, Marshal Pétain and Admiral Darlan. With each of them he yet again raised the question of the fleet.

'France will never in any circumstances surrender her fleet to Germany,' M. Lebrun assured him.

'Orders have been given to every captain in the French fleet to sink his ship rather than let it fall into German hands,' said the Marshal.

Mr Bullitt returned to America enchanted with the reception that he had received and convinced of the sincerity of Admiral Darlan's promises. In New York he told reporters that Marshal Pétain enjoyed the respect of everyone in France: he was 'really the boss'.

In Hanoi General Catroux began talks with General Nishihara. He wished, he said, to treat their discussions as an opportunity for finding an amicable solution to all problems dividing France and Japan.

Their exchanges soon ranged beyond the ultimatum of June 19th. Japan wanted France to acknowledge her as the predominant power in the Far East and to agree to Indo-China's inclusion in what Tokyo called 'the sphere of Asiatic co-prosperity'.

Admiral Decoux writes: 'General Catroux agreed in principle to Indo-China's collaborating politically and militarily with Japan.'

———————◆•◆◆•◆———————

MILITARY SITUATION

Hitler sent for his three service chiefs and asked them to draw up plans for the invasion of Britain.

They were amazed to find themselves entrusted with a task that seemed to belie the widespread peace rumours. One of them asked Hitler whether all hope of concluding an amicable agreement with Britain was to be abandoned.

'No,' replied Hitler. 'But I have little confidence in the success of diplomatic bargaining — I'm sorry to say.'

In Alexandria Admiral Cunningham sent the following letter to Admiral Godfroy, aboard the *Duquesne*:

My dear Admiral,

I have been instructed by the British Admiralty to submit certain proposals to you. Would you be so kind as to come and see me on board the *Warspite* at 9 a.m. tomorrow, Wednesday.

Bring a staff-officer or your flag-officer with you if you like ...

POLITICAL SITUATION

From 11 a.m. to 1.15 p.m. there was a meeting of the inner Cabinet in Vichy. Those attending were Laval, General Weygand, Yves Bouthillier, Paul Baudouin and Adrien Marquet.

After dealing with a number of immediate matters, they turned to Laval's constitutional bill. It was adopted in principle, but discussion of the substance of the bill was held over, by general agreement, till next day.

JULY 3RD

MILITARY SITUATION

Shortly before dawn the British seized the French warships sheltering in Plymouth, Falmouth, Portsmouth and Sheerness. Operation 'Catapult' had begun.

In Plymouth were a 22,000-ton battleship, the *Paris*, the light cruiser *Triomphant*, three destroyers including the *Mistral*, four sloops, the giant submarine *Surcouf* and three smaller submarines, all under the command of Admiral Cayol.

In Portsmouth were the battleship *Courbet*, the light cruiser *Léopard*, the destroyers *Chevreuil*, *Savorgnan de Brazza* and *Pollux*, two torpedo-boats, three sloops, two submarines (*Orion* and *Ondine*, both undergoing repairs), twelve submarine chasers and a number of patrol boats, all under the command of Admiral Gaudin de Villaine.

In Falmouth there were three sloops and two submarines.

In Sheerness there were two sloops and a number of harbour craft (tugs, dredgers, lighters, etc.).

At 3.45 a.m. detachments of armed British soldiers stole aboard in carpet-slippers, overcame the sentries, clubbed those who tried to defend themselves and surprised the sleeping officers and men. Their arrival was so unexpected that resistance was practically impossible. But here and there serious incidents occurred.

The French commanders were handed copies of a note signed by Sir Dunbar Nasmith, C.-in-C. Western Approaches. It stated that, since Britain was still at war with Germany and Italy, it was essential that French naval units in British harbours should not fall into enemy hands; consequently the British government had decided, with the deepest regret, that all such ships must be detained.

How could vessels berthed or anchored in British harbours fall into enemy hands?

Later, groups of French sailors escorted by Royal Marines returned to the ships to pack their belongings. They had been told to help themselves to whatever they wanted, especially food and drink, and they knew it would be a long time before they drank wine again. 'Within a few hours,' writes Muselier, 'our fine crews had become a disorderly, half-drunk rabble.'

In Alexandria, Force X comprised the battleship *Lorraine*, three 10,000-ton cruisers (the *Suffren*, the *Tourville* and the *Duquesne*, the latter flying Admiral Godfroy's flag), the 8,000-ton cruiser *Duguay-Trouin*, three destroyers (the *Fortuné*, the *Basque* and the *Forbin*) and the 1,500-ton submarine *Protée*.

They were anchored in the close harbour and surrounded by the *Warspite*, flying Admiral Cunningham's flag, the *Malaya*, the *Barham*, the *Ramillies*, the *Royal Sovereign*, the aircraft-carrier *Eagle* and a flotilla of destroyers.

At 9 a.m. Admiral Godfroy went aboard the *Warspite* with his Chief of Staff, Post-Captain Tisserand.

Admiral Cunningham met them at the head of the gangway and took them down to the cabin. There, tense-featured, he handed a typewritten document to Admiral Godfroy. Its contents can be summarized as follows:

1. Either agree to place the ships of Force X, manned by volunteers, at the disposal of the British;
2. Or agree to their being disarmed under British supervision — in other words, under constraint;
3. Or sink them.

Having taken stock of these proposals, Admiral Godfroy returned to the *Duquesne* to word his reply. It was ready at 11.30 a.m.:

> ... I should be inclined to accept the second [proposal] if I could recommend it to my superiors, who alone can give me authority to disarm my ships in a foreign port, under constraint from a foreign power.
>
> If I am not allowed to discuss it with them I find myself compelled to choose the third solution, regrettable as it may be for the future, for in these conditions it alone is reconcilable with our sense of honour.

Suddenly Admiral Godfroy was handed signals from the fleet at Mers-el-Kebir. Something tragic seemed to have happened.

He immediately went aboard the *Warspite* to express his indignation to Admiral Cunningham and to inform him that he was countermanding all the conciliatory arrangements that he had made earlier in the afternoon. He heard English officers aboard the British flagship say of the action at Mers-el-Kebir: 'It is simply madness.'

In Mers-el-Kebir lay the French Atlantic fleet, the cream of the French navy: the battleships *Dunkerque*, *Strasbourg*, *Provence* and *Bretagne*, and the cruisers *Volta*, *Mogador*, *Terrible*, *Lynx*, *Tigre* and *Kersaint*.

There were also a number of ships under Admiral Jarry, naval commander at Oran, including the aircraft-carrier *Commandant Teste*, several destroyers and four submarines.

On board all these vessels everything was proceeding as usual. Parties were preparing to go ashore, either for leave or for discharge — for demobilization had started the day before. The ships were no longer on a war footing.

Pierre Varillon writes:

When, at about 7 a.m., the look-outs reported that a British destroyer, the *Foxhound*, had just anchored about a mile from the channel, and when, a little later on, three British capital ships (the 42,000-ton battle-cruiser *Hood*, flying Admiral Somerville's flag, the *Resolution* and the *Valiant*, escorted by two cruisers and a number of destroyers) and shortly afterwards the *Ark Royal*, Britain's most modern aircraft-carrier, appeared on the horizon, most of our men supposed that the British squadron was on its way to engage Italian units and that the first round in the fight for the domination of the Mediterranean was about to begin.

But when they noticed launches plying back and forth between the *Foxhound* and the *Dunkerque* they began to realize that something else might be happening.

Admiral Gensoul had received a message from Admiral Somerville in which the latter stated that he was sending Captain Holland to confer with him. The Royal Navy, he added, hoped that its proposals would allow the French navy to align itself with the British.

Admiral Gensoul sent Lieutenant Dufay to inquire into Admiral Somerville's proposals. About a quarter of an hour later Lieutenant Dufay returned with a sealed envelope. Admiral Gensoul tore it open and was amazed to find himself confronted with a veritable ultimatum:

… His Majesty's Government have instructed me to demand that the French fleet now at Mers-el-Kebir and Oran shall act in accordance with one of the following alternatives:

(a) Sail with us and continue to fight for victory against the Germans and Italians.

(b) Sail with reduced crews under our control to a British port …

(c) Alternatively, if you feel bound to stipulate that your ships should not be used against the Germans or Italians unless these break the armistice, then sail them with us with reduced crews to some French port in the West Indies — Martinique, for instance — where they can be demilitarized to our satisfaction or be perhaps entrusted to the United States and remain safe until the end of the war ...

Admiral Gensoul was immediately convinced that he would be unable to agree to any of these alternatives. He therefore ordered: 'Action stations!' But it was going to take some time for his ships to get up steam and prepare to sail.

He then sent the following telegram to the French Admiralty:

2607   8.45 a.m.
Flagship Dunkerque to French Admiralty
British forces comprising 3 battleships, 1 aircraft-carrier, cruisers and destroyers off Oran. — Ultimatum sent: sink your ships within six hours or we shall force you to. — Reply: French ships will meet force with force.[1]

At 10.50 a.m. Admiral Somerville sent a further message, regretfully informing Admiral Gensoul that he would not be allowed to sail unless the British conditions were accepted and adding that, in Alexandria, Admiral Godfroy was demilitarizing his ships with reduced crews.

Somerville himself was hesitant to use force. Conscious that Admiral Gensoul would not go back on his decision, he telegraphed to London in an attempt to get his orders changed.

In Whitehall Mr Alexander, Sir Dudley Pound, Sir Francis Little and others sat tense-faced at the Admiralty. Their silence was amply expressive of their state of mind: they would much prefer to leave things as they stood rather than carry through Operation 'Catapult' to its bitter conclusion.

Churchill 'sat all the afternoon in the Cabinet Room in frequent contact with my principal colleagues and the First Lord and First Sea Lord'.

Admiral Darlan had followed the government to Vichy. The only senior naval officer left in Nérac was Admiral Le Luc, Chief of General Staff. He telephoned Admiral Négadelle and asked him to inform Admiral Darlan of the news from Mers-el-Kebir with all possible haste.

1 Admiral Gensoul has since been blamed for not sending the full text of Admiral Somerville's proposals to the French Admiralty. His critics have suggested that the French government might have responded to one of them and that the tragedy would thus have been avoided. This seems highly improbable.

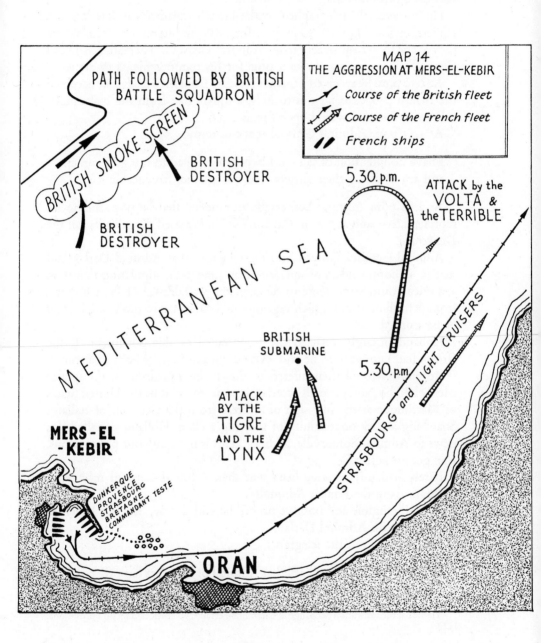

PATH FOLLOWED BY BRITISH BATTLE SQUADRON

MAP 14
THE AGGRESSION AT MERS-EL-KEBIR

Course of the British fleet
Course of the French fleet
French ships

BRITISH SMOKE SCREEN

BRITISH DESTROYER

BRITISH DESTROYER

MEDITERRANEAN SEA

5.30 p.m.

ATTACK by the VOLTA & the TERRIBLE

BRITISH SUBMARINE

5.30 p.m.

STRASBOURG and LIGHT CRUISERS

ATTACK BY THE TIGRE AND THE LYNX

MERS-EL-KEBIR

DUNKERQUE
PROVENCE
STRASBOURG
BRETAGNE
COMMANDANT TESTE

ORAN

An hour later Admiral Négadelle rang back to say that Admiral Darlan was nowhere to be found.[1] Thus Admiral Le Luc had to take the necessary decisions himself.

He immediately telegraphed to the French squadrons in Toulon and Algiers, instructing them to prepare for battle and hasten to Oran, where they were to act on orders from Admiral Gensoul. Thereafter Admiral Gensoul's one aim was to gain time for his reinforcements to arrive.

At 1.30 p.m. he received a further message from the *Hood*: if he accepted the British proposals he was to hoist a square flag from the main mast; otherwise Force H would open fire at 2 p.m.

At 1.45 p.m. Admiral Gensoul sent this reply:

I have no intention of sailing. I have telegraphed to my government and am awaiting their answer. Do not take an irrevocable step.

At 2.12 p.m. Admiral Somerville announced that he was sending his representative, and at 3 p.m. Captain Holland crossed the gangway of the *Dunkerque*.

Admiral Gensoul showed him the telegram that Admiral Darlan had sent to all commanders of squadrons, on June 24th, stipulating that if an armistice commission were to demand the withdrawal of French crews from demobilized ships, such vessels would either sail to the United States or be scuttled.

Holland instantly realized the importance of this document. If the British had known of it, he said, everything might have been different.

Admiral Gensoul then offered to disarm his squadron on the spot at Mers-el-Kebir, and gave his word of honour to sail it to the United States or Martinique at the first sign of a threat from the Germans or Italians. Snatching at any opportunity of averting a clash, Holland signalled this news to Admiral Somerville, adding: 'This is not quite our propositions. Can get no nearer.'

Barely had this message been sent than Admiral Gensoul received a telegram from the French Admiralty.

'Here is tangible and positive proof,' he said slowly, 'that we have not lost touch with Admiral Darlan.'

He then read out the telegram:

Inform British intermediary that Admiral of the Fleet has ordered all French forces in the Mediterranean to rally to you immediately ...

[1] He was at the Institution Monange in Clermont-Ferrand, where he had set up a provisional H.Q.

Holland bowed his head, realizing that the chips were down. In any case, a further signal came from Admiral Somerville immediately afterwards. It stated that unless one or other of the British proposals were accepted by 5.30 p.m., British Summer Time, he would have to sink the French ships.

'Action stations!' ordered Admiral Gensoul.

The signal, hoisted from the *Dunkerque*, was instantly taken up by the ships' buglers.

It would be for the light cruisers to leave harbour first, followed in turn by the *Dunkerque*, the *Strasbourg*, the *Bretagne* and the *Provence*. But they would not stir till the British had fired the first salvo. In this way, they would not provide Admiral Somerville with an excuse.

They had not long to wait. At 4.56 p.m. came a deafening roar: the Royal Navy had opened fire. Four shells landed alongside the jetty, sending jets of water three hundred feet into the air.

The French light cruisers had more than half a mile to cover before they reached the boom. They moved off in line ahead, manoeuvring to avoid the shell-bursts. Every minute twenty-four 15-in. shells landed in the narrow channel that they had to navigate. No armour-plating could have stood up to them at such short range. Then the battleships got under way. They were steered with commendable coolness, but several of them were hit almost as soon as they left the quays. The stern of the *Bretagne* was ablaze. A further salvo tore into her hull, below the water-line. Soon the unfortunate ship was a mass of flames and started to sink from the stern. Suddenly there was a tremendous flash that seemed to rend the sky. The *Bretagne* keeled over, carrying a crew of a thousand and some thirty officers to their deaths.

The *Dunkerque*, too, had been hit in the first minute. One shell caught her aft, on the port side, without causing major damage or affecting her steerage. But then three further 15-in. shells struck her. The first hit one of her turrets, knocking out two guns and killing their crews. The second penetrated the side-engines and put one of the generators out of action. This was serious. The third exploded in a boiler-room, caused a fire in the No. 2 stokehold and destroyed the starboard cable subway, thus totally depriving the ship of electricity. She was paralysed.

At 5 p.m. the *Provence*, bearing Admiral Bouxin's insignia, slid gently away from the quay, taking care not to impede the *Dunkerque*. Two of her turrets were knocked out in swift succession. A severe fire broke out in the stern and a gaping hole was reported below the water-line. The temperature in the bunkers rose so rapidly that they had to be flooded to avoid disaster. The stern was slowly sinking. There was only one way out: to run her gently aground.

Meanwhile the light cruisers were nearing the harbour channel. Suddenly, at about 5.3 p.m., the *Mogador* vanished in the midst of an enormous explosion. Her stern had been torn away by a 15-in. shell setting off her supply of depth-charges. A quarter of the ship had simply disappeared.

The *Terrible* and the *Volta* opened fire on two British destroyers, which made off. At about the same time the *Rigault de Genouilly*, which had left Oran harbour to come to the aid of the main fleet, was caught in the fire of two British cruisers. Firing at maximum range with her three 138-mm. guns, the *Rigault* manoeuvred as much as she could to escape damage. But two 6-in. shells hit her, one in the fore-funnel, the other slightly astern. Aboard, there followed moments of anxious waiting, for there was a chance that the third salvo might obliterate her. Fortunately it landed in the sea. Then, abruptly, the firing ceased. Presumably recalled by their admiral, the British cruisers had turned about.

But at this point cries of joy rang out on every bridge: 'The *Strasbourg*! Here comes the *Strasbourg*!' And, indeed, the great battle-cruiser was speeding majestically out into the open sea.

At the very first salvo she had cut her moorings and started her engines. By the time the third salvo landed — the salvo that finished her neighbour, the *Bretagne* — she was starting to turn. Steaming slowly up the line, she passed alongside the *Bretagne*, now a sheet of flames. She was still abreast of her when she capsized. Amid the terrifying din of the alternating discharges and detonations, the whistling shells and the roar of aircraft circling in the sky, mindless of the jets of water shooting up all round her, she continued on her way, miraculously unscathed. At 5.9 p.m. she reached the opening in the boom. All eyes were upon her. Would she get through the channel? Would she manage to miss the mines? Her stem ploughing the water, she reached the danger zone. Breaths were held. She was going to make it ... she had made it! She, at least, was going to be able to fight back and avenge the dead, the poor dead killed like animals caught in a trap. The moment she was through the boom she accelerated to twenty-eight knots, binoculars and range-finders trained towards the enemy, ready to open fire on the British squadron as soon as she could see it.

But she never saw it. For eight miles westwards a huge black wall rose from the sea. As soon as the *Dunkerque* and the *Provence* had commenced firing, the British ships had covered themselves with a smokescreen.

Alerted by the Fleet Air Arm, the British squadron set off in pursuit of the *Strasbourg*. At 6.5 p.m. her captain learned from one of the French pilots that the British were steering a parallel course, somewhere over in the west. Fifty minutes later a further message reported that they were still there – but now the *Hood* was alone, apart from a few smaller ships. The *Valiant* and the *Resolution* were no longer of an age to take part in such a chase. Finally, at 7.25 p.m., the *Hood* herself gave up, not caring to wander alone and in daylight, in a part of the Mediterranean on which three French battle squadrons were converging.

At 6.30 p.m. Admiral Gensoul wired Admiral Somerville: 'Request you cease fire.'

At 6.35 p.m. the Commander of Force H replied that he would open fire again if he found that the French ships were not sunk.

Admiral Gensoul decided to withdraw the crews of the *Dunkerque* and the *Provence* for the night so as to avoid further slaughter. If nothing happened in the meantime, they could return next day and carry out the most urgent repairs.

POLITICAL SITUATION

In Vichy the news of the British ultimatum had burst like a bombshell in the early afternoon.

When Admiral Négadelle finally managed to contact him in Clermont, Admiral Darlan set out at once; but by the time he reached Vichy the destruction of Force X had begun. At the Cabinet meeting he was quite cool and collected. 'What had happened was so incredible that he could not grasp it,' writes Bouthillier. 'Thus it was with great restraint, without raising his voice, that he related the morning's events.'

More detailed news reached Vichy that evening. It confirmed the extent of French losses. Coupled with the seizures in Britain and Egypt, the sinkings at Mers-el-Kebir constituted a full-scale naval disaster.

'It was a terrible blow to our hopes,' writes de Gaulle. 'The recruitment of volunteers dropped off immediately. Many of those who had been preparing to join us – servicemen and civilians alike – now turned their backs on us. Furthermore, the attitude adopted towards us by the civil authorities in the Empire, and by the naval and military forces guarding it, changed in most cases from hesitation to reprobation.'

THE END OF A REGIME

ARMISTICE NEGOTIATIONS

General von Stulpnagel sent General Huntziger a letter beginning:

In reply to your communication concerning the incidents in the Western Mediterranean I have the honour to inform you that the Führer of the German Reich has expressed approval of the steps taken by the French government ...

JULY 4TH

MILITARY SITUATION

In Oran the *Rigault de Genouilly*, which had barely had time to carry out her repairs, had been ordered to sail to Bizerta. She had put to sea at once, under cover of darkness, hugging the coast as closely as possible. Dawn brought mist, but it soon lifted and was replaced by glorious sunshine. At about 3 p.m. she was hit by two torpedoes. Most of the bow was torn away and there was a heavy fire amidships. There could be no hope of saving her, for the engines, too, were ablaze. The men were ordered to jump overboard.

In Alexandria the situation was quite different. True, Force X could not leave harbour without being sunk; but it could inflict terrible damage on the Royal Navy before going down.

At 11 a.m. the *Warspite* transmitted, in French and in clear, the following message to Admiral Godfroy's crews:

> The British admiral does not want to sink your ships. What is the use of pointlessly sacrificing lives when you are outnumbered? ... All that we ask is that your ships should be rendered unsailable, for if they leave harbour they may fall into enemy hands ...

Admiral Godfroy's initial reaction was rather unfavourable. He was annoyed that the British should have appealed directly to his men, for the broadcast might encourage acts of insubordination. But Admiral Cunningham's intentions, however tactlessly announced, did appear conciliatory.

Admiral Godfroy demanded that the French themselves should be responsible for immobilizing their ships, without supervision, and that the British commander should be content with a statement from himself, the commander of Force X, assuring him that the necessary steps had been taken. Admiral Cunningham agreed to this proposal.

At 4 p.m. Admiral Godfroy sent the following letter of confirmation to the *Warspite*:

July 4th, 1940

Admiral,

I agree to instruct the ships of Force X to unload such fuel oil as they
have aboard, apart from a small quantity to be retained for current
use ... I shall have the breach-plugs removed from the heavy guns
and the firing pins from the smaller ones and deposit them at the
French consulate ...

A few moments later one of *Warspite's* officers brought Admiral
Cunningham's reply, expressing deep gratitude for Admiral Godfroy's
decisions.

It seemed that a repetition of the tragedy at Mers-el-Kebir would be
avoided.

POLITICAL SITUATION

At 10.30 a.m. there was a meeting between the Marshal, Admiral
Darlan, Pierre Laval and Paul Baudouin. The atmosphere was quite
different from that at the closed Cabinet session the day before. Admiral
Darlan, in particular, who had since received detailed news of what had
happened at Mers-el-Kebir, had difficulty in controlling his temper. His
voice was shaking. 'I have been betrayed by my brothers-in-arms,' he
said.

He announced that he had ordered the cruiser squadron previously at
Algiers to spend the night south of the Balearics. It was to be reinforced
by the *Strasbourg* and had been instructed to try to launch a surprise
attack, by way of reprisal, on the British squadron.

'Let us at least allow ourselves time to think,' said Baudouin, hoping that
tempers would cool. 'The attack on our fleet is one thing, war is another.'

By the time the meeting broke up, the ministers had made up their
minds not to engage in any form of reprisal without fully weighing the
consequences.

At 10 a.m. the entire Cabinet met under M. Lebrun. The ministers
decided to delay any form of armed retaliation till further notice. On the
other hand, they approved Baudouin's suggestion that diplomatic
relations should be broken off *de jure*.

Pierre Laval took no part in the discussions. He favoured a forceful
rejoinder of the kind envisaged by Admiral Darlan, but he could see that the
Marshal was opposed to any such action. He therefore reserved his
energies for another task: the reshaping of the Constitution. Towards the

end of the meeting the Deputy Premier broached this subject for the first time before the full Cabinet. He suggested a specific text to his colleagues. Here it is:

Sole article: The National Assembly gives all powers to the government of the Republic, under the signature and authority of Marshal Pétain, the Prime Minister, to promulgate in one or more acts the new Constitution of the French State.

This Constitution shall safeguard the rights of work, of the family and of the nation. It will be ratified by the assemblies that it creates.

Laval did not want the motion discussed at this stage. The atmosphere was not right. He went straight from the Cabinet meeting to the hall of the Society of Medical Sciences, where a group of senators was impatiently awaiting him.

'The attack on our ships is an unforgivable act,' he said gravely. 'We cannot take such things lying down. Yet the government has decided not to declare war on Britain ... '

His words produced both amazement and relief.

'Parliament,' he continued without giving them time to recover, 'is to be dissolved. The Constitution is to be revised. It must be brought in line with that of the totalitarian states. Everything needs reconstructing. An enormous task awaits us ... '

While this was going on in Vichy, Churchill was telling the House of Commons:

... When two nations are fighting together under long and solemn alliance against a common foe, one of them may be stricken down and overwhelmed and may be forced to ask its ally to release it from its obligations. But the least that could be expected was that the French government, in abandoning the conflict and leaving its whole weight to fall upon Great Britain and the British Empire, would have been careful not to inflict needless injury upon their faithful comrade, in whose final victory the sole chance of French freedom lay, and lies.

As the House will remember, we offered to give full release to the French from their treaty obligations, although these were designed for precisely the case which arose, on one condition — namely that the French fleet should be sailed for British harbours before the separate armistice negotiations with the enemy were completed. This was not done ...

It shows how strong were the reasons for the course which we thought it our duty to take that every member of the Cabinet had the same conviction about what should be done ...

Now I turn to the Mediterranean. At Alexandria, where a strong British battle-fleet is lying, there are, besides a French battleship, four French cruisers, three of them modern eight-inch-gun vessels, and a number of smaller ships ... Measures have now been taken to ensure that those ships, which are commanded by a very gallant admiral, shall be sunk or otherwise made to comply with our wishes ...

But the most serious part of the story remains ...

Mr Churchill read out Admiral Somerville's ultimatum to Admiral Gensoul. He continued:

We had hoped that one or other of the alternatives which we presented would have been accepted, without the necessity of using the terrible force of a British battle squadron ... Admiral Gensoul refused to comply and announced his intention of fighting ... I need hardly say that the French ships were fought, albeit in this unnatural cause, with the characteristic courage of the French navy ...

I leave the judgment of our action, with confidence, to Parliament. I leave it to the nation and I leave it to the United States. I leave it to the world and to history ...

During the afternoon Lord Halifax addressed the House of Lords on the same subject. But the tone that he adopted was far more restrained than the Prime Minister's:

... The officers and men of the French navy were placed in a position which must have seemed to them wellnigh intolerable ... It is, I suppose, inevitable that what has passed ... must create sharp resentment in France, where already the distress of war and harsh conditions of the armistice have strained public feeling almost to breaking-point, and it is not difficult to realize what is likely to be the feeling among the officers and men of the French navy, the members of the French government and among the French people ...

Nearly all Britain's newspapers treated the Royal Navy's action as a noble exploit.

JULY 5TH

The victims of the British attack were buried in the cemetery at Mers-el-Kebir. In an emotion-laden speech, delivered beside the line of coffins, Admiral Gensoul said:

> You had promised to obey your superiors in whatever they might command you to do for the honour of the Flag and the greatness of the arms of France. If there is a stain on a flag today, it is certainly not on yours.

POLITICAL SITUATION

The position of Frenchmen in London was becoming more and more precarious as a result of de Gaulle's decision to take command of all French nationals in Britain. Increasing pressure was brought to bear on members of the French navy to get them to enrol in the Free French forces. Paul Morand writes:

> Stung by the part played by our Missions in putting French soldiers, sailors and refugees on their guard against hasty enlistment, the British government had the leading-seamen of the Naval Mission arrested for using the Breton dialect in the street to some of their compatriots; leaflets were seized; two of our officers were put in solitary confinement in Glasgow ...

In Vichy, Jean Taurines, the senator for the Rhône and one of the wounded of the 1914–18 war, called his ex-service colleagues together. There were twenty-five of them, including Senators Paul-Boncour, Maroselli, Jacquy, Chaumié and Dormann.

They had all been somewhat startled by Laval's remarks in the hall of the Society of Medical Sciences. Of course, they were willing to accord Marshal Pétain full powers; but need that entail abolishing the Constitution? They unanimously adopted the following motion:

> The ex-service senators meeting in Vichy on Friday, July 5th, under the chairmanship of M. Jean Taurines, salute with emotion and pride

their revered leader Marshal Pétain who, in tragically painful hours, has bestowed himself on the nation.

They trust in him, within the legitimate framework of the Republic, to reorganize our national strength, stimulate our energies and prepare the moral ground that will reconstruct a France worthy of their sacrifices.

But the Marshal was not to be found. The senators spent all day trying, unsuccessfully, to hand him their statement.

Meanwhile a meeting of deputies was being held in the Petit Casino. The eighty attending it had been warned of Laval's plans by their colleagues from the Senate. So they were on their guard and ready to stand up to him.

The hall had been decked out to suggest the Palais Bourbon. On the stage were a rostrum for the speakers and a presidential chair, to be taken, for this session, by M. Cayrel, deputy for the Gironde. The front row of the orchestra stalls served as the government bench.

Marcel Héraud said he was alarmed to see power passing into the hands of the military. The supremacy of the civil authorities, he argued, had always been one of France's characteristics.

François Chasseigne, Socialist deputy for Issoudun, took the opposite line. He was recently back from Flanders, where he had been wounded. His unit was among those to suffer the first onslaught of German armour, in the Gembloux plain. He backed Laval to the hilt.

When the time came for Laval to reply he did not bother to go up on to the stage. He merely rose from his seat, took a few steps towards the front of the hall and leaned against the front of the stage.

'Everything must be reconstructed on a fresh basis,' he said. 'Either you agree to what we ask, or Hitler will impose it on you by force ... France has never had, and will never have, a more implacable enemy than Great Britain. Our whole history is there to attest it. We have been mere toys in Britain's hands. She has been using us for her own protection. Today we are at the bottom of the abyss into which she has led us ... I am as opposed to a military dictatorship as you are. Otherwise I could simply let things drift. I should not be here, doing my utmost to persuade you. Can you not see that I am the guarantor of civil authority? Help me in my task, instead of thwarting me ... '

On this more soothing note the meeting ended. The deputies spilled out into the corridors where Laval hurried about, busily canvassing those whose feelings he might have bruised.

JULY 6TH

MILITARY SITUATION

In Mers-el-Kebir the wrecked French fleet was the object of a further British attack, apparently provoked by a tactless communiqué broadcast throughout Algeria in which Admiral Sud had claimed that the *Dunkerque* had not been seriously damaged and could soon be repaired.

Three waves of torpedo-bombers appeared in the sky. They were from *Ark Royal*. The first swooped over the jetty and the wreck of the *Mogador*, launched its torpedoes unsuccessfully, banked and headed back out to sea.

The second, approaching from the south-east, ran into heavy anti-aircraft fire from the *Provence* and turned away without dropping its load.

But the third, approaching from the south-west, dived and delivered a double attack on the *Dunkerque*. One torpedo struck the *Estérel*, which sank without loss of life. Another hit the *Terre-Neuve*, with more tragic results. All her depth-charges exploded, opening an enormous gash in the side of the *Dunkerque* and killing or wounding four officers and a hundred and fifty men.

POLITICAL SITUATION

More and more politicians were arriving in Vichy and activity was becoming increasingly intense. Senators and deputies both decided to hold regular 'news meetings': the former in the hall of the Society of Medical Sciences, the latter in the Petit Casino. Laval put his heart and soul into these sessions, drawing on all his powers as an orator and a tactician.

In the Petit Casino, where M. Cayrel again took the chair, Laval spoke of the reasons that had led the government to seek the convocation of the National Assembly.

'The disaster to which we have been brought by the levity of those who led us into the war,' he declared, 'makes it a sacred duty for us to ensure the continuity of France. We are asking Parliament to give us the means. Were it to refuse — but it will not refuse — the responsibilities that would weigh on it would be appalling.'

Later M. Spinasse, deputy for the Corrèze, spoke. He had been a minister in the Popular Front government and was a friend of Léon Blum's. He was visibly moved. He spoke slowly, without emphasis, with a simplicity that added still further to the loftiness of this thinking.

'Parliament,' he said, 'is about to take the sins of the whole nation upon itself. This crucifixion is necessary to prevent France from sinking into violence and anarchy. It is our duty to allow the government to carry out a bloodless revolution ... '

His emotion spread to his entire audience. Their applause was long and loud.

Then Xavier Vallat, Nationalist deputy for the Ardèche, rose to say: 'I rejoice at the prospect of all parties meeting tomorrow in a single national gathering, at which the misunderstandings that we have persistently fostered will fade. Institutions have corrupted men: we must change the institutions. But men have also corrupted institutions: we must change the men too, so that France may live again.'

Deeply moved, Laval thanked both speakers. Their moral support, as spokesmen of the Right and of the Left, was unquestionably a victory for him.

But there were still many obstacles to be overcome and many matters to be determined. Nearly everybody agreed that the Marshal should be accorded full powers; of those who did *not* agree, few had the courage to say so in public. But was the new regime to derive its backing from a one-party system or from a coalition? Was the Constitution to be abolished or merely suspended?

———◆◆◆——◆—

MILITARY SITUATION

In Alexandria the general agreement initialled on July 4th was signed by Admirals Godfroy and Cunningham. It specified that:

1. The French ships would be maintained in their present condition with regard to equipment. They would not be scuttled.
2. No attempt would be made by the British to seize the French ships by force.
3. The disembarkment of personnel would continue till an agreed number of men had been reached.
4. The remaining personnel would undertake no hostile activity against British ships or establishments; nor would the ships try to leave harbour.
5. The upkeep and pay of the ships' personnel would continue to be ensured as at present till the French government was in a position to take over this responsibility.
6. The French ships would be free to return to France as soon as peace returned.

But there was to be no such arrangement in Dakar, where a British battle squadron now arrived, accompanied by the aircraft-carrier *Hermes*. The patrol-ship *Milford* pulled away from the rest of the squadron and headed for the *Richelieu*, which was commanded by Post-Captain Marzin. The British vessel was warned that if she came any nearer the defence would open fire. She stopped and semaphored for permission to send a message to the Commander of the navy in French West Africa. The message offered these alternatives:

1. All ships at Dakar, including the *Richelieu*, were to be sailed to Britain with reduced crews. The crews would afterwards be repatriated to France;
2. The fleet was to be sailed to a West Indies port with reduced crews and there disarmed, or sent to the United States and left under American supervision;

515

3. The fleet was to be disarmed at Dakar itself, within twelve hours;
4. If none of these proposals were accepted, the fleet was to be scuttled within a few hours, on receipt of a signal.

Reluctant to use force, and anxious to give Post-Captain Marzin time to think, the British commander let the night go by without opening fire.

That evening the French Admiralty published the casualty figures for the two British attacks on Mers-el-Kebir: killed and missing, 1,297; wounded, 351.

POLITICAL SITUATION

An important conference was going on in Berlin, where Count Ciano had gone for talks with Herr von Ribbentrop and Chancellor Hitler. The topics listed for discussion were the organization of Europe, the continuation of the war against Britain and the possibilities of peace with France.

The 'peace or war' alternative was examined from all aspects. So far as Britain was concerned, the Führer was now convinced that the peace-drive would not succeed. But his mind was not irrevocably made up. That was why he had deferred his projected Reichstag speech till July 19th; he meant to weigh every word.

The talk then turned to France. Ciano knew that Mussolini was opposed to a rapid settlement of the Franco-German conflict and 'alarmed at seeing France slip imperceptibly into the anti-British camp'.

It was indeed clear that a peace advantageous to France could be achieved only at the expense of Britain or Italy — of Italy alone if Britain were not beaten. Italy's claims to Savoy, Corsica, the county of Nice and Tunisia would not be met. The Duce therefore favoured a continuation of hostilities, which would enable him — or so he hoped — to improve his position in the eyes of his Axis partner.

As for Franco, Herr von Stohrer, German ambassador in Madrid, had informed Herr von Ribbentrop of the Caudillo's wishes. Spain desired:

1. The return of Gibraltar.
2. Protectorate rights over Morocco and the Sahara region north of the 20th Parallel.
3. Jurisdiction over the area between the mouth of the Niger and Cape Lopez.

The Führer thought these demands exorbitant in view of the fact that Spain had in no way contributed to the success of his armies.

All the military and political factors that were to develop in the months ahead — Churchill's grim obstinacy, Hitler's vacillations, Mussolini's assumption of the role of jealous lover, Spain's African aims, France's fate hanging in the balance between these conflicting forces — had their beginnings in this international conference, the importance of which has never, till now, been sufficiently emphasized.

The Führer concluded the meeting by telling Ciano that he would consider making some gesture that would have a psychological impact on London. 'I consider that such a gesture may still be useful,' he said, 'though I am practically convinced that the war with Britain will go on.'

While the Axis leaders examined the respective advantages of war and peace, discussions in Vichy still turned on this dilemma: was the Republic to be retained, or was an authoritarian government to be set up?

The day was marked by a stiffening of opposition to Laval's schemes. The ex-service group of senators drew up the following counter-proposal:

The National Assembly has decided:
1. The application of the constitutional laws of February 24th–25th and July 16th '1875' is suspended till the conclusion of peace;
2. Marshal Pétain has full powers to take, by decrees tantamount to law, necessary steps for the preservation of order, for the life and recovery of the nation and for the liberation of the country;
3. The National Assembly entrusts Marshal Pétain with the mission of preparing, in co-operation with the relevant parliamentary committees, the new Constitutions, which will be subject to the nation's approval as soon as circumstances allow a free referendum.

Laval at once scented danger, and strove to counter it by isolating the Taurines–Boncour group from the rest of the senators.

The Senate met at 3.30 p.m. in the hall of the Medical Society. Laval made a speech that was a masterpiece of adaptability and savoir-faire. On July 4th he had advocated the out-and-out suppression of the parliamentary system. Today he gave his colleagues to understand that Parliament would retain certain of its prerogatives. There was nothing to prevent some of the senators from finding a place in the new government. He hinted that the Senate itself might be kept going, even if the other Assembly ceased to function.

A dangerous rival of Laval's had just arrived in Vichy: Pierre-Étienne Flandin, Deputy for the Yonne. He was perhaps the only leading member of the Chamber with the slightest hope of out-trumping the senator for the Seine. In the first place he had a party: the Democratic Alliance. In the second place, he had not been involved in the declaration of war and was generally known to have been hostile to it. Flandin made a speech:

I have just come from Yonne and have spent the last few weeks in contact with the German authorities. I consider that we are in mortal danger. Unless the government acts without delay, we shall witness a complete Nazification of the country's inhabitants. They are short of everything and the Germans are supplying them. The French authorities have fled and the Germans are taking their place. There is no longer a single representative of the French government in the occupied zone ...

The government has called us together ... to modify or change the Constitution. That seems incredible to those who, like me, know the urgency of the work waiting to be done because, like me, they keep their eyes and ears open ...

There was applause at this. The tide of opinion was turning. A member called out: 'Bravo! At last some realistic talk!' Some deputies, while not daring to admit it, were glad to see a colleague standing up to Laval and trying to check his growing influence. Flandin continued:

Why change the Constitution? Why do we need to alter institutions when we can be charged, first and foremost, with not respecting them?
... Nothing could be simpler ... than to ask M. Lebrun to hand in his resignation and to appoint Marshal Pétain President in his place. Then all we have to do is to grant him plenary powers.

In Laval's view, Flandin's scheme presented nothing but drawbacks. It was a hybrid solution of which nothing good could come. Not only would it bring no innovations to the country: it would preserve the men and institutions that had brought about its ruin.

At 6.30 p.m. M. Flandin went to the Pavillon Sévigné to call on the President of the Republic. He was accompanied by MM. Candace and Mistler.

M. Lebrun received the trio with his usual perfect civility, but he instinctively rebelled on hearing what they had to say, and told them that he disagreed entirely. If the Constitution went, he said, he would go with it — but not before. Faithful to the mission that had been entrusted to him, he would respect traditional procedure to the very end.

When the deputy for the Yonne left, half an hour later, the plan that he had concocted lay virtually in ruins.

JULY 8TH

MILITARY SITUATION

In Dakar, after a night of waiting, the British admiral decided to carry out the orders that he had received. At daybreak, taking advantage of the uncertain light and the haze over the water, a vedette from the *Hermes* fired a torpedo at the stern of the *Richelieu*, fortunately missing its target. Then the battleship was subjected to a fierce air attack. She replied with intensive A.A. fire.

But at that point a torpedo hit one of the stern compartments on the starboard side, damaging a line of shafting and the steering mechanism. The stern sagged twenty inches into the water. This time the great battleship had been hit badly enough to be out of action for some time. Judging its mission accomplished, the British squadron withdrew.

The London newspapers treated this attack as a genuine naval victory.

The French Admiralty published the following communiqué:

A British naval unit arrived off Dakar and presented a shameful ultimatum which the admiral commanding French West African forces saw no point in answering. The port was immediately attacked and bombarded by planes from the British aircraft-carrier *Hermes*. The *Richelieu* is now listing to port, with her stern rather low in the water.

POLITICAL SITUATION

The day saw the beginning of the final phase of Laval's offensive. The next forty-eight hours would either make him or break him. He responded to the challenge with an ardour and energy astonishing in a man who was physically far from strong, and who had only his eloquence and conviction to support him. To achieve his ends he would have to employ every facet of his talent — wiliness, adaptability, vehemence and the power to move an audience — and tax his intelligence and nervous system to the full.

What chiefly enabled him to keep his footing in this whirl of conflicting opinions was the fact that he knew where he was going, whereas most of his opponents were hesitant and wavering. It was the power to fascinate, not intellectual ascendancy, that finally won the day for him. He was helped by his keen tactical sense, his flair for adopting the most persuasive line and his speed in discerning an opponent's weakness, an argument's implications or the atmosphere of a meeting. Parliamentary leaders were silent in his presence — or afraid. Léon Blum, who accused his colleagues of cowardice, did not utter a single dissenting word in public. Flandin had tried to make a stand, but his hopes had been crushed by Lebrun's refusal to resign. After spending two days in Vichy he realized that Laval's position was much stronger than he had supposed. Time had been wholly against him. Now there was nothing for it but to patch things up with his rival — who came more than half-way to meet him.

Laval's Bill was unanimously adopted at the morning Cabinet meeting. The following decree was initialled:

> The draft resolution given below will be presented to the Chamber of Deputies by the Prime Minister, who is instructed to uphold it in debate:
> 'The Chamber of Deputies declares that there are grounds for revising the constitutional laws.'

In the afternoon Laval went to the Petit Casino, where for the first time he read out the text of his Bill. He also outlined his reasons for introducing it. Of France's foreign policy he said: 'We were always at Britain's beck and call. Nothing was more humiliating than the sight of our politicians going to London for permission to be French ministers. At home, we made rash promises to certain countries … We did everything to cause war and neglected nothing to lose it. We can see where that led us … The only course open to us is one of honest collaboration with Germany and Italy. This policy — the only policy compatible with France's interests — must be practised honourably and with dignity.

'I feel no embarrassment at saying this, for I desired such a collaboration before the war. I regret [our] having to practise it in the aftermath of defeat …'

A prolonged ovation greeted the end of this speech. A few diehards protested, but they were shouted down.

Armed with this second success Laval next visited the Society of Medical Sciences. There he encountered a less favourable atmosphere, but he managed to stem the tide, and by the end of the meeting he had won most senators over to his way of thinking.

JULY 9TH

—◆•◆◆•◆—

POLITICAL SITUATION

During the week preceding the meeting of the Assemblies there was a ceaseless flow of manifestoes, leaflets, motions and resolutions. They were not all of equal stature; but there is one text that deserves attention because of its contents and the character of its signatories. It has become known as the 'Motion of the 27'. It ran as follows:

> The undersigned members of parliament ... desire to state solemnly that they are fully aware of what is blameworthy in the present state of affairs ... [and] that they realize the pressing need to bring about the moral and economic recovery of our poor country ...
>
> With this end in view, considering it indispensable to grant Marshal Pétain, who in these grave hours so perfectly embodies the traditional French virtues, all powers to carry out this work of public welfare and peace, but refusing to vote for a Bill that would inevitably lead to the disappearance of the Republican regime, the undersigned proclaim that they remain more than ever attached to the democratic freedoms, for the defence of which the best of our country's sons have fallen.

Vincent Badie, the author of this text, was a game and likeable young radical. He had just returned from service with the 3rd Army, having fought valiantly since the opening days of the German offensive. He had reached Vichy only the night before and was dismayed by the mood prevailing in the town.

President Lebrun's decree convoking the Assemblies was based on Article 8 of the law of February 25th, 1875, which stated:

> The Chambers will have the right, by separate deliberations carried by a majority in each, either of their own accord or at the President's request, to declare that there are grounds for revising the constitutional laws.

It was under the terms of this provision that the Chamber of Deputies

521

and the Senate were to meet and declare whether or not the Constitution should be revised.

At 9.30 a.m. the leader of the Chamber of Deputies, M. Herriot, arrived at the Grand Casino and advanced into the hall in accordance with the usual ceremony. The guards presented arms. The three hundred and ninety-eight deputies reassembled. M. Herriot and the secretaries took their places on stage, while the public crowded into the boxes and galleries. It was just like an ordinary Opening of Parliament.

Laval's Bill was submitted to the Committee for Universal Suffrage. After an adjournment the Committee Chairman, M. Mistler, stated: 'The Committee for Universal Suffrage is unanimously in favour of the proposed resolution ... Today it is a question of undertaking the task of reconstructing the country in orderliness and republican legality, so that France may live again!'

The Bill was then put to the vote, with the following results:

> For: 395 votes.
> Against: 3 votes.

In the afternoon the Senate met in the same hall. M. Jeanneney presided. The atmosphere was slightly more solemn, but the procedure was the same.

'It seems to be France's fate to be regenerated through misfortune,' said M. Jeanneney. 'Never has her misfortune been greater. Let us set to work to forge a new spirit for our country, to imbue it with creative force and faith, to make it muscular too — in short, to re-establish, with the authority of moral values, authority pure and simple ... '

The Senate voted as follows:

> For: 229 votes.
> Against: 1 vote.

JULY 10TH

POLITICAL SITUATION

The decisive day had come at last. At 10.30 a.m., in dazzling sunshine, the deputies and senators assembled in the Grand Casino, where the two Chambers were to combine in secret session. The hall had been minutely inspected by the administrative staffs to ensure that no outsider should be present at the deliberations.

The theatre foyer served as an improvised lobby in which the leading lights of the Third Republic met and conversed. Possibly the dense crowd outside was expecting to see the Marshal. If so, it was disappointed: neither he nor M. Lebrun attended.

Laval was about to deliver the final attack in the grim battle that he had been conducting for the past week. Today it was win or lose. He knew that there might be some rough skirmishing ahead, but he found the prospect far from displeasing. It sharpened his intelligence and redoubled his energies.

Four other speeches were expected: one by M. Taurines, on behalf of the ex-service senators; one by Vincent Badie, the radical deputy, who intended to defend the 'Motion of the 27'; one by Pierre-Étienne Flandin (nobody knew what line he was going to take); and one by Gaston Bergery.

M. Valadier introduced the government Bill.

M. Taurines immediately rose and tabled an amendment on behalf of the ex-service group. It was worded as follows:

The National Assembly has decided:

1. The application of the constitutional laws of February 24th–25th and July 16th, 1875, is suspended till the conclusion of peace;
2. Marshal Pétain has all powers to take, by decrees tantamount to law, necessary steps for the preservation of order, for the life and recovery of the nation and for the liberation of the country;
3. The National Assembly entrusts Marshal Pétain with the mission of preparing, in co-operation with the relevant parliamentary

committees, the new Constitutions, which will be submitted for the nation's approval as soon as circumstances allow a free referendum.

The differences in the two texts were striking. In the first the Marshal was authorized to *promulgate* the Constitution, in the second he was merely called upon to prepare it. In the first he was to be given a free hand, in the second he was to co-operate with the parliamentary committees. In the first the Constitution would be ratified by the *Assemblies that it creates*, in the second it would be *submitted for the nation's approval*.

Laval realized that this amendment constituted a considerable threat. He decided to parry it at once by reading out the letter that Marshal Pétain had handed to him on the evening of July 7th:

Monsieur le Président,
The constitutional Bill tabled by my government will be debated by the Assemblies on Tuesday, July 9th, and Wednesday, July 10th.
As it is difficult for me to attend the meetings I am asking you to represent me at them.
Adoption of the Bill that the government is presenting to the National Assembly seems to me essential to the welfare of our country ...

This letter rocked the meeting. For all its brevity, it made it quite clear that Laval's motion was the Marshal's own, that he recognized no other and that he regarded the Bill's adoption as indispensable.

Laval sensed that this was the moment to explain himself fully. He went up to the rostrum and stared at the faces before him. At this crucial moment Laval was about to deliver one of the finest speeches of his career. One is tempted to call it a masterpiece of oratory, but the phrase suggests a trace of artificiality. Laval's every word was stamped with absolute sincerity, as even his worst enemies were bound to admit.

After replying indirectly to the criticisms voiced by Flandin three days earlier, Laval turned his attention to the causes of the plight in which France now found herself:

... Undoubtedly the greatest crime committed in our country for a very long time was declaring war — and declaring war without preparing for it, either militarily or diplomatically. I do not think there is any greater disaster to be found in the pages of our history ...
It has been said — this was the argument of those politicians who wanted to go abroad — that France was unwilling to admit that she was beaten. Had there been the faintest glimmer of hope, what

Frenchmen could have felt differently? But ... between Clermont-Ferrand and Bordeaux, in the course of the most painful journey that I have experienced, I witnessed the spectacle of an army in flight ... We cannot save France by leaving her soil, I said. I stick to that view. It was our place to remain in the midst of her suffering inhabitants, in order to suffer with them if necessary ...

Britain dragged us into the war, then did nothing that would enable us to achieve victory. Finally France was ravaged; but while we still supposed that we were Britain's associates, how did she treat us French? As mercenaries, more or less ...

Then came the ultimatum addressed to the admiral commanding our battle squadron at Mers-el-Kebir. Our ships were being disarmed, and it would take them at least twelve or eighteen hours to leave harbour; yet the ultimatum said: 'Unless you surrender within six hours we shall fire.' ...

And yesterday, in Dakar, an ultimatum was addressed to the *Richelieu*, which was anchored in the harbour, and to the small number of cruisers beside her. Once again the ultimatum expired after six hours: another instance of attempted murder. The British officers bombarded our ships and machine-gunned our sailors, who only yesterday were sacrificing themselves for Britain ...

Conscious of having captured his audience, he decided to lay the issue squarely before them.

I cannot accept any amendment to the text proposed by the government, and I do not intend making any promises to the Assembly other than those authorized in my conversations with Marshal Pétain ... One cannot, without being frivolous, envisage a Constitution that is not the expression of a country's ways, of its desires, of its will: it would be a waste of time. One would construct something that was purely artificial and that would soon be swept away by events. That is not what we are urging upon you ...

Suddenly certain memories roused his anger again. His voice grew rasping, and it was with a cry of pain that he spoke of the declaration of war: 'From the social point of view the Constitution may be broad, airy, human and generous, but there is one thing you must make no mistake about: never again will the State's authority be flouted! Never again will anyone be able to determine ... the country's fate and plunge it into war without the Assemblies even being consulted.' Then his anger subsided.

' ... We have the luck, the good fortune, to have in France, in these bad times, a victorious soldier, a Marshal of France. The whole world respects this man, who embodies the finest page in our history. We have the good fortune to have him, to be able to shelter behind him and try to secure the nation's welfare. That is what I urge upon you, and I am sure that every vote this evening will be for the Bill's adoption — for it is to France that you will be giving it.'

This peroration was greeted with thunderous applause, which can have given little encouragement to the Bill's opponents. Laval had not even deigned to consider the texts of their amendments.

In the afternoon the senators and deputies reassembled in the same hall. This time members of the public were allowed in.

M. Fernand Bouisson, former leader of the Chamber of Deputies, proposed that the government Bill should be given priority. This meant that the alternative proposals tabled by Boncour, Taurines and Vincent Badie could be examined only if the government's motion were rejected. The Assembly pronounced in favour of this suggestion by a show of hands.

The Bill was then submitted to a special joint committee, composed of the Senate's Committee of Legislation and the Lower Chamber's Committee of Universal Suffrage. The Deputy Premier appeared before it to 'provide its members with all necessary explanations'.

M. Masse was anxious to know whether individual liberties would be protected.

'I am none too clear as to the meaning of your question,' replied Laval. 'If by individual liberty you mean the right of any scruffy foreigner to govern France, don't count on it! I shall specify, for example, that nobody can be a deputy unless his family has been French for several generations. That will be our way — I did understand you aright, didn't I? — of practising racial policy ... '

M. Marx Dormoy asked: 'Who will be responsible for deciding on peace or war?'

'I take it,' said Laval, 'that you are referring to the possibility of our replying to the bombardment of Dakar. I can give you a plain answer. As you can imagine, we are not going to saddle ourselves with complicated legislature that would prevent us from dealing blow for blow. If we find ourselves unable to fire on His Majesty's ships, but are in a position to confiscate something, we shall confiscate it — with or without your permission.'

These questions clearly stung Laval. But he refrained from pressing home his advantage. His parliamentary experience had taught him that a fair compromise was worth more than a victory too brutally won. He therefore agreed to insert a clause in a later text *preventing the Head of State from declaring war without the prior consent of the legislative Assemblies.*

Meanwhile, Laval's followers were busy in the lobbies, trying to win the votes of his few remaining opponents. By the time the public sitting resumed at 5.15 p.m. it was difficult to see who could impede the Bill's passage.

For the last time M. Jeanneney read out the (modified) text on which the deputies and senators were to have to vote:

Constitutional Bill

The President of the French Republic,

In view of Article 8 of the constitutional law of February 25th, 1875,

And in view of the resolutions adopted by the Senate and the Chamber of Deputies,

Decrees:

The Constitutional Bill given below will be presented to the National Assembly by the Prime Minister, who is directed to uphold it in debate:

Sole article: The National Assembly gives all powers to the government of the Republic under the authority and signature of Marshal Pétain to promulgate in one or more acts a new Constitution of the French State. This Constitution shall safeguard the rights of work, the family and the country.

It will be ratified by the nation and put into effect by the Assemblies that it creates.

Given at Vichy, July 10th, 1940.

ALBERT LEBRUN

By the President of the Republic
Marshal of France,
Prime Minister
PHILIPPE PÉTAIN

At that moment M. Vincent Badie climbed on to the stage to defend the 'Motion of the 27'. But M. Bouisson took him violently to task. Grabbing him by the lapels of his jacket, he hustled him off the stage with the help of a pair of ushers, reminding him that the Assembly had accorded the government Bill priority.

Disregarding the objections of the young deputy from Hérault, M. Jeanneney hurriedly put the Constitutional Bill to the vote.

The results were as follows:

Voters	666
Absolute majority	334
For	569
Against	80
Abstained	17

The Constitutional Law was in consequence adopted by the National Assembly. The announcement of the figures was greeted with thunderous applause.

Then M. Laval rose and, turning to the Assembly, said: 'Just one word on Marshal Pétain's behalf: I thank you in the name of France!'

The cry went up: '*Vive la France!*'

M. Marcel Astier, senator for the Ardèche, called out: '*Vive la République quand même!*', but the slogan met with no response.

———————◄••••►———————

The Marshal formed a new government, made up as follows:

Premier:	Marshal Pétain
Deputy Premier:	Pierre Laval
Justice:	Alibert
Interior:	Marquet
Foreign Affairs:	Baudouin
Finance:	Bouthillier
National Defence:	Weygand
Education and Fine Arts:	Mireaux
Youth and Families:	Ybarnegaray
Agriculture and Food:	Caziot
Industrial Production and Labour:	Belin
Communications:	Piétri
Colonies:	Lémery

In the evening the Marshal broadcast to the French people:

Frenchmen!

The National Assembly has invested me with extensive powers.

... To accomplish the huge task confronting us I need your trust. Your representatives have given it to me in your name. Like you and me, they intend that the State's impotence shall no longer paralyse the nation ...

Governors will be placed in charge of the large French provinces. Thus the administration will be, at one and the same time, concentrated and decentralized.

Officials will no longer be hampered by hide-bound regulations or redundant controls ...

Our programme is to give France back the strength that she has lost. She will regain it only by following the simple rules that, from time immemorial, have ensured the life, the health and the prosperity of nations.

We shall construct an organized France in which the discipline of the ruled matches the authority of the rulers, in fairness to all ...

The toil of the French people is our country's chief resource. It must be sacred. The international capitalism and international socialism that exploited and degraded it both belong to the pre-war scene. What made them particularly deadly was that, while apparently opposing each other, they were secretly working hand in glove. We shall no longer tolerate their shady alliance ...

We are renouncing neither the powerful driving force of profit nor the reserves that are accumulated by economy.

But favour will no longer govern the distribution of emoluments. Earnings will remain the recompense of toil and risk. In our reconstructed France, money will be simply the reward of effort ...

French families are the trustees of long centuries of honour. It is their duty to keep alive, from generation to generation, the ancient virtues that make for strong races.

Family discipline will be preserved.

But, as we know, modern youth needs to live with youth, to build up its strength in the open air in a wholesome brotherliness that prepares it for the battle of life. We shall watch over it ...

HISTORY TAKES SHAPE

ONE CAMPAIGN: THREE WARS

What could be more evocative than a plain chronological account of those sixty days? Yet something essential would be lost were I to end there, for my method has entailed arbitrary breaks in my description of events, giving a disjointed quality to military and political moves that developed uninterruptedly. It remains for me to try to draw the threads together.

Inside the quadrilateral formed by the Rhine in the east, the Low Countries and Flanders in the north, the North Sea and the Channel in the west, and the Loire in the south, there occurred a series of military engagements known jointly as the campaign of 1939–40. Beginning at dawn on May 10th, a single battle spread right across this area of Western Europe.

But within that single battle — hence the real interest of the sixty days — three wars, not one, were taking place: a German war, a French war and a British war.

THE GERMAN WAR

The French army of 1940 was from every point of view prematurely old. It had not managed to keep pace with the developments of its time. The Wehrmacht, on the other hand, was a young army, brimming over with energy and vitality. This is not just a figure of speech. The difference was reflected in the manpower of the two armies. The average age of men serving in the French army was about twenty-nine. The average age of members of the Wehrmacht was under twenty-three.

A second characteristic of the Wehrmacht was its extreme mobility. Overcoming the conservatism of generals of the old school, a handful of young officers — Guderian, Manstein, Milch, Sperrle and Kesselring — convinced that 'whoever first conquers the stagnation of positional warfare will win the next war', had fashioned the tool of the new strategy: the co-ordination of tanks and planes, followed by powerful motorized infantry units.

A third factor played a large part in the German success: the methodical concentration of resources, both on land and in the air, as opposed to the tragic dispersal of strength on the Allied side.

There has been much talk of the attacks of the 4th Armoured Division in the Montcornet area and its efforts to absorb the Abbeville bridge-head, of the 2nd Armoured Division's offensive in the same sector and its delaying action between Poix and Crèvecœur, of the sortie by British armour south of Arras, and of the great-hearted effort of the young Saumur cadets in defending the Gennes and Montsoreau bridges with the aid of the few guns available at the school. All these actions deserve praise, but they were incapable of altering the course of events: the Germans viewed them as mere local engagements.

Whereas the whole French army — including the last of its reserves — was flung into the line, the operations were so swiftly accomplished that for the Germans the campaign was little more than a series of vanguard actions. The bulk of the Wehrmacht was never fully engaged.

That Germany had admirably thought out the war of 1939–40 and had been able to forge the army capable of waging it was due to the fact that she was run by a taut, compact regime. The uncheckable advance of the mechanized units on the battlefield was just another aspect of the dynamism that the National Socialist government had managed to infuse into the country.

But in the course of these sixty days the German High Command committed three cardinal errors which may be said to have been at the root of her subsequent defeat.

The first was halting the armour before it reached Dunkirk. Whatever the motives that may have inspired Hitler — whether it was his desire to handle the British with kid gloves, or his concern that the Luftwaffe should be allowed to bring the battle to its victorious conclusion — this was undoubtedly a serious mistake.

The second, as has been pointed out many times, was the armistice. Germany would have stood a far greater chance of winning the war had her armoured divisions thrust onwards to North Africa and continued their advance to Casablanca and Alexandria.

The third error lay in Hitler's hesitations in the course of the German-Italian conference of July 7th, 1940. It was essential, that day, to decide firmly on either war or peace. Deciding on war meant carrying through Operation 'Sea Lion' and invading Britain, whatever the cost. Deciding on peace meant concluding generous treaties with Norway, Holland, Belgium and France.

Whereas Germany had thought out the campaign in every detail, France was content to fall blindly back on formulae borrowed from the 1914–18 war.

The ruling concept in French military circles was that defensive warfare, based on the theory of the continuous front, was of prime importance. 'The continuous front is the great revelation of the war,' wrote Marshal Pétain in 1939. ' ... At the start of operations the continuous front emerges as the best means whereby the weaker side can defend its territory.'

The offensive, when finally launched, was to be cautious and planned to the last detail. The *Instruction on the Tactical Use of Large Units*, compiled in 1936 by a committee of eleven generals under General Georges, painstakingly stipulated how it was to be carried out. The offensive was divided into *tranches* (segments), which were in turn broken down into *temps* (phases) and *bonds* (rushes).

'And the attack will be carried out in accordance with this brief,' wrote Colonel Goutard. 'Troops will advance from objective to objective, often with intermediate objectives, all carefully geared to the terrain — for naturally the aim must be to attack, rake in, mop up the *terrain* — not to manoeuvre the *enemy*. And troops will dig in on reaching each objective pending orders to move on, which will be given from the rear — for it is not the front that leads, it is the rear that pushes!'

One can only gasp at all this wariness and complication.

Since the tank's invention two main roles had been assigned to it:

1. An aggressive role: achieving a break-through in an offensive;
2. Reconnaissance, holding actions, exploitation, pursuit; in short, those missions that had been the cavalry's prerogative for a hundred and fifty years.

The infantry had been naturally inclined to use its tank units aggressively, while the cavalry had adopted the opposite approach. No organization had considered the problem in its entirety. The tank had been torn between infantry and cavalry.

Article 236 of the *Instruction on the Tactical Use of Large Units* stipulated: 'When combined forces of infantry and support-tanks are preceded by tactically employed tanks, it is the latter that receive artillery backing. In this case ... artillery fire takes the form of a series of box-barrages, providing "enclosures" within which first the tactically employed tanks, then the combinations of infantry and support-tanks, advance in rushes.'

This meant that tanks were not allowed to leave the artillery 'enclosures'; in other words, they were prevented from advancing more than four or five miles beyond their starting-points.

Turning our attention to the air force, we find the same incoherence and the same wide dispersal of resources. Whereas all German military aircraft (more numerous and more modern than their French counterparts) were massed in two autonomous 'Fleets' under a single command and were 'ready to strike the enemy at the selected point', the French northern front was divided into 'air operation zones' tied to the Groups of Armies. These zones were subject to the orders of the Army Group Commanders *as well as* to those of General Têtu, General Vuillemin's representative at General Georges's headquarters.

There was the same muddle over the use of airborne troops. The Luftwaffe had a division of paratroops under General Student (they were to drop in huge clusters over Rotterdam and the fortress of Eben-Emaël), and 100,000 young Germans had qualified for the parachutist's badge. But the French had only two air infantry groups — the 601st and 602nd, respectively stationed in Rheims and Algiers. Only three hundred and sixty men in all, and to their air force colleagues they were despised outsiders. The idea of a large-scale attack behind enemy lines had never occurred to France's leaders.

The fact is that France was no more capable than any other country of forming an army that did not resemble her system of government. And since her system of government was lax and uncoordinated, how could it foster vigorous and victorious fighting services? The government must take final responsibility for the tragedy: it had allowed France to stagnate.

The plans of the French General Staff, like the programmes of the nation's political leaders, were constantly outpaced by events. To suppose that the German tanks could be separated from the units that they were escorting was a dangerous illusion. It was based on the idea that there was a vacuum between armour and infantry. But this was a mistake. Tanks, motorized infantry and standard infantry followed each other without pause.[1]

In a country where politics had become merely a series of experiments, was it not to be expected that military leaders should come to regard war not as a trial of strength but simply as a choice between various

[1] General Perré records: 'The type of formation with which we clashed when attacking a German position would vary from day to day. Where there were tanks on May 18th we met with motorized infantry on May 20th and standard infantry, solidly supported by artillery, on May 23rd.'

'plans'? The battle in the north began with the execution of the 'Dyle plan' — in other words, with a move worked out in every detail in November 1939, and executed blindly in May 1940 without any attempt to ascertain whether the Belgians had really erected a defensive position, or whether the Germans had redistributed their forces in the previous six months.

THE BRITISH WAR

When the war started in September 1939, Britain was far less well prepared even than France. Her armament level was lower than in 1914. She was so badly off for armour that she asked France for the plans of her 'B' tanks, and later of her 'Hotchkiss' tanks, so that she could mass-produce them.

Luckily for her, she had an excellent air force, and a navy that was still supreme. But the latter did not play a particularly glorious part in the sixty days: its activities consisted mainly of covering the British withdrawal from Dunkirk and attacking the helpless French fleet.

That Britain had made so little effort in the sphere of land armaments was due to the fact that she was counting on the French army to shield her.

Gort made no fuss when he was told that Gamelin had decided to delegate direct command of the British to General Georges. What bothered him was the news that Gamelin was still to remain Commander-in-Chief.

Britain knew that she held a high trump: distance. Why should she not add the natural complement of time? The spring campaign might seal France's fate: it must in no circumstances be allowed to seal the United Kingdom's. Her military leaders therefore adopted a strategy that ran directly counter to Weygand's. It consisted of retiring behind the French shield and scurrying from the sinking ship that Flanders had become. It was, in short, the strategy of a maritime power. As Dunkirk vanished behind the smoke and flames, the outlines of the future war took shape in British minds — the war which Britain would wage in three or four years' time, God willing, and which would be quite different from this undignified scramble. The image sprang from past experience, from the recognition of a recurring factor in her history. Back in Napoleon's day, at the time of the continental blockade, she had owed her security to the Channel. And by gaining time she might gain far more: America would certainly throw off her isolationism one day, and there was always a chance that Russia might change sides.

One thing is certain. Britain's long-term plan could never have been realized had France followed the same course. It was only because the French divisions at Dunkirk formed a shield and prevented the Germans from thrusting straight into the harbour that the B.E.F. could be evacuated without great loss. For the men at the War Office it was essential that the Frenchmen should stay behind and die so that the British troops might one day triumph. 'Lord Gort and General Billotte will work hand in hand,' they said. But next day, without warning Billotte, Lord Gort withdrew north of Arras. 'Our troops will leave France *bras-dessus, bras-dessous!*', promised Churchill. But at that very moment British boats were refusing to take French soldiers aboard. 'Britain demands the honour of forming part of the rearguard!' But by then the commander of the B.E.F. had left the perimeter, and General Alexander, having embarked the last of his troops, decided to halt the evacuation. 'Let Paris be defended district by district, house by house,' proposed Churchill. But Weygand replied vehemently that reducing Paris to ashes would in no way affect the outcome of the battle. Really, these French had no conception of global strategy!

Three wars did indeed go on side by side in those sixty days. Three such dissimilar wars that it is hard to detect anything in common between them. One understands better than ever Marshal Foch's remark: 'I have far less admiration for Napoleon now that I know what a coalition is.'

BIBLIOGRAPHY

arranged under: 1. French sources; 2. Other sources.

A complete bibliography for this book appears in the three-volume French edition, *Soixante Jours qui Ébranlèrent L'Occident*, published by Albin Michel, Paris, in 1956; where it will be found on pages 649-75 of the third volume.

A short list of references is given here, mainly of those works which are quoted in the English edition.

FRENCH SOURCES

ARON, ROBERT, *The Vichy Regime, 1940–1944*, Putnam, London, 1958.

AUPHAN, P., *Histoire de mes trahisons*, N.P. Paris, 1946.

BARDIES, RAPHAËL DE, *La campagne de 39–40*, Fayard, Paris, 1947.

BAUDOUIN, PAUL, *Reflexions sur l'Armistice (1940)*, unpublished.

BAUDOUIN, PAUL, *La vérité sur l'Armistice (1941)*, unpublished.

BAUDOUIN, PAUL, *Neuf mois au gouvernement. Mémoires*, La Table Ronde, Paris, 1948.

BIDOU, HENRI, *La bataille de France*, Éditions du Milieu du Monde, Génève, 1941.

BOURGET, P. A., *De Beyrouth à Bordeaux. La guerre de 1939–1940 vue du P.C. du Général Weygand*, Berger-Levrault, Paris, 1946.

BOUTHILLIER, YVES, *Mémoires. vol. 1. Face à l'ennemi, face à l'allié*, Plon, Paris, 1950.

DARLAN, ALAIN, *L'amiral Darlan parle*, Amiot-Dumont. Paris, 1953.

FABRE-LUCE, ALFRED, *Journal de la France, I: mars 1939–juillet 1940*, Imprimerie de Trevoux, Trevoux, 1940.

FABRE-LUCE, ALFRED, *Une tragédie royale: L'affaire Léopold III*, Flammarion, Paris, 1948.

FABRE-LUCE, ALFRED, *La fumée d'un cigare*, L'élan, Paris, 1949.

GALIMAND, LUCIEN, *Vive Pétain ... Vive de Gaulle!* Éditions de la Couronne, Paris, 1948.

GAMELIN, MARIE GUSTAVE, *Servir. (Mémoires)*, 3 vols., Plon, Paris, 1946–1947.

GAUCHÉ (Général), *Le Deuxième Bureau au travail, 1935–1940*, Amiot-Dumont, Paris, 1954.

GAULLE, CHARLES DE, *War memoirs. vol. 1, The call to honour*, Weidenfeld and Nicolson, London, 1955.

GEORGES (Général), *Rapport au Général Weygand sur les opérations en France, mai-juin 1940*.

GIRARD, LOUIS-DOMINIQUE, *Montoire, Verdun diplomatique*, Bonne, Paris, 1948.

GODFROY, R. E., *Mémoires. L'aventure de la Force X à Alexandrie*, Plon, Paris, 1953.

GOUTARD, A., *1940. La guerre des occasions perdues*, Hachette, Paris, 1956.

HERRIOT, ÉDOUARD, *Episodes 1940–1944*, Flammarion, Paris, 1944.

KAMMERER, ALBERT, *La vérité sur l'Armistice*, Éditions Médicis, Paris, 1944.

BIBLIOGRAPHY

LAURE, E., *Pétain*, Berger-Levrault, Paris, 1941.

LEBRUN, ALBERT, *Témoignage*, Plon, Paris, 1945.

MASSENON, LÉO, *Les leçons de la guerre*, Ecrits de Paris, mai-juin, 1951.

MONZIE, ANATOLE DE, *Ci-devant (souvenirs)*, Flammarion, Paris, 1941.

MORAND, PAUL, *Rélation sommaire de la situation à Londres, du 17 juillet au 20 juillet 1940*, N.P.n.d.

MOURIN, MAXIME, *Les tentatives de paix dans la deuxième guerre mondiale*, Payot, Paris, 1949.

MUSELIER, E. H. D., *De Gaulle contre le Gaullisme*, Éditions du Chêne, 1946.

NOËL, LÉON, *Il y a dix ans était signé l'armistice de 1940*, Historia, mai 1950.

OBERLÉ, JEAN, *Jean Oberlé vous parle ...*, La Jeune Parque, Paris, 1945.

PERRÉ, JEAN, & CHAZAL, JACQUES, *La IIe Division cuirassée à la bataille*, unpublished.

PERTINAX, ANDRÉ, *The Gravediggers of France*, Doubleday, New York, 1944.

PEYREFITTE, ROGER, *La fin des Ambassades*, Flammarion, Paris, 1953.

PEYROUTON, MARCEL, *Du service publique à la prison commune*, Plon, Paris, 1950.

PRIOUX, R., *Souvenirs de guerre, 1939–1940*, Flammarion, Paris, 1947.

PRIOUX, R., *Le procés du Maréchal Pétain*, 2 vols., Albin Michel, Paris, 1945.

REYNAUD, PAUL, *In the thick of the fight*, Cassell, London, 1955.

ROTON, G., *Les années cruciales*, Lavauzelle, Paris, 1947.

WEYGAND, MAXIME, *En lisent les mémoires de Général de Gaulle*, Flammarion, Paris, 1945.

WEYGAND, MAXIME, *Recalled to Service*, Heinemann, London, 1952.

OTHER SOURCES

ABETZ, OTTO, *Histoire d'un politique franco-allemande*, Stock, Paris, 1953.

BADOGLIO, PIETRO, *Italy in the Second World War. Memories and documents*, O.U.P., London, 1948.

BLUMENTRITT, GUENTHER, *Von Rundstedt, the soldier and the man*, Odhams, London, 1952.

BROOKE, ALAN FRANCIS (1st Viscount Alanbrooke), *Operations of the British Expeditionary Force, France, from June 12th to June 19th*, Supplement to London Gazette, May 22nd, 1946.

CHURCHILL, SIR WINSTON, *The Second World War*, Cassell, London, 1949.

CIANO, COUNT GALEAZZO, *Ciano's diary 1939–1943*, Heinemann, London, 1947.

GUDERIAN, HEINZ, *Panzer Leader*, Michael Joseph, London, 1952.

HITLER, ADOLF, *Hitler's Table Talk*, Weidenfeld and Nicolson, 1953.

HITLER, ADOLF, *Aufrufe, Tagesbefehle und Reden des Fuhrers im Krieg, 1939–1941*, Karlsruhe, 1941.

HITLER, ADOLF, *Lettres sécrètes échangées par Hitler et Mussolini*, Édition du Pavois, 1946.

JODL, ALFRED, *Campaign diary*, unpublished.

KESSELRING, ALBERT, *The Memoirs of Field Marshal Kesselring*, Kimber, London, 1953.

LANGER, WILLIAM L., *Our Vichy Gamble*, Harper, New York, 1946.

LIDDELL HART, B. H., *The Other Side of the Hill*, Cassell, London, 1951.

BIBLIOGRAPHY

MANSTEIN, F. E., *Lost Victories*, Methuen, London, 1958.

MICHIELS (Général), *Rapport à S.M. le Roi Léopold III sur les opérations de l'Armée belge (10 mai–28 mai, 1940)*. No publisher given.

MUSSOLINI, BENITO, *Scritti e discorsi*, Annual volumes.

PAGET, R. T., *Field-Marshal von Manstein, his campaigns and his trial*, Collins, London, 1951.

ROMMEL, ERWIN, *The Rommel Papers*, Collins, London, 1953.

ROOSEVELT, FRANKLIN D., *Public papers and addresses. 1939 volume: War and neutrality. 1940 volume: War and aid to democracies*, Macmillan, London, 1941.

SCHAUB, KONRAD JOACHIM (Editor), *Die Behrichte des Oberkommandos der Wehrmacht. Vol. 1. September bis zum Waffenstillstand in Frankriech*, Deutsche Verlagsgesellschaft, Berlin, 1940.

SHERWOOD, ROBERT E. , *The White House Papers of Harry L. Hopkins. An intimate history, vol. I*, Eyre and Spottiswoode, London, 1948.

SPEARS, SIR EDWARD, *Assignment to catastrophe, 2 vols.*, Heinemann, London, 1953–4.

VEREKER, JOHN (6th Viscount Gort), *Despatches. First despatch covering the period from September 3rd, 1939 to May 31st, 1940. Second despatch, covering the period from 1st of February to 31st May, 1940, with an appendix covering operations of the 1st Corps from 6 p.m. 31st May to midnight 2/3rd June*, Supplement to the London Gazette, October 17th, 1941.

ACKNOWLEDGMENTS

Grateful acknowledgment is made to the following authors, executors and publishers for permission to use copyrighted material:

AMIOT-DUMONT: *L'amiral Darlan parle* by Alain Darlan; *Le Deuxième Bureau au travail, 1935–1940* by Général Gauché; we are grateful to Mme A. Gauché, Général Gauché's executor; *Mers el Kebir* by Pierre Varillon.

BERGER-LEVRAULT: *De Beyrouth à Bordeaux* by P. A. Bourget. *Pétain* by E. Laure.

ÉDITIONS ANDRÉ BONNE: *Montoire, Verdun diplomatique* by Louis-Dominique Girard.

CASSELL & CO. LTD: *The Second World War Vol. II* by Sir Winston Churchill; *The Other Side of the Hill* by B. H. Liddell Hart; *In the Thick of the Fight* by Paul Reynaud.

CHARLES-LAVAUZELLE ET CIE: *Les années cruciales* by G. Roton.

ÉDITIONS DU CHÊNE: *De Gaulle contre le Gaullisme* by E. H. D. Muselier.

CHICAGO DAILY NEWS: *Journal 1940–43* by Count Galeazzo Ciano.

WILLIAM COLLINS SONS & CO. LTD: *The Rommel Papers.*

DOUBLEDAY & CO.: *The Gravediggers of France* by André Pertinax.

LES ÉDITIONS DE L'ÉLAN: *La fumée d'un cigare* by Alfred Fabre-Luce.

EYRE & SPOTTISWOODE LTD: *The White House Papers of Harry L. Hopkins* by Robert E. Sherwood.

ARTHÈME FAYARD ET CIE: *La campagne de 39–40* by Raphaël de Bardies.

LIBRAIRIE FLAMMARION: *Une tragédie royal: L'affaire Léopold III* by Alfred Fabre-Luce; *Épisodes 1940–1944* by Édouard Herriot; *Ci-devant (souvenirs)* by Anatole de Monzie; *La fin des Ambassades* by Roger Peyrefitte; *Souvenirs de guerre, 1939–1940* by R. Prioux; *En lisent les mémoires de Général de Gaulle* and *Recalled to Service* both by Maxime Weygand.

LIBRAIRIE HACHETTE: *1940. La guerre des occasions perdues* by A. Goutard.

HARPER & BROS: *Our Vichy Gamble* by William L. Langer.

WILLIAM HEINEMANN LTD: *Assignment to Catastrophe* by Sir Edward Spears.

LA JEUNE PARQUE: *Jean Oberlé vous parle …* by Jean Oberlé.

MICHAEL JOSEPH LTD: *Panzer Leader* by Heinz Guderian.

WILLIAM KIMBER & CO. LTD: *The Memoirs of Field Marshal Kesselring* by Albert Kesselring.

MACMILLAN & CO. LTD: *Puplic papers and addresses. 1939 volume: War and neutrality. 1940 volume: War and aid to democracies* by Franklin D. Roosevelt.

LIBRAIRIE MÉDICIS: *La vérité sur l'Armistice* by Albert Kammerer.

METHUEN & CO. LTD: *Lost Victories* by F. E. Manstein.

ÉDITIONS ALBIN MICHEL: *Le procés du Maréchal Pétain* by R. Prioux.

ÉDITIONS DU MILIEU DE MONDE: *La bataille de France* by Henri Bidou.

ODHAMS PRESS: *Von Rundstedt, the soldier and the man* by Guenther Blumentritt.

ÉDITIONS PAYOT: *Les tentatives de paix dans la deuxième guerre mondial* by Maxime Mourin.

ACKNOWLEDGMENTS

LIBRAIRIE PLON : *Les grimaces de l'histoire* by P. Auphan; *Mémoires. vol. 1. Face à l'ennemie, face à l'allie* by Yves Bouthillier; *Servir (Mémoires)* by Marie Gustave Gamelin; *Mémoires. L'aventure de la Force X à Alexandrie* by R. E. Godfroy; *Témoignage* by Albert Lebrun; *Du service publique à la prison commune* by Marcel Peyrouton.

LIBRAIRIE STOCK : *Histoire d'un politique franco-allemànde* by Otto Abetz.

LA TABLE RONDE : *Neuf mois au governement* by Paul Baudouin.

GEORGE WEIDENFELD & NICOLSON LTD : *War Memoirs, vol 1. The call to honour* by Charles de Gaulle; *Hitler's Table Talk.*

Italy in the Second World War by Pietro Badoglio; we are grateful to the executors. *Revue Historique de l'armée* No. 4 (1946).

INDEX

N.B. *Nationals of the various countries concerned are indexed under their names. Warships are given in italics.*

INDEX

INDEX

INDEX

INDEX

INDEX

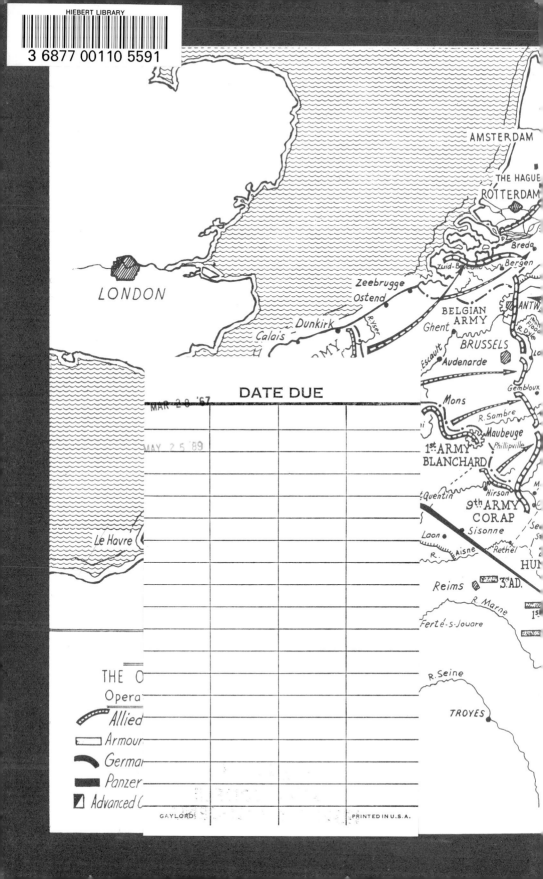